Learn from Scratch

Unlocking AI with PHP

Sharanam Shah
Vaishali Shah

Learn from Scratch

Unlocking AI with PHP

Sharanam Shah
Vaishali Shah

THE X TEAM

SPD®

SHROFF PUBLISHERS & DISTRIBUTORS PVT. LTD.
Navi Mumbai

Learn from Scratch: Unlocking AI with PHP
by Sharanam Shah and Vaishali Shah

First Edition: September 2025

ISBN : 978-93-6808-256-9

Printed at Decora Book Prints Pvt. Ltd., Mumbai • Published by Shroff Publishers and Distributors Pvt. Ltd. B-103, Railway Commercial Complex, Sector 3, Sanpada (E), Navi Mumbai 400705 • Tel: (91 22) 4158 4158 WhatsApp +91 7304487700 4158 4141 • E-mail: spdorders@shroffpublishers.com • URL: www.shroffpublishers.com

Kick off your PHP and AI journey

Welcome to Unlocking AI with PHP! This book is your definitive guide to mastering the world's most popular server-side language, PHP, and elevating your skills by integrating the transformative power of Artificial Intelligence. Starting from the absolute fundamentals and progressing to building sophisticated, real-world applications, this book is engineered to turn you from a beginner into a confident, modern PHP developer.

Critically, in today's tech landscape, we dive deep into a topic rarely covered in PHP literature: bridging the gap between PHP and Python to unlock a world of AI possibilities. You will learn to integrate modern APIs like Gemini and leverage Python's powerful libraries directly within your PHP projects.

This journey culminates in a monumental finale project—ConnectSphere, a complete AI-enhanced social networking site. Here, you'll learn to translate requirements into a fully functional system, taking you on the ultimate development adventure. If you're ready to build robust, dynamic, and intelligent web solutions that employers are actively seeking, your transformation begins now.

This book is dedicated to our kids. Thank you for coming to this world as our kids. You both are the most precious we could ever ask for. We love you both more than our life

About this book

This book serves as your complete roadmap to the powerful world of PHP, from foundational principles to advanced AI integration. We guide you through the essential concepts and tools, ensuring you build a solid foundation in modern web development while embracing cutting-edge AI capabilities that will set you apart.

From understanding basic syntax to deploying a full-stack, AI-powered social network, each chapter is crafted with practical examples and hands-on projects to accelerate your learning. We aim to ensure that by the end of this book, you can confidently code not only standard data-driven PHP applications but also those enhanced with powerful AI and Python-integrated features that give you a competitive edge in today's job market.

What you'll learn?

Our book is thoughtfully structured into logical sections that build upon each other:

- **Foundation - Crafting Your Playground:** We start with the essentials: What is PHP, setting up your XAMPP development environment, mastering Visual Studio Code, and structuring your first multi-page projects with Git for version control.

- **Core PHP Mastery - From Variables to CRUD:** Dive deep into the heart of PHP. Master variables, data types, control structures, loops, functions, and arrays. Learn to handle user input securely through forms, manipulate strings and files, and manage user state with sessions and cookies.
- **Database Onboarding - Meet MySQL:** You will learn to work with databases, the backbone of any dynamic web application. We cover everything from basic SQL commands (CREATE, INSERT, SELECT, UPDATE, DELETE) to building full CRUD applications and designing database schemas.
- **The AI Revolution - PHP Meets Python:** A dedicated section that sets this book apart! Understand how to call Python scripts from PHP to perform complex tasks. You will integrate public AI APIs like Gemini, explore machine learning concepts, and build applications that can analyze sentiment, recommend content, and even "see" with image-to-text recognition.
- **AI-Powered Coding - Your New Assistant:** Learn how to use AI as a partner in your development workflow. We show you how to set up AI code assistants, write effective prompts to generate code, refactor messy scripts, and even design application architecture with AI's help.
- **Grand Culmination - The ConnectSphere Social Network:** The crescendo of your learning journey features a comprehensive finale project where you will build a complete social networking application from the ground up, integrating user authentication, profiles, a friend system, posts, and AI-powered friend suggestions.

Special focus: AI-powered PHP applications with Python

In today's competitive tech landscape, the ability to integrate AI separates good developers from great ones. This book emphasizes getting you ahead of the curve by bridging the PHP and Python ecosystems:

- **Why Python?** Understand why Python is the language of choice for AI and how you can leverage its power without leaving your PHP environment.
- **The Client-Server Model:** Learn to architect applications where PHP acts as the front-end controller and Python works as a back-end AI service, communicating seamlessly with JSON.
- **Direct API Integration:** Master calling external AI services for tasks like sentiment analysis, natural language processing, and image recognition directly from your PHP code.
- **Practical AI Projects:** Build functional AI-powered applications step-by-step, from an intelligent contact form to a smart guestbook and a language translator integrated directly into your ConnectSphere project.

- This ensures you're learning PHP in the context of modern, AI-driven development—exactly what the industry demands.

Learning reinforcement structure

We believe in learning by doing and explicitly connecting theory to practice through our proven methodology:

- **What you'll learn** - Each chapter starts with clear, actionable goals.
- **Examples** - Chapters are packed with practical, real-world code.
- **Hands-on project** - Most chapters include a comprehensive project to apply concepts immediately.
- Crucially, these project sections feature dedicated topics:
- **Bridging the gap: Learned concepts and application implementation** - Explicitly shows how the concepts taught in the chapter are mapped and used within the project code.
- **Exploring application behaviour: A practical run-through** - Demonstrates how the application works in real-time, reinforcing the practical impact of the learned features.
- **Harnessing features in real-world contexts** - Discusses the relevance and application of the features in broader, real-world scenarios.

This structure ensures you not only learn what a feature does, but how and where to apply it effectively in your career.

Hands-on projects

Theory meets practice! You'll gain invaluable experience by building:

- **Core PHP projects:** A dynamic calculator, a temperature converter, an interactive quiz game, a personal portfolio website, and a digital diary.
- **Database & CRUD projects:** A contact book, a task manager, and a complete Mini Content Management System (CMS) for a blog.
- **AI Integration projects:**
    - AI sentiment analysis for a feedback form
    - An AI Help Desk with Gemini
    - An AI-powered Reading Recommender
    - A visual gallery that uses AI for image tagging
    - An Image-to-Text (OCR) extractor
- **PHP & Python Integration projects:**
    - A QR Code Generator built with a Python backend
    - A language translator integrated into the ConnectSphere app
- **Grand Finale project:**
    - **ConnectSphere - An AI-Enhanced Social Network:** A complete social media platform with user registration, login, profiles, a friend request system, posts, and AI-powered friend suggestions.

Who should dive in?

This book is perfect for:

- **Absolute beginners** wanting a structured, comprehensive path to web development with PHP and cutting-edge AI integration.
- **Students and hobbyists** looking to build a strong portfolio with real-world projects, including a full-scale social network.
- **Developers transitioning** from other frameworks who want to quickly master modern PHP and its unique AI capabilities.
- **Career changers** looking to enter the high-demand field of web development with a unique and powerful skill set.
- **Anyone aiming** to build robust, modern, intelligent web applications that solve real-world problems.

Our story

Based in Mumbai, India, my journey into technical writing has been anything but conventional. With experience in application development and tech project management, I discovered a passion for simplifying complex concepts through clear, engaging documentation at a leading technology firm. Today, I blend my love for technology and writing to create accessible developer materials.

Together with my wife, Vaishali, we have co-authored over 30 technical books. We both relish exploring emerging technologies and, once we master them, sharing our insights with the world through our books.

For more about us, please visit www.sharanamshah.com.

Downloadable resources

All examples and projects, including complete AI integrations and the finale ConnectSphere application, are available for download.

Visit: https://www.sharanamshah.com/books/unlockingaiwithphp/bookcodes.zip
Password: **codesbysharanamvaishali**

Gratitude and acknowledgments

This book is the result of passion, persistence, and the unwavering support of our families, peers, and the vibrant PHP community. We are especially grateful to our publisher, Mr. Aziz Shroff, whose support and vision were instrumental in bringing this book to life. Your encouragement and feedback have been invaluable in shaping this book into a resource we hope will inspire and empower you.

If you have any questions, comments or just feel like communicating, please contact us at enquiries@sharanamshah.com.

Dive in and enjoy your journey into PHP and Artificial Intelligence—each line of code brings you closer to building powerful, intelligent solutions, culminating in your own social network built from requirements to reality.

The future of web development is intelligent and interconnected. Happy coding!

Sharanam & Vaishali Shah

Table Of Contents

Section II: Foundations of great code - PHP basics in action

Section IV: Smarter workflows - Functions, Arrays, and Authenticity

Chapter 1

Section 01: Ready, set, code! – Your modern developer toolkit

Welcome to PHP: Why it still rules the Web

What you'll learn

- What is PHP?
- How dynamic pages work?
- Its role on the web
- Inspiring project examples

Welcome to the world of web development! This chapter kicks off your journey by introducing you to PHP, a cornerstone technology of the internet. Think about your favorite social media site, online store, or blog. Behind the scenes, there's a good chance PHP is working hard to deliver the content you see.

PHP has been powering the web for over three decades, and despite predictions of its demise, it continues to dominate the server-side programming landscape. With over 75% of all websites using PHP as their primary backend language, from small blogs to massive platforms, PHP proves that longevity and reliability matter in web development.

We'll explore what PHP is, why it's still so popular after decades, and how it transforms simple, static web pages into powerful, interactive applications. By the end, you'll understand how PHP generates content on the fly and see inspiring examples of what you'll soon be able to build.

What is PHP? - The story, then and now

PHP originally stood for **Personal Home Page**, but it now stands for **PHP: Hypertext Preprocessor**. It's a **server-side scripting language**. This means that unlike HTML or CSS, which your browser reads directly, PHP code runs on a web server ***before*** a page is ever sent to you. It processes instructions, connects to databases, and generates a final HTML document that your browser can display.

PHP began its journey in 1994 when Danish-Canadian programmer Rasmus Lerdorf created a simple set of Common Gateway Interface (CGI) scripts to track visitors to his personal website. What started as a modest collection of tools for managing a homepage has evolved into one of the world's most influential programming languages.

The language grew organically, with Lerdorf himself admitting he never intended to create a programming language at all. In 1995, he released the source code publicly, allowing other developers to contribute improvements and new features. This collaborative approach set the foundation for PHP's community-driven development model that continues today.

PHP 3, released in 1998, marked a major milestone when Zeev Suraski and Andi Gutmans rewrote the parser, officially changing the name to the recursive acronym we know today. This version introduced object-oriented programming capabilities and established PHP as a serious tool for web development.

The release of PHP 4 in 2000 brought significant performance improvements and new features like sessions and improved database support.

PHP 5, launched in 2004, revolutionized the language with the new Zend Engine 2, introducing enhanced object-oriented programming, improved error handling, and the PHP Data Objects (PDO) extension for database access.

PHP 7, released in 2015, represented a quantum leap in performance, delivering nearly twice the speed of its predecessor while using significantly less memory. The introduction of scalar type declarations, return type declarations, and the null coalescing operator made PHP code more robust and maintainable.

Today's PHP 8.4 continues this evolution with powerful new features like Property Hooks, further performance optimizations through a revamped Just-In-Time (JIT) compiler, and enhanced error handling. The language has matured from a simple scripting tool into a sophisticated platform capable of handling enterprise-level applications with millions of users.

Why PHP still dominates the web

Despite numerous predictions of its demise, PHP continues to maintain its position as the web's most popular server-side language. Current statistics show that PHP powers 75.8% of all websites where the server-side technology can be determined, far ahead of competitors like Ruby (6.0%), ASP.NET (5.8%), and Java (5.0%).

Several factors contribute to PHP's enduring success. First, its widespread hosting support makes deployment incredibly simple – virtually every web hosting provider supports PHP out of the box, often at minimal cost. This accessibility has made PHP the go-to choice for small businesses, startups, and individual developers who need to get online quickly without complex infrastructure requirements.

The language's evolution has addressed many historical criticisms. Modern PHP is fast, secure, and feature-rich, with performance improvements in **PHP 8.4** making it more competitive than ever with newer languages. The introduction of JIT compilation, improved memory management, and optimized array handling has transformed PHP from a "slow" scripting language into a high-performance platform capable of handling massive traffic loads.

PHP's ecosystem remains unmatched in the web development space. WordPress, built entirely in PHP, powers over 40% of all websites globally. Popular content management systems like Drupal and Joomla, e-commerce platforms like Magento and WooCommerce, and frameworks like Laravel and Symfony all rely on PHP, creating a vast network of interconnected tools and resources. The language's learning curve remains gentle for beginners while offering advanced features for experienced developers.

Dynamic page generation

A **static website** is like a printed brochure. Every visitor sees the exact same content because the HTML files are pre-written and don't change.

A **dynamic website**, powered by a language like PHP, is like a digital assistant that creates a custom page for each visitor on demand.

When you request a PHP page, the web server doesn't just send a file:

1. It executes the PHP script first.
2. The script might fetch the latest news from a database, check if you're logged in, or calculate the current time.
3. It then weaves that information into an HTML template.
4. The final result is a freshly generated HTML page sent to your browser.

You never see the PHP code itself—only its output.

Let's see this in action. Here is a simple script that displays a welcome message along with the current date and time:

- **PHP code (index.php)**

```
<?php
    // Set the timezone to get accurate local time
    date_default_timezone_set('Asia/Kolkata');
    // Store the current date and time in a variable
    $current_time = date('F j, Y, g:i a');
?>
```

- **HTML and Embedded PHP (index.php)**

```
<!DOCTYPE html>
<html lang="en">
<head>
    <meta charset="UTF-8">
    <meta name="viewport" content="width=device-width, initial-scale=1.0">
    <title>Welcome to PHP!</title>
    <link rel="stylesheet" href="style.css">
</head>
<body>
    <div class="container">
        <h1>Welcome to Our Website!</h1>
        <p>This page is powered by PHP.</p>
        <p class="time-display">
            Current server time is: <?php echo $current_time; ?>
        </p>
    </div>
</body>
</html>
```

- **CSS (style.css)**

```
body {
    font-family: -apple-system, BlinkMacSystemFont, "Segoe UI", Roboto,
                 Helvetica, Arial, sans-serif;
```

```
    background-color: #f0f2f5;
    display: flex;
    justify-content: center;
    align-items: center;
    height: 100vh;
    margin: 0;
}
.container {
    text-align: center;
    background-color: #ffffff;
    padding: 40px;
    border-radius: 12px;
    box-shadow: 0 4px 12px rgba(0, 0, 0, 0.1);
}
h1 {
    color: #1c1e21;
    font-size: 2.5rem;
}
p {
    color: #606770;
    font-size: 1.1rem;
}
.time-display {
    background-color: #e7f3ff;
    color: #1877f2;
    font-weight: bold;
    padding: 10px 20px;
    border-radius: 8px;
    margin-top: 20px;
    display: inline-block;
}
```

When you open index.php in a browser (through your local web server), you won't see any PHP tags. Instead, the **<?php echo $current_time; ?>** part is replaced by its actual value. If you refresh the page a minute later, the time updates automatically because the PHP script runs again, generating a brand-new HTML page with the new time. That's dynamic content in action!

The modern PHP ecosystem

Today's PHP ecosystem is vibrant and sophisticated, offering developers a comprehensive toolkit for building everything from simple websites to complex enterprise applications.

The ecosystem centres around several key components that work together to create a powerful development environment:

- **Frameworks and Libraries:**
    - **Laravel** leads the PHP framework landscape with its elegant syntax and comprehensive feature set, including built-in authentication, routing, sessions, and caching.
    - **Symfony** provides enterprise-grade components used by many other frameworks.
    - **CodeIgniter** offers simplicity for rapid development.
    - The **Composer** package manager gives developers access to thousands of reusable libraries, eliminating the need to reinvent common functionality.
- **Development tools:** Modern PHP development relies on sophisticated tools that enhance productivity and code quality.
    - **PHPStorm** and **Visual Studio Code** provide intelligent code completion, debugging capabilities, and integration with version control systems.
    - Command-line tools like **PHPStan** and **Psalm** perform static analysis to catch errors before they reach production.
    - **PHPUnit** enables comprehensive testing of applications.
- **Performance and Deployment:**
    - Contemporary PHP applications benefit from advanced deployment strategies including containerization with **Docker**, cloud-native development on platforms like **AWS** and **Google Cloud**, and integration with CI/CD pipelines for automated testing and deployment.
    - Tools like **RoadRunner** and **PHP-FPM** optimize application performance, bringing PHP closer to the speed of compiled languages.
- **Community and Support:** PHP's community remains one of its greatest strengths. The language benefits from active development by core contributors, extensive documentation, and countless tutorials and resources.
    - Major conferences like **PHP[World]** and community-driven initiatives ensure knowledge sharing and continued innovation.

What can you build? - Inspiring examples

PHP is incredibly versatile. It's not just for one type of project; it's a multi-purpose tool for solving countless web challenges. As you progress through this book, you'll gain the skills to build sophisticated, real-world applications.

Here's a glimpse of what you can create with PHP:

- **Content Management Systems (CMS):** Build a blog or a news site where you can create, edit, and delete articles through a secure admin panel.
- **E-commerce platforms:** Develop a complete online store with product catalogues, shopping carts, user accounts, and payment processing.
- **Social networks:** Create a community site where users can create profiles, connect with friends, post updates, and interact with each other.
- **SaaS (Software as a Service) applications:** Build subscription-based tools like project management systems, invoicing platforms, or booking calendars.
- **Forums and Membership sites:** Construct online communities with restricted content areas, user roles, and discussion boards.
- **AI-powered tools:** Integrate with AI APIs to build smart applications like a support ticket system that analyses sentiment or a guestbook that automatically tags uploaded images.

The skills you learn here are the foundation for all these projects and more.

Wrapping up

This chapter gave you a high-level tour of PHP and its place in the web development landscape. We covered the most important foundational concepts to get you started on the right foot:

- **PHP is a server-side language:** Its code runs on the web server, not in the user's browser.
- **It creates dynamic pages:** PHP generates HTML on the fly, allowing content to change based on user interaction, database information, or other conditions.
- **It powers much of the web:** From blogs on WordPress to massive social platforms, PHP is a dominant and reliable technology.
- **HTML,CSS, and PHP work together:** HTML provides structure, CSS adds style, and PHP delivers the dynamic logic and data.
- **PHP is a versatile tool:** You can use it to build almost any type of web application imaginable.

Congratulations on taking your first step! You now understand what PHP is and the critical role it plays in creating the interactive web we use every day. You've seen how a few lines of code can bring a static page to life. This fundamental knowledge is the perfect launching pad for your coding adventure.

In the next *Chapter 2: Crafting your playground – Installing PHP & Web servers,* we'll get our hands dirty by setting up your local development environment.

Chapter 2

Section 01: Ready, set, code! – Your modern developer toolkit

Crafting your playground – Installing PHP & Web Servers

What you'll learn

- Local web servers
- Running PHP files
- Browser output
- Installing XAMPP
- Creating project folders
- Basic PHP syntax

Every great web application, from global social networks to your favorite online store, starts on a developer's personal computer.

This chapter is all about setting up your private workshop—a local development environment. We create a space on your own machine that mimics a live web server, allowing you to build, test, and experiment with PHP code safely and efficiently. Think of it as a painter's studio or a mechanic's garage; it's your dedicated area to craft and perfect your work before sharing it with the world. By the end of this chapter, you'll have this essential playground running and will have already built your very first dynamic web page.

Introduction to local development environments

Before writing a single line of PHP, we need a place for our code to run. Unlike static HTML and CSS files, which a browser can open directly, PHP code needs to be processed by a special program called a **PHP interpreter**. This interpreter lives on a web server. A local development environment is simply a web server that you run on your own computer.

What is a Web Server?

A **web server** is software that listens for requests from web browsers. When you type a URL like google.com into your browser, you are sending a request to Google's web server. The server finds the right files (HTML, CSS, images, and in our case, PHP scripts), processes them, and sends the final result back to your browser to display.

The two most important components for us are the **Apache Web Server**, which handles the requests, and the **PHP interpreter**, which executes the PHP code.

Why use a Local Server?

Using a local server is faster, more secure, and completely free. It lets you:

- **Work offline:** Build and test your entire application without an internet connection.
- **Test privately:** Make mistakes and experiment without anyone seeing your work in progress.
- **Instantaneous changes:** See the results of your code edits instantly by simply refreshing your browser.

Introducing XAMPP: Our chosen tool

Setting up a web server, a PHP interpreter, and a database separately can be tricky. Thankfully, all-in-one packages handle this for us. We will use **XAMPP**, a free and popular tool that bundles everything we need:

- **X (Cross-platform):** Works on Windows, macOS, and Linux.
- **Apache:** The web server software.
- **MySQL:** The database (which we'll explore in later chapters).
- **PHP:** The programming language itself.

- **Perl:** Another programming language (which we won't be using).

Installing and configuring XAMPP

Getting XAMPP set up is a straightforward process. It acts as the foundation for all the PHP projects we will build in this book.

Downloading the installer

1. Visit the official **Apache Friends** website at **apachefriends.org**.
2. Download the installer for your operating system (Windows, macOS, or Linux). We are using **Windows installer** for our book.
3. Always choose the version that includes the latest stable release of PHP.

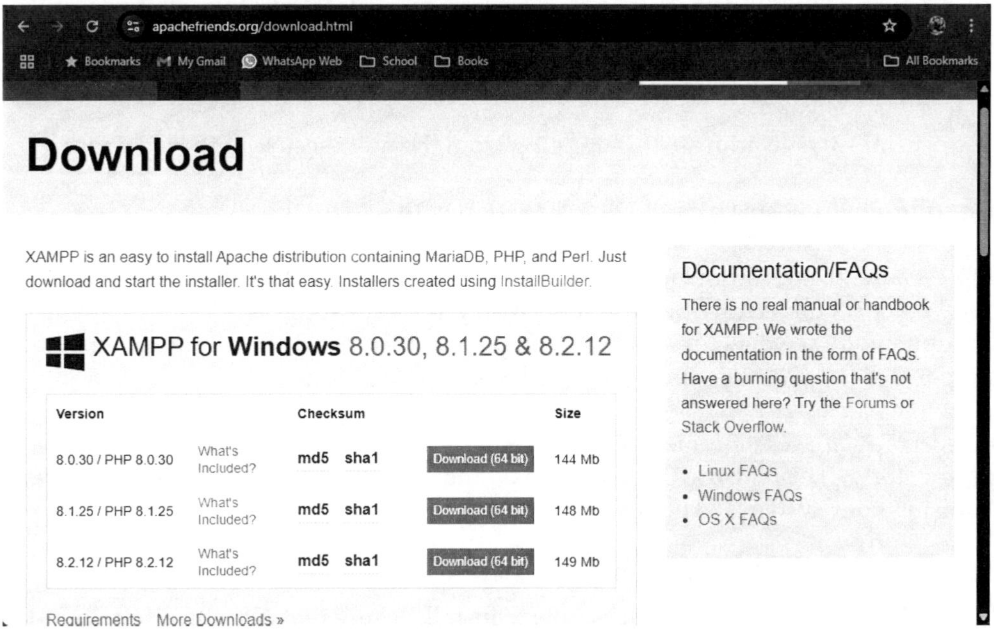

Running the setup wizard

1. Once the download is complete, run the installer.
2. A warning of **User Account Control** may crop up before XAMPP starts installation.

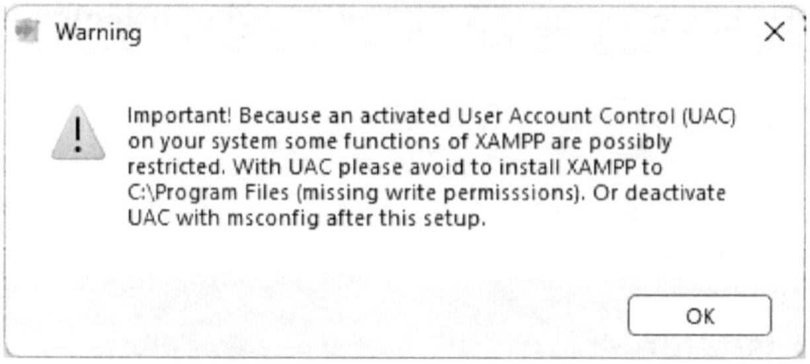

What is UAC and why this warning?

User Account Control (UAC) is a security feature in Windows that helps prevent unauthorized changes to your computer. When you install XAMPP on Windows 11, you might encounter a UAC warning message. This happens because XAMPP needs to write files and services to a location on your hard drive that Windows protects, such as the Program Files folder. The UAC warning is a heads-up that XAMPP's functionality might be limited if installed in a protected location.

There are several ways to address this, ranging from the most secure to the least secure.

The best solution: Choosing a different installation path

The simplest and most recommended solution is to install XAMPP in a directory outside of the protected Windows folders. By default, the XAMPP installer suggests **C:\xampp**, which is an ideal location. If you see the UAC warning, simply ensure you are installing to a directory like C:\xampp instead of C:\Program Files.

This approach avoids UAC issues entirely because the C:\xampp folder is not a protected system directory. This ensures XAMPP has the necessary write permissions without compromising your system's overall security.

3. You can accept the default settings for all steps.
4. The installer asks you which components to install; ensure that **Apache**, **PHP**, and **MySQL** are checked.

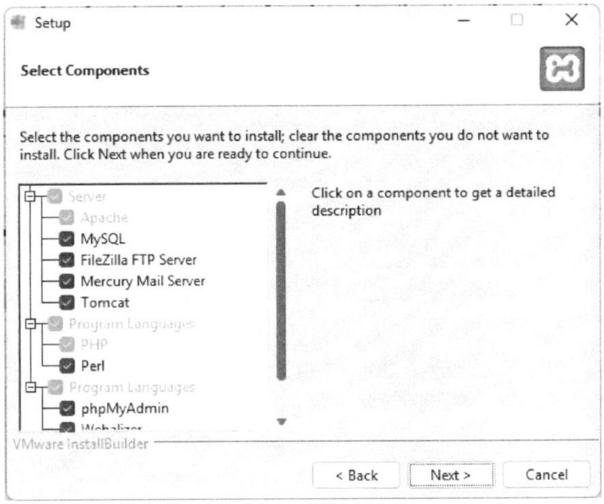

5. **Windows Security** alert appears, which requests you to allow some of the blocked features of Apache HTTP Server by **Windows Firewall**. Click **Allow**.
6. It also asks where to install the software. On Windows, this is typically **C:\xampp**.

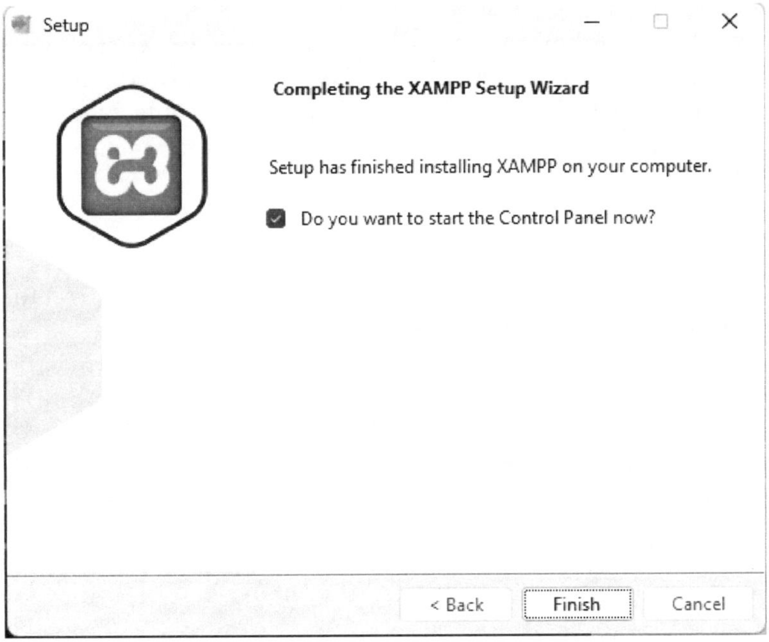

7. Click **Finish** and the XAMPP installation is complete.

Understanding the XAMPP control panel

Once you click **Finish** in the **Setup** dialog box, the installer opens **XAMPP Control Panel**.

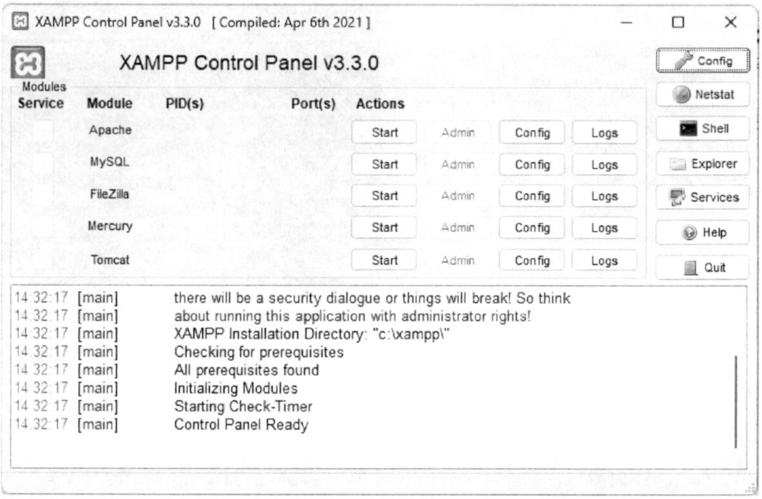

This is your command center for managing the local server. You see a list of services (modules) like Apache and MySQL. Next to each is a **Start** button. This is how you turn your local server on and off. You don't need to have it running all the time—only when you are actively developing your PHP applications.

Your first PHP script

With our server ready, let's write some code. This involves finding the correct folder where the web server looks for files and creating our first project.

Finding the htdocs folder

Apache, the web server inside XAMPP, serves files from a specific directory. This directory is called the **web root**. In XAMPP, the web root is a folder named **htdocs**.

- **On Windows:** You'll find it at C:\xampp\htdocs
- **On macOS:** It's located at /Applications/XAMPP/htdocs

Any folder or file you place inside htdocs will be accessible through your web browser.

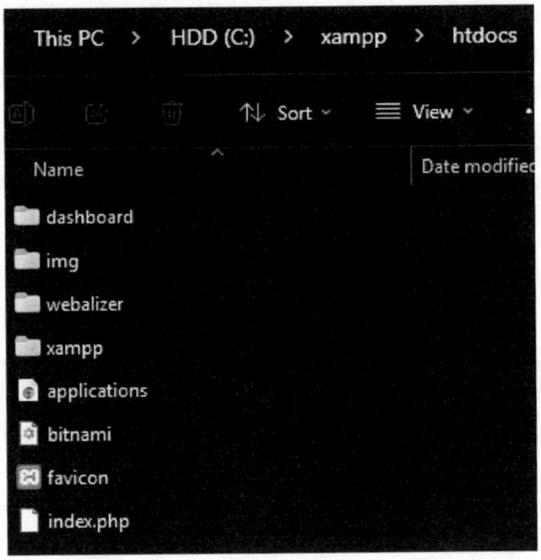

Creating your project folder

It's a best practice to create a dedicated folder for each project. Let's create one for our book exercises:

1. Navigate to the **htdocs** folder.
2. Create a new folder inside **htdocs** and name it **codes**. This is where we will build this book's application.

Writing "Hello, World!" in PHP

Now, let's create our very first PHP file.

1. Open your **text editor**, Notepad or any other text editor.
2. Add the following code:

```
<?php
  echo "Hello, World!";
?>
```

3. Save the file as **hello.php** inside your **C:\xampp\htdocs\codes** folder.

This simple script uses the **echo** command, which is PHP's primary tool for outputting text.

Viewing your work in the browser

We've written the code; now let's see it in action. This is the moment where our local server does its magic.

Starting Apache server

1. Go back to your **XAMPP Control Panel**.
2. Click the **Start** button next to the **Apache** module.

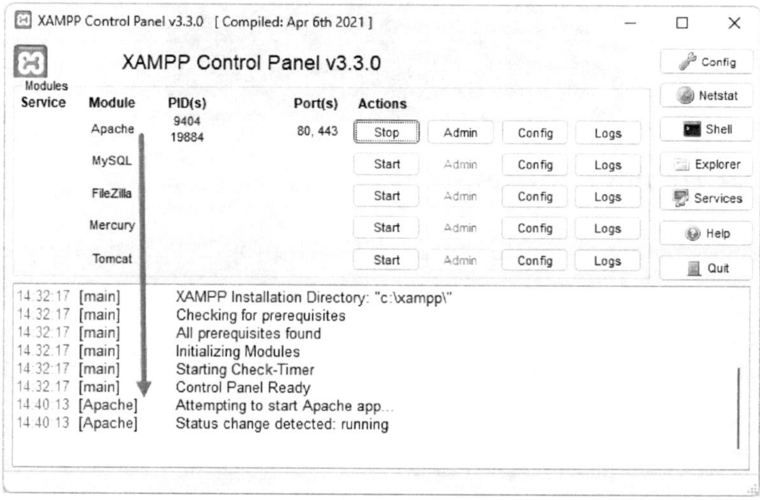

3. It should turn **green**, indicating the web server is now running.

Accessing localhost

1. Open your web browser. In the address bar, type **localhost** and press **Enter**.
2. You see the default XAMPP dashboard page. The term **localhost** is a special name that always points to your own computer. When you type it in the browser, you are talking directly to your local Apache server.

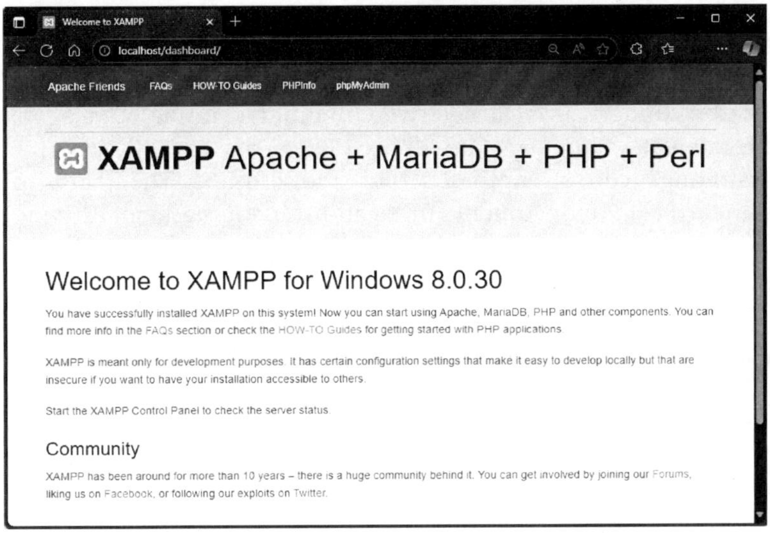

Running your PHP file

To run our specific PHP script, we need to point the browser to its location relative to the **htdocs** folder.

1. In your browser's address bar, type: **http://localhost/codes/hello.php**.
2. Press **Enter**.
3. The browser displays a plain white page with the text:

```
Hello, World!
```

Congratulations! You just created and executed your first PHP script. The server processed the PHP code, found the echo statement, and sent the resulting text back to your browser.

Hands-on: My first web page

To bring together everything we've learned, we will build a simple but elegant Digital Diary entry page. This is not just a static page; it will use PHP to dynamically insert the current date and time, demonstrating a core strength of server-side scripting. The goal is to see how PHP works inside a standard HTML document and to add some professional styling with CSS.

Building the application

We will create a single file that contains our HTML, CSS, and PHP, all working together.

Create the main file

1. Inside the **codes** folder (C:\xampp\htdocs\codes), create a new file named **index.php**.
2. Using **index.php** as the filename is special; web servers will automatically load this file if you only navigate to the folder's URL.

Add the HTML structure

1. Open the **index.php** file in any text editor.
2. Add the following HTML boilerplate, which sets up the basic structure of our page:

```
<!DOCTYPE html>
<html lang="en">
<head>
    <meta charset="UTF-8">
    <meta name="viewport" content="width=device-width, initial-scale=1.0">
    <title>My Digital Diary</title>
</head>
<body>
    <main class="diary-container">
        <h1>My Digital Diary</h1>
        <div class="entry">
            <p>Today's entry is for...</p>
            <textarea placeholder="Start writing..."></textarea>
            <button>Save Entry</button>
        </div>
    </main>
</body>
</html>
```

At this point, if you save and view **http://localhost/codes/** in your browser, you will see a basic, unstyled HTML page.

Add CSS for styling

Now, let's make it look like a real application. We'll add the CSS directly into the <head> section of our HTML using a <style> block:

```
<style>
    body {
        background-color: #f0f2f5;
        font-family: -apple-system, BlinkMacSystemFont, "Segoe UI", Roboto,
                     Helvetica, Arial, sans-serif;
        display: flex;
        justify-content: center;
        align-items: center;
        height: 100vh;
        margin: 0;
    }
    .diary-container {
        background-color: #ffffff;
        padding: 40px;
        border-radius: 12px;
        box-shadow: 0 4px 12px rgba(0, 0, 0, 0.1);
        width: 100%;
        max-width: 500px;
        text-align: center;
    }
    h1 {
        color: #1c1e21;
        margin-bottom: 8px;
    }
    .entry p {
        color: #606770;
        font-size: 1rem;
        margin-bottom: 24px;
    }
    textarea {
        width: 100%;
        height: 150px;
        border: 1px solid #dddfe2;
        border-radius: 8px;
        padding: 12px;
        font-size: 1rem;
        resize: vertical;
        margin-bottom: 16px;
    }
    button {
        background-color: #1877f2;
        color: #ffffff;
        border: none;
        border-radius: 8px;
        padding: 12px 24px;
```

```
        font-size: 1.1rem;
        font-weight: bold;
        cursor: pointer;
        transition: background-color 0.3s;
    }
    button:hover {
        background-color: #166fe5;
    }
</style>
```

Place this entire <style> block inside the <head> section of index.php, right before the closing </head> tag.

Integrate the PHP code

This is where the magic happens. We will replace the placeholder text in our paragraph with a PHP script that outputs the current date and time.

Find this line:

```
            <p>Today's entry is for...</p>
```

And replace it with this PHP block:

```
<p>
  Today's Entry: <strong><?php echo date("l, F j, Y - h:i A"); ?></strong>
</p>
```

Now, your final index.php file should look like this:

```
<!DOCTYPE html>
<html lang="en">
<head>
    <meta charset="UTF-8">
    <meta name="viewport" content="width=device-width, initial-scale=1.0">
    <title>My Digital Diary</title>
    <style>
        body {
            background-color: #f0f2f5;
            font-family: -apple-system, BlinkMacSystemFont, "Segoe UI", Roboto,
                         Helvetica, Arial, sans-serif;
            display: flex;
            justify-content: center;
            align-items: center;
            height: 100vh;
            margin: 0;
        }
        .diary-container {
```

```
            background-color: #ffffff;
            padding: 40px;
            border-radius: 12px;
            box-shadow: 0 4px 12px rgba(0, 0, 0, 0.1);
            width: 100%;
            max-width: 500px;
            text-align: center;
        }
        h1 {
            color: #1c1e21;
            margin-bottom: 8px;
        }
        .entry p {
            color: #606770;
            font-size: 1rem;
            margin-bottom: 24px;
        }
        .entry strong {
            color: #0d1a49;
        }
        textarea {
            width: 100%;
            height: 150px;
            border: 1px solid #dddfe2;
            border-radius: 8px;
            padding: 12px;
            font-size: 1rem;
            resize: vertical;
            margin-bottom: 16px;
        }
        button {
            background-color: #1877f2;
            color: #ffffff;
            border: none;
            border-radius: 8px;
            padding: 12px 24px;
            font-size: 1.1rem;
            font-weight: bold;
            cursor: pointer;
            transition: background-color 0.3s;
        }
        button:hover {
            background-color: #166fe5;
        }
    </style>
</head>
<body>
    <main class="diary-container">
        <h1>My Digital Diary</h1>
        <div class="entry">
            <p>Today's Entry: <strong><?php echo date("l, F j, Y - h:i A");
```

```
                ?></strong></p>
            <textarea placeholder="Start writing..."></textarea>
            <button>Save Entry</button>
        </div>
    </main>
</body>
</html>
```

Bridging the gap: Learned concepts and application implementation

- **Local server (localhost):** We accessed the entire application by navigating to http://localhost/codes/. This proves our local server is correctly configured and serving files from the **htdocs** directory.
- **PHP processing:** When the browser requested **index.php**, the Apache server didn't just send the file. It saw the .php extension and handed it to the PHP interpreter first.
- **PHP tags (<?php ... ?>):** The interpreter only executed the code found inside these tags. Everything outside the tags was treated as plain HTML and ignored by the interpreter.
- **echo statement:** Our script used **echo** to output a dynamic string—the current date and time.
- **Dynamic content:** The **date()** function is a built-in PHP command. Every time you refresh the page, PHP re-runs this function and inserts the current timestamp, making the page dynamic.

Running and testing

1. Make sure your **Apache** server is running in the **XAMPP Control Panel**.
2. Open your web browser.
3. Navigate to **http://localhost/codes/**. Because we named our file index.php, we don't need to type the filename.
4. You see your **Digital Diary** page.
5. Notice the date and time are perfectly current. If you wait a minute and refresh the page, the time will update automatically. The expected output in your browser looks like this:

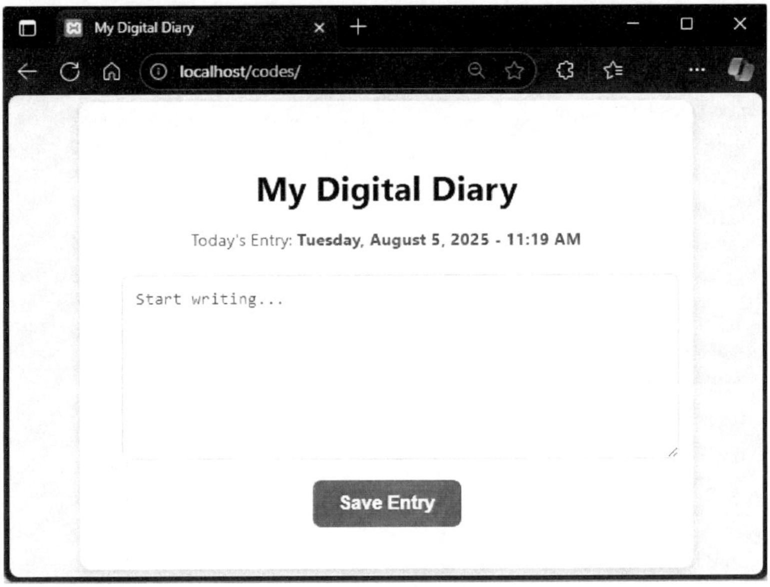

Exploring application behaviour: A practical run-through

- **Valid scenario:** When a user loads the page, the PHP script runs successfully on the server. The user sees a clean, formatted page with the current date, such as **Today's Entry: Tuesday, August 5, 2025 - 11:19 AM**. The browser's **View Page Source** shows the final HTML output, not the PHP code that generated it:

```
<!DOCTYPE html>
<html lang="en">
<head>
    <meta charset="UTF-8">
    <meta name="viewport" content="width=device-width, initial-scale=1.0">
    <title>My Digital Diary</title>
    <style>
        body {
            background-color: #f0f2f5;
            font-family: -apple-system, BlinkMacSystemFont, "Segoe UI", Roboto,
                         Helvetica, Arial, sans-serif;
            display: flex;
            justify-content: center;
            align-items: center;
            height: 100vh;
            margin: 0;
        }
        .diary-container {
            background-color: #ffffff;
            padding: 40px;
```

```
            border-radius: 12px;
            box-shadow: 0 4px 12px rgba(0, 0, 0, 0.1);
            width: 100%;
            max-width: 500px;
            text-align: center;
        }
        h1 {
            color: #1c1e21;
            margin-bottom: 8px;
        }
        .entry p {
            color: #606770;
            font-size: 1rem;
            margin-bottom: 24px;
        }
        textarea {
            width: 100%;
            height: 150px;
            border: 1px solid #dddfe2;
            border-radius: 8px;
            padding: 12px;
            font-size: 1rem;
            resize: vertical;
            margin-bottom: 16px;
        }
        button {
            background-color: #1877f2;
            color: #ffffff;
            border: none;
            border-radius: 8px;
            padding: 12px 24px;
            font-size: 1.1rem;
            font-weight: bold;
            cursor: pointer;
            transition: background-color 0.3s;
        }
        button:hover {
            background-color: #166fe5;
        }
    </style>
</head>
<body>
    <main class="diary-container">
        <h1>My Digital Diary</h1>
        <div class="entry">
            <p>
                Today's Entry: <strong><?php echo date("l, F j, Y - h:i A"); ?>
                </strong>
            </p>
            <textarea placeholder="Start writing..."></textarea>
            <button>Save Entry</button>
```

```
        </div>
    </main>
</body>
</html>
```

- **Error case (What if Apache is off?):** If you stop the Apache server in XAMPP and try to access localhost, your browser shows an error like **This site can't be reached** or **Unable to connect**. This confirms that the browser needs a running web server to process the request:

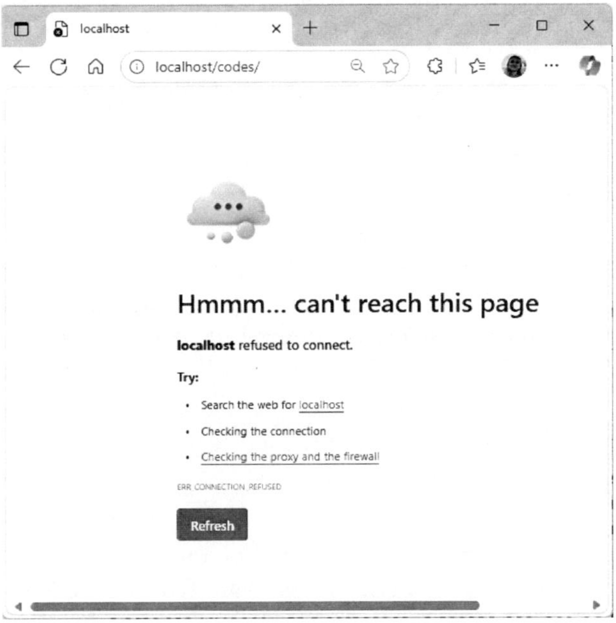

Harnessing dynamic content in real-world contexts

The simple act of displaying today's date is a building block for countless real-world features.

- News websites use it to timestamp articles.
- E-commerce sites use it to show "Order placed on..." confirmations.
- Social media platforms use it to show when a post was published.

This dynamic capability is the core reason PHP is so powerful: it builds web pages that are alive with fresh, relevant information.

Basic PHP syntax essentials

Let's quickly recap the fundamental syntax rules we saw in our application.

PHP tags

All PHP code must be enclosed within PHP tags. The server uses these to distinguish PHP instructions from other content like HTML. The most common form is:

```
<?php
    . . .
?>.
```

The echo statement

echo is used to send output to the browser. It can be a string of text, a number, or the result of a function. While it looks like a function, it's technically a **language construct**, meaning it's a core part of the language. You can use it with or without parentheses:

```
echo "Hello";
echo("Hello");
```

Adding comments in PHP

Comments are lines in your code that are ignored by the PHP interpreter. They are for humans to read, helping to explain what the code does. There are two main types:

```
<?php
// This is a single-line comment. It's great for short notes.
# This is also a single-line comment. (Less common but works)
/*
  This is a multi-line comment block.
  It's perfect for longer explanations that span several lines.
*/
echo "Hello with comments!"; // Comments can also be placed at the end of a line.
?>
```

Adding comments is a critical habit for writing clean, maintainable code that you and others can understand later.

Wrapping up

- **Web Server fundamentals:** We learned that a web server like Apache is needed to process and run PHP code.
- **Local environment:** Setting up a local server with XAMPP allows for fast, private, and offline web development.
- **The htdocs folder:** This is the web root directory where all our web-accessible projects must live.
- **Executing PHP:** We run PHP scripts by starting the Apache server and navigating to the file's URL via localhost.
- **PHP in HTML:** PHP code can be embedded directly into an HTML file to create dynamic content, like inserting the current date.
- **Core syntax:** We were introduced to the essential PHP tags (<?php ?>), the echo statement for output, and how to write comments.

Fantastic work! You have successfully transformed your computer from a simple machine into a powerful web development studio. You've installed and configured a professional-grade server environment, written your first lines of PHP, and built a dynamic web page that combines HTML, CSS, and PHP. This foundation is the single most important step in your journey. You are now equipped with the essential tools and understanding to start building real applications.

In the next *Chapter 3: Level up your coding – Visual Studio Code (VS Code) setup*, we will dive into the Visual Studio Code setup and installing necessary extensions.

Chapter 3

Section 01: Ready, set, code! – Your modern developer toolkit

Level up your coding – Visual Studio Code (VS Code) setup

What you'll learn

- Why VS Code is essential?
- Installing VS Code
- Navigating the interface
- Adding powerful extensions
- Organizing project workspaces
- Integrating Git for version control

Welcome to your new digital workshop! Think of a professional chef. They don't just use any old pot or pan; they have a specific set of tools that help them work efficiently, cleanly, and creatively. For a web developer, your most important tool is your code editor. It's where you'll write, organize, debug, and manage every line of code for your web applications.

In this chapter, we're setting up **Visual Studio Code** (**VS Code**), an industry-leading editor that is powerful yet friendly for beginners. Mastering your editor is the first step toward writing clean, professional code with confidence. It will be our central hub for building everything from simple scripts to the complex AI-powered applications that lie ahead, all running on your XAMPP server.

Why choose VS Code?

You have many choices for code editors, so why does nearly everyone, from beginners to seasoned professionals at companies like Google and Microsoft, recommend VS Code? The answer is simple: it hits the perfect balance of power, simplicity, and flexibility.

- **It's free and open source:** VS Code is completely free, with no hidden costs. It's built by Microsoft and improved by a massive community of developers, meaning it's constantly updated with new features and security patches.
- **Lightweight but powerful:** Unlike older, heavier programs called IDEs (Integrated Development Environments), VS Code starts fast and stays responsive. But don't let its speed fool you; it has powerful features like built-in debugging, Git version control, and an integrated terminal.
- **Endless extensibility:** The real magic of VS Code is its Marketplace. You can install extensions—small add-ons—that give the editor new capabilities. Need better PHP code suggestions? There's an extension for that. Want to connect to a database? There's an extension for that, too. This means you can tailor your editor to fit your exact needs.

In short, VS Code is the perfect companion for your PHP journey because it grows with you. It's simple enough for your first **Hello, World!** script but powerful enough for the final, AI-driven project we'll build in this book.

Downloading and installing VS Code

Let's get the tool installed. The process is straightforward and only takes a few minutes.

1. **Visit the official website:** Open your web browser and navigate to the official Visual Studio Code download page: **https://code.visualstudio.com/download**.

2. **Choose your operating system:** Click the **big blue button** according to the operating operator you are working on to download it. We will be using Windows based VS Code.
3. **Run the installer:**
   a. **On Windows:** Double-click the downloaded **.exe** file. **Accept the license agreement** and **proceed** through the installation wizard. On the **Select Additional Tasks** screen, we highly recommend checking all the boxes, especially **Add to PATH** (which is usually on by default) and the **Open with Code** options. This will let you right-click on a folder and open it directly in VS Code, which is incredibly useful.

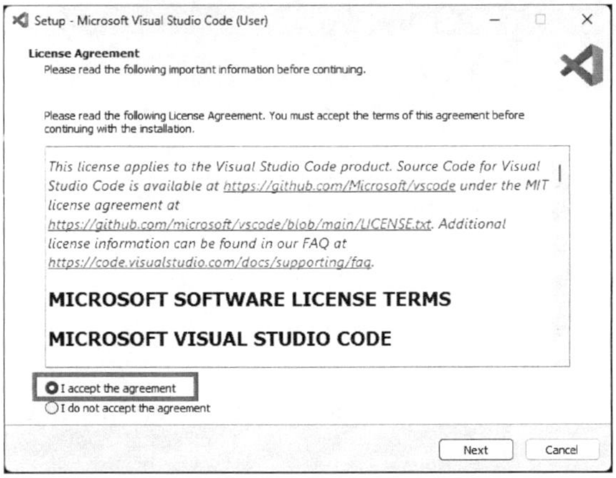

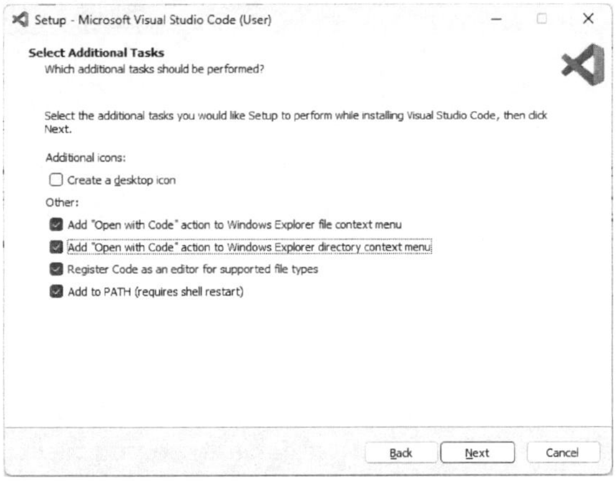

   b. **On Mac:** Double-click the downloaded **.zip** file to extract the application. Then, drag the Visual Studio Code.app file into your Applications folder.

   c. **On Linux:** You likely downloaded a **.deb** (for Debian/Ubuntu) or **.rpm** (for Fedora/Red Hat) file. You can typically install it by double-clicking the file or by using your distribution's software installation tool.

4. Once the installation is complete, go ahead and launch Visual Studio Code for the first time. You are greeted with a **Welcome** screen, which you can close to see the main editor interface.

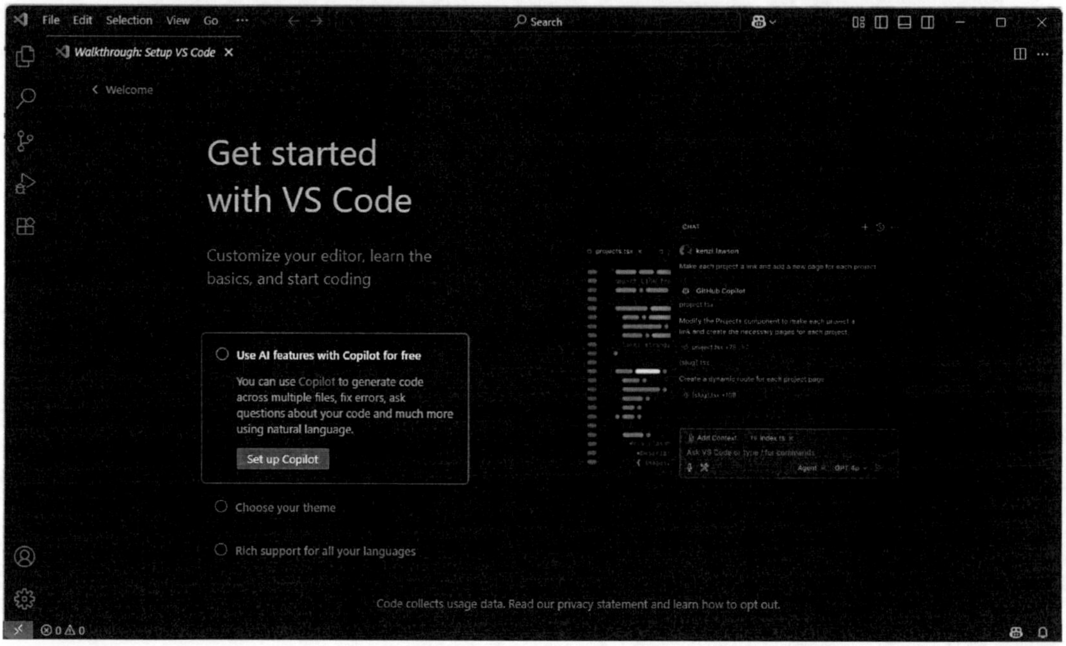

From now on, you'll be creating your project folders inside the **htdocs\codes** directory of your XAMPP installation (e.g., C:\xampp\htdocs\codes\my-first-project) and opening them here in VS Code.

Navigating the interface

At first glance, the VS Code interface might look a bit busy, but it's logically organized into five main areas. Let's take a quick tour so you feel right at home:

- **Activity Bar (far left):** This is your main navigation bar. Each icon switches the context of the Side Bar next to it.
    - **Explorer:** Shows all the files and folders in your current project. You'll spend most of your time here.

- **Search:** A powerful tool to find and replace text across your entire project.
- **Source Control:** Where you'll interact with Git for version control.
- **Run and Debug:** Your hub for debugging PHP scripts.
- **Extensions:** The gateway to the VS Code Marketplace, where you'll install add-ons.

- **Side Bar (left panel):** This panel changes based on what you've selected in the Activity Bar. If you click the Explorer icon, it shows your project files. If you click the Extensions icon, it becomes the Marketplace browser. You can toggle it open and closed by pressing Ctrl+B (or Cmd+B on Mac).
- **Editor Group (center):** This is the main area where you'll write your code. You can have multiple files open at once in different tabs. You can even split your view to see two or more files side-by-side—a great feature for comparing code or looking at an HTML file and its CSS at the same time.
- **Panel (bottom):** This area can be toggled open (Ctrl+`` or Cmd+``) and serves multiple purposes. It contains:
    - **Terminal:** A built-in command line. This is extremely useful for running Git commands or other tools without leaving your editor.
    - **Problems:** Shows any errors, warnings, or hints detected in your code.
    - **Output:** Displays messages from various extensions and tasks.
    - **Debug Console:** Shows output from your debugging sessions.
- **Status Bar (bottom edge):** The blue bar at the very bottom provides at-a-glance information about your project, such as the current Git branch, file encoding, and any errors or warnings.

Spend a minute clicking each icon in the Activity Bar to see how it changes the Side Bar. Open and close the bottom Panel. Getting comfortable with this layout will make your coding workflow much smoother.

Installing must-have extensions

This is where we turn VS Code from a great text editor into a super-smart PHP development environment. We're going to install a few key extensions that will provide code completion, debugging help, and quality checks.

To get started, click on the **Extensions** icon in the **Activity Bar** (it looks like four squares, with one flying off). This opens the **Marketplace** search bar.

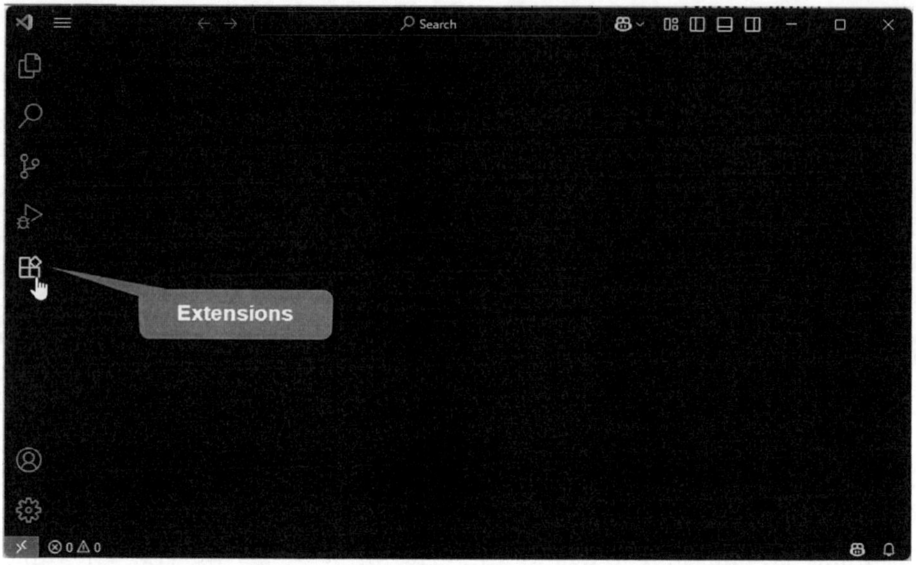

PHP Intelephense

This is arguably the most important extension for any PHP developer using VS Code. It gives you **IntelliSense** for your PHP code, which means it intelligently suggests variable names, functions, and more as you type. It also helps you quickly navigate your code by letting you jump to the definition of a function or class.

1. In the **Extensions** search bar, type **PHP Intelephense**.
2. The top result is the one by **Ben Mewburn**.

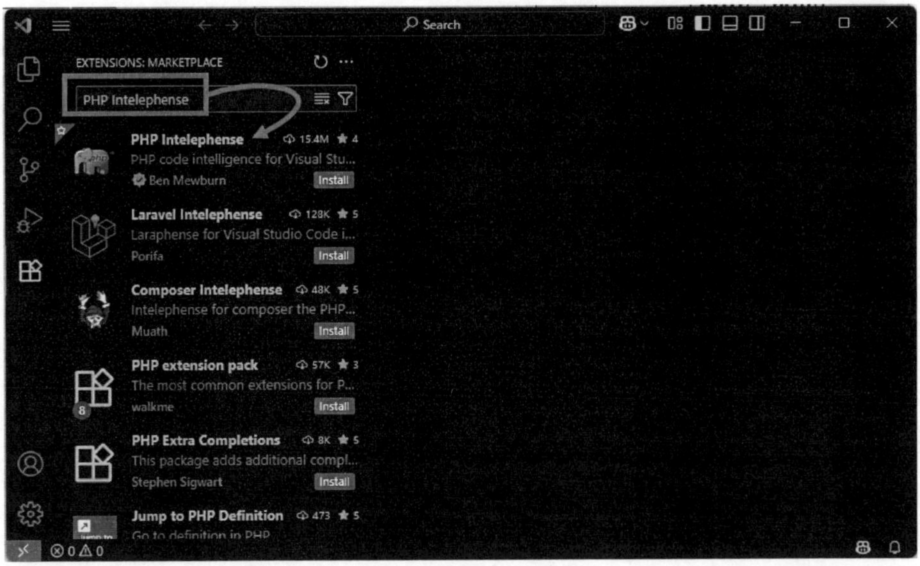

3. Click the **blue Install** button.
4. An **alert** dialog box appears asking you whether you trust the publisher, since VS Code has no control over the behaviour of the extension. Click **Trust Publisher & Install**.

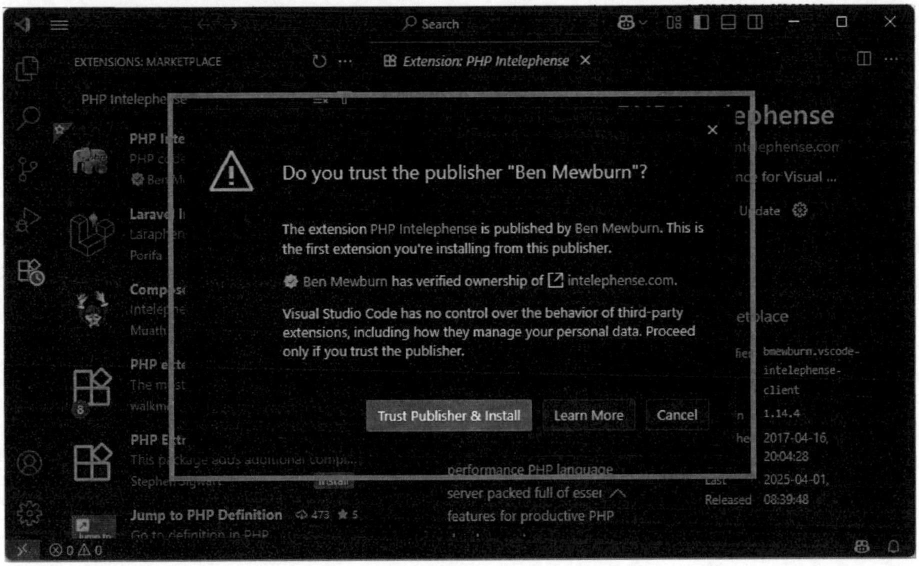

5. It installs globally, so you only need to do this once.

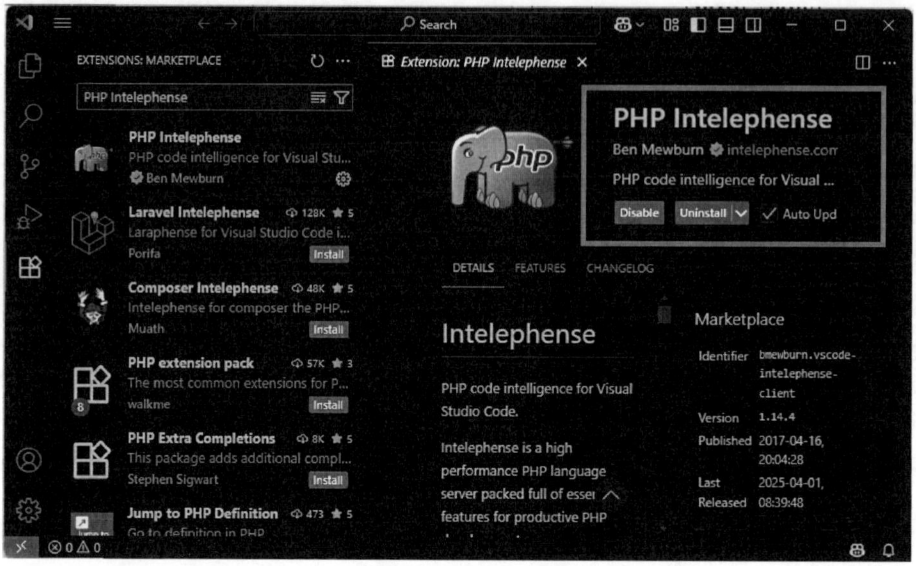

Now, when you start writing PHP code, you'll see helpful pop-ups and suggestions that will save you from typos and looking up function names.

PHP Debug

In the past, many developers would debug their code by littering it with **echo** or **var_dump()** statements. This is messy and inefficient. A real debugger lets you pause your code's execution, inspect variables, and step through logic line by line. The **PHP Debug** extension integrates this capability right into VS Code.

1. In the **Extensions** search bar, type **PHP Debug**.
2. The top result is the one by **Xdebug**.

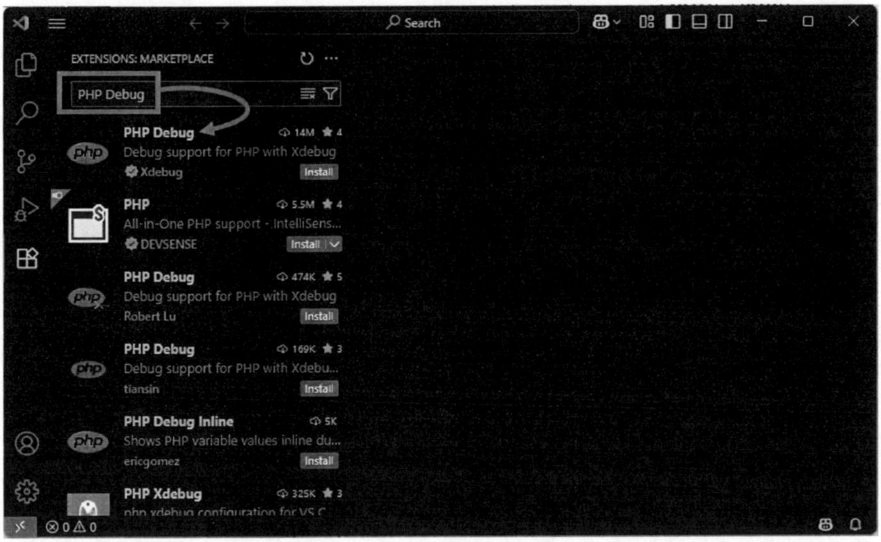

3. Click **Install**. Again, an alert dialog box appears asking you whether you trust the publisher, since VS Code has no control over the behaviour of the extension. Click **Trust Publisher & Install**.

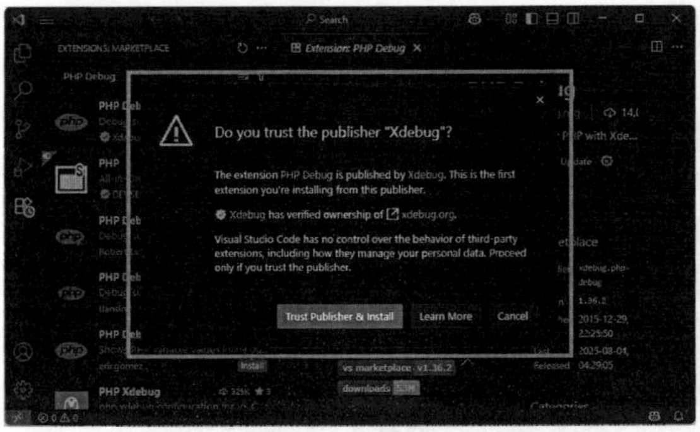

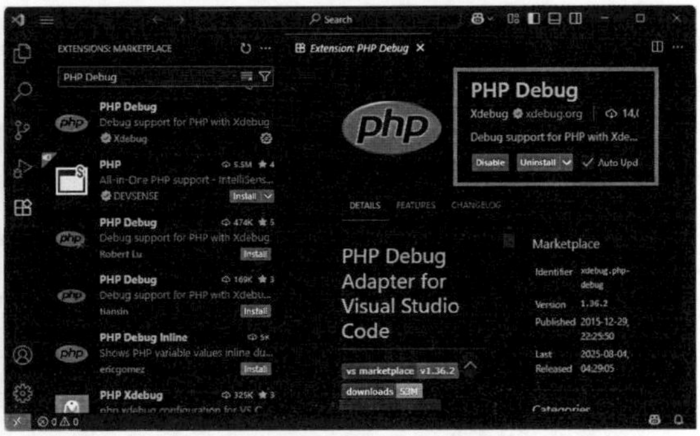

For this extension to work, it needs to connect to the Xdebug module that comes with PHP in your XAMPP installation. This requires a small configuration change in your php.ini file, which is located in your C:\xampp\php directory.

Live Server for HTML/CSS/PHP

A **live server** automatically reloads your browser when you save a file. While many extensions provide this for static HTML and CSS, our setup is even simpler. Since you set up XAMPP in Chapter 2, you already have a powerful Apache web server running.

Our workflow will be:

1. Ensure your **Apache server** is **running** in the **XAMPP Control Panel**.
2. Write your PHP and HTML code in **VS Code** in a project folder located at **C:\xampp\htdocs\codes\your-project-name**.
3. Open your browser and navigate to **http://localhost/codes/your-project-name**.
4. After you save a change in VS Code, simply switch to your browser and press **refresh** (F5 or Ctrl+R) to see the result.

This is the most direct and reliable way to test your PHP applications and is the standard practice we will use throughout this book. No extension is needed for this core functionality.

CodeSniffer and linting tools

A **linter** is a tool that analyzes your code for potential errors and stylistic inconsistencies. A **CodeSniffer** checks if your code adheres to a specific coding standard (like PSR-12, the community standard for PHP). This helps you write cleaner, more professional code from day one.

The most popular extension for this is phpcs.

1. In the **Extensions** search bar, type **phpcs**.

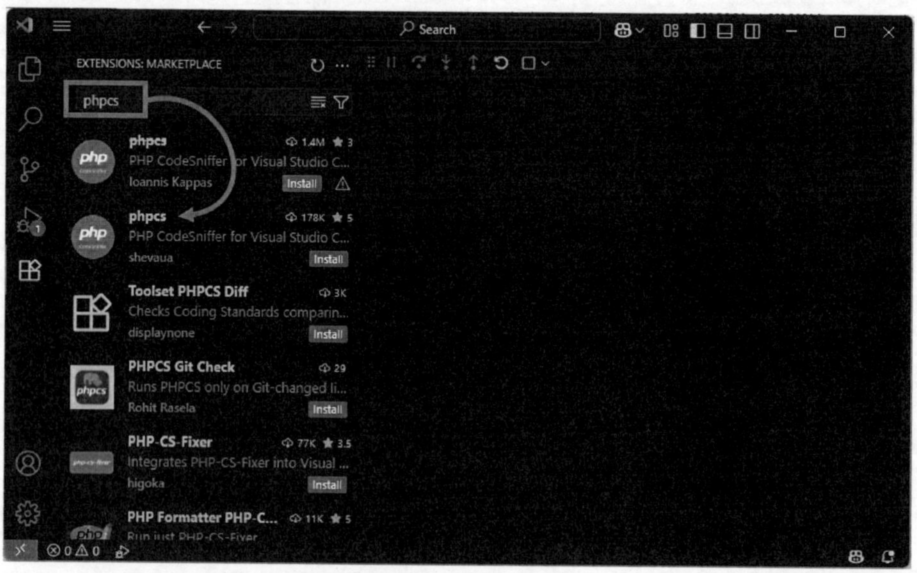

2. Find the extension by **shevaua** and click **Install**.

This tool will underline messy or non-standard code right in your editor, often with a message explaining the problem, helping you learn best practices as you go.

Customizing themes and shortcuts

A comfortable environment is a productive one. VS Code lets you change its entire color scheme with just a few clicks.

1. Go to **File → Preferences → Theme → Color Theme** (or use the shortcut Ctrl+K Ctrl+T).

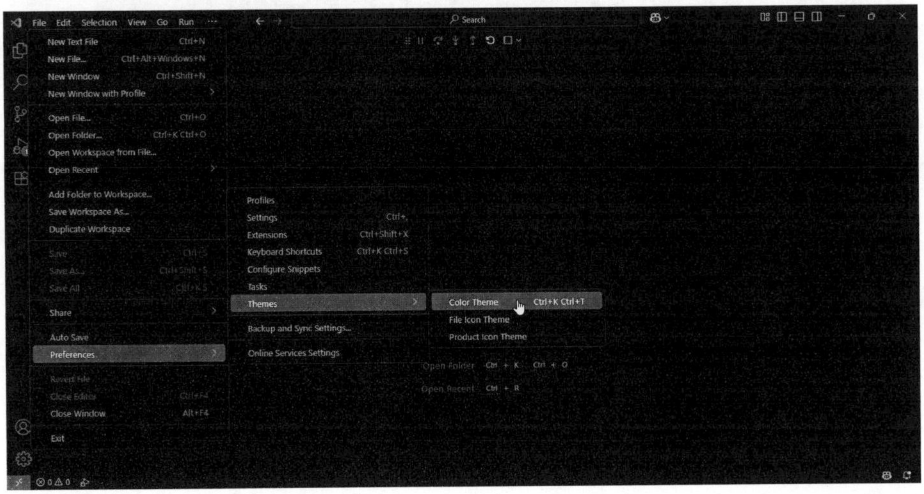

2. A **dropdown** menu appears with a list of built-in themes. Use your arrow keys to preview them in real-time.

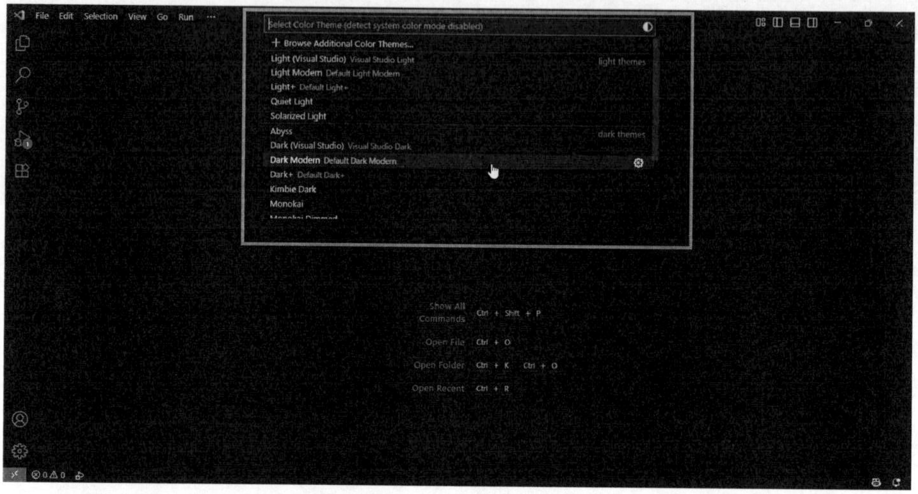

3. Popular choices include **Dark Modern (the default)**, **Light Modern**, and **Monokai**. Find one that is easy on your eyes and click to select it.
4. You can also download thousands of other themes from the Marketplace. Just search for **theme** in the **Extensions** view.

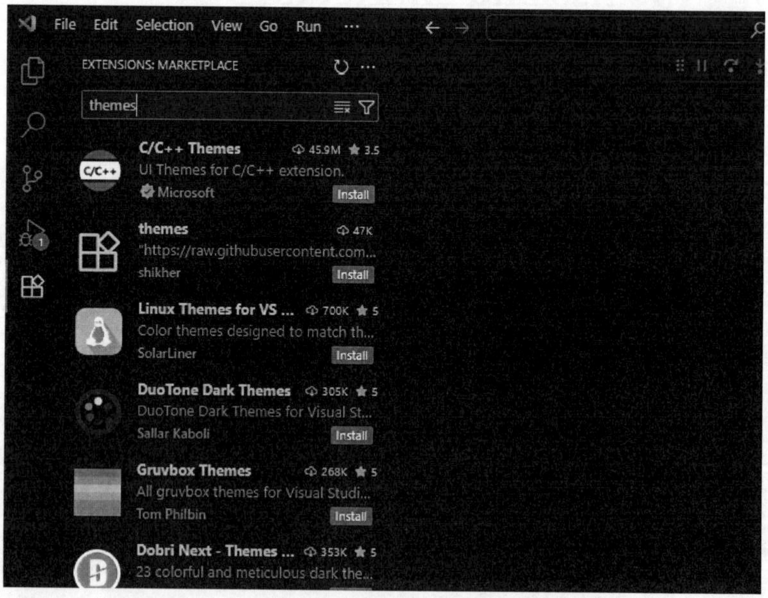

For shortcuts, VS Code has a handy graphical interface for viewing and changing them. Go to **File → Preferences → Keyboard Shortcuts**.

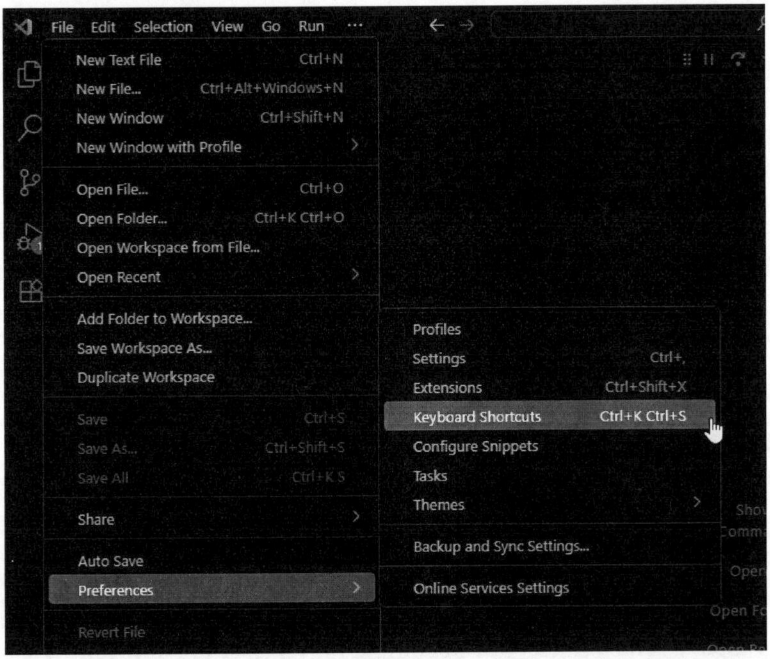

Here you can search for any command (e.g., **Save File**) and see or change its associated **keybinding**. For now, the defaults are excellent, but it's good to know where this is for the future.

Setting up PHP, HTML, and CSS integration

Modern web pages are a mix of languages, and VS Code handles this blend seamlessly. You don't need to do much to set it up; it just works.

When you open a project folder from your htdocs/codes directory, you'll have files like index.php and style.css. VS Code knows what to do with each one:

- In your **.php** files, you can write PHP code inside **<?php ... ?>** tags and standard HTML outside of them. The editor will provide the correct syntax highlighting for both.
- The **PHP Intelephense extension** will only activate its suggestions on PHP code.

- VS Code has **built-in Emmet support**, a massive time-saver for writing HTML. For example, in an HTML or PHP file, type **nav>ul>li*3>a** and press **Tab**. It will instantly expand to:

```
<nav>
    <ul>
        <li><a href=""></a></li>
        <li><a href=""></a></li>
        <li><a href=""></a></li>
    </ul>
</nav>
```

This makes building out your page structure incredibly fast. When you link a CSS file in your HTML using a **<link>** tag, VS Code can even provide suggestions for your CSS class names right in your HTML file. This deep integration is what makes it so powerful for web development.

Crafting workspaces for multi-file projects

As your projects grow, you might be working with multiple related folders. A VS Code **Workspace** lets you group multiple project folders together in one window.

A more common use for beginners, however, is to simply save your single project folder's settings as a workspace. This saves your specific UI layout, extension settings, and open files for that project.

Here's how to do it:

1. Open your main project folder (**File → Open Folder...**).

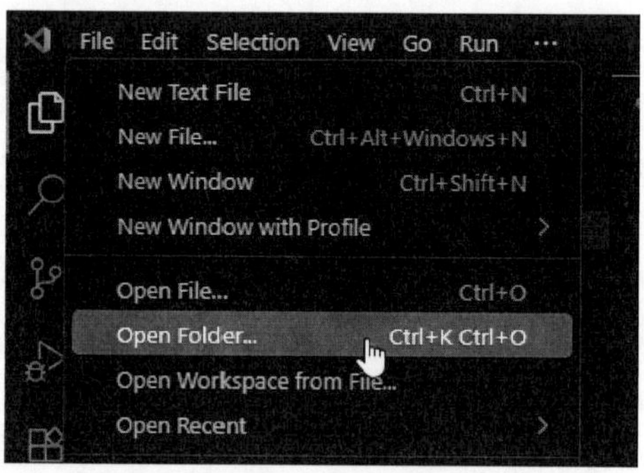

2. Arrange your editor panels exactly how you like them. Maybe you have two files open side-by-side.
3. Go to **File → Save Workspace As...**.

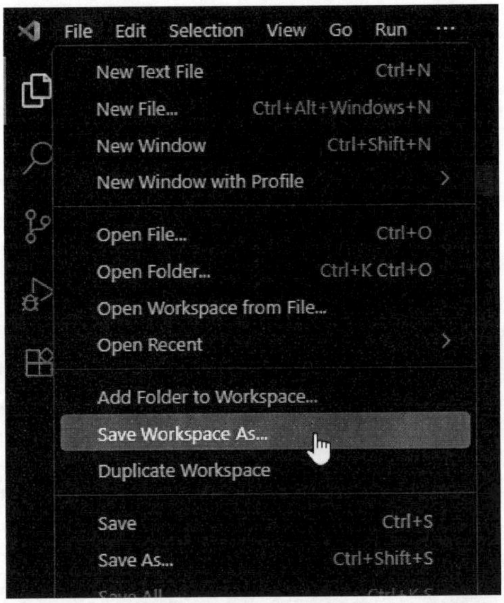

4. Give the workspace file a name (e.g., my-first-project.code-workspace) and save it outside of your project folder (e.g., in your main Documents or Development folder).

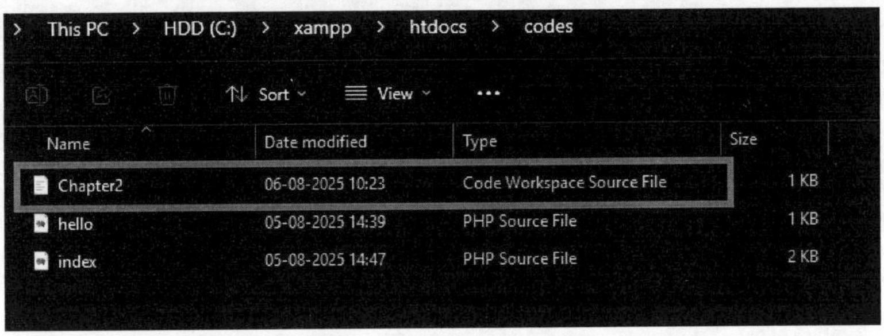

Now, instead of opening the folder, you can just double-click that **.code-workspace** file. VS Code will launch and restore your entire setup—all the right folders, files, and panel layouts—instantly. It's a small step that makes managing bigger projects much tidier.

Version control: Git in VS Code basics

Version control is one of the most crucial skills for a modern developer. Think of it as a time machine for your code. It tracks every single change you make to your project, allowing you to revert to a previous working version if you make a mistake, see exactly who changed what, and collaborate seamlessly with other developers. The industry-standard tool for this is **Git**, and VS Code has incredible, built-in support for it.

Let's get you set up from scratch.

Download and install Git

Before VS Code can use Git, it needs to be installed on your computer.

1. **Navigate to the official Git website:** Open your browser and go to **https://git-scm.com/downloads**. The site detects your operating system and shows the appropriate download link.

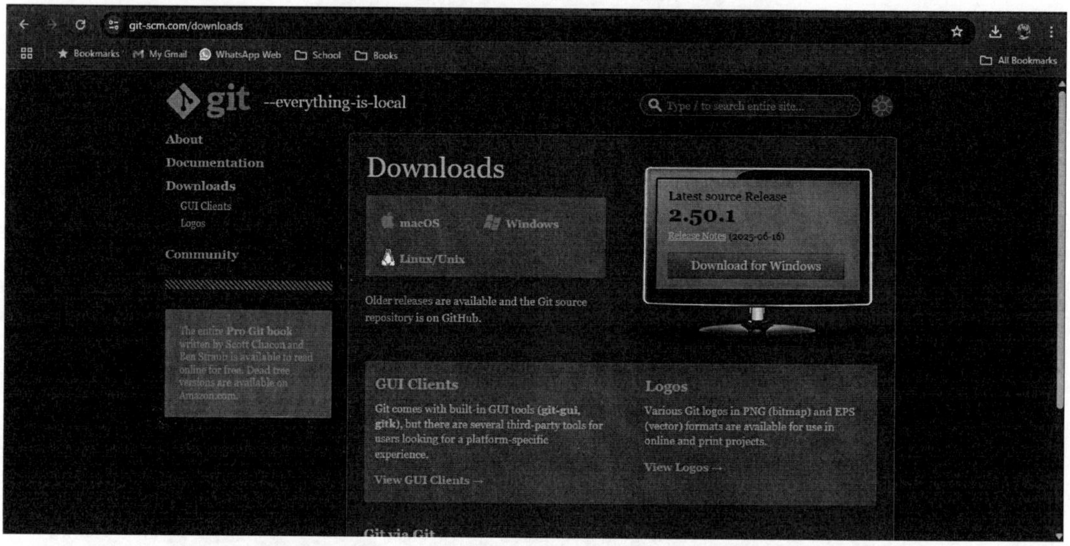

2. **Download the Installer:** Click the button to download the installer for your system (Windows, macOS, or Linux).
3. **Run the Installer (Windows walkthrough):** The Git installer for Windows has many options, but for our purposes, the default settings are almost always what you need.
    - Launch the downloaded **.exe** file.
    - When prompted, accept the **GNU General Public License**.

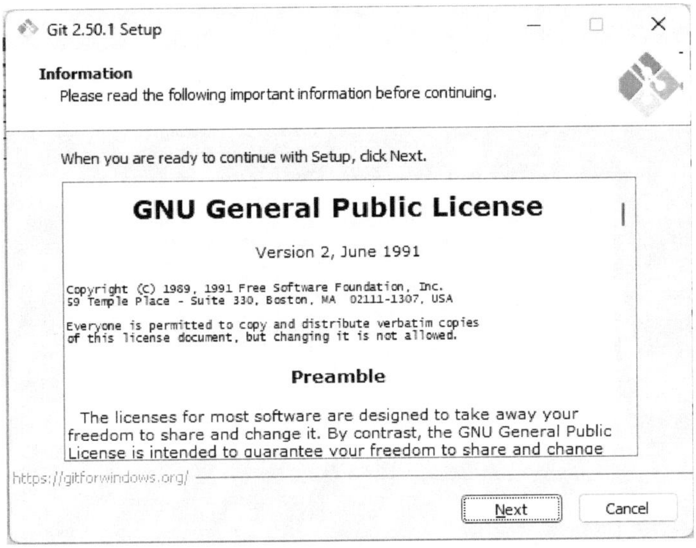

- **Select Components:** You can leave the default components checked.

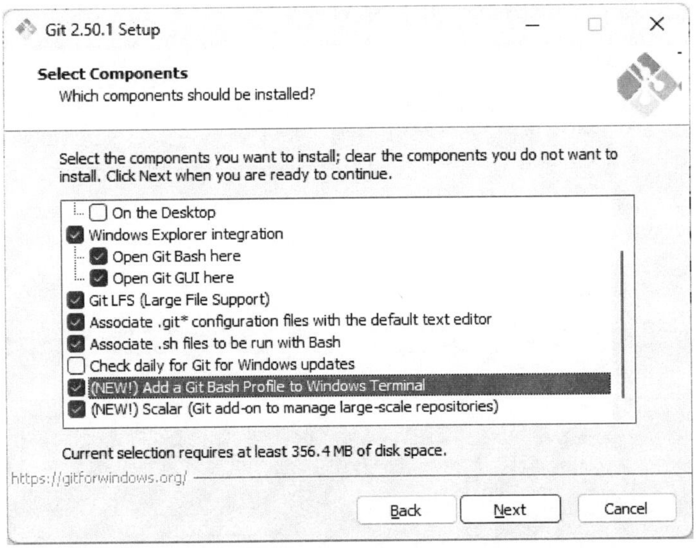

- **Choosing the default editor used by Git:** The installer may ask you to choose a default text editor. The default is often **Vim**, which is a powerful but complex command-line editor. For simplicity, it's a good idea to select **Use Visual Studio Code as Git's default editor** from the dropdown list.

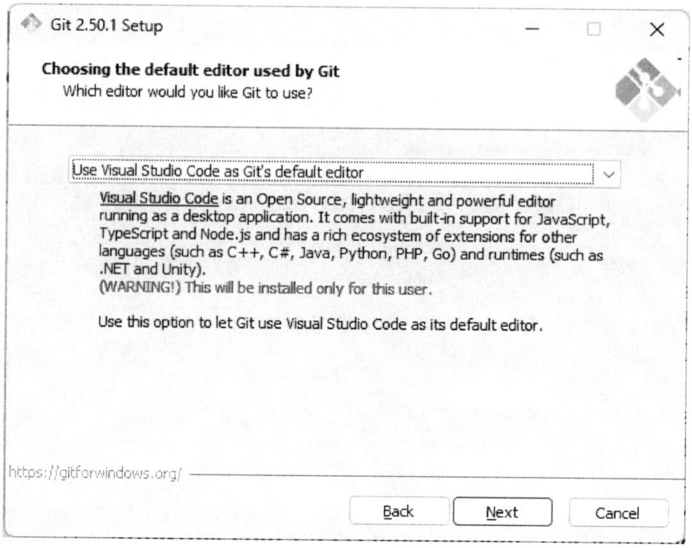

- **Adjusting the name of the initial branch: Let Git decide**. The default is "main." This is the modern standard, so just click **Next**.

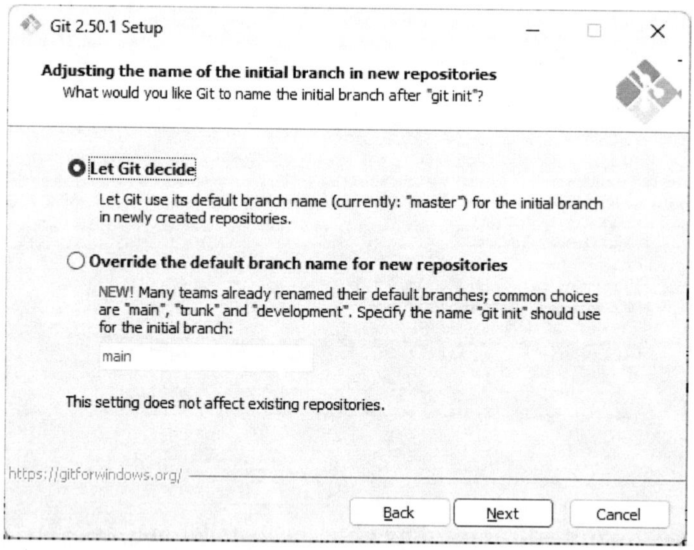

- **Adjusting your PATH environment:** This is the most important step. Ensure you select **Git from the command line and also from 3rd-party software.** This is what allows VS Code to find and use Git automatically.

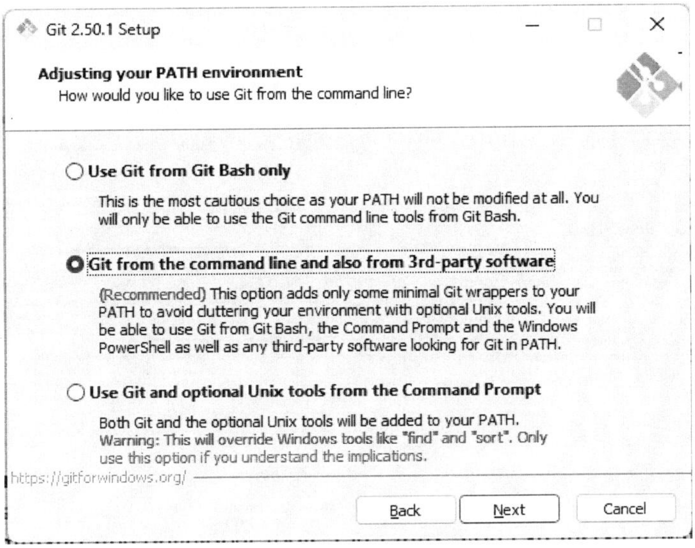

- Continue clicking **Next** through the remaining steps (SSH executable, HTTPS transport backend, line ending conversions, etc.). The default options are perfect for our needs.

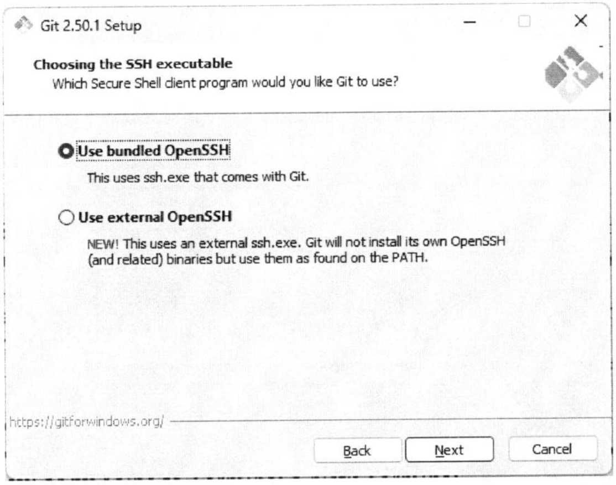

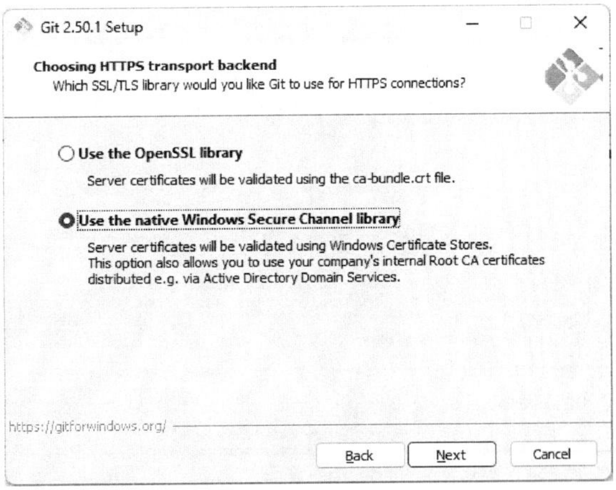

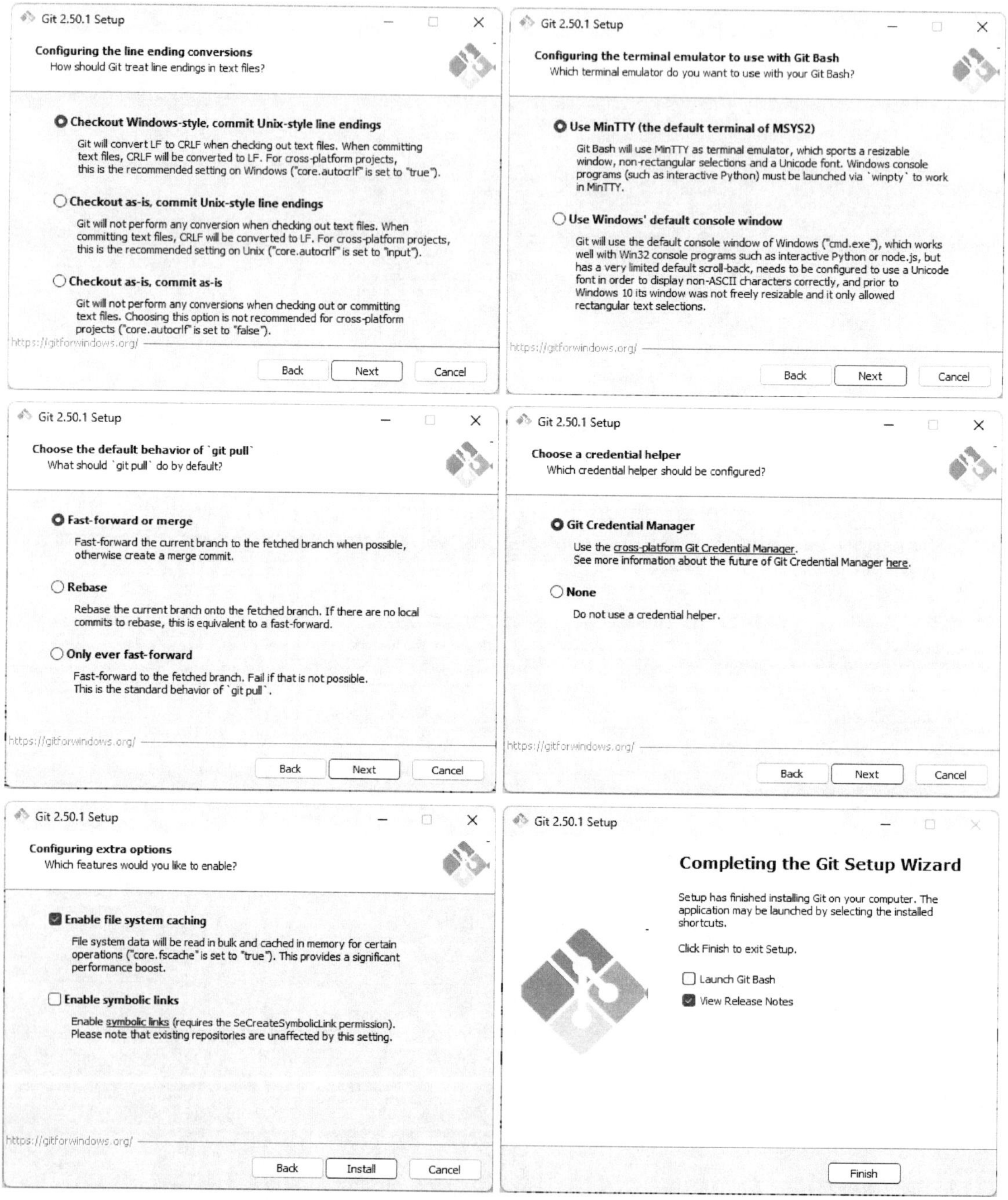
Git 2.50.1 Setup
Configuring the line ending conversions
How should Git treat line endings in text files?
Checkout Windows-style, commit Unix-style line endings
Git will convert LF to CRLF when checking out text files. When committing text files, CRLF will be converted to LF. For cross-platform projects, this is the recommended setting on Windows ("core.autocrlf" is set to "true").
Checkout as-is, commit Unix-style line endings
Git will not perform any conversion when checking out text files. When committing text files, CRLF will be converted to LF. For cross-platform projects, this is the recommended setting on Unix ("core.autocrlf" is set to "input").
Checkout as-is, commit as-is
Git will not perform any conversions when checking out or committing text files. Choosing this option is not recommended for cross-platform projects ("core.autocrlf" is set to "false").
https://gitforwindows.org/
Back
Next
Cancel
Git 2.50.1 Setup
Configuring the terminal emulator to use with Git Bash
Which terminal emulator do you want to use with your Git Bash?
Use MinTTY (the default terminal of MSYS2)
Git Bash will use MinTTY as terminal emulator, which sports a resizable window, non-rectangular selections and a Unicode font. Windows console programs (such as interactive Python) must be launched via `winpty` to work in MinTTY.
Use Windows' default console window
Git will use the default console window of Windows ("cmd.exe"), which works well with Win32 console programs such as interactive Python or node.js, but has a very limited default scroll-back, needs to be configured to use a Unicode font in order to display non-ASCII characters correctly, and prior to Windows 10 its window was not freely resizable and it only allowed rectangular text selections.
https://gitforwindows.org/
Back
Next
Cancel
Git 2.50.1 Setup
Choose the default behavior of `git pull`
What should `git pull` do by default?
Fast-forward or merge
Fast-forward the current branch to the fetched branch when possible, otherwise create a merge commit.
Rebase
Rebase the current branch onto the fetched branch. If there are no local commits to rebase, this is equivalent to a fast-forward.
Only ever fast-forward
Fast-forward to the fetched branch. Fail if that is not possible. This is the standard behavior of `git pull`.
https://gitforwindows.org/
Back
Next
Cancel
Git 2.50.1 Setup
Choose a credential helper
Which credential helper should be configured?
Git Credential Manager
Use the cross-platform Git Credential Manager.
See more information about the future of Git Credential Manager here.
None
Do not use a credential helper.
https://gitforwindows.org/
Back
Next
Cancel
Git 2.50.1 Setup
Configuring extra options
Which features would you like to enable?
Enable file system caching
File system data will be read in bulk and cached in memory for certain operations ("core.fscache" is set to "true"). This provides a significant performance boost.
Enable symbolic links
Enable symbolic links (requires the SeCreateSymbolicLink permission). Please note that existing repositories are unaffected by this setting.
https://gitforwindows.org/
Back
Install
Cancel
Git 2.50.1 Setup
Completing the Git Setup Wizard
Setup has finished installing Git on your computer. The application may be launched by selecting the installed shortcuts.
Click Finish to exit Setup.
Launch Git Bash
View Release Notes
Finish

- Finally, click **Install.**

For **macOS** and **Linux** users, Git is often already installed. You can check by opening your terminal and typing git --version. If it's not installed, macOS will typically prompt you to install the command line developer tools. On Linux, you can install it with a simple command like sudo apt-get install git (for Debian/Ubuntu) or sudo yum install git (for CentOS/Fedora).

Configure Git for the first time

After installation, you need to introduce yourself to Git. It needs to know your name and email address so it can label every change you make.

1. Open **Visual Studio Code**.
2. Open the integrated terminal by going to **Terminal → New Terminal**.

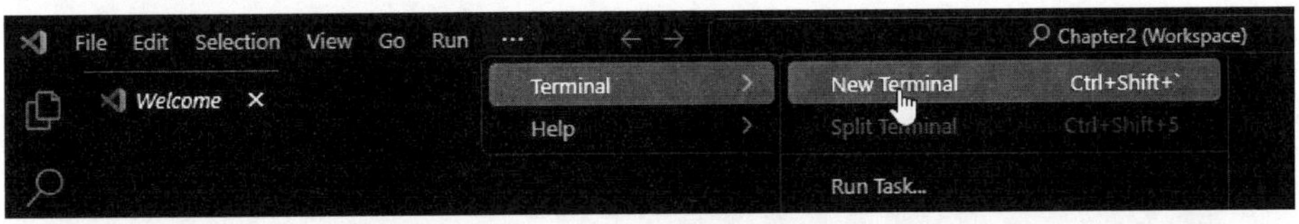

3. In the **terminal panel** that appears at the **bottom**, type the following two commands, pressing **Enter** after each one. Replace **Your Name** and **youremail@example.com** with your actual name and email:

```
<Command Prompt> git config --global user.name "YourName"
<Command Prompt> git config --global user.email "YourEmail@example.com"
```

The **--global** flag means this setting will apply to every Git project on your computer. You only need to do this once!

Using Git inside your VS Code project

Now for the fun part! Let's put Git to work on a project.

1. **Create and open your project folder:** In your XAMPP installation, navigate to the **htdocs\codes** folder (e.g., C:\xampp\htdocs\codes). Create a new folder for this project called **git-chapter3-project**. Now, in VS Code, go to **File → Open Folder...** and open **git-chapter3-project**.
2. **Initialize the Repository:** Click on the **Source Control** icon in the **Activity Bar** on the left (it looks like a branching path). Since this folder isn't being tracked by Git yet, you can see a blue button that says **Initialize Repository**.

3. Click **Initialize Repository**. VS Code runs the git init command in the background. Your project is now a Git repository! The Source Control panel now shows your project files.
4. **The "Change, Stage, Commit" cycle:** This is the fundamental workflow of Git.
   - **Make a change:** Let's create our first file. In the **Explorer** panel, right-click and select **New File**. Name it **index.php**.

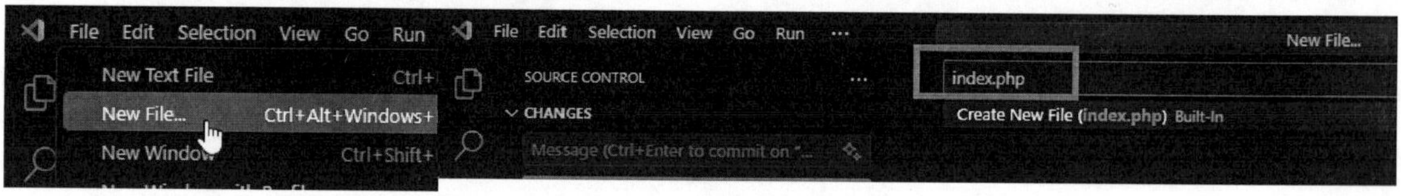

   - Add the following code to it and save the file (Ctrl+S):

```
<!DOCTYPE html>
<html lang="en">
<head>
    <meta charset="UTF-8">
    <title>Git Test Page</title>
</head>
<body>
    <h1>Welcome to My Git-Powered Project!</h1>
    <?php
        echo "<p>PHP is working!</p>";
    ?>
</body>
</html>
```

   - **See the change:** Look at the **Source Control** icon. It now has a **blue badge** with the number '**1**' on it, indicating one untracked change. In the **Explorer**, the index.php file is marked with a '**U**' for "Untracked."

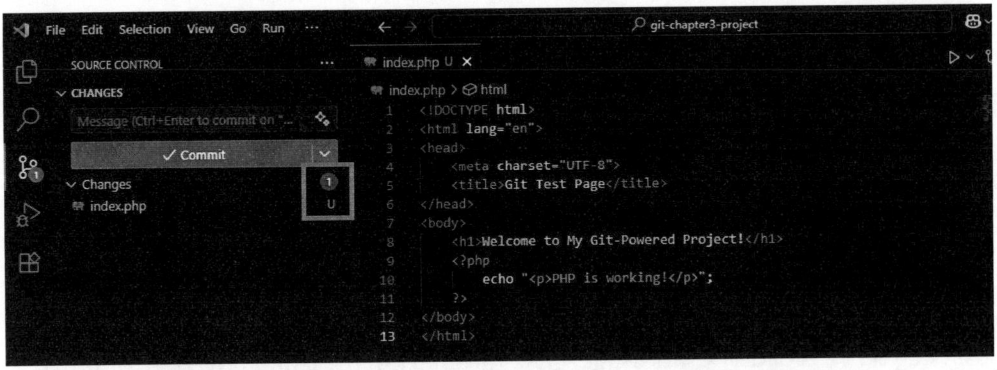

- Stage the change: Go back to the **Source Control** panel. You can see index.php listed under **Changes**. Staging a change tells Git, **I want to include this change in my next save point**. Hover over index.php and click the + icon (**Stage Changes**).

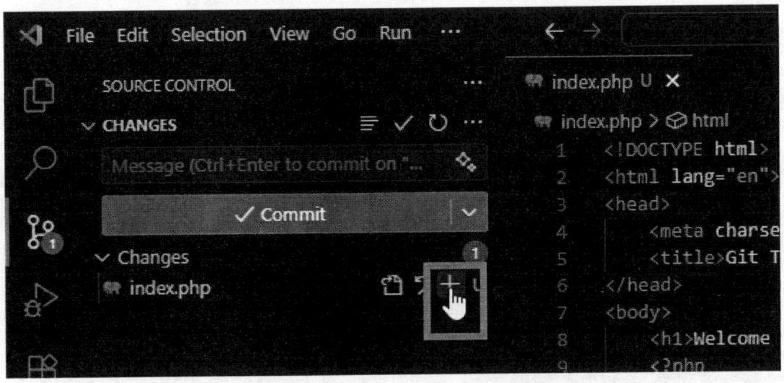

- The file now moves up to a new section called **Staged Changes**, and its status badge will change to an '**A**' for "Added."

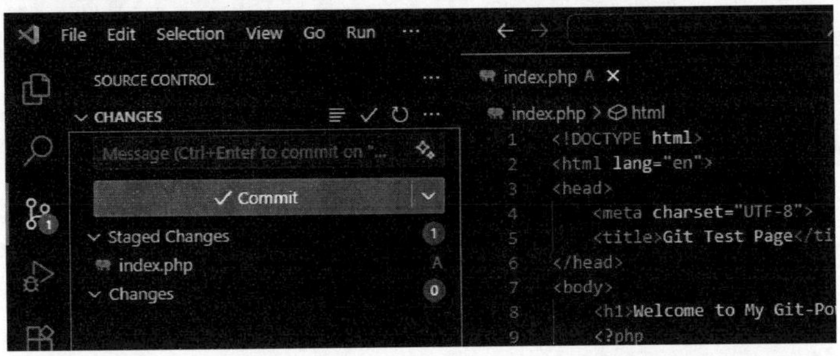

- **Commit the change:** A commit is the official **save point**. In the **message** box at the top of the Source Control panel, type a short, descriptive message about what this save point contains. For your first one, a great message is **Initial commit: Create index.php**.

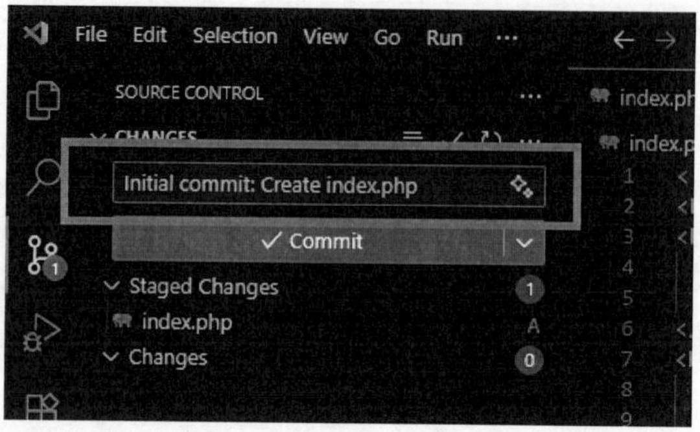

- Once you've typed your message, click the **checkmark icon** above it (**Commit**).
- Congratulations! You've just made your first commit. The file list in the **Source Control** panel is now empty because there are no more un-saved changes. You have a permanent record of your project at this exact moment.

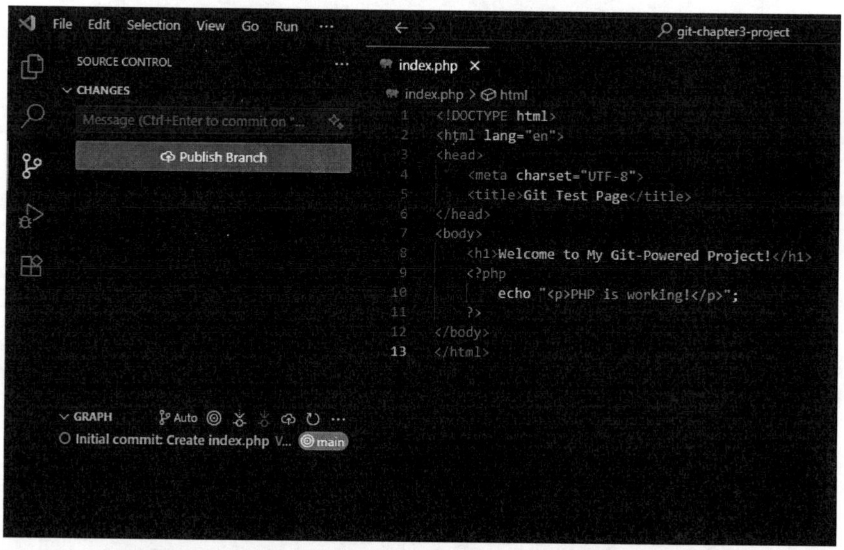

5. **Repeating the cycle:** Let's make another change to see the workflow for modifications. Add a little CSS to your index.php file inside the <head> section and save it.

```
<head>
    <meta charset="UTF-8">
    <title>Git Test Page</title>
    <style>
        body { font-family: sans-serif; background-color: #f0f0f0; }
        h1 { color: #333; }
    </style>
</head>
```

- Look at your **Source Control** panel again. index.php is back under **Changes**, but this time it's marked with an '**M**' for "Modified."

- **Stage** the change by clicking the **+** icon.
- **Commit** the change with a new message, like **Feat: Add basic page styling**. ("Feat" is a common prefix for a new feature).

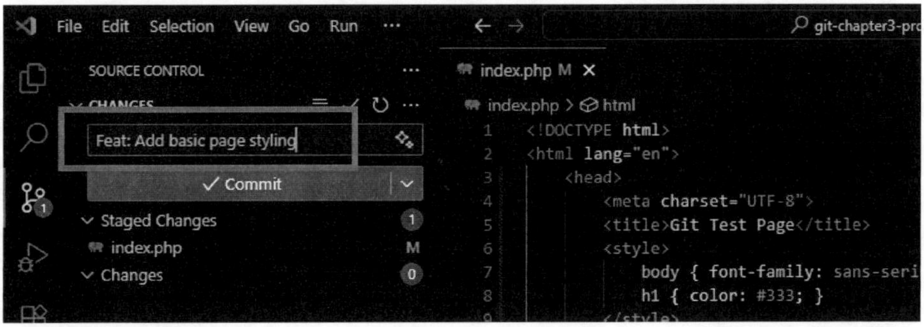

- Click the **checkmark**.

You've now saved a second snapshot of your project's history. This simple "change, stage, commit" cycle is something you will do dozens of times a day as a developer. It provides an incredible safety net and is the foundation for all modern software development.

Wrapping up

In this chapter, we transformed a plain text editor into a professional-grade development environment, fully integrated with our XAMPP server. You're now equipped with the same core toolset that developers around the world use to build fast, secure, and reliable web applications.

- **VS Code fundamentals:** You learned why VS Code is a top choice and how to install it.
- **Interface navigation:** You can now confidently navigate the Activity Bar, Side Bar, Editor, and Panels.

- **Essential extensions:** You installed PHP Intelephense for smart code completion and PHP Debug for future troubleshooting, supercharging your editor for PHP development.
- **XAMPP workflow:** You understand the simple and effective process of coding in VS Code and refreshing the browser to see changes served by Apache.
- **Project workspaces:** You learned how to save your project setup for easy access later.
- **Git integration:** You performed your first Git commit, the foundational skill for modern version control.

Congratulations on setting up your developer cockpit! You've moved beyond simply writing code to thinking about your workflow, efficiency, and code quality. Having a well-configured editor that communicates with your local XAMPP server will pay huge dividends in the chapters to come, making coding feel less like a chore and more like a creative process.

In the next *Chapter 4: Coding with confidence – Building your first project structure*, we'll put this new setup to use by creating a clean, organized folder structure for our very first multi-page web application.

Chapter 4

Section 01: Ready, set, code! – Your modern developer toolkit

Coding with confidence - Building your first project structure

What you'll learn

- Organizing project files
- Building multipage websites
- Saving work with Git
- Professional naming conventions
- Linking a shared stylesheet
- Creating a portfolio site

Welcome to one of the most important chapters for your future as a developer! Think about building a house. Would you just start throwing bricks and wood into a pile? Of course not. You'd start with a blueprint—a plan that shows where the kitchen, bedrooms, and bathrooms go. A good project structure is the blueprint for your web application. It keeps your code organized, easy to find, and simple to update.

In this chapter, we'll move beyond single-file scripts and build a clean, professional foundation for a complete, multipage website. This organized approach is what separates hobbyists from professional developers, and it's a skill that will serve you every single day.

The importance of project structure

Before we write another line of code, let's talk about organization. When your project only has one or two files, it's easy to keep track of everything. But what happens when you have ten pages, twenty images, and multiple stylesheets? It becomes a mess.

A logical project structure offers three huge benefits:

- **It's easy to maintain**. When you need to update your site's navigation menu or change a colour, you'll know exactly which file to open. You won't have to hunt through dozens of disorganized files.
- **It's scalable**. As your project grows, a good structure grows with it. Adding new pages, features, or sections is simple because you already have a designated place for everything.
- **It's collaborative**. If you ever work with another developer, they will be able to understand your project instantly because you're using a standard, logical layout.

Starting with a clean structure now will save you countless hours of frustration down the road. It's a habit of a professional developer.

Creating folders

Let's establish a simple, powerful folder structure that you can use for most of your web projects. For our purposes, we'll start with two primary folders:

- **public:** This folder will contain all the files that a user's browser can access directly. Your main PHP files, like index.php, about.php, and contact.php, will live here. Think of it as the public-facing part of your website.
- **assets:** This folder is for all the supporting files that your PHP pages will use, but that users don't need to access directly. This includes your CSS for styling, JavaScript for interactivity, and images. We will create sub-folders inside assets to keep things even tidier (css, js, images).
- **includes** and **views**, we will introduce them later in the book when our applications become more complex. For now, public and assets are all we need.

Let's create this structure. First, open your XAMPP installation folder:

1. Go into the **htdocs/codes** directory, and create a new folder for our project called **my-website**.
2. Now, in **VS Code** open this empty **my-website** folder by selecting **File → Open Folder...**.

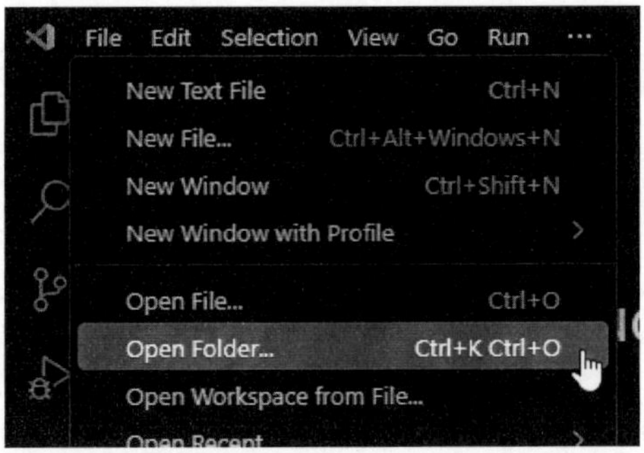

3. In the **Explorer** panel on the left side of VS Code, right-click in the empty space of the **Explorer** panel and select **New Folder**.

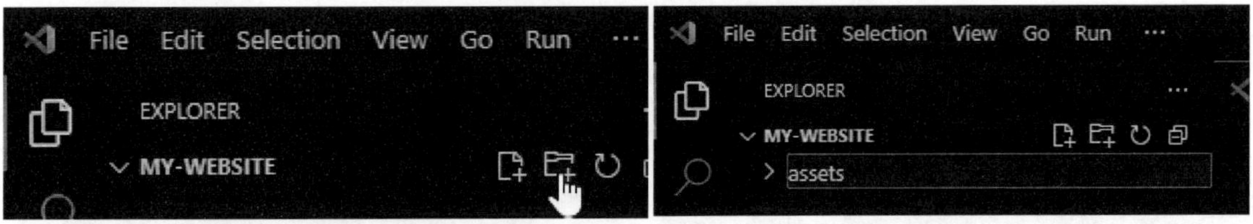

4. Name this folder **assets** and press **Enter**.
5. Right-click again in the empty space below **assets** and select **New Folder**.
6. Name this folder **public** and press **Enter**.
7. Now, right-click directly on the **assets** folder you just created, select **New Folder**, and name it **css**.

Your VS Code Explorer should now look like this:

```
/MY-WEBSITE/
|-- /assets/
|   |-- /css/
|-- /public/
```

Naming conventions and file management

How you name your files and folders is just as important as where you put them. Clear, consistent names make your project easy to understand at a glance. Here are the simple rules we'll follow throughout this book:

- **Use lowercase letters**. about.php is better than About.PHP. This avoids issues on different operating systems, some of which are case-sensitive.

- **Separate words with hyphens**. If a file name needs multiple words, use a hyphen (-). For example, contact-form-handler.php is much easier to read than contactformhandler.php. This style is often called **kebab-case**.
- **Be descriptive but concise**. A file named contact.php is perfect. A file named the-page-where-users-can-contact-us.php is not.
- **Never use spaces**. Spaces in file names can cause unexpected errors on web servers. Always use hyphens instead.

Stick to these rules, and your projects will be clean and professional from day one.

Your first multipage app

Now let's create the actual PHP files for our site inside the public folder.

1. **Create index.php:** In the VS Code **Explorer**, right-click on the **public** folder and select **New File...**. Type **index.php** and press **Enter**. An empty editor tab opens.

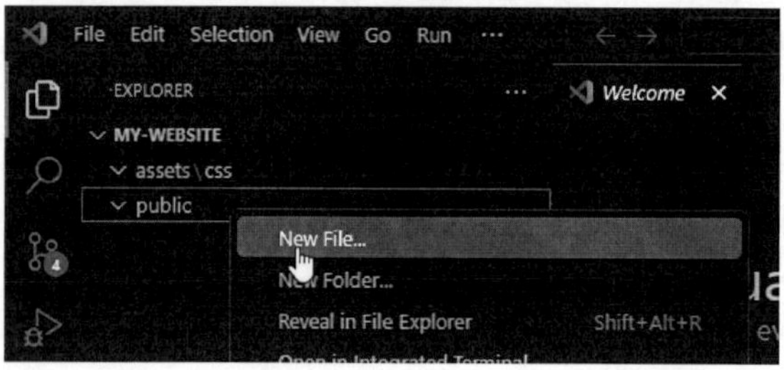

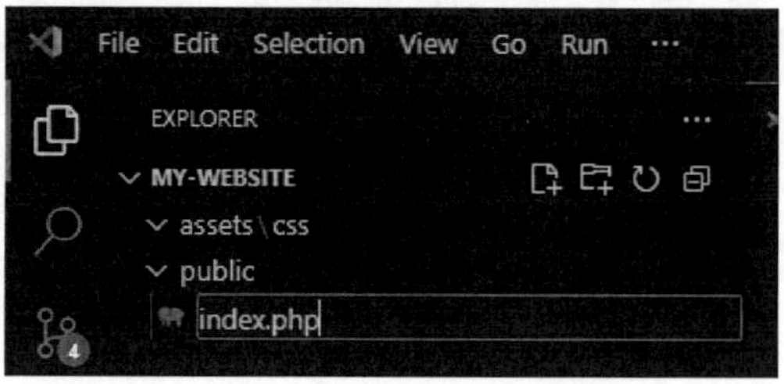

2. **Add code to index.php:** Add the following code in the index.php editor window:

```
<!DOCTYPE html>
<html lang="en">
<head>
    <meta charset="UTF-8">
    <meta name="viewport" content="width=device-width, initial-scale=1.0">
    <title>Welcome to Our Website</title>
</head>
<body>
    <h1>Home Page</h1>
</body>
</html>
```

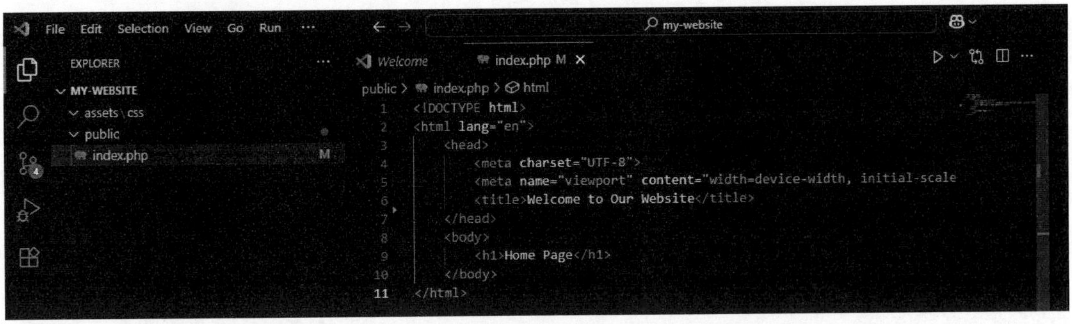

3. **Create about.php:** Right-click on the **public** folder again and select **New File...**. Type **about.php** and press **Enter**.
4. **Add code to about.php:** Add the following code in the about.php editor window:

```
<!DOCTYPE html>
<html lang="en">
<head>
    <meta charset="UTF-8">
    <meta name="viewport" content="width=device-width, initial-scale=1.0">
    <title>About Us</title>
</head>
<body>
    <h1>About Our Company</h1>
</body>
</html>
```

5. **Create contact.php:** Right-click one more time on the **public** folder and select **New File...**. Type **contact.php** and press **Enter**.
6. **Add code to contact.php:** Add this last block of code in the contact.php editor window:

```
<!DOCTYPE html>
<html lang="en">
<head>
    <meta charset="UTF-8">
    <meta name="viewport" content="width=device-width, initial-scale-1.0">
    <title>Contact Us</title>
</head>
<body>
    <h1>Contact Information</h1>
</body>
</html>
```

You now have the three core pages of your website ready. Save your work by pressing **Ctrl+S** (or **Cmd+S** on Mac) in each file tab.

Right now, these are just separate pages. If you open them in your browser (e.g., **http://localhost/codes/my-website/public/**), you see each one works, but they don't look like a unified site yet, and you can't navigate between them. That's what we'll fix next.

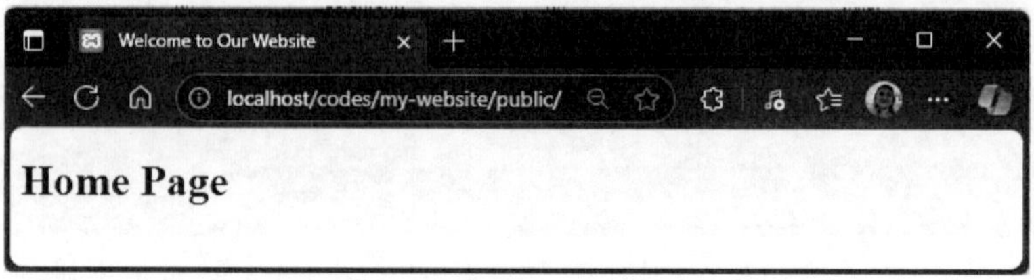

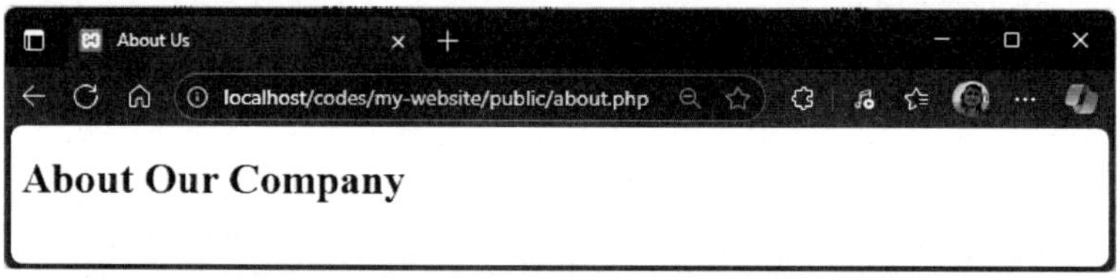

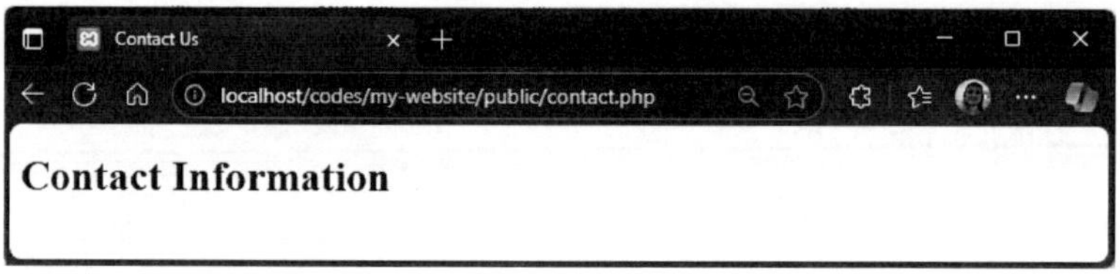

Linking CSS across pages

A consistent look and feel are key to a professional website. You achieve this by using a single stylesheet for all your pages. This is a perfect example of why our assets folder is so useful.

Let's create it and link it to our pages.

1. **Create the CSS file:** In the VS Code **Explorer**, find the **css** folder (which is inside **assets** folder). Right-click on **css** and select **New File...**. Name it **style.css** and press Enter.

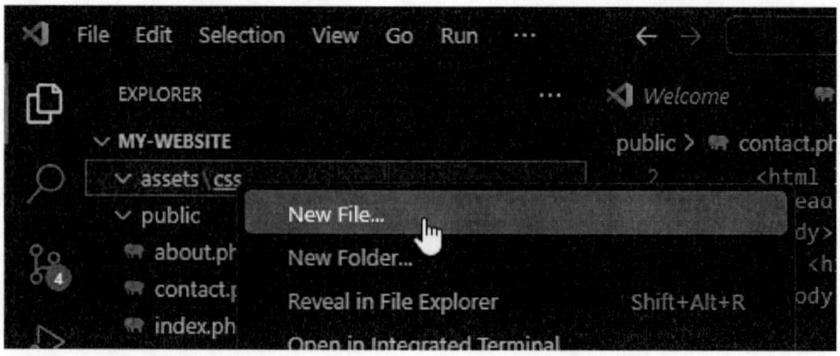

2. **Add the CSS rules:** Add the following code in the **style.css** editor window. This will set a clean background colour and style our main heading.

```
body {
    font-family: -apple-system, BlinkMacSystemFont, "Segoe UI", Roboto,
                 Helvetica, Arial, sans-serif;
    background-color: #f0f2f5;
    color: #1c1e21;
    line-height: 1.6;
    margin: 0;
    padding: 20px;
}
h1 {
    color: #0056b3;
}
```

3. **Link the stylesheet to your pages:** Now we must tell each PHP page to use this file. We will add a **<link>** tag to the **<head>** section of all three pages.
   - **Open index.php**. In the editor, find the line that says **<title>....** On the next line, before the closing **</head>** tag, paste the following line of code:

```
<link rel="stylesheet" href="../assets/css/style.css">
```

   - **Open about.php** and do the exact same thing: paste the <link> tag inside the <head> section.
   - **Open contact.php** and do the same one last time.

The path **../assets/css/style.css** is crucial. It tells the browser to go "up" one directory level (from public) to find the assets folder. Now, all three pages share one style source.

Now, when you refresh any of the pages in your browser, you'll see the new font and colours applied. We've styled our entire website from a single, central file!

Tracking changes with Git

As you build projects, you'll make hundreds of changes. What if you make a mistake and want to go back to a version that worked? That's where version control comes in. Git is the industry-standard tool for tracking changes in code, and VS Code has amazing built-in support for it.

Let's save the current state of our project. Think of this as creating a permanent, named save point.

1. **Initialize repository:** Click the **Source Control** icon on the left **Activity Bar** (it looks like a branching path). Click **Initialize Repository**. This tells Git to start tracking changes in this folder.
2. **Stage changes:** You see all your new files (index.php, style.css, etc.) listed under **Changes**. **Staging** means preparing changes for the next save point. Hover over the **Changes** title and click the + icon to stage all files.

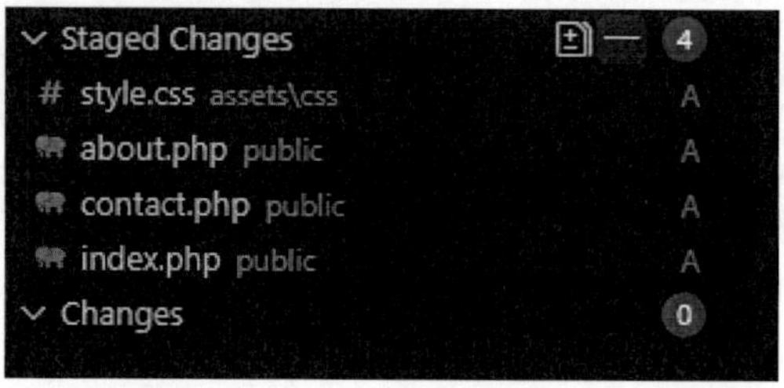

3. **Commit changes:** A **commit** is the save point. In the **message** box at the top of the **Source Control** panel, type a short, descriptive message like **Initial project structure and styling**.

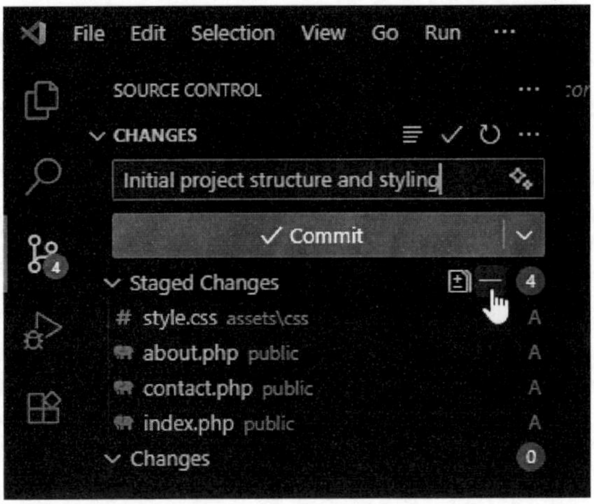

4. **Click commit:** Click the **checkmark** (**✓ Commit**) icon above the message box to finalize the commit.

That's it! You've just saved a snapshot of your entire project. You can now confidently make changes, knowing you can always return to this stable version.

For now, you have mastered local version control, your personal safety net.

Hands-on: My Personal Portfolio

Now, let's combine everything we've learned into a single, polished project. We will build a clean, professional-looking three-page personal portfolio website.

This project will create a simple yet elegant personal portfolio site with a Home, About, and Contact page. It will feature a consistent navigation bar and a clean, modern design. By building this, you will solidify your understanding of project structure, file linking, and the power of shared CSS.

Building the application

We'll use a new folder for this project but, first, ensure you have VS Code closed.

1. Go to your **C:\xampp\htdocs\codes** folder using Windows Explorer (or Finder on Mac).
2. Create a new folder named **my-portfolio**.
3. Now, launch VS Code and go to **File → Open Folder...**.
4. Select the **my-portfolio** folder you just created.

5. Your VS Code window should now be dedicated to this new project.

Create the folder structure

We need to create the following folders inside **my-portfolio**.

/my-portfolio/
|-- /assets/
| |-- /css/
|-- /public/

Just as we did before, let's create the folders in the VS Code Explorer:

1. Right-click in the empty **Explorer** area and select **New Folder...**. Name it **public** and press **Enter**.
2. Right-click in the empty **Explorer** area again and select **New Folder...**. Name it **assets** and press **Enter**.
3. Right-click directly on the **assets** folder and select **New Folder...**. Name it **css** and press **Enter**.

Create and populate the CSS file

Let's create a beautiful, modern theme for our portfolio. This CSS provides a clean layout, a stylish navigation bar, and responsive behavior for different screen sizes.

1. Right-click the **css** folder and select **New File**. Name it **style.css** and press **Enter**.
2. An empty editor for **style.css** opens. Add the following block of CSS code directly in this file:

```
/* General Body and Typography */
body {
    font-family: 'Segoe UI', Tahoma, Geneva, Verdana, sans-serif;
    margin: 0;
    background-color: #f4f4f9;
    color: #333;
}
/* Main Container */
.container {
    max-width: 960px;
    margin: 20px auto;
    padding: 0 20px;
    background-color: #ffffff;
    border-radius: 8px;
    box-shadow: 0 4px 8px rgba(0,0,0,0.1);
}
/* Header and Navigation */
```

```
.main-header {
    background-color: #2c3e50;
    color: #ecf0f1;
    padding: 1rem 0;
    text-align: center;
}
.main-nav ul {
    padding: 0;
    list-style: none;
    background-color: #34495e;
    text-align: center;
}
.main-nav ul li {
    display: inline;
}
.main-nav ul li a {
    display: inline-block;
    padding: 15px 20px;
    text-decoration: none;
    color: #ecf0f1;
    transition: background-color 0.3s;
}
.main-nav ul li a:hover, .main-nav ul li a.active {
    background-color: #e74c3c;
}
/* Page Content */
.content {
    padding: 20px 0;
}
.content h1 {
    color: #2c3e50;
    border-bottom: 2px solid #e74c3c;
    padding-bottom: 10px;
}
.content p {
    line-height: 1.7;
}
```

Create and build the main pages

Now we'll create the three pages of our site. Notice how they all link to the same style.css file and share a common navigation structure for a seamless user experience.

Create and code index.php

1. Right-click the **public** folder and select **New File**. Name it **index.php** and press **Enter**.

2. Add the following HTML block in the empty index.php editor:

```
<!DOCTYPE html>
<html lang="en">
<head>
    <meta charset="UTF-8">
    <meta name="viewport" content="width=device-width, initial-scale=1.0">
    <title>Home | My Portfolio</title>
    <link rel="stylesheet" href="../assets/css/style.css">
</head>
<body>
    <div class="container">
        <header class="main-header">
            <h1>Sharanam and Vaishali's Portfolio</h1>
        </header>
        <nav class="main-nav">
            <ul>
                <li><a href="index.php" class="active">Home</a></li>
                <li><a href="about.php">About Me</a></li>
                <li><a href="contact.php">Contact</a></li>
            </ul>
        </nav>
        <main class="content">
            <h1>Welcome!</h1>
            <p>Welcome to my official portfolio website. Here you will find
               information about my projects, skills, and how to get in touch with
               me. I am passionate about building modern and efficient web
               applications.</p>
        </main>
    </div>
</body>
</html>
```

Create and code about.php

1. Right-click the **public** folder and select **New File**. Name it **about.php** and press **Enter**.
2. Add the following code into the about.php editor:

```
<!DOCTYPE html>
<html lang="en">
<head>
    <meta charset="UTF-8">
    <meta name="viewport" content="width=device-width, initial-scale=1.0">
    <title>About Me | My Portfolio</title>
    <link rel="stylesheet" href="../assets/css/style.css">
</head>
<body>
    <div class="container">
        <header class="main-header">
            <h1>Sharanam and Vaishali's Portfolio</h1>
```

```
        </header>
        <nav class="main-nav">
            <ul>
                <li><a href="index.php">Home</a></li>
                <li><a href="about.php" class="active">About Me</a></li>
                <li><a href="contact.php">Contact</a></li>
            </ul>
        </nav>
        <main class="content">
            <h1>About Me</h1>
            <p>I am a budding web developer with a strong foundation in
               HTML, CSS, and PHP. I specialize in creating dynamic and
               user-friendly websites. My goal is to leverage technology to
               solve real-world problems and create beautiful digital
               experiences.</p>
        </main>
    </div>
</body>
</html>
```

Create and code contact.php

1. Right-click the **public** folder and select **New File**. Name it **contact.php** and press **Enter**.
2. Add the following code into the contact.php editor:

```
<!DOCTYPE html>
<html lang="en">
<head>
    <meta charset="UTF-8">
    <meta name="viewport" content="width=device-width, initial-scale=1.0">
    <title>Contact | My Portfolio</title>
    <link rel="stylesheet" href="../assets/css/style.css">
</head>
<body>
    <div class="container">
        <header class="main-header">
            <h1>Sharanam and Vaishali's Portfolio</h1>
        </header>
        <nav class="main-nav">
            <ul>
                <li><a href="index.php">Home</a></li>
                <li><a href="about.php">About Me</a></li>
                <li><a href="contact.php" class="active">Contact</a></li>
            </ul>
        </nav>
        <main class="content">
            <h1>Get In Touch</h1>
            <p>You can reach me via email at: <strong>
               sharanam.vaishali@example.com</strong>.</p>
```

```
            <p>I am always open to discussing new projects, creative ideas,
               or opportunities to be part of an amazing team.</p>
        </main>
    </div>
</body>
</html>
```

Notice the **class="active"** on the navigation links. This is a simple but effective trick to highlight which page the user is currently on, using the CSS we wrote earlier.

Remember to save each file (**Ctrl+S** or **Cmd+S**). Your project is now complete!

Bridging the gap: Learned concepts and application implementation

This portfolio project is a direct application of everything covered in this chapter:

- **Project structure:** We created a clean **my-portfolio** directory with **assets** and **public** folders to organize our code logically.
- **Naming conventions:** All files and folders use lowercase letters and hyphens, making them easy to read and web-friendly.
- **Multipage app:** We built a functional three-page website (index.php, about.php, contact.php) with a shared navigation menu, forming the core of a real-world site.
- **Linked CSS:** The entire look and feel of the site is controlled by a single style.css file, ensuring consistency and making future design changes incredibly easy.

Running and testing

1. Make sure your **XAMPP Control Panel** has the **Apache** module started.
2. Open your web browser (Chrome, Firefox, etc.).
3. In the address bar, type **http://localhost/codes/my-portfolio/public/** and press **Enter**.
4. You see the **Home** page of your portfolio, beautifully styled by our CSS.

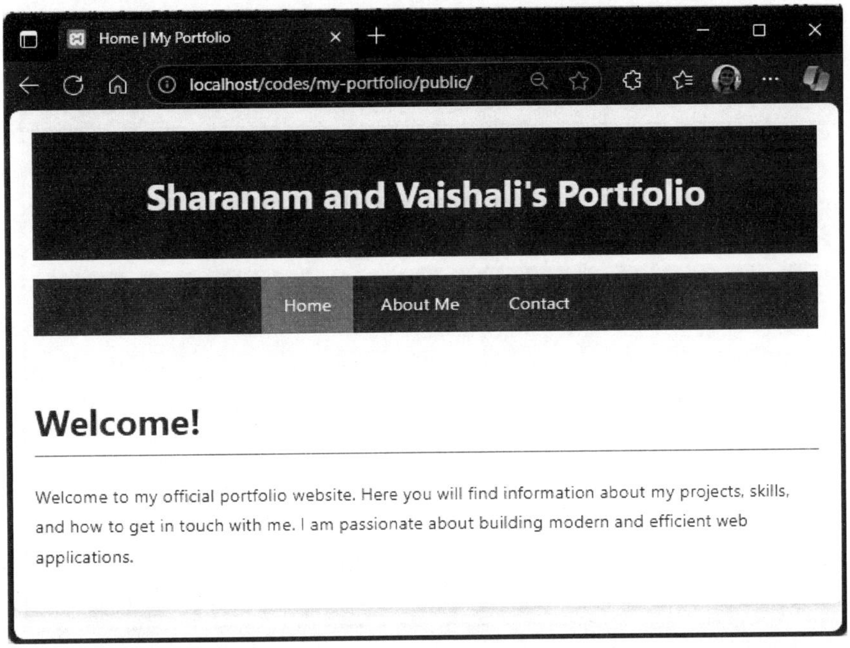

5. Click the **About Me** link in the navigation bar. The browser loads the about.php page, and the styling remains consistent. The **About Me** link is highlighted in **red**.

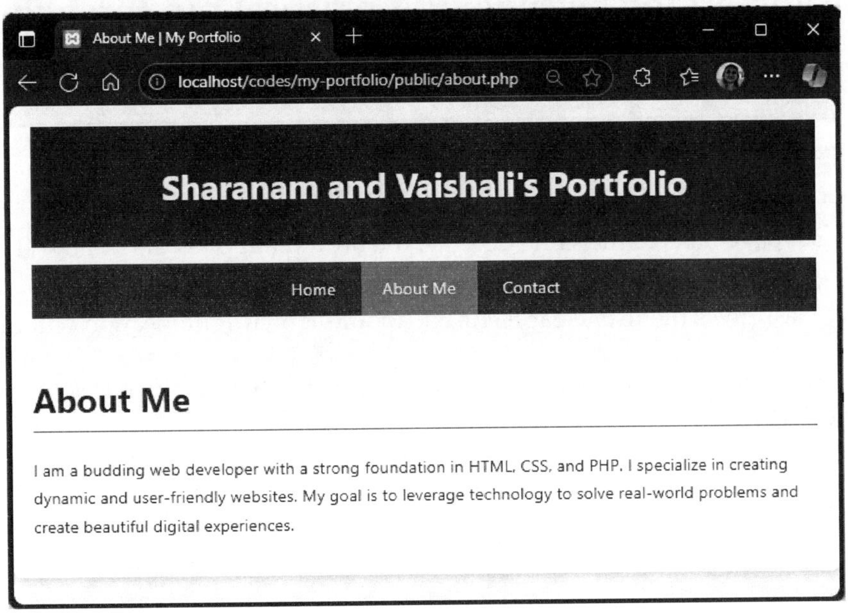

6. Click the **Contact** link to see the contact page.

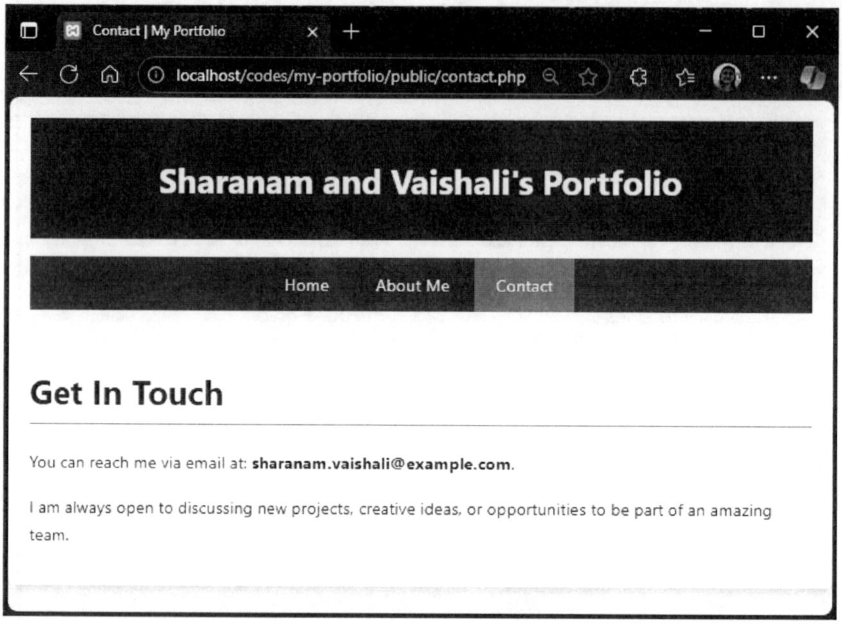

7. Everything should work seamlessly.

Exploring application behaviour: A practical run-through

The application behaves like a standard professional website:

- When a user clicks a navigation link, the browser sends a request to the server for the corresponding PHP file (e.g., about.php).
- The server processes the file and sends back the HTML content.
- Because each page links to the same CSS file, the browser applies the same styles, creating a consistent visual identity.
- The active class gives the user clear feedback about their current location within the site.

This simple, static site forms the perfect foundation for the dynamic features we will add in the upcoming chapters.

Harnessing multipage structures in real-world contexts

This fundamental structure—multiple pages linked together with shared assets—is the backbone of over 90% of websites on the internet. Corporate websites, blogs, e-commerce stores, and documentation sites all use this model. By mastering this simple portfolio project, you have already built something that uses the same core architectural principles as massive, complex web platforms.

Wrapping up

In this chapter, you took a giant leap from writing simple scripts to building structured, professional web projects. This foundation is critical for everything that comes next.

- **Project structure is key:** You learned to organize files into public and assets folders for maintainability.
- **Consistency matters:** You adopted professional naming conventions for files and folders.
- **Websites have multiple pages:** You created a functional, three-page site with linked navigation.
- **CSS provides the theme:** You saw how a single, shared stylesheet can define the look and feel of an entire application.
- **Git is your safety net:** You learned the basics of version control by staging and committing your work in VS Code.
- **You built a real project:** You created a polished, multipage portfolio—your first complete web application!

Congratulations! You are no longer just writing code; you are now an architect of web applications. You have built a clean, professional, and fully functional multipage website from scratch. The skills you learned in this chapter—organization, structure, and consistency—are the habits that will define your career as a developer. You have built the house; now it's time to put things inside it.

In the next chapter, we dive into the heart of PHP. Get ready for ***Chapter 5: Variables unleashed - Storing data with style***, where you'll learn how to make your websites truly dynamic.

Chapter 5

Section 02: Foundations of great code - PHP basics in action

Variables unleashed - Storing data with style

What you'll learn

- Storing information in variables
- Understanding different data types
- Using operators for math and logic
- How to find and fix bugs with debugging tools

Welcome to the true beginning of your journey as a programmer! Imagine you ask a friend to remember a phone number for you. Their brain stores that information so they can recall it a moment later. A website or application needs to do the exact same thing, but it doesn't have a brain. Instead, it uses temporary, digital containers called **variables**.

Every time you see your username on a website, add an item to a shopping cart, or see a personalized greeting, variables are working hard behind the scenes, holding onto that information just for you.

In this chapter, you'll learn how to create and manage these essential containers in PHP. We'll move beyond static text and start making web pages that can remember, calculate, and interact in truly dynamic ways.

Declaring variables

In PHP, a **variable** is like a labeled box where you can place a piece of information to use later. Creating one is simple. The **label** for the box must always start with a dollar sign ($), followed by a name you choose. To place something inside the box, you use the equals sign (=), which we call the **assignment operator**.

Let's create our very first variable. Think of it as creating a box, labeling it **pageTitle**, and putting a piece of paper inside that says **My Awesome Website**:

```
<?php
  // Let's create a variable to hold the title of our page.
  $pageTitle = "My Awesome Website";
  // Now, let's use the 'echo' command to open the box and display its contents.
  echo $pageTitle;
?>
```

What's happening here:

- **$pageTitle** creates the variable (our labeled box).
- = assigns the value on the right to the variable on the left.
- **My Awesome Website** is the piece of information—a **string** of text—that we are storing.
- **echo $pageTitle;** tells PHP: "Find the variable named $pageTitle, read the value stored inside it, and print that value to the browser screen."

When you run this PHP script, the browser won't show the PHP code itself. It only shows the final output that echo produced.

Naming rules and case sensitivity

PHP is flexible, but it has a few strict rules for naming your variables. Getting this right is crucial to avoid errors.

- A variable name **must** start with a letter (a-z, A-Z) or an underscore (_). It **cannot** start with a number.

- After the first character, a variable name can contain any combination of letters, numbers, and underscores. No spaces or special characters like ! or - are allowed.
- Most importantly, variable names in PHP are **case-sensitive**. This is a common trip-up for beginners! It means that $name, $Name, and $NAME are three completely different and unrelated variables.

Let's see a practical example of case sensitivity. Imagine we are storing colours for different items:

```
<?php
  $color = "blue";
  $Color = "red";
  // The <br> tag is simple HTML to create a line break for cleaner output.
  echo "The car is " . $color . "<br>";
  echo "The house is " . $Color;
?>
```

As you can see, PHP fetched the value from the lowercase **$color** variable for the first line and the capitalized **$Color** variable for the second.

To keep your code clean and avoid confusion, developers often adopt a naming convention. A very popular one is **camelCase**, where the first word is all lowercase and every subsequent word starts with a capital letter. Examples: $userFirstName, $itemsInShoppingCart, $pageTitle.

Basic data types

Variables can hold different types of data. While you don't have to tell PHP the type in advance, understanding these categories is essential for writing logical and error-free code.

- **String:** A sequence of characters, like a word, a sentence, or any text. You must wrap strings in single (') or double (") quotes.
  - ***Analogy:*** Think of it as any text you'd write down on paper.

- **Integer:** A whole number without any decimal places. It can be positive, negative, or zero.
    - *Analogy:* Used for counting things you can't split, like the number of people in a room (5) or steps you've walked (1200).
- **Float:** A number that *does* have a decimal point. Also known as a **floating-point number** or **double**.
    - *Analogy:* Used for measurements you *can* split, like a price ($19.99) or a rating (4.7).
- **Boolean:** The simplest type. It can only have one of two possible values: **true** or **false**.
    - *Analogy:* It's like a light switch—it's either on (true) or off (false). There is no in-between. Booleans are the foundation of decision-making in code.

Let's create a variable for each type, imagining we are describing a book for an online store:

```
<?php
  $bookTitle = "PHP for Beginners"; // String
  $pageCount = 350;                 // Integer
  $price = 49.99;                   // Float
  $isPublished = true;              // Boolean
  echo "Book Title: " . $bookTitle . "<br>";
  echo "Pages: " . $pageCount . "<br>";
  echo "Price: $" . $price . "<br>";
  echo "Is Published? " . $isPublished;
?>
```

Wait, why did Is Published? show a 1 instead of true? This is an interesting quirk of PHP. When you use **echo** on a **boolean**, **true** is converted to the string **1**, and **false** is converted to an **empty** string (nothing). It's technically correct, but not very descriptive. To see the *real* type and value, we need special debugging tools, which we'll cover in just a moment!

Variable scope

Scope is a crucial concept that defines *where* in your code a variable is accessible. Think of it like rooms in a house.

- **Global scope:** A variable declared outside of any function is a global variable. It's like an announcement on a public bulletin board in the main hallway of the house. Anyone in the hallway can see it.
- **Local scope:** A variable declared *inside* a function is a local variable. It's like a secret whispered between two people inside a locked room. It only exists and is only known within that room (the function). Once you leave the function, the variable vanishes.

Let's illustrate with an example:

```
<?php
  // This variable is in the GLOBAL scope.
  $appName = "My Calculator";
  // This is a function. We'll learn more about them later.
  function showAppName() {
    // This variable is in the LOCAL scope, it only exists inside this function.
    $message = "Welcome to ";
    echo $message; // This works, because we are inside the function.
    // echo $appName; // If you uncomment this line, it will cause an error!
    // PHP can't see the global $appName from inside the function's "room".
  }
  // We call the function to make it run.
  showAppName();
  // This works, because we are back in the global scope.
  echo $appName;
  // echo $message; // This would also cause an error!
  // The local $message variable was destroyed when the function finished.
?>
```

This code successfully runs because we are only ever accessing variables within their correct scope. If you were to uncomment the lines that try to access variables from the wrong "room," PHP would halt and show you an **Undefined variable** error message.

There's also a special category called **Superglobals**. These are built-in PHP variables (like $_GET and $_POST) that are always accessible from anywhere—global or local scope. They are like a master key that works on any door in the house. We'll use these extensively starting in Chapter 8.

Type casting and auto-juggling

PHP is known as a **loosely typed** language. This sounds technical, but it simply means that PHP is very clever and tries to be helpful by automatically converting data types for you when it makes sense. This process is called **type juggling**.

For instance, if you have a number stored as a string and you try to use it in a math calculation, PHP won't crash. It will **juggle** the string into a number type on the fly:

```
<?php
  $itemsInCart = "5"; // Note: this is a STRING because of the quotes.
  // PHP sees you're doing math and automatically converts "5" to the number 5.
  $totalPrice = $itemsInCart * 10;
  echo "Total price is: $" . $totalPrice;
?>
```

While type juggling is handy, sometimes you need to be explicit and *force* a variable into a specific type. This is called **type casting**. You do this by writing the type you want in parentheses directly before the variable:

```
<?php
  $rating = "4.5 stars"; // A string containing numbers and text.
  // We are forcing PHP to treat $rating as a float (a number with decimals).
  $numericRating = (float) $rating;
  echo "The numeric rating is: " . $numericRating;
?>
```

When casting a string to a number, PHP is smart enough to read the number from the beginning of the string and simply stop when it encounters the first character that isn't part of a number.

Operators in depth

Operators are the action symbols of PHP. They are what allow you to add numbers, compare values, and combine logic. Let's explore the main categories.

Mathematical Operators

These are your standard arithmetic operators for performing calculations:

```
<?php
   $x = 10;
   $y = 4;
   echo "Addition (10 + 4): " . ($x + $y) . "<br>";
   echo "Subtraction (10 - 4): " . ($x - $y) . "<br>";
   echo "Multiplication (10 * 4): " . ($x * $y) . "<br>";
   echo "Division (10 / 4): " . ($x / $y) . "<br>";
   echo "Modulus (10 % 4): " . ($x % $y);
?>
```

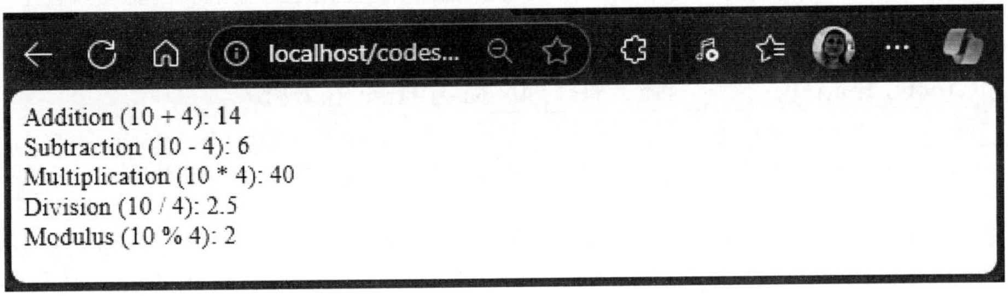

Assignment Operators

These are convenient shortcuts to modify a variable's value based on its current value:

```
<?php
   $score = 100;
   $score += 50; // This is a shortcut for $score = $score + 50;
   echo "New score: " . $score . "<br>";
   $greeting = "Hello";
   $greeting .= ", World!"; // For strings, '.=' concatenates (joins) the text.
   echo $greeting;
?>
```

Comparison Operators

These are the foundation of all decision-making in your code. They compare two values and the entire expression evaluates to a boolean (true or false).

Operator	Name	Example	Explanation
==	Equal	$a == $b	Is the *value* of $a the same as $b? (e.g., 5 == "5" is true)
===	Identical	$a === $b	Is the *value* AND *type* of $a the same as $b? (e.g., 5 === "5" is false)
!=	Not equal	$a != $b	Is the value of $a different from $b?
!==	Not identical	$a !== $b	Is the value OR type of $a different from $b?
<	Less than	$a < $b	Is $a less than $b?
>	Greater than	$a > $b	Is $a greater than $b?
<=	Less than or equal to	$a <= $b	Is $a less than or equal to $b?
>=	Greater than or equal to	$a >= $b	Is $a greater than or equal to $b?

The distinction between **== (equal)** and **=== (identical)** is vital. As a best practice, you should almost always use the strict, triple-equals === comparison to avoid unexpected bugs from PHP's type juggling.

Logical Operators

These are used to create more complex conditions by combining multiple true/false checks.

Operator	Name	Example	Result
&&	And	$x && $y	true only if *both* $x and $y are true
`		`	Or
!	Not	!$x	Flips the value: true becomes false, and false becomes true

Finally, there are **Bitwise operators** (&, |, ^). These perform operations on the individual bits that make up an integer. They are used in highly specialized, low-level programming and are beyond the scope of this beginner's guide. It's just good to know they exist.

String interpolation and concatenation

When you need to combine variables with plain text into a single string, PHP gives you two great options.

Concatenation

This method uses the **dot** (.) **operator** to **glue** different pieces together. It's explicit and works whether your string is in single quotes (') or double quotes ("):

```
<?php
  $username = 'Sharanam';
  // We are joining three pieces: a string, a variable, and another string.
  $message = 'Welcome back, ' . $username . '!';
  echo $message;
?>
```

Interpolation

This is a convenient shortcut where PHP automatically finds and replaces variables directly inside a string. This powerful feature only works with double quotes (`"):

```
<?php
  $username = 'Vaishali';
  // PHP sees the $username variable inside the double quotes and inserts its value.
  $message = "Welcome back, $username!";
  echo $message;
?>
```

Which one should you use? **Interpolation** is often faster to write and easier to read for simple cases. **Concatenation** is sometimes clearer for very complex strings and is necessary if your original string must use single quotes.

Debugging variable values

Sooner or later, your code won't do what you expect. The #1 cause of bugs is variables not containing the data you *think* they contain. PHP provides three essential tools to help you peek inside your variables and see what's really going on.

Let's personify them:

- **echo:** Your straightforward friend. It just tells you the simple value. Quick and easy, but not very detailed. It will fail with an error if you try to echo a complex type like an array.
- **print_r():** Your organized friend. It "prints human-readable" information. It's great for looking inside arrays and objects, showing you their contents in a clean list.
- **var_dump():** Your super-detailed, slightly obsessive friend. This is the most powerful debugging tool. It tells you *everything*: the variable's type, its size or length, and its value. When you are truly stuck, var_dump() is your best friend.

Let's create a more complex variable (an "associative array," which is a collection of key-value pairs) and see how each tool describes it:

```
<?php
  // This array holds information about a user.
  $user = [
    'name' => 'Sharanam Shah',
    'age' => 44,
    'is_active' => true
  ];
  echo "<h3>Using print_r:</h3>";
  // We wrap the output in HTML's <pre> tag. This tells the browser to
  // preserve whitespace and line breaks, making the output much easier to read.
  echo '<pre>';
  print_r($user);
  echo '</pre>';
  echo "<h3>Using var_dump:</h3>";
  echo '<pre>';
  var_dump($user);
  echo '</pre>';
?>
```

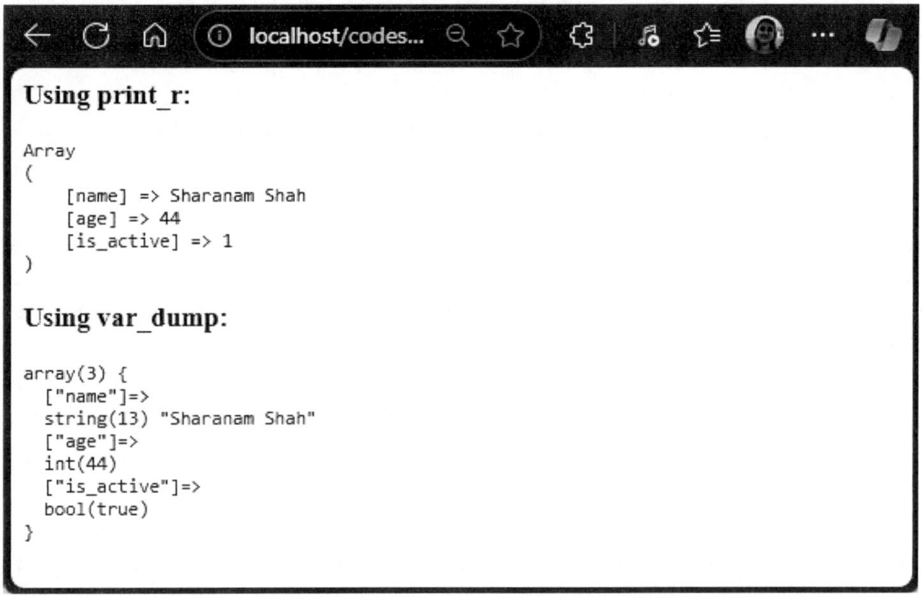

Look at the difference! **print_r()** gives a nice, clean overview. But **var_dump()** gives us the critical details: **name** is a **string** with a length of **13** characters, **age** is an **integer**, and **is_active** is a true **boolean**, not the number 1. This level of detail is invaluable for finding bugs.

Real-world use: Where variables matter most

Variables are not an abstract academic exercise; they are the lifeblood of virtually every website you use.

- **Contact forms:** When you fill out a contact form, the website stores your input in variables like $name, $email, and $message before processing it.
- **E-commerce sites:** Your shopping cart is a collection of variables holding product IDs, quantities ($quantity), prices ($price), and a final $totalCost.
- **Social media:** When you log in, your user ID is stored in a variable to fetch your profile, posts, and friends. The content of a post you're writing is held in a variable until you click the Submit button.
- **Personalization:** When a site says "Welcome back, Sarah!", it's because it retrieved your name from a database and placed it into a $userName variable before printing it to the page.

Any piece of information that changes from user to user or from one moment to the next is managed with variables.

Hands-on: Building a dynamic Calculator interface

Alright, enough theory! It's time to build something real and useful. We are going to apply everything we've just learned to create a fully functional, interactive web Calculator. This project is the perfect way to see variables in action. We'll use them to capture the numbers a user types in, store the mathematical operation they choose, and then hold the final calculated result to display it back to them. And of course, we'll use CSS to make it look fantastic.

Building the application

Let's get our project environment set up correctly.

- Using your computer's file explorer, navigate to your XAMPP installation folder. Inside, find and open the **htdocs\codes** directory (this is usually at C:\xampp\htdocs). This is the root folder for all your web projects.
- Inside **htdocs\codes**, create a new folder and name it **calculator**.
- Now, open **Visual Studio Code**. Go to **File → Open Folder...** and select the **calculator** folder you just created.
- In the VS Code Explorer panel on the left, create two new files by clicking **File → New File...**:
    - index.php (this will hold all our PHP logic and HTML structure)
    - style.css (this will hold all our visual styles)

Create the HTML skeleton

First, let's build the user interface with standard HTML. This form is how the user will provide their input to our PHP script. It needs two fields for numbers, a dropdown menu (<select>) for the operator, and a Submit button.

Copy the following code in your index.php file:

```
<!DOCTYPE html>
<html lang="en">
<head>
    <meta charset="UTF-8">
    <meta name="viewport" content="width=device-width, initial-scale=1.0">
    <title>Dynamic PHP Calculator</title>
    <link rel="stylesheet" href="style.css">
```

```
</head>
<body>
    <div class="calculator-container">
        <h1>PHP Calculator</h1>
        <form action="index.php" method="post">
            <input type="number" name="num1" class="input-field"
                   placeholder="Enter first number" required>
            <select name="operator" class="input-field">
                <option value="add">+</option>
                <option value="subtract">-</option>
                <option value="multiply">*</option>
                <option value="divide">/</option>
            </select>
            <input type="number" name="num2" class="input-field"
                   placeholder="Enter second number" required>
            <button type="submit" name="submit" class="submit-btn">Calculate
            </button>
        </form>
    </div>
</body>
</html>
```

Save this file. At this point, you can test it! Make sure XAMPP's Apache server is running, then open your browser and go to **http://localhost/codes/calculator/**. You can see the raw, unstyled HTML form. It works, but it doesn't look great yet.

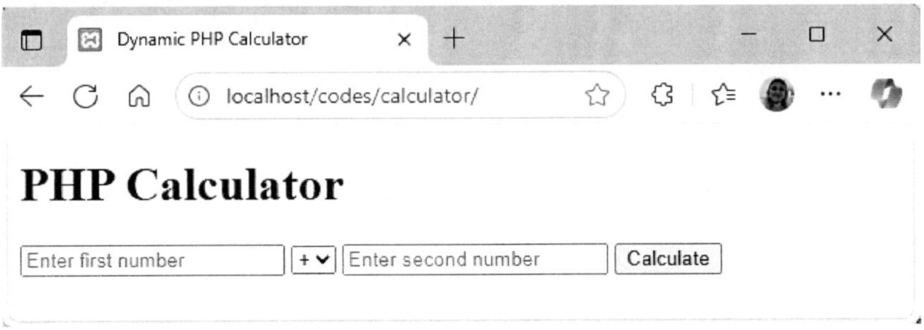

Add the CSS styling

Now let's give our calculator a professional and clean design. This CSS will center the calculator on the page, add colors, spacing, and a modern feel to the input fields and button.

Add the following code in your style.css file:

```
body {
    font-family: -apple-system, BlinkMacSystemFont, 'Segoe UI', Roboto,
                 'Helvetica Neue', Arial, sans-serif;
```

```
    background-color: #f0f2f5;
    display: flex;
    justify-content: center;
    align-items: center;
    height: 100vh;
    margin: 0;
}
.calculator-container {
    background-color: #ffffff;
    padding: 30px 40px;
    border-radius: 12px;
    box-shadow: 0 6px 20px rgba(0, 0, 0, 0.08);
    text-align: center;
    width: 340px;
}
h1 {
    color: #1c1e21;
    margin-bottom: 25px;
    font-weight: 600;
}
.input-field {
    width: 100%;
    padding: 12px;
    margin-bottom: 18px;
    border: 1px solid #dddfe2;
    border-radius: 6px;
    box-sizing: border-box; /* Ensures padding doesn't affect the width */
    font-size: 16px;
}
.input-field:focus {
    outline: none;
    border-color: #007bff;
    box-shadow: 0 0 0 2px rgba(0, 123, 255, 0.25);
}
.submit-btn {
    width: 100%;
    padding: 12px;
    background-color: #007bff;
    color: white;
    border: none;
    border-radius: 6px;
    cursor: pointer;
    font-size: 18px;
    font-weight: 500;
    transition: background-color 0.2s ease-in-out;
}
.submit-btn:hover {
    background-color: #0069d9;
}
.result {
    margin-top: 25px;
```

```
    padding: 15px;
    background-color: #e7f3ff;
    border: 1px solid #b3d7ff;
    border-radius: 6px;
    font-size: 22px;
    color: #004085;
    font-weight: 500;
}
.error {
    margin-top: 25px;
    padding: 15px;
    background-color: #f8d7da;
    border: 1px solid #f5c6cb;
    border-radius: 6px;
    font-size: 18px;
    color: #721c24;
}
```

Save the file and refresh **http://localhost/codes/calculator/** in your browser. Voilà! The calculator should now look polished and modern. The final step is to make it actually *calculate*.

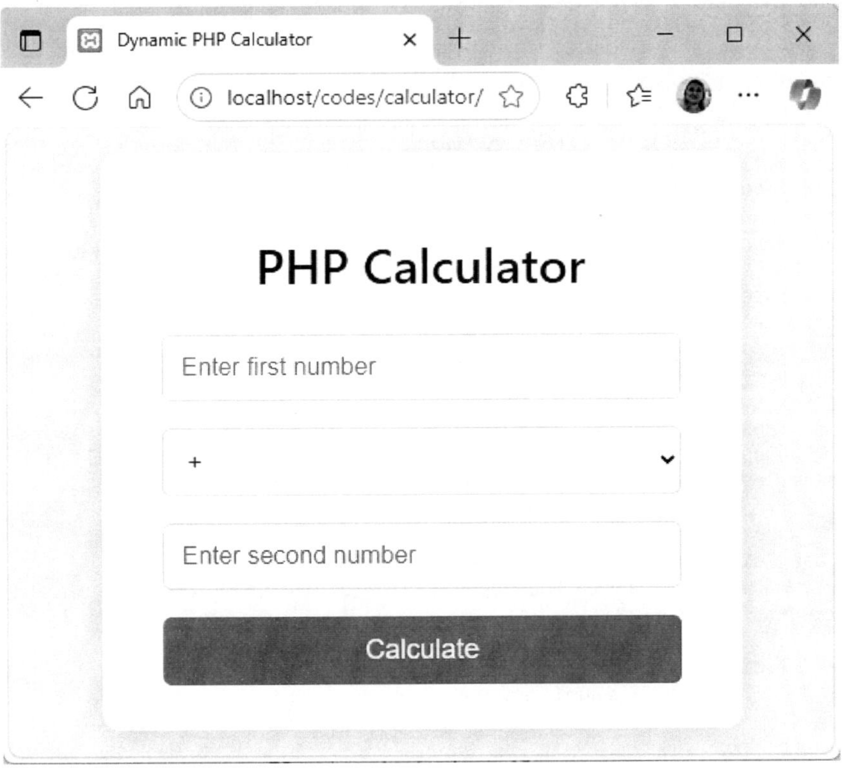

Add the PHP processing logic

This is where the brain of our application comes to life. We will add a PHP script at the very top of our index.php file. This script will execute on the server *before* any HTML is sent to the browser. It will check if the user has submitted the form, grab the inputs, do the math, and save the result (or an error message) in a variable.

Replace the entire content of your index.php with the following complete code. This version integrates the PHP logic with the HTML structure:

```
<?php
  // It's a good practice to define our output variables at the start.
  // We initialize them as empty strings. This prevents errors on the first
  // page load.
  $result = "";
  $error = "";
  // This is our gatekeeper. The code inside this 'if' block will ONLY run
  // after the user clicks the 'submit' button. 'isset' checks if a variable exists.
  if (isset($_POST['submit'])) {
    // Grab the user's input from the $_POST superglobal array and store
    // it in our own variables.
    $num1 = $_POST['num1'];
    $num2 = $_POST['num2'];
    $operator = $_POST['operator'];
    // Input validation and type casting. We ensure the inputs are numbers.
    // We use floatval() to handle both integers and decimals correctly.
    $num1 = floatval($num1);
    $num2 = floatval($num2);
    // The switch statement is a clean way to handle multiple choices.
    // It checks the value of $operator and runs the corresponding code block.
    switch ($operator) {
        case "add":
            $result = $num1 + $num2;
            break; // 'break' exits the switch statement.
        case "subtract":
            $result = $num1 - $num2;
            break;
        case "multiply":
            $result = $num1 * $num2;
            break;
        case "divide":
            // We must handle the edge case of dividing by zero.
            if ($num2 == 0) {
                $error = "Error: Cannot divide by zero!";
            } else {
                $result = $num1 / $num2;
            }
            break;
        default:
```

```
            $error = "An unknown error occurred.";
    }
  }
?>
<!DOCTYPE html>
<html lang="en">
<head>
    <meta charset="UTF-8">
    <meta name="viewport" content="width=device-width, initial-scale=1.0">
    <title>Dynamic PHP Calculator</title>
    <link rel="stylesheet" href="style.css">
</head>
<body>
    <div class="calculator-container">
        <h1>PHP Calculator</h1>
        <form action="index.php" method="post">
            <input type="number" step="any" name="num1" class="input-field"
                   placeholder="Enter first number" required>
            <select name="operator" class="input-field">
                <option value="add">+</option>
                <option value="subtract">-</option>
                <option value="multiply">*</option>
                <option value="divide">/</option>
            </select>
            <input type="number" step="any" name="num2" class="input-field"
                   placeholder="Enter second number" required>
            <button type="submit" name="submit" class="submit-btn">Calculate
            </button>
        </form>
        <?php
          // This is the display logic. It runs every time the page loads. We use a
          // strict check to see if our $result variable contains a numeric value.
          // is_numeric() is safer than just checking if it's not an empty string.
          if (is_numeric($result)) {
            echo "<div class='result'>Result: " . $result . "</div>";
          } elseif ($error !== "") {
            // If there's no result, we check if an error message was set.
            echo "<div class='error'>" . $error . "</div>";
          }
        ?>
    </div>
</body>
</html>
```

The **step="any"** attribute is added to our number inputs. This is a small but important HTML5 detail that tells the browser to allow decimal values. PHP logic is also slightly improved by using floatval() for casting and is_numeric() for checking the result, which are more robust methods.

Bridging the gap: Learned concepts and application implementation

Let's pause and explicitly connect our hands-on project back to the core concepts of this chapter. Seeing the theory in a real application is how learning sticks.

- **Declaring variables:** At the top of our script, we declared **$result** = ""; and **$error** = "";. Inside our main logic, we created **$num1**, **$num2**, and **$operator** to hold the data coming from the user.
- **Basic data types:** The data from the HTML form **($_POST['num1'])** always arrives as a string. This is a critical point! We immediately use **type casting** with **floatval($num1)** to convert that string into a float number, allowing us to perform accurate math. Our **$result** is a **number** (float or integer), and our **$error** is a **string**.
- **Operators in action:** This app is a festival of operators!
  - We used the **assignment operator** (=) dozens of times to store values in our variables.
  - The core of the app uses the **mathematical operators** (+, -, *, /) inside the switch statement.
  - We used the **comparison operator** (==) in our special check: if ($num2 == 0).
- **String concatenation:** To display our final output, we used the **dot** (.) to join our static text with our dynamic variable: **echo "<div class='result'>Result: " . $result . "</div>";**.
- **Superglobals:** We used the **$_POST** superglobal array, our **mailbag** for receiving all the data from the form that was submitted using the POST method. **$_POST['num1']** is how we accessed the specific value from the input field that had **name="num1"**.

Running and testing

It's time for the moment of truth! Let's test our fully functional application.

1. Confirm that your **Apache** server is running from the **XAMPP Control Panel**.
2. Open your favourite web browser (Chrome, Firefox, etc.).
3. In the address bar, type **http://localhost/codes/calculator/** and press **Enter**.
4. The stylish calculator interface appears.

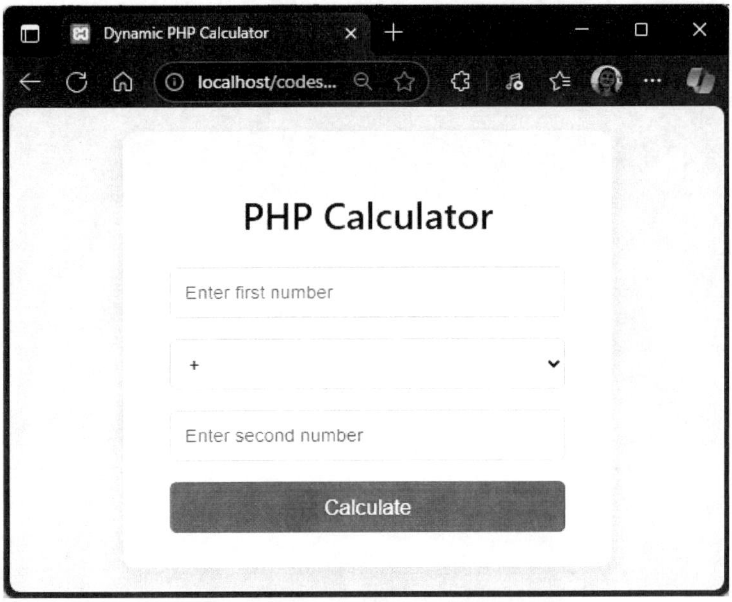

5. Let's perform a calculation:
   - Enter a **number** in the **first number field** as well as in the **second number field**.
   - Select the **operator** from the **dropdown list**.

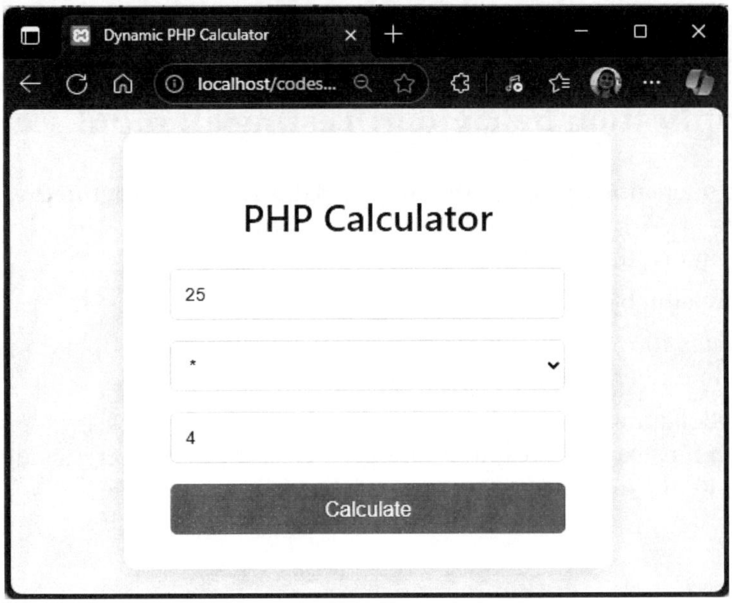

6. Click the big blue **Calculate** button. The page instantly reloads. Below the button, a styled blue box appears containing the correct answer.

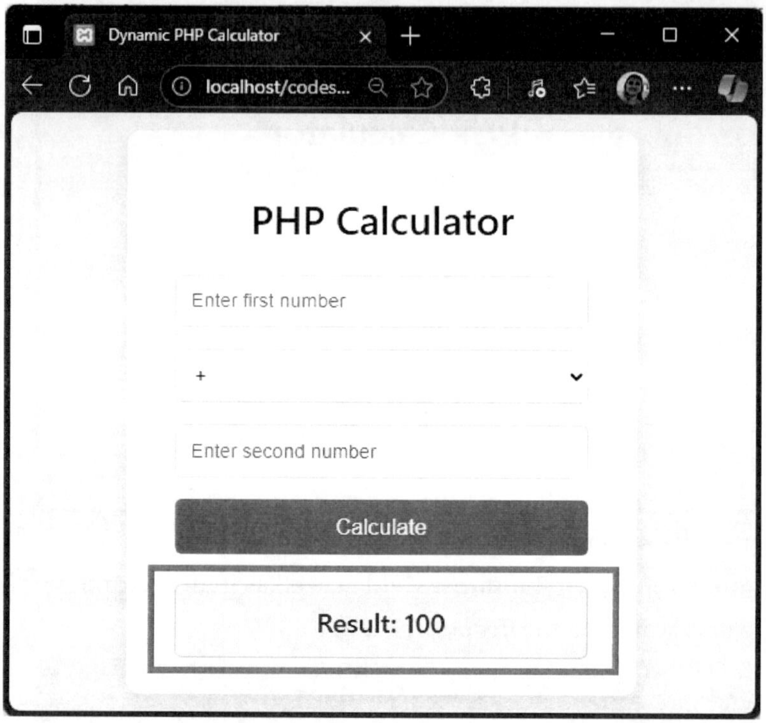

Exploring application behaviour: Testing all input scenarios

Professional developers don't just test the "happy path" (where everything works perfectly); they actively try to break their own code to find and fix weaknesses. This is called testing for **edge cases**. Let's put on our tester hats.

1. **Scenario 1: Division by Zero**
    - **Action:** Enter **100** for the first number, select the **division (/)** operator, and enter **0** for the second number. Click **Calculate**.
    - **Expected Behaviour:** Our if **($num2 == 0)** logic should kick in perfectly. The page reloads, and instead of a result or an ugly PHP error, our user-friendly red error box appears with the message: **Error: Cannot divide by zero!**

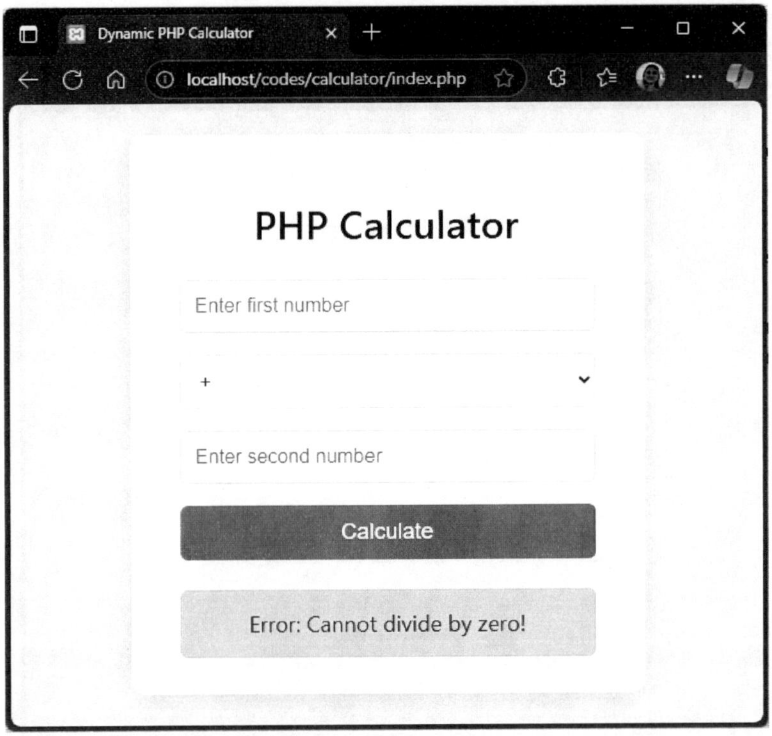

2. **Scenario 2: Decimal Numbers (Floats)**
    - **Action:** Enter **10.5** and **5.5**. Select the **addition (+)** operator. Click **Calculate**.
    - **Expected Behaviour:** Because we used **floatval()** and **<input type="number" step="any">**, the calculator handles decimals flawlessly. The result box should show **Result: 16**.

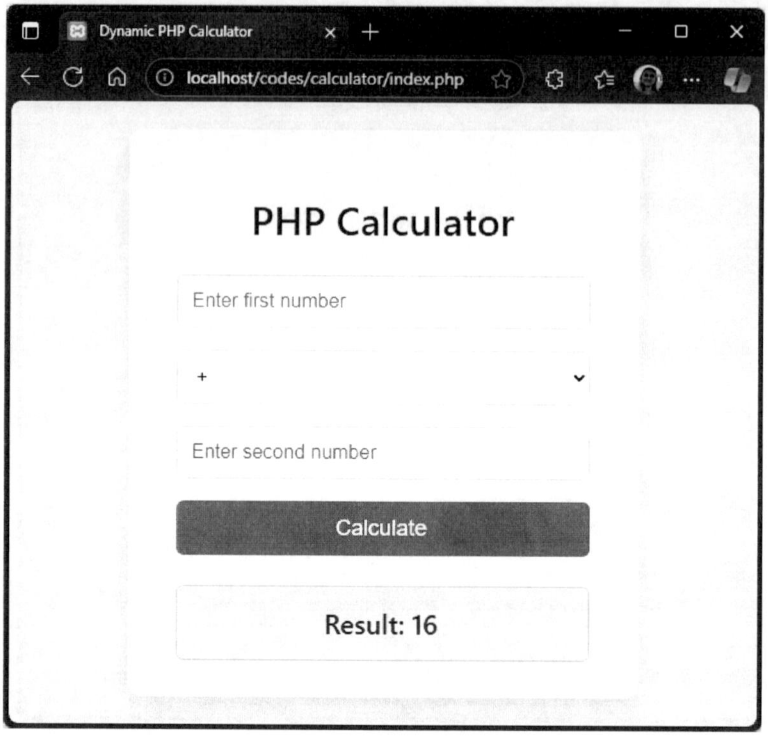

3. **Scenario 3: Empty Inputs**
   - **Action:** Leave one or both number fields empty and click **Calculate**.
   - **Expected Behaviour:** The required attribute we added to our HTML <input> tags provides *client-side validation*. The browser itself will stop the form from being submitted and pop up a little message like **Please fill out this field**. This is a great first line of defence that prevents bad data from ever reaching our PHP script.

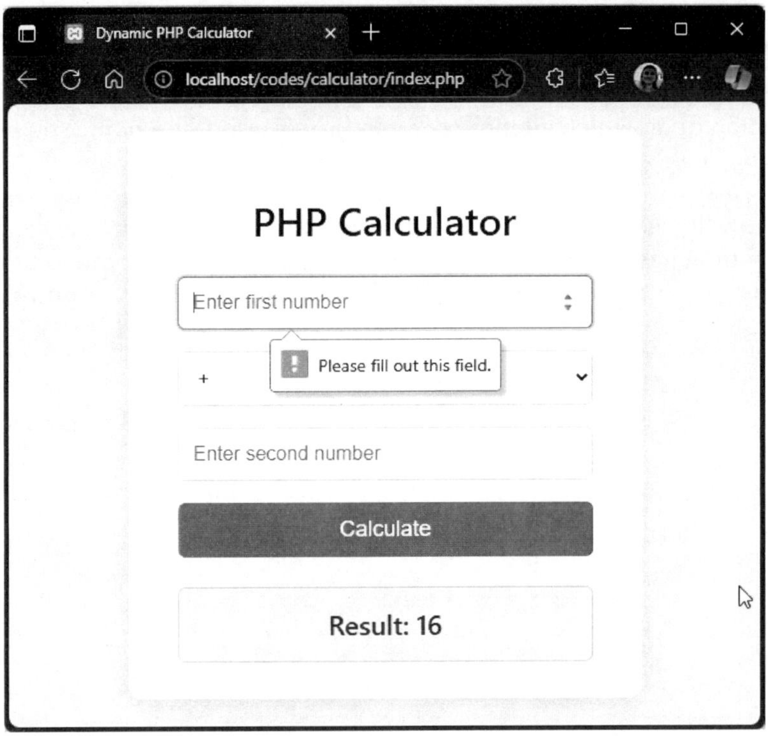

Wrapping up

In this chapter, we covered a massive amount of ground and you mastered the absolute fundamentals of programming. Let's recap the key takeaways.

- **Variables are labeled boxes:** They start with a $ and store information for later use.
- **Data has different types:** We worked with Strings (text), Integers (whole numbers), Floats (decimal numbers), and Booleans (true/false).
- **PHP is a "loosely typed" language:** It often converts types for you automatically (type juggling), but you can force a conversion with type casting (e.g., floatval()).
- **Operators are action words:** We used mathematical (+, *), assignment (=), and comparison (==) operators to bring our calculator to life.
- **Debugging is a superpower:** var_dump() is your most trusted tool for inspecting a variable's true type and value to solve problems.
- **Theory to practice:** We successfully applied all these concepts to build a complete, interactive, and good-looking web application from scratch.

Incredible work! You've officially moved beyond simply displaying static content. You can now write code that remembers, calculates, and responds to user input. Mastering variables is a huge milestone, and the skills you built in this chapter—especially in the hands-on project—form the foundation upon which all more complex applications are built. You should be very proud of what you've accomplished.

Now that you know how to manage data, the next logical step is to learn how to make decisions and perform repetitive tasks based on that data. Get ready to take command of your code's execution flow as we dive into ***Chapter 6: Think Like a programmer - Control structures & loops***.

Chapter 6

Section 02: Foundations of great code – PHP basics in action

Think like a programmer – Control structures & loops

What you'll learn

- Making decisions with code
- Handling different conditions
- Repeating tasks automatically
- Building complex program flows

Welcome to the brain of your web application! Imagine you're following a recipe. Some instructions are simple: **add flour**. But others depend on the situation: ***If* the dough is too sticky, add more flour**. Some instructions are repetitive: **Knead the dough *for* 10 minutes**. This is exactly how programming works! So far, you've learned to store ingredients (data) in containers (variables). Now, you're going to learn how to write the recipe itself.

This chapter is all about **control structures**, the fundamental building blocks that allow your code to make decisions and perform repetitive tasks. They are the logic that directs the flow of your program, turning a static, boring page into a dynamic, interactive experience. By the end of this chapter, you'll be able to write code that intelligently responds to user input, just like a real web application.

Conditional statements

At its very heart, programming is about making decisions. The most basic and powerful tool for this is the **if** statement. It asks a simple question that can be answered with a **yes** or **no** (in programming, this is true or false). If the answer is true, it runs a specific block of code inside its **curly braces {}**.

You can make this even more powerful by adding an **else** block. This is the **otherwise** part of your logic—if the if condition is false, the code inside the else block will run instead.

What if you have more than two possibilities? That's where **elseif** comes in. It allows you to chain multiple conditions together, creating a clear and readable decision-making process.

Let's build a simple script that greets the user with a different message based on the time of day. This is a classic example of how websites personalize the user experience.

First, we'll write the PHP logic to determine the correct greeting:

```
<?php
// Let's find out the current hour. The date() function is a built-in PHP tool.
// 'H' tells it we want the hour in 24-hour format (00 to 23).
    $hour = date('H');
// We'll prepare an empty variable to hold our final greeting message.
    $greeting = '';
// Now, let the decision-making begin! First check: is it before 12 PM (noon)?
    if ($hour < 12) {
    // If true, this is our message. The other checks will be skipped.
        $greeting = 'Good Morning!';
   // If the first check was false, let's try another one: is it before
   // 6 PM (18:00)?
    } elseif ($hour < 18) {
    // If true, this is our message.
        $greeting = 'Good Afternoon!';
// If all previous checks were false, we don't need another condition.
// This else block will catch any other possibility (any time from 18:00 onwards).
    } else {
        $greeting = 'Good Evening!';
    }
?>
```

Now that our PHP has figured out the correct greeting, we need some HTML and CSS to display it beautifully in the browser:

```
<!DOCTYPE html>
<html lang="en">
<head>
```

```
    <meta charset="UTF-8">
    <meta name="viewport" content="width=device-width, initial-scale=1.0">
    <title>Dynamic Greeting</title>
    <style>
        body {
            font-family: Arial, sans-serif;
            display: flex;
            justify-content: center; /* Horizontally center */
            align-items: center;     /* Vertically center */
            height: 100vh;           /* Full viewport height */
            background-color: #f0f8ff; /* A nice light blue background */
        }
        .greeting-box {
            padding: 2rem 4rem;
            background-color: #ffffff;
            border-radius: 10px;
            box-shadow: 0 4px 10px rgba(0,0,0,0.1);
            font-size: 2rem;
            color: #333;
        }
    </style>
</head>
<body>
    <div class="greeting-box">
        <?php echo $greeting; ?>
    </div>
</body>
</html>
```

When you save this file in your XAMPP **htdocs/codes** folder and open it in the browser, you'll see a clean, centered box. Depending on the time you run it, the message inside change automatically.

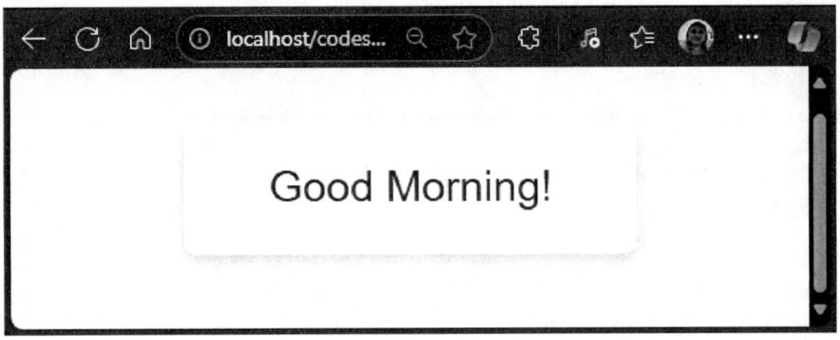

The switch statement

Sometimes, you have one variable that you need to compare against a long list of specific values. You could use a lengthy if-elseif-elseif-else structure, but it can get messy and hard to read. A **switch** statement is a much cleaner and more elegant solution for this exact scenario.

Think of it like a button panel on an elevator. You press one button (your variable's value), and it takes you to a specific floor (the matching case).

The switch statement has three key parts:

- **case:** This is one of the possible values you want to check for.
- **break:** This is crucial! It tells PHP to stop checking and exit the switch block once a match is found. If you forget it, the code will **fall through** and execute the code in the next case as well, which is usually not what you want.
- **default:** This is a **safety net**. If none of the case values match, the default block will be executed. It's like the else in an if statement.

Let's build a simple feedback system where a user's numerical rating (1-5) generates a specific text response:

```
<!DOCTYPE html>
<html lang="en">
<head>
    <title>Rating Feedback</title>
    <style>
        body {
            font-family: Arial, sans-serif; display: flex;
            justify-content: center; align-items: center;
             height: 100vh; background-color: #f0f8ff;
        }
        .feedback-box {
            padding: 2rem 4rem; background-color: #fff;
            border-radius: 10px;
            box-shadow: 0 4px 10px rgba(0,0,0,0.1);
            text-align: center;
        }
        .rating {
            font-size: 2rem; font-weight: bold;
            margin-bottom: 1rem;
        }
        .message {
            font-size: 1.2rem; color: #555;
        }
    </style>
</head>
```

```
<body>
    <div class="feedback-box">
        <?php
         // In a real app, this is where a user clicks a star.
         $userRating = 4; // But we'll set it manually.
         $message = '';
         // The switch statement evaluates our $userRating variable.
         switch ($userRating) {
             case 5: // Is the rating 5?
                 $message = 'Excellent! We are thrilled you enjoyed it.';
                 break; // Stop here.
             case 4: // Is the rating 4?
                 $message = 'Great! Thank you for the positive feedback.';
                 break; // Stop here.
             case 3: // Is the rating 3?
                 $message = 'Good. We appreciate you taking the time to rate.';
                 break; // Stop here.
             case 2:
             case 1: // We can stack cases for a shared response!
                 $message = 'We are sorry to hear that. Please let us know how we
                            can improve.';
                 break; // Stop here.
             default: // If the rating is none of the above...
                 $message = 'Invalid rating. Please choose a value from 1 to 5.';
                 break; // Stop here.
         }
         ?>
        <div class="rating">Your Rating: <?php echo $userRating; ?> ★</div>
        <div class="message"><?php echo $message; ?></div>
    </div>
</body>
</html>
```

The browser displays a styled box showing:

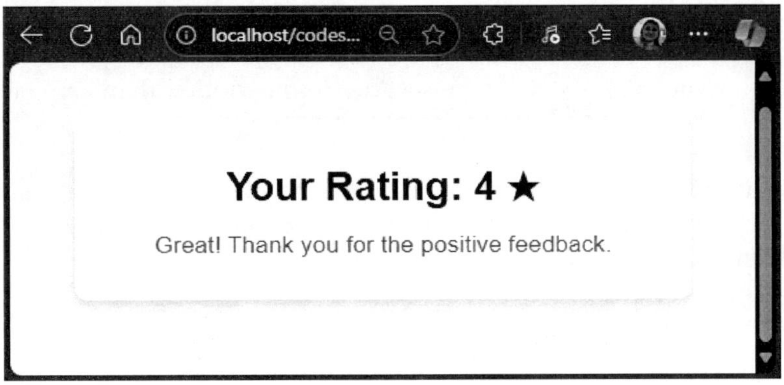

If you change the **$userRating** variable to **1**, then the message changes to the one we set for cases 1 and 2. If you set it to **99**, the default message appears.

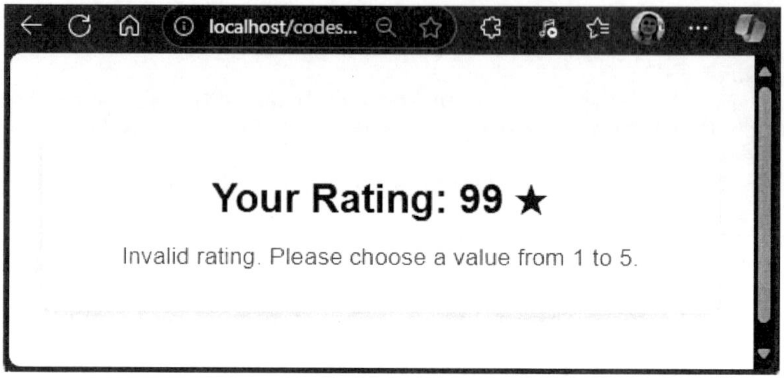

Truthy and falsy

This is a simple but incredibly powerful concept in PHP. In an if statement, PHP doesn't just look for the literal boolean values true or false. It can evaluate almost *any* value in a boolean context to see if it's "truthy" or "falsy."

- **Falsy values** are the ones that behave like false in a condition. There are only a few to remember:
  - The integer 0
  - The float 0.0
  - An empty string ''
  - A string containing only a zero "0"
  - An empty array []
  - The special value NULL (meaning "no value")
- **Truthy values** are literally everything else! Any number other than zero, any non-empty string, and any array with items in it is considered true.

This is extremely useful for writing quick and readable checks. For instance, instead of writing if ($username !== ''), you can just write if ($username). It's shorter and does the same thing: it checks if the $username variable actually contains something:

```
<!DOCTYPE html>
<html lang="en">
<head>
    <title>Truthy Falsy Check</title>
    <style>
        body {
```

```
            font-family: sans-serif; padding: 2em;
            line-height: 1.6;
        }
        .check {
            margin-bottom: 1em; padding: 1em;
            border-left: 5px solid #ccc;
        }
        .check.truthy {
            background-color: #eaf7ec; border-color: #28a745;
        }
        .check.falsy {
            background-color: #fbe9ea; border-color: #dc3545;
        }
    </style>
</head>
<body>
    <h1>Truthy vs. Falsy Demo</h1>
    <?php
    $username = "Admin"; // This is a non-empty string, so it is TRUTHY.
    // This `if` statement checks if $username is truthy.
    if ($username) {
        echo "<div class='check truthy'>Welcome back, <strong>$username
             </strong>! (The variable contains a string, which is TRUTHY)</div>";
    } else {
        echo "<div class='check falsy'>No user is logged in. (The variable
             is empty or falsy)</div>";
    }
    $itemsInCart = 0; // This is the integer 0, which is FALSY.
    // This `if` statement checks if $itemsInCart is truthy.
    if ($itemsInCart) {
        echo "<div class='check truthy'>You have items in your cart. (The
             variable is a non-zero number, which is TRUTHY)</div>";
    } else {
        echo "<div class='check falsy'>Your shopping cart is empty. (The
             variable is 0, which is FALSY)</div>";
    }
    ?>
</body>
</html>
```

The browser displays two distinct messages. This clearly demonstrates how different values are evaluated.

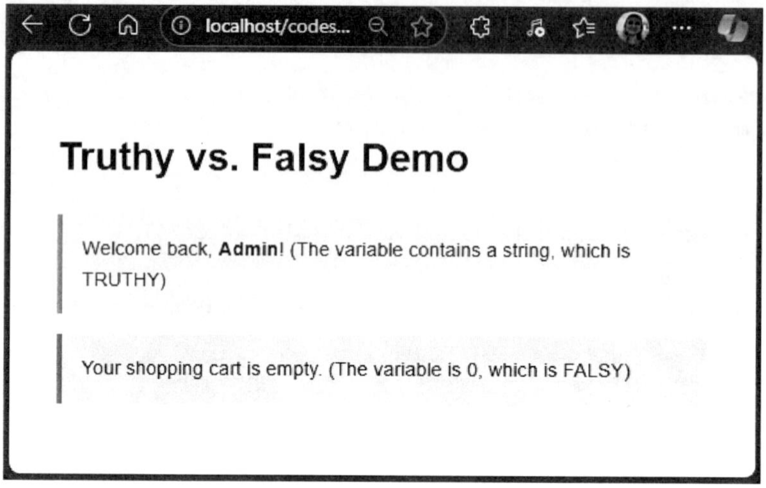

Repetition

Loops are the ultimate time-savers in programming. They are designed to execute the same block of code over and over again, so you don't have to. PHP provides a few different kinds of loops; each suited for a specific kind of repetitive task.

- **for loop:** The perfect tool when you know *exactly* how many times you need to repeat an action. Think of it as telling someone to run exactly 5 laps around a track. It has three parts in its parentheses:
    - **Initializer ($i = 1):** A counter variable is set up once at the very beginning.
    - **Condition ($i <= 5):** This is checked *before* every single loop. If it's true, the loop runs. If it's false, the loop stops.
    - **Increment ($i++):** This runs *after* every loop, usually to increase the counter.
- **while loop:** Use this when you need a loop to run as long as a condition is true, but you don't know ahead of time how many repetitions that will take. It's like waiting for a download to finish; you just keep waiting *while* it's not at 100%. The condition is always checked *before* the code runs.
- **do-while loop:** This is a close cousin of the while loop, with one critical difference: the condition is checked *after* the code runs. This means a do-while loop is **guaranteed to run at least once**, even if its condition is false from the start.
- **foreach loop:** This is the modern, easy, and preferred way to work with arrays. It gracefully iterates over each element in an array, giving you access to it without needing to manage a counter variable. It's like going through a checklist item by item.

Let's see them all in action:

```
<!DOCTYPE html>
<html lang="en">
<head>
    <title>PHP Loops Demo</title>
    <style>
        body {
            font-family: monospace; padding: 2em;
            background-color: #fdfdff;
        }
        h2 {
            border-bottom: 2px solid #eee; padding-bottom: 5px;
            color: #333;
        }
        .loop-output {
            background-color: #f9f9f9; padding: 1em;
            border-radius: 5px; margin-bottom: 2em;
            border: 1px solid #eee;
        }
    </style>
</head>
<body>
    <h1>Demonstrating PHP Loops</h1>
    <div class="loop-output">
        <h2>for loop (Countdown)</h2>
        <?php
        // Start at 5; loop as long as i > 0; decrease i by 1 each time.
        for ($i = 5; $i > 0; $i--) {
            echo "Countdown: $i...<br>";
        }
        echo "<strong>Liftoff!</strong>";
        ?>
    </div>
    <div class="loop-output">
        <h2>while loop (Random Roll)</h2>
        <?php
        $roll = 0;
        $count = 0;
        // The loop continues as long as the roll is NOT a 6.
        while ($roll != 6) {
            $roll = rand(1, 6); // Generate a random number between 1 and 6.
            $count++; // Increment our roll counter.
            echo "Roll #$count: You rolled a $roll.<br>";
        }
        echo "<strong>It took $count rolls to get a 6!</strong>";
        ?>
    </div>
    <div class="loop-output">
        <h2>foreach loop (Team Roster)</h2>
        <?php
```

```
        $team = ['Sharanam', 'Vaishali', 'Janya', 'Dhrish'];
        echo "<ul>";
        // For each item in the $team array, temporarily call it $member
        // and run the code.
        foreach ($team as $member) {
            echo "<li>Welcome, $member!</li>";
        }
        echo "</ul>";
        ?>
    </div>
</body>
</html>
```

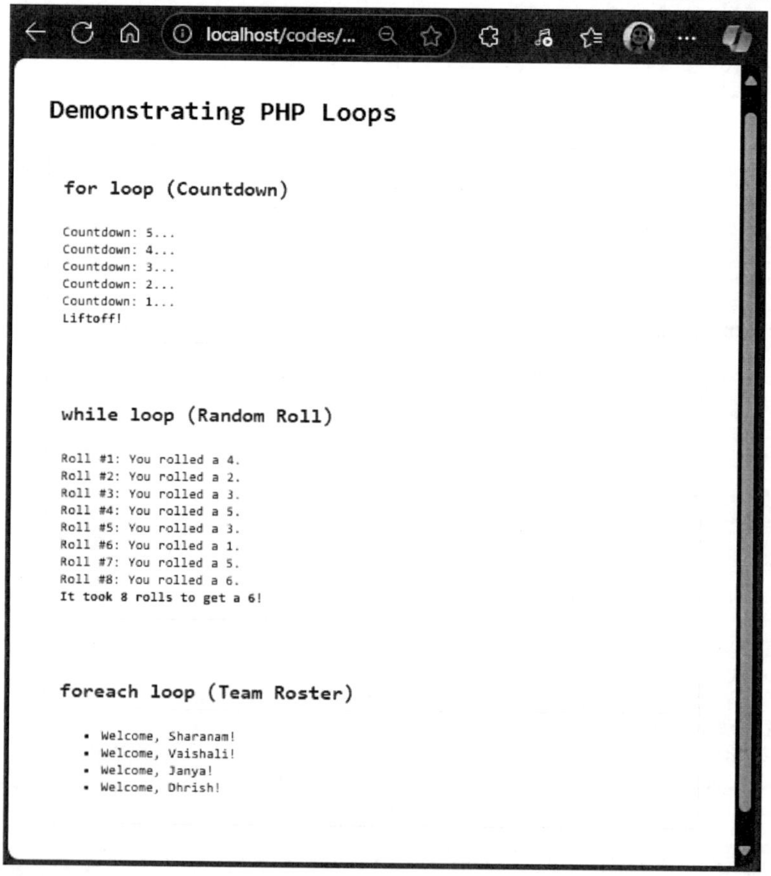

Your browser renders three distinct sections:

- **for loop (Countdown):** This prints a countdown from 5 down to 1 neatly, ending with a bold "Liftoff!".

- **while loop (Random roll):** This part is fun because it's unpredictable! It shows a list of simulated dice rolls, and it stops only when a 6 is rolled. The number of rolls is different almost every time you refresh the page.
- **foreach loop (Team roster):** This displays a clean, bulleted list containing a welcome message for each person in our $team array.

Looping through arrays and ranges

The **foreach** loop is your best friend when it comes to arrays. It has two handy forms. The one we just saw **(foreach ($array as $value))** is great for when you only care about the values. But what if the array's *keys* are also important? For that, there's a slightly different syntax:

```
foreach ($array as $key => $value)
```

This is perfect for associative arrays where the key has meaning, like a product's SKU or a user's ID.

The **range()** function is another useful tool. It quickly generates an array of numbers or letters between two points, which is perfect for creating things like year selection dropdowns in a form.

For example:

```
<!DOCTYPE html>
<html lang="en">
<head>
    <title>Looping Techniques</title>
    <style>
        body {
            font-family: sans-serif; padding: 2em;
            background-color: #fafafa;
        }
        .card {
            border: 1px solid #ddd; border-radius: 8px;
            padding: 1em; margin-bottom: 1em;
            box-shadow: 0 2px 4px rgba(0,0,0,0.05);
            background-color: #fff;
        }
        h2 {
            margin-top: 0;
        }
        select {
            padding: 8px; font-size: 1rem;
        }
    </style>
</head>
```

```
<body>
    <div class="card">
        <h2>Product Inventory (using foreach with key and value)</h2>
        <?php
        // An associative array where keys (SKUs) and values (Product Names)
        // are both important.
        $inventory = [
            'SKU100' => 'T-Shirt',
            'SKU200' => 'Mug',
            'SKU300' => 'Sticker'
        ];
        echo "<ul>";
        // Here we capture BOTH the key (as $sku) and the value (as $product).
        foreach ($inventory as $sku => $product) {
            echo "<li>Item <strong>$sku</strong> is a <strong>$product
                 </strong>.</li>";
        }
        echo "</ul>";
        ?>
    </div>
    <div class="card">
        <h2>Generating Years (using foreach and range)</h2>
        <select name="birth_year">
            <option>-- Select a Year --</option>
            <?php
            // Let's get the current year dynamically.
            $currentYear = date('Y');
            // Use range() to create an array of years from now back to
            // 100 years ago.
            $years = range($currentYear, $currentYear - 100);
            // Now, loop through our newly created $years array to build
            // the options.
            foreach ($years as $year) {
                echo "<option value='$year'>$year</option>";
            }
            ?>
        </select>
    </div>
</body>
</html>
```

You see two clean cards on the page:

- The first card list your product inventory, clearly showing how the foreach loop extracted both the SKU and the product name from the associative array.
- The second card features a dropdown menu. If you click on it, you see it's perfectly populated with a list of years, starting with the current year and going back a century. This is a common and professional feature on registration forms.

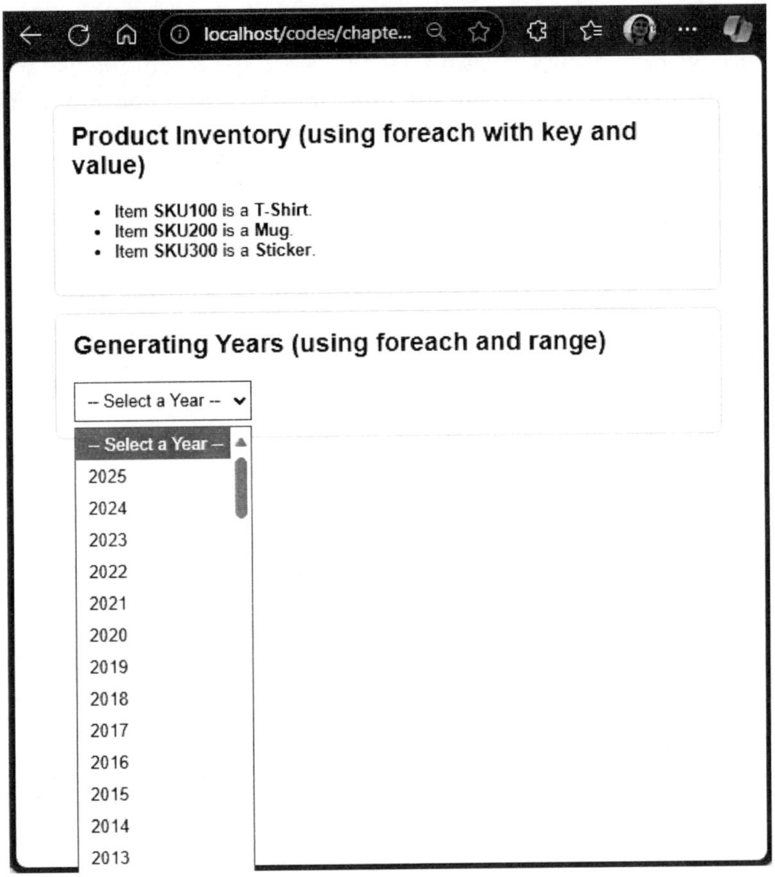

Breaking and continuing flows

Even inside a loop, you sometimes need more control. What if you want to stop the loop early, or just skip one particular iteration? PHP gives you two commands for this:

- **break:** This is the emergency stop. The moment PHP encounters break, it immediately terminates the current loop and continues with the code that comes after it.
- **continue:** This is less drastic. It tells PHP to stop the *current iteration* right where it is, skip to the end of the loop block, and start the *next iteration*.

Let's use an example. Imagine we are searching through a list of users to find the first administrator. Once we find them, there's no need to check the rest of the list, so we can break. In a separate task, we might want to create a mailing list of only non-admin users. For that, we can continue to skip over the admins:

```
<!DOCTYPE html>
<html lang="en">
<head>
    <title>Break and Continue</title>
    <style>
        body {
            font-family: sans-serif; padding: 2em;
        }
        .output {
            background: #f4f4f4; padding: 1em;
            border-radius: 5px; margin-top: 1em;
            font-family: monospace;
        }
        .highlight {
            color: #d9534f; font-weight: bold;
        }
    </style>
</head>
<body>
    <h1>Using `break` to find the first admin</h1>
    <div class="output">
    <?php
    $users = [
        ['name' => 'Vaishali', 'role' => 'user'],
        ['name' => 'Janya', 'role' => 'user'],
        ['name' => 'Sharanam', 'role' => 'admin'], // The one we're looking for!
        ['name' => 'Dhrish', 'role' => 'user']
    ];
    $foundAdmin = '';
    foreach ($users as $user) {
        echo "Checking user: {$user['name']}...<br>";
        // If this user's role is 'admin', we've found our target.
        if ($user['role'] === 'admin') {
            $foundAdmin = $user['name'];
            break; // Mission complete! Exit the loop immediately.
        }
    }
    echo "<p>Search stopped. First admin found: <span class='highlight'>
         $foundAdmin</span></p>";
    ?>
    </div>
    <h1>Using `continue` to list non-admins</h1>
    <div class="output">
    <p>The following users are not admins:</p>
    <ul>
```

```
    <?php
    foreach ($users as $user) {
        // If this user's role is 'admin', skip the rest of this iteration.
        if ($user['role'] === 'admin') {
            continue; // Go to the next user immediately.
        }
        // This line of code will ONLY be reached if the continue was not triggered.
        echo "<li>{$user['name']}</li>";
    }
    ?>
    </ul>
    </div>
</body>
</html>
```

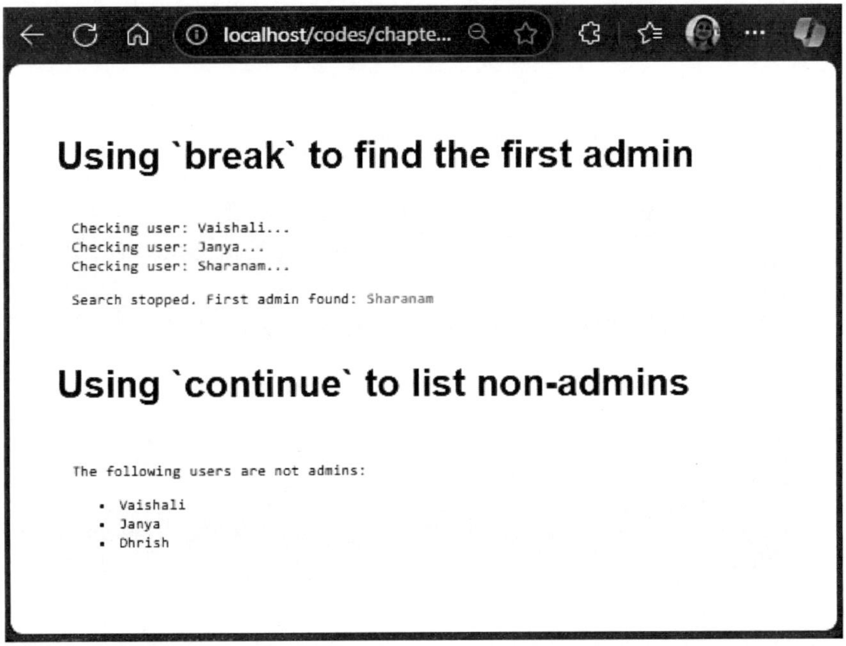

- The first output box shows the search in progress. As soon as it checks Sharanam, it stops and displays the final message: "Search stopped. First admin found: **Sharanam**". Notice it never even checks Dhrish, because break ended the process efficiently.
- The second output box shows a bulleted list containing "Vaishali", "Janya", and "Dhrish". It perfectly excluded Sharanam because the continue statement skipped the part of the code that would have printed his name.

Nested structures: Building complex logic

To build truly powerful applications, you'll often need to place control structures inside one another. This is called **nesting**. You can put an if statement inside a for loop, or a foreach loop inside another foreach loop.

Think of it like a set of Russian nesting dolls. Opening one reveals another inside. A great practical example is creating a calendar grid. You need an outer loop to handle the rows (weeks) and an inner loop to handle the columns (days of the week).

Let's build a simple grid for a 31-day month. We'll nest an if statement inside the for loop to highlight the weekends:

```
<!DOCTYPE html>
<html lang="en">
<head>
    <title>Nested Loops - Calendar</title>
    <style>
        .calendar {
            display: grid;
            grid-template-columns: repeat(7, 1fr); /* Creates a 7-column grid */
            gap: 5px;
            width: 100%;
            max-width: 500px;
            margin-top: 1em;
        }
        .day {
            background: #e9ecef;
            text-align: center;
            padding: 15px 10px;
            border-radius: 4px;
        }
        .header {
            font-weight: bold;
            background: #343a40;
            color: white;
        }
        .highlight {
            background: #ffc107; /* A nice yellow for weekends */
            color: #333;
        }
    </style>
</head>
<body>
    <h2>Simple Monthly Grid</h2>
    <div class="calendar">
        <?php
        $daysOfWeek = ['Sun', 'Mon', 'Tue', 'Wed', 'Thu', 'Fri', 'Sat'];
```

```
        // First, let's loop through the headers and print them.
        foreach ($daysOfWeek as $day) {
            echo "<div class='day header'>$day</div>";
        }
        // Now, the main loop to generate the day numbers from 1 to 31.
        for ($i = 1; $i <= 31; $i++) {
            // NESTED LOGIC: Inside our loop, an 'if' statement checks for
            // weekends. The modulo operator (%) gives the remainder of a
            // division. We'll pretend the 1st, 7th, 8th, 14th etc. are weekends
            // for this simple example.
            if ($i % 7 == 1 || $i % 7 == 0) {
                echo "<div class='day highlight'>$i</div>"; // Weekend style!
            } else {
                echo "<div class='day'>$i</div>"; // Weekday style.
            }
        }
        ?>
    </div>
</body>
</html>
```

This code produces a beautiful, responsive grid. The top row contains the days of the week on a dark background. Below it, you can see numbers from 1 to 31 filling out the grid, with every 1st, 7th, 8th, etc., day highlighted in yellow, clearly marking them as weekends.

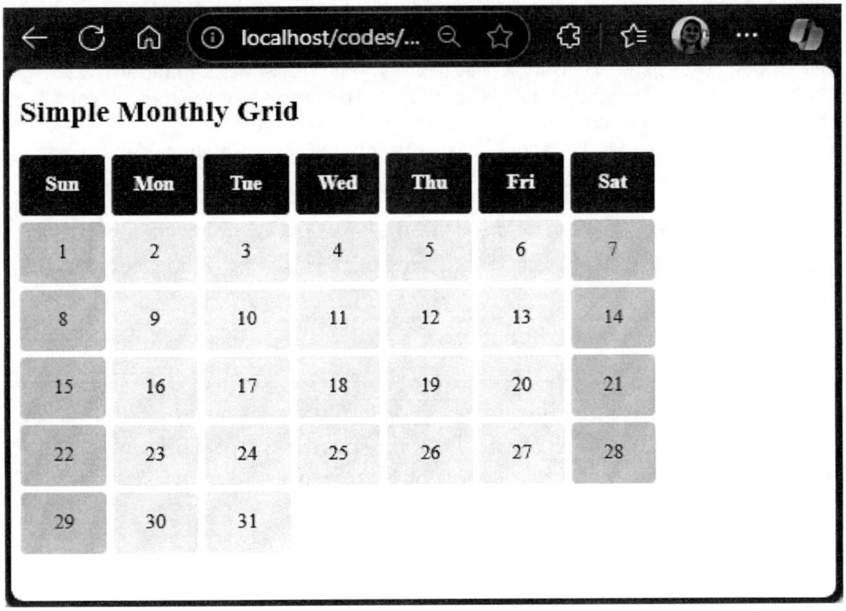

Debugging and visualizing logic paths

As your logic becomes more complex with nested structures, it becomes easier to make mistakes. One of the most common and frustrating bugs is the **infinite loop**. This happens when a loop's condition is never met, causing it to run forever and crash your script. For example, a **while** loop that says **while ($counter > 0)** but inside the loop you accidentally increment the counter **($counter++)** instead of decrementing it.

The best way to find and fix such problems is to **visualize the logic path**. You can do this by strategically placing **echo** or **var_dump()** statements inside your loops and conditionals. This acts like an X-ray, showing you the exact value of your variables at each step of the execution, making it much easier to spot where your logic went wrong.

Let's look at that buggy loop and how a simple echo makes the problem obvious (with a deliberate bug):

```
<?php
// BUGGY CODE - This is for demonstration only.
$counter = 1;
echo "Starting a countdown... or so we thought.<br>";
// The intention is to count DOWN to 0.
// But we are INCREMENTING the counter, so it will never be less than 0.
while ($counter > 0) {
    // This debugging line is our X-ray! It shows us what's happening.
    echo "Current counter value is: $counter. The loop continues...<br>";
    $counter++; // The bug is here! It should be $counter--
    // To prevent this example from actually crashing your browser,
    // we'll add a safety 'break' that stops it after 10 loops.
    if ($counter > 10) {
        echo "<strong style='color:red;'>SAFETY BREAK! The loop was infinite.
             The counter was going up, not down.</strong>";
        break;
    }
}
?>
```

By looking at the output, you would immediately see "Current counter value is: 1", "...value is: 2", "...value is: 3", and realize your "countdown" is counting up! The simple echo statement inside the loop makes the bug's behavior completely transparent.

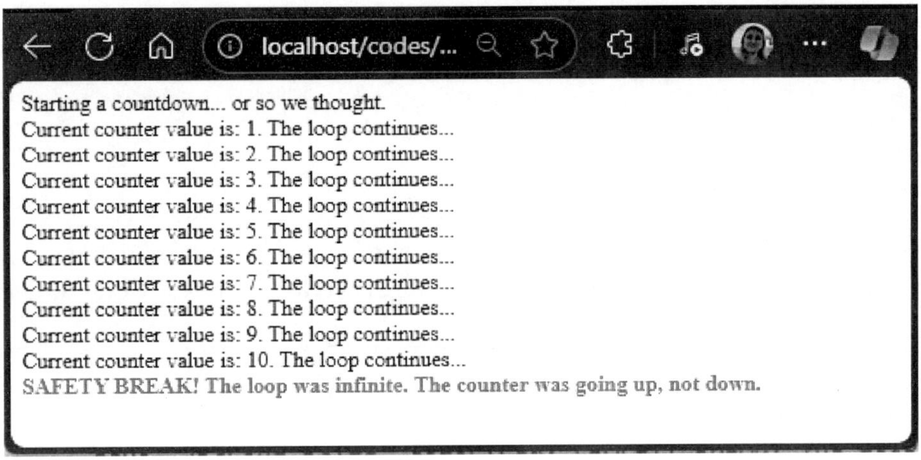

Hands-on: Creating a Temperature Converter web app

It's time to combine everything we've just learned into a single, polished, and practical web application. We are going to build a **Temperature Converter**. This useful tool will allow a user to enter a number, choose a conversion type (like Celsius to Fahrenheit), and instantly see the calculated result.

This project is the perfect way to solidify your understanding of control structures. You'll see firsthand how an if/elseif statement can take input from an HTML form and intelligently decide which mathematical operation to perform, creating a seamless and interactive experience for the user. Let's get building!

Building the application

We'll start by setting up our project folder inside XAMPP's **htdocs/codes** directory. This organization is key to managing your projects. Inside this folder, we'll create our PHP file for logic and our CSS file for styling.

Create the folder and files

1. Using your file explorer, navigate to your XAMPP installation folder (usually C:\xampp on Windows). Open the **htdocs** directory—this is the root folder for all your local web projects.
2. Inside **htdocs\codes**, create a new folder and name it **temperature-converter**.
3. Open this new folder in **Visual Studio Code**.

4. In VS Code's file explorer panel, create two new files:
    - index.php
    - style.css

Write the CSS for styling

A great user experience starts with a clean design. Let's write the CSS first so that when we build our HTML, it will look good right away. Open **style.css** in **VS Code** and add the following code:

```
body {
    font-family: 'Segoe UI', Tahoma, Geneva, Verdana, sans-serif;
    background-color: #eef1f5;
    display: flex;
    justify-content: center;
    align-items: center;
    height: 100vh;
    margin: 0;
}
.converter-wrapper {
    background: #ffffff;
    padding: 2.5rem;
    border-radius: 12px;
    box-shadow: 0 8px 30px rgba(0, 0, 0, 0.1);
    width: 100%;
    max-width: 400px;
    text-align: center;
}
h1 {
    color: #333;
    margin-bottom: 2rem;
}
.form-group {
    margin-bottom: 1.5rem;
    text-align: left;
}
label {
    display: block;
    margin-bottom: 0.5rem;
    color: #555;
    font-weight: 600;
}
input[type="text"], select {
    width: 100%;
    padding: 12px;
    border: 1px solid #ccc;
    border-radius: 8px;
    font-size: 1rem;
```

```
    box-sizing: border-box; /* Ensures padding doesn't affect final width */
}
button {
    width: 100%;
    padding: 15px;
    background-color: #007bff;
    color: white;
    border: none;
    border-radius: 8px;
    font-size: 1.1rem;
    font-weight: bold;
    cursor: pointer;
    transition: background-color 0.3s ease;
}
button:hover {
    background-color: #0056b3;
}
.result-box {
    margin-top: 2rem;
    padding: 1.5rem;
    border-radius: 8px;
    font-size: 1.2rem;
    font-weight: bold;
    display: none; /* The result is hidden until there's something to show */
}
.result-box.show {
    display: block; /* We'll use PHP to add this class to show the box */
    animation: fadeIn 0.5s;
}
.result-box.success {
    background-color: #d4edda;
    color: #155724;
    border: 1px solid #c3e6cb;
}
.result-box.error {
    background-color: #f8d7da;
    color: #721c24;
    border: 1px solid #f5c6cb;
}
@keyframes fadeIn {
    from { opacity: 0; transform: translateY(-10px); }
    to { opacity: 1; transform: translateY(0); }
}
```

This CSS creates a modern, centered layout with pleasing colors and even a subtle animation for the result box.

Write the PHP and HTML

This is where the magic happens. Open **index.php** in **VS Code**. We will structure this file logically: the PHP processing code will go at the very top, and the HTML structure that the user sees will go below it:

```
<?php
// === PART 1: INITIALIZATION ===
// It's good practice to declare the variables we'll use at the top. This prevents
// errors and makes the code easier to read.
$result = null; // Will hold our final message, e.g., "100 °C is 212 °F".
$inputValue = ''; // Will hold the number the user typed in.
$conversionType = 'c_to_f'; // Default conversion type.
// === PART 2: PROCESSING FORM SUBMISSION ===
// This `if` block is the gatekeeper. The code inside only runs if the form was
// submitted. `$_SERVER['REQUEST_METHOD']` is a PHP superglobal that tells us
// how the page was requested.
if ($_SERVER['REQUEST_METHOD'] === 'POST') {
    // Get the data the user sent from the form. We use an `if` statement with
    // `isset()` to make sure the data actually exists before we use it.
    if (isset($_POST['temperature']) && isset($_POST['conversion_type'])) {
        $inputValue = $_POST['temperature'];
        $conversionType = $_POST['conversion_type'];
        // === PART 3: VALIDATION ===
        // Before we do math, we MUST validate! Is the input actually a number? `is_
        // numeric()` is a handy PHP function for this. It's a "truthy/falsy" check!
        if (is_numeric($inputValue)) {
            $temp = floatval($inputValue); // Convert the input string to a number.
            // === PART 4: THE CORE LOGIC (DECISION MAKING) ===
            // Here's our if/elseif statement doing its job. It checks which
            // conversion to perform.
            if ($conversionType === 'c_to_f') {
              // Celsius to Fahrenheit formula: (°C × 9/5) + 32
              $convertedTemp = ($temp * 9 / 5) + 32;
              // Create the success message. `round()` makes the result neat.
              $result = "$temp °C is equal to " . round($convertedTemp, 2) . " °F.";
            } elseif ($conversionType === 'f_to_c') {
              // Fahrenheit to Celsius formula: (°F − 32) × 5/9
              $convertedTemp = ($temp - 32) * 5 / 9;
              $result = "$temp °F is equal to " . round($convertedTemp, 2) . " °C.";
            }
        } else {
          // If the `is_numeric()` check failed, we create an error message instead.
          $result = "Please enter a valid number for the temperature.";
        }
    }
}
?>
<!DOCTYPE html>
<html lang="en">
```

```
<head>
    <meta charset="UTF-8">
    <meta name="viewport" content="width=device-width, initial-scale=1.0">
    <title>Temperature Converter</title>
    <link rel="stylesheet" href="style.css">
</head>
<body>
    <div class="converter-wrapper">
        <h1>Temperature Converter</h1>
        <form action="index.php" method="POST">
            <div class="form-group">
                <label for="temperature">Enter Temperature:</label>
                <input type="text" id="temperature" name="temperature"
                       value="<?php echo htmlspecialchars($inputValue); ?>"
                       required>
            </div>
            <div class="form-group">
                <label for="conversion_type">Select Conversion:</label>
                <select id="conversion_type" name="conversion_type">
                    <option value="c_to_f" <?php if ($conversionType === 'c_to_f')
                            echo 'selected'; ?>>Celsius to Fahrenheit</option>
                    <option value="f_to_c" <?php if ($conversionType === 'f_to_c')
                            echo 'selected'; ?>>Fahrenheit to Celsius</option>
                </select>
            </div>
            <button type="submit">Convert</button>
        </form>
        <?php if ($result !== null): ?>
            <div class="result-box
                <?php echo (is_numeric($inputValue) || $inputValue === '') ?
                          'success' : 'error'; ?>
                show">
                <?php echo $result; ?>
            </div>
        <?php endif; ?>
    </div>
</body>
</html>
```

Bridging the gap: Learned concepts and application implementation

Let's pause and admire our work. This application beautifully demonstrates the core concepts of this chapter:

- **if ($_SERVER['REQUEST_METHOD'] === 'POST'):** This is the master control gate. It ensures our calculation logic only runs in response to a user action (clicking the button), not on the initial page load.

- **if (is_numeric($inputValue)):** Here we see a "truthy/falsy" check in a real-world validation scenario. It protects our code from trying to do math on text, which would cause an error.
- **if ($conversionType === 'c_to_f') { ... } elseif ($conversionType === 'f_to_c') { ... }:** This is the heart of our application's intelligence. It's a clear decision-making structure that looks at the user's choice and executes the one, correct block of code.
- **<?php if ($result !== null): ?> ... <?php endif; ?>:** This is a sophisticated way to control HTML output. The entire div for the result box doesn't even exist in the HTML source code until our PHP code has a result to display. This keeps our page clean.
- **The Ternary operator (condition ? value_if_true : value_if_false):** We used this clever shorthand if/else statement to dynamically add either the success or error CSS class to our result box. This is what makes the box green for good results and red for errors, providing excellent user feedback.

You have now personally experienced the most fundamental partnership in web development: the HTML form and PHP control structures. The form acts as the messenger, collecting information from the user and delivering it to the server. The PHP control structures act as the command center, receiving that message, validating it, making decisions based on it, and formulating a response.

This pattern of **Check → Validate → Process** is something you will use in every single web application you build:

- **Check:** if ($_SERVER['REQUEST_METHOD'] === 'POST')
- **Validate:** if (is_numeric($input))
- **Process:** if ($type === 'a') { do_this; } else { do_that; }

Mastering this flow is a huge step toward becoming a proficient web developer.

Running and testing

Let's bring our application to life!

1. Make sure your **XAMPP Control Panel** shows that the **Apache** module is running (it should have a green background).
2. Open your favourite web browser (like Chrome, Firefox, or Edge).
3. In the address bar, type in the path to your project: **http://localhost/codes/temperature-converter/** and press **Enter**.

4. If everything is correct, you can see your beautifully styled Temperature Converter form. If you see a **Not Found** error, double-check that your folder is named correctly and is inside the htdocs/codes directory.

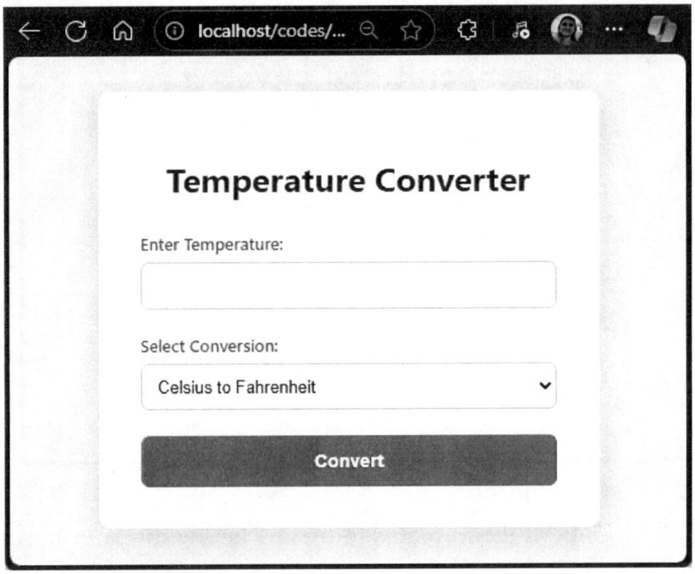

5. Now, let's test its functionality:
6. **Test Scenario 1:** Celsius to Fahrenheit (A boiling point!)
   - In the **temperature** field, type **100**.
   - Ensure the dropdown is set to "**Celsius to Fahrenheit**".

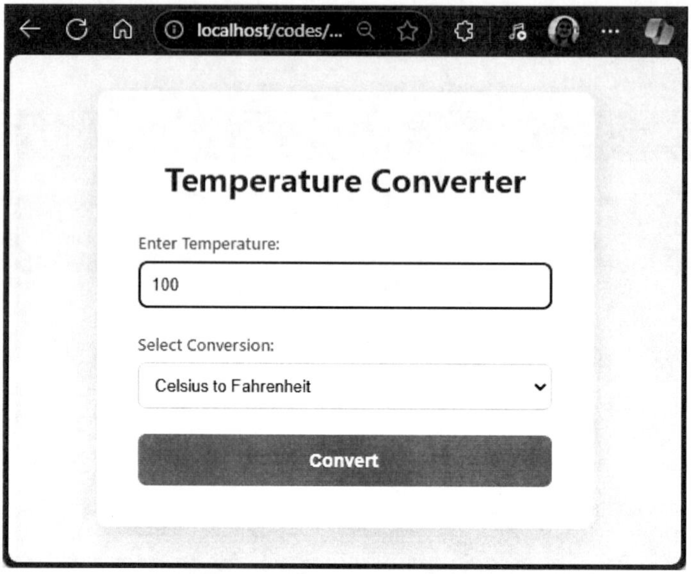

- Click the blue **Convert** button.
- A green result box smoothly animates into view below the button, containing the text: "**100 °C is equal to 212 °F.**"

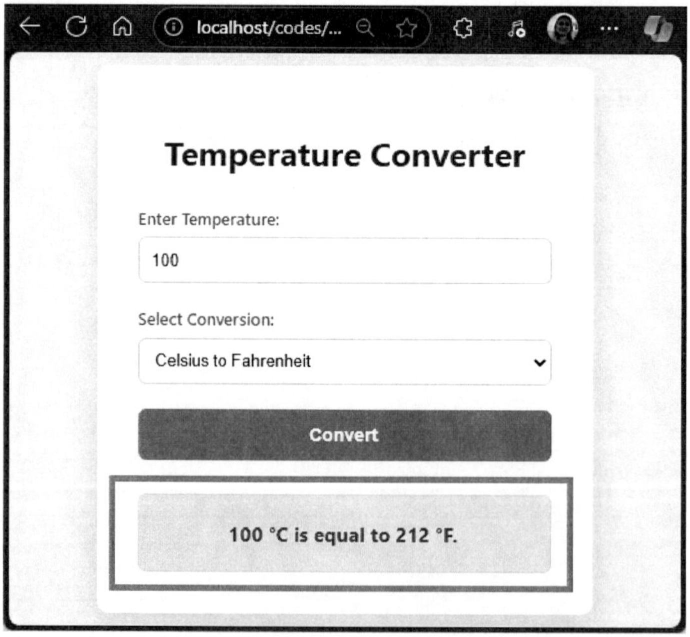

7. **Test Scenario 2:** Fahrenheit to Celsius (A freezing point!)
    - In the **temperature** field, type **32**.
    - Change the dropdown selection to "**Fahrenheit to Celsius**".
    - Click **Convert**.
    - The green result box appears with the text: "**32 °F is equal to 0 °C.**"

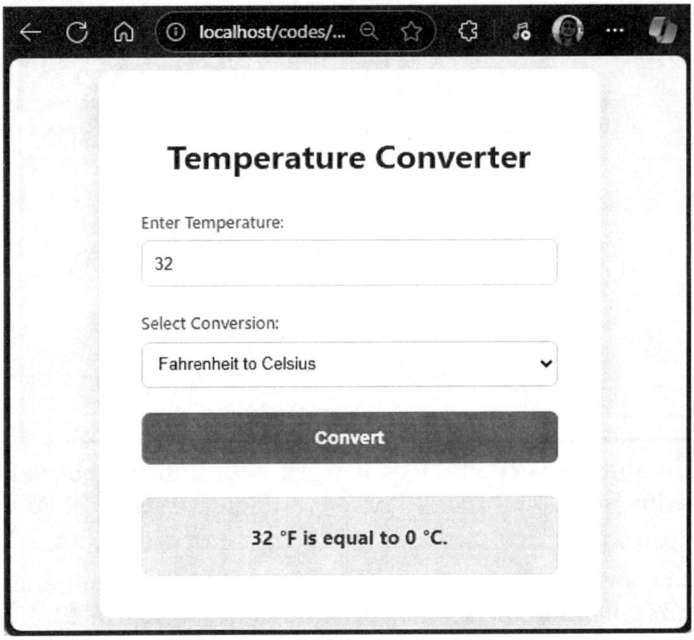

Exploring application behaviour: A practical run-through

A good developer thinks not just about the "happy path" but about all the ways a user might interact with the application. Let's explore:

- **Invalid input:** What happens if a user types their name, **hello**, into the temperature field and clicks convert?
    - **Your app's behaviour:** Our is_numeric() check evaluates to false. The logic then skips the calculations and jump straight to the else block, setting our $result variable to the error message.
    - **The visual result:** The user instantly sees a red error box appear with the clear message: **Please enter a valid number for the temperature**. This is excellent, user-friendly design.

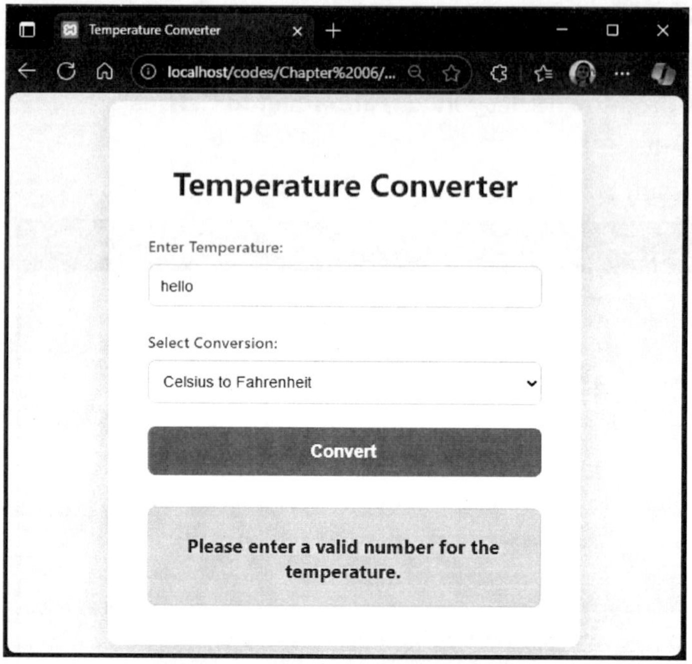

- **Edge cases (Zero and Negatives):** Does it work with unusual but valid numbers? Try converting 0 Celsius (should be 32 °F). Try converting -40 Celsius (should be -40 °F—a fun trivia fact!).
  - **Your app's behaviour:** Our mathematical formulas are sound and handle positive, negative, and zero values perfectly. The calculations are correct.
  - **The visual result:** The app confidently displays the correct converted values in the green success box.

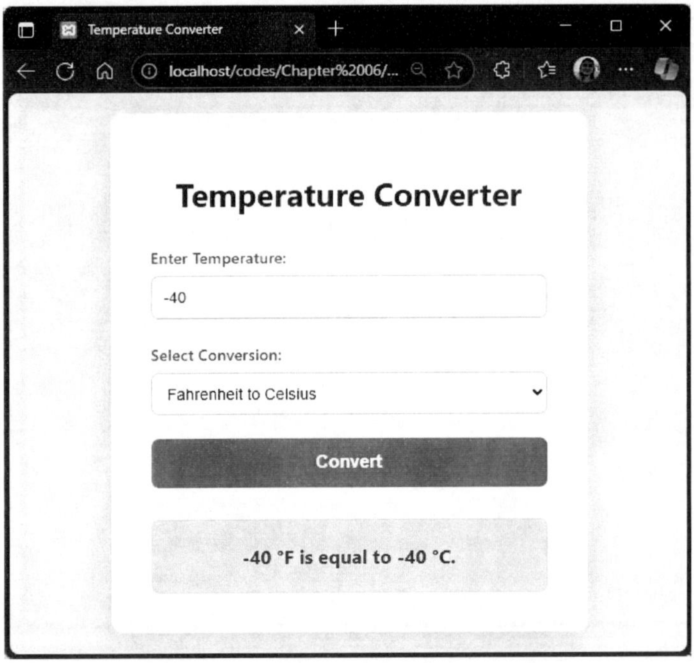

- **Empty submission:** What if a user clicks the **Convert** button without typing anything?
    - **Your app's behaviour:** The required attribute we placed in the HTML <input> tag provides client-side validation. Most modern browsers stops the form from even being submitted and prompts the user to fill out the field. This saves our server from doing unnecessary work.

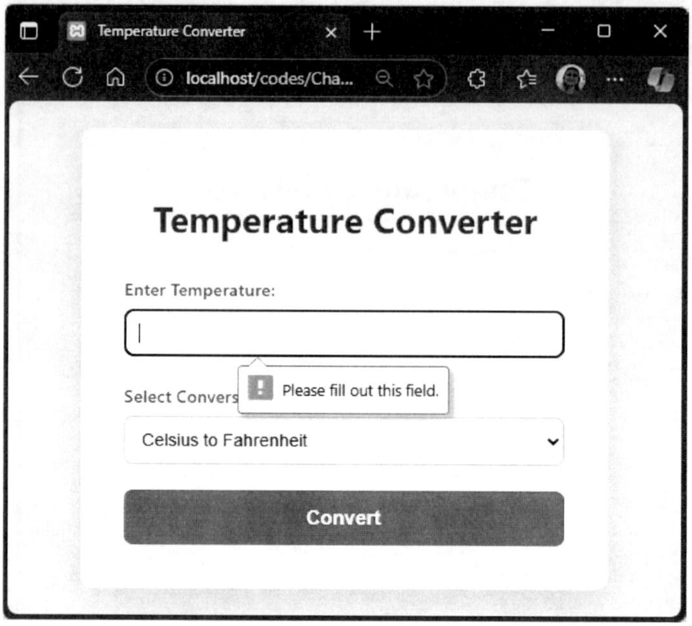

Harnessing control structures in real-world contexts

The simple but powerful logic you just built is a miniature version of what drives the world's biggest websites. Control structures are absolutely everywhere:

- **E-commerce (like Amazon):** if an item is in stock, show the "Add to Cart" button, else show "Out of Stock." foreach item in the cart, calculate the total price.
- **Social media (like Facebook):** if the user is logged in, show their news feed, else show the login page. if a user has permission, show the "delete post" button.
- **Content Management Systems (like WordPress):** switch based on the user's role ('admin', 'editor', 'subscriber') to show different dashboard options. foreach post in the database, display it on the blog page.

Wrapping up

In this chapter, you've made a monumental leap. You've gone from simply storing data to commanding your code to think, decide, and act. You now possess the foundational tools to control the flow and logic of any application.

- You learned to empower your code to make decisions using if, elseif, else, and switch.

- You discovered the power of automation by repeating tasks with for, while, and foreach loops.
- You understood the practical, time-saving concept of "truthy" and "falsy" values.
- You saw how nesting structures allows you to build sophisticated logic for complex tasks.

Give yourself a huge pat on the back! You have successfully mastered the core logic that breathes life into virtually every website on the internet. These control structures are the brain of your programs, and you are now officially qualified to be the director of that brain. You built a real, working utility that takes user input, processes it intelligently, and provides a useful result. That is the very essence of web development.

Carry this confidence and momentum forward. In our next ***Chapter 7: Culmination - Quiz master – Interactive flashcards game***, we're going to use these new skills to build something even more fun and interactive, putting everything you've learned to the test.

Chapter 7

Section 02: Foundations of great code – PHP basics in action

Culmination: Quiz master – Interactive flashcards game

What you'll learn

- Designing application flow
- Handling user input
- Styling with CSS
- Structuring data with arrays
- Calculating results
- Managing state with sessions

Welcome to your first mini-project! This is a milestone chapter where we transition from learning individual concepts to building a complete, interactive web application. We're going to combine everything you've mastered so far—variables, control structures, and arrays—to create a fun and engaging **Quiz master flashcards game**.

Think about any online quiz you've ever taken. It presents a question, you pick an answer, and it immediately tells you if you were right before moving on. That simple, satisfying loop is the heart of countless web applications, from e-learning platforms to customer feedback forms.

In this chapter, we are going to build that exact mechanism from the ground up. Don't worry, I will be with you every step of the way. Let's start building!

Recap

Before we start coding, let's open our developer toolkit and remind ourselves of the three essential tools we'll be using for this project. Mastering how they work together is the key to building this application.

- **Variables:** Think of a variable as a labelled storage box where you can keep one piece of information. For our quiz, we'll need several boxes: one to hold the current question, one to hold the user's answer, and a very important one to keep track of the user's score (e.g., $score = 0;).
- **Control structures:** These are the decision-makers in our code. An if statement acts like a fork in the road, allowing our program to follow a different path based on a condition. For our quiz, the main decision is: "Is the user's answer correct?" The if statement will check this and guide the program to either show a "Correct!" message or an "Incorrect" one. We'll also use a loop (foreach) which tells our program to repeat an action, like displaying every single answer option for a given question.
- **Arrays:** Imagine a filing cabinet. An array is the programming equivalent. Instead of having dozens of separate variable "boxes" all over the place, an array lets us store a whole collection of related items in one organized place. For our quiz, this is a lifesaver! We'll use a **multidimensional array**—think of a filing cabinet with multiple drawers. Each drawer will represent a single question and will contain folders for the question text, the possible answer options, and the single correct answer.

By weaving these three tools together, we can create a dynamic experience that feels alive and responds intelligently to the user's actions.

Designing the quiz flow

A great builder always starts with a blueprint. In web development, our blueprint is the **application flow**. Planning this out before writing any code is a crucial habit that saves countless hours of confusion later. Let's map out the journey a user will take through our Quiz master game.

Here is the step-by-step flow:

- **Start:** The user opens the webpage. The application's first job is to get ready. This means setting the score to 0 and preparing the very first question.

- **Display question:** The application shows the user the question and a set of clickable answer options.
- **User input:** This is the interactive part! The user chooses an answer by clicking one of the options. This click is the **input** that our application needs to process.
- **Process answer:** The application takes the user's submitted answer and compares it to the correct answer stored in our "filing cabinet" (the array).
- **Provide feedback & update score:** This is the output.
    - If the answer is **correct**, the application displays a "Correct!" message and adds one point to the user's score.
    - If the answer is **incorrect**, it shows a "Sorry..." message and tells the user what the correct answer was. The score remains unchanged.
- **Check for more questions:** The application checks: are there any more question "drawers" left in our filing cabinet?
    - If **yes**, it gets the next question ready and the flow repeats from Step 2.
    - If **no**, the quiz is over, and it's time for the grand finale.
- **Show final results:** The application displays the user's final score (e.g., "You got 3 out of 4 correct!") and provides a "Play Again" button to restart the entire process.

This clear, logical flow ensures a predictable and user-friendly experience.

Building the question bank

The heart of our quiz is the content—the questions and answers. As we planned, a multidimensional array is the perfect tool for this job. It allows us to bundle all the information for a single question into one neat package.

Let's build our question bank in PHP. This is the "filing cabinet" we discussed, where each item in the main $questions array is a "drawer" containing another array of information:

```
<?php
$questions = [
    [
        'question' => 'What does PHP stand for?',
        'options' => ['Personal Home Page', 'PHP: Hypertext Preprocessor',
                      'Private Home Page'],
        'answer' => 'PHP: Hypertext Preprocessor'
    ],
    [
        'question' => 'Which symbol is used to declare a variable in PHP?',
        'options' => ['$', '#', '&'],
```

```
            'answer' => '$'
        ],
        [
            'question' => 'Which of the following is a control structure?',
            'options' => ['if/else', 'echo', 'array()'],
            'answer' => 'if/else'
        ]
];
?>
```

Let's break down this structure:

- **$questions = [...]** is our main array, our filing cabinet.
- Each **[...]** block inside it is an associative array, our question drawer.
- Inside each drawer, we have three labeled folders (keys):
    - **'question'** stores the question text as a string.
    - **'options'** stores another array—a simple list of the multiple-choice answers.
    - **'answer'** stores the one correct answer as a string.

This organized structure is incredibly powerful. If we want to add ten more questions later, we just add ten more "drawers" to our cabinet. The rest of our application code won't need to change at all!

Handling user answers

When a user clicks an answer, how does that information get from their browser back to our PHP script on the server? This happens through an HTML form. Think of the $_POST superglobal variable as a special **digital delivery truck**. When a user submits a form, the browser packages up the data and sends it to the server. Our PHP script can then open the cargo delivered by the $_POST truck to see what the user sent.

Let's look at the logic for how our script will handle this delivery:

```
<?php
// Let's assume our $questions array from above is available here. The server
// receives the delivery from the browser. We get the question number the user was
// on (we'll see how this is sent later).
$question_number = $_POST['question_id'];
// We get the answer the user clicked on.
$user_answer = $_POST['answer'];
// Now, we look up the correct answer in our own records (the array).
$correct_answer = $questions[$question_number]['answer'];
// Finally, we compare the user's answer to the correct one.
```

```
if ($user_answer === $correct_answer) {
    echo "<h1>Correct! You're a star!</h1>";
    // In our real app, we'll also add a point to the score here.
} else {
    echo "<h1>Sorry, the correct answer was: " . $correct_answer . "</h1>";
    // No points added, but we provide helpful feedback.
}
?>
```

This simple if/else block is the brain of our quiz. It takes the user's input, makes a decision, and produces an immediate, helpful output.

Calculating scores and feedback

Here we face a classic challenge in web development. The web is **stateless**. This means that every time you load a page, the server has no memory of your previous visit. It's like having a conversation with someone who forgets everything you said the moment you finish a sentence. So, when a user answers question #1 and the page reloads to show question #2, how does the server remember their score? We have to remind it! We will use PHP **sessions** for this. A session is like giving the user a temporary name tag. The server gives the browser a unique ID, and for as long as the browser is open, the server can store information linked to that ID (like a score).

Here's how our scoring logic will work using a session:

- **Start the session:** At the very beginning of the quiz, we tell the server, "Hey, we need to track this user."
- **Initialize the score:** We create a spot in the session's memory for the score and set it to 0. $_SESSION['score'] = 0;
- **Increment the score:** If the user's answer is correct, we update the score in the session's memory: $_SESSION['score']++;.
- **Display the score:** Because the score is stored on the server in the session, we can access and display it on any page, at any time during the quiz.

When the quiz is over, we simply display the final value stored in $_SESSION['score']. This elegant solution overcomes the "memoryless" nature of the web and allows for a continuous user experience.

UI/UX: Enhancing with CSS

Functionality is king, but a beautiful and intuitive **User Interface (UI)** and **User Experience (UX)** make an application a pleasure to use. We will use simple CSS to transform our quiz from plain HTML into something that looks polished and professional.

Our styling goals are:

- **Layout:** A clean, centered quiz box that focuses the user's attention.
- **Typography:** A modern, easy-to-read font for all text.
- **Interaction:** Buttons that look and feel clickable.
- **Feedback:** Using colour to provide instant understanding. Green is universally understood as "go" or "correct," while red signals "stop" or "incorrect." This visual cue is faster to process than reading text alone.

We'll place all our styles in a dedicated style.css file to keep our project tidy. This is a best practice known as **separation of concerns**—keeping our structure (HTML), logic (PHP), and presentation (CSS) in different files.

Here's a preview of the CSS that will bring our quiz to life:

```
.quiz-container {
    background-color: #fff;
    padding: 2rem;
    border-radius: 10px;
    box-shadow: 0 4px 8px rgba(0,0,0,0.1);
    width: 500px;
    text-align: center;
}
/* Style for the "Correct!" message */
.feedback.correct {
    color: #28a745; /* A friendly green */
    font-weight: bold;
}
/* Style for the "Sorry..." message */
.feedback.incorrect {
    color: #dc3545; /* A clear red */
    font-weight: bold;
}
```

With just a little CSS, we can dramatically improve the entire experience for our users.

Hands-on: The Quiz master app

Alright, it's time to get our hands dirty and build this thing! This is the most exciting part. We will now construct the Quiz Master application from a blank slate. Follow these steps carefully, and by the end, you'll have a fully functional web app running on your own computer. Let's begin.

Building the application

First things first, let's create our project folder. Navigate to your XAMPP installation folder, find the **htdocs/codes** directory, and create a new folder inside **/codes** called **quiz-master**.

Inside this new **quiz-master** folder, we'll use VS Code to create two empty files:

- index.php (for our main logic and HTML)
- style.css (for our styling)

Your project structure should be clean and simple:

```
xampp/htdocs/codes/quiz-master/
├──index.php
└──style.css
```

Create the CSS file

Let's paint the canvas before we add the actors. Open the style.css file in VS Code and paste in the following code:

```
body {
    font-family: -apple-system, BlinkMacSystemFont, "Segoe UI", Roboto, Helvetica,
                 Arial, sans-serif;
    background-color: #f0f2f5;
    display: flex;
    justify-content: center;
    align-items: center;
    min-height: 100vh;
    margin: 0;
}
.container {
    background: #ffffff;
    padding: 2rem 3rem;
    border-radius: 15px;
    box-shadow: 0 10px 25px rgba(0, 0, 0, 0.1);
    width: 100%;
    max-width: 600px;
```

```
    text-align: center;
}
h1 {
    color: #333;
    margin-bottom: 0.5rem;
}
h2 {
    color: #555;
    margin-bottom: 2rem;
    font-weight: 400;
}
.question {
    font-size: 1.2rem;
    margin-bottom: 2rem;
}
.options-form {
    display: flex;
    flex-direction: column;
    gap: 1rem;
}
.option-btn {
    padding: 1rem;
    border: 2px solid #ddd;
    background-color: #fafafa;
    color: #333;
    border-radius: 8px;
    cursor: pointer;
    text-align: center;
    font-size: 1rem;
    transition: background-color 0.2s, border-color 0.2s;
}
.option-btn:hover {
    background-color: #e9ecef;
    border-color: #adb5bd;
}
.feedback-container {
    padding: 1.5rem;
    margin: 2rem 0;
    border-radius: 8px;
    font-size: 1.2rem;
    font-weight: bold;
}
.feedback-container.correct {
    background-color: #d4edda;
    color: #155724;
    border: 1px solid #c3e6cb;
}
.feedback-container.incorrect {
    background-color: #f8d7da;
    color: #721c24;
    border: 1px solid #f5c6cb;
```

```
}
.final-score {
    font-size: 1.5rem;
    color: #007bff;
    margin-bottom: 2rem;
}
.restart-btn {
    background-color: #007bff;
    color: white;
    padding: 1rem 2rem;
    border: none;
    border-radius: 8px;
    font-size: 1rem;
    cursor: pointer;
    text-decoration: none;
    display: inline-block;
    transition: background-color 0.2s;
}
.restart-btn:hover {
    background-color: #0056b3;
}
```

This CSS will create the modern, card-like appearance for our quiz, style the buttons, and set up the colors for our feedback messages.

Create the main PHP file

This file is the engine of our application. It will contain our PHP logic and the HTML structure that gets displayed in the browser. Open index.php in VS Code and carefully enter the following code:

```
<?php
// This MUST be the very first line. It tells PHP to start or resume a session.
session_start();
// --- 1. The Question Bank ---
// Our single source of truth for all quiz content.
$questions = [
    [
        'question' => 'What is the primary function of CSS?',
        'options' => ['To structure web content', 'To style web pages',
                      'To program server logic'],
        'answer' => 'To style web pages'
    ],
    [
        'question' => 'Which PHP superglobal variable is used to collect form
                       data after submitting an HTML form with method="post"?',
        'options' => ['$_GET', '$_SERVER', '$_POST'],
        'answer' => '$_POST'
```

```
    ],
    [
        'question' => 'What does `var_dump()` function do in PHP?',
        'options' => ['Prints a variable', 'Deletes a variable', 'Dumps information
                     about a variable'],
        'answer' => 'Dumps information about a variable'
    ],
    [
        'question' => 'In HTML, which tag is used to create a hyperlink?',
        'options' => ['<link>', '<a>', '<href>'],
        'answer' => '<a>'
    ]
];
// --- 2. Initialize Quiz State ---
// We check if a question index was sent via the form. If not, it's the start of
// the quiz. The (int) part ensures we are dealing with a number, which is good
// practice.
$current_question_index = isset($_POST['question_index']) ?
(int)$_POST['question_index'] : 0;
$feedback = null;
// If this is the very first page load (no answer submitted yet), initialize
// the score.
if ($current_question_index === 0 && !isset($_POST['answer'])) {
    $_SESSION['score'] = 0;
}
// --- 3. Process User Answer ---
// This block only runs if a form was submitted (i.e., the user clicked an answer).
if (isset($_POST['answer'])) {
    $user_answer = $_POST['answer'];
    // The index of the question they *just* answered is one less than the
    // current one.
    $previous_question_index = $current_question_index - 1;
    // Compare the submitted answer with the correct answer from our array.
    if ($user_answer === $questions[$previous_question_index]['answer']) {
        // Correct! Increment score and prepare positive feedback.
        $_SESSION['score']++;
        $feedback = [
            'message' => 'Correct!',
            'class' => 'correct'
        ];
    } else {
        // Incorrect. Prepare helpful feedback.
        $feedback = [
            'message' => 'Sorry, the correct answer was: ' . htmlspecialchars(
                        $questions[$previous_question_index]['answer']),
            'class' => 'incorrect'
        ];
    }
}
// Determine if the quiz is over by comparing the current index to the total
// number of questions.
```

```
$is_quiz_over = ($current_question_index >= count($questions));
?>
<!DOCTYPE html>
<html lang="en">
<head>
    <meta charset="UTF-8">
    <meta name="viewport" content="width=device-width, initial-scale=1.0">
    <title>Quiz Master - Flashcards Game</title>
    <link rel="stylesheet" href="style.css">
</head>
<body>
    <div class="container">
        <h1>Quiz Master</h1>
        <?php if ($is_quiz_over): ?>
            <h2>Quiz Complete!</h2>
            <p class="final-score">Your final score is: <?php echo
               $_SESSION['score']; ?> out of <?php echo count($questions);?></p>
            <a href="index.php" class="restart-btn">Play Again</a>
        <?php else: ?>
            <?php if ($feedback): ?>
                <div class="feedback-container <?php echo $feedback['class']; ?>">
                    <p><?php echo $feedback['message']; ?></p>
                </div>
            <?php endif; ?>
            <p class="question"><?php echo htmlspecialchars($questions[$current_
                     question_index]['question']); ?></p>
            <form action="index.php" method="post" class="options-form">
                <input type="hidden" name="question_index"
                       value="<?php echo $current_question_index + 1; ?>">
                <?php foreach ($questions[$current_question_index]['options']
                      as $option): ?>
                    <button type="submit" name="answer"
                            value="<?php echo htmlspecialchars($option); ?>"
                            class="option-btn">
                        <?php echo htmlspecialchars($option); ?>
                    </button>
                <?php endforeach; ?>
            </form>
            <p style="margin-top: 2rem; color: #777;">Question <?php echo
               $current_question_index + 1; ?> of <?php echo
               count($questions); ?></p>
        <?php endif; ?>
    </div>
</body>
</html>
```

Let's walk through the index.php file together, piece by piece.

- **session_start():** This function is our memory switch. It *must* be the very first line of code, before any HTML is sent to the browser. It tells PHP to wake up its session handling system, either creating a new memory slot for a new user or reconnecting to an existing one.
- **The PHP logic block (top section):**
  - **$questions array:** This is our self-contained database for the quiz.
  - **Initializing state**: The line $current_question_index = isset($_POST['question_index']) ? ... is a compact if/else statement. It asks, "Did the form submission include a question_index?" If yes, use that number. If no (meaning it's the first visit), start with 0. The isset() function is a safety check to prevent errors by making sure a variable exists before we try to use it. We also initialize the $_SESSION['score'] to 0 only on the very first load.
  - **Processing the answer:** The if (isset($_POST['answer'])) block is the core of our quiz's brain. It only runs after the user has clicked an answer. It retrieves the user's answer, compares it to the correct one, updates the score in the session, and prepares a $feedback array with a message and a CSS class (correct or incorrect).
  - **htmlspecialchars():** This is a crucial security function. It converts special HTML characters (like < and >) into plain text. This prevents a user from injecting malicious HTML into our page. We use it whenever we display data that originated from our array or from a user.
  - **$is_quiz_over:** This boolean (true/false) variable acts as a simple flag. We calculate it once and then use it in our HTML below to decide which section to show.
- **The HTML display block (bottom section):**
  - **The main if/else:** The <?php if ($is_quiz_over): ?> statement is the master controller of our page's content. If our $is_quiz_over flag is true, PHP will only render the "Quiz Complete!" HTML. If it's false, it will only render the HTML for showing a question.
  - **The form:** The <form> is how we send data back to the server. Notice action="index.php" and method="post". This tells the browser to send the data right back to this same file using the $_POST "delivery truck."
  - **The hidden input:** The line <input type="hidden" ...> is the clever trick that makes the quiz advance. The user doesn't see it, but when they submit the form, it sends the *next* question's index along for the ride. This is how the script knows which question to display after processing the answer.

- **The foreach loop:** This loop is beautifully efficient. It iterates over the options array for the current question and generates a <button> for each one, preventing us from having to write the HTML for each button manually.

Bridging the gap: Learned concepts and application implementation

Let's take a moment to connect the dots and see how the theory we learned came to life in our application:

- **Variables and arrays in action:** Our $questions array is a perfect real-world example of how to structure complex, related data. It's clean, readable, and scalable. The variables like $current_question_index and the $_SESSION['score'] weren't just for storing data; they were for managing the *state* of our application—its memory of what's happening right now.
- **Control structures at work:** The if/else logic was the application's brain, making decisions at every step. The foreach loop was a workhorse, building our user interface dynamically. This is what reusability is all about. We wrote the button-making code once, and it works for every question, no matter how many options it has.
- **Code organization:** By creating separate index.php and style.css files, we practiced the fundamental principle of **separation of concerns**. Our logic (PHP) is not messy and tangled up with our presentation (CSS). This makes our project infinitely easier to debug, maintain, and expand in the future.

Running and testing

The moment of truth! Let's fire up the application and see our code in action:

1. Open your **XAMPP Control Panel** and ensure that the **Apache** service is started (it should have a green highlight).
2. Open your favourite web browser (like Chrome or Firefox).
3. In the address bar, navigate to **http://localhost/codes/quiz-master/**.
4. You see the first question of your quiz, presented in a clean, styled container. It's alive!

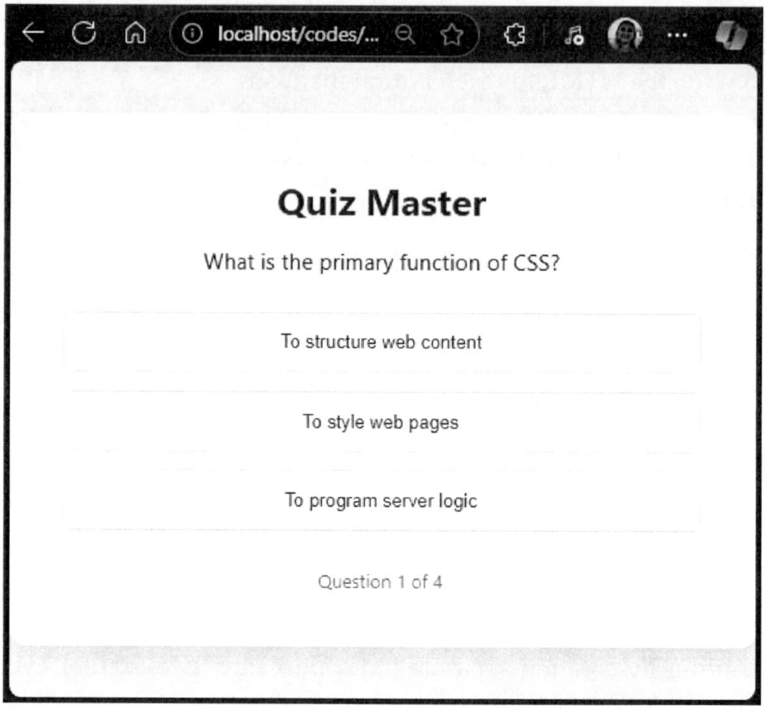

5. Follow this user journey:
    - **Answer a question:** Click on one of the answer buttons. The page reloads instantly.
    - **See your feedback:** You are now on the second question, but at the top of the container, you see the feedback message ("Correct!" in green or "Sorry..." in red) from the question you just answered. Your score has been updated silently in the session.

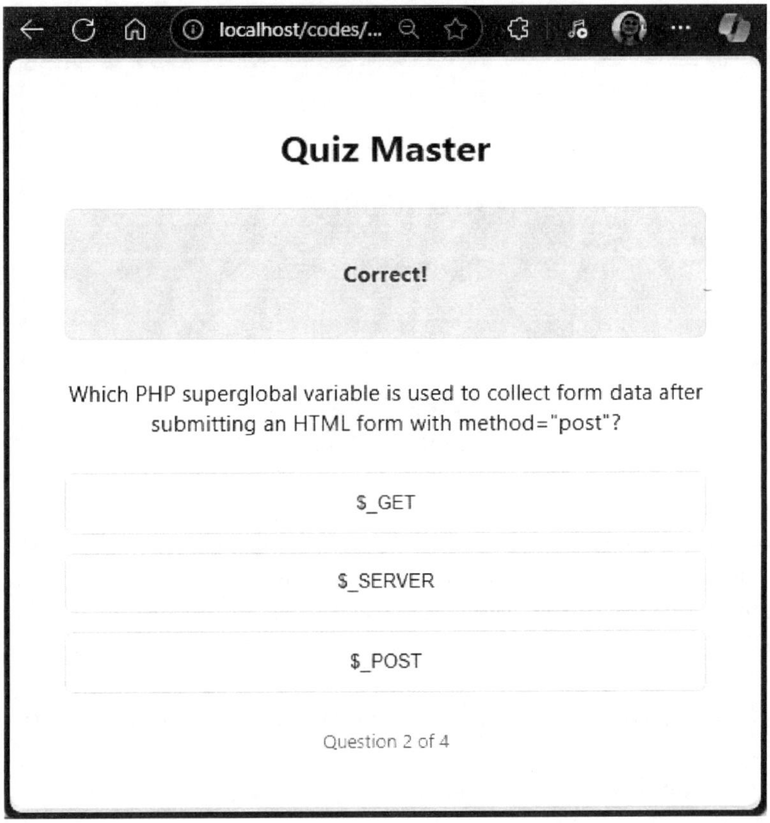

6. **Complete the Quiz:** Continue this process for all four questions. After you answer the final question, the page changes to display your final score.

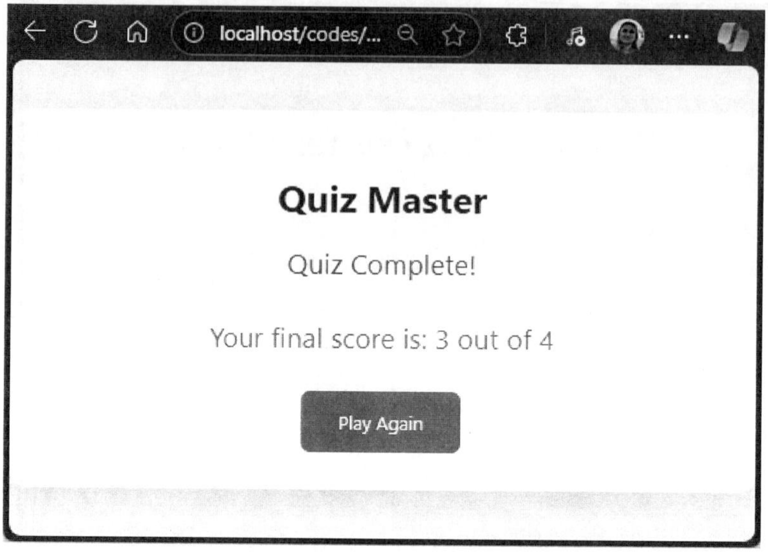

7. **Play again:** Click the **Play Again** button. This link simply reloads index.php without any form data, which our script interprets as a fresh start, resetting the score and taking you back to question #1.

Exploring application behaviour: A practical run-through

A robust application handles various scenarios gracefully. Let's consider a few:

- **Replayability:** Our **Play Again** link is just a simple <a> tag pointing to index.php. When clicked, the browser makes a new request without sending any POST data. Our script's logic (!isset($_POST['answer'])) correctly identifies this as the start of a new quiz and resets the score. It just works!
- **Adding new questions:** The true beauty of our data-driven design is how easy it is to expand. Open index.php and simply add a new array block to the $questions list.

```
// Add this to the $questions array, maybe at the end
[
    'question' => 'What is the file extension for a PHP file?',
    'options' => ['.html', '.css', '.php'],
    'answer' => '.php'
]
```

Save the file and refresh the quiz. The new question is now part of the game! The code automatically adjusts the question count and loops through it without any other changes. This is the power of writing smart, reusable code.

- **What if a user reloads the page?:** If a user is on question #2 and hits the browser's refresh button, what happens? The page reloads, but since no form was submitted, isset($_POST['answer']) is false. The script won't process an answer, and it will simply re-display question #2. No errors, no crashes. Our application is stable.

Harnessing quizzes in real-world contexts

This quiz master project, while small, is a direct model of features you see on the web every day.

- **E-learning & education:** Sites like Khan Academy or Coursera use this exact model for exercises and tests to verify learning.
- **Corporate training:** New employees are often onboarded with interactive quizzes about company policies or software tools.
- **Marketing & user engagement:** Fun "personality quizzes" on sites like BuzzFeed are a massively popular way to increase user engagement and drive traffic.
- **Surveys & feedback:** A customer satisfaction survey follows the same pattern: present a question, collect an answer, and move to the next one.

Wrapping up

In this chapter, you've made a giant leap from a learner to a builder. You created a complete, interactive web application from scratch. Let's recap all the amazing skills you put into practice:

- You designed the logical flow of an application before writing code.
- You used a multidimensional array to create a clean, scalable data source.
- You successfully handled user input using an HTML form and the $_POST superglobal.
- You managed the application's "memory" across page loads using PHP Sessions ($_SESSION).
- You used control structures (if/else, foreach) to intelligently control the quiz flow and display data dynamically.
- You enhanced the entire user experience with an external CSS stylesheet for a professional look and feel.

Take a moment and be proud of what you've accomplished. You are no longer just writing lines of code; you are building real web applications. You've seen firsthand how fundamental programming concepts are woven together to create a dynamic and interactive user experience. You are, officially, a web application developer.

The journey doesn't stop here. Now that you've built a way to *present* information and get simple feedback, it's time to learn how to collect more complex data from users. In the next chapter, we will master one of the most essential components of the web. Get ready for ***Chapter 8: Connecting with the world - Smart forms and secure input***. Keep that curiosity burning!

Chapter 8

Section 03: User power – Forms, strings, and file magic

Connecting with the world – Smart forms and secure input

What you'll learn

- Building HTML forms
- Handling user input securely
- Preventing common attacks
- Using GET vs. POST
- Validating and sanitizing data

Welcome to one of the most exciting and transformative parts of your web development journey! Until now, our web pages have been like television broadcasts—they present information one-way, from us to the user. This chapter is where we turn that television into a telephone. We're opening up a line of communication, allowing users to talk back to our application. This two-way street is made possible by **forms**.

Think about it: every time you log into a website, search on Google, post a photo on social media, or leave a product review, you're using a web form. They are the fundamental bridge between a user's intent and an application's action.

In this chapter, we'll learn how to build that bridge, how to listen for what users are saying, and, most critically, how to handle their messages safely and securely. By the time we're done, you'll have built a fully functional, professional, and secure contact form—a cornerstone of nearly every website on the internet.

Introduction to HTML forms

At its core, a web form is simply a designated area on an HTML page designed to collect information. The magic begins with the **<form>** tag. Think of this tag like a physical suggestion box. It tells the browser, "Everything I'm wrapping around—all these text boxes, buttons, and labels—belongs together. When the user is ready, bundle it all up and send it off to the address I specify."

Inside our <form> tag, we place various input elements. The most common are:

- **<input type="text">:** A single-line text box for things like names or usernames.
- **<textarea>:** A multi-line text box for longer messages or comments.
- **<button type="submit">:** A special button that, when clicked, tells the browser to package up the form data and send it.

Let's look at the blueprint for a simple form.

```
<!DOCTYPE html>
<html lang="en">
<head>
    <meta charset="UTF-8">
    <meta name="viewport" content="width=device-width, initial-scale=1.0">
    <title>Simple HTML Form</title>
</head>
<body>
    <h2>My First Form</h2>
    <form action="/submit-data.php" method="post">
        <label for="name">Name:</label><br>
        <input type="text" id="name" name="visitor_name">
        <br><br>
        <label for="message">Message:</label><br>
        <textarea id="message" name="visitor_message" rows="4" cols="50"></textarea>
        <br><br>
        <button type="submit">Send</button>
    </form>
</body>
</html>
```

If you save this as an HTML file and open it in your browser, you'll see a clean, simple form. Pay close attention to the attributes:

- The **action** tells the form which file on the server should handle the data.
- The **method** defines how the data is sent.
- And most importantly for us, the **name** attribute of each input acts like a label on a package; it's how PHP will identify each piece of data it receives.

GET vs. POST methods: Pros and Cons

The **method** attribute is a critical choice. It's like deciding whether to send information via a postcard or a sealed envelope. Both get the message there, but in very different ways.

- **GET (The postcard):** The GET method bundles up all the form data and appends it directly to the URL. If you filled out a form with your name as **Tom** and a search query of **PHP**, the URL would look something like this:

```
http://example.com/search.php?name=Tom&query=PHP
```

  The data is visible to anyone who can see the screen, the browser history, or server logs.

  - **Pros:** Great for things that aren't secret. Think of a Google search. You can bookmark the results page or share the URL with a friend, and they'll see the exact same thing you did. It's perfect for search, filtering, or sorting.
  - **Cons:** Terribly insecure for private information. You would never write your password or credit card number on a postcard, right? The same logic applies here. GET requests also have a length limit, so they're not suitable for long messages.

- **POST (The sealed envelope):** The POST method sends the form data inside the body of the HTTP request itself. It's hidden from the URL, tucked away from prying eyes. This is the secure, private way to send information.

  - **Pros:** This is the standard for any sensitive data. Login credentials, personal information, financial details—anything you wouldn't want to be seen in a URL should use POST. It also has no limit on the amount of data you can send.
  - **Cons:** Because the data isn't in the URL, you can't bookmark the result of a POST request. If you've ever submitted a form and then hit the **back** button, your browser might warn you about **resubmitting form data**. That's because it needs to send that sealed envelope again.

The Golden Rule:
Use GET when a user is **requesting** or **filtering** data. Use POST when a user is **submitting**, **creating**, or **changing** data, especially if it's sensitive. For our contact form, POST is the only correct choice.

Accessing user data

Alright, the user has filled out our form and clicked **Submit**. The browser has sent the data to our PHP script. How do we retrieve it? PHP makes this incredibly easy with special built-in variables called **superglobals**. Think of them as PHP's magical, pre-filled inboxes.

- **$_GET:** This is an associative array that acts as the inbox for any data sent via the GET method.
- **$_POST:** This is the inbox for data sent via the POST method. This is the one we'll be using most often for forms.
- **$_REQUEST:** This is a **combined inbox** that contains data from $_GET, $_POST, and another source called $_COOKIE. While it might seem convenient, it's considered bad practice to use it. Why? Because it makes your code ambiguous. You no longer know for sure if the data came from a secure POST request or an insecure GET request. Always be specific!

Let's build a tiny application to see $_POST in action. Inside your **xampp/htdocs/codes** folder, create a new folder called **form-test**. Open the **form-test** folder in Visual Studio Code. Inside that folder, create these two files:

1. index.html:

```
<!DOCTYPE html>
<html lang="en">
<head>
    <title>POST Test</title>
</head>
<body>
    <form action="handler.php" method="post">
        <label for="name">Your Name:</label>
        <input type="text" id="name" name="user_name">
        <button type="submit">Submit</button>
    </form>
</body>
</html>
```

2. handler.php

```
<?php
// First, it's good practice to check if the data even exists. isset() checks if a
```

```
// variable or array key has been set and is not null.
if (isset($_POST['user_name'])) {
    // If it exists, retrieve the value from the $_POST 'inbox' using the key
    // 'user_name' (from the input's 'name' attribute).
    $name = $_POST['user_name'];
    // Now we can use this variable!
    echo "<h1>Hello, " . $name . "!</h1>";
} else {
    // If someone visits handler.php directly without submitting the form.
    echo "<h1>Welcome! Please go back and enter your name.</h1>";
}
// For learning purposes, let's see what the entire $_POST array contains. The <pre>
// tags just make the output nicely formatted.
echo "<pre>";
print_r($_POST);
echo "</pre>";
?>
```

1. Now start the **Apache** engine in **XAMPP Control Panel**.
2. Next, point your browser to **http://localhost/codes/form-test/**.

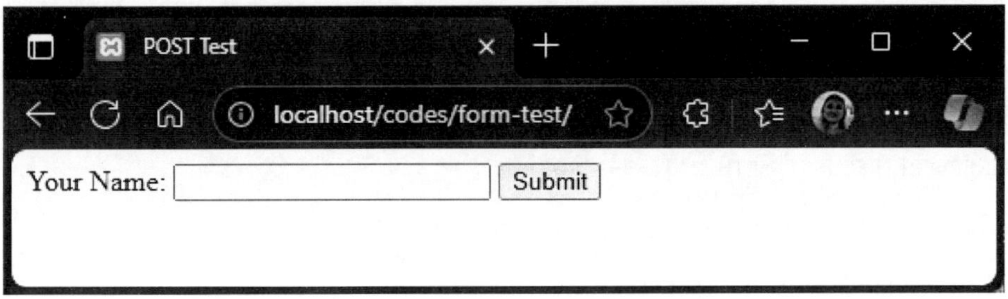

3. Type your name in the box and hit **Submit**. You are taken to handler.php, and you see a personalized greeting! Below it, the print_r() output shows you the exact structure of the array PHP received:

4. Look at that! The **name="user_name"** attribute from our HTML has become the **key** in PHP's associative $_POST array. This direct link is the foundation of handling form data.

Input validation

This is perhaps the most important lesson in this chapter: **Never, ever trust user input.** Think of your PHP script as a secure building and the form as the front door. You need a bouncer—your validation logic—to check everyone who tries to enter. Users will make mistakes. They'll forget to fill out fields, they'll type their phone number in the email box, and sometimes, malicious users will intentionally try to break your application.

Validation is the process of enforcing your rules. Our bouncer's checklist might look like this:

- ❑ Did the user provide everything we require? (e.g., Is the name field blank?)
- ❑ Is the data they provided in the correct format? (e.g., Is this actually a valid email address?)

Let's upgrade our handler.php to be a much stricter bouncer:

```
<?php
// We'll use an array to collect any error messages.
$errors = [];
// Only run this logic if the form was submitted. $_SERVER['REQUEST_METHOD'] tells
// us if it was 'GET', 'POST', etc.
if ($_SERVER['REQUEST_METHOD'] === 'POST') {
    // --- Validation for Name ---
    $name = $_POST['user_name']; // Get the data first
    if (empty(trim($name))) { // trim() removes whitespace from the start and end
        $errors[] = "Name is required.";
    }
    // --- Validation for Email ---
    $email = $_POST['user_email'];
    if (empty(trim($email))) {
        $errors[] = "Email is required.";
    } elseif (!filter_var($email, FILTER_VALIDATE_EMAIL)) {
        // filter_var() is a powerful PHP function for checking data formats.
        // FILTER_VALIDATE_EMAIL is a built-in "filter" that knows what an email
        // should look like.
        $errors[] = "The email format you entered is not valid.";
    }
    // --- Decision Time ---
    // After all checks, we see if our errors array is still empty.
    if (empty($errors)) {
        // If it's empty, we're good to go!
        echo "<h1>Success!</h1>";
        echo "<p>Thank you, " . $name . ". Your information has been
             processed.</p>";
    } else {
```

```
        // If the errors array has items in it, we must display them.
        echo "<h1>Oops! Please fix the following issues:</h1>";
        echo "<ul>";
        foreach ($errors as $error) {
            echo "<li>" . $error . "</li>";
        }
        echo "</ul>";
    }
}
?>
```

Of course, we need to add an email field to our index.html to test this:

```
<!DOCTYPE html>
<html lang="en">
<head>
    <title>Validation Test</title>
</head>
<body>
    <form action="handler.php" method="post">
        <label for="name">Your Name:</label>
        <input type="text" id="name" name="user_name">
        <br><br>
        <label for="email">Your Email:</label>
        <input type="email" id="email" name="user_email">
        <br><br>
        <button type="submit">Submit</button>
    </form>
</body>
</html>
```

1. Now, go back and try to submit the form. If you leave it blank, our bouncer stops you and lists the errors.

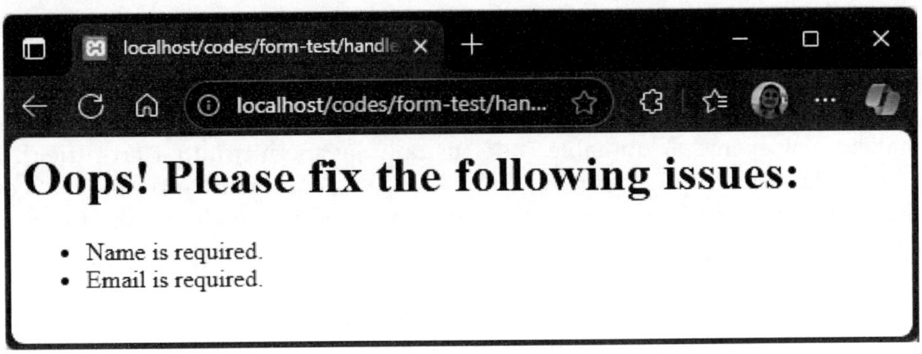

2. If you enter an invalid email like **my Name**, filter_var() catches it.

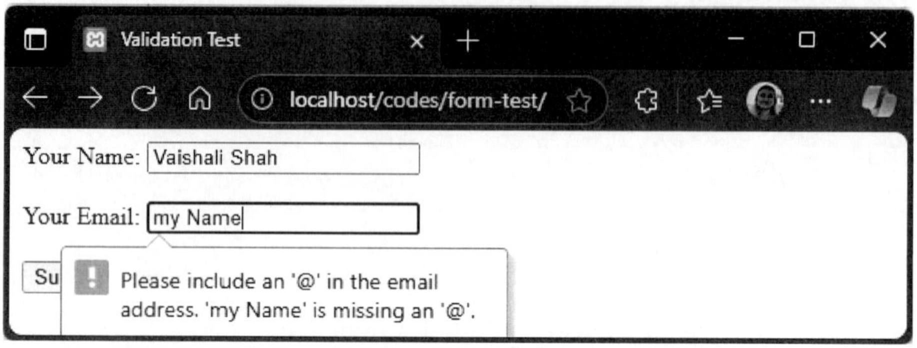

3. Only when you satisfy all the rules, you see the success message.

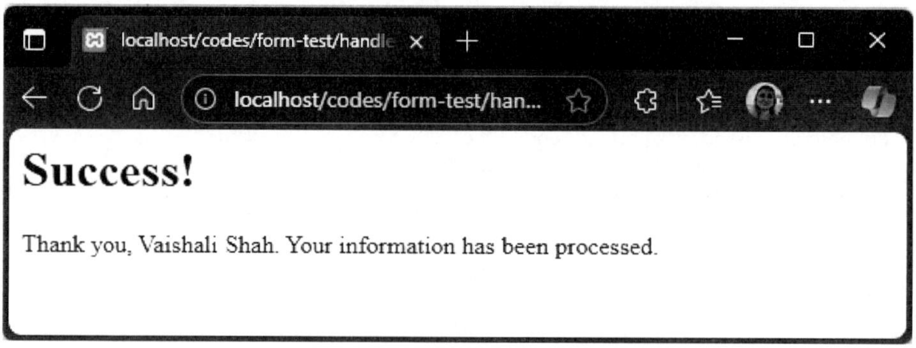

Preventing injection and sanitizing input

Our bouncer (validation) checks that the input looks right. But there's a second, equally important step: **sanitization**. This is the process of cleaning the data to make it safe. Think of it like this: validation checks the guest's ID, but sanitization makes sure they don't track mud into the building.

The biggest threat we're protecting against here is **Cross-Site Scripting (XSS)**. This is an attack where a malicious user injects runnable code (usually JavaScript) into a form field. If your website then displays that input somewhere else—like in a comments section—that code will run in the browser of every other user who visits the page, potentially stealing their data or performing actions on their behalf.

The solution is wonderfully simple. PHP gives us a golden shield: the **htmlspecialchars()** function. It takes any text you give it and converts characters that are special in HTML into their harmless, text-only equivalents.

- < becomes < (the entity for **less than**)

- > becomes > (the entity for **greater than**)
- " becomes " (the entity for **double quote**)
- & becomes & (the entity for **ampersand**)

Imagine an attacker submits this as their name:

```
<script>alert('XSS Attack!');</script>
```

Insecure code (Extremely dangerous!):

```
$name = $_POST['user_name'];
echo "<h2>Welcome back, $name</h2>";
// The browser will see a <script> tag and execute the JavaScript inside. A popup
// will appear.
```

Secure code (The right way!)

```
// Sanitize the data BEFORE you display it!
$name = htmlspecialchars($_POST['user_name'], ENT_QUOTES, 'UTF-8');
echo "<h2>Welcome back, $name</h2>";
// The browser will see the text "<script>alert(...", which it knows how to display
// as plain text, not execute as code. The user will literally see the script tag
// written out on the page, completely neutralized.
```

The second Golden Rule:
Any time you are about to echo data that originally came from a user, wrap it in htmlspecialchars(). No exceptions.

Inline validation with CSS/JS

Our PHP validation is the ultimate source of truth—it's the security that *must* happen on the server. However, waiting for a full page reload just to find out you missed a field is a poor user experience. We can provide a friendlier, instant layer of feedback right in the browser using HTML5 and CSS.

Modern HTML gives us helpful attributes like **required** (which tells the browser a field must be filled) and input types like **type="email"** (which lets the browser do a basic format check).

CSS gives us special **pseudo-classes** that act like little spies, reporting on the current state of an input.

- **:valid:** The input's content meets the browser's rules (e.g., a required field is filled with a valid email).
- **:invalid:** The input's content *fails* to meet the rules.

Let's create a form that uses this for instant visual feedback:

```
<!DOCTYPE html>
<html lang="en">
<head>
    <title>CSS Inline Validation</title>
    <style>
        body { font-family: sans-serif; }
        input {
            padding: 8px;
            border: 2px solid #ccc; /* A slightly thicker border to make the
                                       color change obvious */
            border-radius: 4px;
            width: 250px;
            transition: border-color 0.3s ease-in-out; /* Smooth transition */
        }
        /* By default, let's not have any color until the user interacts. But when
           it's invalid, show a clear error state. */
        input:invalid {
            border-color: #e53e3e; /* A noticeable red */
        }
        /* And when it's valid, show a success state. */
        input:valid {
            border-color: #48bb78; /* A calming green */
        }
    </style>
</head>
<body>
    <h2>Sign Up</h2>
    <form action="#" method="post">
        <label for="email">Email:</label><br>
        <input type="email" id="email" name="user_email" required
               placeholder="you@example.com">
        <br><br>
        <label for="password">Password (min 8 chars):</label><br>
        <input type="password" id="password" name="user_password" required
               minlength="8">
        <br><br>
        <button type="submit">Register</button>
    </form>
</body>
</html>
```

Open this file and start interacting with the form. The email field starts with a red border because it's required but empty. As soon as you type a valid email address, the border snaps to green. The password field stays red until you've typed at least 8 characters. This is a fantastic, user-friendly feature that complements, but *never replaces*, our essential PHP validation.

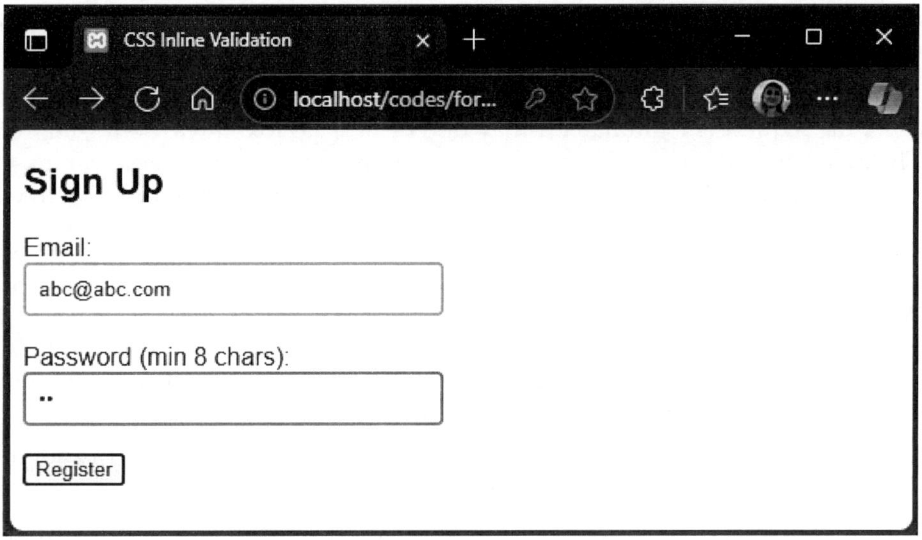

Security: CSRF and basic protections

Let's discuss one more sneaky attack: **Cross-Site Request Forgery (CSRF)**, pronounced **sea-surf**. Imagine this story:

- You log into your favourite social media site, social.com. The site gives your browser a cookie to remember you're logged in.
- You get an email with a link to a **funny cat pictures** website. You click it.
- Unbeknownst to you, that cat website has a hidden, invisible form. That form's **action** points to **http://social.com/post-status** and its **method** is **POST**. It has a **hidden field** with the value **I love spam! Visit my site!**. Using JavaScript, the malicious site automatically submits this form the moment you land on the page.
- Because you're still logged into social.com, your browser helpfully attaches your login cookie to this request.
- social.com receives a valid request to post a new status, from you! It has no idea the request was **forged** by the **cat** website. Your status is updated with the spam message.

The defense against this is a **CSRF token**. It's like a secret, single-use password for every form:

- When your server shows a form, it generates a long, random, secret string (the token). It saves this token in the user's session and also places it in a hidden **<input type="hidden">** field in the form.
- When the user submits the form, that secret token is sent back to the server.

- The server's first check is: "Does the token I just received match the one I stored in the session?"

If they match, the request is legitimate. If they don't—or if no token was sent—the request is rejected. The attacker's cat website has no way of knowing or guessing the secret token, so its forged request will fail. We'll implement this powerful technique in Chapter 14 when we cover sessions.

Practical uses

You've now been introduced to the core mechanics that power the most common interactive features on the web. Everything you've learned is directly applicable to:

- **Login & sign up forms:** They use POST to send credentials, require strict validation, and are the primary entry point for a user's session.
- **Feedback & contact forms:** The perfect real-world application of our concepts. They gather user messages and are a prime target for spam and XSS, making validation and sanitization essential.
- **E-commerce checkout:** This is just a complex, multi-page form that needs extreme security and validation for addresses and payment information.
- **Search bars:** The classic example of a simple GET form.

Hands-on: Build a contact/feedback form

Alright, it's time to put all of this knowledge together into a single, polished project. We're going to build a beautiful, secure, and user-friendly contact form. This single-page application will handle its own submissions, provide clear success or error messages, and be resilient against common attacks. This is a project you can be proud of and a piece of code you will reuse throughout your career.

Building the application

Let's start with a clean workspace. In your **xampp/htdocs/codes** directory, create a new folder called **feedback-app**. Inside this folder, we'll create just two files:

- **index.php:** This will be our all-in-one file, containing both the PHP processing logic and the HTML form itself.
- **style.css:** This will hold all the presentation rules to make our form look professional.

The PHP brain

The very first thing in our index.php file will be the PHP block. It's good practice to put the processing logic before any HTML output. This code will act as the **brain** of our page, deciding what to do when a user submits the form:

```
<?php
// We start by declaring our variables. It's good practice to initialize them so
// they exist, even if the form hasn't been submitted yet.
$name = '';
$email = '';
$message = '';
$errors = []; // An array to hold all our validation error messages.
$successMessage = ''; // A variable to hold our success message.
// The core of our logic: only run this code if the page was accessed via a POST
// request.
if ($_SERVER['REQUEST_METHOD'] === 'POST') {
    // --- VALIDATE AND SANITIZE NAME ---
    // trim() removes any accidental whitespace from the beginning or end of the
    // input. htmlspecialchars() makes the input safe to display.
    $name = htmlspecialchars(trim($_POST['name']));
    if (empty($name)) {
        $errors[] = 'Name is a required field.';
    }
    // --- VALIDATE AND SANITIZE EMAIL ---
    $email = htmlspecialchars(trim($_POST['email']));
    if (empty($email)) {
        $errors[] = 'Email is a required field.';
    } elseif (!filter_var($email, FILTER_VALIDATE_EMAIL)) {
        $errors[] = 'Please enter a valid email address.';
    }
    // --- VALIDATE AND SANITIZE MESSAGE ---
    $message = htmlspecialchars(trim($_POST['message']));
    if (empty($message)) {
        $errors[] = 'Message is a required field.';
    }
    // --- FINAL CHECK ---
    // After running all our checks, we see if the $errors array is still empty.
    if (empty($errors)) {
        // If it's empty, everything was perfect!
        $successMessage = "Thank you, {$name}! Your message has been
                          received. We'll be in touch shortly.";
        // In a real application, this is where you would:
        // 1. Save the data to a database.
        // 2. Send an email notification.
        // For our project, we'll clear the variables to reset the form.
        $name = '';
        $email = '';
        $message = '';
    }
```

```
}
?>
```

The HTML body

Now that our brain is ready, let's build the skeleton. This HTML will create the visual form and include special PHP if blocks to conditionally display our success or error messages:

```
<!DOCTYPE html>
<html lang="en">
<head>
    <meta charset="UTF-8">
    <meta name="viewport" content="width=device-width, initial-scale=1.0">
    <title>Contact Us</title>
    <link rel="stylesheet" href="style.css">
    <link rel="preconnect" href="https://fonts.googleapis.com">
    <link rel="preconnect" href="https://fonts.gstatic.com" crossorigin>
    <link href="https://fonts.googleapis.com/css2?family=Poppins:wght@400;600
               &display=swap" rel="stylesheet">
</head>
<body>
    <div class="container">
        <h1>Contact Us</h1>
        <p>Have a question or some feedback? We'd love to hear from you!</p>
        <?php if (!empty($successMessage)): ?>
            <div class="message success">
                <?= $successMessage; ?>
            </div>
        <?php endif; ?>
        <?php if (!empty($errors)): ?>
            <div class="message error">
                <strong>Please fix the following issues:</strong>
                <ul>
                    <?php foreach ($errors as $error): ?>
                        <li><?= $error; ?></li>
                    <?php endforeach; ?>
                </ul>
            </div>
        <?php endif; ?>
        <form action="index.php" method="POST" novalidate>
            <div class="form-group">
                <label for="name">Your Name</label>
                <input type="text" id="name" name="name"
                       value="<?= htmlspecialchars($name); ?>" required>
            </div>
            <div class="form-group">
                <label for="email">Your Email</label>
                <input type="email" id="email" name="email"
                       value="<?= htmlspecialchars($email); ?>" required>
```

```
            </div>
            <div class="form-group">
                <label for="message">Your Message</label>
                <textarea id="message" name="message" rows="6" required>
                          <?= htmlspecialchars($message); ?></textarea>
            </div>
            <button type="submit" class="btn">Send Message</button>
        </form>
    </div>
</body>
</html>
```

A few very important details here:

- **Self-submitting form:** The **action="index.php"** tells the form to send its data right back to the very page it's on. This is a common and powerful pattern for single-page applications.
- **Sticky form:** The **value="<?= htmlspecialchars($name); ?>"** part is a huge user experience win. Imagine you fill out a long form, make one typo in your email, and hit submit. If the form comes back completely blank, it's frustrating! This code ensures that any valid data the user entered is put right back into the form for them.
- **Conditional HTML:** The **<?php if (!empty($successMessage)): ?>** block is a fantastic feature of PHP. It allows us to embed logic directly into our HTML, ensuring that the success and error divs are only rendered when they actually have content.

The stylish suit

A great application isn't just functional; it's also pleasant to use. This CSS will give our form a modern, clean, and responsive design:

```
body {
    font-family: 'Poppins', sans-serif;
    background-color: #f4f7f6;
    color: #333;
    display: flex;
    justify-content: center;
    align-items: center;
    min-height: 100vh;
    margin: 0;
    padding: 20px;
    box-sizing: border-box;
}
.container {
    background-color: #ffffff;
    padding: 40px;
    border-radius: 8px;
    box-shadow: 0 4px 20px rgba(0, 0, 0, 0.08);
    width: 100%;
```

```
    max-width: 550px;
}
h1 {
    color: #2c3e50;
    margin-top: 0;
    margin-bottom: 10px;
    font-weight: 600;
}
p {
    color: #7f8c8d;
    margin-bottom: 30px;
}
.form-group {
    margin-bottom: 20px;
}
label {
    display: block;
    margin-bottom: 8px;
    font-weight: 600;
    color: #34495e;
    font-size: 14px;
}
input[type="text"], input[type="email"], textarea {
    width: 100%;
    padding: 12px;
    border: 1px solid #dcdcdc;
    border-radius: 5px;
    font-size: 16px;
    font-family: 'Poppins', sans-serif;
    box-sizing: border-box;
    transition: border-color 0.3s, box-shadow 0.3s;
}
input[type="text"]:focus, input[type="email"]:focus, textarea:focus {
    outline: none;
    border-color: #3498db;
    box-shadow: 0 0 0 3px rgba(52, 152, 219, 0.2);
}
textarea {
    resize: vertical;
    min-height: 120px;
}
.btn {
    background-color: #3498db;
    color: #ffffff;
    border: none;
    padding: 15px 25px;
    border-radius: 5px;
    font-size: 16px;
    font-weight: 600;
    cursor: pointer;
    width: 100%;
```

```
    transition: background-color 0.3s;
}
.btn:hover {
    background-color: #2980b9;
}
.message {
    padding: 15px;
    margin-bottom: 20px;
    border-radius: 5px;
    border: 1px solid transparent;
    font-size: 15px;
}
.message.success {
    background-color: #d4edda;
    color: #155724;
    border-color: #c3e6cb;
}
.message.error {
    background-color: #f8d7da;
    color: #721c24;
    border-color: #f5c6cb;
}
.message.error ul {
    margin: 0;
    padding-left: 20px;
}
.message.error strong {
    display: block;
    margin-bottom: 5px;
}
```

Bridging the gap: Learned concepts and application implementation

Let's pause and connect the dots. This project is a living demonstration of every concept from this chapter:

- **HTML forms:** We used a <form> with a POST method, along with <label>, <input>, and <textarea> to build the user interface.
- **POST method:** We chose POST because this is a data submission.
- **$_SERVER and $_POST:** Our PHP logic is wrapped in an if ($_SERVER['REQUEST_METHOD'] === 'POST') block, and we access user data with $_POST['name'].

- **Validation:** The code checks if (empty($name)) and uses filter_var() for the email. This is our bouncer.
- **Sanitization:** We are consistently using htmlspecialchars() whenever we retrieve data from $_POST and whenever we echo data back into the HTML value attributes. This is our security shield.
- **Custom UI feedback:** By disabling browser validation (novalidate) and using our own styled divs, we are providing a superior user experience.

Running and testing

The moment of truth!

1. Ensure your **Apache** server is running from the **XAMPP Control Panel**.
2. Open your favourite web browser (like Chrome or Firefox).
3. Navigate to the project's URL: **http://localhost/codes/feedback-app/index.php**.
4. You are greeted by your beautiful, professional contact form.

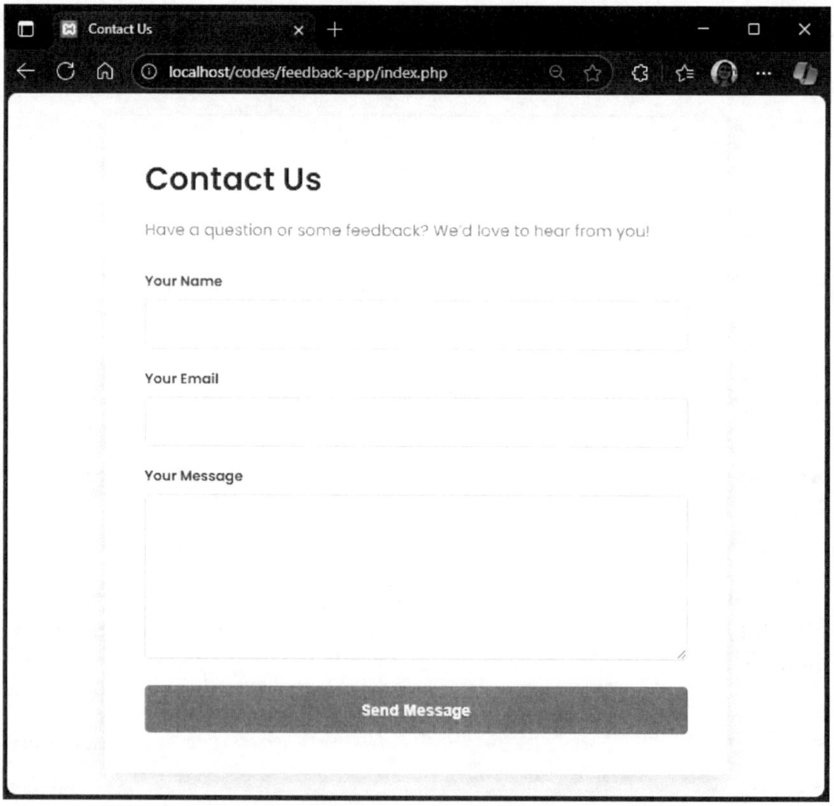

5. **Test case 1:** The "Happy Path" (Perfect submission)
    - Fill in your **name** and a **valid email**.
    - Write a message: **Just writing to say that this form looks and works great!**
    - Click the **Send Message** button.
6. The page reloads. The form fields are now empty, and a friendly **green success message** appears at the top:

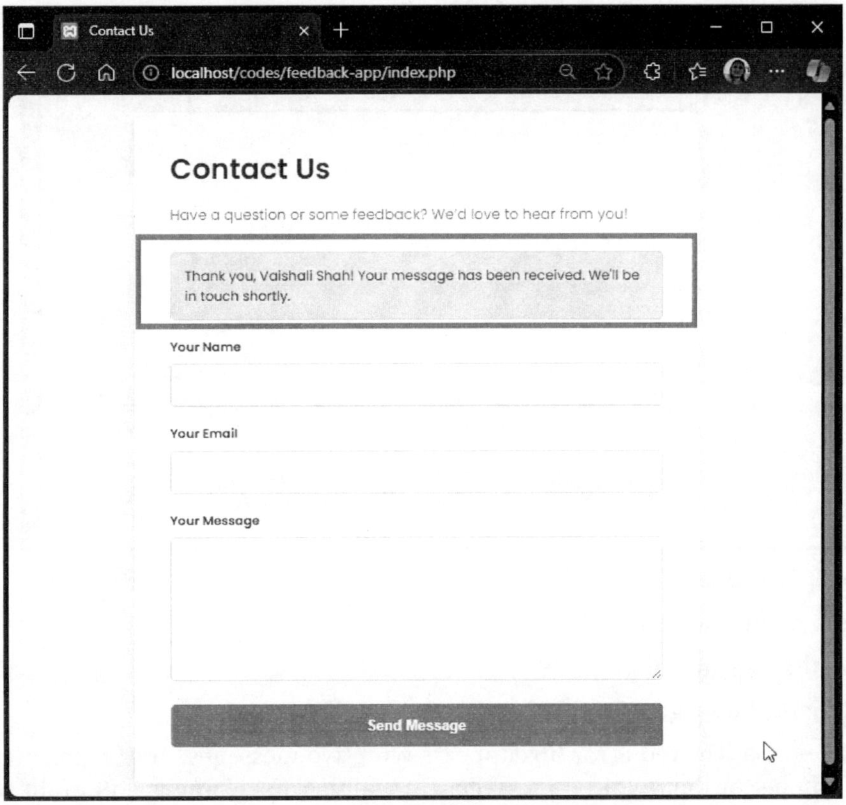

7. **Test case 2:** The "Oops, I forgot something" Path (Validation errors)
    - Go to the form and click **Send Message** without filling anything in.
8. The page reloads. A **red error box** appears at the top with a list of all three required fields. The form itself remains empty.

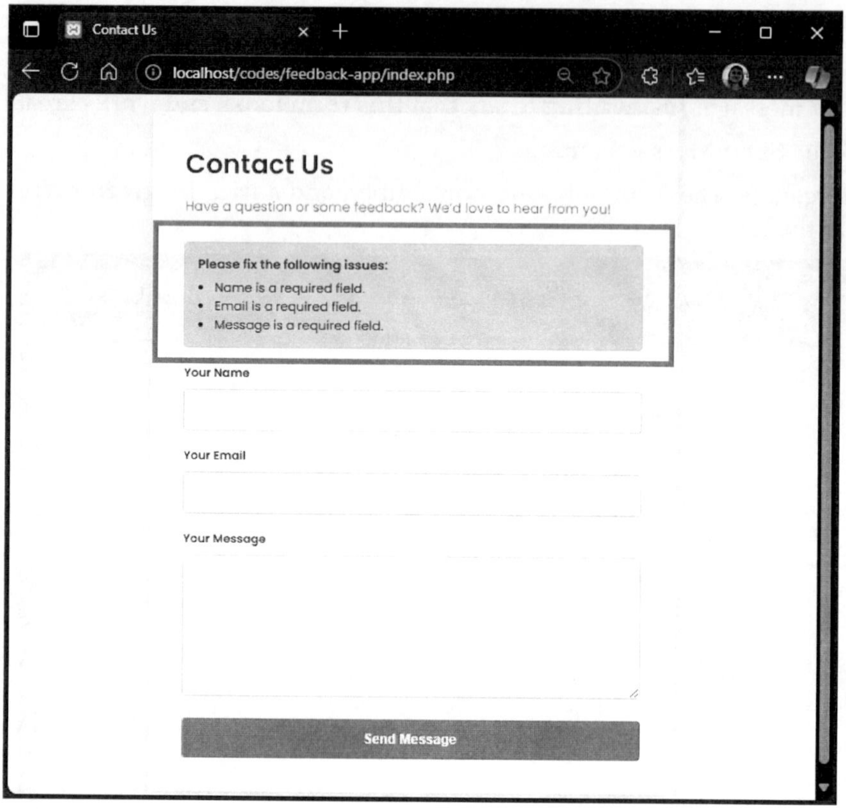

9. **Test case 3:** The "Sticky Form" Test
   - Enter a **name** and an ***invalid* email**.
   - Leave the message **blank**.
   - Click **Send Message**.
10. The page reloads. The **red error box** appears with two messages: one for the invalid email format and one for the required message. Crucially, **Your Name** is still in the name field and **Your Invalid Email** is still in the email field, waiting to be corrected. This is our sticky form in action!

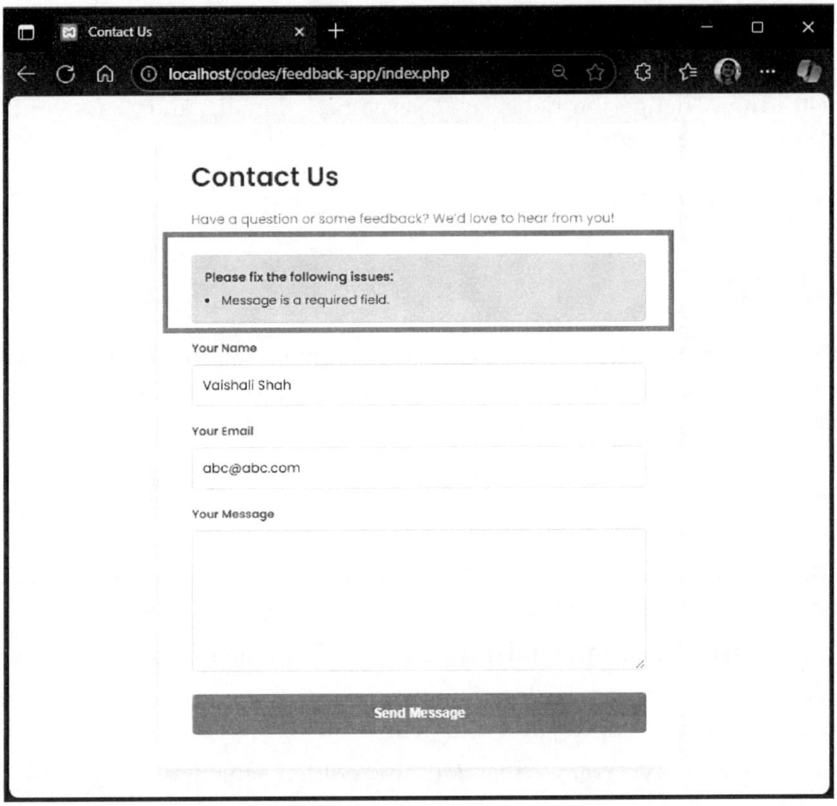

Exploring application behaviour: A practical run-through

Let's put on our tester hats and really probe the application.

- **Valid input:** We've confirmed this works perfectly. The feedback is clear and positive.
- **Invalid input:** Our validation logic catches all our rules. The error messages are specific and helpful, guiding the user to fix their mistakes. The sticky form prevents user frustration.

Harnessing feedback form in real-world contexts

This isn't just a toy project. The code you just wrote is 90% of what you need for many real-world features. Imagine how you could adapt this:

- **Support ticket system:** Add a "Subject" field and a "Priority" dropdown. Instead of showing a success message, INSERT the data into a tickets table in a database.

- **Product review form:** Add a 1-5 star rating input. Save the review to be displayed on a product page.
- **User registration:** Change the fields to "Username," "Email," and "Password," and add password confirmation logic.

The core pattern—Receive, Validate, Sanitize, Process—is universal.

Wrapping up

What a chapter! We've moved from simply displaying content to actively engaging with users. This is a monumental step in your journey as a developer. You have acquired a vital set of skills for building interactive, safe, and user-friendly web applications. Let's quickly review the key takeaways:

- **Forms are the bridge:** You now know how to build the HTML structure of a form, the essential bridge for user communication.
- **POST is for privacy:** You understand the crucial difference between GET and POST and can choose the correct method for the job.
- **PHP is the recipient:** You can confidently use $_POST to catch data on the server-side.
- **Validate first, always:** You've built a "bouncer" for your application, checking that input follows your rules using empty() and filter_var().
- **Sanitize before display:** You've wielded the golden shield of htmlspecialchars() to neutralize XSS threats and keep your application and users safe.
- **User experience matters:** You've built a polished application that provides clear feedback for both success and errors and uses "sticky" fields to reduce user friction.

Take a moment to congratulate yourself. You have built a complete, secure, and professional web application feature from scratch. You are no longer just a coder; you are an architect of interaction. The security-first mindset you've begun to cultivate—validate everything, sanitize everything—is one of the most valuable traits of a professional developer. It will serve you well in every project you ever build.

This is just the beginning of what you can do with user data. Now that we know how to receive it safely, what else can we do with it? In the next chapter, we will focus on transforming and manipulating that data. Get ready for *Chapter 9: Text transformers - Powerful string manipulation*, where you'll learn to slice, search, replace, and reformat text like a pro to unlock even more dynamic possibilities. Onward!

Chapter 9

Section 03: User power - Forms, strings, and file magic

Text transformers - Powerful string manipulation

What you'll learn

- Safely handle text
- Use powerful text functions
- Find and replace words
- Comine and split strings
- Format text for display
- Protect against XSS attacks

Welcome back! In the last chapter, we built a fully functional contact form and learned how to handle user input securely. Now, it's time to learn what to *do* with that text data. The web is built on text—from usernames and comments to blog posts and product descriptions. Knowing how to manipulate, clean, and format this text is a superpower for any developer. This chapter is all about transforming plain strings into smart, safe, and dynamic content for your applications.

Every time you see your username displayed on a website, fill out a profile, or see a post's word count, you're witnessing string manipulation in action. **Strings** are simply pieces of text, and PHP gives us an amazing toolbox to work with them.

In this chapter, we'll move beyond just receiving data and start actively shaping it. We'll learn how to combine variables into sentences, count words, find specific phrases, and sanitize text to prevent common security vulnerabilities. These skills are essential for creating dynamic, user-friendly web pages that can process and present information effectively, from a simple welcome message to a complex content management system.

String assignment and escaping

In PHP, you create a string by enclosing text in quotes. But what if your text *itself* contains a quote? This can confuse PHP, as it might think the string has ended prematurely. To solve this, we use the **backslash** (\) character to **escape** the inner quote, telling PHP to treat it as a literal part of the text.

You can use either **single quotes** (') or **double quotes** ("). Double quotes are special because they allow for *variable interpolation*. Let's see how to assign a string and escape a character.

Let's create a file to demonstrate this.

1. Inside your **htdocs/codes** folder in XAMPP, create a new folder named **chapter-9**.
2. Inside **chapter-9**, create a new file named **01_assignment_escaping.php**.
3. Open this file in VS Code and add the following code:

```
<?php
// Using a backslash to escape the single quote
$message1 = 'It\'s a beautiful day for coding!';
// Using double quotes allows you to have unescaped single quotes inside
$message2 = "She said, 'PHP is fun!' and she was right.";
// To use a double quote inside double quotes, you must escape it
$message3 = "He responded, \"I agree completely!\"";
?>
<!DOCTYPE html>
<html lang="en">
<head>
    <meta charset="UTF-8">
    <meta name="viewport" content="width=device-width, initial-scale=1.0">
    <title>String Assignment</title>
    <style>
        body {
            font-family: sans-serif; background-color: #f0f2f5;
            color: #333; padding: 20px;
        }
        .container {
            background-color: #fff; padding: 20px;
            border-radius: 8px; box-shadow: 0 2px 4px rgba(0,0,0,0.1);
        }
```

```
        p {
            font-size: 1.1em; line-height: 1.6;
        }
    </style>
</head>
<body>
    <div class="container">
        <h1>String Examples</h1>
        <p><?php echo $message1; ?></p>
        <p><?php echo $message2; ?></p>
        <p><?php echo $message3; ?></p>
    </div>
</body>
</html>
```

When you navigate to **http://localhost/codes/chapter-9/01_assignment_escaping.php** in your browser, you see the following output, perfectly rendered without any errors:

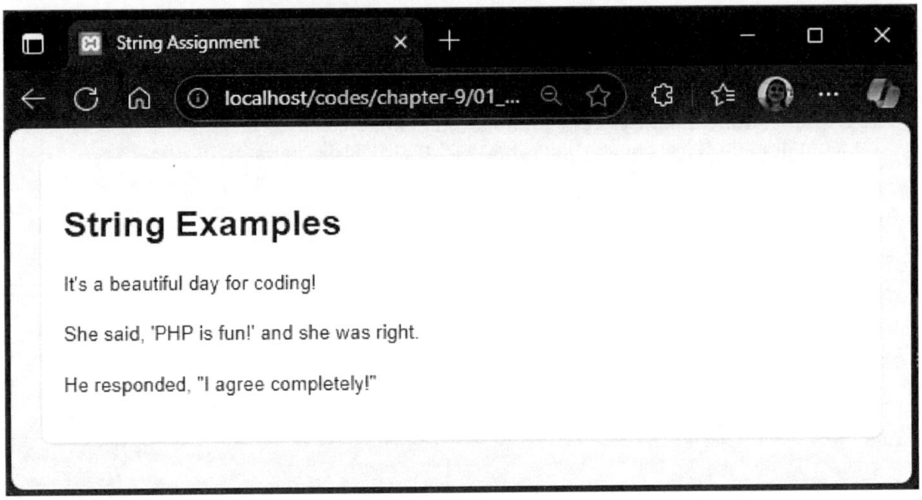

Concatenation and interpolation

Static text is boring. To build dynamic web pages, you need to combine strings with variables. PHP gives you two primary ways to do this:

- **Concatenation** uses the **dot** (.) operator to join strings and variables together. It's explicit and works with both single and double quotes.
- **Interpolation** is a **magic** feature that only works with **double-quoted** strings. You can place variables directly inside the string, and PHP will automatically replace them with their values. It often makes code cleaner and easier to read.

Let's create a new file **02_concat_interp.php** in your **chapter-9** folder:

```
<?php
$username = "Sharanam";
$login_hour = 10;
// 1. Concatenation using the dot (.) operator
$greeting_concat = 'Hi, ' . $username . '. You logged in at ' . $login_hour .
                    ' AM.';
// 2. Interpolation using double quotes. Braces are optional but good practice
$greeting_interp = "Hi, $username. You logged in at {$login_hour} AM.";
?>
<!DOCTYPE html>
<html lang="en">
<head>
    <meta charset="UTF-8">
    <title>Concatenation and Interpolation</title>
    <style>
        body {
            font-family: sans-serif; background-color: #f0f2f5;
            color: #333; padding: 20px;
        }
        .container {
            background-color: #fff; padding: 20px;
            border-radius: 8px; box-shadow: 0 2px 4px rgba(0,0,0,0.1);
        }
        .method {
            margin-bottom: 15px;
        }
        h2 {
            border-bottom: 2px solid #ddd; padding-bottom: 5px;
        }
    </style>
</head>
<body>
    <div class="container">
        <div class="method">
            <h2>Using Concatenation:</h2>
            <p><?php echo $greeting_concat; ?></p>
        </div>
        <div class="method">
            <h2>Using Interpolation:</h2>
            <p><?php echo $greeting_interp; ?></p>
        </div>
    </div>
</body>
</html>
```

Open **http://localhost/codes/chapter-9/02_concat_interp.php**. Both methods produce the exact same result for the user, demonstrating two different developer techniques to achieve the same goal:

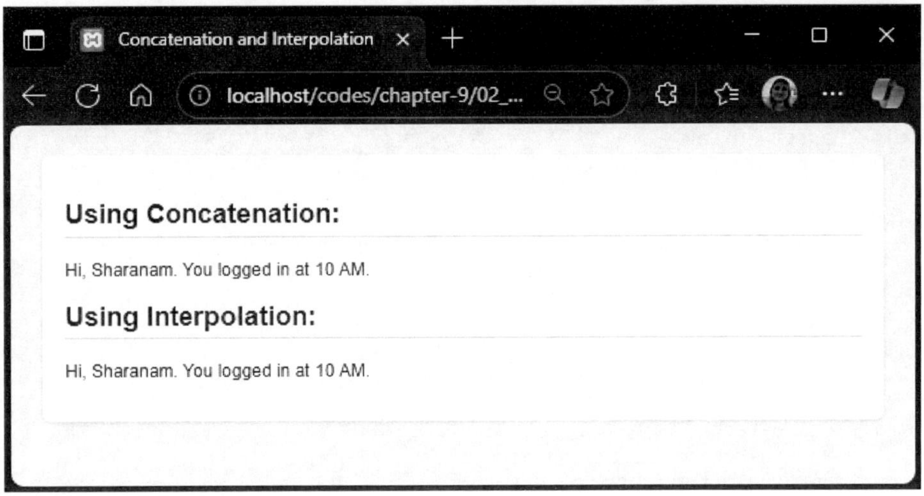

Useful string functions

PHP comes packed with hundreds of functions, and its string functions are among the most useful. They allow you to analyze, transform, and search within text effortlessly. Let's look at five essential ones:

- **strlen():** Returns the **len**gth of a **str**ing (how many characters it has).
- **strtoupper():** Converts a **str**ing **to upper**case.
- **substr():** Gets a **sub-str**ing (a portion of a string).
- **strpos():** Finds the **pos**ition of the first occurrence of a **str**ing inside another.
- **str_replace(): Replace**s all occurrences of a search **str**ing with a replacement string.

Create a new file **03_string_functions.php** in your **chapter-9 directory**. We will apply each of these functions to a sample sentence:

```
<?php
$original_string = "The quick brown fox jumps over the lazy dog.";
// 1. Get the length of the string
$length = strlen($original_string);
// 2. Convert to uppercase
$uppercase_string = strtoupper($original_string);
// 3. Get a substring (from index 4, for 11 characters). Indices start at 0
$substring = substr($original_string, 4, 11); // "quick brown"
// 4. Find the position of the word "fox"
$position = strpos($original_string, "fox");
// 5. Replace "dog" with "cat"
$replaced_string = str_replace("dog", "cat", $original_string);
```

```
?>
<!DOCTYPE html>
<html lang="en">
<head>
    <meta charset="UTF-8">
    <title>Powerful String Functions</title>
    <style>
        body {
            font-family: sans-serif; background-color: #f0f2f5;
            color: #333; padding: 20px;
        }
        .container {
            background-color: #fff; padding: 20px;
            border-radius: 8px; box-shadow: 0 2px 4px rgba(0,0,0,0.1);
        }
        .function-test {
            margin-bottom: 10px; padding-bottom: 10px;
            border-bottom: 1px solid #eee;
        }
        code {
            background-color: #e8e8e8; padding: 2px 5px;
            border-radius: 4px;
        }
        .result {
            font-weight: bold; color: #d63384;
        }
    </style>
</head>
<body>
    <div class="container">
        <h1>Original String: "<?php echo $original_string; ?>"</h1>
        <div class="function-test">
            <p><code>strlen()</code>: The length of the string is <span
               class="result"><?php echo $length; ?></span> characters.</p>
        </div>
        <div class="function-test">
            <p><code>strtoupper()</code>: The uppercase version is " <span
               class="result"><?php echo $uppercase_string; ?></span>".</p>
        </div>
        <div class="function-test">
            <p><code>substr(4, 11)</code>: The substring starting at index 4 is "
               <span class="result"><?php echo $substring; ?></span>".</p>
        </div>
        <div class="function-test">
            <p><code>strpos("fox")</code>: The word "fox" starts at index<span
               class="result"><?php echo $position; ?></span>.</p>
        </div>
        <div class="function-test">
            <p><code>str_replace("dog", "cat")</code>: The modified sentence is "
               <span class="result"><?php echo $replaced_string; ?></span>".</p>
        </div>
```

```
    </div>
</body>
</html>
```

Visiting **http://localhost/codes/chapter-9/03_string_functions.php** shows a clear breakdown of what each function did:

Formatting output for display

Raw data is rarely pretty. When you pull data from a database or a user, it might contain extra whitespace or have line breaks represented as **\n (a newline character)**. PHP provides functions to clean this up for a polished front-end display.

- **trim():** Removes whitespace (or other specified characters) from the beginning and end of a string. This is crucial for handling user input, as people often accidentally add extra spaces.
- **nl2br():** Converts **n**ewline characters (\n) into HTML **br**eak tags (<br>). This is perfect for displaying multi-line text from a <textarea> form field.

Let's create **04_formatting_output.php** in our project folder:

```
<?php
// 1. User input with extra whitespace
$raw_username = "    shah.shah@example.com    ";
$trimmed_username = trim($raw_username);
// 2. A multi-line comment from a textarea
```

```
$comment = "This is the first line.\nThis is the second line.\nAnd a third one!";
$formatted_comment = nl2br($comment);
?>
<!DOCTYPE html>
<html lang="en">
<head>
    <meta charset="UTF-8">
    <title>Formatting Output</title>
    <style>
        body {
            font-family: sans-serif;
            background-color: #f0f2f5;
            color: #333;
            padding: 20px;
        }
        .container {
            background-color: #fff;
            padding: 20px;
            border-radius: 8px;
            box-shadow: 0 2px 4px rgba(0, 0, 0, 0.1);
        }
        .before-after {
            display: grid;
            grid-template-columns: 1fr 1fr;
            gap: 20px;
        }

        .box {
            border: 1px solid #ddd;
            padding: 15px;
            border-radius: 5px;
        }
        h2 {
            margin-top: 0;
        }
        pre {
            background-color: #eee;
            padding: 10px;
            white-space: pre-wrap;
            font-family: monospace;
        }
    </style>
</head>
<body>
    <div class="container">
        <h1>Using <code>trim()</code></h1>
        <div class="before-after">
            <div class="box">
                <h2>Before trim()</h2>
                <pre>"<?php echo $raw_username; ?>"</pre>
            </div>
```

```
            <div class="box">
                <h2>After trim()</h2>
                <pre>"<?php echo $trimmed_username; ?>"</pre>
            </div>
        </div>
        <h1 style="margin-top: 30px;">Using <code>nl2br()</code></h1>
        <div class="before-after">
            <div class="box">
                <h2>Before nl2br()</h2>
                <p><?php echo $comment; ?></p>
            </div>
            <div class="box">
                <h2>After nl2br()</h2>
                <p><?php echo $formatted_comment; ?></p>
            </div>
        </div>
    </div>
</body>
</html>
```

Navigating to **http://localhost/codes/chapter-9/04_formatting_output.php** clearly demonstrates the **before and after** for both functions. Notice how the extra spaces are gone from the username and how the comment's line breaks are now rendered correctly in HTML:

Regular expressions

Regular expressions, or **regex**, are a mini-language for finding complex patterns in strings. They can seem intimidating at first, but they are incredibly powerful. A common use case is validation: does this string *look like* an email address? Does this password contain at least one number?

PHP's **preg_match()** function checks if a string matches a regex pattern. It returns **1** if it finds a match and **0** if it doesn't.

Let's test a simple pattern: checking if a string contains only letters and spaces. The pattern **/^[a-zA-Z\s]+$/** means:

- **/** : The start and end delimiters for the pattern.
- **^** : Asserts the start of the string.
- **[a-zA-Z\s]** : Matches any character that is a lowercase letter (a-z), an uppercase letter (A-Z), or a whitespace character (\s).
- **+** : Means the previous character set must appear one or more times.
- **$** : Asserts the end of the string.

Create a new file, **05_regex_basics.php**:

```
<?php
$name1 = "Sharanam Shah";
$name2 = "SharanamShah123";
// Regex pattern to allow only letters and whitespace
$pattern = '/^[a-zA-Z\s]+$/';
$result1_match = preg_match($pattern, $name1); // This will match
// This will NOT match (due to numbers)
$result2_match = preg_match($pattern, $name2);
function get_result_text($match_value)
{
    if ($match_value === 1) {
        return '<span class="valid">Valid Name (Matches Pattern)</span>';
    } else {
        return '<span class="invalid">Invalid Name (Does Not Match Pattern)
               </span>';
    }
}
?>
<!DOCTYPE html>
<html lang="en">
<head>
    <meta charset="UTF-8">
    <title>Regular Expression Basics</title>
```

```
    <style>
        body {
            font-family: sans-serif;
            background-color: #f0f2f5;
            color: #333;
            padding: 20px;
        }
        .container {
            background-color: #fff;
            padding: 20px;
            border-radius: 8px;
            box-shadow: 0 2px 4px rgba(0, 0, 0, 0.1);
        }
        .test-case {
            padding: 10px;
            border: 1px solid #ddd;
            margin-top: 10px;
        }
        .valid {
            color: #198754;
            font-weight: bold;
        }
        .invalid {
            color: #dc3545;
            font-weight: bold;
        }
        code {
            background-color: #e8e8e8;
            padding: 2px 5px;
            border-radius: 4px;
        }
    </style>
</head>
<body>
    <div class="container">
        <h1>Regex Pattern: <code><?php echo $pattern; ?></code></h1>
        <p>This pattern checks for strings containing only letters (a-z, A-Z)
           and spaces.</p>
        <div class="test-case">
            <p>Testing string: "<?php echo $name1; ?>"</p>
            <p>Result: <?php echo get_result_text($result1_match); ?></p>
        </div>
        <div class="test-case">
            <p>Testing string: "<?php echo $name2; ?>"</p>
            <p>Result: <?php echo get_result_text($result2_match); ?></p>
        </div>
    </div>
</body>
</html>
```

When you run **http://localhost/codes/chapter-9/05_regex_basics.php**, you see how **preg_match()** validates our strings against the pattern. **Sharanam Shah passes**, but **SharanamShah123 fails** because of the numbers.

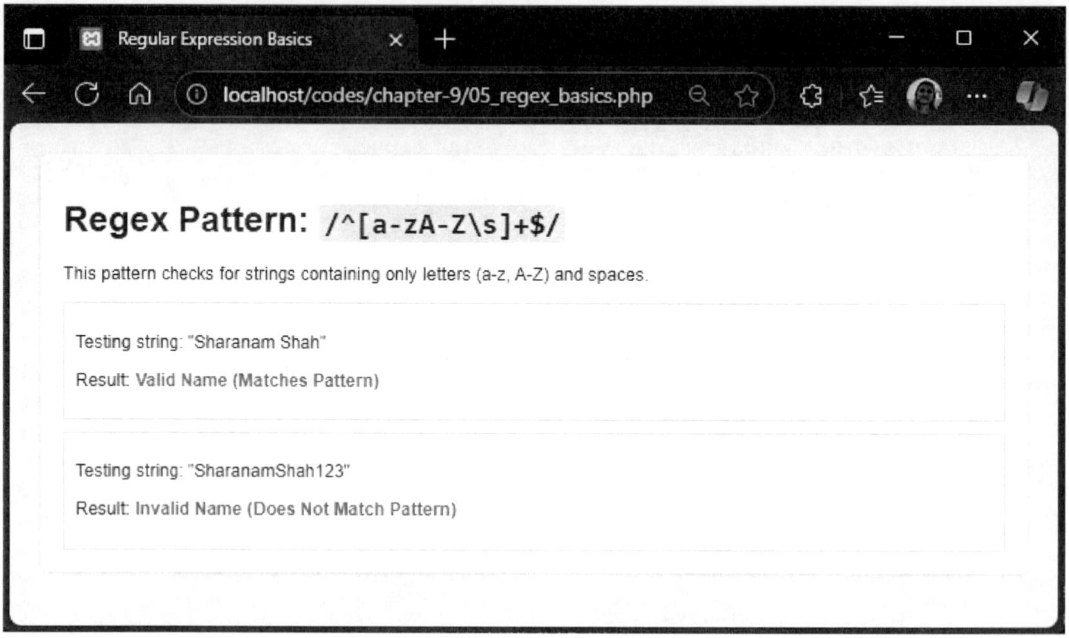

HTML entities and XSS protection

This is one of the most important security concepts in web development. Imagine a user submits a comment containing this text:

```
<script>alert('You have been hacked!');</script>
```

If you simply **echo** that comment onto your page, the browser won't just *display* the text. It will execute it as JavaScript! This is a **Cross-Site Scripting (XSS)** attack, and it's extremely dangerous.

To prevent this, you must **always** sanitize user-provided output with the **htmlspecialchars()** function. This function converts special HTML characters (like <, >, &, ") into their **entity** equivalents (<, >, &, "). These entities *look* like the original characters to a human, but the browser treats them as plain text, not code.

Let's create 06_xss_protection.php to see the danger and the solution:

```
<?php
// A malicious string submitted by a user
$malicious_comment = "<script>alert('XSS Attack!');</script>";
// The safe, sanitized version of the string
$safe_comment = htmlspecialchars($malicious_comment);
?>
<!DOCTYPE html>
<html lang="en">
<head>
    <meta charset="UTF-8">
    <title>XSS Protection</title>
    <style>
        body {
            font-family: sans-serif;
            background-color: #f0f2f5;
            color: #333;
            padding: 20px;
        }
        .container {
            background-color: #fff;
            padding: 20px;
            border-radius: 8px;
            box-shadow: 0 2px 4px rgba(0, 0, 0, 0.1);
        }
        .box {
            padding: 15px;
            border-radius: 5px;
            margin-top: 15px;
        }
        .unsafe {
            border: 2px solid #dc3545;
            background-color: #f8d7da;
        }
        .safe {
            border: 2px solid #198754;
            background-color: #d1e7dd;
        }
        h2 {
            margin-top: 0;
        }
        code {
            display: block;
            white-space: pre;
            background-color: rgba(0, 0, 0, 0.05);
            padding: 10px;
        }
    </style>
</head>
<body>
```

```
    <div class="container">
        <h1>HTML Entities and XSS Protection</h1>
        <div class="box unsafe">
            <h2>Unsafe Output (Vulnerable!)</h2>
            <p>If we just <code>echo</code> the raw input, the script will run!</p>
            <p><strong>Output:</strong> <?php /* echo $malicious_comment; */ ?>
               (Code commented out for safety)</p>
            <p style="font-weight: bold;">If this were not commented out, you
               would see a JavaScript alert pop up right now.</p>
        </div>
        <div class="box safe">
            <h2>Safe Output (Using <code>htmlspecialchars()</code>)</h2>
            <p>By using <code>htmlspecialchars()</code>, we convert the script tags
               to harmless text.</p>
            <p><strong>Raw Sanitized String:</strong></p>
            <code><?php echo $safe_comment; ?></code>
            <p><strong>Rendered Safe Output:</strong></p>
            <p><?php echo $safe_comment; ?></p>
        </div>
    </div>
</body>
</html>
```

Go to **http://localhost/codes/chapter-9/06_xss_protection.php**. We have commented out the dangerous echo to prevent the alert from actually running in your own environment. The output shows how htmlspecialchars() transforms the dangerous code into displayable, safe text.

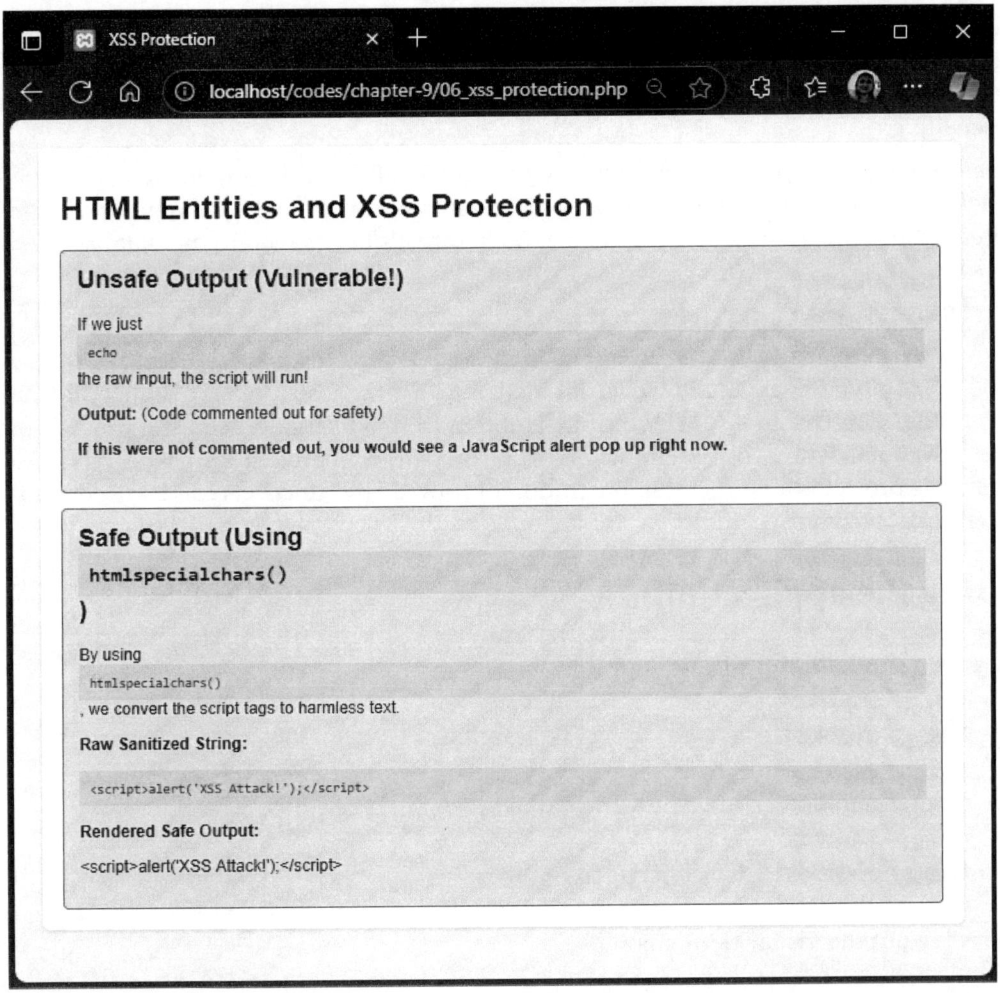

Real-world uses

String manipulation isn't just an academic exercise; it's the engine behind many features you use daily.

- **Clean URLs:** When you see a URL like mysite.com/blog/my-first-post instead of mysite.com/blog.php?id=123, that's string manipulation at work. Developers use functions to replace spaces with hyphens, convert text to lowercase, and remove special characters to create SEO-friendly and human-readable links.

- **Search**: When you search for "brown fox" on a site, the backend code uses string functions like strpos() or str_contains() to check product descriptions or articles for that phrase. It might also convert both your query and the content to lowercase to make the search case-insensitive.
- **Usernames:** When you sign up for a service, it often tells you "Usernames can only contain letters, numbers, and underscores." This rule is enforced using a regular expression (preg_match()) to ensure your input is valid before it's ever saved to the database.

Hands-on: Text analyzer

It's time to combine everything we've learned into a practical tool. We will build a Text Analyzer web app. This tool will take a block of text from a user and instantly provide useful statistics: the total word count, character count, and how many times a specific keyword appears. This project is a perfect demonstration of how string functions can be used to extract meaningful data from user input.

Building the application

We'll create a single-file application for this.

Create the project file

In your **chapter-9** folder, create a new file named **text_analyzer.php**.

Set up the HTML and CSS structure

First, let's lay out the visual elements:

- A title
- A form with a textarea and a text input for the keyword
- A section to display our results

The form will POST the data back to this same file for processing. Add the following code to text_analyzer.php:

```
<!DOCTYPE html>
<html lang="en">
<head>
    <meta charset="UTF-8">
    <meta name="viewport" content="width=device-width, initial-scale=1.0">
    <title>Text Analyzer</title>
```

```
    <style>
        body {
            font-family: -apple-system, BlinkMacSystemFont, "Segoe UI", Roboto,
                          "Helvetica Neue", Arial, sans-serif;
            background-color: #f4f7f9;
            color: #333;
            margin: 0;
            padding: 20px;
            display: flex;
            justify-content: center;
            align-items: center;
            min-height: 100vh;
        }
        .container {
            width: 100%;
            max-width: 600px;
            background-color: #fff;
            padding: 30px;
            border-radius: 12px;
            box-shadow: 0 8px 16px rgba(0, 0, 0, 0.1);
        }
        h1 {
            color: #2c3e50;
            text-align: center;
            margin-bottom: 20px;
        }
        form textarea, form input[type="text"] {
            width: 100%;
            padding: 12px;
            margin-bottom: 15px;
            border: 1px solid #ccc;
            border-radius: 6px;
            font-size: 16px;
            box-sizing: border-box;
            /* Important for padding */
        }
        form button {
            width: 100%;
            padding: 12px;
            background-color: #3498db;
            color: white;
            border: none;
            border-radius: 6px;
            font-size: 16px;
            cursor: pointer;
            transition: background-color 0.3s;
        }
        form button:hover {
            background-color: #2980b9;
        }
        .results {
```

```
            margin-top: 30px;
            background-color: #ecf0f1;
            padding: 20px;
            border-radius: 8px;
            /* Use PHP to conditionally display this block */
            display: <?php echo $show_results ? 'block' : 'none'; ?>;
        }
        .results h2 {
            margin-top: 0;
            color: #2c3e50;
            border-bottom: 2px solid #bdc3c7;
            padding-bottom: 10px;
        }
        .results p {
            font-size: 1.1em;
            line-height: 1.6;
        }
        .results span {
            font-weight: bold;
            color: #e74c3c;
        }
    </style>
</head>
<body>
    <div class="container">
        <h1>Text Analyzer</h1>
        <form action="text_analyzer.php" method="POST">
            <textarea name="main_text" rows="10" placeholder="Paste your text
                      here..."> </textarea>
            <input type="text" name="keyword" placeholder="Enter keyword to
                   search for..." . . .>
            <button type="submit">Analyze Text</button>
        </form>
        <div class="results">
            <h2>Analysis Results</h2>
            <p>Character Count: <span>. . .</span></p>
            <p>Word Count: <span>. . .</span></p>
            <p>Keyword Count for . . .: <span>. . .</span></p>
        </div>
    </div>
</body>
</html>
```

If you open this file in your browser (http://localhost/codes/chapter-9/text_analyzer.php), you see the styled form, but it doesn't do anything yet. The results are hidden.

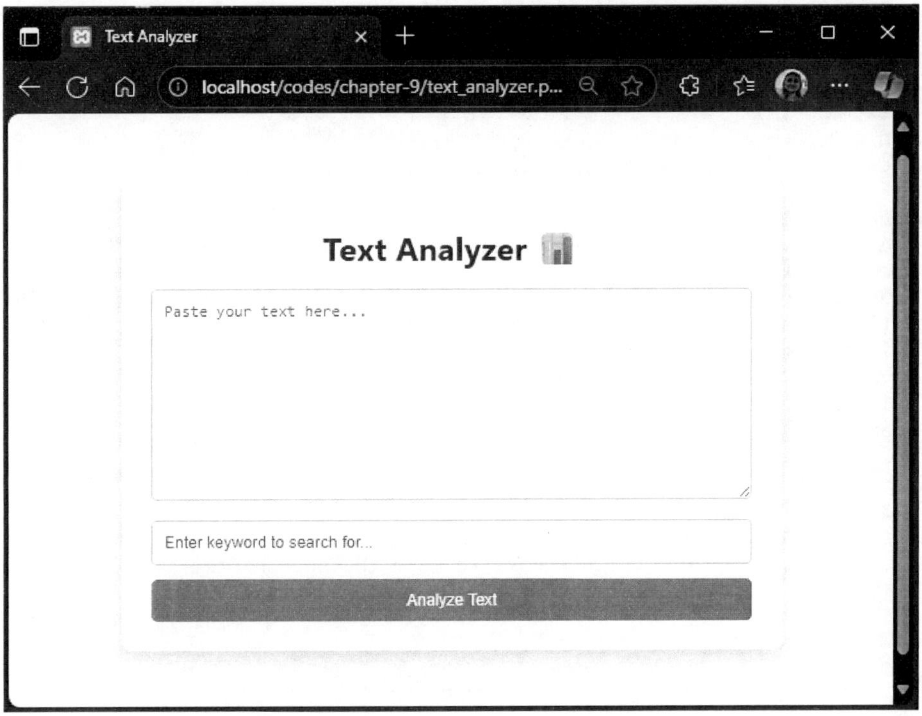

Add the PHP processing logic

Now, let's add the PHP code to the top of the file. This code will:

- Check if the form was submitted ($_SERVER['REQUEST_METHOD'] == 'POST').
- Grab the text and keyword from the $_POST superglobal.
- Use htmlspecialchars() to ensure the input is safe to display.
- Use strlen() to count characters.
- Use str_word_count() (a new handy function!) to count words.
- Use substr_count() (another great one!) to count the keyword occurrences, making it case-insensitive by first converting both the main text and keyword to lowercase.
- Store these results in variables.

Add the following PHP block at the **very top** of text_analyzer.php, before the <!DOCTYPE html> line:

```
<?php
// Initialize variables to hold results and input
```

```
$char_count = 0;
$word_count = 0;
$keyword_count = 0;
$main_text = '';
$keyword = '';
$show_results = false;
// Check if the form has been submitted
if ($_SERVER['REQUEST_METHOD'] == 'POST') {
    // A form was submitted, so we should show the results div
    $show_results = true;
    // Get the raw text from the form fields. Use the null coalescing operator
    // (??) as a shortcut to avoid errors if the field is empty.
    $main_text = $_POST['main_text'] ?? '';
    $keyword = $_POST['keyword'] ?? '';
    // 1. Calculate character count
    $char_count = strlen($main_text);
    // 2. Calculate word count
    $word_count = str_word_count($main_text);
    // 3. Calculate keyword count (case-insensitive)
    if (!empty($main_text) && !empty($keyword)) {
        // We convert both to lowercase to make the search case-insensitive
        $keyword_count = substr_count(strtolower($main_text), strtolower($keyword));
    }
}
?>
```

Connect PHP variables to the HTML

Our final step is to make the HTML dynamic. We need to:

- Make the results div visible only after the form is submitted.
- Display the calculated counts ($char_count, $word_count, $keyword_count).
- Use htmlspecialchars() on our input variables ($main_text, $keyword) to "re-fill" the form fields after submission. This is good UX!
- Use htmlspecialchars() on any output we display to prevent XSS.

Modify the HTML part of your file to integrate the PHP variables.

- Find the <textarea> and <input> tags and set their content to the PHP variables.
- Find the div with the class results and add a style attribute to display it conditionally.
- Update the <span> tags in the results div to echo the calculated values.

Here is the **complete, final code** for text_analyzer.php:

```
<?php
// Initialize variables to hold results and input
```

```
$char_count = 0;
$word_count = 0;
$keyword_count = 0;
$main_text = '';
$keyword = '';
$show_results = false;
// Check if the form has been submitted
if ($_SERVER['REQUEST_METHOD'] == 'POST') {
    // A form was submitted, so we should show the results div
    $show_results = true;
    // Get the raw text from the form fields
    // Use the null coalescing operator (??) as a shortcut to avoid errors
    // if the field is empty
    $main_text = $_POST['main_text'] ?? '';
    $keyword = $_POST['keyword'] ?? '';
    // 1. Calculate character count
    $char_count = strlen($main_text);
    // 2. Calculate word count
    $word_count = str_word_count($main_text);
    // 3. Calculate keyword count (case-insensitive)
    if (!empty($main_text) && !empty($keyword)) {
        // We convert both to lowercase to make the search case-insensitive
        $keyword_count = substr_count(strtolower($main_text),
                                      strtolower($keyword));
    }
}
?>
<!DOCTYPE html>
<html lang="en">
<head>
    <meta charset="UTF-8">
    <meta name="viewport" content="width=device-width, initial-scale=1.0">
    <title>Text Analyzer</title>
    <style>
        body {
            font-family: -apple-system, BlinkMacSystemFont, "Segoe UI", Roboto,
                         "Helvetica Neue", Arial, sans-serif;
            background-color: #f4f7f9;
            color: #333;
            margin: 0;
            padding: 20px;
            display: flex;
            justify-content: center;
            align-items: center;
            min-height: 100vh;
        }
        .container {
            width: 100%;
            max-width: 600px;
            background-color: #fff;
            padding: 30px;
```

```
            border-radius: 12px;
            box-shadow: 0 8px 16px rgba(0, 0, 0, 0.1);
        }
        h1 {
            color: #2c3e50;
            text-align: center;
            margin-bottom: 20px;
        }
        form textarea, form input[type="text"] {
            width: 100%;
            padding: 12px;
            margin-bottom: 15px;
            border: 1px solid #ccc;
            border-radius: 6px;
            font-size: 16px;
            box-sizing: border-box;
            /* Important for padding */
        }
        form button {
            width: 100%;
            padding: 12px;
            background-color: #3498db;
            color: white;
            border: none;
            border-radius: 6px;
            font-size: 16px;
            cursor: pointer;
            transition: background-color 0.3s;
        }
        form button:hover {
            background-color: #2980b9;
        }
        .results {
            margin-top: 30px;
            background-color: #ecf0f1;
            padding: 20px;
            border-radius: 8px;
            /* Use PHP to conditionally display this block */
            display: <?php echo $show_results ? 'block' : 'none'; ?>;
        }
        .results h2 {
            margin-top: 0;
            color: #2c3e50;
            border-bottom: 2px solid #bdc3c7;
            padding-bottom: 10px;
        }
        .results p {
            font-size: 1.1em;
            line-height: 1.6;
        }
        .results span {
```

```
            font-weight: bold;
            color: #e74c3c;
        }
    </style>
</head>
<body>
    <div class="container">
        <h1>Text Analyzer</h1>
        <form action="text_analyzer.php" method="POST">
            <textarea name="main_text" rows="10"
                      placeholder="Paste your text here...">
                      <?php echo htmlspecialchars($main_text); ?></textarea>
            <input type="text" name="keyword"
                   placeholder="Enter keyword to search for..."
                   value="<?php echo htmlspecialchars($keyword); ?>">
            <button type="submit">Analyze Text</button>
        </form>
        <div class="results">
            <h2>Analysis Results</h2>
            <p>Character Count: <span><?php echo $char_count; ?></span></p>
            <p>Word Count: <span><?php echo $word_count; ?></span></p>
            <p>Keyword Count for "<?php echo htmlspecialchars($keyword);
               ?>": <span><?php echo $keyword_count; ?></span></p>
        </div>
    </div>
</body>
</html>
```

Bridging the gap: Learned concepts and application implementation

- **HTML forms & $_POST:** This application is built around an HTML form that uses the POST method. Our PHP code checks $_SERVER['REQUEST_METHOD'] to see if the form was submitted and then uses $_POST['main_text'] and $_POST['keyword'] to access the data.
- **String functions:** The core logic relies entirely on the string functions from this chapter. We use strlen() for character count, str_word_count() for word count, and substr_count() combined with strtolower() for a case-insensitive keyword search.
- **htmlspecialchars() for security and UX:** We use this function in two critical places. First, we wrap the output ($keyword in the results heading) to prevent XSS. Second, we use it to pre-fill the <textarea> and <input> fields with the user's previous submission. This is both secure and user-friendly.

- **Conditional display:** We use a PHP variable ($show_results) and a simple echo in a style attribute (display: <?php echo $show_results ? 'block' : 'none'; ?>;) to control whether the results div is visible. This is a common technique for showing content only after an action has been taken.

Running and testing

1. Make sure XAMPP is running (**Apache** module).
2. Open your browser and navigate to **http://localhost/codes/chapter-9/text_analyzer.php**.
3. You see the form interface.

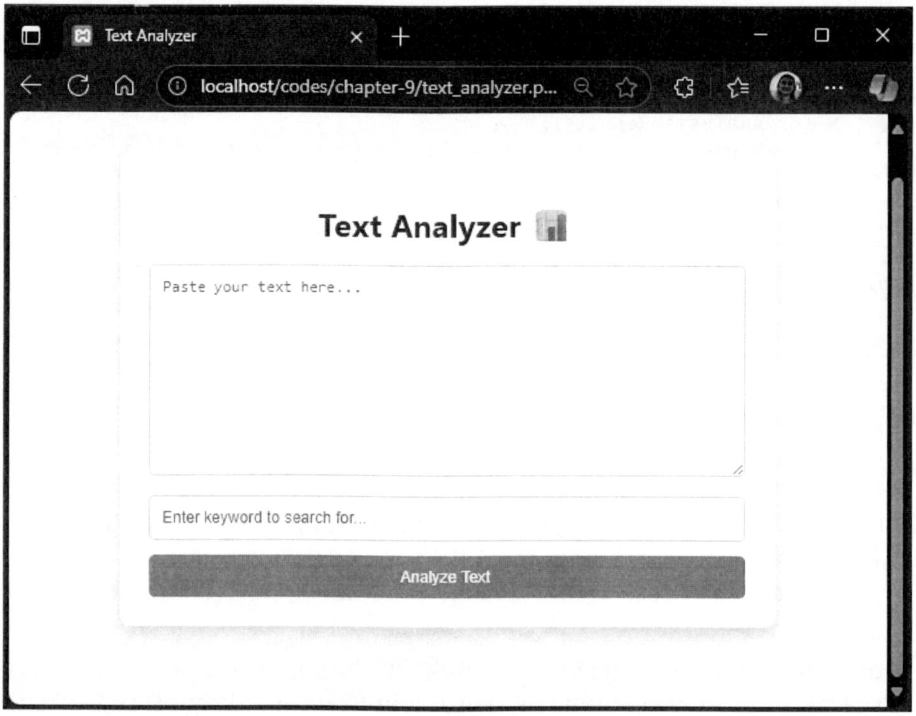

4. In the **textarea**, type the following text: **PHP is a powerful language. Many developers love PHP for its simplicity and speed.** And in the **keyword** input, type **PHP**.

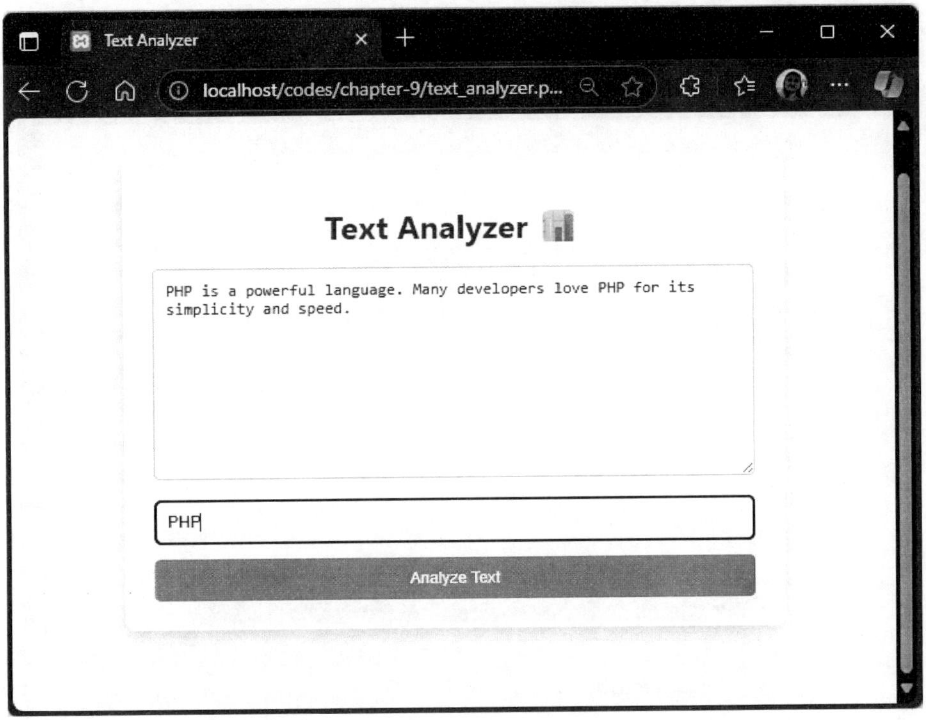

5. Click the **Analyze Text** button.
6. The page reloads. The form still contains the text you entered, and below it, the **Analysis Results** box is now be visible.

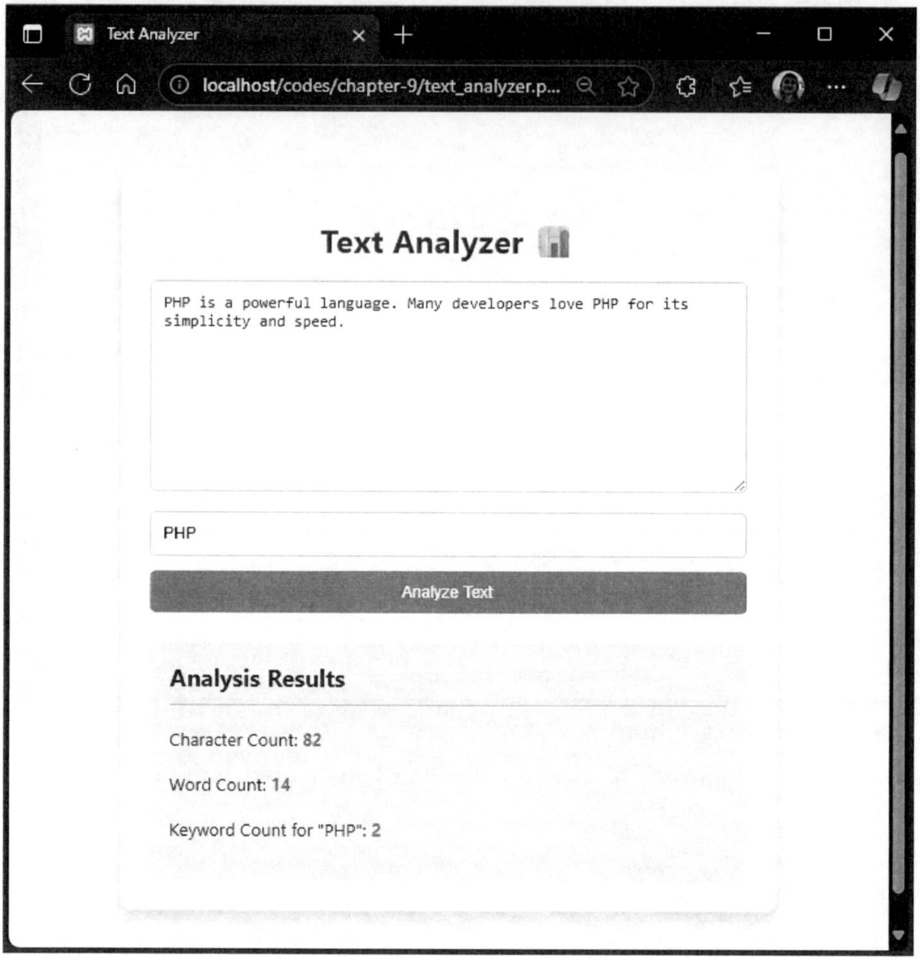

Exploring application behaviour: A practical run-through

- **Valid input:** As seen above, with normal text and a keyword, the app works perfectly. Try it with a different keyword like **language** (should be 1) or **php** in lowercase (should still be 2, because our search is case-insensitive).

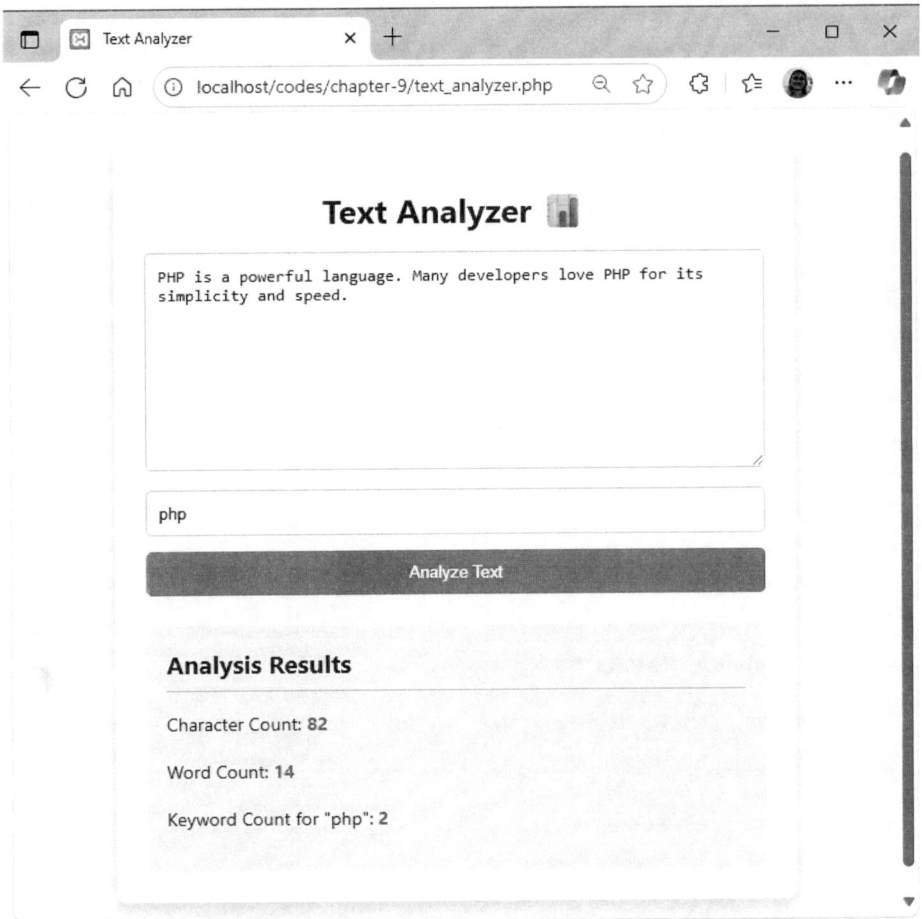

- **Empty input:** If you click **Analyze Text** with both fields empty, the results will correctly show 0 for all counts. The app doesn't break.

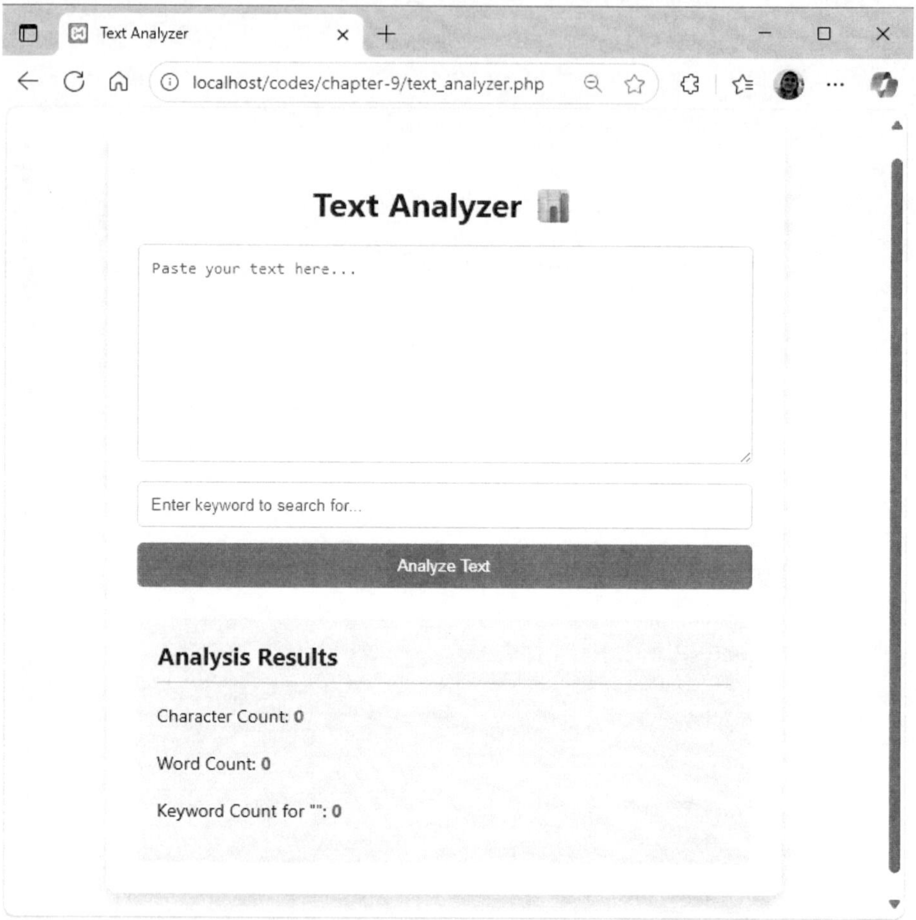

- **No keyword:** If you provide text but no keyword, the character and word counts will be calculated correctly, and the keyword count will be 0.

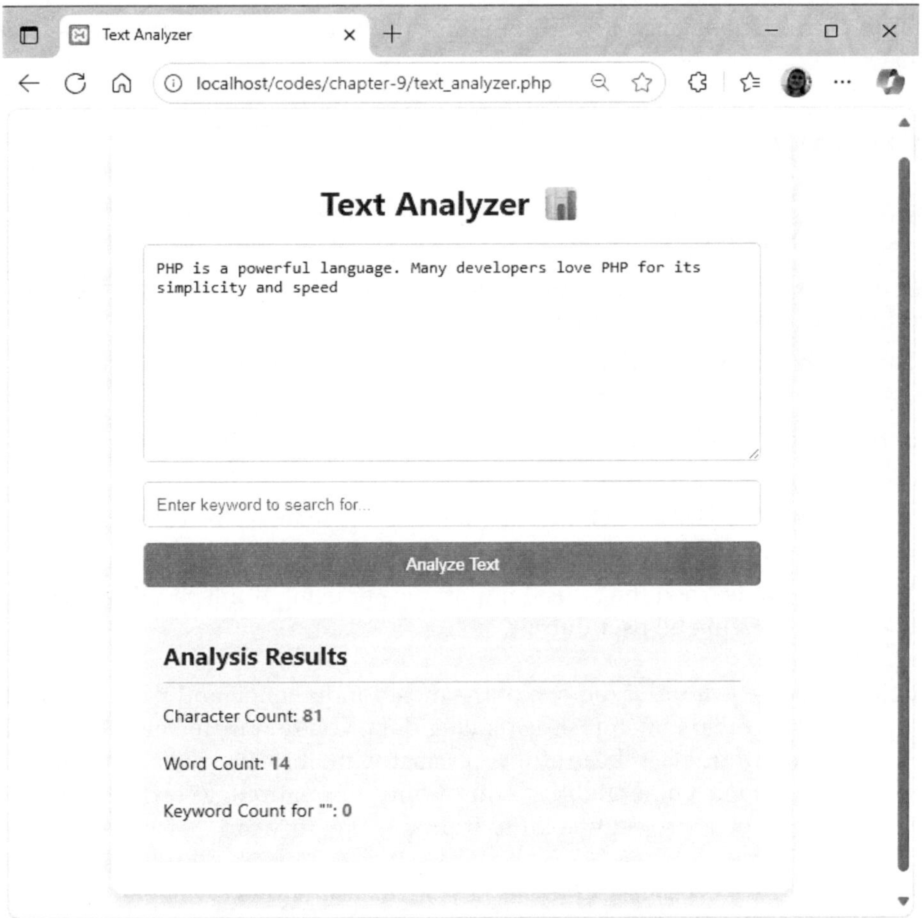

- **Malicious input:** Try pasting **<script>alert('test');</script>** into the textarea's **value** attribute and script as the keyword. Click **Analyze Text**. The page will reload, the script text will be safely displayed back in the textarea, and the results will be shown without any pop-up alerts. This proves our htmlspecialchars() defence is working!

Harnessing the Text analyzer in real-world contexts

This simple tool uses the same principles as many professional features:

- SEO analysis tools use this to calculate keyword density in articles.
- Content management systems use it to show authors a word count as they type.
- Social media sites use it to enforce character limits on posts and comments.

This project is a foundational step toward building any feature that needs to understand and quantify text.

Wrapping up

- **String creation:** We learned to create strings with single and double quotes and how to escape special characters.
- **Combining strings:** We explored joining strings with the concatenation operator (.) and embedding variables directly with interpolation.
- **Core functions:** We used strlen(), strtoupper(), substr(), and str_replace() to measure, transform, and modify text.
- **Output formatting:** We used trim() to clean whitespace and nl2br() to preserve line breaks for display.
- **Pattern matching:** We had a brief introduction to preg_match() for validating strings with regular expressions.
- **Security is key:** We learned the critical importance of using htmlspecialchars() to prevent XSS attacks by sanitizing all user output.

Congratulations! You've just unlocked one of the most fundamental and powerful skill sets in web development. You're no longer just displaying data; you're transforming it. You can now clean up user input, format it beautifully, extract valuable insights, and protect your applications from common vulnerabilities. This ability to manipulate text is something you will use in every single PHP project you build from this day forward.

In the next chapter, we'll solve a major puzzle: how to make our data last. Get ready for ***Chapter 10: Files and Bytes – Saving and retrieving user data,*** where we'll learn to save information permanently in files on the server!

Chapter 10

Section 03: User power - Forms, strings, and file magic

Files and Bytes - Saving and retrieving user data

What you'll learn

- Filesystem permissions and paths
- Reading and writing files
- Handling file uploads
- Validating user files
- Securing file operations: Preventing common attacks

Welcome to one of the most exciting steps in your journey! So far, our web apps have had a short memory. When a user closes their browser, all the information—like their name, calculator results, or quiz score—vanishes. This chapter changes everything.

We're going to give our applications the power to **remember** by saving data directly onto the server's filesystem. This is called **data persistence**, and it's the magic behind everything from simple guestbooks and contact forms to complex document storage systems. You'll learn how to read, write, and manage files, enabling you to build applications that can save user progress, store notes, log important events, and even handle file uploads like resumés or profile pictures. Let's start building apps that leave a lasting impression!

Filesystem permissions and paths

Before we can ask PHP to write a file, we need to make sure it has permission to do so. Think of your computer's filesystem like an office building. Not everyone is allowed to open every door; some are locked and require a key. Web servers work the same way. For security, web servers (like Apache in our XAMPP installation) run as a specific user, and that user has limited permissions.

If you want PHP to create or modify a file in a folder, you must grant that folder **write** permissions for the server's user. If you don't, you'll get a frustrating **Permission denied** error.

File paths

A **path** is an address that tells PHP where to find a file or folder. There are two types:

- **Absolute path:** A full address starting from the root of the filesystem. For example, C:\xampp\htdocs\codes\my-project\data on Windows or /Users/YourName/Sites/my-project/data on a Mac.
- **Relative path:** A partial address that starts from the location of the currently running PHP script (e.g., data/notes.txt).

For simplicity and portability, we will often use relative paths.

Let's create a dedicated folder for our data:

1. Inside your XAMPP **htdocs/codes** folder, create a new project folder called **php-file-magic**.
2. Inside **php-file-magic**, create another folder named **data**. This is where we'll store our files.

On most systems, the permissions XAMPP sets will be sufficient, but if you encounter errors, this is the first place to check.

Opening, reading, and writing files

PHP gives us several powerful tools to interact with files. The most common are

- **file_put_contents()** for easily writing to a file (it even creates the file if it doesn't exist!).
- **file_get_contents()** for reading an entire file into a string.

For more control, you can use a three-step process:

1. fopen() (open)

2. fwrite() (write) or fread() (read)
3. fclose() (close)

Let's start with the simplest method.

Writing a file with file_put_contents()

This function is a fantastic shortcut. It handles opening, writing, and closing the file all in one command.

Create a new file in your **php-file-magic** folder called **create_note.php** and add the following code:

```
<?php
// 1. Define the path and filename
$filePath = 'data/note.txt';
// 2. Define the content to save
$content = "Hello, world! This is my first note saved with PHP. "
           . date('Y-m-d H:i:s');
// 3. Write the content to the file
// The function returns the number of bytes written, or false on failure.
$result = file_put_contents($filePath, $content);
// 4. Give the user feedback
if ($result !== false) {
    echo "<h1>Success!</h1>";
    echo "<p>Your note has been saved to <strong>{$filePath}</strong>.</p>";
    echo "<p>Go check the 'data' folder to see your new file!</p>";
} else {
    echo "<h1>Error!</h1>";
    echo "<p>Could not write to the file. Check folder permissions.</p>";
}
?>
```

To run this file,

1. Start Apache engine available in **XAMPP Control Panel**.
2. Make sure the **data** folder is already created under the **php-file-magic** folder.
3. Open your browser and navigate to **http://localhost/codes/php-file-magic/create_note.php**.

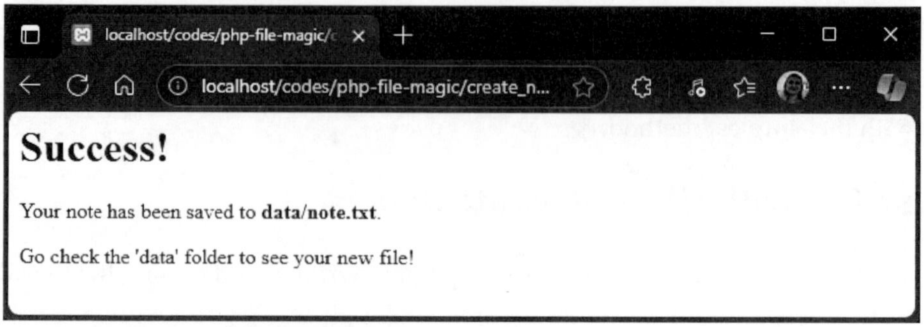

4. Now, look inside the **php-file-magic/data/** folder.

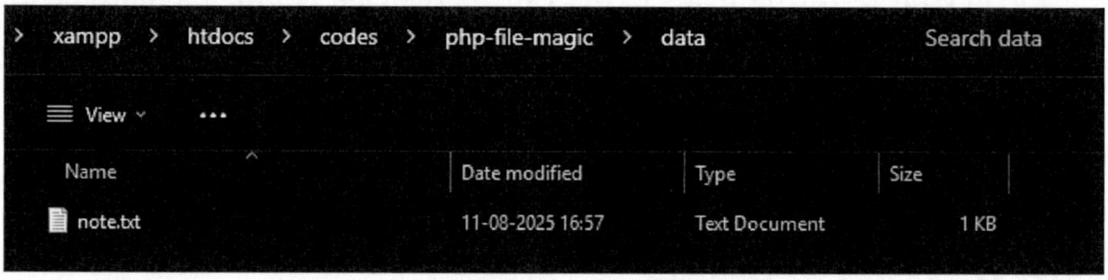

5. You see a new file, **note.txt**, containing the text we defined!

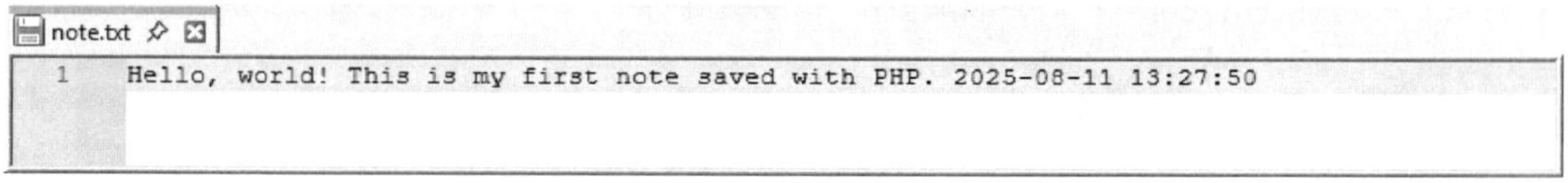

Reading a file with file_get_contents()

Now let's retrieve that data and display it on a web page. Create another file called **read_note.php**:

```
<?php
// 1. Define the path to the file we want to read
$filePath = 'data/note.txt';
// 2. Check if the file actually exists before trying to read it
if (file_exists($filePath)) {
    // Read the entire contents of the file into a variable
    $noteContent = file_get_contents($filePath);
    // Display the content in a nicely formatted way
    echo "<h1>My Saved Note</h1>";
    echo "<p style='font-family: monospace; background-color: #f0f0f0;
          padding: 15px; border-radius: 5px;'>";
    echo htmlspecialchars($noteContent); // Security first!
    echo "</p>";
} else {
```

```
    // If the file doesn't exist, show a friendly error message
    echo "<h1>Oops!</h1>";
    echo "<p>No note found. Please run <strong>create_note.php
        </strong> first.</p>";
}
?>
```

Navigate to **http://localhost/codes/php-file-magic/read_note.php** in your browser.

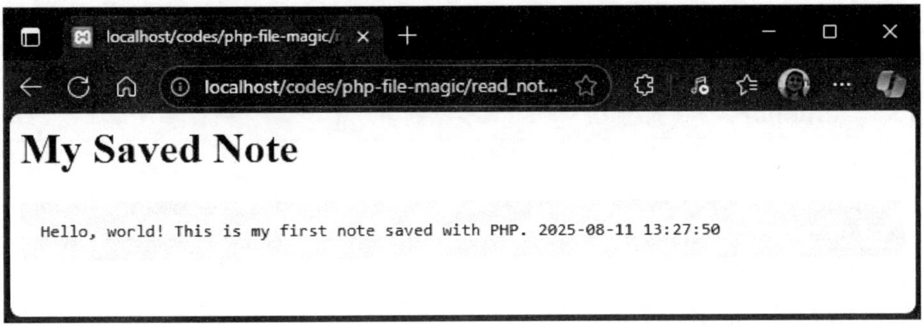

Notice the use of **htmlspecialchars()**. This is a crucial security function. If the text file contained HTML code (e.g., <script>alert('hacked!');</script>), htmlspecialchars() converts it into plain text that the browser will display safely instead of executing. Always use it when echoing user-provided content.

Every variable and piece of data in your scripts was ephemeral—it existed only for the fraction of a second it took for the page to load. By using functions like file_put_contents() and file_get_contents(), you have created a bridge between your application's temporary memory and the server's permanent storage. This concept of **persistence** is what separates static web pages from dynamic web applications. You've given your app a memory, allowing it to store and retrieve information across different visits and different users.

Handling file uploads: Setup and security

Allowing users to upload files is a powerful feature, but it's also a major security risk if not handled correctly. A malicious user could try to upload a dangerous PHP script or a virus.

First, your PHP installation needs to be configured to allow uploads. This is controlled in a file called **php.ini**. In XAMPP, you can find php.ini in **<Drive>\xampp\php** folder.

Two key settings are:

- file_uploads = On (This is usually on by default)

- upload_max_filesize = 2M (You can increase this, e.g., to 8M for larger files)

After changing php.ini, you must restart the Apache server for the changes to take effect.

Now, let's create the HTML form. The form tag needs two special attributes:

- **method="POST":** File uploads must use the POST method.
- **enctype="multipart/form-data":** This tells the browser to encode the file data in a way the server can understand.

Create **upload_form.php**:

```
<!DOCTYPE html>
<html lang="en">
<head>
    <meta charset="UTF-8">
    <title>File Upload</title>
    <style>
        body {
           font-family: sans-serif; max-width: 500px;
           margin: 50px auto;
        }
        .form-container {
           padding: 20px; border: 1px solid #ccc;
           border-radius: 8px;
        }
        .feedback {
           margin-top: 15px; padding: 10px; border-radius: 5px;
        }
        .success {
           background-color: #e8f5e9; color: #2e7d32;
        }
        .error {
           background-color: #ffebee; color: #c62828;
        }
    </style>
</head>
<body>
    <div class="form-container">
        <h2>Upload Your Resumé</h2>
        <p>Please upload a PDF or DOCX file (max 2MB).</p>
        <form action="upload_handler.php" method="POST"
              enctype="multipart/form-data">
            <input type="file" name="resumeFile" required>
            <br><br>
            <button type="submit">Upload File</button>
        </form>
    </div>
</body>
```

```
</html>
```

Now, let's create the PHP script to handle the uploaded file, **upload_handler.php**. When a file is uploaded, PHP stores its information in a special superglobal array called $_FILES:

```
<?php
// Define the directory where files will be stored
$uploadDirectory = 'uploads/';
// Ensure the upload directory exists
if (!is_dir($uploadDirectory)) {
    mkdir($uploadDirectory, 0755, true);
}
// Check if a file was uploaded
if (isset($_FILES['resumeFile']) && $_FILES['resumeFile']
            ['error'] === UPLOAD_ERR_OK) {
    // Get file details from the $_FILES superglobal
    $tempFilePath = $_FILES['resumeFile']['tmp_name'];
    $originalFileName = basename($_FILES['resumeFile']['name']);
    $destinationPath = $uploadDirectory . $originalFileName;
    // Move the uploaded file from its temporary location to the final destination
    if (move_uploaded_file($tempFilePath, $destinationPath)) {
        echo "<h1 style='color: green;'>Success!</h1>";
        echo "<p>The file <strong>" . htmlspecialchars($originalFileName) .
              "</strong> has been uploaded.</p>";
        echo "<a href='upload_form.php'>Upload another file</a>";
    } else {
        echo "<h1 style='color: red;'>Error!</h1>";
        echo "<p>There was an error moving the uploaded file.</p>";
    }
} else {
    // Handle potential upload errors
    echo "<h1 style='color: red;'>Upload Failed!</h1>";
    $errorCode = $_FILES['resumeFile']['error'] ?? 'Unknown';
    echo "<p>An error occurred. Error code: " . $errorCode . "</p>";
    echo "<a href='upload_form.php'>Try again</a>";
}
?>
```

How it works:

- We define an **uploads/** directory. The **mkdir()** function creates it if it doesn't exist.
- PHP first receives the uploaded file into a temporary, hidden folder on the server.
- We access the file's details through **$_FILES['resumeFile']**. The name **'resumeFile'** matches the name attribute of our **<input type="file">** tag.
- The most important step is **move_uploaded_file()**. This function safely moves the file from its temporary location to our desired uploads/ directory. It's the only secure way to handle uploaded files in PHP.

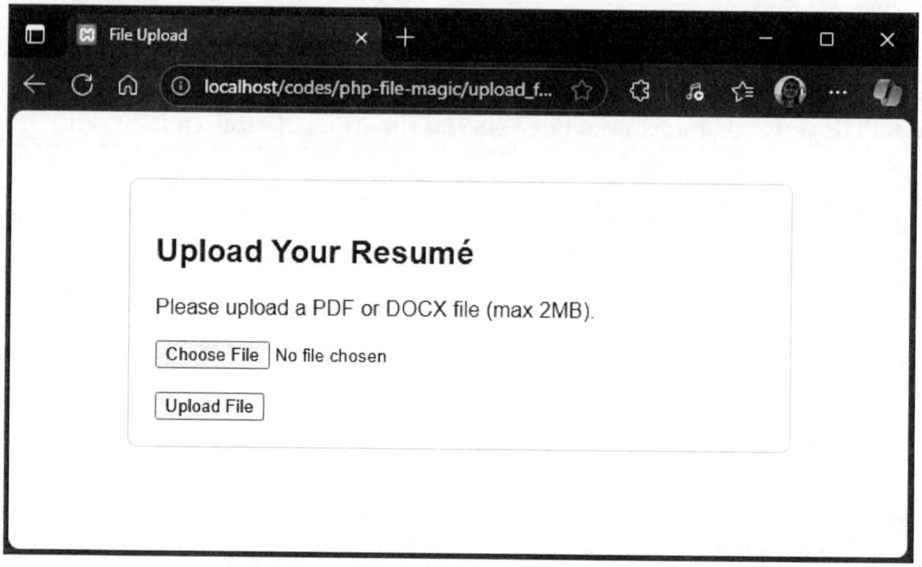
File Upload
localhost/codes/php-file-magic/upload_f...
Upload Your Resumé
Please upload a PDF or DOCX file (max 2MB).
Choose File
No file chosen
Upload File

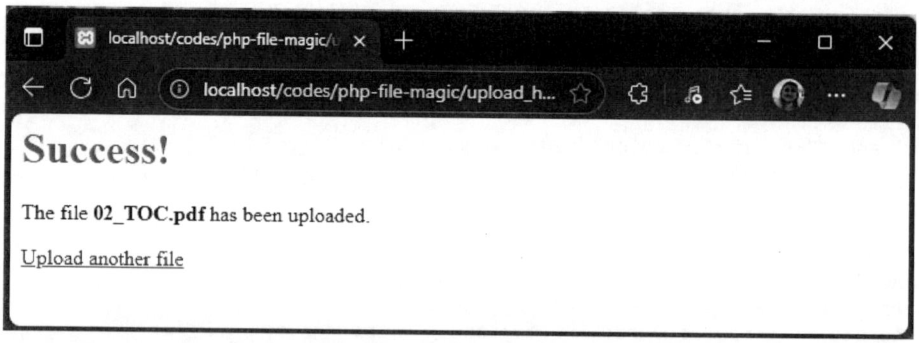
localhost/codes/php-file-magic/u
localhost/codes/php-file-magic/upload_h...
Success!
The file 02_TOC.pdf has been uploaded.
Upload another file

xampp
htdocs
codes
php-file-magic
uploads
View
Name
Date modified
Type
Size
02_TOC.pdf
11-08-2025 17:07
Adobe Acrobat D...
130 KB

Validating uploaded files

The previous example was insecure because it accepted *any* file. Let's add validation to only allow specific file types and sizes.

We'll modify upload_handler.php to be much smarter:

```
<?php
// File: php-file-magic/upload_handler.php (Version 2 - Secure)
$uploadDirectory = 'uploads/';
if (!is_dir($uploadDirectory)) {
    mkdir($uploadDirectory, 0755, true);
}
// --- Validation Constants ---
$allowedMimeTypes = ['application/pdf', 'application/vnd.openxmlformats-
                     officedocument.wordprocessingml.document'];
$maxFileSize = 2 * 1024 * 1024; // 2 MB in bytes
// Check if a file was uploaded and there's no initial error
if (isset($_FILES['resumeFile']) && $_FILES['resumeFile']
['error'] === UPLOAD_ERR_OK) {
    // --- 1. Size Validation ---
    if ($_FILES['resumeFile']['size'] > $maxFileSize) {
        die("<h1 style='color: red;'>Error: File is too large.</h1> <p>
             Maximum size is 2MB.</p>");
    }
    // --- 2. Type Validation ---
    $fileMimeType = mime_content_type($_FILES['resumeFile']['tmp_name']);
    if (!in_array($fileMimeType, $allowedMimeTypes)) {
        die("<h1 style='color: red;'>Error: Invalid file type.</h1> <p>Only
             PDF and DOCX are allowed.</p>");
    }
    // --- 3. Secure Filename ---
    $originalFileName = $_FILES['resumeFile']['name'];
    $fileExtension = pathinfo($originalFileName, PATHINFO_EXTENSION);
    // Create a unique, safe filename to prevent overwrites and path
    // traversal issues
    $safeFileName = uniqid('resume_', true) . '.' . $fileExtension;
    $destinationPath = $uploadDirectory . $safeFileName;
    // --- Move the file ---
    if (move_uploaded_file($_FILES['resumeFile']['tmp_name'], $destinationPath)) {
        echo "<h1 style='color: green;'>Success!</h1>";
        echo "<p>The file <strong>" . htmlspecialchars($originalFileName) .
              "</strong> has been uploaded as " . htmlspecialchars($safeFileName)
              . ".</p>";
        echo "<a href='upload_form.php'>Upload another file</a>";
    } else {
        echo "<h1 style='color: red;'>Error!</h1> <p>Could not move the file.</p>";
    }
} else {
```

```
    // Handle initial upload errors
    die("<h1 style='color: red;'>Upload Failed!</h1> <p>Please select a file and
        try again.</p>");
}
?>
```

Key improvements:

- **Size check:** We check **$_FILES['resumeFile']['size']** (in bytes) against our **$maxFileSize**.
- **Type check:** We use **mime_content_type()** to check the *actual* content of the file. This is much more reliable than just checking the file extension (.pdf), which a user can easily fake. We check if the detected MIME type is in our **$allowedMimeTypes** array.
- **Secure filename:** We no longer trust the user's original filename. **pathinfo()** extracts the file extension safely. We then generate a new, unique filename using **uniqid()** to prevent users from overwriting existing files or attempting to traverse directories (e.g., uploading a file named ../../error.php).

Directory manipulation and cleanup

Your application might need to create folders for new users, list files in a directory, or delete temporary files.

- **is_dir('folder'):** Checks if a directory exists.
- **mkdir('folder'):** Creates a new directory.
- **scandir('folder'):** Returns an array containing the names of all files and folders inside a directory.
- **unlink('file.txt'):** Deletes a file.
- **rmdir('folder'):** Deletes an *empty* directory.

Let's build a simple file explorer that lists all uploaded files and provides a delete link for each.

Create a new file, **file_manager.php**:

```
<?php
$uploadDirectory = 'uploads/';
// --- Handle Deletion Request ---
if (isset($_GET['delete'])) {
    $fileToDelete = basename($_GET['delete']); // Sanitize input
    $filePath = $uploadDirectory . $fileToDelete;
    // Security check: ensure the file is within our upload directory
    if (file_exists($filePath) && strpos(realpath($filePath),
             realpath($uploadDirectory)) === 0) {
        unlink($filePath);
        echo "<p style='color: green; font-weight: bold;'>File "
             . htmlspecialchars($fileToDelete) . " deleted successfully!</p>";
    } else {
        echo "<p style='color: red; font-weight: bold;'>Error: File not
             found or invalid path.</p>";
    }
}
?>
<!DOCTYPE html>
<html lang="en">
<head>
    <meta charset="UTF-8">
    <title>File Manager</title>
    <style>
        body {
           font-family: sans-serif; max-width: 800px;
           margin: 50px auto;
        }
        table {
           width: 100%; border-collapse: collapse;
        }
        th, td {
           padding: 10px; border: 1px solid #ccc;
           text-align: left;
        }
        th {
           background-color: #f2f2f2;
         }
        .delete-link {
           color: #c62828; text-decoration: none;
        }
        .delete-link:hover {
           text-decoration: underline;
        }
    </style>
</head>
<body>
    <h1>Uploaded Resumés</h1>
    <table>
```

```
        <thead>
            <tr>
                <th>Filename</th>
                <th>File Size (KB)</th>
                <th>Action</th>
            </tr>
        </thead>
        <tbody>
            <?php
            if (is_dir($uploadDirectory)) {
                // Scan the directory for files
                $files = scandir($uploadDirectory);
                // Filter out '.' and '..' which represent current and parent
                // directories
                $files = array_diff($files, ['.', '..']);
                if (count($files) > 0) {
                    foreach ($files as $file) {
                        $filePath = $uploadDirectory . $file;
                        // Get size in KB
                        $fileSize = round(filesize($filePath) / 1024, 2);
                        echo "<tr>";
                        echo "<td>" . htmlspecialchars($file) . "</td>";
                        echo "<td>" . $fileSize . " KB</td>";
                        echo "<td><a class='delete-link' href='?delete="
                             . urlencode($file) . "' onclick='return
                             confirm(\"Are you sure you want to delete
                             this file?\");'>Delete</a></td>";
                        echo "</tr>";
                    }
                } else {
                    echo "<tr><td colspan='3'>No files uploaded yet.</td></tr>";
                }
            } else {
                echo "<tr><td colspan='3'>Upload directory does not exist.
                      </td></tr>";
            }
            ?>
        </tbody>
    </table>
    <br>
    <a href="upload_form.php">Upload a new file</a>
</body>
</html>
```

This script first checks if a delete parameter exists in the URL. If so, it attempts to delete the specified file after a crucial security check. Then, it scans the **uploads/** directory, lists each file in an HTML table, and provides a formatted delete link for each one. The onclick JavaScript adds a confirmation dialog to prevent accidental deletions.

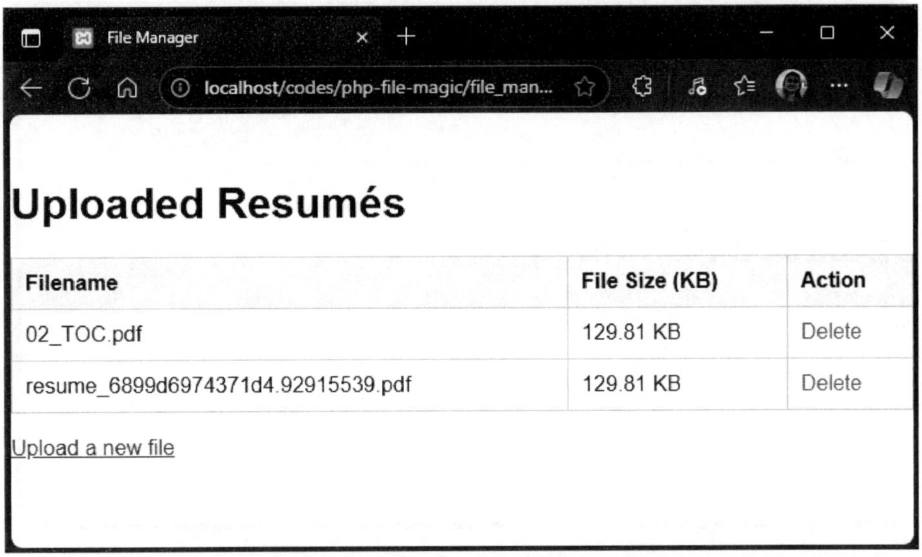
File Manager
localhost/codes/php-file-magic/file_man...
Uploaded Resumés
Filename
File Size (KB)
Action
02_TOC.pdf
129.81 KB
Delete
resume_6899d6974371d4.92915539.pdf
129.81 KB
Delete
Upload a new file

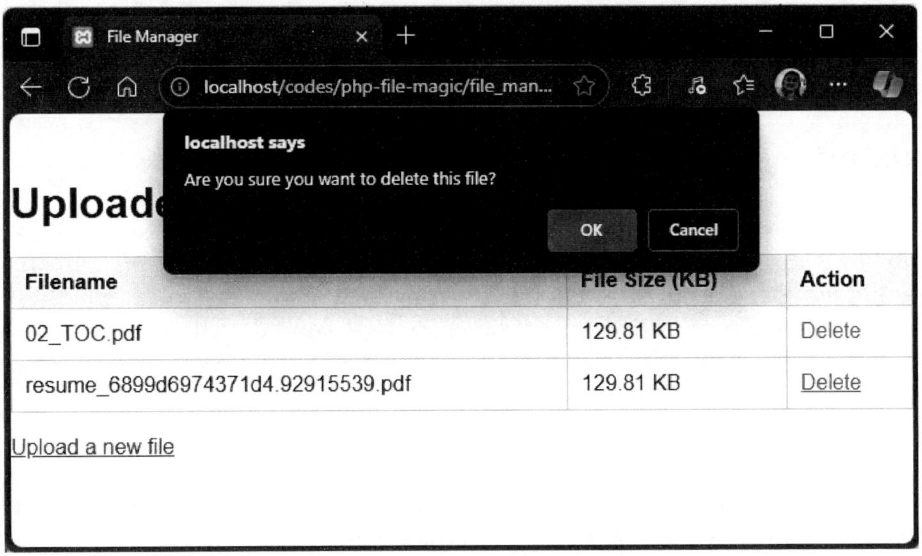
File Manager
localhost/codes/php-file-magic/file_man...
localhost says
Are you sure you want to delete this file?
OK
Cancel
Filename
Action
02_TOC.pdf
129.81 KB
Delete
resume_6899d6974371d4.92915539.pdf
129.81 KB
Delete
Upload a new file

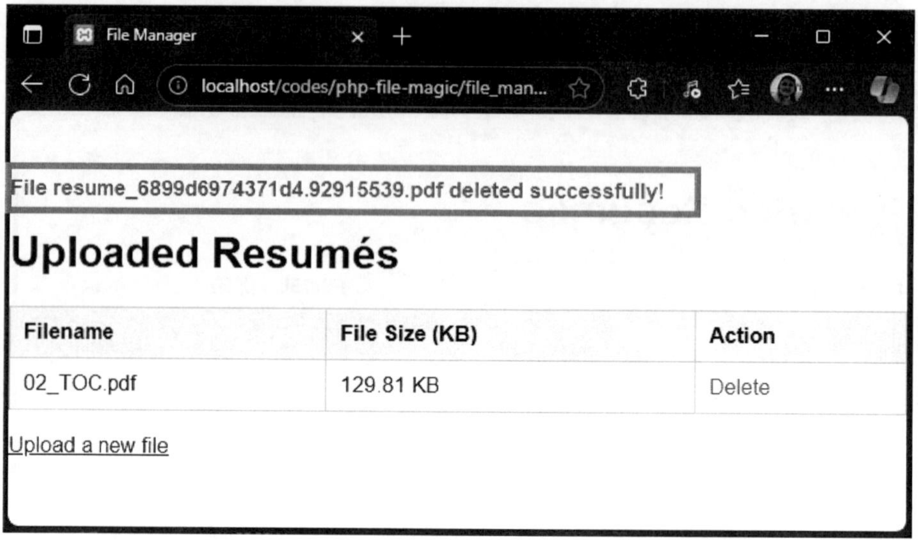

Security tips

We've already implemented some key security measures, but let's formalize them.

Sandboxing

Sandboxing means isolating your file operations within a **safe** directory. Never allow users to upload files to a directory that contains executable code (like your main .php files). Our **uploads/** folder is a perfect sandbox. Even better, on a real server, this folder should be placed outside the public web root (htdocs) if possible, so users can't directly navigate to uploaded files.

Path traversal

A path traversal attack happens when a user tricks your script into accessing files outside the intended sandbox directory. For example, an attacker might submit **../../../../etc/passwd** as a filename.

How we prevent it:

- **basename($_GET['delete']):** This function strips out any directory information, so ../../file.txt becomes file.txt. It's a simple but effective first line of defense.

- **Generating safe filenames:** As we did in ***Section: Validating uploaded files***, creating our own unique filenames (uniqid()) completely removes this risk, as the user's input is never used in the file path.
- **Real path check:** The check strpos(realpath($filePath), realpath($uploadDirectory)) === 0 in our file manager is a robust way to verify that the absolute path of the file to be deleted genuinely starts with the absolute path of our allowed upload directory.

Real uses

Now you understand the mechanics, think about the possibilities!

- **Resumés & cover letters:** Job application portals use these techniques to securely receive, validate (PDF/DOCX only, max 5MB), and store candidate documents.
- **Guestbooks & comments:** While databases are better for this, a simple guestbook can be built by appending each new entry to a text file. Each entry is a new line.
- **Application logs:** You can create a logging system that writes important events (like a user login, a failed payment, or a critical error) to a log file (app_events.log). This is invaluable for debugging.

Hands-on: Digital diary

Let's combine everything we've learned into a single, useful application: a **Digital Diary**. This app will allow you to write diary entries, save them as individual text files, and then list all your past entries. It will be the perfect showcase of your new file handling skills. We'll build the interface, the logic to save new entries, and the code to read and display existing ones.

Building the application

First, let's set up our project structure:

1. Inside your **php-file-magic** folder, create a new folder named **digital-diary**.
2. Inside **digital-diary** folder, create another folder named **entries**.

Your structure should look like this:

```
/php-file-magic
  /digital-diary
    /entries
    index.php
```

style.css

Create the HTML and CSS

We will build a single-file application. The top of the file will contain the PHP logic for saving and listing entries, and the bottom will contain the HTML form and display area.

Create **digital-diary/index.php**:

```
<?php
// PHP logic will go here in the next step
?>
<!DOCTYPE html>
<html lang="en">
<head>
    <meta charset="UTF-8">
    <meta name="viewport" content="width=device-width, initial-scale=1.0">
    <title>Digital Diary</title>
    <link rel="stylesheet" href="style.css">
</head>
<body>
    <div class="container">
        <header>
            <h1>My Digital Diary</h1>
            <p>Your thoughts, saved forever.</p>
        </header>
        <main>
            <section class="entry-form">
                <h2>New Entry</h2>
                <form action="index.php" method="POST">
                    <label for="title">Title:</label>
                    <input type="text" id="title" name="title" required>
                    <label for="content">Today's Thoughts:</label>
                    <textarea id="content" name="content" rows="8" required>
                    </textarea>
                    <button type="submit">Save Entry</button>
                </form>
            </section>
            <section class="entries-list">
                <h2>Past Entries</h2>
            </section>
        </main>
    </div>
</body>
</html>
```

Next, create **digital-diary/style.css** to make our diary look great:

```
body {
```

```
    font-family: 'Segoe UI', Tahoma, Geneva, Verdana, sans-serif;
    background-color: #fdfdfd;
    color: #333;
    line-height: 1.6;
    margin: 0;
    padding: 0;
}
.container {
    max-width: 800px;
    margin: 20px auto;
    padding: 20px;
    background: #fff;
    box-shadow: 0 0 15px rgba(0,0,0,0.05);
    border-radius: 8px;
}
header {
    text-align: center;
    border-bottom: 2px solid #f0f0f0;
    padding-bottom: 15px;
    margin-bottom: 20px;
}
header h1 {
    color: #4a4a4a;
}
.entry-form h2, .entries-list h2 {
    color: #5a5a5a;
    border-bottom: 1px solid #eee;
    padding-bottom: 5px;
}
form {
    display: flex;
    flex-direction: column;
}
form label {
    margin-top: 10px;
    font-weight: bold;
}
form input[type="text"], form textarea {
    padding: 10px;
    margin-top: 5px;
    border: 1px solid #ccc;
    border-radius: 4px;
    font-size: 1rem;
}
form button {
    margin-top: 15px;
    padding: 12px;
    background-color: #007bff;
    color: white;
    border: none;
```

```
    border-radius: 4px;
    cursor: pointer;
    font-size: 1.1rem;
    transition: background-color 0.2s;
}
form button:hover {
    background-color: #0056b3;
}
.message {
    padding: 15px;
    margin-bottom: 20px;
    border-radius: 5px;
    text-align: center;
    font-weight: bold;
}
.message.success {
    background-color: #d4edda;
    color: #155724;
}
.entries-list {
    margin-top: 30px;
}
.entry {
    background-color: #f9f9f9;
    border: 1px solid #e0e0e0;
    border-left: 5px solid #007bff;
    padding: 15px;
    margin-bottom: 15px;
    border-radius: 5px;
}
.entry h3 {
    margin: 0 0 5px 0;
    color: #0056b3;
}
.entry p {
    margin: 0;
    white-space: pre-wrap; /* Preserves whitespace and line breaks */
}
.entry small {
    display: block;
    margin-top: 10px;
    color: #777;
    font-style: italic;
}
```

Add the PHP logic to index.php

Now, let's add the PHP code to the very top of index.php. This code will handle two things: saving a new post if the form was submitted, and reading all existing posts from the entries/ directory:

```
<?php
$entriesDir = 'entries/';
$message = ''; // To store success/error messages
// Ensure the entries directory exists
if (!is_dir($entriesDir)) {
    mkdir($entriesDir, 0755, true);
}
// --- Part 1: Handle Form Submission to SAVE a new entry ---
if ($_SERVER['REQUEST_METHOD'] === 'POST' &&
isset($_POST['title'], $_POST['content'])) {
    $title = trim($_POST['title']);
    $content = trim($_POST['content']);
    // Basic validation
    if (!empty($title) && !empty($content)) {
        // Create a safe and unique filename from the title and current timestamp
        $timestamp = time();
        $safeTitle = preg_replace('/[^A-Za-z0-9-]+/', '-', strtolower($title));
        $filename = $timestamp . '_' . $safeTitle . '.txt';
        $filePath = $entriesDir . $filename;
        // Prepare the content to be saved (Title + Content)
        $fileContent = "Title: " . $title . "\n\n" . $content;
        // Save the content to the file
        if (file_put_contents($filePath, $fileContent)) {
            $message = "<div class='message success'>Entry saved
                        successfully!</div>";
        } else {
            $message = "<div class='message error'>Failed to save entry.
                        Please check permissions.</div>";
        }
    } else {
        $message = "<div class='message error'>Title and content
                    cannot be empty.</div>";
    }
}
// --- Part 2: Read and prepare existing entries to DISPLAY them ---
function getDiaryEntries($dir) {
    $entries = [];
    $files = scandir($dir);
    // Sort files by name in descending order to show newest first
    rsort($files);
    foreach ($files as $file) {
        if ($file !== '.' && $file !== '..') {
            $filePath = $dir . $file;
            $fileContent = file_get_contents($filePath);
```

```
            // Extract title and content
            // We use a simple format, so we can parse it back
            $title = 'Untitled';
            $content = $fileContent;
            if (strpos($fileContent, "\n\n") !== false) {
                list($titleLine, $contentPart) = explode("\n\n", $fileContent, 2);
                $title = substr($titleLine, strlen('Title: '));
                $content = $contentPart;
            }
            // Extract timestamp from filename for display
            $timestamp = (int) substr($file, 0, strpos($file, '_'));
            $entries[] = [
                'title' => htmlspecialchars($title),
                'content' => htmlspecialchars($content),
                'date' => date('l, F j, Y \a\t g:i a', $timestamp)
            ];
        }
    }
    return $entries;
}
$diaryEntries = getDiaryEntries($entriesDir);
?>
<!DOCTYPE html>
<html lang="en">
<head>
    <meta charset="UTF-8">
    <meta name="viewport" content="width=device-width, initial-scale=1.0">
    <title>Digital Diary</title>
    <link rel="stylesheet" href="style.css">
</head>
<body>
    <div class="container">
        <header>
            <h1>My Digital Diary</h1>
            <p>Your thoughts, saved forever.</p>
        </header>
        <main>
            <?php echo $message; // Display success/error message here ?>
            <section class="entry-form">
                <h2>New Entry</h2>
                <form action="index.php" method="POST">
                    <label for="title">Title:</label>
                    <input type="text" id="title" name="title" required>
                    <label for="content">Today's Thoughts:</label>
                    <textarea id="content" name="content" rows="8" required>
                    </textarea>
                    <button type="submit">Save Entry</button>
                </form>
            </section>
            <section class="entries-list">
                <h2>Past Entries</h2>
```

```
                <?php if (empty($diaryEntries)): ?>
                    <p>No entries yet. Write your first one above!</p>
                <?php else: ?>
                    <?php foreach ($diaryEntries as $entry): ?>
                        <div class="entry">
                            <h3><?php echo $entry['title']; ?></h3>
                            <small>Posted on <?php echo $entry['date']; ?></small>
                            <p><?php echo nl2br($entry['content']); ?></p>
                        </div>
                    <?php endforeach; ?>
                <?php endif; ?>
            </section>
        </main>
    </div>
</body>
</html>
```

Bridging the gap: Learned concepts and application implementation

Let's connect our code to the concepts from this chapter:

- **Directory manipulation:** The code first checks **is_dir($entriesDir)** and uses **mkdir($entriesDir)** to create our **sandbox** directory if it doesn't exist. This prevents errors on the first run.
- **Writing files:** When you submit the form, **file_put_contents($filePath, $fileContent)** is used to save your note. This is the core **save** functionality.
- **Secure filenames:** We don't use the user's title directly as the filename. We create a safe, URL-friendly version and prepend it with time() to ensure every entry has a unique filename and to avoid overwrites.
- **Reading files:** The **getDiaryEntries()** function uses **scandir()** to get a list of all saved note files. It then loops through them, using **file_get_contents()** to read the content of each entry.
- **Data persistence:** This is the key takeaway. You can close your browser, restart your computer, and when you come back to http://localhost/codes/php-file-magic/digital-diary/, your entries will still be there, read directly from the text files you saved.

Running and testing

1. Open your browser and navigate to **http://localhost/codes/php-file-magic/digital-diary/**.
2. You see the form to add a new entry and a message saying **No entries yet**.

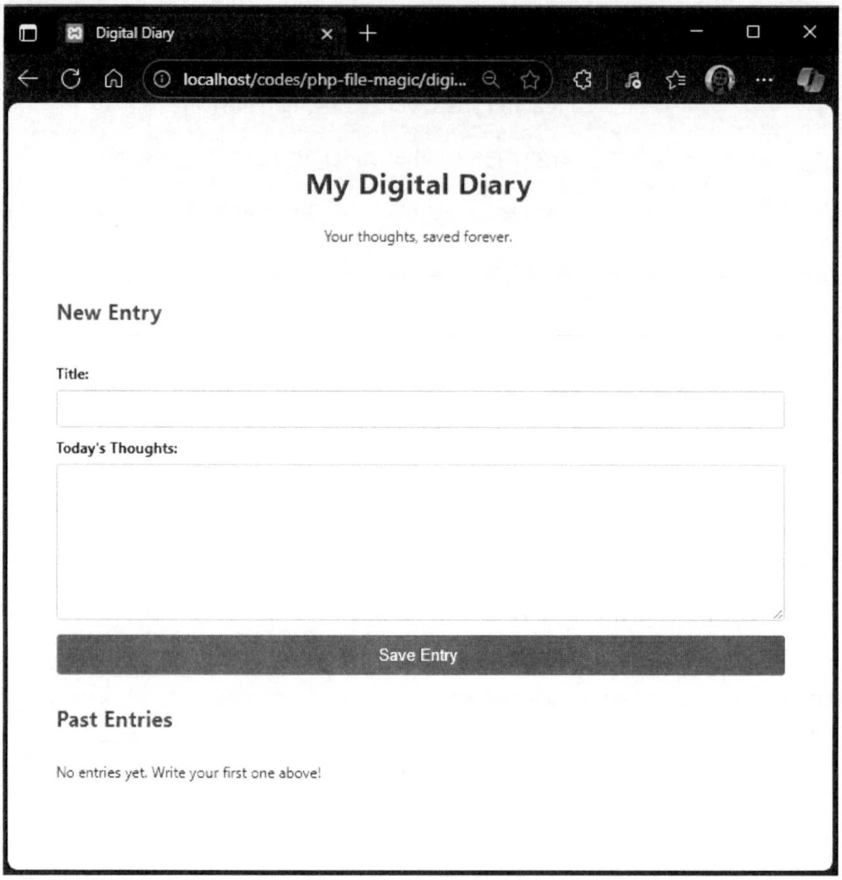

3. Fill in the **Title** field with **My First Day with PHP** and the **Today's Thoughts** field with **Today I learned how to save data to files. It feels like a superpower! I can build apps that remember things**.
4. Click the **Save Entry** button.
5. The page reloads. You see a green success message: **Entry saved successfully!**.
6. Below the form, your newly created entry appears under **Past Entries**, beautifully styled and formatted.

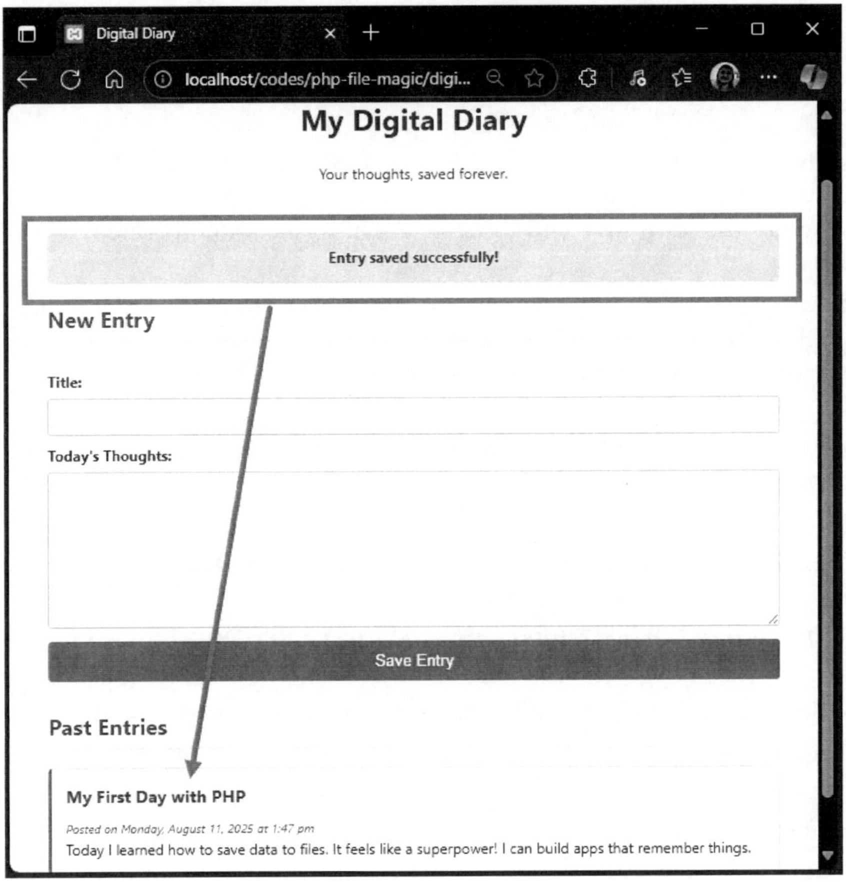

7. Add another entry, for example, with the **title**: **Future Ideas** and some content. You see it appear at the top of the list, as the entries are sorted by newest first.

Exploring application behaviour: A practical run-through

- **Valid input:** As we just tested, entering a title and content works perfectly. The entry is saved, and the list updates.
- **Invalid input (empty fields):** Try clicking **Save Entry** without filling in the title or content. The page will reload and show the red error message: **Title and content cannot be empty**. No file will be created.
- **Line breaks:** Write an entry with multiple paragraphs or line breaks. When it's displayed in the **Past Entries** list, the line breaks will be preserved thanks to the nl2br() PHP function, which converts newline characters into HTML <br> tags.

- **File system check:** Open the **php-file-magic/digital-diary/entries/** folder. You see the **.txt** files that the script created. Their names look something like **1754912872_my-first-day-with-php.txt**. This confirms that our application is physically writing data to the server's disk.
- **Permissions error:** If the **entries** folder was not writable by the web server, the **file_put_contents()** function would fail and return **false**. Our code handles this gracefully by showing the **Failed to save entry** message. This is a common issue when deploying to live servers.
- **File not found:** If someone manually deleted a text file from the entries folder, our **getDiaryEntries()** function would simply not see it on the next **scandir()** call, and it would disappear from the list without causing an error. This is robust behaviour.
- **Large files:** While not an issue for our text-based diary, if we were handling uploads, an excessively large file would be stopped by PHP's **upload_max_filesize()** setting before our script even runs, or caught by our custom size validation.

Harnessing file storage in real-world contexts

This Digital Diary project, while simple, uses the exact same principles as many real-world applications.

- **Guestbooks**, where users leave public messages, work this way.
- **Simple logging systems** that track errors or user activity append messages to a log file.
- Even some simple **Content Management Systems (CMS)** might store blog posts or pages as individual files, especially when a full database is overkill.

Understanding how to manage files gives you a lightweight and powerful tool for data persistence.

Wrapping up

- **Persistent data:** You learned how to save data that lasts beyond a single page load.
- **File I/O:** You mastered the core PHP functions for writing (file_put_contents) and reading (file_get_contents) files.
- **File uploads:** You built a secure form and handler for user-submitted files.
- **Crucial validation:** You know how to validate files by size, type (mime_content_type), and how to create safe filenames.

- **Directory management:** You can now create (mkdir), scan (scandir), and manage directories and files (unlink).
- **Security first:** You understand the risks of path traversal and the importance of sandboxing file operations.

Congratulations on mastering one of the most fundamental skills in web development! You have officially broken through the barrier of stateless web pages and can now build applications with memory. The Digital Diary project is more than just an exercise; it's a fully functional application that demonstrates your ability to handle user input, process it, and store it securely for later retrieval. This is a massive step forward.

In the next chapter, we'll build on this foundation by creating a more complex and feature-rich application. Get ready for ***Chapter 11: Culmination - Journal Pro - Your personal multimedia diary***, where we'll combine everything, you've learned about forms, strings, and files to build an impressive portfolio project.

Chapter 11

Section 03: User power – Forms, strings, and file magic

Culmination: Journal Pro – Your personal multimedia diary

What you'll learn

- Integrating core skills
- Building dynamic forms
- Styling with advanced CSS
- Handling file uploads
- Creating a search feature
- Structuring a complete app

Welcome to your first major project milestone! In the last few chapters, you mastered the three pillars of user interaction: handling forms, manipulating text, and working with files. Now, it's time to assemble those skills into a single, powerful application: Journal Pro. This personal multimedia diary will let you save your thoughts, upload important documents or images, and find past entries with a quick search.

This chapter is all about integration—seeing how individual concepts come together to create a seamless, useful tool, much like a simple version of popular note-taking apps like Evernote or Google Keep.

Planning the app

Before writing a single line of code, great developers pause to plan. A good plan acts as a blueprint, preventing confusion and saving time later. For Journal Pro, we need to decide what it will do and how it will store information.

Our app will have the following key features:

- **Create new entries:** A user can write a title and the main text for a diary entry.
- **Attach a file:** Each entry can have one optional file (an image or a document) uploaded with it.
- **View all entries:** The main page will display all saved entries, with the newest one first.
- **Search and filter:** A user can search through all entries to find specific ones based on a keyword.

Next, let's consider the **data design**. Since we haven't covered databases yet, we'll use a simple and effective file-based system. Each journal entry will be saved as a separate file on the server. To keep things organized, we will create two folders:

- **entries/:** This will store the text content of our journal entries.
- **uploads/:** This will store the images and documents we attach to our entries.

To link an entry's text with its uploaded file, we'll use a data format called **JSON (JavaScript Object Notation)**. It's a lightweight, human-readable way to store structured data. Each entry file in the **entries/** directory will be a **.json** file containing the title, content, the path to the associated uploaded file (if any), and a timestamp.

Implementing forms, strings, and file handling

This is where our previous lessons connect. We'll build an HTML form (Chapter 8) to collect the user's input, use PHP string functions (Chapter 9) to safely process the text, and leverage file handling functions (Chapter 10) to save everything to the server.

Let's start by creating the main HTML form that the user will interact with. This form will include fields for a title, the main content, and a file upload button:

```
<form action="index.php" method="post" enctype="multipart/form-data">
    <label for="title">Entry Title:</label>
    <input type="text" id="title" name="title" required>
    <label for="content">Your Thoughts:</label>
    <textarea id="content" name="content" rows="5" required></textarea>
```

```
    <label for="media">Attach a File (Image or Doc):</label>
    <input type="file" id="media" name="media">
    <button type="submit">Save Entry</button>
</form>
```

A crucial detail:

The **enctype="multipart/form-data"** attribute on the <form> tag is essential. It tells the browser to prepare the data for a file upload. Without it, the file will not be sent to the server.

When this form is submitted, our PHP script will receive the data in the **$_POST** and **$_FILES** superglobals. We will then sanitize the text to prevent security issues and prepare it for storage.

Adding file uploads

Handling file uploads is a multi-step process that requires careful validation to ensure security and stability. We can't just trust any file a user sends us. Our PHP script will perform these checks:

- **Check if a file was uploaded:** The user might not attach a file, and our app should handle that gracefully.
- **Check for errors:** PHP reports any issues during the upload process, like a file being too large.
- **Validate file type and size:** We will only allow specific file types (e.g., JPEG, PNG, PDF) and set a reasonable size limit (e.g., 5MB) to prevent users from filling up our server's storage.

Here is a PHP snippet demonstrating how we access the file data from the $_FILES superglobal and move it to our uploads/ directory:

```
<?php
// A simplified look at the file handling logic
$upload_dir = 'uploads/';
$uploaded_file_path = ''; // Will hold the final path if upload is successful
// Check if a file was uploaded and there are no errors
if (isset($_FILES['media']) && $_FILES['media']['error'] === UPLOAD_ERR_OK) {
    $file_info = $_FILES['media'];
    // Create a unique name
    $file_name = uniqid() . '-' . basename($file_info['name']);
    $target_path = $upload_dir . $file_name;
    // Move the temporary file to its final destination
    if (move_uploaded_file($file_info['tmp_name'], $target_path)) {
        $uploaded_file_path = $target_path;
```

```
    } else {
        echo "There was an error moving the uploaded file.";
    }
}
?>
```

In this code:

- **$_FILES['media']** contains information about the uploaded file.
- We generate a unique filename using **uniqid()** to prevent file name collisions if two users upload files with the same name.
- **move_uploaded_file()** is the PHP function that securely moves the file from its temporary location to our desired uploads/ folder.

Search and filter functionality

A diary isn't very useful if you can't find old entries. We'll add a simple search bar that filters the displayed entries. The logic is straightforward:

- Add a search form to the top of our page. This form will use the GET method.
- When the page loads, the PHP script will check if a search query is present in the URL (e.g., index.php?search=meeting).
- If a search term exists, the script will read all the .json entry files from the entries/ directory.
- It will then loop through each entry and check if the search term appears in either the title or the content. str_contains() is a perfect, case-sensitive function for this.
- Only the entries that match the query will be displayed.

Here's the HTML for the search form:

```
<form action="index.php" method="get">
    <input type="text" name="search" placeholder="Search entries...">
    <button type="submit">Search</button>
</form>
```

The PHP logic to handle the filtering will be integrated directly into the part of our script that displays the journal entries, making our page dynamic.

Upgrading display with advanced CSS

Functionality is key, but presentation matters. We want our diary to be pleasant to look at and easy to read. We'll use CSS to style our application, focusing on a clean, card-based layout for each journal entry.

Our CSS will achieve the following:

- A clean, centered layout for the main content.
- Well-styled form inputs that are easy to use.
- A **card** design for each journal entry, with a clear separation between title, content, and the attached file.
- Responsive design so it looks good on both desktop and smaller screens.

Here is a sneak peek at the CSS for an entry card:

```
/* CSS for a single journal entry card */
.entry-card {
    background-color: #ffffff;
    border: 1px solid #e0e0e0;
    border-radius: 8px;
    padding: 20px;
    margin-bottom: 20px;
    box-shadow: 0 2px 4px rgba(0,0,0,0.05);
}
.entry-card h3 {
    margin-top: 0;
    color: #333;
}
.entry-card .attachment img {
    max-width: 100%;
    border-radius: 4px;
    margin-top: 10px;
}
```

This CSS creates a visually distinct container for each entry, making the whole page feel organized and professional.

Hands-on: Journal Pro app

It's time to build the complete Journal Pro application. In this section, we will create all the necessary files and write the code from start to finish. By the end, you will have a fully functional, beautifully styled multimedia diary running in your local XAMPP environment.

Building the application

Follow these steps carefully. We'll create one folder and two files to house our entire application.

Create the project structure

First, we need to set up our folders.

1. Open the **htdocs\codes** folder inside your XAMPP installation directory (this is usually at C:\xampp\htdocs\codes on Windows).
2. Inside **htdocs\codes**, create a main folder named **journal-pro**.
3. Open the new **journal-pro** folder.
4. Inside **journal-pro**, create two more folders: one named **entries** and another named **uploads**.

Your final structure within htdocs\codes should look like this:

```
C:\xampp\htdocs\codes
└── journal-pro\
    ├── entries\
    └── uploads\
```

The **entries** folder will hold our journal text files, and **uploads** will hold the images and documents.

Create the main application file

This single file will contain all our PHP logic and HTML structure.

1. In your VS Code editor, create a new file.
2. Save it as **index.php** inside the **journal-pro** folder (at the same level as the entries and uploads folders).
3. Replace the following code into your index.php file:

```
<?php
// --- CONFIGURATION ---
$entries_dir = 'entries/';
$uploads_dir = 'uploads/';
$allowed_extensions = ['jpg', 'jpeg', 'png', 'gif', 'pdf', 'docx'];
$max_file_size = 5 * 1024 * 1024; // 5 MB
// --- INITIALIZATION ---
$message = ''; // To store feedback messages for the user
```

```
// --- FORM HANDLING (POST REQUEST) ---
if ($_SERVER['REQUEST_METHOD'] === 'POST') {
    // 1. Get and sanitize form data
    $title = trim($_POST['title'] ?? '');
    $content = trim($_POST['content'] ?? '');
    if (empty($title) || empty($content)) {
        $message = '<div class="message error">Title and content are required.
                    </div>';
    } else {
        // 2. Handle file upload
        $uploaded_file_path = '';
        if (isset($_FILES['media']) && $_FILES['media']['error']
                  === UPLOAD_ERR_OK) {
            $file_tmp_name = $_FILES['media']['tmp_name'];
            $file_name = $_FILES['media']['name'];
            $file_size = $_FILES['media']['size'];
            $file_ext = strtolower(pathinfo($file_name,
                                        PATHINFO_EXTENSION));
            // Validate file
            if ($file_size > $max_file_size) {
                $message = '<div class="message error">Error: File is too
                            large (Max 5MB).</div>';
            } elseif (!in_array($file_ext, $allowed_extensions)) {
                $message = '<div class="message error">Error: Invalid file
                            type.</div>';
            } else {
                $new_file_name = uniqid('', true) . '.' . $file_ext;
                $destination = $uploads_dir . $new_file_name;
                if (move_uploaded_file($file_tmp_name, $destination)) {
                    $uploaded_file_path = $destination;
                } else {
                    $message = '<div class="message error">Failed to move
                                uploaded file.</div>';
                }
            }
        }
        // 3. Save the entry (if no errors occurred)
        if (empty($message)) {
            $entry_data = [
                'title' => htmlspecialchars($title),
                'content' => htmlspecialchars($content),
                'timestamp' => time(),
                'attachment' => $uploaded_file_path
            ];
            $entry_filename = $entries_dir . time() . '.json';
            file_put_contents($entry_filename, json_encode($entry_data,
                                JSON_PRETTY_PRINT));
            $message = '<div class="message success">Journal entry saved
                        successfully!</div>';
        }
    }
```

```
}
// --- DISPLAY LOGIC (GET REQUEST) ---
function get_journal_entries() {
    global $entries_dir;
    $entries = [];
    $files = glob($entries_dir . '*.json');
    // Sort files by name (timestamp) in descending order
    rsort($files);
    foreach ($files as $file) {
        $json_data = file_get_contents($file);
        $entries[] = json_decode($json_data, true);
    }
    return $entries;
}
$all_entries = get_journal_entries();
// Filter entries based on search query
$search_query = trim($_GET['search'] ?? '');
if (!empty($search_query)) {
    $filtered_entries = [];
    foreach ($all_entries as $entry) {
        if (str_contains(strtolower($entry['title']), strtolower($search_query)) ||
          str_contains(strtolower($entry['content']), strtolower($search_query))) {
            $filtered_entries[] = $entry;
        }
    }
    // Replace all entries with filtered ones
    $all_entries = $filtered_entries;
}
?>
<!DOCTYPE html>
<html lang="en">
<head>
    <meta charset="UTF-8">
    <meta name="viewport" content="width=device-width, initial-scale=1.0">
    <title>Journal Pro</title>
    <link rel="stylesheet" href="style.css">
</head>
<body>
    <div class="container">
        <header>
            <h1><a href="index.php">Journal Pro</a></h1>
            <p>Your Personal Multimedia Diary</p>
        </header>
        <main>
            <section class="new-entry-form">
                <h2>Add a New Entry</h2>
                <?php echo $message; // Display feedback message ?>
                <form action="index.php" method="post"
                      enctype="multipart/form-data">
                    <label for="title">Entry Title:</label>
                    <input type="text" id="title" name="title" required>
```

```
                    <label for="content">Your Thoughts:</label>
                    <textarea id="content" name="content" rows="6" required>
                    </textarea>
                    <label for="media">Attach a File (Image, PDF, DOCX):</label>
                    <input type="file" id="media" name="media">
                    <button type="submit">Save Entry</button>
                </form>
            </section>
            <section class="entries-section">
                <h2>Your Entries</h2>
                <form action="index.php" method="get" class="search-form">
                    <input type="text" name="search"
                           placeholder="Search by keyword..."
                           value="<?= htmlspecialchars($search_query) ?>">
                    <button type="submit">Search</button>
                    <?php if (!empty($search_query)): ?>
                        <a href="index.php" class="clear-search">Clear</a>
                    <?php endif; ?>
                </form>
                <div class="entries-list">
                    <?php if (empty($all_entries)): ?>
                        <p>No journal entries found. Why not write one?
                        </p>
                    <?php else: ?>
                        <?php foreach ($all_entries as $entry): ?>
                            <div class="entry-card">
                                <h3><?= htmlspecialchars($entry['title']) ?></h3>
                                <p class="entry-meta">
                                    Saved on: <?= date('F j, Y, g:i a', $entry['
                                    timestamp']) ?>
                                </p>
                                <div class="entry-content">
                                    <?= nl2br(htmlspecialchars($entry['
                                        content'])) ?>
                                </div>
                                <?php if (!empty($entry['attachment'])):
                                    $file_ext = strtolower(pathinfo(
                                                           $entry['attachment'],
                                                           PATHINFO_EXTENSION));
                                    $image_extensions = ['jpg', 'jpeg',
                                                         'png', 'gif'];
                                ?>
                                    <div class="attachment">
                                        <h4>Attachment:</h4>
                                        <?php if (in_array($file_ext,
                                                   $image_extensions)): ?>
                                            <a href="<?= $entry['attachment'] ?>"
                                               target="_blank">
                                                <img src="<?= $entry['
                                                          attachment'] ?>"
                                                     alt="Attached Image">
```

```
                                            </a>
                                        <?php else: ?>
                                            <a href="<?= $entry['attachment'] ?>"
                                               target="_blank">
                                                Download File (<?= strtoupper(
                                                               $file_ext) ?>)
                                            </a>
                                        <?php endif; ?>
                                    </div>
                                <?php endif; ?>
                            </div>
                        <?php endforeach; ?>
                    <?php endif; ?>
                </div>
            </section>
        </main>
    </div>
</body>
</html>
```

Create the stylesheet

This file will contain all the visual styling for our application.

1. In VS Code, create another new file.
2. Save it as **style.css** in the same **journal-pro** folder.
3. Replace the following code into your style.css file:

```
/* --- General Body & Typography --- */
body {
    font-family: -apple-system, BlinkMacSystemFont, "Segoe UI", Roboto,
Helvetica, Arial, sans-serif;
    background-color: #f4f7f9;
    color: #333;
    line-height: 1.6;
    margin: 0;
    padding: 20px;
}
.container {
    max-width: 800px;
    margin: 0 auto;
    background-color: #ffffff;
    padding: 30px;
    border-radius: 10px;
    box-shadow: 0 4px 15px rgba(0,0,0,0.1);
}
header {
    text-align: center;
    border-bottom: 2px solid #e9ecef;
```

```
    padding-bottom: 20px;
    margin-bottom: 30px;
}
header h1 a {
    text-decoration: none;
    color: #0056b3;
}
header p {
    color: #6c757d;
    font-size: 1.1em;
}
/* --- Forms --- */
form label {
    display: block;
    margin-bottom: 8px;
    font-weight: bold;
    color: #495057;
}
form input[type="text"], form textarea, form input[type="file"] {
    width: 100%;
    padding: 12px;
    margin-bottom: 20px;
    border: 1px solid #ced4da;
    border-radius: 5px;
    box-sizing: border-box; /* Important */
    font-size: 1em;
}
form input[type="file"] {
    padding: 5px;
}
form button {
    display: inline-block;
    background-color: #007bff;
    color: white;
    padding: 12px 20px;
    border: none;
    border-radius: 5px;
    cursor: pointer;
    font-size: 1em;
    font-weight: bold;
    transition: background-color 0.2s;
}
form button:hover {
    background-color: #0056b3;
}
/* --- Feedback Messages --- */
.message {
    padding: 15px;
    margin-bottom: 20px;
    border-radius: 5px;
    font-weight: bold;
```

```
    text-align: center;
}
.message.success {
    background-color: #d4edda;
    color: #155724;
    border: 1px solid #c3e6cb;
}
.message.error {
    background-color: #f8d7da;
    color: #721c24;
    border: 1px solid #f5c6cb;
}
/* --- Entries Section --- */
.entries-section {
    margin-top: 40px;
}
.search-form {
    display: flex;
    gap: 10px;
    margin-bottom: 20px;
}
.search-form input[type="text"] {
    flex-grow: 1; /* Take up available space */
    margin-bottom: 0;
}
.clear-search {
    padding: 10px 15px;
    background-color: #6c757d;
    color: white;
    text-decoration: none;
    border-radius: 5px;
    font-size: 0.9em;
    display: flex;
    align-items: center;
}
/* --- Entry Card --- */
.entry-card {
    background-color: #fff;
    border: 1px solid #e0e0e0;
    border-radius: 8px;
    padding: 20px;
    margin-bottom: 20px;
    box-shadow: 0 2px 4px rgba(0,0,0,0.05);
}
.entry-card h3 {
    margin-top: 0;
    color: #0056b3;
}
.entry-meta {
    font-size: 0.85em;
    color: #888;
```

```
    margin-bottom: 15px;
}
.entry-content {
    white-space: pre-wrap; /* Preserves line breaks */
}
/* --- Attachments --- */
.attachment {
    margin-top: 15px;
    border-top: 1px solid #eee;
    padding-top: 15px;
}
.attachment h4 {
    margin: 0 0 10px 0;
    color: #555;
}
.attachment img {
    max-width: 200px;
    height: auto;
    border-radius: 4px;
    border: 1px solid #ddd;
}
.attachment a {
    display: inline-block;
    padding: 8px 12px;
    background-color: #f0f0f0;
    border-radius: 4px;
    text-decoration: none;
    color: #333;
    font-weight: bold;
}
```

Bridging the gap: Learned concepts and application implementation

This project is the perfect summary of ***Section 3*** of our book. Let's see how:

- **Smart forms:** The core of our application is the HTML form. We use the POST method for creating data and the GET method for our search functionality. We access user input securely using the $_POST, $_GET, and $_FILES superglobals.
- **String manipulation:** We use trim() to clean up user input, htmlspecialchars() to prevent XSS attacks by neutralizing any HTML characters, strtolower() and str_contains() for our case-insensitive search, and pathinfo() to safely extract a file's extension.

- **File handling:** This is the star of the show. We use file_put_contents() to save our entries as JSON files, file_get_contents() to read them back, and glob() to get a list of all entry files. The entire file upload mechanism—from checking $_FILES to validation and using move_uploaded_file().

This chapter was less about learning new syntax and more about **synthesis**. We took the separate tools from your developer toolbox—forms, strings, and files—and integrated them into a cohesive whole. You will see how a single user action, like clicking **Save Entry**, triggers a chain of events: form data is received, text is sanitized, a file is validated and moved, and a structured data file is written to the server. This integration is the essence of web application development.

Running and testing

Now for the exciting part! Let's run Journal Pro.

1. **Start XAMPP:** Open the **XAMPP Control Panel** and click the **Start** button for the **Apache** module.
2. **Open browser:** Open your web browser (like Chrome or Firefox).
3. **Navigate to the project:** In the address bar, type **http://localhost/codes/journal-pro/** and press **Enter**.
4. **You should see:** The main page with the **Add a New Entry** form and the **Your Entries** section, which currently says **No journal entries found.**

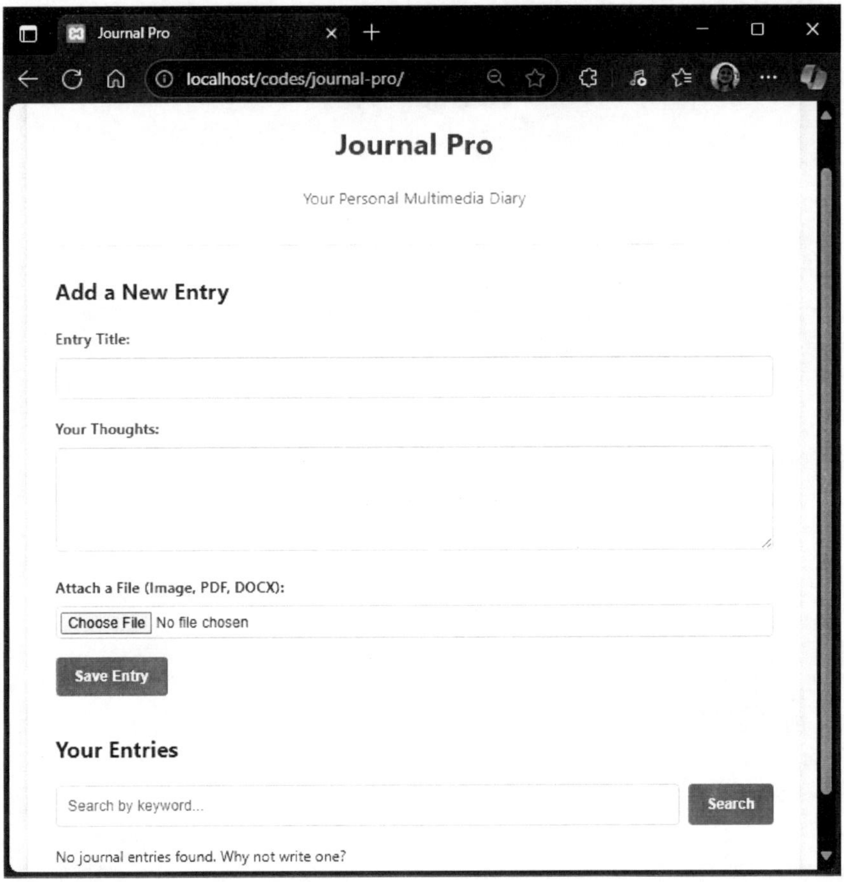

5. **Create an entry:** Fill in the title (My First Day with PHP) and content (Today, I built a full web application!). Click **Save Entry**. You see a **green success message**, and your new entry appears below.

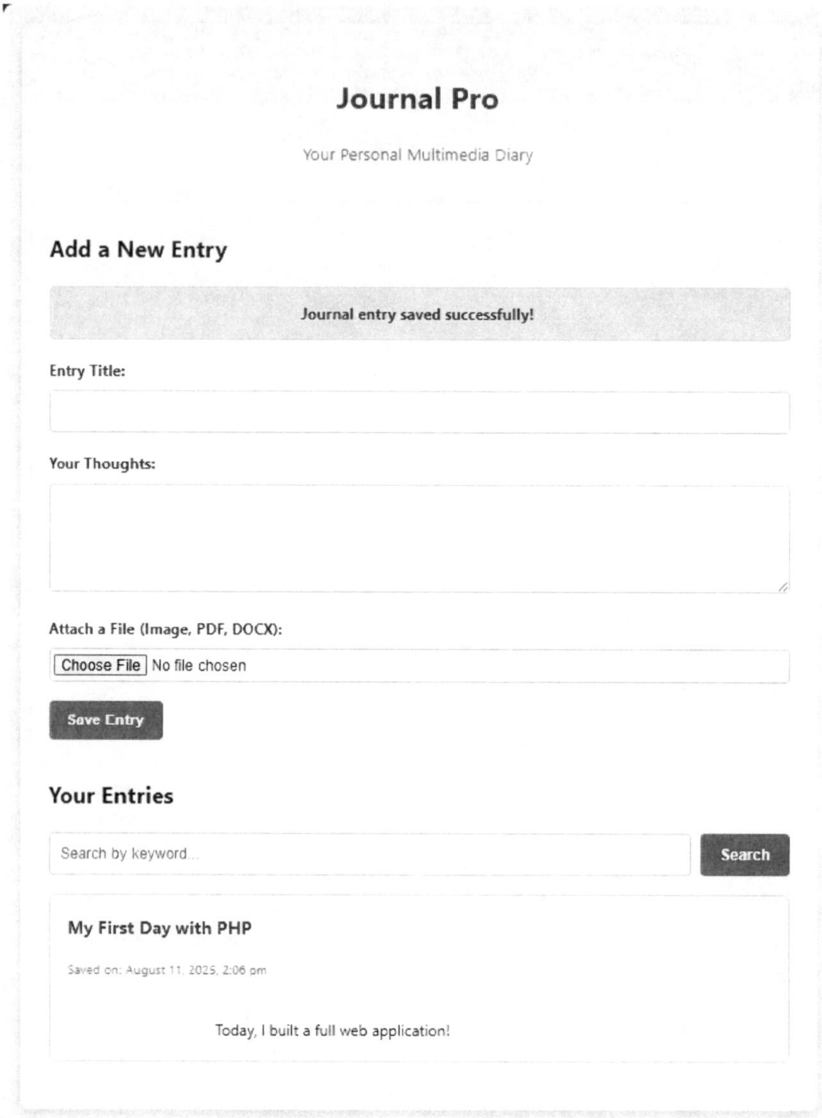

6. **Create an entry with an image:** Create another entry titled **Project Snapshot**. Add some text and use the **Choose File** button to select a JPEG or PNG image from your computer. Save it. The new entry appears at the top, now with a preview of your uploaded image.

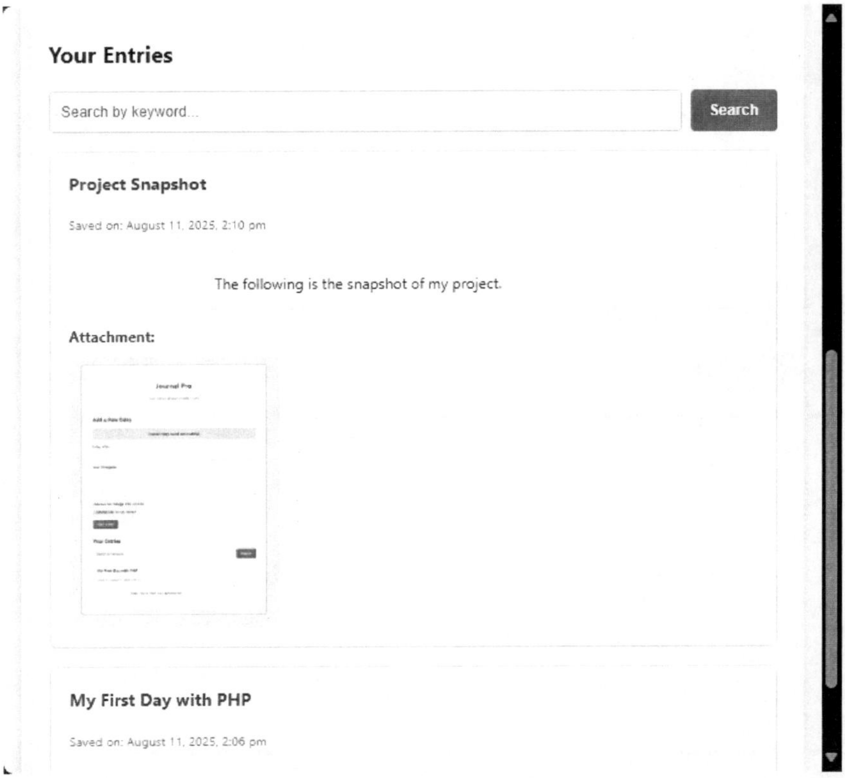

7. **Search for an entry:** In the search bar, type **PHP** and click **Search**. The page reloads, showing only the **My First Day with PHP** entry. Click the **Clear** button to see all entries again.

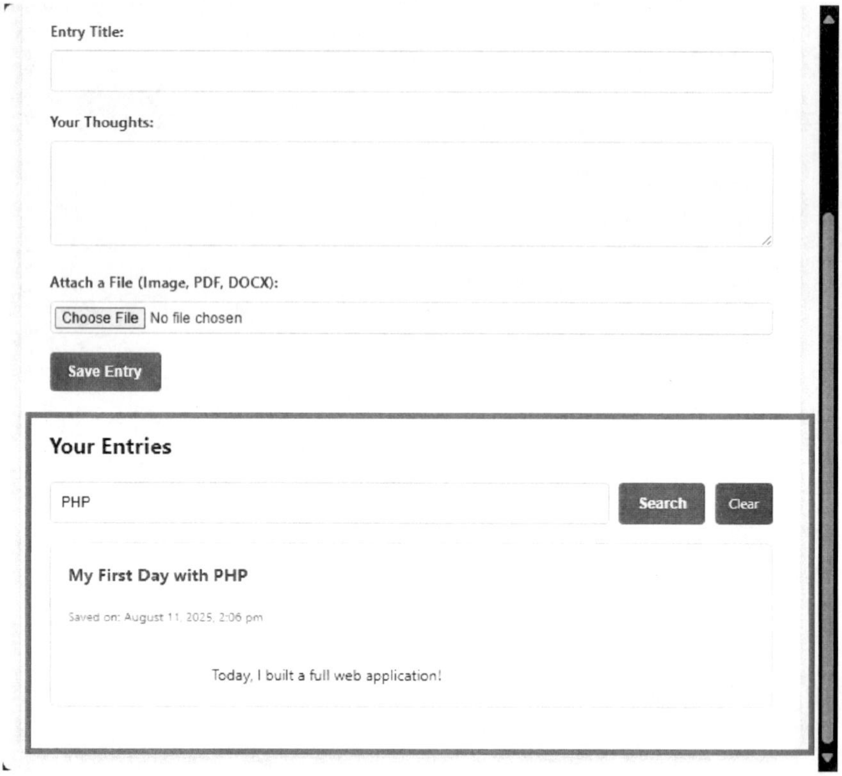

Exploring application behaviour: A practical run-through

A robust application handles both expected and unexpected user actions. Let's see how Journal Pro behaves:

- **Invalid input:** If you try to save an entry with an empty title or content, the PHP script will catch it and display a red error message without saving anything.

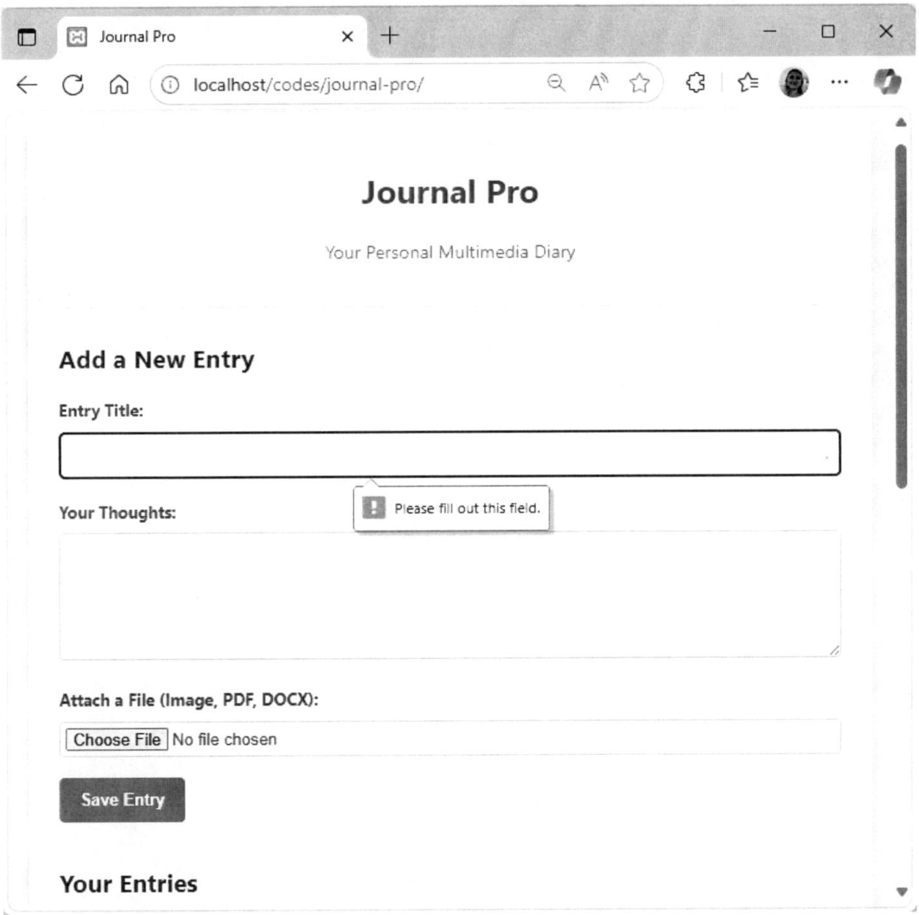

- **Invalid file upload:** Try uploading a very large file (e.g., a 10MB video) or a disallowed file type (like a .exe file). Our validation logic will kick in, showing a specific error message ("File is too large" or "Invalid file type") and will not save the entry.

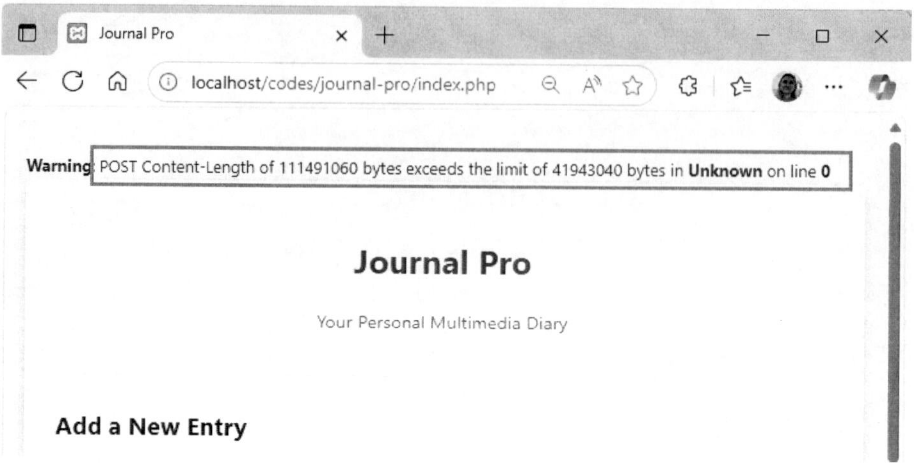

- **No search results:** If you search for a word that doesn't exist in any entry (e.g., "zxyqwr"), the page will correctly display the message: "No journal entries found."

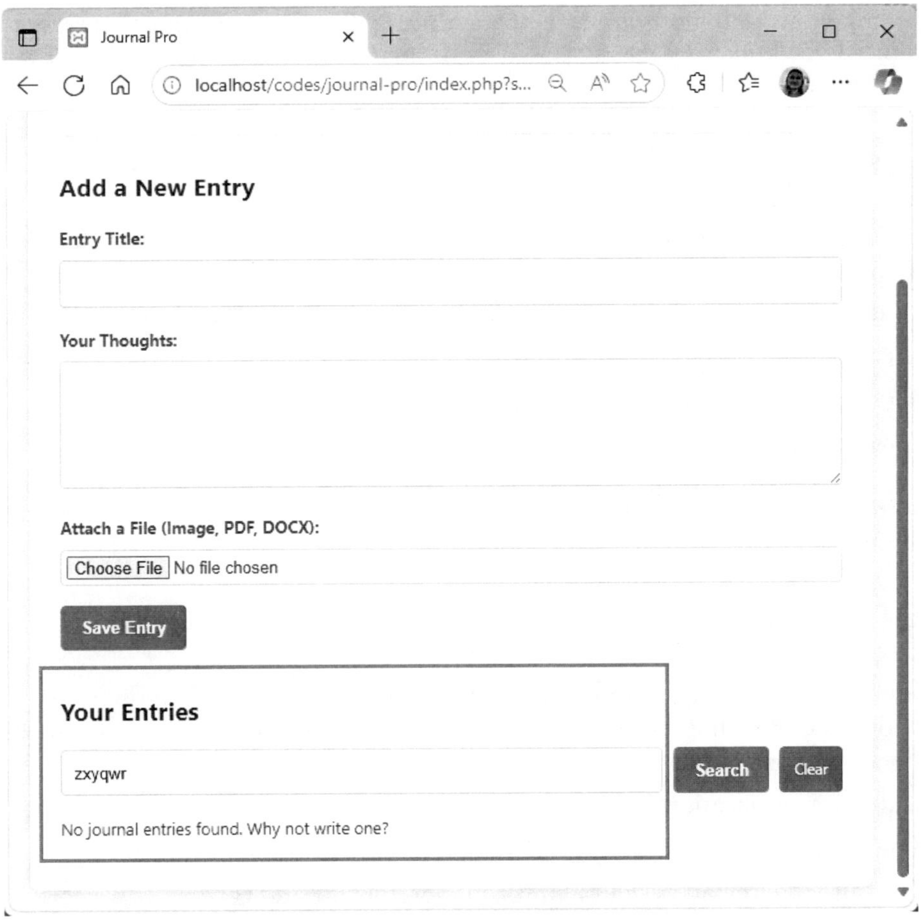

Our current version of Journal Pro is perfect for a single user on a local machine. However, it's important to understand its limitations in a broader context:

- **Multi-user issues:** If two people tried to save an entry at the exact same second, our time() based filename could potentially cause a conflict. A real multi-user app would need a database with unique IDs to solve this. Furthermore, there is no privacy; all entries are visible to anyone who accesses the page.
- **Storage limits:** We implemented a 5MB file size limit, which is a critical practice. Without it, a user could easily upload huge files and crash the server or fill up the available disk space. In a real-world application, these limits are essential for stability and cost management.

Understanding these limitations is a sign of a maturing developer. It helps you recognize why more advanced tools like databases and user authentication (which we'll cover soon!) are necessary for building larger, more complex platforms.

Harnessing Journal Pro in real-world contexts

While our Journal Pro is a personal project, the skills you've used are fundamental to countless real-world applications. Almost every web app needs to:

- Accept user input via forms (contact forms, registration pages, comment sections).
- Process and store that data safely.
- Allow users to upload files (profile pictures, résumés, project files).
- Provide a way to search or filter through existing data.

This project is a direct, albeit simplified, model for a personal blog, a simple document management system, or a support ticket system.

Wrapping up

In this chapter, you successfully built a complete, feature-rich web application from the ground up. You should be incredibly proud of what you've accomplished. Let's recap the key skills and concepts you mastered:

- Planned a web application's features and data structure.
- Combined form handling, string processing, and file I/O into one script.
- Built a secure file upload system with validation for size and type.
- Implemented a dynamic search feature to filter content.
- Used advanced CSS to create a professional, responsive user interface.
- Learned how to test for and handle various user inputs and edge cases.

Congratulations! You have officially graduated from learning isolated PHP concepts to building an integrated, functional web application. Journal Pro is more than just a project; it's a testament to your growing skills and a solid piece for your developer portfolio. You've taken the fundamental building blocks of the web and created something tangible and useful.

Keep this momentum going! In our next section, ***Section 04: Smarter workflows – Functions, Arrays, and Authenticity***, we will start making our code more organized, powerful, and reusable by diving into the world of functions.

Chapter 12

Section 04: Smarter workflows – Functions, Arrays, and Authenticity

Code as building blocks – Functions for everything

What you'll learn

- Creating reusable code
- Understanding variable scope
- Passing data around
- Writing safer code

Welcome to one of the most powerful concepts in all of programming: **Functions**. Think of them as mini-programs or specialized tools you create once and use forever. Imagine you have a complex recipe, like baking a cake. You don't re-invent how to **whisk eggs** or **preheat the oven** every time; you just perform those standard actions. Functions are the programming equivalent.

In this chapter, you'll learn how to bundle your logic into these neat, reusable blocks, making your code cleaner, more efficient, and much easier to manage. This is the secret to building complex applications without getting lost in a sea of repeated code.

What are functions? when and why?

A **function** is a self-contained block of code that performs a specific task. You give it a name, and you can **call** that name whenever you need to execute that task.

The main reason to use functions is to follow the **DRY** principle: **Don't Repeat Yourself**. If you find yourself writing the same lines of code in multiple places, it's a perfect candidate for a function.

Why is this so important?

- **Reusability:** Write it once, use it a hundred times.
- **Readability:** Giving a block of code a name, like calculateTotalPrice(), makes it immediately clear what it does.
- **Maintainability:** If you need to fix a bug or update the logic, you only have to change it in one place—the function itself.

Let's see a simple example. Imagine we want to display a copyright notice on several pages of our website.

- PHP code:

```
<?php
// Define a function to display a copyright notice
function displayCopyright() {
  echo "<p>© 2025 SmartEvents Inc. All rights reserved.</p>";
}
?>
```

- HTML Code:

```
<!DOCTYPE html>
<html lang="en">
<head>
    <meta charset="UTF-8">
    <title>Functions Demo</title>
</head>
<body>
    <h1>Welcome to Our Homepage</h1>
    <p>This is the main content of our site.</p>
    <footer>
        <?php displayCopyright(); // Call the function here ?>
    </footer>
    <h1>About Us</h1>
    <p>Here is some information about our company.</p>
    <footer>
```

```
        <?php displayCopyright(); // Call the function again! ?>
    </footer>
</body>
</html>
```

In this example, instead of writing the <p> tag twice, we just call displayCopyright(). If we ever need to change the year or the company name, we only have to edit it inside the function.

Defining, calling, and returning data

Defining a function means creating it. **Calling** it means executing it. So far, our function only *did* something (echo text). But the real power comes when functions can process data and give you a result back. This is done with the **return** keyword.

A function that returns a value doesn't display anything itself; it just hands a result back to the code that called it.

Let's create a function that calculates the area of a rectangle:

```
<?php
// This function takes two numbers, calculates the area, and returns the result.
function calculateArea(int $length, int $width): int {
  $area = $length * $width;
  return $area;
}
// Let's call the function and store its result in a variable. The result (50) is
// now in $rectangleArea
$rectangleArea = calculateArea(10, 5);
?>
<!DOCTYPE html>
<html lang="en">
<head>
    <meta charset="UTF-8">
    <title>Returning Data</title>
</head>
<body>
    <h1>Calculating Area</h1>
    <p>The area of a 10x5 rectangle is: <?php echo $rectangleArea; ?></p>
    <p>We can also use it directly: The area of a 20x3 rectangle is:
    <?php echo calculateArea(20, 3); ?></p>
</body>
</html>
```

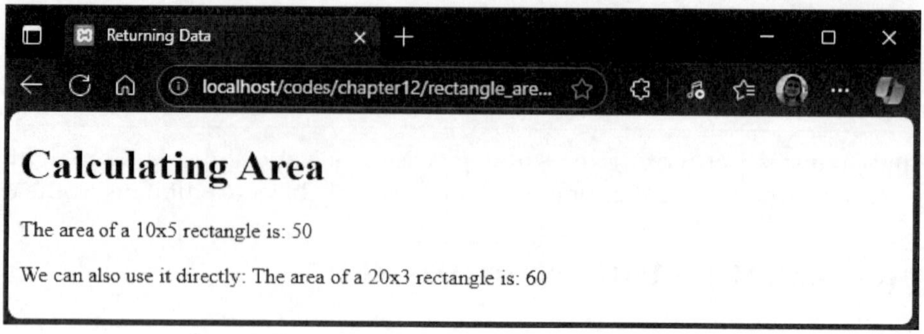

Notice the **: int** after the parentheses? This is a **return type declaration**. It tells PHP that this function is *expected* to return an integer. It helps prevent bugs by making our code more predictable.

Arguments

Arguments (or **parameters**) are the pieces of data you pass *into* a function for it to work with. In the last example, **$length** and **$width** were **required** arguments. You can't call calculateArea() without them.

Sometimes, an argument might be **optional**. You can achieve this by giving it a **default value**. If the caller doesn't provide a value for that argument, the **default** is used instead.

Let's create a function to generate a welcome message. The name is required, but a title (like "Dr." or "Ms.") is optional:

```
<?php
// $name is required. $title is optional and defaults to an empty string if not
// provided.
function createWelcomeMessage(string $name, string $title = ''): string {
    if ($title) {
        // If a title was provided, include it.
        return "Hello, $title $name! Welcome to our website.";
    } else {
        // Otherwise, use a simpler message.
        return "Hello, $name! Welcome to our website.";
    }
}
// Call the function with and without the optional argument
$message1 = createWelcomeMessage("Vaishali");
$message2 = createWelcomeMessage("Sharanam", "Dr.");
?>
<!DOCTYPE html>
<html lang="en">
```

```
<head>
    <meta charset="UTF-8">
    <title>Function Arguments</title>
</head>
<body>
    <h1>Welcome Messages</h1>
    <p><?php echo $message1; ?></p>
    <p><?php echo $message2; ?></p>
</body>
</html>
```

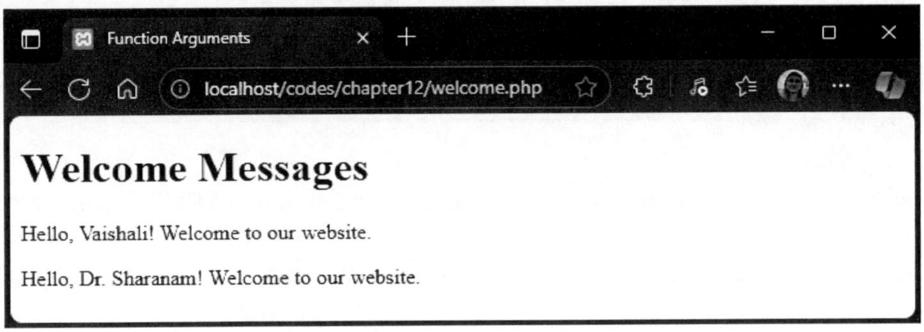

This makes our function more flexible. Optional arguments should always come *after* required arguments in the function definition.

Scope

Scope is a critical concept that defines where a variable can be accessed.

Local scope

By default, any variable declared inside a function is **local** to that function. It is born there, it lives there, and it dies there. It is completely invisible to any code outside the function:

```
<?php
function myFunction() {
    $local_variable = "I am local!";
    echo $local_variable; // This works fine.
}
myFunction();
// This will cause an error because $local_variable doesn't exist here.
// echo $local_variable;
?>
```

Global scope

A variable declared outside of any function has **global** scope. However, functions cannot see global variables by default. To access a global variable from inside a function, you must use the **global** keyword:

```
<?php
$global_variable = "I am global!";
function anotherFunction() {
    global $global_variable; // Now the function can see it.
    echo $global_variable;
}
anotherFunction(); // Outputs: I am global!
?>
```

Heads Up!
Using the **global** keyword is generally discouraged in modern PHP. It can make code hard to debug because it's not clear where a variable is being changed. A better practice is to pass variables into functions as arguments.

Superglobals

Superglobals are special built-in PHP variables that are always accessible from any scope. You don't need the global keyword for them. We've already used them! $_GET, $_POST, and $_REQUEST are all superglobals. This is why you can access form data from anywhere in your script.

Passing by value vs by reference

This is a subtle but important distinction.

- **Passing by Value (default):** When you pass a variable to a function, PHP makes a *copy* of that variable's value and gives it to the function. Any changes the function makes are to the *copy*, not the original variable. This is the safest and most common way.
- **Passing by Reference:** When you pass by reference, you are not passing a copy. You are passing a direct pointer to the original variable's location in memory. Any changes the function makes will permanently alter the original variable. You do this by adding an ampersand (&) before the argument name.

Let's see this in action:

```
<?php
// This function receives the variable BY VALUE (a copy).
```

```
function addFiveByValue($number) {
    $number += 5;
}
// This function receives the variable BY REFERENCE (the original).
function addFiveByReference(&$number) {
    $number += 5;
}
// --- Test Case 1: Pass by Value ---
$my_num_1 = 10;
// The function works on a copy of $my_num_1.
addFiveByValue($my_num_1);
// --- Test Case 2: Pass by Reference ---
$my_num_2 = 10;
// The function works on the original $my_num_2.
addFiveByReference($my_num_2);
?>
<!DOCTYPE html>
<html lang="en">
<head>
    <title>Value vs. Reference</title>
</head>
<body>
    <h1>Pass by Value vs. Pass by Reference</h1>
    <p>Original Number: 10</p>
    <p>Variable pass BY VALUE: <?php echo $my_num_1; ?>
       (The original is unchanged)</p>
    <p>Variable pass BY REFERENCE: <?php echo $my_num_2; ?>
       (The original has been modified)</p>
</body>
</html>
```

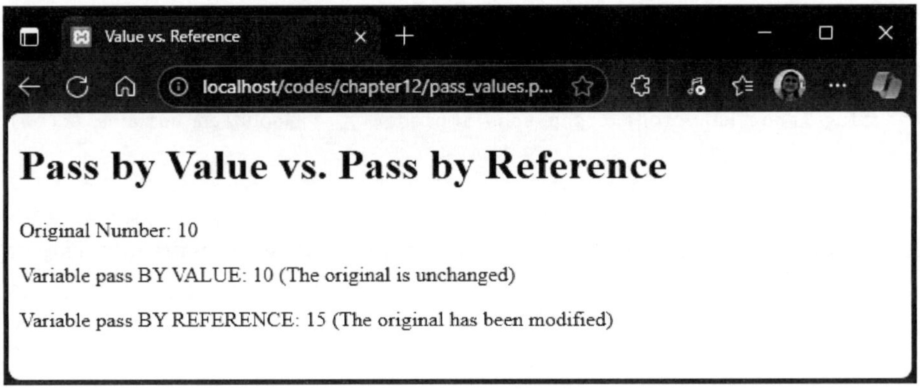

Passing by reference can be useful, but use it with caution as it can lead to unexpected behavior if you're not careful.

Anonymous and arrow functions

PHP also allows for functions that don't have a name. These are called **anonymous functions** (or **closures**). They are useful for quick, one-off tasks and are often used as arguments to other functions that process arrays.

An **arrow function** is a shorter, more convenient syntax for simple anonymous functions, introduced in PHP 7.4.

Let's imagine we have an array of numbers and we want to create a new array where each number is doubled:

```
<?php
$numbers = [1, 2, 3, 4];
// Example 1: Using an anonymous function with array_map. It applies a function to
// every element of an array
$doubled_numbers_anon = array_map(function($number) {
    return $number * 2;
}, $numbers);
// Example 2: Using a shorter arrow function (does the exact same thing)
$doubled_numbers_arrow = array_map(fn($number) => $number * 2, $numbers);
?>
<!DOCTYPE html>
<html lang="en">
<head>
    <title>Anonymous & Arrow Functions</title>
</head>
<body>
    <h1>Doubling Numbers</h1>
    <p>Original Array: <?php echo implode(', ', $numbers); ?></p>
    <p>Using Anonymous Function: <?php echo implode(', ', $doubled_numbers_anon); ?>
    </p>
    <p>Using Arrow Function: <?php echo implode(', ', $doubled_numbers_arrow); ?>
    </p>
</body>
</html>
```

The **implode()** function is a handy PHP function that joins array elements into a string.

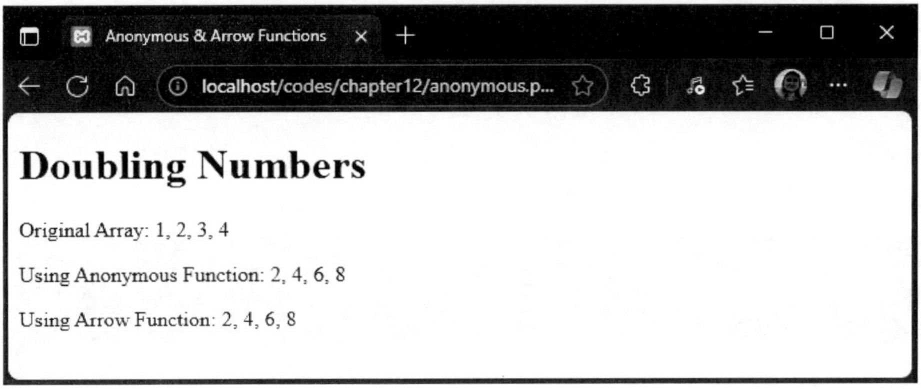

Arrow functions are great for making your code more concise when the logic is simple.

Error handling and defensive coding

A robust function doesn't just work for perfect inputs; it anticipates and handles bad inputs gracefully. This is called **defensive coding**. You should always check your inputs before you process them.

A classic example is a function that performs division. What happens if the denominator is zero? You can't divide by zero—it will crash your script with a fatal error. A defensive function checks for this:

```
<?php
// A defensive function to handle division.
function safeDivide(float $numerator, float $denominator): string {
    // Check for the "bad" input first.
    if ($denominator == 0) {
        return "Error: Cannot divide by zero.";
    }
    // If the input is safe, proceed with the calculation.
    $result = $numerator / $denominator;
    return "The result is: $result";
}
// Let's test it with both good and bad inputs.
$good_result = safeDivide(10, 2);
$bad_result = safeDivide(10, 0);
?>
<!DOCTYPE html>
<html lang="en">
<head>
    <title>Defensive Coding</title>
</head>
```

```
<body>
    <h1>Safe Division</h1>
    <p>Dividing 10 by 2: <?php echo $good_result; ?></p>
    <p>Dividing 10 by 0: <?php echo $bad_result; ?></p>
</body>
</html>
```

Instead of a fatal error, our page displays a user-friendly message:

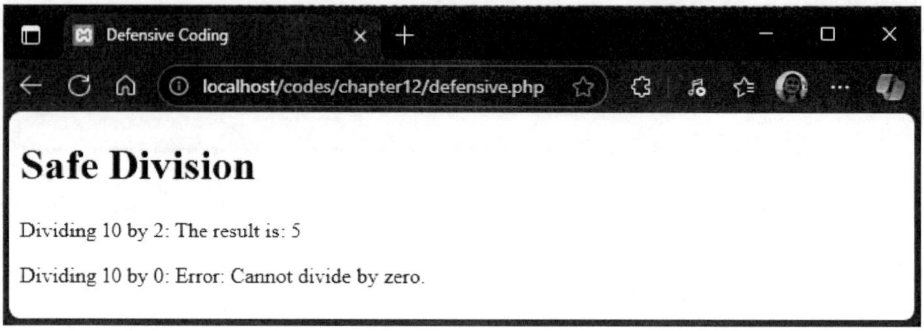

This is a fundamental practice. Always think about the **edge cases**—the weird, invalid, or unexpected inputs your function might receive.

Hands-on: Math library

Now, let's combine everything we've learned into a practical, interactive web application. We are going to build a **Math Library** tool. This tool will take a single number from a user and perform three different calculations using dedicated functions:

- **Sum:** Calculate the sum of all integers from 1 up to the given number.
- **Average:** Calculate the average of all integers from 1 up to the given number.
- **Factorial:** Calculate the factorial of the number.

This project will solidify your understanding of defining functions, handling user input via $_POST, returning values, and performing defensive coding.

Building the application

We will create a project folder containing two files: index.php for our logic and HTML, and style.css for the design.

Create the project directory and files

For every new project, it's best practice to create a dedicated folder. We will use Visual Studio Code's built-in file explorer to manage our project files, which is a fast and efficient workflow.

1. **Open your web root in VS Code:**
   - Launch VS Code.
   - Go to **File → Open Folder....**
   - Navigate to your XAMPP installation directory and select the **htdocs\codes** folder (usually located at C:\xampp\htdocs\codes).
   - Click **Select Folder**.
   - The **Explorer** panel on the left side of VS Code should now show the **htdocs\codes** directory.
2. **Create the project folder:**
   - In the VS Code **Explorer** panel, right-click on an empty area (not on any existing folder name) and select **New Folder...**.
   - A text box appears.
   - Type **math-library** and press **Enter**.
   - You've just created your project folder.
3. **Create the project files:**
   - Now, right-click on your new **math-library** folder in the **Explorer** panel.
   - Select **New File...**. Name the file **index.php** and press **Enter**. The file automatically opens in the editor.
   - Right-click on the **math-library** folder again.
   - Select **New File...**. Name this one **style.css** and press **Enter**.

When you're done, your VS Code Explorer should look exactly like this, ensuring the files are *inside* the math-library folder:

```
htdocs\codes
 └─ math-library
    ├─ index.php
    └─ style.css
```

This organized structure is crucial for keeping your project assets together.

Write the CSS for the user interface

Open **style.css** in VS Code and add the following code. This will give our application a clean, modern look with a card-based layout, nice fonts, and colorful feedback:

```
body {
    font-family: -apple-system, BlinkMacSystemFont, "Segoe UI", Roboto,
                 Helvetica, Arial, sans-serif;
    background-color: #f0f2f5;
    color: #333;
    display: flex;
    justify-content: center;
    align-items: center;
    height: 100vh;
    margin: 0;
}
.container {
    background: #ffffff;
    padding: 2rem 3rem;
    border-radius: 12px;
    box-shadow: 0 8px 25px rgba(0, 0, 0, 0.1);
    width: 100%;
    max-width: 450px;
    text-align: center;
}
h1 {
    color: #1e3a8a; /* A nice deep blue */
    margin-bottom: 1.5rem;
}
.form-group {
    margin-bottom: 1.5rem;
}
label {
    display: block;
    font-weight: 600;
    margin-bottom: 0.5rem;
    color: #555;
}
input[type="number"] {
    width: 100%;
    padding: 0.75rem;
    border: 1px solid #ccc;
    border-radius: 8px;
    font-size: 1rem;
    box-sizing: border-box; /* Important for padding */
}
.button-group {
    display: flex;
    gap: 1rem;
    justify-content: center;
```

```
}
button {
    flex-grow: 1;
    padding: 0.75rem 1rem;
    font-size: 1rem;
    font-weight: 600;
    color: #fff;
    background-color: #2563eb; /* A vibrant blue */
    border: none;
    border-radius: 8px;
    cursor: pointer;
    transition: background-color 0.2s;
}
button:hover {
    background-color: #1d4ed8; /* A darker blue for hover */
}
.result {
    margin-top: 2rem;
    padding: 1rem;
    border-radius: 8px;
    font-size: 1.1rem;
    font-weight: 500;
}
.result.success {
    background-color: #dcfce7; /* Light green for success */
    color: #166534;
    border: 1px solid #4ade80;
}
.result.error {
    background-color: #fee2e2; /* Light red for error */
    color: #991b1b;
    border: 1px solid #f87171;
}
```

Write the PHP logic and HTML structure

Now for the main event. Open **index.php** in VS Code. We will write the PHP functions at the top, followed by the logic to handle the form submission, and finally the HTML to display the page:

```
<?php
// --- Part 1: Function Definitions ---
/**
 * Calculates the sum of integers from 1 to n.
 * Includes defensive checks for non-positive numbers.
 */
function calculateSum(int $n): int|string {
    if ($n <= 0) {
        return "Please enter a positive number.";
```

```
    }
    // Formula for sum of first n integers: n * (n + 1) / 2
    return array_sum(range(1, $n));
}
/**
 * Calculates the average of integers from 1 to n.
 * Reuses the calculateSum function!
 */
function calculateAverage(int $n): float|string {
    if ($n <= 0) {
        return "Please enter a positive number.";
    }
    $sum = calculateSum($n);
    return $sum / $n;
}
/**
 * Calculates the factorial of n (n!).
 * Includes defensive checks for negative numbers and a reasonable
 * upper limit.
 */
function calculateFactorial(int $n): int|string {
    if ($n < 0) {
        return "Factorial is not defined for negative numbers.";
    }
    if ($n == 0) {
        return 1; // Factorial of 0 is 1
    }
    if ($n > 17) { // Factorials get very big, very fast!
        return "Number is too large to calculate factorial accurately.";
    }
    $factorial = 1;
    for ($i = 1; $i <= $n; $i++) {
        $factorial *= $i;
    }
    return $factorial;
}
// --- Part 2: Form Handling Logic ---
$result = '';
$result_class = '';
// Check if the form was submitted
if ($_SERVER["REQUEST_METHOD"] == "POST") {
    // Get the number from the form, ensuring it's an integer
    $number = isset($_POST['number']) ? (int)$_POST['number'] : 0;
    // Check which button was clicked and call the appropriate function
    if (isset($_POST['calculate_sum'])) {
        $output = calculateSum($number);
        $result = "Sum: " . $output;
    } elseif (isset($_POST['calculate_average'])) {
        $output = calculateAverage($number);
        // Using number_format to make the average look nice
        $result = "Average: " . (is_numeric($output) ? number_format(
```

```
                  $output, 2) : $output);
    } elseif (isset($_POST['calculate_factorial'])) {
        $output = calculateFactorial($number);
        $result = "Factorial: " . $output;
    }
    // Set the CSS class for the result box based on whether we got a number or
    // an error string
    $result_class = is_numeric($output) ? 'success' : 'error';
}
?>
<!DOCTYPE html>
<html lang="en">
<head>
    <meta charset="UTF-8">
    <meta name="viewport" content="width=device-width, initial-scale=1.0">
    <title>PHP Math Library</title>
    <link rel="stylesheet" href="style.css">
</head>
<body>
    <div class="container">
        <h1>PHP Math Library</h1>
        <form action="index.php" method="post">
            <div class="form-group">
                <label for="number">Enter a Number</label>
                <input type="number" id="number" name="number" required>
            </div>
            <div class="button-group">
                <button type="submit" name="calculate_sum">Sum</button>
                <button type="submit" name="calculate_average">Average</button>
                <button type="submit" name="calculate_factorial">Factorial</button>
            </div>
        </form>
        <?php if ($result): ?>
            <div class="result <?php echo $result_class; ?>">
                <?php echo htmlspecialchars($result); ?>
            </div>
        <?php endif; ?>
    </div>
</body>
</html>
```

Bridging the gap: Learned concepts and application implementation

Let's break down how this hands-on project connects directly to the concepts we learned earlier in the chapter:

- **Defining functions:** We created three distinct, well-named functions: calculateSum(), calculateAverage(), and calculateFactorial(). Each has a single, clear purpose. This makes our code easy to read and manage.
- **Arguments and return values:** Each function accepts a single required argument, **$n**. They all return a value—either the calculated number or an error string. This separation of calculation and display is a core principle of good programming.
- **Function reusability:** Notice how calculateAverage() calls calculateSum() inside it. This is a brilliant example of reusing code! We didn't need to write the summing logic twice.
- **Scope:** The variables inside our functions (like $factorial or $i) are all **local**. The main script logic uses the **superglobal** $_POST to get user data safely.
- **Defensive coding:** This is the most critical part.
  - calculateSum() and calculateAverage() check if $n is positive.
  - calculateFactorial() checks for negative numbers (which are invalid) and also for very large numbers that could cause issues, returning a user-friendly error in both cases.
- **HTML & CSS integration:** The PHP logic generates a result, and that result is then cleanly embedded into our HTML structure. The **$result_class** variable dynamically changes the CSS to give the user immediate visual feedback (green for success, red for error).

When you move from single-file scripts to a large, multi-file project, functions become absolutely essential. You can't just have hundreds of lines of code in one file. It becomes impossible to manage.

Instead, you organize your code into files of related functions. For example, you might have:

- **user-functions.php:** Contains functions like loginUser(), registerUser(), updateProfile().
- **database-functions.php:** Contains functions for connecting to the database, fetching records, and inserting data.
- **validation-functions.php:** A whole library of functions like isEmail(), isStrongPassword(), sanitizeInput().

This approach, known as **procedural programming**, allows you to build complex systems by assembling simple, well-tested building blocks. It makes your project scalable and allows teams to work on different parts of the application simultaneously.

Running and testing

Now let's see our creation in action!

1. Make sure your **XAMPP Control Panel** is running and the **Apache** module is started.
2. Open your web browser (Chrome, Firefox, etc.).
3. In the address bar, type: **http://localhost/codes/math-library/** and press **Enter**.
4. You see our **PHP Math Library** interface.

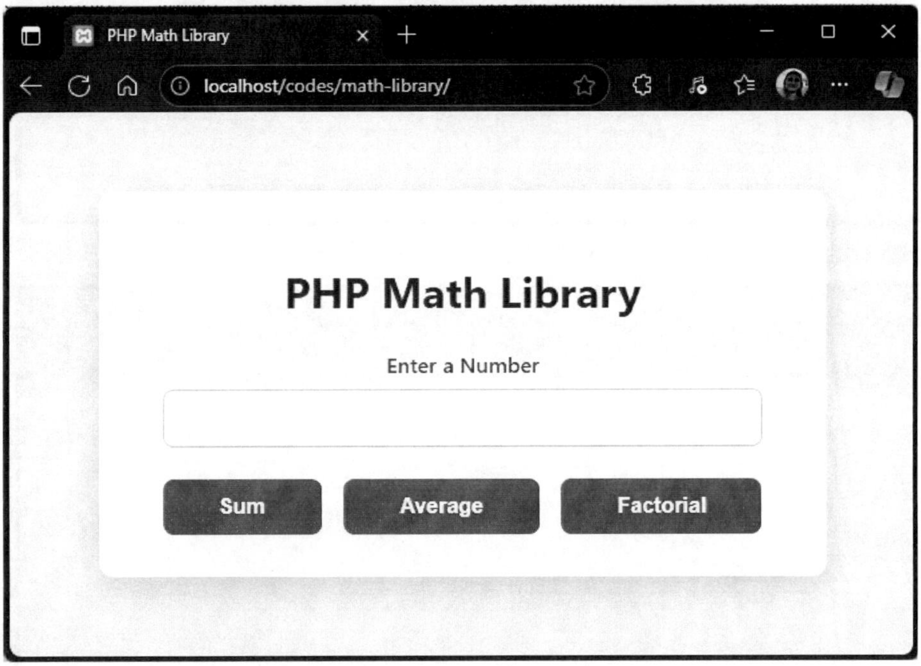

5. Enter a number into the input box.
6. Click **Sum**. The page reloads, and a green box appears below with the text:

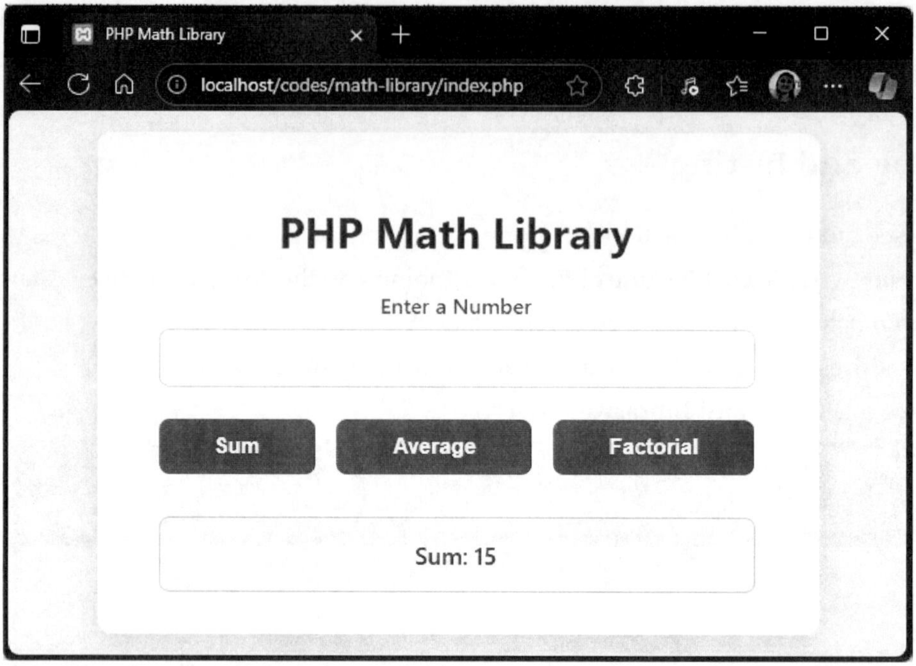

7. Click **Average**. The box now says:

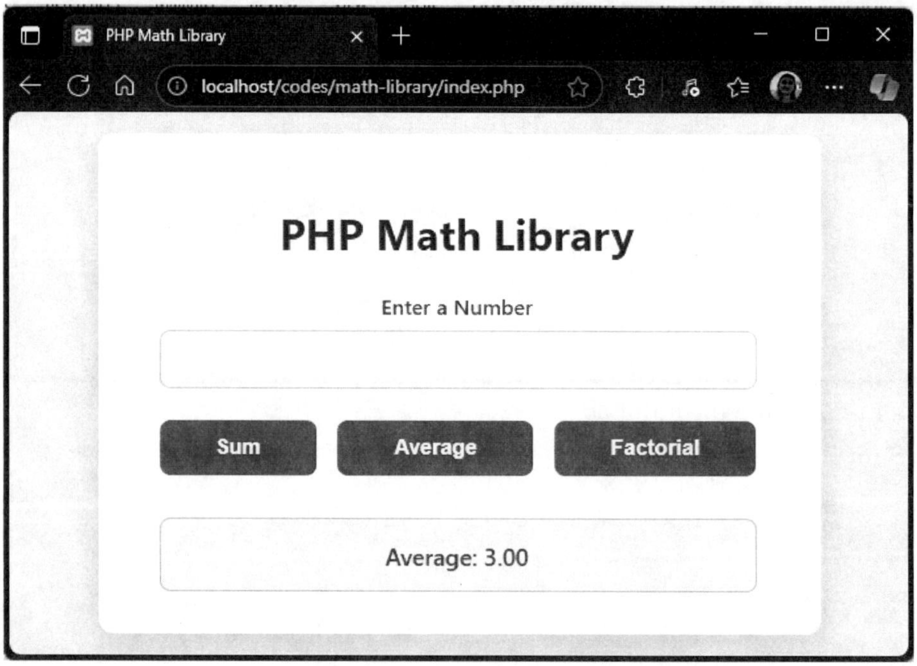

8. Click **Factorial**. The box now says:

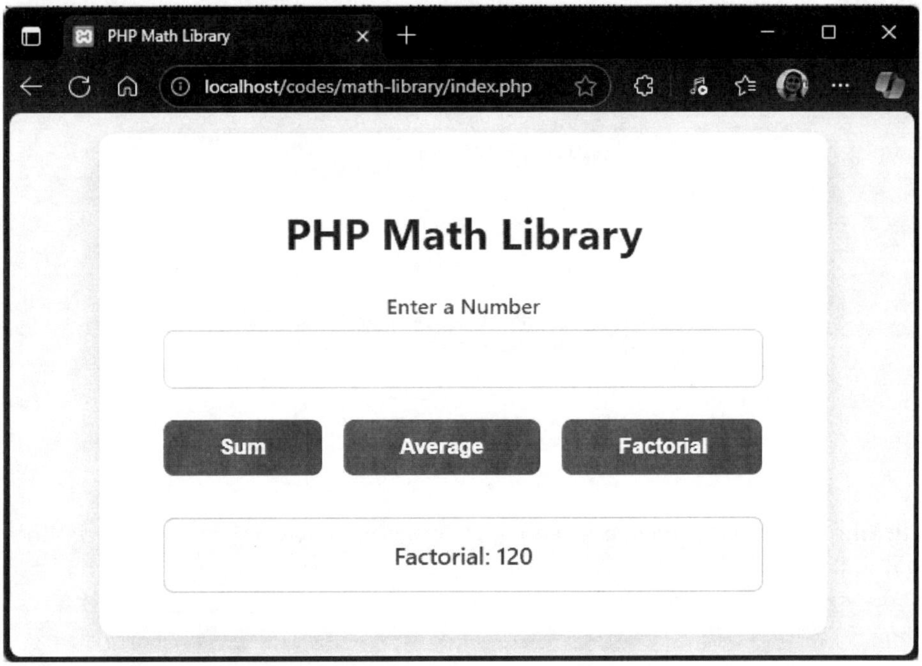

Exploring application behaviour: A practical run-through

A professional developer doesn't just test the "happy path." They test the edge cases. Let's see how our defensive coding holds up.

- **Scenario 1:** Entering zero.
    - Enter **0** and click **Sum**. You can see a red error box: **Sum: Please enter a positive number**. This is our defensive check in action.

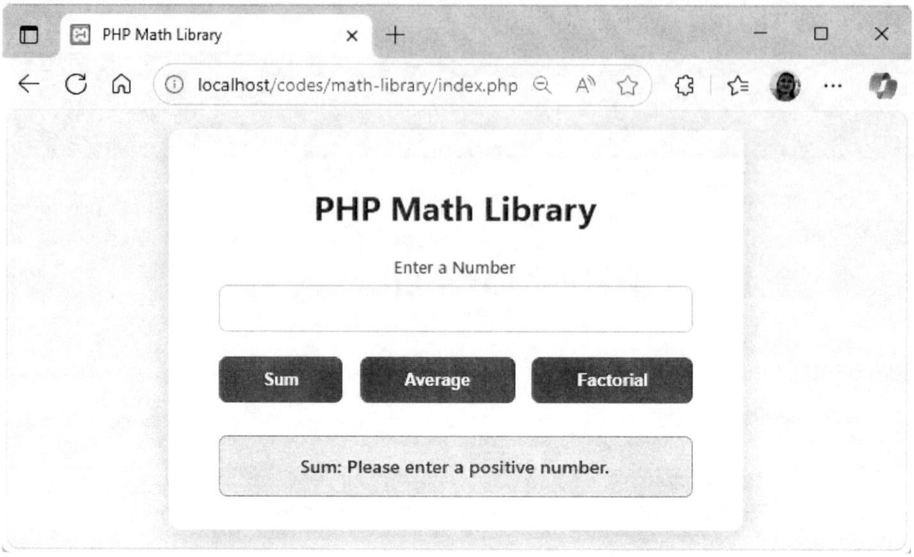

- Clicking **Factorial** gives a green success box: Factorial: 1, which is the correct mathematical definition.

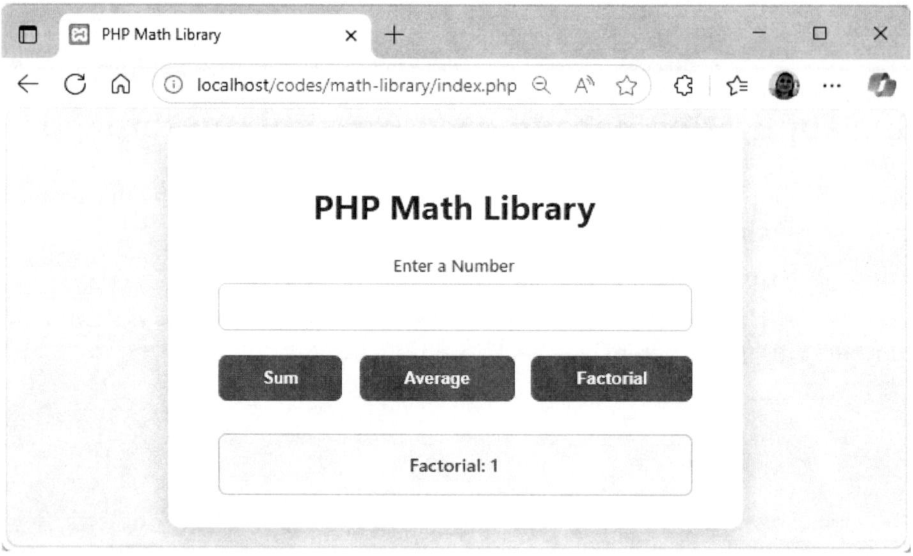

- **Scenario 2:** Entering a negative number.
  - Enter **-5** and click **Average**. You get the red error box: **Average: Please enter a positive number**.

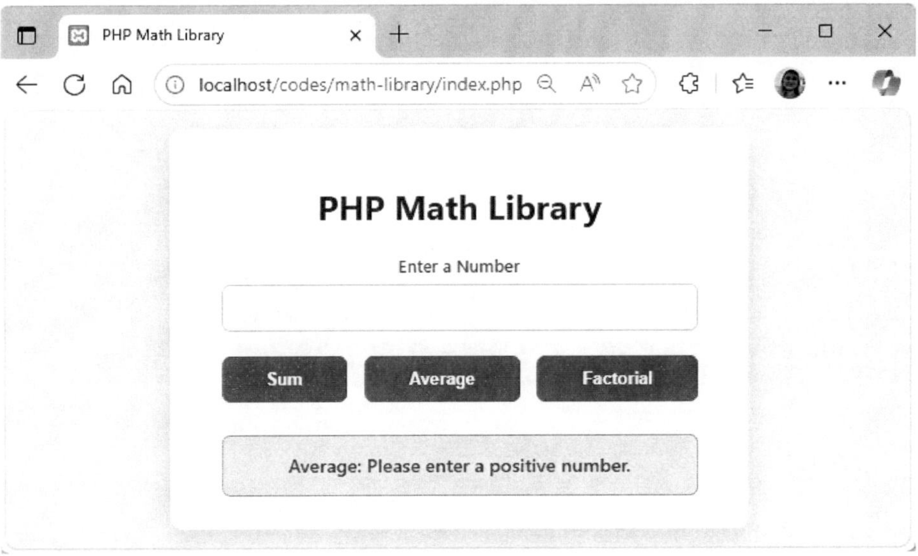

- Click **Factorial**. You get the red error box: **Factorial: Factorial is not defined for negative numbers**. Perfect!

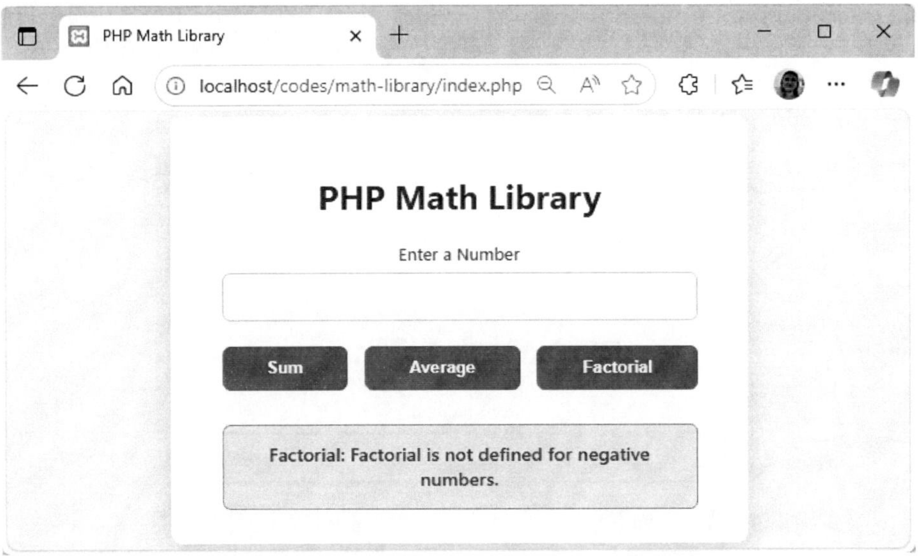

- **Scenario 3:** Entering a large number.
  - Enter 20 and click **Factorial**. You get a red error box: **Factorial: Number is too large to calculate factorial accurately**. This prevents our script from crashing or producing a nonsensical result.

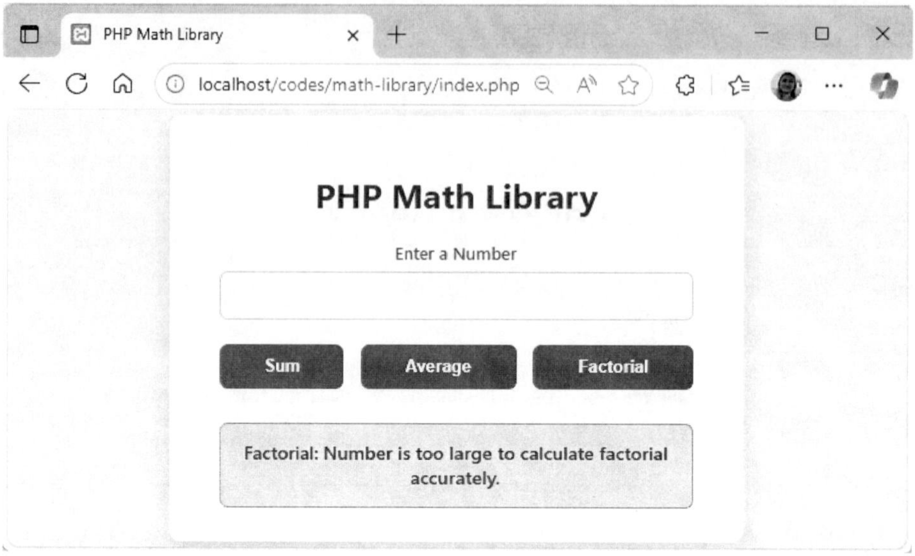

- **Scenario 4:** Submitting an empty form.
  - Because we used the required attribute in our HTML input tag, the browser itself will likely prevent submission. If it gets through, our PHP code (int)$_POST['number'] would treat it as 0, and our defensive checks would handle it gracefully.

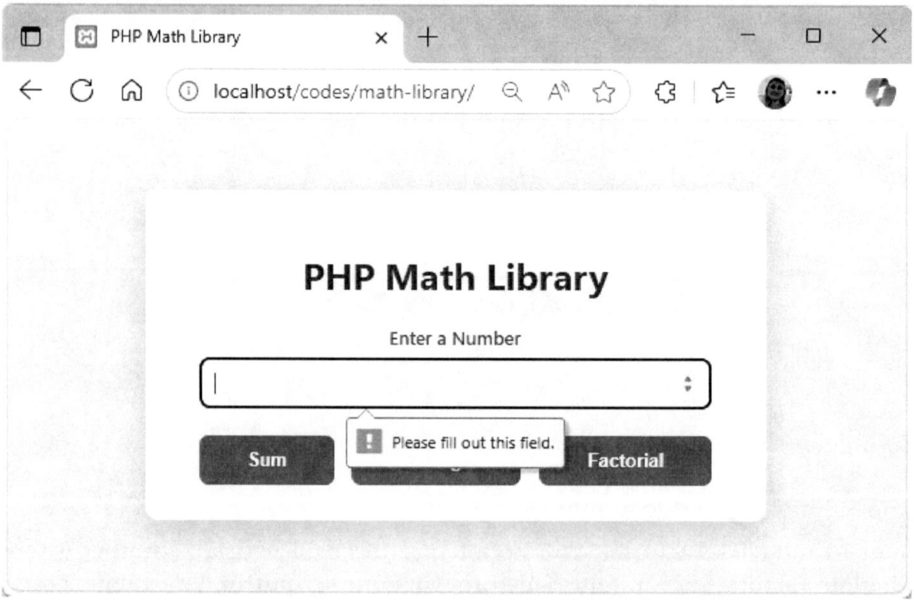

Our hands-on project gave us a taste of handling edge cases. This mindset is what separates a beginner from a professional. When writing any function, always ask yourself:

- What if the input is null or empty? ('')
- **What if it's zero?** (Especially for division or loops)
- What if it's negative?
- **What if it's the wrong data type?** (e.g., the string "hello" instead of a number)
- **What if it's a ridiculously large number?** (Could it exceed memory or time limits?)

Handling these cases inside your function makes it a robust and reliable tool. Your function should either handle the edge case gracefully (like factorial of 0 being 1) or return a clear error message that the calling code can use to inform the user. This practice prevents bugs, improves security, and leads to a much better user experience.

Harnessing functions in real-world contexts

The small calculator we just built demonstrates a pattern used in every major web application:

- **E-commerce:** A calculateShippingCost() function might take a weight, destination, and shipping method as arguments.
- **Social media:** A validateUsername() function would check if a new username meets criteria (length, allowed characters, not already taken).
- **Content Management Systems:** A generateArticleSlug() function would take a blog post title like "My First Day at a New Job!" and turn it into a URL-friendly string like my-first-day-at-a-new-job.

By mastering functions, you've learned how to create reliable, reusable, and readable code—the foundation of professional web development.

Wrapping up

- **Functions as tools:** We learned that functions are named, reusable blocks of code that follow the DRY (Don't Repeat Yourself) principle.
- **Data flow:** Functions can accept data through **arguments** and send results back using the **return** keyword.
- **Variable scope:** We explored how variables are either **local** to a function or **global**, and how **superglobals** like $_POST are always available.

- **Defensive coding:** We practiced writing robust functions that anticipate and handle bad inputs or edge cases gracefully.
- **Practical application:** We built a complete, interactive Math Library web app, applying all the core concepts from the chapter.
- **Modern syntax:** We saw how **anonymous and arrow functions** can make code more concise for specific tasks.

Congratulations! You've just mastered one of the most fundamental pillars of programming. You've moved beyond writing simple, linear scripts and can now create your own "building blocks" of logic. This ability to encapsulate, reuse, and organize code is what will allow you to build applications of ever-increasing complexity without losing control. You've developed the mindset of a true programmer—thinking about reusability, readability, and reliability.

Keep this momentum going! In the next ***Chapter 13: Tables turned - Mastering Arrays***, we'll explore the best way to handle lists and collections of data, a perfect companion to the functions you now know how to build.

Chapter 13

Section 04: Smarter workflows - Functions, Arrays, and Authenticity

Tables turned - Mastering Arrays

What you'll learn

- Array types and uses
- Looping through data
- Essential array functions
- Building dynamic tables

Welcome to Chapter 13! So far, we've worked with single pieces of data—a username, a number, a message. But what happens when you need to handle a *list* of items? A list of products in a shopping cart, comments on a blog post, or students in a class? This is where arrays come in. They are the foundation for managing collections of data, and mastering them is a huge leap forward in your journey as a developer.

Think of a variable as a single box that can hold one item. An **array**, on the other hand, is like a cabinet with multiple, labeled drawers. Each drawer can hold its own item, but they are all part of the same cabinet. This structure allows us to store and organize related information together under a single variable name. In web development, arrays are everywhere. They power everything from a simple list of navigation links to complex data sets that are displayed in tables, like a list of products on an e-commerce site or, as we'll build in this chapter, a student gradebook.

Array types

PHP arrays are incredibly flexible and come in a few flavours. Understanding each type helps you choose the right tool for the job.

Indexed arrays

The simplest type of array is an **indexed array**. It uses numeric keys (or **indexes**) to organize its values, starting from 0. Think of it as a numbered list.

Let's create an array of our favourite programming languages. In VS Code, create a new file named **arrays.php** in your project folder within XAMPP's **htdocs\codes\chapter 13** directory and add the following code:

```
<?php
// An indexed array of strings
$languages = ["PHP", "JavaScript", "Python", "HTML", "CSS"];
// To see the structure and contents of the array, we use print_r()
echo '<pre>';
print_r($languages);
echo '</pre>';
// Accessing a single element using its index
echo "The first language is: " . $languages[0]; // Outputs: PHP
?>
```

When you run this script in your browser, you'll see the following output. The <pre> tags make the print_r() output readable.

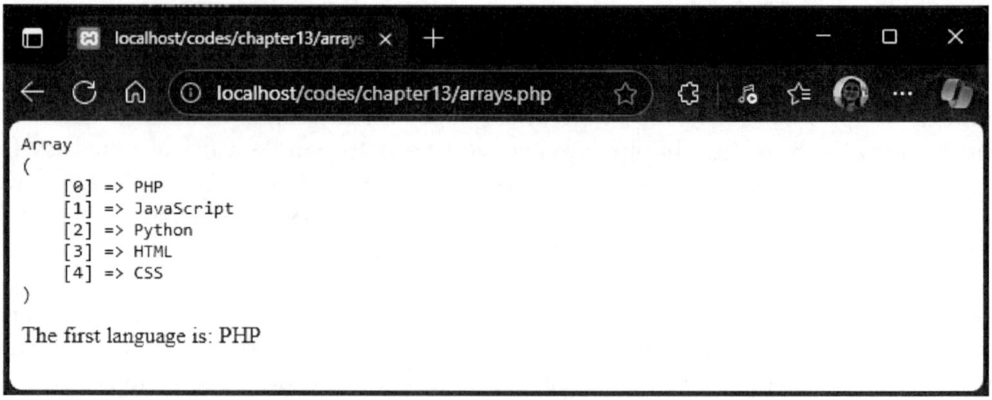

Notice how each language is assigned an index, starting from 0. We can retrieve any value by referencing its index number inside square brackets.

Associative arrays

What if a numbered list isn't descriptive enough? An **associative array** lets you use custom strings (called keys) to label your values. This is incredibly useful for storing record-like data, where each piece of information has a specific name.

Let's store information about a single student:

```
<?php
// An associative array representing a student
$student = [
    'firstName' => 'Sharanam',
    'lastName'  => 'Shah',
    'grade'     => 92,
    'subject'   => 'PHP'
];
echo '<pre>';
print_r($student);
echo '</pre>';
// Accessing a single element using its key
echo "Student Name: " . $student['firstName'] . " " . $student['lastName'];
?>
```

The output clearly shows the key-value pairs:

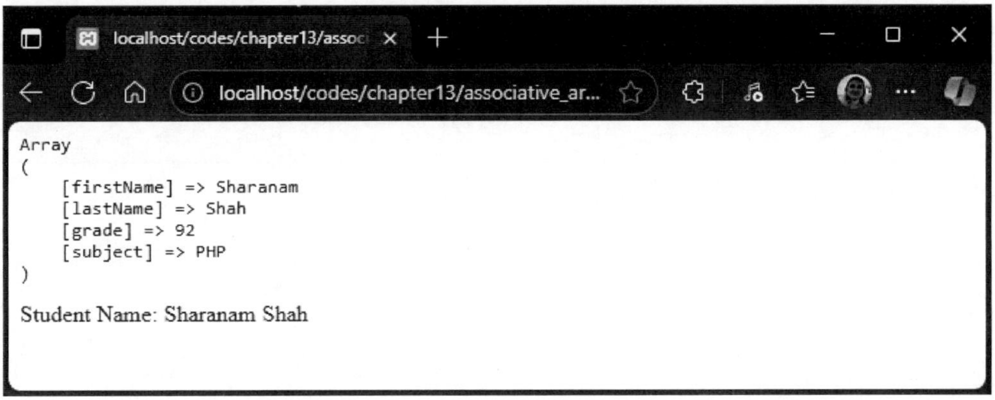

This is far more readable and manageable than trying to remember if the grade was at index 2 or 3.

Multidimensional arrays

Now, let's combine these concepts. A **multidimensional array** is an array that contains other arrays. This is how you create complex data structures, like a list of records.

Let's create a list of students, where each student is an associative array. This is the exact structure we'll use for our hands-on project:

```
<?php
// A multidimensional array: an indexed array of associative arrays
$students = [
    [
        'firstName' => 'Sharanam',
        'lastName'  => 'Shah',
        'grade'     => 92,
        'subject'   => 'PHP'
    ],
    [
        'firstName' => 'Vaishali',
        'lastName'  => 'Shah',
        'grade'     => 85,
        'subject'   => 'JavaScript'
    ],
    [
        'firstName' => 'Janya',
        'lastName'  => 'Shah',
        'grade'     => 98,
        'subject'   => 'PHP'
    ]
];
echo '<pre>';
print_r($students);
echo '</pre>';
// Accessing a specific piece of data. This gets the first name of the second
// student (index 1)
echo "The second student is: " . $students[1]['firstName'];
?>
```

The output shows our neatly organized list of students:

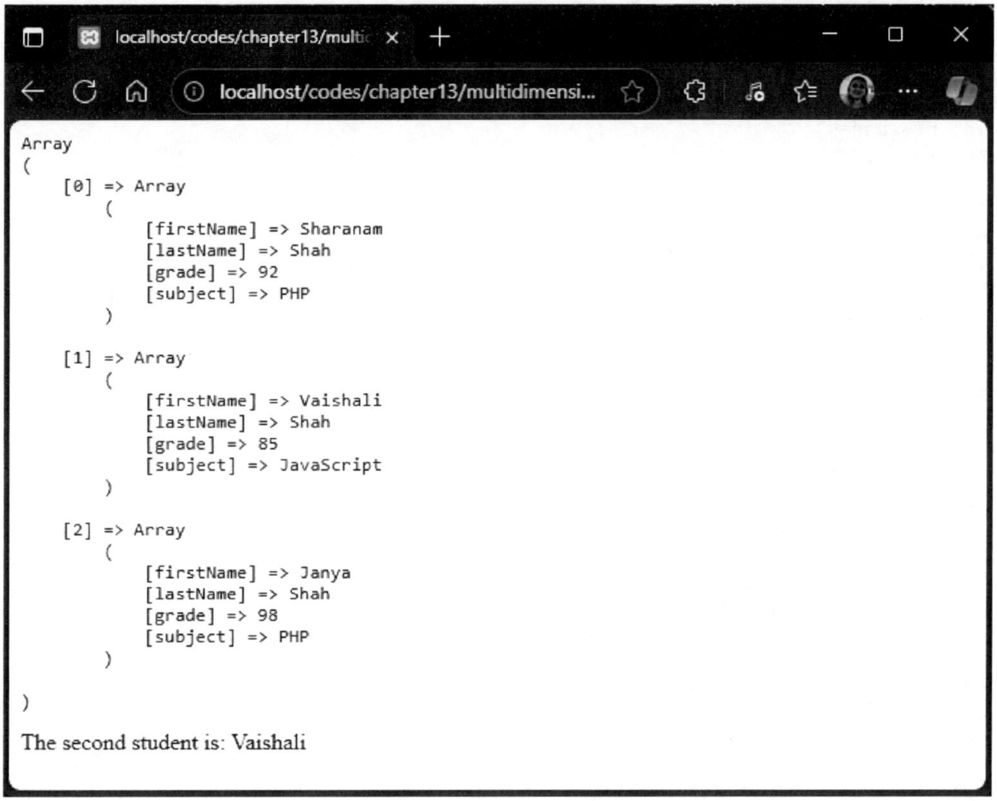

Array functions

PHP provides hundreds of functions to work with arrays. Here are five essential ones you'll use constantly:

- **sort():** Sorts an indexed array in ascending order.
- **array_merge():** Combines two or more arrays into one.
- **in_array():** Checks if a value exists in an array.
- **explode():** Splits a string into an array based on a delimiter.
- **implode():** Joins array elements into a single string.

Let's see them in action:

```
<?php
// 1. sort() - Sorts an array
$grades = [88, 92, 75, 100, 85];
```

```
echo "Original grades: ";
print_r($grades);
sort($grades);
echo "<br>Sorted grades: ";
print_r($grades);
echo "<hr>";
// 2. array_merge() - Merges two arrays
$firstHalf = ["a", "b", "c"];
$secondHalf = ["d", "e"];
$fullAlphabet = array_merge($firstHalf, $secondHalf);
echo "Merged array: ";
print_r($fullAlphabet);
echo "<hr>";
// 3. in_array() - Checks if a value exists
$haystack = ["PHP", "JavaScript", "Python"];
$needle = "PHP";
if (in_array($needle, $haystack)) {
    echo "'$needle' exists in the array.";
} else {
    echo "'$needle' does not exist in the array.";
}
echo "<hr>";
// 4. explode() - Splits a string into an array
$csvString = "sharanam,shah,shah.shah@email.com";
$userData = explode(",", $csvString);
echo "User data from string: ";
print_r($userData);
echo "<hr>";
// 5. implode() - Joins an array into a string
$tags = ["php", "web-development", "beginner"];
$tagString = implode(", ", $tags);
echo "Tag string: " . $tagString;
?>
```

Here's the browser output for that script, demonstrating each function's purpose:

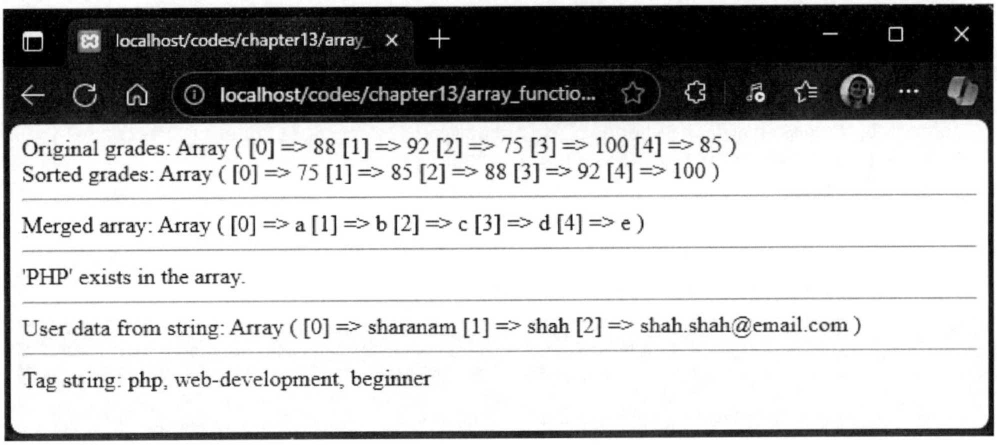

Iterating arrays

Displaying the whole array with print_r() is useful for debugging, but it's not what you want to show your users. To process and display each item in an array, we need to **iterate** (or loop) through it. The foreach loop is perfectly designed for this.

The basic syntax is:

```
foreach ($array as $value)
```

For associative arrays, you can get both the key and the value:

```
foreach ($array as $key => $value)
```

Let's loop through our $students array:

```
<?php
$students = [
    [
        'firstName' => 'Sharanam',
        'lastName'  => 'Shah',
        'grade'     => 92,
        'subject'   => 'PHP'
    ],
    [
        'firstName' => 'Vaishali',
        'lastName'  => 'Shah',
        'grade'     => 85,
        'subject'   => 'JavaScript'
    ]
];
echo "<h3>Student Report</h3>";
```

```
// This is a nested loop! The outer loop gets each student (which is an array).
foreach ($students as $student) {
    echo "<p>";
    // The inner logic processes the associative array for one student.
    echo "<b>Name:</b> " . $student['firstName'] . " " . $student['lastName'];
    echo " | <b>Grade:</b> " . $student['grade'];
    echo "</p>";
}
?>
```

This code produces a clean, user-friendly output:

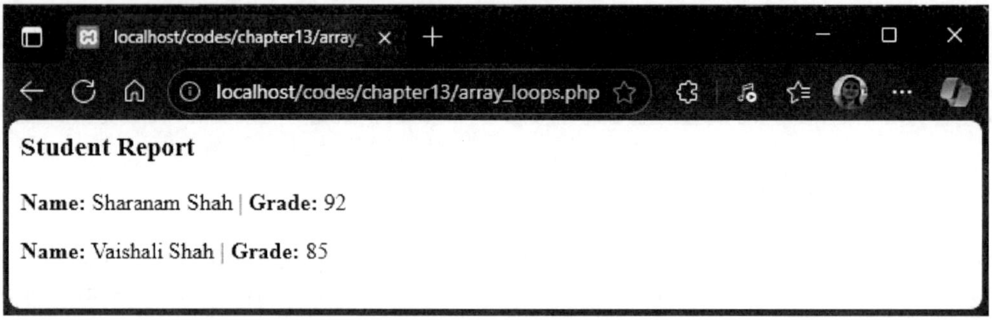

We used a **nested loop** concept here. The foreach iterates through the main $students array. Inside the loop, the $student variable is itself an associative array, which we then access using its keys ('firstName', 'grade').

Searching and filtering arrays

Often, you don't need the entire array; you need a subset of it that matches certain criteria. For example, finding all students who passed, or all students studying PHP.

The **array_filter()** function is perfect for this. It iterates over an array and passes each value to a callback function. If the callback function returns true, the value is kept; otherwise, it's discarded.

Let's find all the students who scored 90 or above:

```
<?php
$students = [
    ['name' => 'Sharanam', 'grade' => 92],
    ['name' => 'Vaishali', 'grade' => 85],
    ['name' => 'Janya', 'grade' => 98],
    ['name' => 'Dhrish', 'grade' => 89]
];
```

```
// Define the filtering logic in a function. This is a simple "callback" function.
$passing_students = array_filter($students, function($student) {
    // Return true only if the student's grade is 90 or higher
    return $student['grade'] >= 90;
});
echo "<h3>High-Achievers (90+)</h3>";
echo '<pre>';
print_r($passing_students);
echo '</pre>';
?>
```

The output shows a new array containing only the students who met our condition:

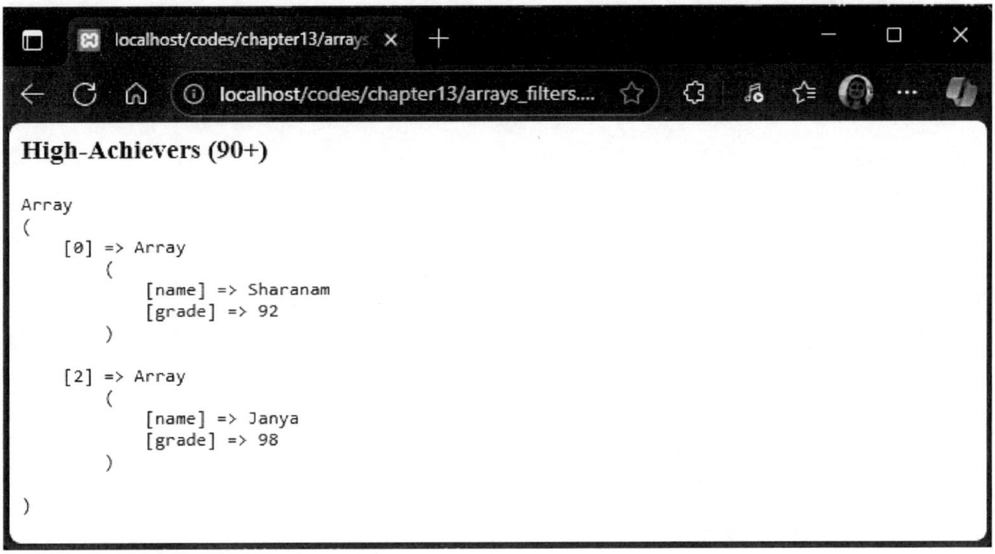

Note that the original array keys (0 and 2) are preserved.

Constructing array-based data tables

The most common way to display a multidimensional array is in an HTML <table>. This is a powerful combination of PHP's logic and HTML's structure. We'll use a foreach loop to generate the table rows (<tr>) and table data cells (<td>).

Let's turn our full $students array into a proper HTML table:

```
<?php
$students = [
    [
        'firstName' => 'Sharanam',
```

```
        'lastName'  => 'Shah',
        'grade'     => 92,
        'subject'   => 'PHP'
    ],
    [
        'firstName' => 'Vaishali',
        'lastName'  => 'Shah',
        'grade'     => 85,
        'subject'   => 'JavaScript'
    ],
    [
        'firstName' => 'Janya',
        'lastName'  => 'Shah',
        'grade'     => 98,
        'subject'   => 'PHP'
    ]
];
?>
<!DOCTYPE html>
<html lang="en">
<head>
    <meta charset="UTF-8">
    <title>Student List</title>
</head>
<body>
    <h1>Student Roster</h1>
    <table border="1">
        <thead>
            <tr>
                <th>First Name</th>
                <th>Last Name</th>
                <th>Grade</th>
                <th>Subject</th>
            </tr>
        </thead>
        <tbody>
            <?php foreach ($students as $student): ?>
                <tr>
                    <td><?php echo $student['firstName']; ?></td>
                    <td><?php echo $student['lastName']; ?></td>
                    <td><?php echo $student['grade']; ?></td>
                    <td><?php echo $student['subject']; ?></td>
                </tr>
            <?php endforeach; ?>
        </tbody>
    </table>
</body>
</html>
```

This script generates a structured HTML table. In the browser, you'll see a clean, organized table—though it won't be very pretty until we add CSS in our hands-on project:

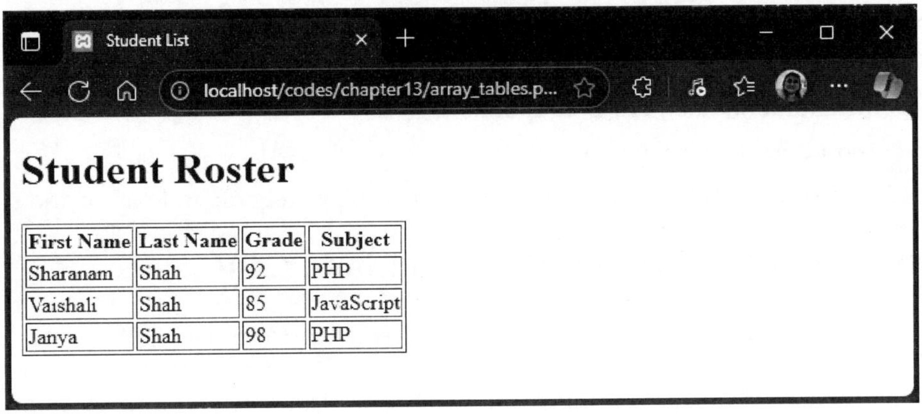

Practical uses

You now have the theoretical knowledge, but where do you apply it?

- **Configuration files:** Associative arrays are perfect for storing website settings. You can have a config.php file with an array holding your database credentials, site name, and other constants. This keeps your settings organized and easy to change.
- **Managing records:** As we've seen, a multidimensional array is the ideal structure for holding a set of records before they are saved to a database. When a user submits a form with multiple items, you'll often build an array like this first.
- **Dynamic data tables:** This is the most visible use case. Any time you see a list of users, products, comments, or posts on a website, there's a very high chance that the data was first stored in an array in the backend before being looped over to generate an HTML table or list.

Hands-on: Student Gradebook (CRUD with Arrays)

It's time to put everything together. We will build a fully functional Student Gradebook application. This single-page app will allow us to **C**reate (add), **R**ead (view), **U**pdate, and **D**elete student records. While real-world applications use a database for this, we will simulate persistence by holding our data in an array. This project perfectly demonstrates the logic of data manipulation that is central to web development.

Building the application

First, let's set up our project folder.

1. Navigate to your XAMPP installation folder, and open the **htdocs\codes** directory.
2. Create a new folder named **c13-gradebook**.
3. Open **c13-gradebook** in **VS Code**.
4. In VS Code Explorer Panel, create two files inside **c13-gradebook**: index.php and style.css.

Initial data and HTML structure (The 'Read' in CRUD)

Let's start by creating our initial data and the HTML structure to display it.

Open **index.php** in VS Code and add the following code. This sets up our student array and uses a foreach loop to display it in a table:

```
<?php
// Our "database" - a multidimensional array of student records
$students = [
    ['id' => 1, 'name' => 'Sharanam Shah', 'grade' => 92, 'subject' => 'PHP'],
    ['id' => 2, 'name' => 'Vaishali Shah', 'grade' => 85,
      'subject' => 'JavaScript'],
    ['id' => 3, 'name' => 'Janya Shah', 'grade' => 98, 'subject' => 'PHP'],
];
?>
<!DOCTYPE html>
<html lang="en">
<head>
    <meta charset="UTF-8">
    <meta name="viewport" content="width=device-width, initial-scale=1.0">
    <title>Student Gradebook</title>
    <link rel="stylesheet" href="style.css">
</head>
<body>
    <div class="container">
        <h1>Student Gradebook</h1>
        <table class="gradebook-table">
            <thead>
                <tr>
                    <th>ID</th>
                    <th>Name</th>
                    <th>Grade</th>
                    <th>Subject</th>
                    <th>Actions</th>
                </tr>
            </thead>
            <tbody>
```

```
                <?php foreach ($students as $student): ?>
                    <tr>
                        <td><?php echo $student['id']; ?></td>
                        <td><?php echo htmlspecialchars($student['name']); ?></td>
                        <td><?php echo htmlspecialchars($student['grade']); ?></td>
                        <td><?php echo htmlspecialchars($student['subject']); ?>
                        </td>
                        <td>
                            <a href="#" class="btn btn-delete">Delete</a>
                        </td>
                    </tr>
                <?php endforeach; ?>
            </tbody>
        </table>
        <hr>
    </div>
</body>
</html>
```

Styling the table with CSS

An unstyled table is hard to read. Open **style.css** and add the following CSS to make our gradebook clean and professional:

```
body {
    font-family: -apple-system, BlinkMacSystemFont, "Segoe UI", Roboto,
                 Helvetica, Arial, sans-serif;
    background-color: #f4f7f6;
    color: #333;
    line-height: 1.6;
    margin: 0;
    padding: 20px;
}
.container {
    max-width: 800px;
    margin: 20px auto;
    padding: 20px;
    background-color: #fff;
    border-radius: 8px;
    box-shadow: 0 4px 8px rgba(0,0,0,0.1);
}
h1 {
    color: #0056b3;
    text-align: center;
    margin-bottom: 20px;
}
.gradebook-table {
    width: 100%;
    border-collapse: collapse;
```

```
    margin-bottom: 20px;
}
.gradebook-table th, .gradebook-table td {
    border: 1px solid #ddd;
    padding: 12px;
    text-align: left;
}
.gradebook-table th {
    background-color: #007bff;
    color: white;
    font-weight: bold;
}
.gradebook-table tbody tr:nth-child(even) {
    background-color: #f2f2f2; /* Zebra striping */
}
.gradebook-table tbody tr:hover {
    background-color: #e9ecef;
}
.btn {
    display: inline-block;
    padding: 6px 12px;
    border: none;
    border-radius: 4px;
    color: white;
    text-decoration: none;
    font-size: 14px;
    cursor: pointer;
}
.btn-delete {
    background-color: #dc3545;
}
.btn-delete:hover {
    background-color: #c82333;
}
hr {
    border: 0;
    height: 1px;
    background-color: #ccc;
    margin: 30px 0;
}
```

Now, if you open **http://localhost/codes/c13-gradebook/index.php** in your browser, you should see a beautifully styled table with your three students.

Adding a new student (The 'Create' in CRUD)

Now let's add the form to create new students.

- HTML Form (in index.php):

```
<div class="form-container">
    <h2>Add New Student</h2>
    <form action="index.php" method="POST">
        <div class="form-group">
            <label for="name">Name:</label>
            <input type="text" id="name" name="name" required>
        </div>
        <div class="form-group">
            <label for="grade">Grade:</label>
            <input type="number" id="grade" name="grade" required>
        </div>
        <div class="form-group">
            <label for="subject">Subject:</label>
            <input type="text" id="subject" name="subject" required>
        </div>
        <button type="submit" name="add_student" class="btn btn-submit">Add Student
        </button>
    </form>
</div>
```

- CSS for the form (add to style.css):

```
/* Form styling */
.form-container {
    background-color: #fdfdfd;
    padding: 20px;
    border-radius: 8px;
    border: 1px solid #eee;
}
.form-container h2 {
    margin-top: 0;
    color: #333;
}
.form-group {
    margin-bottom: 15px;
}
.form-group label {
    display: block;
    margin-bottom: 5px;
    font-weight: bold;
}
.form-group input {
    width: 100%;
    padding: 10px;
    border: 1px solid #ccc;
    border-radius: 4px;
    box-sizing: border-box; /* Important for padding */
}
.btn-submit {
```

```
    background-color: #28a745;
    width: 100%;
    padding: 12px;
    font-size: 16px;
}
.btn-submit:hover {
    background-color: #218838;
}
```

- Now, to make the form work, we need to add the PHP processing logic. **At the very top of index.php**, before the <!DOCTYPE html> line, add this PHP block:

```
<?php
// IMPORTANT: This session_start() is needed for our data to "survive" page reloads.
// We will cover sessions in detail in the next chapter.
session_start();
// Initialize the students array in the session if it doesn't exist
if (!isset($_SESSION['students'])) {
    $_SESSION['students'] = [
        ['id' => 1, 'name' => 'Sharanam Shah', 'grade' => 92, 'subject' => 'PHP'],
        ['id' => 2, 'name' => 'Vaishali Shah', 'grade' => 85,
         'subject' => 'JavaScript'],
        ['id' => 3, 'name' => 'Janya Shah', 'grade' => 98, 'subject' => 'PHP'],
    ];
}
// Handle form submission for adding a new student
if ($_SERVER['REQUEST_METHOD'] === 'POST' && isset(
$_POST['add_student'])) {
    // Basic validation
    if (!empty($_POST['name']) && !empty($_POST['grade']) &&
            !empty($_POST['subject'])) {
        // Find the highest existing ID and add 1
        $new_id = 0;
        foreach ($_SESSION['students'] as $student) {
            if ($student['id'] > $new_id) {
                $new_id = $student['id'];
            }
        }
        $new_id++;
        // Create the new student array
        $new_student = [
            'id'      => $new_id,
            'name'    => $_POST['name'],
            'grade'   => $_POST['grade'],
            'subject' => $_POST['subject']
        ];
        // Add the new student to our session array
        $_SESSION['students'][] = $new_student;
    }
}
```

```
// Point our local $students variable to the session data
$students = $_SESSION['students'];
?>
```

- Finally, we need to update our foreach loop to use the $_SESSION['students'] array. Find this line:

```
<?php foreach ($students as $student): ?>
```

And it's already correct since we set **$students = $_SESSION['students'];**. Perfect!

Deleting a student (The 'Delete' in CRUD)

To delete a student, we need a way to identify *which* student to remove. We will pass the student's unique id in the URL.

First, update the **Delete** link in the table in index.php:

```
<a href="index.php?action=delete&id=<?php echo $student['id']; ?>"
   class="btn btn-delete">Delete</a>
```

Now, add the processing logic for this action. In the PHP block at the top of index.php, add the following code right before the add_student logic:

```
// Handle deletion of a student
if (isset($_GET['action']) && $_GET['action'] === 'delete' && isset($_GET['id'])) {
    $id_to_delete = (int)$_GET['id'];
    // Filter the array, keeping only students that DO NOT match the ID
    $_SESSION['students'] = array_filter($_SESSION['students'],
                                         function($student) use ($id_to_delete) {
        return $student['id'] !== $id_to_delete;
    });
    // Redirect to clean the URL
    header('Location: index.php');
    exit;
}
```

We use **array_filter()** here for a safe deletion. It creates a new array containing only the elements that don't match the ID we want to delete. The **header()** redirect is a common practice to prevent accidental re-submissions if the user reloads the page.

Your gradebook is now a fully functional CRUD application!

Bridging the gap: Learned concepts and application implementation

Let's connect what we just built to the concepts from this chapter:

- **Multidimensional array:** Our **$students** array, stored in the **$_SESSION**, is the heart of our application. It's a classic indexed array of associative arrays, perfect for storing records.
- **foreach loop:** We use this **loop** in the HTML section to iterate through the **$students** array and dynamically generate a **<tr>** for each student. This is how data is transformed into a visual display.
- **Associative array keys:** We access specific data points like **echo $student['name'];**. This readable, key-based access is what makes associative arrays so powerful.
- **Array manipulation:** When we add a new student, we are simply adding a new element to the **$_SESSION['students']** array. When we delete, we use **array_filter()** to create a new array without the unwanted element. This is the essence of data management in PHP.

Running and testing

Let's test all the features of our new application.

1. **Start your environment:** Make sure **Apache** is running in your **XAMPP control panel**.
2. **Open the app:** Navigate your browser to **http://localhost/codes/c13-gradebook/index.php**. You see the initial list of three students.

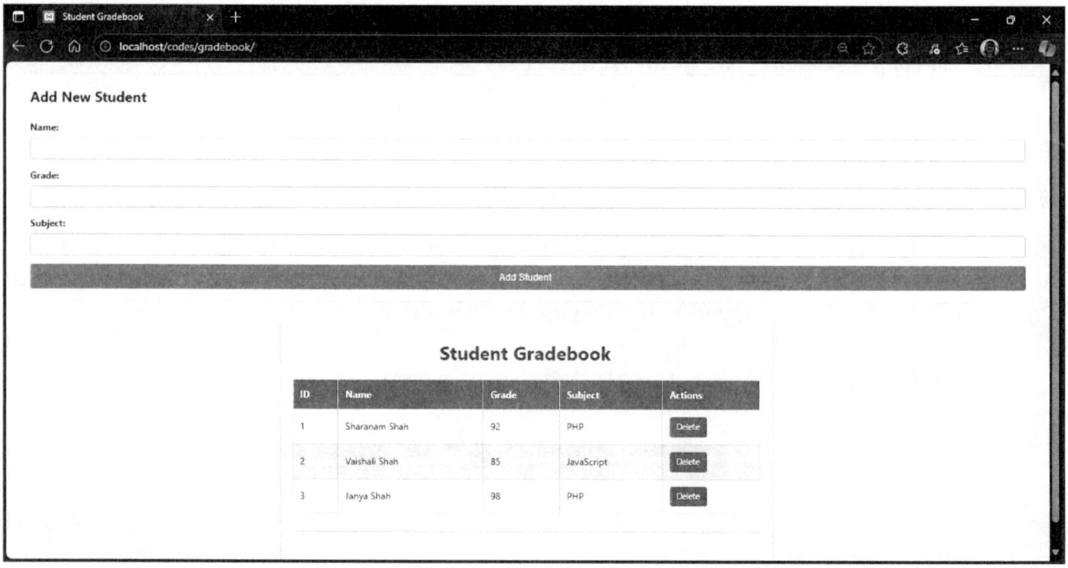

3. **Add a student:** Enter a name, a grade, and a subject. Click **Add Student**.
4. **Verify creation:** The page reloads, and you now see the fourth student details in the table.

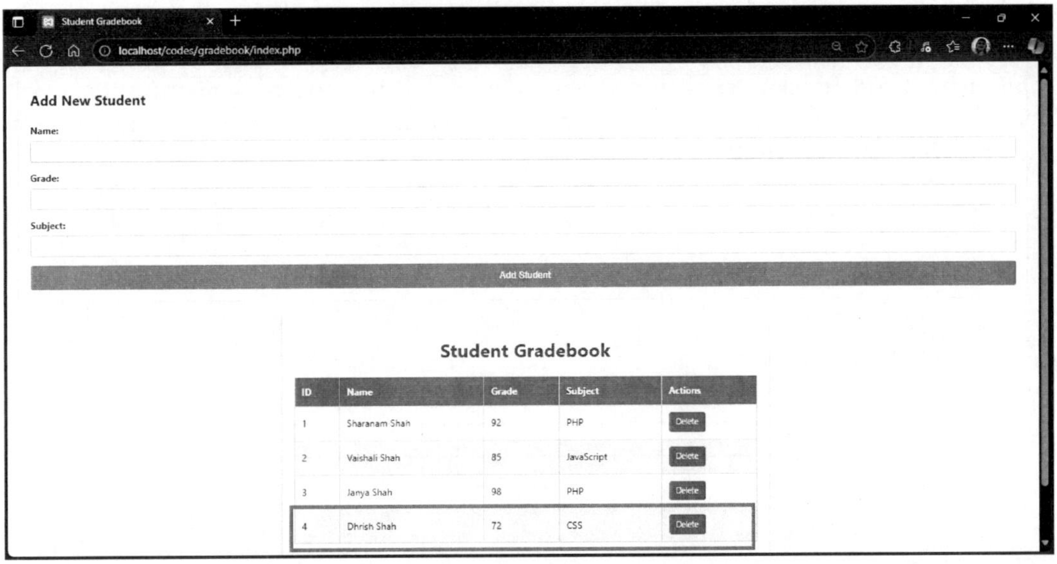

5. **Delete a student**: Find the name of the student you want to delete and click the red **Delete** button.
6. **Verify deletion**: The page reloads, and the name is gone from the list.

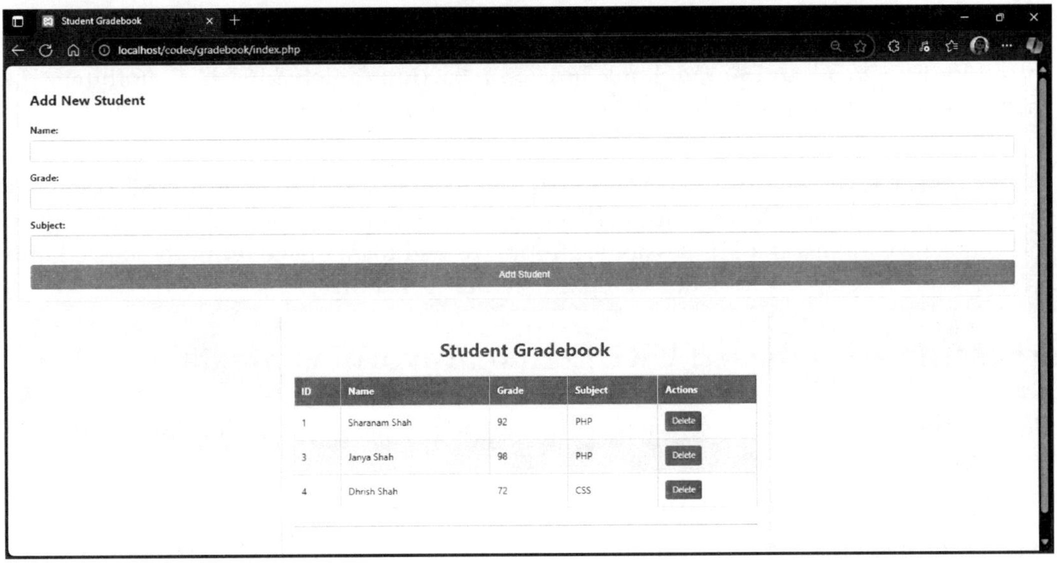

Exploring application behaviour: A practical run-through

What about edge cases? A robust application handles them gracefully.

- **Invalid input:** What happens if you try to submit the **Add Student** form with empty fields? Our current code doesn't explicitly show an error, but because of the **!empty()** checks, it simply does nothing, which is safe. A more advanced version would display a message like **All fields are required**.

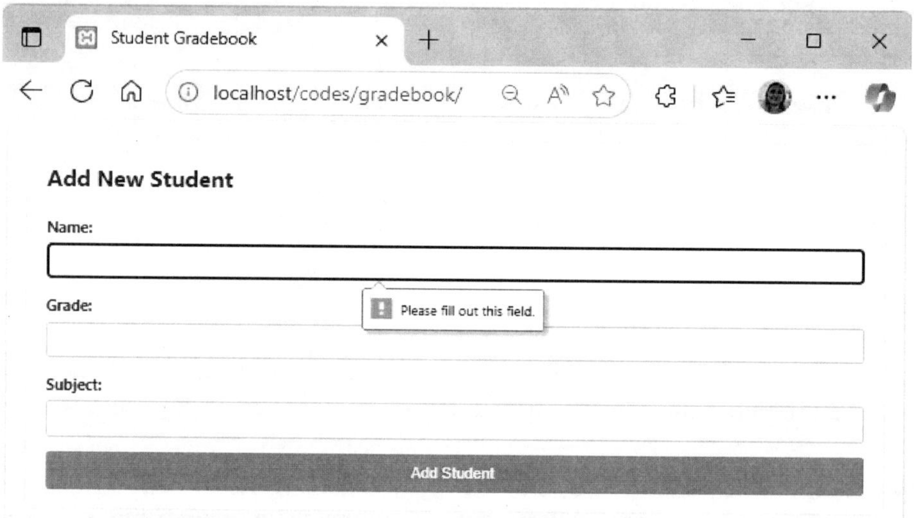

- **Deleting non-existent student:** If you manually change the URL to **http://localhost/codes/c13-gradebook/index.php?action=delete&id=99**, nothing bad happens. **array_filter()** simply does not find a matching student to remove, and the array remains unchanged.
- **Data persistence:** Close the browser tab and reopen http://localhost/codes/c13-gradebook/index.php. Your changes (the new student and the deletion) are still there! This is because we are using PHP Sessions, a topic we will formally cover in the next chapter. It's a sneak peek at how to make web pages **remember** things.

Harnessing array-based CRUD in real-world contexts

While this gradebook doesn't use a permanent database, the logic is **identical** to how real-world applications work. The process of:

- Receiving user input from a form.
- Validating and packaging that input into an associative array.

- Adding, updating, or removing that array from a larger collection.
- Looping through the collection to display it.

This pattern is the absolute core of most web applications, from managing products in an online store to posting comments on social media. Mastering it with arrays is the first, most critical step.

Wrapping up

In this chapter, we turned a simple variable concept into a powerful tool for data management. You learned how to handle not just one piece of data, but entire collections of it in a structured and scalable way.

- Arrays store lists of data using **indexed** (numeric) or **associative** (named) keys.
- **Multidimensional arrays** are arrays of arrays, perfect for holding records like our list of students.
- The **foreach** loop is the essential tool for iterating over an array to display its contents.
- PHP's built-in functions like **array_filter()**, **sort()**, and **implode()** allow you to easily manipulate array data.
- Combining HTML forms and PHP array logic allows for full **CRUD** (Create, Read, Update, Delete) operations.
- **CSS** is critical for transforming raw array data into a visually appealing and user-friendly table.

Congratulations! You have just built your first dynamic data-driven application. You've taken a fundamental programming concept, the array, and used it to create, read, and delete data—a huge milestone. This logical foundation is something you will use in every single project you build from here on out.

In the next chapter, we'll officially explore the magic that made our gradebook "remember" our changes across page loads. Get ready for ***Chapter 14: Safe spaces – Sessions and Cookies for dynamic user experience***!

Chapter 14

Section 04: Smarter workflows – Functions, Arrays, and Authenticity

Safe spaces – Sessions and Cookies for dynamic user experience

What you'll learn

- HTTP statelessness
- Working with cookies
- Access control
- PHP sessions
- Building a login system
- Common security pitfalls

Welcome to one of the most exciting parts of your web development journey. So far, the pages we have built are powerful but have one major limitation: they have no memory. Every time a user visits a new page, the server treats them like a complete stranger. This chapter solves that problem by introducing sessions and cookies, the technologies that allow our applications to remember users, create personalized experiences, and secure exclusive content areas.

Have you ever wondered how an e-commerce site remembers the items in your shopping cart even when you navigate to different product pages? Or how a social media platform keeps you logged in as you browse your feed? The magic behind this is the ability to maintain a "state"—a memory of who the user is and what they have done across multiple requests.

By default, the protocol that powers the web, HTTP, is **stateless**. This means each request a browser makes to a server is an isolated, independent event. The server has no built-in way to know that the request for about.php is from the same person who just visited index.php.

In this chapter, we will master PHP sessions and cookies, the two primary tools for overcoming this limitation. You will learn how to build applications that offer personalized greetings, remember user preferences, and, most importantly, create secure login systems that protect content for authorized users only.

HTTP statelessness and the role of Sessions

As we just mentioned, HTTP is stateless. Think of it like a conversation with someone who has no short-term memory. Every time you speak, you have to reintroduce yourself. On the web, this would be incredibly frustrating. Imagine having to log in again for every single page you visit on a site.

Sessions are the server's way of creating that memory. Here's how it works in a nutshell:

- A user visits your site for the first time.
- PHP creates a unique random string of characters called a **session ID**.
- The server stores any data you want to save for that user in a special temporary file on the server, linked to that session ID.
- The server sends the session ID back to the user's browser, where it is stored for the duration of the visit (often as a special kind of cookie).
- On every subsequent page request, the browser sends the session ID back to the server.
- PHP uses this ID to retrieve the correct data file, **remembering** everything about that user's visit.

This entire process is mostly invisible to the user but gives our application a continuous memory, or **state**, for each visitor.
#

Setting, reading, and destroying sessions

Working with sessions in PHP is straightforward once you know the core functions. It all revolves around the **session_start()** function and the **$_SESSION** superglobal array.

A critical rule to remember is that you must call **session_start()** at the very beginning of any PHP script that needs access to session data, before any HTML or even a single space is sent to the browser.

Setting and reading session data

Let's create a simple script that sets a session variable and then reads it back.

1. In your VS Code, inside your **htdocs\codes** (or www) folder, create a new folder named **c14-sessions**.

- Open the **c14-sessions** folder in VS Code.
- Inside **c14-sessions**, create a new file named **create_session.php**.
- Add the following code:

```
<?php
// Step 1: Start the session
session_start();
// Step 2: Set session variables
$_SESSION['username'] = 'admin';
$_SESSION['favorite_color'] = 'blue';
echo "Session variables have been set.";
?>
```

In this script, we first initialize the session system. Then, we add two key-value pairs to the $_SESSION array, just like any other PHP array. When you run this script by navigating to **http://localhost/codes/c14-sessions/create_session.php** in your browser, it won't show much—just the confirmation message. But on the server, PHP has created a file and stored that data.

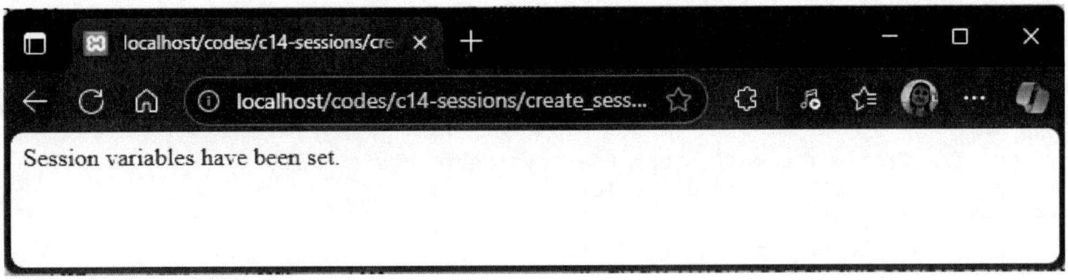

Now, let's create another page to read this data.

1. In the same **c14-sessions** folder, create a new file named **read_session.php**.
2. Add the following code:

```
<?php
```

```
// Step 1: You must start the session to access the data
session_start();
// Step 2: Read the session variables
if (isset($_SESSION['username'])) {
    $username = $_SESSION['username'];
    $color = $_SESSION['favorite_color'];
    echo "Welcome back, " . htmlspecialchars($username) . "!<br>";
    echo "Your favorite color is " . htmlspecialchars($color) . ".";
} else {
    echo "No session data found.";
}
?>
```

Now, open **http://localhost/codes/c14-sessions/read_session.php** in your browser. Because you previously visited create_session.php in the same browser session, PHP retrieves your stored data and you see the personalized greeting.

Destroying sessions

When a user logs out, we need a way to completely destroy their session data. This is a two-step process for maximum security.

1. In the **c14-sessions** folder, create **destroy_session.php**.
2. Add the following code:

```
<?php
session_start(); // You must start the session to destroy it
// Step 1: Unset all session variables
$_SESSION = array();
// Step 2: Destroy the session completely
session_destroy();
echo "You have been logged out and the session is destroyed.";
// Optional: Redirect to a public page
// header('Location: create_session.php');
// exit;
?>
```

session_unset() (or setting **$_SESSION = array();**) removes all the data from the session, but the session ID might still exist. **session_destroy()** finishes the job by removing the session itself.

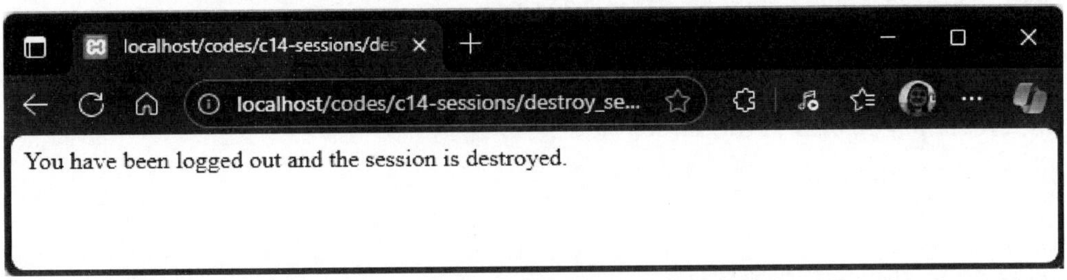

Now, if you revisit read_session.php, it shows **No session data found**.

Passing data between pages securely

The real power of sessions shines when you use them to create a seamless experience across multiple pages. Unlike passing data in a URL with the GET method, session data is never visible to the user in the address bar. It is handled securely between the browser and the server.

Let's demonstrate this with a simple two-page example.

1. Inside your **c14-sessions** folder, create a file named **page1.php**.
2. Add the following code:

```
<?php
session_start();
// Store a piece of information
$_SESSION['user_step'] = 'Visited Page 1';
?>
<!DOCTYPE html>
<html lang="en">
<head>
    <meta charset="UTF-8">
    <title>Page 1</title>
</head>
<body>
```

```
    <h1>This is Page 1</h1>
    <p>We have saved a value to your session.</p>
    <a href="page2.php">Go to Page 2</a>
</body>
</html>
```

3. Now, create **page2.php** in the same folder.
4. Add the following code:

```
<?php
session_start();
// Check for the data from Page 1
if (isset($_SESSION['user_step'])) {
    $message = "The session confirms that you " . htmlspecialchars($_SESSION['
                user_step']) . ".";
} else {
    $message = "It seems you haven't visited Page 1 yet.";
}
?>
<!DOCTYPE html>
<html lang="en">
<head>
    <meta charset="UTF-8">
    <title>Page 2</title>
</head>
<body>
    <h1>This is Page 2</h1>
    <p><?php echo $message; ?></p>
</body>
</html>
```

5. First, navigate to **http://localhost/codes/c14-sessions/page1.php**.

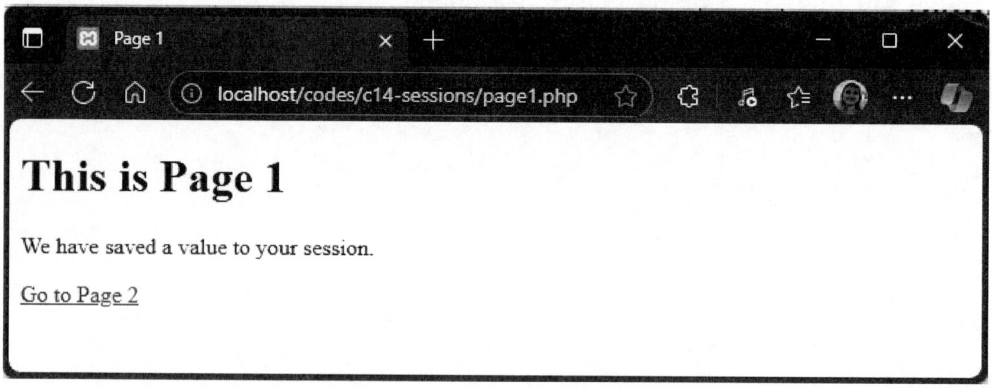

6. Then, click the link to go to **Page 2**. Page 2 successfully retrieves the data set on Page 1, proving that the "memory" persists across the navigation.

7. If you try to visit page2.php directly in a new browser (or after destroying the session), it will show the alternate message.

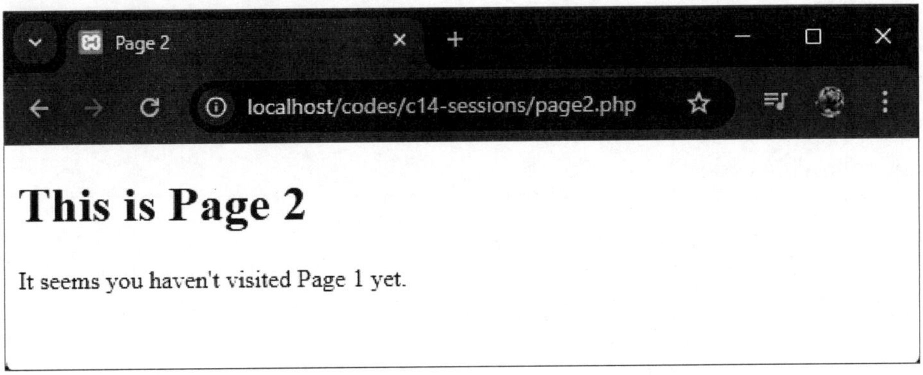

Cookie basics

While sessions handle server-side data, **cookies** are small pieces of data that your script tells the browser to store on the user's computer. The browser then sends this data back to the server with every request.

Cookies are best used for non-sensitive, persistent data, like remembering a user's preference for a light or dark theme, or storing a **Remember Me** token.

Setting a cookie

We use the **setcookie()** function to create a cookie. Like session_start(), this function must be called before any output is sent to the browser.

Syntax:

```
setcookie(name, value, expiry_timestamp, path, domain, secure, httponly);
```

Here,

- **name:** The name of the cookie.
- **value:** The data you want to store.
- **expiry_timestamp:** A Unix timestamp indicating when the cookie should expire. A common practice is to use **time() + number_of_seconds**. If omitted, the cookie expires when the browser closes.
- **httponly:** A crucial security flag. When set to **true**, it prevents client-side scripts like JavaScript from accessing the cookie, mitigating certain types of attacks. **You should almost always set this to true**.

Let's create a cookie to remember a user's preferred theme.

1. In your **c14-sessions** folder, create a file named **set_cookie.php**.
2. Add the following code:

```php
<?php
// Set a cookie that expires in 30 days
$cookie_name = "theme_preference";
$cookie_value = "dark";
$expiry = time() + (86400 * 30); // 86400 = 1 day
// "/" means available sitewide
setcookie($cookie_name, $cookie_value, $expiry, "/", "", false, true);
echo "Cookie has been set!";
?>
```

Reading a cookie

To read a cookie's value, you use the **$_COOKIE** superglobal array.

1. In the **c14-sessions** folder, create **read_cookie.php**.
2. Add the following code:

```php
<?php
if(isset($_COOKIE['theme_preference'])) {
    $theme = htmlspecialchars($_COOKIE['theme_preference']);
    echo "Your saved theme preference is: " . $theme;
} else {
    echo "No theme preference cookie found.";
}
?>
```

Visit **set_cookie.php** first, then **read_cookie.php**. The second page correctly reads the value. Even if you close and reopen your browser, the cookie persists until the 30-day lifetime is up.

Best practices

- **Never store sensitive data in cookies.** Passwords, personal information, or user roles should never be in a cookie. Users can easily view and edit their cookies.
- **Always use the httponly flag.** This is your first line of defense against cross-site scripting (XSS) attacks that try to steal cookie data.
- **Use sessions for authentication.** Sessions are stored on the server and are far more secure for managing login states.

Designing access control with sessions

Now we can combine our knowledge to build the core logic of a members-only area. The concept is simple: on any protected page, we first check if a specific session variable exists and holds the correct value. If it does, we show the page content. If not, we redirect the user to the login page.

Let's imagine we have a **dashboard.php** that should only be accessible to logged-in users. We will decide that when a user logs in successfully, we will set **$_SESSION['loggedin']** to **true**.

Here is the code that would go at the very top of dashboard.php:

```
<?php
// Always start the session first
```

```
session_start();
// Check if the user is logged in. If not, redirect to the login page.
if (!isset($_SESSION['loggedin']) || $_SESSION['loggedin'] !== true) {
    header('Location: login.php'); // Assuming you have a login.php
    exit; // Important to stop the script from continuing
}
// If the script reaches this point, the user is authenticated.
// You can now show the protected content.
?>
<!DOCTYPE html>
<html lang="en">
<head>
    <title>Secret Dashboard</title>
</head>
<body>
    <h1>Welcome to the Members-Only Area!</h1>
    <p>This content is highly confidential.</p>
</body>
</html>
```

This simple **if** statement is the gatekeeper for our protected content. The **header('Location: ...')** function performs a redirect, and **exit;** ensures that no part of the confidential HTML is ever sent to an unauthorized user.

Common pitfalls

While sessions are secure, there are common pitfalls that beginners should be aware of.

Session fixation

Session fixation is an attack where an attacker tricks a user into using a session ID that the attacker already knows. If the user then logs in, the attacker can use that same session ID to gain access to the user's account.

The fix is simple and crucial: always regenerate the session ID immediately after a successful login.

PHP has a function for this: **session_regenerate_id(true);**. The **true** parameter tells PHP to delete the old session file associated with the previous ID, making it useless to an attacker. We will implement this in our hands-on project.

Cookie tampering

As mentioned earlier, cookies are stored on the user's machine in plain text. A savvy user can find these files and change their values. For example, if you stored a user's access level in a cookie like **access_level=user**, they could try changing it to **access_level=admin**.

This is why you **must never trust cookie data for authorization or to store sensitive information**. Always store this kind of data in server-side sessions, which the user cannot access or modify.

Hands-on: Login and personalized dashboard

Let's put all this theory into practice by building a complete, working login system. Our application will have a public login page, a private dashboard that greets the user by name, and a secure logout function.

This project will create a simple authentication system. A user can visit a login page and enter credentials. If they are correct, they are taken to a personalized dashboard. If they try to access the dashboard directly without logging in, they are redirected back to the login page. This project perfectly demonstrates how sessions manage state and control access in a real-world scenario.

Building the application

First, let's set up our project folder.

1. Navigate to your XAMPP **htdocs\codes** directory.
2. Create a new folder named **c14-auth-app**.
3. We will create three files inside this folder: login.php, dashboard.php, and logout.php.

Create the login page

This file contains the HTML form for logging in and the PHP logic to process the submission. Create **login.php** inside **c14-auth-app** and add the following code:

```
<?php
// Start the session at the very beginning
session_start();
// If the user is already logged in, redirect them to the dashboard
if (isset($_SESSION['loggedin']) && $_SESSION['loggedin'] === true) {
    header('Location: dashboard.php');
```

```
    exit;
}
// Define dummy credentials for this example
define('CORRECT_USERNAME', 'admin');
define('CORRECT_PASSWORD', 'password123');
$error_message = '';
// Check if the form has been submitted
if ($_SERVER['REQUEST_METHOD'] === 'POST') {
    $username = $_POST['username'];
    $password = $_POST['password'];
    // Validate credentials
    if ($username === CORRECT_USERNAME &&
           $password === CORRECT_PASSWORD) {
        // --- SECURITY: Regenerate session ID on login ---
        session_regenerate_id(true);
        // Set session variables
        $_SESSION['loggedin'] = true;
        $_SESSION['username'] = 'Guest'; // A friendly name for the user
        // Redirect to the protected dashboard
        header('Location: dashboard.php');
        exit;
    } else {
        $error_message = "Invalid username or password.";
    }
}
?>
<!DOCTYPE html>
<html lang="en">
<head>
    <meta charset="UTF-8">
    <meta name="viewport" content="width=device-width, initial-scale=1.0">
    <title>Login Page</title>
    <style>
        body {
            font-family: -apple-system, BlinkMacSystemFont, "Segoe UI", Roboto,
                         "Helvetica Neue", Arial, sans-serif;
            background-color: #f4f7f6;
            display: flex;
            justify-content: center;
            align-items: center;
            height: 100vh;
            margin: 0;
        }
        .login-container {
            background-color: #ffffff;
            padding: 40px;
            border-radius: 8px;
            box-shadow: 0 4px 10px rgba(0, 0, 0, 0.1);
            width: 100%;
            max-width: 400px;
        }
```

```
        h2 {
            text-align: center;
            color: #333;
            margin-bottom: 25px;
        }
        .form-group {
            margin-bottom: 20px;
        }
        label {
            display: block;
            margin-bottom: 5px;
            color: #555;
            font-weight: 500;
        }
        input[type="text"], input[type="password"] {
            width: 100%;
            padding: 12px;
            border: 1px solid #ccc;
            border-radius: 4px;
            box-sizing: border-box;
        }
        .btn {
            background-color: #007bff;
            color: white;
            padding: 12px 20px;
            border: none;
            border-radius: 4px;
            cursor: pointer;
            width: 100%;
            font-size: 16px;
            font-weight: bold;
        }
        .btn:hover {
            background-color: #0056b3;
        }
        .error {
            color: #d9534f;
            background-color: #f2dede;
            border: 1px solid #ebccd1;
            padding: 10px;
            border-radius: 4px;
            text-align: center;
            margin-top: 20px;
        }
    </style>
</head>
<body>
    <div class="login-container">
        <h2>Member Login</h2>
        <form action="login.php" method="POST">
            <div class="form-group">
```

```
                <label for="username">Username</label>
                <input type="text" id="username" name="username" required>
            </div>
            <div class="form-group">
                <label for="password">Password</label>
                <input type="password" id="password" name="password"
                       required>
            </div>
            <button type="submit" class="btn">Login</button>
        </form>
        <?php if (!empty($error_message)): ?>
            <div class="error"><?php echo $error_message; ?></div>
        <?php endif; ?>
    </div>
</body>
</html>
```

This code does a lot:

- It starts the session and checks if the user is *already* logged in, redirecting them if so.
- It defines a correct username and password (in a real app, this would come from a database).
- When the form is submitted via POST, it checks the credentials.
- On success, it regenerates the session ID, sets the loggedin and username session variables, and redirects to the dashboard.
- On failure, it prepares an error message to be displayed below the form.
- The CSS provides a clean, modern form style.

Create the personalized dashboard

This is our protected, members-only page. Create **dashboard.php** in the **c14-auth-app** folder and add the following code:

```
<?php
// Always start the session first
session_start();
// This is our gatekeeper. If the user is not logged in, redirect them to
// the login page.
if (!isset($_SESSION['loggedin']) || $_SESSION['loggedin'] !== true) {
    header('Location: login.php');
    exit;
}
// Get the username from the session for a personalized welcome
$username = isset($_SESSION['username']) ?
                  htmlspecialchars($_SESSION['username']) : 'Valued Member';
?>
```

```
<!DOCTYPE html>
<html lang="en">
<head>
    <meta charset="UTF-8">
    <meta name="viewport" content="width=device-width, initial-scale=1.0">
    <title>Dashboard</title>
    <style>
        body {
            font-family: -apple-system, BlinkMacSystemFont, "Segoe UI", Roboto,
                         "Helvetica Neue", Arial, sans-serif;
            background-color: #f4f7f6;
            color: #333;
            margin: 0;
            padding: 40px;
        }
        .dashboard-container {
            max-width: 800px;
            margin: auto;
            background: #fff;
            padding: 30px;
            border-radius: 8px;
            box-shadow: 0 4px 10px rgba(0, 0, 0, 0.1);
        }
        h1 {
            color: #007bff;
        }
        p {
            line-height: 1.6;
        }
        .logout-link {
            display: inline-block;
            margin-top: 20px;
            padding: 10px 15px;
            background-color: #d9534f;
            color: white;
            text-decoration: none;
            border-radius: 4px;
            font-weight: bold;
        }
        .logout-link:hover {
            background-color: #c9302c;
        }
    </style>
</head>
<body>
    <div class="dashboard-container">
        <h1>Welcome, <?php echo $username; ?>!</h1>
        <p>This is your personalized and secure dashboard. Only logged-in users can
           see this content. Congratulations on building a secure authentication
           system!</p>
        <p>From here, you could display user-specific information, settings, or
```

```
            exclusive content.</p>
        <a href="logout.php" class="logout-link">Logout</a>
    </div>
</body>
</html>
```

This script is much simpler. Its primary job is to act as a gatekeeper. If the session check passes, it displays a welcome message using the username we stored in the session and provides a link to log out.

Create the logout script

This script will securely end the user's session. Create **logout.php** in the **c14-auth-app** folder and add the following code:

```
<?php
// Always start the session to be able to access and destroy it
session_start();
// Unset all of the session variables
$_SESSION = array();
// Destroy the session
session_destroy();
// Redirect to the login page
header('Location: login.php');
exit;
?>
```

This is the cleanup crew. It ensures no session data is left behind and sends the user back to the public login page, completing the authentication cycle.

Bridging the gap: Learned concepts and application implementation

Let's connect the theory to our hands-on project:

- **HTTP statelessness:** We overcame this by using **session_start()** on every page, creating a persistent state for each user.
- **Setting and reading sessions:** In login.php, we set **$_SESSION['loggedin']** and **$_SESSION['username']**. In dashboard.php, we read these variables to control access and personalize the content.

- **Designing access control:** The **if (!isset($_SESSION['loggedin']))** block in dashboard.php is the direct implementation of our access control design. It acts as a bouncer, checking for the **logged in** ticket before allowing entry.
- **Destroying sessions:** logout.php properly implements the session destruction process we learned, ensuring a secure exit.
- **Security pitfalls:** We addressed session fixation by using **session_regenerate_id(true)** in login.php right after verifying the password, making the login process much more secure.

Running and testing

Now, let's test the complete user journey.

1. Open your browser and navigate to the login page: **http://localhost/codes/c14-auth-app/login.php**. You see the login form.

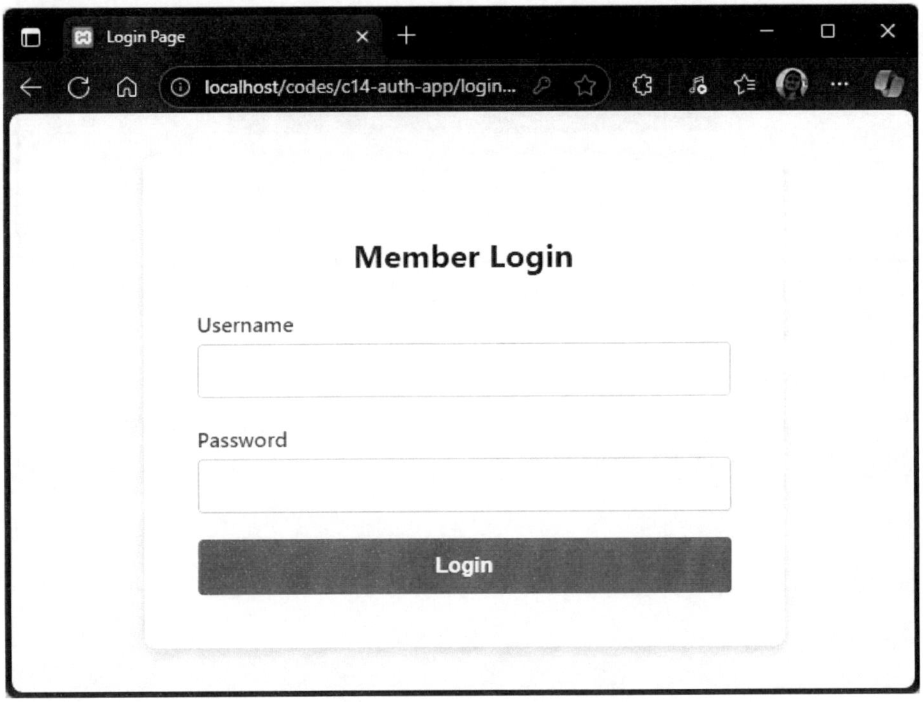

2. **Test the protection:** Try to access the dashboard directly by typing **http://localhost/codes/c14-auth-app/dashboard.php** into the address bar. The server should immediately redirect you back to login.php. This proves our gatekeeper is working.

3. **Test invalid login:** On the login page, enter an incorrect username or password. Click the **Login** button. The page reloads and displays the **Invalid username or password** error message.

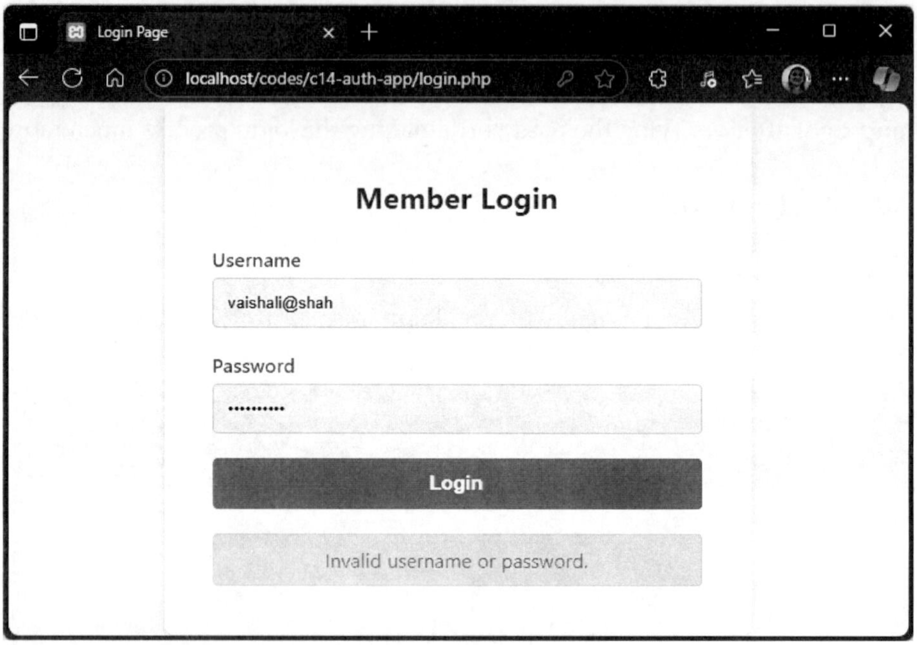

4. **Test successful login:** Now, enter the correct credentials:
   - **Username:** admin
   - **Password**: password123
   - Click the **Login** button. You are instantly redirected to dashboard.php and see the personalized welcome message.

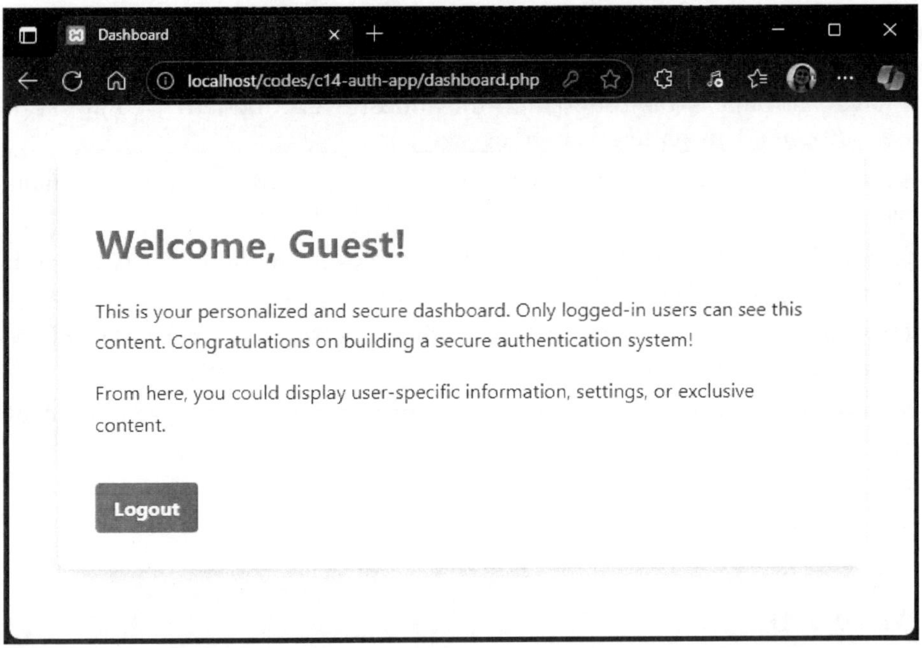

5. **Test logout:** On the dashboard, click the **Logout** link. You are redirected back to the login.php page. If you try to access the dashboard URL again, you will be blocked. The session was successfully destroyed.

Exploring application behaviour: A practical run-through

- **Session expiry:** By default, a session lasts until the user closes their browser completely. If you log in, close the tab (but not the whole browser), and then reopen the dashboard URL, you will likely still be logged in. If you close the entire browser application and then reopen it, the session will be gone, and you will need to log in again.
- **Simulated multi-user access:** Open a different browser (e.g., Firefox if you were using Chrome) or an Incognito/Private window in your current browser. Navigate to http://localhost/codes/c14-auth-app/dashboard.php. You will be redirected to the login page. This demonstrates that each browser (or private session) maintains its own separate session with the server, preventing users from seeing each other's data.

Harnessing sessions in real-world contexts

What you have just built is the foundation for almost every modern web application that requires user accounts. This pattern is used everywhere:

- **E-commerce sites:** To keep track of shopping carts, view order history, and manage user profiles.
- **Online portals:** For students to check grades, employees to view internal documents, or patients to see medical records.
- **Social media:** To keep users logged in so they can see their personalized feed, post updates, and interact with others.
- **Subscription services:** To ensure only paying members can access premium content like articles or videos.

Mastering sessions is a fundamental skill for building dynamic, secure, and user-friendly web applications.

Wrapping up

In this chapter, we tackled the challenge of the web's stateless nature and emerged with powerful tools to create stateful, personalized experiences. You now understand the fundamental difference between server-side sessions and client-side cookies and when to use each one effectively.

- **HTTP is stateless:** Each request is independent and has no memory of past requests.
- **Sessions create memory:** PHP sessions store data on the server, linked by a unique session ID, to track a user's journey.
- **session_start() is mandatory:** It must be called at the top of any script using sessions.
- **$_SESSION is your data store:** Use this superglobal array to set and get user-specific data.
- **Cookies for persistence:** Cookies store non-sensitive data on the client's machine, ideal for preferences.
- **Authentication is key:** You built a complete, secure login, dashboard, and logout system—a core skill for any web developer.

Congratulations! You have successfully implemented one of the most critical features of modern web applications: user authentication. You have built a secure space where only authorized users can enter, and you now possess the skills to create applications that remember and respond to users personally. This ability to maintain state is what transforms a collection of static pages into a truly interactive web application.

You are well-equipped to manage user data securely across multiple pages. In the next ***Chapter 15: Culmination - Student success lounge,*** we will integrate everything you have learned about functions, arrays, and sessions to build a more comprehensive and feature-rich project.

Chapter 15

Section 04: Smarter workflows – Functions, Arrays, and Authenticity

Culmination: Student success lounge

What you'll learn

- Application blueprinting
- Session-based navigation
- CSS theme personalization
- Integrating core concepts
- Testing access control

Welcome to a major milestone in your PHP journey! In the previous chapters, you mastered the essential building blocks of programming: functions to create reusable code, arrays to manage lists of data, and sessions to give your web applications a memory. Now, it's time to assemble these pieces into a complete, practical application. This chapter is a culmination of everything you have learned in Section 4, where we transition from writing isolated scripts to building a cohesive, multi-page user experience.

We are about to build the Student success lounge, a personalized dashboard where users can log in to access exclusive content. This project is not just an exercise; it mirrors the core functionality of countless real-world websites, from social media platforms and online banking portals to e-commerce stores and membership sites. By building this, you are taking your first big step toward developing professional, dynamic web applications.

App blueprint

Before writing a single line of code, professional developers create a blueprint. This plan ensures that what they build matches the project's goals. A **blueprint** consists of defining the features, writing user stories to understand the user's perspective, and identifying the data the application needs to function.

Features are the specific things our application does. For our Student success lounge, the features are:

- A secure login page for registered students.
- A private dashboard page visible only after logging in.
- A personalized welcome message on the dashboard.
- A logout mechanism to securely end the user's session.

User stories help us frame these features from a user's point of view. They typically follow the format: "As a [type of user], I want to [perform an action] so that I can [achieve a goal]."

- As a student, I want to log in with my credentials so that I can access my private dashboard.
- As a logged-in student, I want to see a personalized welcome message so that I feel recognized by the system.
- As a logged-in student, I want to log out easily so that I can secure my account on a shared computer.

Data needs refer to the information our application must manage. Since we are not yet using a database (that's coming in the next part!), we will simulate a user database with a PHP array.

- **User credentials:** We need a list of valid usernames and passwords to check against.
- **Session data:** We need to store a flag in the session to indicate that a user is logged in, along with their name for personalization.

Planning this way turns a vague idea into a clear, actionable roadmap.

Integrating functions, arrays, sessions, UI

This project is where the concepts from our previous chapters come together to form a complete system. Think of it like building with Lego bricks—each piece has a purpose, but they only become something amazing when connected correctly.

- **Arrays:** An associative array will act as our temporary user database. The array keys will be usernames, and the values will be their corresponding passwords and full names.
- **Functions:** We will create functions for repetitive tasks to keep our code clean and organized. For example, a function to check if a user is logged in can be called on every private page. This is much better than writing the same checking logic over and over.
- **Sessions:** Sessions are the **glue** that holds the user experience together across multiple pages. When a user logs in successfully, we will start a session and store their identity. This session data acts as a keycard, granting them access to protected areas.
- **UI (User Interface):** The UI is what the user sees and interacts with. It consists of our HTML forms and the visual output styled with CSS. Our PHP logic will dynamically change the UI, for instance, by showing a welcome message with the user's name fetched from the session.

Here is a small conceptual example of how these parts interact:

```
<?php
// 1. Session is started on every page
session_start();
// 2. An array holds our user data
$users = [
    'student1' => ['password' => 'pass123', 'name' => 'Alice']
];
// 3. A function checks if the user is authenticated
function is_user_logged_in() {
    return isset($_SESSION['username']);
}
// On the dashboard page, we use the function
if (is_user_logged_in()) {
    // 4. The UI is personalized using session data
    echo "Welcome, " . htmlspecialchars($_SESSION['name']) . "!";
} else {
    echo "Access denied.";
}
?>
```

In this snippet, the array, function, and session all work together to control and personalize the UI.

Building the navigation and user personalization

A key feature of a dynamic application is navigation that adapts to the user's status. A visitor should see a **Login** link, while a logged-in user should see a **Dashboard** and **Logout** link. This is achieved by using conditional PHP logic directly within our HTML.

We use the $_SESSION superglobal to check the user's state. When the user successfully logs in, we set a session variable, like $_SESSION['username']. On every page, we can check if this variable exists.

Personalization goes beyond just showing the right links. It's about making the user feel that the application is *for them*. The simplest and most effective way to do this is by addressing them by name. We can store the user's name in the session upon login and then display it on the dashboard.

Consider this navigation bar logic:

```
<nav>
    <a href="/index.php">Home</a>
    <?php if (isset($_SESSION['username'])): ?>
        <a href="/dashboard.php">Dashboard</a>
        <a href="/logout.php">Logout</a>
    <?php else: ?>
        <a href="/login.php">Login</a>
    <?php endif; ?>
</nav>
```

This code checks whether the user is logged in or not. If the user is not logged in then the browser renders the navigation with a Login link. If the user is logged in then the browser renders the navigation with Dashboard and Logout links.

This dynamic rendering is controlled entirely by the state of the session, providing a seamless and context-aware experience for the user.

Testing access, sessions, edge cases

A secure application must protect its private areas. It's not enough to simply hide the link to the dashboard; we must actively block unauthorized users from accessing it directly. What if someone who is not logged in tries to visit the dashboard.php URL by typing it into their browser?

Our application must be ready for this. On every protected page, the very first thing we do (after starting the session) is check for the session variable that confirms the user's identity. If it's not there, we immediately redirect them to the login page using the PHP header() function:

```
<?php
// Start the session to access session variables
session_start();
// Check if the 'username' key is NOT set in the session
if (!isset($_SESSION['username'])) {
```

```
    // If they aren't logged in, redirect them to the login page
    header('Location: login.php');
    // It's crucial to call exit() after a redirect to stop script execution
    exit();
}
// The rest of the dashboard code goes here...
// This part will only be reached by authenticated users.
?>
```

Edge cases are scenarios that are not part of the normal workflow but can happen. We need to consider them:

- **Session expiry:** What happens if a user leaves their dashboard open for a long time? PHP sessions have a limited lifetime. When it expires, our check will fail, and they will be properly redirected to the login page upon their next action.
- **Logout:** A user must be able to log out. Our logout.php script will handle this by destroying the session data completely, ensuring no one can use the back button to see the previous user's dashboard.

Advanced CSS personalization (themes)

We can take personalization a step further by allowing users to select a visual theme, such as **light mode** or **dark mode**. PHP can facilitate this beautifully. While we won't build the theme-switching mechanism just yet, we can easily set up our CSS to support it and use PHP to apply a theme dynamically.

The strategy is to add a CSS class to the <body> element of our HTML based on a session variable. Our CSS file will then contain rules that apply different styles based on this body class.

For example, our PHP could set a theme like this:

```
<?php
// Let's assume the user's theme preference is stored in the session
$_SESSION['theme'] = 'dark';
$themeClass = isset($_SESSION['theme']) ? 'theme-' .
              $_SESSION['theme'] : 'theme-light';
?>
<body class="<?php echo $themeClass; ?>">
</body>
```

Our CSS file would then contain rules for both themes:

```
/* --- Default (Light Theme) Styles --- */
body.theme-light {
```

```
    background-color: #f4f4f9;
    color: #333;
}
.theme-light .widget {
    background-color: #ffffff;
    border: 1px solid #ddd;
}
/* --- Dark Theme Styles --- */
body.theme-dark {
    background-color: #2c3e50;
    color: #ecf0f1;
}
.theme-dark .widget {
    background-color: #34495e;
    border: 1px solid #5d6d7e;
}
```

By changing the class on the <body> element, we can dramatically alter the entire look and feel of the page with a single line of PHP, providing a rich, personalized experience.

Hands-on: Building the Student success lounge

It's time to build! We will now create the Student success lounge from scratch. This project will tie together everything we've discussed: an array for user data, a login form, a protected dashboard that displays personalized content, a secure logout script, and stylish CSS for a great user experience. By the end of this section, you will have a fully functional, multi-page web application.

Building the application

First, let's set up our project structure. Inside your XAMPP htdocs/codes folder, create a new folder named **student-lounge**. All our files will go inside this folder:

```
/xampp/htdocs/codes/student-lounge/
├── login.php
├── dashboard.php
├── logout.php
└── style.css
```

Create the project folder

1. Navigate to your XAMPP installation directory, and open the **htdocs/codes** folder.
2. Create a new folder and name it **student-lounge**.

3. Open this folder in **Visual Studio Code**.

Create the stylesheet

Let's start with the CSS so our application looks good from the beginning. Create a new file named **style.css** inside the **student-lounge** folder and add the following code. This file defines styles for our login form, the dashboard, and a dark theme:

```
/* General Body & Theme Styling */
body {
    font-family: -apple-system, BlinkMacSystemFont, "Segoe UI", Roboto,
                 Helvetica, Arial, sans-serif;
    margin: 0;
    padding: 40px;
    transition: background-color 0.3s, color 0.3s;
}
/* --- Light Theme (Default) --- */
body.theme-light {
    background-color: #eef2f7;
    color: #333;
}
.theme-light .container {
    background-color: #ffffff;
    box-shadow: 0 4px 12px rgba(0, 0, 0, 0.1);
}
.theme-light h1 {
    color: #2c3e50;
}
.theme-light .btn {
    background-color: #3498db;
}
.theme-light .btn:hover {
    background-color: #2980b9;
}
.theme-light .error {
    color: #e74c3c;
    background-color: #fbe2e2;
    border-left: 4px solid #e74c3c;
}
.theme-light .logout-link {
    color: #3498db;
}
/* --- Dark Theme --- */
body.theme-dark {
    background-color: #2c3e50;
    color: #ecf0f1;
}
.theme-dark .container {
    background-color: #34495e;
```

```
    box-shadow: 0 4px 12px rgba(0, 0, 0, 0.2);
    border: 1px solid #4a627a;
}
.theme-dark h1 {
    color: #ecf0f1;
}
.theme-dark .btn {
    background-color: #5dade2;
}
.theme-dark .btn:hover {
    background-color: #85c1e9;
}
.theme-dark .error {
    color: #f1a59d;
    background-color: #5d3a3a;
    border-left: 4px solid #e74c3c;
}
.theme-dark .logout-link {
    color: #5dade2;
}
/* Common Styles */
.container {
    max-width: 500px;
    margin: 0 auto;
    padding: 30px;
    border-radius: 8px;
}
h1 {
    text-align: center;
    margin-bottom: 25px;
}
.form-group {
    margin-bottom: 20px;
}
label {
    display: block;
    margin-bottom: 8px;
    font-weight: 600;
}
input[type="text"], input[type="password"] {
    width: 100%;
    padding: 12px;
    border: 1px solid #ccc;
    border-radius: 5px;
    box-sizing: border-box;
    /* Important for padding */
}
.btn {
    width: 100%;
    padding: 12px;
    border: none;
```

```
    border-radius: 5px;
    color: white;
    font-size: 16px;
    font-weight: 700;
    cursor: pointer;
    transition: background-color 0.3s;
}
.error {
    padding: 15px;
    margin-bottom: 20px;
    border-radius: 5px;
    text-align: center;
}
.dashboard-header {
    display: flex;
    justify-content: space-between;
    align-items: center;
    border-bottom: 2px solid #bdc3c7;
    padding-bottom: 10px;
    margin-bottom: 20px;
}
.theme-dark .dashboard-header {
    border-bottom-color: #4a627a;
}
.logout-link {
    text-decoration: none;
    font-weight: 600;
}
```

Create the Login page

This is the entry point for our users. It contains an HTML form and the PHP logic to process the login attempt. Create a file named **login.php** and add the following code:

```
<?php
// Always start the session at the very beginning of the script
session_start();
// If the user is already logged in, redirect them to the dashboard
if (isset($_SESSION['username'])) {
    header('Location: dashboard.php');
    exit();
}
// Our pretend database of users. In a real application, this comes from
// a database.
$users = [
    'student1' => [
        'password' => 'jshah',
        'name' => 'Janya Shah',
        'theme' => 'light'
```

```
    ],
    'student2' => [
        'password' => 'dshah',
        'name' => 'Dhrish Shah',
        'theme' => 'dark'
    ]
];
$error_message = '';
// Check if the form was submitted using the POST method
if ($_SERVER['REQUEST_METHOD'] === 'POST') {
    $username = $_POST['username'];
    $password = $_POST['password'];
    // Check if the username exists in our array and if the password matches
    if (isset($users[$username]) && $users[$username]['password'] === $password) {
        // Correct credentials! Store user info in the session.
        $_SESSION['username'] = $username;
        $_SESSION['name'] = $users[$username]['name'];
        $_SESSION['theme'] = $users[$username]['theme'];
        // Redirect to the protected dashboard page
        header('Location: dashboard.php');
        exit();
    } else {
        // Invalid credentials, set an error message
        $error_message = "Invalid username or password.";
    }
}
?>
<!DOCTYPE html>
<html lang="en">
<head>
    <meta charset="UTF-8">
    <meta name="viewport" content="width=device-width, initial-scale=1.0">
    <title>Student Login</title>
    <link rel="stylesheet" href="style.css">
</head>
<body class="theme-light">
    <div class="container">
        <h1>Student Success Lounge</h1>
        <?php if ($error_message): ?>
            <div class="error"><?php echo $error_message; ?></div>
        <?php endif; ?>
        <form action="login.php" method="POST">
            <div class="form-group">
                <label for="username">Username</label>
                <input type="text" id="username" name="username" required>
            </div>
            <div class="form-group">
                <label for="password">Password</label>
                <input type="password" id="password" name="password" required>
            </div>
            <button type="submit" class="btn">Login</button>
```

```
        </form>
    </div>
</body>
</html>
```

Create the Dashboard page

This is the protected page that only logged-in users can see. It checks for a valid session and displays personalized content. Create a file named **dashboard.php** and add the following code:

```
<?php
// This must be the first line to access session variables
session_start();
// This is our security guard. If the user is not logged in,
// send them to the login page.
if (!isset($_SESSION['username'])) {
    header('Location: login.php');
    exit();
}
// Get user data from the session to personalize the page
$name = htmlspecialchars($_SESSION['name']);
$theme = isset($_SESSION['theme']) ? 'theme-' .
               $_SESSION['theme'] : 'theme-light';
?>
<!DOCTYPE html>
<html lang="en">
<head>
    <meta charset="UTF-8">
    <meta name="viewport" content="width=device-width, initial-scale=1.0">
    <title>Your Dashboard</title>
    <link rel="stylesheet" href="style.css">
</head>
<body class="<?php echo $theme; ?>">
    <div class="container">
        <div class="dashboard-header">
            <h1>Welcome, <?php echo $name; ?>!</h1>
            <a href="logout.php" class="logout-link">Logout</a>
        </div>
        <p>This is your private dashboard. Here you can find exclusive
           resources and tools to help you succeed.</p>
        <div class="widget">
            <h2>Announcements</h2>
            <p>The final project deadline has been extended to next Friday.
               Good luck!</p>
        </div>
        <div class="widget">
            <h2>Quick Links</h2>
            <ul>
                <li>Course Materials</li>
```

```
                <li>Grades Portal</li>
                <li>Submit Assignment</li>
            </ul>
        </div>
    </div>
</body>
</html>
```

Create the Logout script

This simple script securely ends the user's session. Create a file named **logout.php** and add the following code:

```
<?php
// Always start the session to be able to modify it
session_start();
// Unset all session variables
$_SESSION = [];
// Destroy the session completely
session_destroy();
// Redirect the user to the login page
header('Location: login.php');
exit();
?>
```

Your application is now complete!

Bridging the gap: Learned concepts and application implementation

Let's connect this project back to the core concepts you've learned:

- **Functions:** While we didn't create custom functions in this specific build to keep it simple, the entire application relies on built-in PHP functions like session_start(), isset(), htmlspecialchars(), and header(). The login.php script's logic could easily be refactored into authenticate_user() and redirect() functions in a larger project.
- **Arrays:** The $users associative array in login.php is a perfect example of using an array to store structured data. We access user details with a key ($users[$username]) to retrieve their password and name, demonstrating the power of associative arrays.
- **Sessions:** Sessions are the star of this chapter. We use session_start() to initiate them, $_SESSION['username'] = $username; to store data, isset($_SESSION['username']) to check for authentication, and session_destroy() to log the user out. You have now seen a full, end-to-end implementation of session-based access control.

- **Forms and $_POST:** The login form uses the POST method. Our PHP script safely retrieves the submitted data from the $_POST superglobal to perform the authentication check.

Running and testing

Now, let's see our application in action.

1. Ensure your **Apache** server is running from the **XAMPP Control Panel**.
2. Open your web browser and navigate to **http://localhost/codes/student-lounge/login.php**.
3. You see the stylish login form.

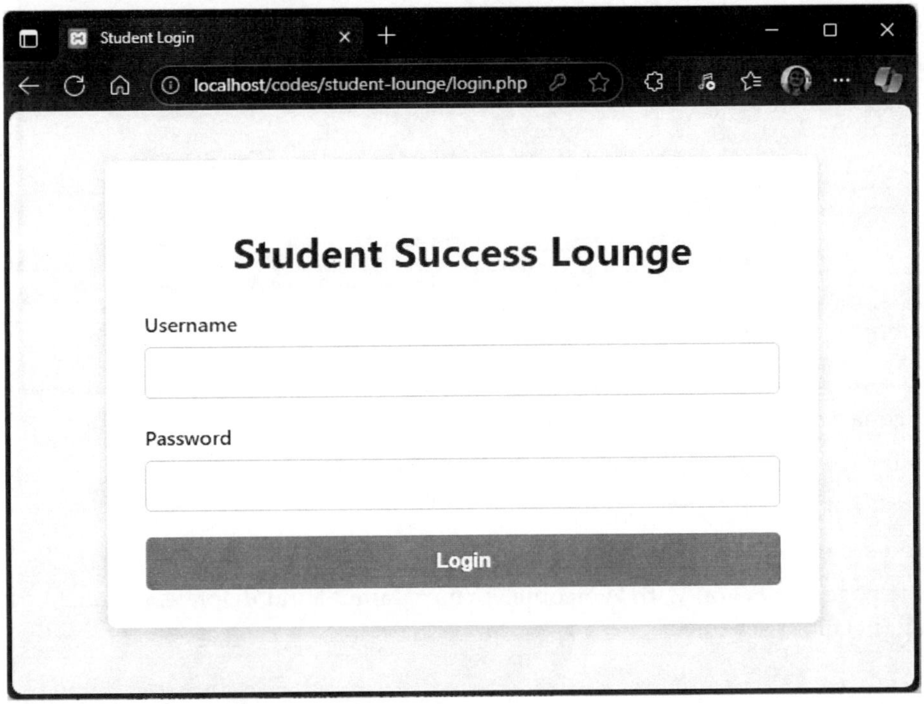

4. **Test Scenario 1:** Invalid login
   - Enter a wrong username like **test** and any password.
   - Click **Login**.
   - The page reloads, and you see the **Invalid username or password**. error message displayed above the form.

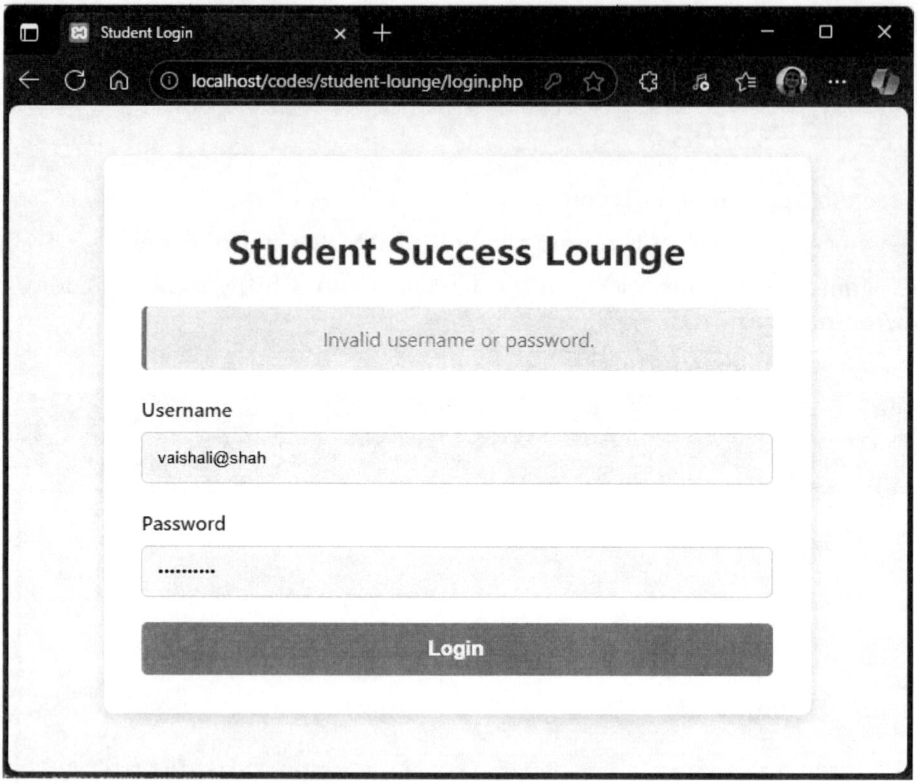

5. **Test Scenario 2:** Successful login (Light Theme)
    - Enter the username **student1** and the password **jshah**.
    - Click **Login**.
    - You are redirected to dashboard.php. Notice the URL has changed.
    - The page greets you with **Welcome, <Your Name>!** and displays the dashboard with a light colour scheme.

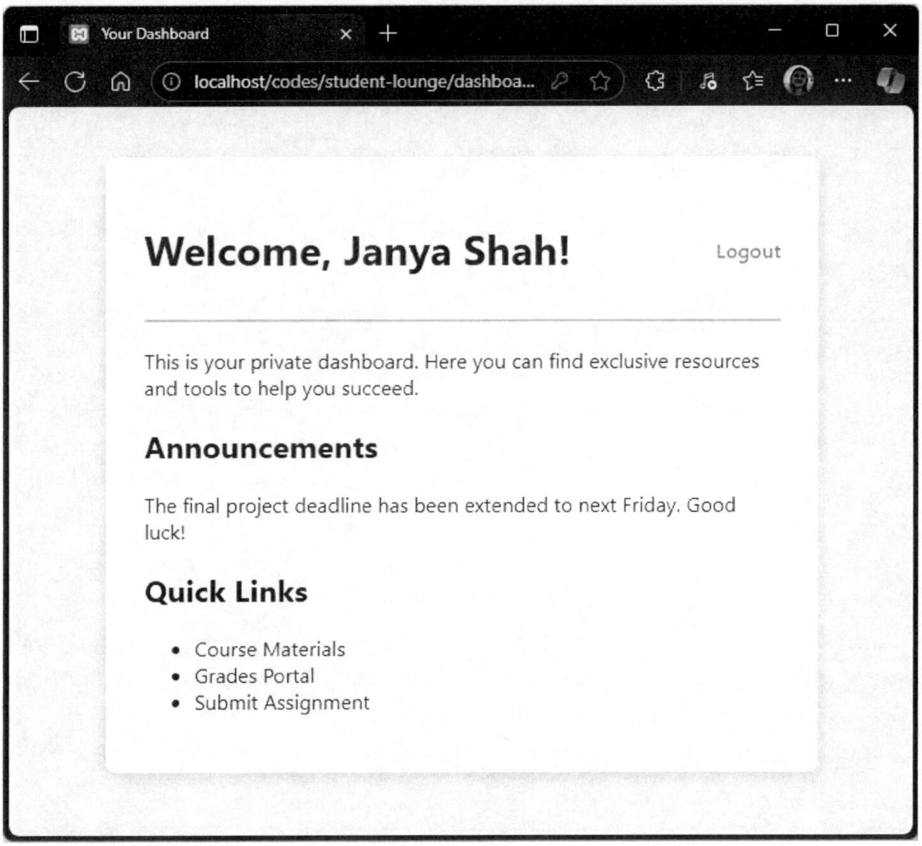

6. **Test Scenario 3:** Successful login (Dark Theme)
   - Click **Logout** on the dashboard. You are sent back to the login page.
   - Now, log in with the username **student2** and the password **dshah**.
   - You are redirected to the dashboard again. This time, it greets you with **Welcome, <Your Name>!** and the entire page uses the dark theme defined in our CSS.

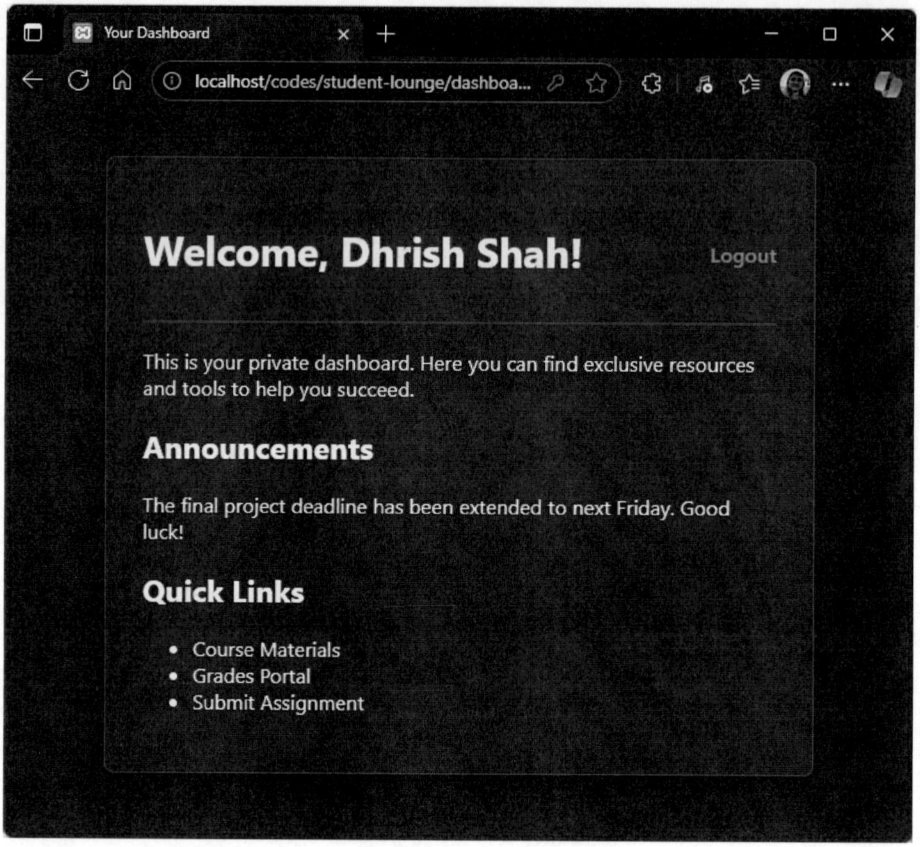

7. **Test Scenario 4:** Unauthorized access
   - Make sure you are logged out. You are on the login.php page.
   - Now, manually change the URL in your browser's address bar to **http://localhost/codes/student-lounge/dashboard.php** and press **Enter**.
   - Instead of seeing the dashboard, you are instantly redirected back to the login page. Our security guard (**!isset($_SESSION['username'])**) is working perfectly!

Exploring application behaviour: A practical run-through

Our application behaves intelligently in different situations:

- **Valid inputs:** When correct credentials are provided, the session is created, and the user gains access. The UI is personalized with their name and preferred theme, demonstrating a successful workflow.

- **Invalid inputs:** When incorrect credentials are used, the system does not crash. Instead, it provides clear, helpful feedback to the user (Invalid username or password.) without revealing *which* part was wrong (a good security practice).
- **Simulated multi-user environment:** By having two different users (student1 and student2) with different names and themes, we simulate how the application would serve multiple people. The session ensures that each user's data (name, theme) is kept separate, providing a unique experience for everyone.

Harnessing personalization in real-world contexts

The session-based personalization and access control you just built is one of the most fundamental and valuable skills in web development. This pattern is the foundation for:

- **E-commerce sites:** Remembering what's in a user's shopping cart and keeping them logged in as they browse.
- **Social media:** Displaying a personalized news feed and ensuring only you can post to your profile.
- **Online banking:** Protecting sensitive financial information and ensuring all activity is tied to a verified, logged-in user.
- **SaaS (Software as a Service) applications:** Providing access to paid features and personal project dashboards.

Mastering this concept means you can now build applications that don't just present information, but create secure, interactive, and personalized experiences.

Wrapping up

In this chapter, we combined our knowledge of functions, arrays, and sessions to build a complete, real-world application. You have taken a significant step from writing simple scripts to engineering a cohesive user experience.

- **Blueprint planning:** You learned to plan applications by defining features, user stories, and data needs.
- **Concept integration:** You saw how arrays, functions, and sessions work together to power a dynamic web app.
- **Access control:** You implemented a secure login system that protects pages from unauthorized access.
- **User personalization:** You used session data to display a user's name and dynamically change the website's theme.

- **Logout and security:** You built a secure logout mechanism that properly destroys the session.

Congratulations on completing the Student success lounge! You have successfully built a multi-page, secure, and personalized web application—a truly impressive accomplishment. You've proven that you can take individual PHP concepts and weave them together to create something functional and meaningful. This project serves as the capstone for our work with fundamental PHP structures.

However, our application currently relies on a hardcoded array for user data. This isn't scalable or practical for real-world use. What if we need thousands of users? Or what if we want to store more complex information? To solve that, we need a database.

In the next *Chapter 16: Database onboarding - Meet MySQL & phpMyAdmin*, you will learn how to store, retrieve, and manage data professionally using a powerful database system. Get ready to unlock the next level of web development!

Chapter 16

Section 05: Dynamic data - Databases and CRUD essentials

Database onboarding - Meet MySQL & phpMyAdmin

What you'll learn

- What databases are?
- Writing basic SQL
- Using phpMyAdmin
- Using MySQL
- Connecting PHP to MySQL
- Handling connection errors

Welcome to a pivotal moment in your web development journey. So far, we have built amazing things by storing information in files. While that works for simple applications like a personal diary, it has its limits. Imagine a website like Facebook or Amazon trying to manage millions of users and products using text files—it would be slow, chaotic, and insecure.

This chapter introduces the solution: databases. We move from simple file storage to a structured, powerful, and efficient way of managing data, paving the way for the complex and dynamic applications you are destined to build.

What is a database? Why use MySQL?

Think of a **database** as a highly organized digital filing cabinet. Instead of stuffing documents into random folders, a database uses a structured system of tables, rows, and columns to store information. This organization makes it incredibly fast to find, add, update, and remove data.

A **table** is like a single spreadsheet, dedicated to one type of information (e.g., users, products, or blog posts). Each **row** in the table represents a single item (one user, one product), and each **column** defines a specific piece of information about that item (name, email, price).

MySQL is a Relational DataBase Management System (RDBMS). It is the software that manages these databases. It's the most popular open-source database system in the world, especially for web applications. Why?

- **It's fast and reliable:** Built for speed and to handle large amounts of data without breaking a sweat.
- **It's free and open-source:** You can use it without paying any licensing fees.
- **It's secure:** It includes robust features to protect your data.
- **It works perfectly with PHP:** PHP has excellent built-in support for MySQL, making them a powerhouse duo for web development.

By learning to use a database like MySQL, you are unlocking the ability to build applications that can grow, manage complex information, and serve many users at once.

Installing and launching MySQL & phpMyAdmin

The great news is that if you have followed along and installed XAMPP as recommended in Chapter 2, you already have MySQL and a fantastic tool called **phpMyAdmin** installed. There is no need for a separate installation.

phpMyAdmin is a web-based graphical user interface for managing your MySQL databases. Instead of typing commands in a terminal, you can create databases, design tables, and manage data with a few clicks. It is the perfect tool for beginners.

Let's get them running.

1. Open the **XAMPP Control Panel**.
2. In the **Control Panel**, you see a list of modules. Find **Apache** and **MySQL**.
3. Click the **Start** button for **Apache**. It should turn green.

4. Click the **Start** button for **MySQL**. It should also turn green.

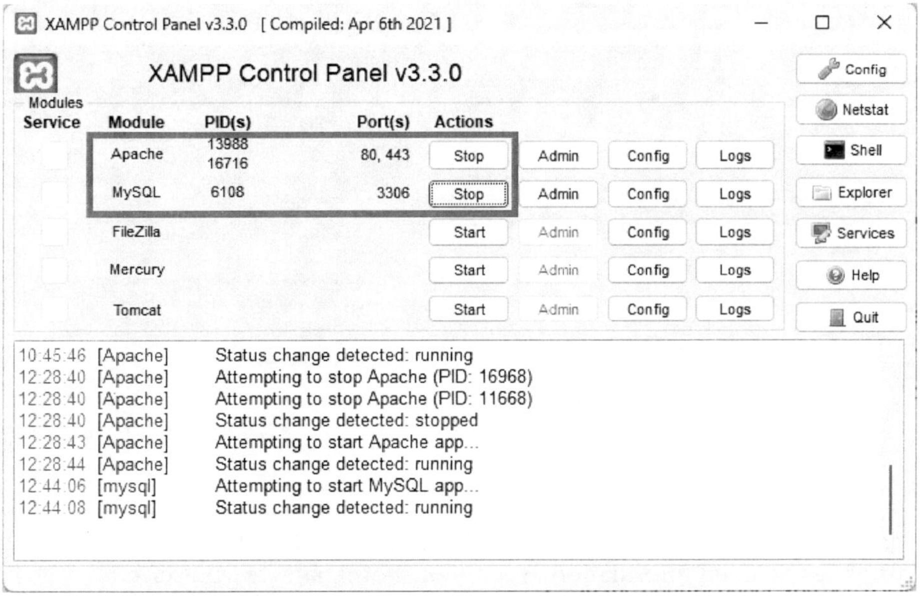

5. That's it! Your web server and database server are now running.

To access phpMyAdmin:

1. Open your web browser.
2. Navigate to the address **http://localhost/phpmyadmin/**.
3. You are now looking at the **phpMyAdmin dashboard**. This is your command center for everything related to your databases.

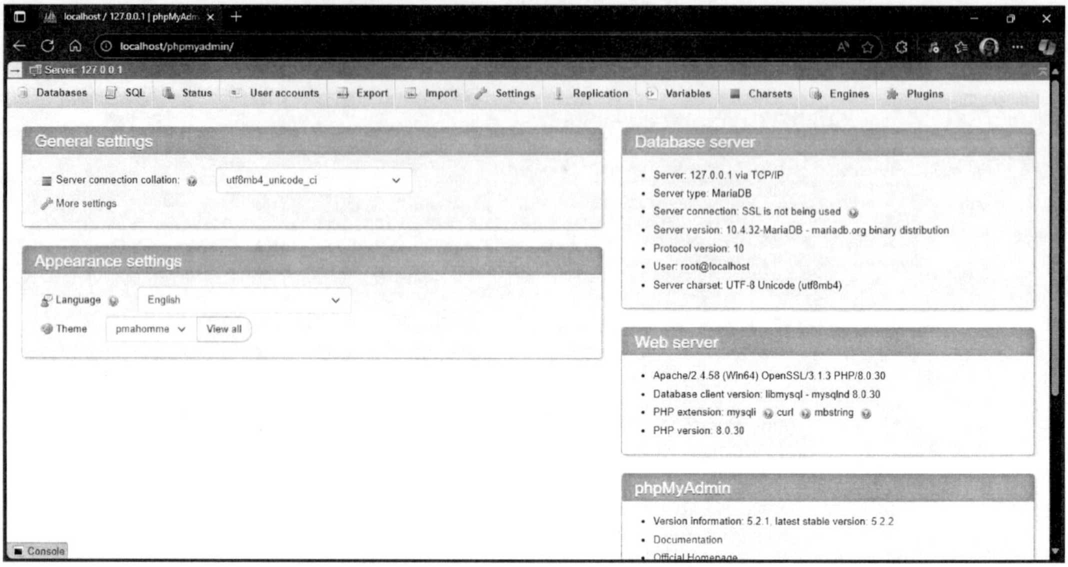

4. Take a moment to look around. On the left, you see a list of default databases. The main panel provides detailed information and options for whatever you select.

Basic SQL

SQL (Structured Query Language) is the language we use to talk to databases like MySQL. It is a standardized language for performing tasks like retrieving, adding, and managing data. With phpMyAdmin, you can run SQL queries directly.

Let's create a database for our upcoming projects.

1. In **phpMyAdmin**, click on the **Databases** tab at the top.

2. Under **Create database**, enter a name for our database. Let's call it **contact_app**.

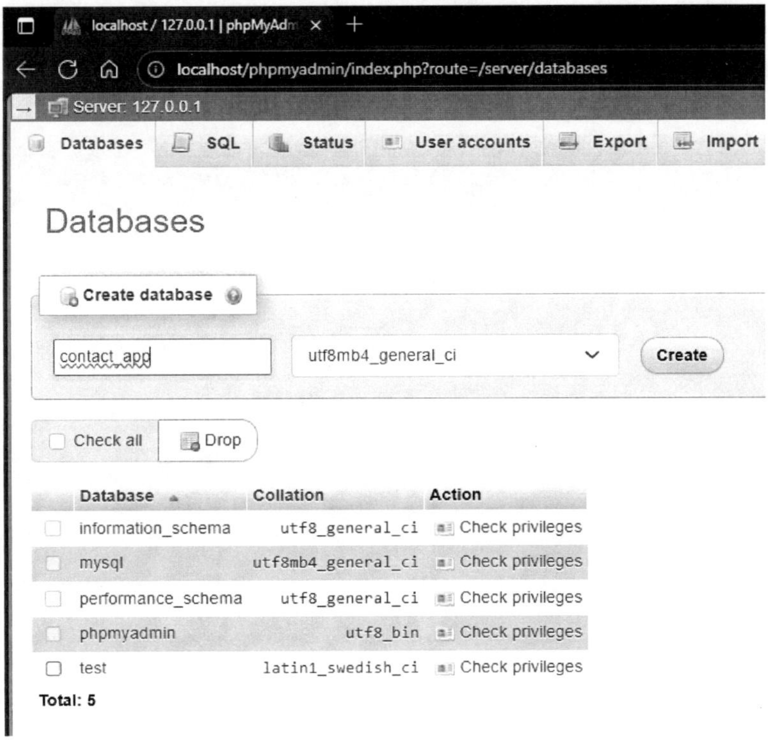

3. Leave the dropdown next to it as **utf8mb4_general_ci** (a standard character encoding) and click **Create**.

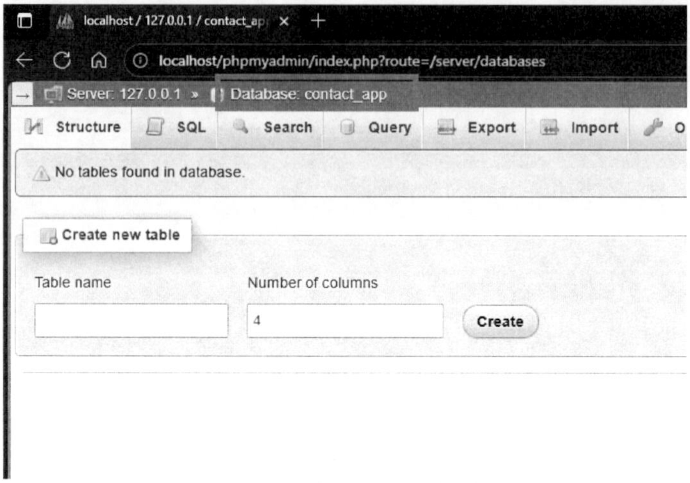

4. You have just executed your first command without writing any code! You can see **contact_app** on top. Click on it. phpMyAdmin now prompts you to create a table.

Let's explore the five fundamental SQL commands. Click on the **SQL** tab at the top of the main panel to get a query editor where you can type these commands.

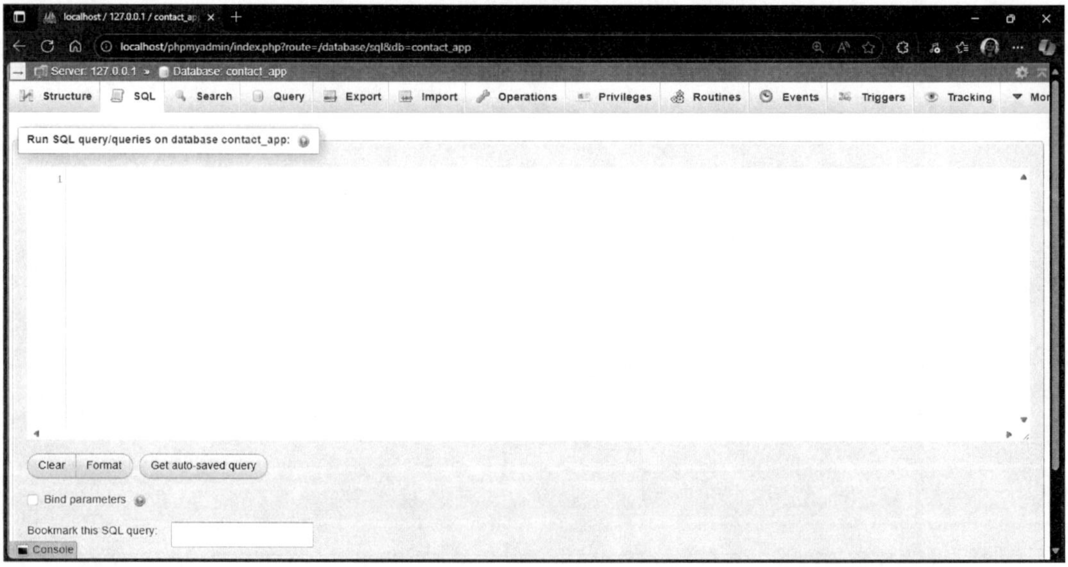

CREATE

The CREATE TABLE command builds the structure for our data. Let's create a contacts table with columns for an ID, name, email, and phone number:

```
CREATE TABLE contacts (
    id INT(11) AUTO_INCREMENT PRIMARY KEY,
    name VARCHAR(100) NOT NULL,
    email VARCHAR(100) NOT NULL,
    phone VARCHAR(50),
    created_at TIMESTAMP DEFAULT CURRENT_TIMESTAMP
);
```

Explanation

- **CREATE TABLE contacts:** This tells MySQL to create a new table named contacts.
- **id INT(11) AUTO_INCREMENT PRIMARY KEY:** Creates a column named id to hold an integer. It is the PRIMARY KEY, meaning it uniquely identifies each row. AUTO_INCREMENT tells MySQL to automatically assign a new, unique number for each record we add.
- **VARCHAR(100):** A variable-length string that can hold up to 100 characters.
- **NOT NULL:** This ensures that the name and email fields cannot be left empty.
- **TIMESTAMP DEFAULT CURRENT_TIMESTAMP:** This automatically records the date and time when a contact is created.

1. Select the **SQL** tab of the **contact_app** database.
2. Type the above table creation SQL into the **SQL** query box in **phpMyAdmin**, scroll the page down and click the **Go** button.
3. After running the query, phpMyAdmin confirms that the table was created.

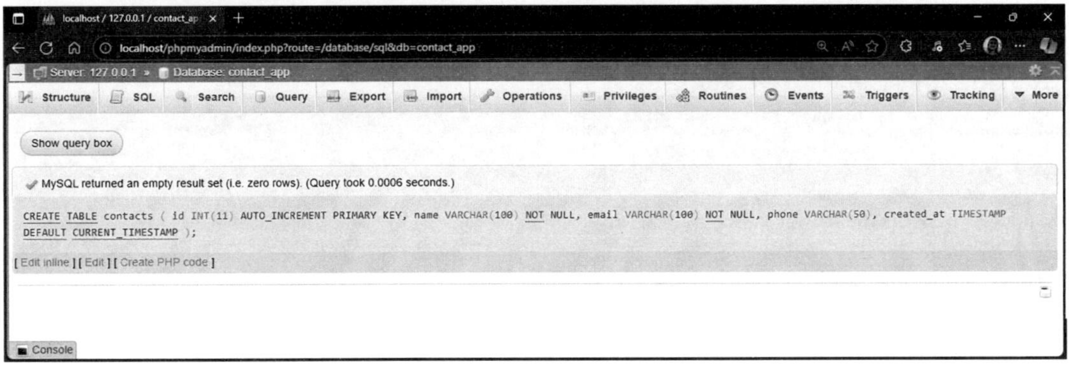

4. Click on the **Structure** tab to see your new table's design.

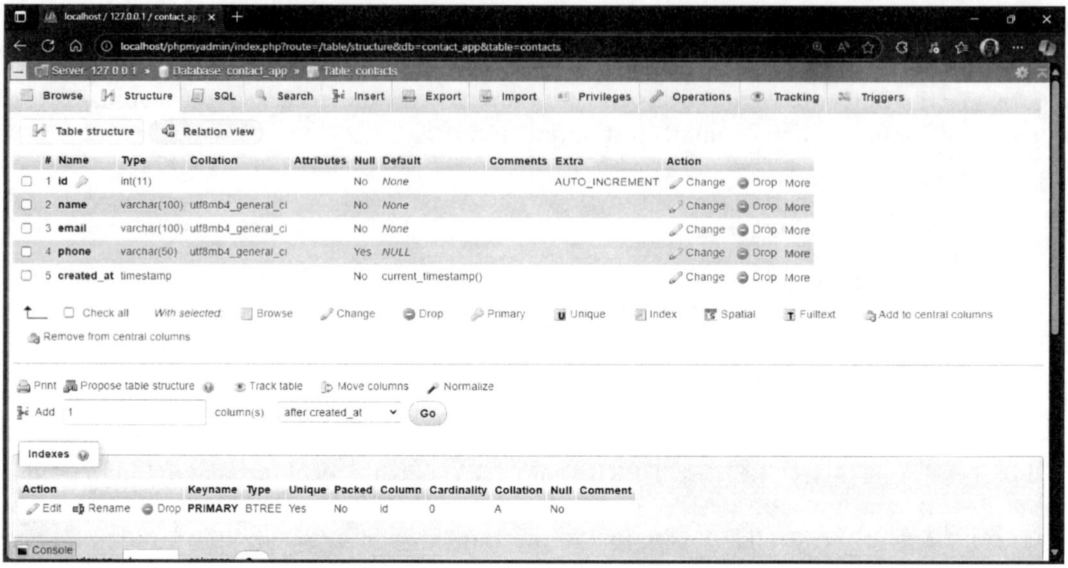

INSERT

The INSERT INTO command adds a new row of data to a table:

```
INSERT INTO contacts (name, email, phone)
VALUES ('Sharanam Shah', 'shah.shah@example.com', '123-456-7890');
```

Explanation

- **INSERT INTO contacts (...):** Specifies the table and the columns we are providing data for.
- **VALUES (...):** Provides the actual data. The values must be in the same order as the column names.

1. Run this query in the **SQL** tab.

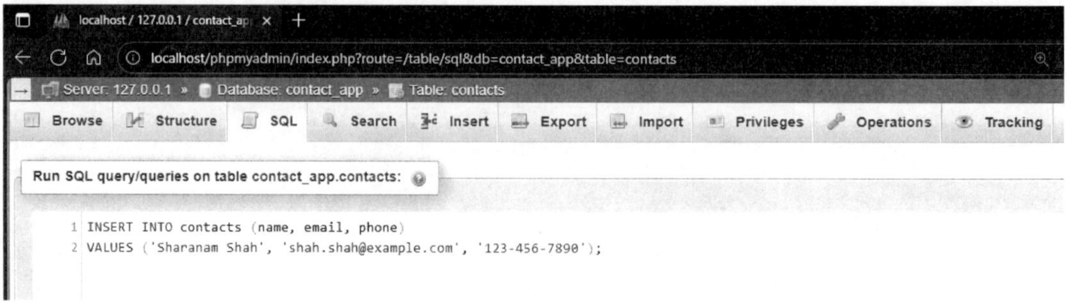

2. After running it, phpMyAdmin reports **1 row inserted**.

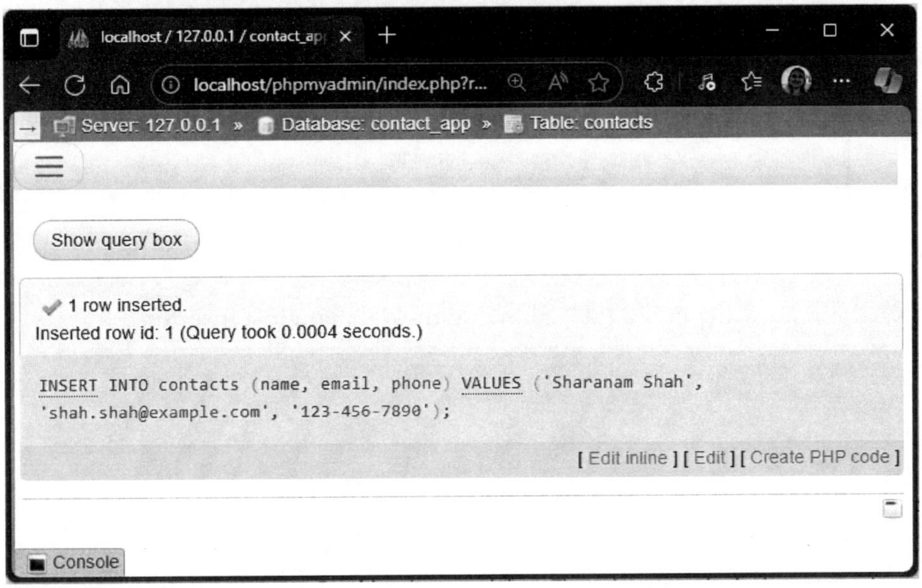

SELECT

The SELECT command retrieves data from a table. This is the command you will use most often:

```
SELECT id, name, email FROM contacts;
```

Explanation

- **SELECT id, name, email:** Specifies which columns you want to retrieve.
- **SELECT *:** A common shortcut to select *all* columns.
- **FROM contacts:** Specifies the table to retrieve data from.

1. Run this query.

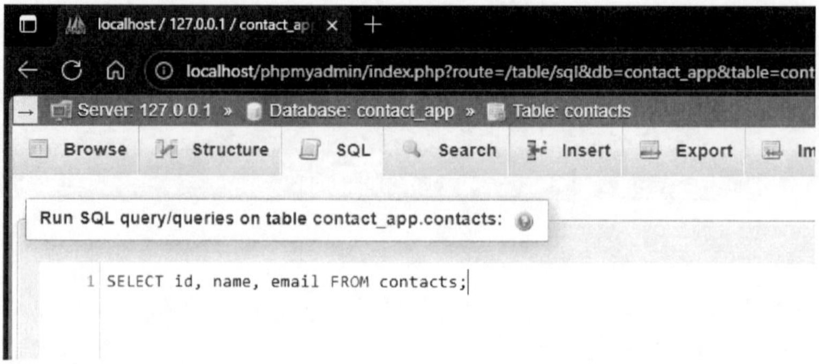

2. phpMyAdmin now displays a table showing the data you just inserted.

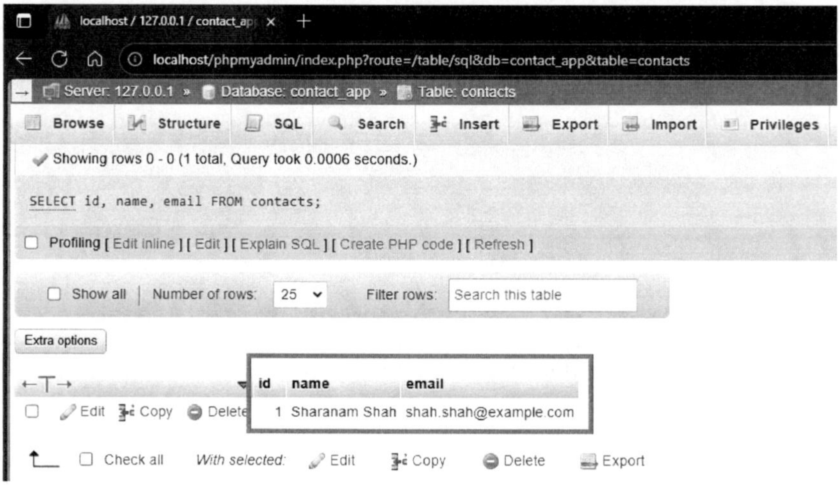

UPDATE

The UPDATE command modifies existing records. You must use a WHERE clause to specify *which* record to update, otherwise you will update all of them!

```
UPDATE contacts
SET phone = '987-654-3210'
WHERE name = 'Sharanam Shah';
```

Explanation

- **UPDATE contacts:** Specifies the table.
- **SET phone = '...':** The column and the new value to set.

- **WHERE name = 'Sharanam Shah':** This is the crucial part. It tells MySQL to only update the row where the name column has the value 'Sharanam Shah'.

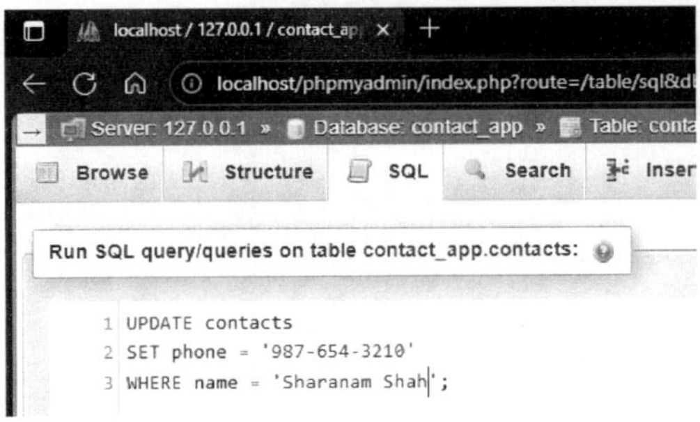

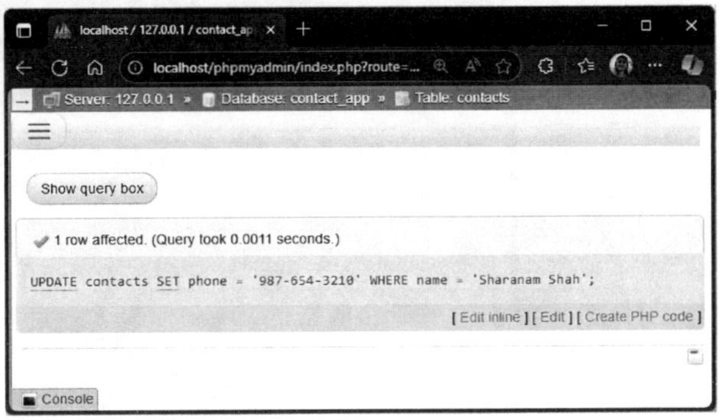

DELETE

The DELETE command removes records. Like UPDATE, it requires a WHERE clause to target specific rows:

```
DELETE FROM contacts
WHERE name = 'Sharanam Shah';
```

1. Run the query.

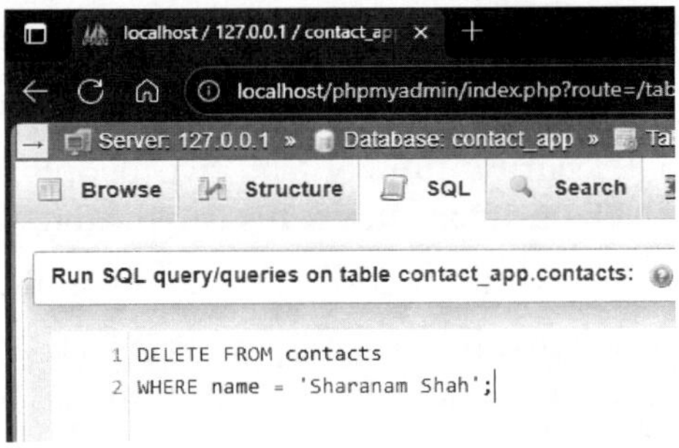

2. phpMyAdmin displays a dialog box to confirm whether you want to delete the record or not.

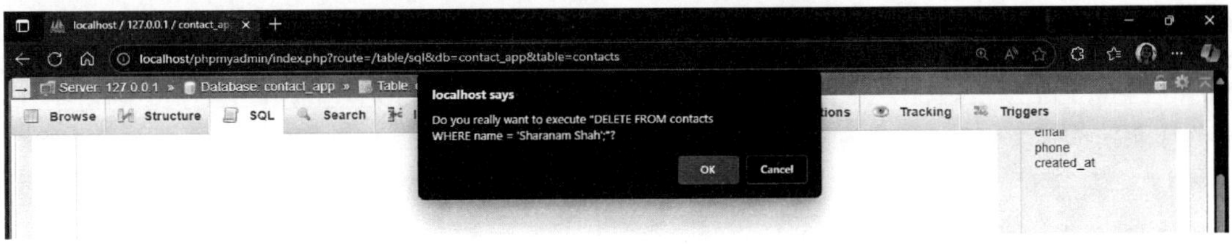

3. Click **OK**. The record is deleted.

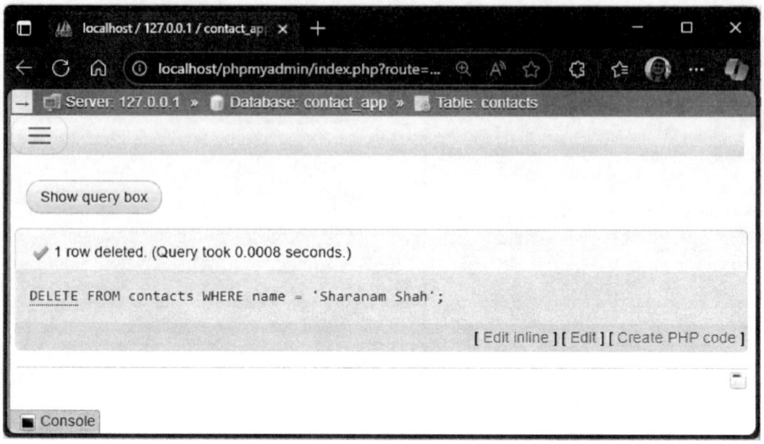

4. After running this, use the **SELECT * FROM contacts;** query again. The table will be empty.

Database structure

We already used PRIMARY KEY and AUTO_INCREMENT when creating our table, but let's formalize why they are so important.

A **Primary Key** is a constraint that uniquely identifies each record in a table. Think of it as a student ID number or a social security number—no two people have the same one. In our **contacts** table, the **id** column is the **primary key**. This is critical for a few reasons:

- **Uniqueness:** It guarantees that you can never have two identical rows.
- **Targeting:** It allows you to reliably UPDATE or DELETE a specific row without any ambiguity. WHERE id = 5 is much safer than WHERE name = 'John Doe', as there could be multiple people named John Doe.

Auto Increment is an attribute that you can apply to a numeric primary key. When you INSERT a new record without specifying a value for the id column, MySQL automatically assigns the next available integer. This saves you the trouble of figuring out what the last ID was and manually incrementing it. It is simple, foolproof, and highly recommended for primary keys.

Connecting PHP and MySQL

Now that we have a database, we need a way for our PHP scripts to communicate with it. PHP provides two main extensions for this:

- **mysqli (MySQL Improved):** This extension is specific to MySQL. It is relatively easy to learn and offers both a procedural style (using simple functions) and an object-oriented style. It is a great choice when you know you will only be using MySQL.
- **PDO (PHP Data Objects):** This is a more abstract and versatile extension. It provides a consistent interface for connecting to many different types of databases (MySQL, PostgreSQL, SQLite, etc.). If you write your code using PDO, you can switch your database system with minimal code changes. It is generally considered the modern standard, but has a slightly steeper learning curve.

For this chapter, we will use **mysqli** in its procedural form because its functions are very clear and easy for beginners to understand.

Here is the PHP code to connect to the contact_app database we created. Create a new folder **c:\xampp\htdocs\codes\db-test**. Inside it, create a file named **connect.php**:

```php
<?php
// Database credentials
$hostname = "localhost";
$username = "root";
$password = ""; // Default XAMPP password is empty
$database = "contact_app";
// Create a database connection
$conn = mysqli_connect($hostname, $username, $password, $database);
// Check the connection
if (!$conn) {
    die("Connection failed: " . mysqli_connect_error());
}
echo "Connected successfully to the database!";
mysqli_close($conn);  // Always close the connection when you're done
?>
```

Code explanation

- We define four variables to hold our connection details. For a default XAMPP setup, the username is **root** and there is no password.
- **mysqli_connect()** is the function that attempts to establish a connection. It returns a connection object if successful, or false if it fails.
- We use an **if** statement to check if the connection failed. **!$conn** is **true** if the connection variable is **false**.

- **die()** is a function that immediately stops the script and prints a message. We use **mysqli_connect_error()** to get the specific reason why the connection failed.
- If the script gets past the if block, it means the connection was a success.
- **mysqli_close()** is good practice to release the connection resources back to the server.

Save this file and navigate to **http://localhost/codes/db-test/connect.php** in your browser.

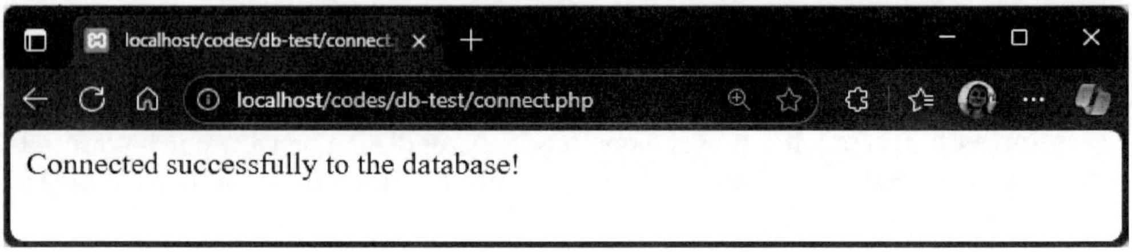

Handling connection errors and security

Our connect.php script already includes basic error handling with die("Connection failed: " . mysqli_connect_error()). This is crucial. Without it, if the database is offline or if you mistype a credential, your script would produce ugly PHP errors that could confuse users and potentially expose sensitive information about your server's file structure.

For example, if you change the database name to contact_app_wrong, you will see this output:

```
Connection failed: Unknown database 'contact_app_wrong'
```

This is a user-friendly error. It tells you exactly what is wrong without breaking the page layout or revealing system internals.

A note on Security:
In our example, we put the database password directly in the script. In a real-world application, this is risky. Best practice is to store credentials in a separate configuration file outside of the public web root (htdocs) and include it in your scripts. This prevents anyone from accessing it even if your server is misconfigured. For our learning purposes, keeping it in the script is fine.

Hands-on: Contact Book—Save/view contact info

It's time to put everything together. We will build a simple but fully functional **Contact Book** web application. This application allows a user to submit a contact's name, email, and phone number through a form. The data is saved to our MySQL database. Below the form, the application displays a neatly formatted table of all the contacts currently in the database.

This project perfectly demonstrates the **Create** and **Read** operations, which are the foundation of most web applications.

Building the application

Create the project folder

1. Navigate to your **c:\xampp\htdocs\codes** directory.
2. Create a new folder named **contact-book**.
3. All our files for this project will go inside this folder.

Create the database and table

1. If you skipped the earlier section, go to **http://localhost/phpmyadmin/**.
2. Create a database named **contact_app**.
3. Run the following SQL query to create the contacts table:

```
CREATE TABLE contacts (
    id INT(11) AUTO_INCREMENT PRIMARY KEY,
    name VARCHAR(100) NOT NULL,
    email VARCHAR(100) NOT NULL,
    phone VARCHAR(50),
    created_at TIMESTAMP DEFAULT CURRENT_TIMESTAMP
);
```

Create the main application file

Inside the **contact-book** folder, create a new file in VS Code and name it **index.php**. This single file will contain our HTML form, the PHP logic to handle form submissions, the database connection, and the logic to display the contacts.

Open index.php and add the following code into it:

```
<?php
// --- DATABASE CONNECTION ---
$hostname = "localhost";
$username = "root";
$password = "";
$database = "contact_app";
$conn = mysqli_connect($hostname, $username, $password, $database);
if (!$conn) {
    die("Connection failed: " . mysqli_connect_error());
}
// --- FORM HANDLING ---
$message = ""; // To store success or error messages
if ($_SERVER["REQUEST_METHOD"] == "POST") {
    // Check if form fields are not empty
    if (!empty($_POST['name']) && !empty($_POST['email'])) {
        $name = mysqli_real_escape_string($conn, $_POST['name']);
        $email = mysqli_real_escape_string($conn, $_POST['email']);
        $phone = mysqli_real_escape_string($conn, $_POST['phone']);
        $sql = "INSERT INTO contacts (name, email, phone) VALUES ('$name',
                '$email', '$phone')";
        if (mysqli_query($conn, $sql)) {
            $message = "New contact added successfully!";
        } else {
            $message = "Error: " . $sql . "<br>" . mysqli_error($conn);
        }
    } else {
        $message = "Name and Email are required fields.";
    }
}
// --- DATA FETCHING ---
$contacts = [];
$sql_select = "SELECT id, name, email, phone, created_at FROM contacts
               ORDER BY created_at DESC";
$result = mysqli_query($conn, $sql_select);
if (mysqli_num_rows($result) > 0) {
    while($row = mysqli_fetch_assoc($result)) {
        $contacts[] = $row;
    }
}
// Close connection at the end of the script
mysqli_close($conn);
?>
<!DOCTYPE html>
<html lang="en">
<head>
    <meta charset="UTF-8">
    <meta name="viewport" content="width=device-width, initial-scale=1.0">
    <title>Contact Book</title>
```

```
    <link rel="stylesheet" href="style.css">
</head>
<body>
    <div class="container">
        <h1>My Contact Book</h1>
        <div class="form-container">
            <h2>Add a New Contact</h2>
            <?php if (!empty($message)): ?>
                <p class="message"><?php echo $message; ?></p>
            <?php endif; ?>
            <form action="index.php" method="POST">
                <div class="form-group">
                    <label for="name">Name:</label>
                    <input type="text" id="name" name="name" required>
                </div>
                <div class="form-group">
                    <label for="email">Email:</label>
                    <input type="email" id="email" name="email" required>
                </div>
                <div class="form-group">
                    <label for="phone">Phone:</label>
                    <input type="text" id="phone" name="phone">
                </div>
                <button type="submit" class="btn">Add Contact</button>
            </form>
        </div>
        <div class="table-container">
            <h2>Saved Contacts</h2>
            <table>
                <thead>
                    <tr>
                        <th>Name</th>
                        <th>Email</th>
                        <th>Phone</th>
                        <th>Date Added</th>
                    </tr>
                </thead>
                <tbody>
                    <?php if (!empty($contacts)): ?>
                        <?php foreach ($contacts as $contact): ?>
                            <tr>
                                <td><?php echo htmlspecialchars($contact['name']);
                                    ?></td>
                                <td><?php echo htmlspecialchars($contact['email']);
                                    ?></td>
                                <td><?php echo htmlspecialchars($contact['phone']);
                                    ?></td>
                                <td><?php echo date("M d, Y", strtotime($contact[
                                    'created_at'])); ?></td>
                            </tr>
```

```
                        <?php endforeach; ?>
                    <?php else: ?>
                        <tr>
                            <td colspan="4">No contacts found.</td>
                        </tr>
                    <?php endif; ?>
                </tbody>
            </table>
        </div>
    </div>
</body>
</html>
```

Add the CSS for styling

Now, create a new file named **style.css** in the same contact-book folder. This will make our application look professional:

```
body {
    font-family: -apple-system, BlinkMacSystemFont, "Segoe UI", Roboto,
                 Helvetica, Arial, sans-serif;
    background-color: #f4f7f9;
    color: #333;
    line-height: 1.6;
    margin: 0;
    padding: 20px;
}
.container {
    max-width: 800px;
    margin: 0 auto;
    background: #fff;
    padding: 20px 30px;
    border-radius: 8px;
    box-shadow: 0 4px 10px rgba(0,0,0,0.1);
}
h1 {
    color: #2c3e50;
    text-align: center;
    margin-bottom: 20px;
}
h2 {
    color: #34495e;
    border-bottom: 2px solid #ecf0f1;
    padding-bottom: 10px;
    margin-top: 30px;
}
/* Form Styles */
.form-container {
```

```
    margin-bottom: 40px;
}
.form-group {
    margin-bottom: 15px;
}
label {
    display: block;
    margin-bottom: 5px;
    font-weight: bold;
}
input[type="text"], input[type="email"] {
    width: 100%;
    padding: 10px;
    border: 1px solid #ccc;
    border-radius: 4px;
    box-sizing: border-box; /* Important for padding */
}
.btn {
    display: inline-block;
    background-color: #3498db;
    color: #fff;
    padding: 10px 20px;
    border: none;
    border-radius: 4px;
    cursor: pointer;
    font-size: 16px;
    transition: background-color 0.3s ease;
}
.btn:hover {
    background-color: #2980b9;
}
.message {
    padding: 10px;
    background-color: #e8f5e9;
    color: #2e7d32;
    border: 1px solid #a5d6a7;
    border-radius: 4px;
    margin-bottom: 15px;
}
/* Table Styles */
.table-container {
    overflow-x: auto; /* For responsive behavior on small screens */
}
table {
    width: 100%;
    border-collapse: collapse;
    margin-top: 20px;
}
th, td {
    padding: 12px 15px;
    text-align: left;
```

```
    border-bottom: 1px solid #ddd;
}
thead th {
    background-color: #ecf0f1;
    color: #34495e;
    font-weight: bold;
}
tbody tr:nth-child(even) {
    background-color: #f9f9f9;
}
tbody tr:hover {
    background-color: #f1f1f1;
}
td[colspan="4"] {
    text-align: center;
    color: #777;
    padding: 20px;
}
```

Bridging the gap: Learned concepts and application implementation

Let's connect the PHP code in index.php to the concepts we learned.

- **Database connection (mysqli):** The code at the top of the script uses **mysqli_connect()** to establish communication with our contact_app database, exactly as we practiced.
- **Handling form submissions ($_POST):** The block **if ($_SERVER["REQUEST_METHOD"] == "POST")** checks if the user has submitted the form. This is the same technique we used in previous chapters to handle user input.
- **Creating data (SQL INSERT):** Inside the form handling block, we build an **INSERT** query. Notice the **mysqli_real_escape_string()** function. This is a vital security measure that "escapes" special characters in the user's input, helping to prevent a common attack called **SQL Injection**. We then run the query using **mysqli_query()**.
- **Reading data (SQL SELECT):** Further down, we define a **SELECT** query to get all contacts, ordered by the newest first (**ORDER BY created_at DESC**).
- **Fetching and displaying data:** We use a **while** loop with **mysqli_fetch_assoc($result)** to go through each row returned by our **SELECT** query. It converts each row into an associative array (e.g., $row['name']), which we store in a $contacts array. Finally, in the HTML part, we loop through the **$contacts** array with a **foreach** loop to build the table rows. **htmlspecialchars()** is another crucial security function that prevents XSS attacks by ensuring user input is displayed as plain text.

Running and testing

1. Ensure your **Apache** and **MySQL** modules are running in the **XAMPP Control Panel**.
2. Open your browser and navigate to **http://localhost/codes/contact-book/**.
3. You see the **My Contact Book** page with the form and an empty table that says **No contacts found**.

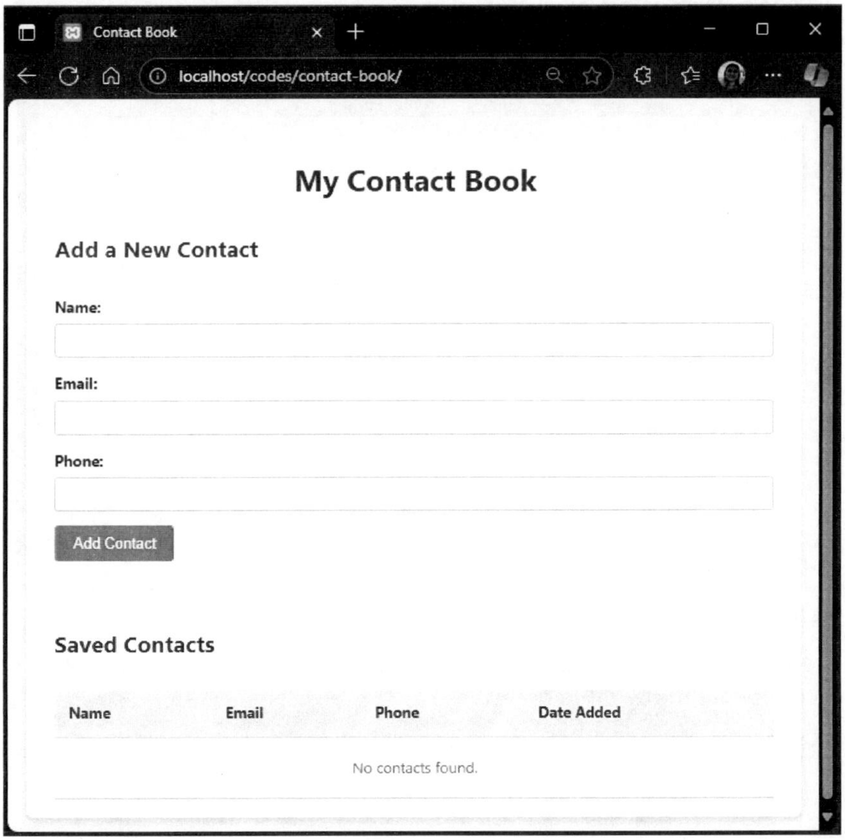

4. **Add a contact**: Fill in the form with a sample name, email, and phone number.

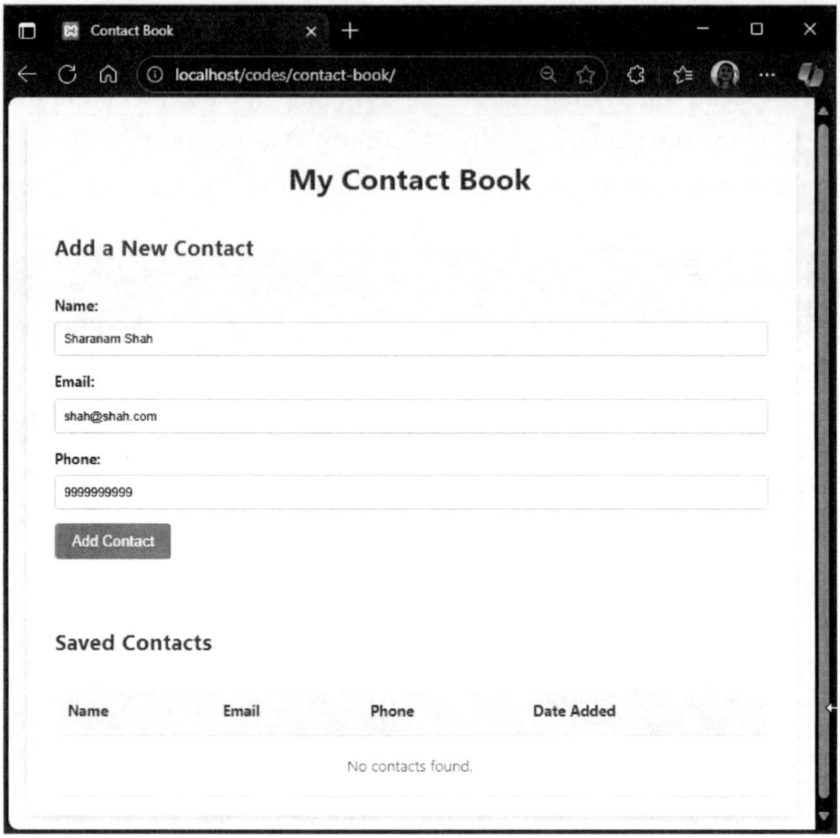

5. Click the **Add Contact** button.
6. The page reloads. You see the success message **New contact added successfully!** and your new contact appears in the table below.

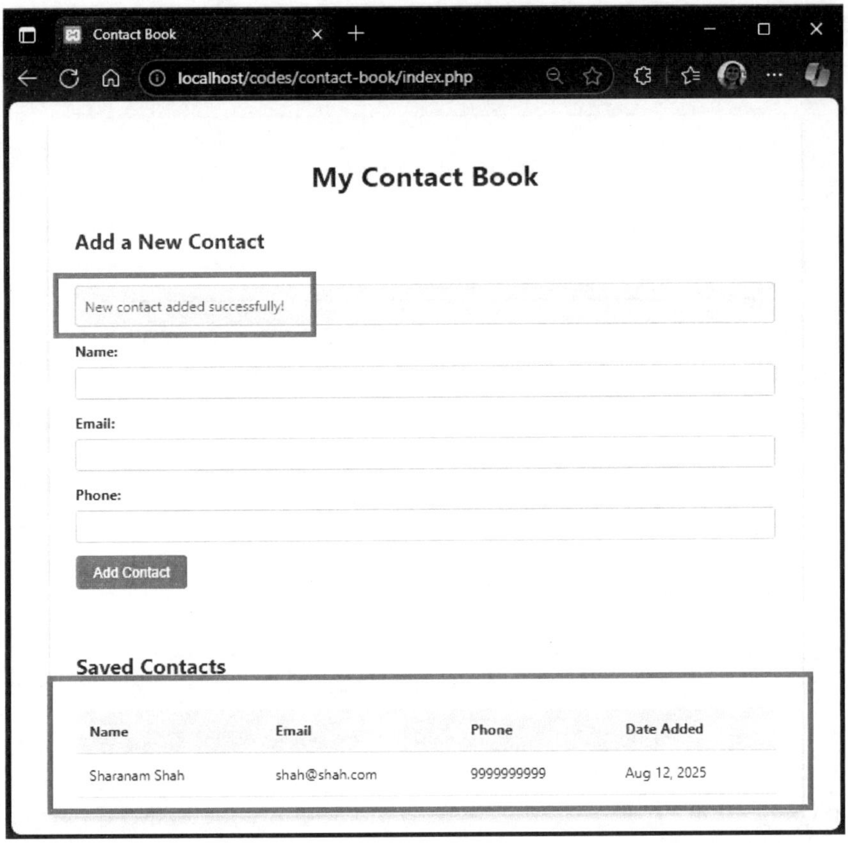

7. Add a few more contacts to see how the list grows. The newest ones will always appear at the top.

Exploring application behaviour: A practical run-through

- **Valid input:** When you provide a name and email and submit, the PHP script connects to MySQL, inserts the data, re-fetches the complete list, and displays it. The process is seamless.
- **Invalid input (Missing fields):** Try submitting the form with the **Name** field empty. The message **Please fill out this field**. appears, and the data is not inserted into the database. Our basic validation works.

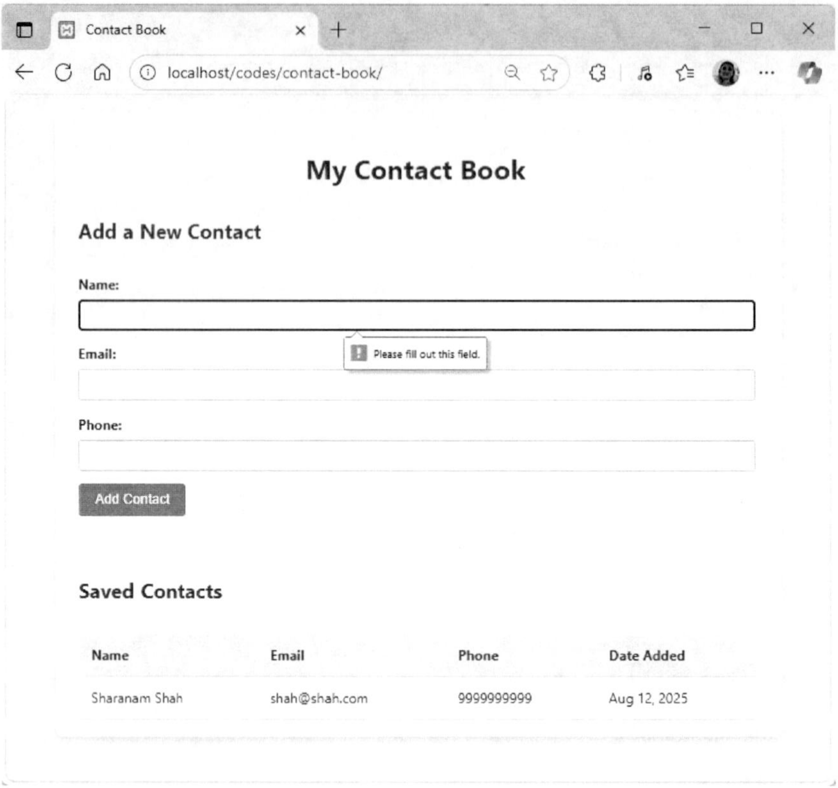

- **Database connection error:** Stop the MySQL module in your XAMPP panel and refresh the page. You will see an error message. This shows our error handling is effective. Remember to restart MySQL to get the app working again.

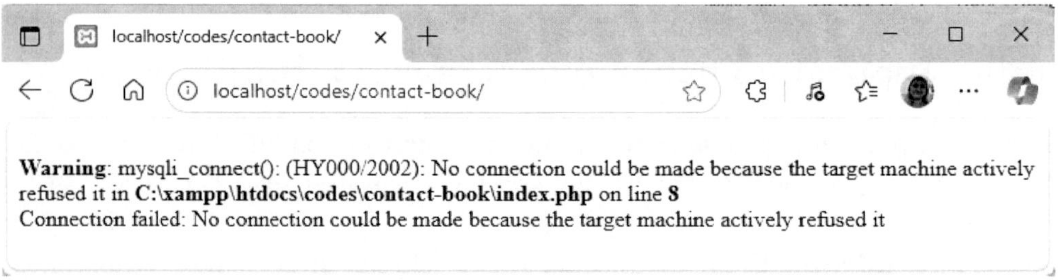

Harnessing database skills in real-world contexts

This simple Contact Book demonstrates a pattern used in almost every significant web application. A user registration system, an e-commerce product list, a blog's post archive, a comments section—they all boil down to this fundamental process of accepting user input, saving it to a structured database, and retrieving it for display. Mastering this workflow is one of the most important steps toward becoming a professional developer.

Wrapping up

This chapter was a giant leap forward. You have successfully transitioned from storing data in simple files to using a professional-grade database system. This skill is the key to building scalable, robust, and dynamic web applications.

- **Databases are organized:** They use tables, rows, and columns for efficient data management.
- **MySQL is the standard:** It is a powerful and free database choice for PHP applications.
- **phpMyAdmin is your friend:** It provides an easy-to-use web interface for managing your databases.
- **SQL is the language:** CREATE, INSERT, SELECT, UPDATE, and DELETE are the core commands.
- **PHP connects via mysqli:** The mysqli extension allows your scripts to talk to the database.
- **Error handling is critical:** Always check for connection failures to create robust applications.

Congratulations! You have successfully built your first database-driven web application. You learned how to design a data structure, write SQL to manipulate it, and connect everything with PHP to create a dynamic user experience. This is a massive milestone and a skill set that is highly valued in the industry.

You now understand how to create and read data. But what about updating and deleting it? In the next *Chapter 17: The CRUD experience - Putting data to work*, we will complete the picture by building the functionality to edit and remove records, giving you full control over your application's data.

Chapter 17

Section 05: Dynamic data – Databases and CRUD essentials

The CRUD experience - Putting data to work

What you'll learn

- CRUD operations
- Prepared statements
- Secure form handling
- Data update and deletion

Welcome back! In the previous chapter, we explored the world of databases, connecting PHP to MySQL and running our first SQL queries. We took a massive leap from storing data in temporary files to using a professional, scalable database system. Now, it's time to put that knowledge to work and build the interactive web applications that are the backbone of the internet.

This chapter is all about **CRUD**—the four fundamental operations that power almost every data-driven application you use, from social media to e-commerce. We will master the techniques to create, read, update, and delete data, transforming our static pages into dynamic and responsive experiences.

CRUD: Web's core interactions

CRUD is an acronym that stands for **Create**, **Read**, **Update**, and **Delete**. These are the four essential functions for managing data in any persistent storage system, like a database. Think about your favorite social media app:

- **Create:** You write a new post and click **Submit**. A new record is created in the database.
- **Read:** You scroll through your feed. The application reads post records from the database and displays them.
- **Update:** You spot a typo in your post and edit it. The application updates the existing record in the database.
- **Delete:** You decide you no longer want the post and delete it. The application removes the record from the database.

These four operations form a complete cycle for managing the lifecycle of any piece of data. In web development, we map these actions to user interactions, typically through HTML forms and links.

CRUD operation	SQL command	Typical web interaction
Create	INSERT	Submitting a "New User" or "Add Post" form.
Read	SELECT	Viewing a list of products, articles, or comments.
Update	UPDATE	Editing your user profile or changing an item in your cart.
Delete	DELETE	Removing a photo, a comment, or an account.

Mastering CRUD is not just about learning four operations; it's about understanding the fundamental pattern for building dynamic, interactive websites.

Creating form interfaces for CRUD

To allow users to create and update data, we need to provide them with an interface. The most common tool for this is the HTML <form>. A single form can be used for creating new records, while a slightly modified version, often pre-filled with existing data, is used for updating them.

Let's imagine a form for adding a new task to a to-do list:

```
<!DOCTYPE html>
<html lang="en">
<head>
    <meta charset="UTF-8">
    <title>Add a New Task</title>
</head>
```

```
<body>
    <h2>Add a New Task</h2>
    <form action="add_task.php" method="POST">
        <label for="task_name">Task Name:</label><br>
        <input type="text" id="task_name" name="task_name" required><br><br>
        <button type="submit">Add Task</button>
    </form>
</body>
</html>
```

This is a simple form for the **Create** operation. It sends the data entered into the **task_name** input field to a PHP script (add_task.php) using the POST method.

For the **Update** operation, the form is very similar, but it would be pre-populated with the task's current data. We would also need a hidden input field to keep track of which specific task we are editing, usually by its unique ID:

```
<!DOCTYPE html>
<html lang="en">
<head>
    <meta charset="UTF-8">
    <title>Edit Task</title>
</head>
<body>
    <h2>Edit Task</h2>
    <form action="update_task.php" method="POST">
        <input type="hidden" name="task_id" value="123"> <label for="task_name">
               Task Name:</label><br>
        <input type="text" id="task_name" name="task_name"
               value="My existing task name" required><br><br>
        <button type="submit">Update Task</button>
    </form>
</body>
</html>
```

Notice the two key differences: the hidden input with **name="task_id"** and the **value** attribute of the text input, which is filled with the data we are editing.

Prepared statements for secure input

When we accept user input and use it in database queries, we expose our application to a serious security risk called **SQL Injection**. An attacker could enter malicious SQL code into a form field, tricking our database into running unintended commands, like deleting all our data or exposing sensitive user information.

To prevent this, we must **never** insert user-provided data directly into our SQL strings. Instead, we use **prepared statements**.

A prepared statement is a pre-compiled SQL template. We send the template to the database server first, and then we send the user data separately. The database engine combines them safely, ensuring that user data is treated only as data, not as executable code.

Let's see how to safely INSERT data using mysqli with prepared statements.

```
<?php
// Assume $db is our mysqli connection object from the previous chapter.
// $db = new mysqli('localhost', 'root', '', 'my_database');
// 1. Get user input from the form (for demonstration) e.g., "Learn PHP prepared
// statements"
$task_name = $_POST['task_name'];
// 2. Prepare the SQL template with placeholders (?)
$sql = "INSERT INTO tasks (task_name) VALUES (?)";
$stmt = $db->prepare($sql);
if ($stmt === false) {
    die("Error preparing the statement: " . $db->error);
}
// 3. Bind the user data to the placeholder "s" means the data is a string.
$stmt->bind_param("s", $task_name);
// 4. Execute the statement
if ($stmt->execute()) {
    echo "New task created successfully!";
} else {
    echo "Error: " . $stmt->error;
}
// 5. Close the statement
$stmt->close();
?>
```

In this process:

- The SQL query contains a **?** placeholder instead of the actual user data.
- **$db->prepare()** sends this template to the database to be compiled.
- **$stmt->bind_param()** securely attaches the **$task_name** variable to the placeholder. The "**s**" tells the database to expect a string. If it were an integer, we would use "**i**".
- **$stmt->execute()** runs the query with the bound data.

This method completely neutralizes the threat of SQL injection for this query.

Updating and deleting records safely

Updating and deleting records also require prepared statements and, crucially, a WHERE clause to target the correct record. Without a WHERE clause, an UPDATE or DELETE query would affect **all rows** in the table! We always use the record's unique primary key (like task_id) to ensure we are modifying exactly one record.

Updating a record

Here's how to safely update a task's name using the task_id we passed in our hidden form field:

```
<?php
// Assume $db is our mysqli connection object. Assume we received data from our
// "Edit Task" form.
$task_id = $_POST['task_id']; // e.g., 123
$task_name = $_POST['task_name']; // e.g., "Finish Chapter 17"
// Prepare the statement
$sql = "UPDATE tasks SET task_name = ? WHERE id = ?";
$stmt = $db->prepare($sql);
if ($stmt === false) {
    die("Error preparing statement: " . $db->error);
}
// Bind parameters. "si" means string first, then integer.
$stmt->bind_param("si", $task_name, $task_id);
// Execute and check for success
if ($stmt->execute()) {
    echo "Task updated successfully!";
} else {
    echo "Error updating task: " . $stmt->error;
}
$stmt->close();
?>
```

Deleting a record

Deleting is even simpler. We only need to bind the id of the record we want to remove. A delete action is often triggered by a link or button, not a full form. For security, it's best to use a form with a POST request to prevent accidental deletion from search engine crawlers or other automated tools:

```
<?php
// Assume $db is our mysqli connection object. Assume we received the ID from a
// POST request.
$task_id_to_delete = $_POST['task_id']; // e.g., 123
```

```
// Prepare the statement
$sql = "DELETE FROM tasks WHERE id = ?";
$stmt = $db->prepare($sql);
if ($stmt === false) {
    die("Error preparing statement: " . $db->error);
}
// Bind the ID. "i" means integer.
$stmt->bind_param("i", $task_id_to_delete);
// Execute and check for success
if ($stmt->execute()) {
    echo "Task deleted successfully!";
} else {
    echo "Error deleting task: " . $stmt->error;
}
$stmt->close();
?>
```

Pagination for larger data sets

Imagine a blog with thousands of articles or a store with thousands of products. If we tried to SELECT and display all of them on a single page, the page would take forever to load and be impossible for a user to navigate.

Pagination is the solution. It is the process of dividing a large set of results into smaller, manageable pages. To implement it, we need two key pieces of information:

- **Results per page:** How many items we want to show at once (e.g., 10).
- **Current page number:** Which page the user is currently viewing (e.g., page 3).

In SQL, we achieve this with the LIMIT and OFFSET clauses:

- **LIMIT** specifies the maximum number of rows to return.
- **OFFSET** specifies how many rows to skip before starting to return rows.

The formula to calculate the offset is:

```
($current_page - 1) * $results_per_page
```

Let's say we want to show 10 results per page and the user is on page 3:

- **LIMIT** will be 10.
- **OFFSET** will be (3 - 1) * 10 = 20.

Our query would be:

```
SELECT * FROM tasks LIMIT 10 OFFSET 20;
```

This query skips the first 20 tasks and returns the next 10 (tasks 21 through 30). This is exactly what we need for the third page of our results.

Reusable CRUD functions and error handling

As our application grows, we will find ourselves writing the same prepared statement logic over and over. This is a perfect opportunity to create **reusable functions**. By wrapping our CRUD logic in functions, we make our main code cleaner, easier to read, and much simpler to maintain. If we need to change how we connect to the database, we only have to change it in one place.

Let's refactor our previous examples into a set of functions:

```php
<?php
// Function to get all tasks (could be modified for pagination)
function getAllTasks($db) {
    $sql = "SELECT id, task_name, created_at FROM tasks
            ORDER BY created_at DESC";
    $result = $db->query($sql);
    return $result->fetch_all(MYSQLI_ASSOC);
}
// Function to add a new task
function addTask($db, $task_name) {
    $sql = "INSERT INTO tasks (task_name) VALUES (?)";
    $stmt = $db->prepare($sql);
    $stmt->bind_param("s", $task_name);
    return $stmt->execute(); // Returns true on success, false on failure
}
// Function to get a single task by its ID
function getTaskById($db, $id) {
    $sql = "SELECT id, task_name FROM tasks WHERE id = ?";
    $stmt = $db->prepare($sql);
    $stmt->bind_param("i", $id);
    $stmt->execute();
    $result = $stmt->get_result();
    return $result->fetch_assoc(); // Returns the task or null if not found
}
// Function to update a task
function updateTask($db, $id, $task_name) {
    $sql = "UPDATE tasks SET task_name = ? WHERE id = ?";
    $stmt = $db->prepare($sql);
    $stmt->bind_param("si", $task_name, $id);
    return $stmt->execute();
}
```

```
// Function to delete a task
function deleteTask($db, $id) {
    $sql = "DELETE FROM tasks WHERE id = ?";
    $stmt = $db->prepare($sql);
    $stmt->bind_param("i", $id);
    return $stmt->execute();
}
?>
```

Now, in our main application file, instead of writing out the full prepared statement logic, we can simply call these functions. For example, to add a task, we would just write:

```
addTask($db, $_POST['task_name']);
```

This approach dramatically simplifies our main application logic and separates concerns, which is a core principle of good software design.

Hands-on: Task manager

It's time to put all this theory into practice! We are going to build a complete, single-page **Task manager** application. This app will allow us to create, read, update, and delete tasks from a database. We will build the interface, write the PHP logic to handle all four CRUD operations, and add some nice CSS for user feedback messages.

Building the application

Follow these steps carefully to build the Task Manager from the ground up.

Set up the database and table

First, we need a place to store our tasks.

1. Open your **XAMPP Control Panel** and ensure **Apache** and **MySQL** are running.
2. Navigate to **http://localhost/phpmyadmin** in your browser.
3. Click on the **Databases** tab.
4. In the **Create database** input field, type **task_manager_db** and click **Create**.
5. Click on the new **task_manager_db** database in the left-hand sidebar.
6. Click on the **SQL** tab.

7. Copy and paste the following SQL code into the text area and click **Go**:

```
CREATE TABLE tasks (
  id int(11) NOT NULL AUTO_INCREMENT,
  task_name varchar(255) NOT NULL,
  created_at timestamp NOT NULL DEFAULT current_timestamp(),
  PRIMARY KEY (id)
) ENGINE=InnoDB DEFAULT CHARSET=utf8mb4 COLLATE=utf8mb4_general_ci;
```

This creates a **tasks** table with three columns:

- A unique **id** that increments automatically
- The **task_name**, and
- A **created_at** timestamp that defaults to the current time

Create the project structure

Now, let's create the folder and files for our project in **VS Code**.

1. Open **VS Code**.
2. Click **File → Open Folder**.
3. Navigate to your XAMPP installation directory, and open the **htdocs\codes** folder (usually C:/xampp/htdocs/codes).
4. Create a new folder named **task-manager**. Select this folder to open it in **VS Code**.
5. Inside the **task-manager** folder, create three new files:
   - db.php (for our database connection)
   - index.php (our main application file)
   - style.css (for our styling)

Your project structure should look like this:

```
/htdocs/codes
└── /task-manager
    ├── db.php
    ├── index.php
    └── style.css
```

Create the database connection

Open **db.php** and add the following code. This script will connect to our new database and will be included in our main file:

```
<?php
```

```
// Database connection details
$hostname = 'localhost';
$username = 'root'; // Default XAMPP username
$password = '';     // Default XAMPP password
$database = 'task_manager_db';
// Create a new mysqli connection
$db = new mysqli($hostname, $username, $password, $database);
// Check for a connection error
if ($db->connect_error) {
    die("Connection failed: " . $db->connect_error);
}
?>
```

Build the main application

This is where all the magic happens. We will write the PHP to handle form submissions and the HTML to display the interface. Open index.php and add the following code:

```
<?php
// Include the database connection
require_once 'db.php';
// Initialize variables for messaging and editing
$message = '';
$message_type = '';
$task_to_edit = null;
$edit_mode = false;
// --- LOGIC FOR HANDLING ACTIONS (CREATE, UPDATE, DELETE) ---
// Handle DELETE request
if (isset($_POST['delete_task'])) {
    $id_to_delete = $_POST['task_id'];
    $sql = "DELETE FROM tasks WHERE id = ?";
    $stmt = $db->prepare($sql);
    $stmt->bind_param("i", $id_to_delete);
    if ($stmt->execute()) {
        $message = "Task deleted successfully!";
        $message_type = "success";
    } else {
        $message = "Error deleting task.";
        $message_type = "error";
    }
    $stmt->close();
}
// Handle EDIT request (to fetch the task)
if (isset($_POST['edit_task'])) {
    $edit_mode = true;
    $id_to_edit = $_POST['task_id'];
    $sql = "SELECT id, task_name FROM tasks WHERE id = ?";
    $stmt = $db->prepare($sql);
```

```
    $stmt->bind_param("i", $id_to_edit);
    $stmt->execute();
    $result = $stmt->get_result();
    $task_to_edit = $result->fetch_assoc();
    $stmt->close();
}
// Handle form submission for CREATE or UPDATE
if (isset($_POST['submit_task'])) {
    $task_name = trim($_POST['task_name']);
    if (empty($task_name)) {
        $message = "Task name cannot be empty.";
        $message_type = "error";
    } else {
        // If in edit mode, UPDATE the task
        if (isset($_POST['edit_id']) && !empty($_POST['edit_id'])) {
            $id_to_update = $_POST['edit_id'];
            $sql = "UPDATE tasks SET task_name = ? WHERE id = ?";
            $stmt = $db->prepare($sql);
            $stmt->bind_param("si", $task_name, $id_to_update);
            if ($stmt->execute()) {
                $message = "Task updated successfully!";
                $message_type = "success";
            } else {
                $message = "Error updating task.";
                $message_type = "error";
            }
            $stmt->close();
        } else {
            // Otherwise, CREATE a new task
            $sql = "INSERT INTO tasks (task_name) VALUES (?)";
            $stmt = $db->prepare($sql);
            $stmt->bind_param("s", $task_name);
            if ($stmt->execute()) {
                $message = "New task added successfully!";
                $message_type = "success";
            } else {
                $message = "Error adding task.";
                $message_type = "error";
            }
            $stmt->close();
        }
    }
    // Redirect to clear POST data and prevent form resubmission
    header("Location: index.php?message=" . urlencode($message) . "&type=" .
            $message_type);
    exit();
}
// Check for messages from redirect
if (isset($_GET['message'])) {
    $message = $_GET['message'];
```

```
    $message_type = $_GET['type'];
}
// --- LOGIC FOR READING TASKS ---
$tasks_result = $db->query("SELECT id, task_name, created_at FROM tasks
                            ORDER BY created_at DESC");
?>
<!DOCTYPE html>
<html lang="en">
<head>
    <meta charset="UTF-8">
    <meta name="viewport" content="width=device-width, initial-scale=1.0">
    <title>Task Manager</title>
    <link rel="stylesheet" href="style.css">
</head>
<body>
    <div class="container">
        <h1>Task Manager</h1>
        <?php if (!empty($message)): ?>
            <div class="message <?php echo $message_type; ?>">
               <?php echo htmlspecialchars($message); ?></div>
        <?php endif; ?>
        <form action="index.php" method="POST" class="task-form">
            <?php if ($edit_mode): ?>
                <input type="hidden" name="edit_id"
                       value="<?php echo $task_to_edit['id']; ?>">
            <?php endif; ?>
                 <input type="text" name="task_name" class="task-input"
                        placeholder="Enter a new task" value="<?php echo
                        $edit_mode ? htmlspecialchars($task_to_edit['task
                        _name']) : ''; ?>" required>
            <button type="submit" name="submit_task" class="btn submit-btn">
                <?php echo $edit_mode ? 'Update Task' : 'Add Task'; ?>
            </button>
        </form>
        <table class="task-table">
            <thead>
                <tr>
                    <th>Task</th>
                    <th>Added On</th>
                    <th>Actions</th>
                </tr>
            </thead>
            <tbody>
                <?php while ($row = $tasks_result->fetch_assoc()): ?>
                <tr>
                    <td><?php echo htmlspecialchars($row['task_name']); ?></td>
                    <td><?php echo date('M d, Y', strtotime($row['created
                                        _at'])); ?></td>
                    <td class="actions">
                        <form action="index.php" method="POST"
```

```
                                    style="display:inline;">
                                <input type="hidden" name="task_id"
                                       value="<?php echo $row['id']; ?>">
                                <button type="submit" name="edit_task"
                                        class="btn edit-btn">Edit</button>
                            </form>
                            <form action="index.php" method="POST"
                                    style="display:inline;">
                                <input type="hidden" name="task_id"
                                       value="<?php echo $row['id']; ?>">
                                <button type="submit" name="delete_task" class="btn
                                        delete-btn" onclick="return confirm('Are you
                                        you sure you want to delete this task?');">
                                        Delete</button>
                            </form>
                        </td>
                    </tr>
                    <?php endwhile; ?>
                </tbody>
            </table>
        </div>
</body>
</html>
<?php
// Close the database connection
$db->close();
?>
```

Code explanation

- **PHP logic block:** The top section handles all the logic. It checks which button was pressed (**Add Task**, **Update Task**, **Edit**, or **Delete**) by looking at the **$_POST superglobal**. Based on the action, it prepares and executes the correct SQL query (INSERT, UPDATE, or DELETE).
- **Redirection:** After creating or updating a task, the line **header("Location: index.php?...");** is very important. It redirects the user back to the main page. This is a common pattern called **Post/Redirect/Get (PRG)** that prevents the same form from being submitted again if the user refreshes the page. The feedback message is passed as a URL parameter.
- **Read logic:** The line **$tasks_result = $db->query(...)** fetches all existing tasks from the database so we can display them.
- **Feedback message:** The **div** with the **class message** only appears if a **$message** variable is set, showing the user a success or error message.
- **Dynamic form:** The form cleverly adapts for both creating and editing. If **$edit_mode** is **true**, it includes a hidden input with the task's ID and changes the button text to **Update Task**. The input field is also pre-filled with the task name.

- **Task table:** A **while** loop iterates through the **$tasks_result** and creates a new table row <tr> for each task. **htmlspecialchars()** is used to prevent XSS attacks by ensuring any HTML in the task name is displayed as text, not rendered by the browser.
- **Action buttons:** Each row has its own tiny form for the **Edit** and **Delete** buttons. This is a secure way to pass the specific **task_id** for the action using the **POST** method. The delete button also includes a JavaScript confirmation dialog **(onclick="...")** as a simple safety measure.

Add the CSS for styling

Finally, let's make our application look good. Open **style.css** and add the following code. This CSS will style the container, form, table, buttons, and our special feedback messages:

```
body {
    font-family: -apple-system, BlinkMacSystemFont, "Segoe UI", Roboto,
                 "Helvetica Neue", Arial, sans-serif;
    background-color: #f4f7f6;
    color: #333;
    margin: 0;
    padding: 20px;
}
.container {
    max-width: 800px;
    margin: 40px auto;
    padding: 30px;
    background-color: #fff;
    border-radius: 12px;
    box-shadow: 0 4px 15px rgba(0, 0, 0, 0.1);
}
h1 {
    text-align: center;
    color: #2c3e50;
    margin-bottom: 30px;
}
/* --- Feedback Messages --- */
.message {
    padding: 15px;
    margin-bottom: 20px;
    border-radius: 8px;
    font-size: 16px;
    text-align: center;
    border: 1px solid transparent;
}
.message.success {
    background-color: #d4edda;
    color: #155724;
    border-color: #c3e6cb;
```

```
}
.message.error {
    background-color: #f8d7da;
    color: #721c24;
    border-color: #f5c6cb;
}
/* --- Task Form --- */
.task-form {
    display: flex;
    margin-bottom: 30px;
    gap: 10px;
}
.task-input {
    flex-grow: 1;
    padding: 12px 15px;
    font-size: 16px;
    border: 2px solid #ddd;
    border-radius: 8px;
    transition: border-color 0.3s;
}
.task-input:focus {
    outline: none;
    border-color: #3498db;
}
/* --- Buttons --- */
.btn {
    padding: 12px 20px;
    border: none;
    border-radius: 8px;
    font-size: 16px;
    font-weight: bold;
    color: #fff;
    cursor: pointer;
    transition: background-color 0.3s, transform 0.2s;
}
.btn:hover {
    transform: translateY(-2px);
}
.submit-btn {
    background-color: #2980b9;
}
.submit-btn:hover {
    background-color: #3498db;
}
.edit-btn {
    background-color: #f39c12;
    padding: 6px 12px;
    font-size: 14px;
}
.edit-btn:hover {
```

```
    background-color: #f1c40f;
}
.delete-btn {
    background-color: #c0392b;
    padding: 6px 12px;
    font-size: 14px;
}
.delete-btn:hover {
    background-color: #e74c3c;
}
/* --- Task Table --- */
.task-table {
    width: 100%;
    border-collapse: collapse;
}
.task-table th, .task-table td {
    padding: 15px;
    text-align: left;
    border-bottom: 1px solid #eee;
}
.task-table th {
    background-color: #ecf0f1;
    font-weight: bold;
    color: #34495e;
}
.task-table tr:last-child td {
    border-bottom: none;
}
.task-table tr:hover {
    background-color: #f9f9f9;
}
.task-table .actions {
    text-align: right;
}
```

Bridging the gap: Learned concepts and application implementation

Let's connect what we just built to the concepts from earlier in the chapter.

- **Create:** Our **if (isset($_POST['submit_task']))** block handles the "Create" operation. When the form is submitted without an **edit_id**, it runs an **INSERT** query using a prepared statement to safely add the new task.
- **Read:** The **SELECT** query right before the HTML begins is our "Read" operation. It fetches all tasks, and the **while** loop in the <tbody> displays them in the table.

- **Update:** The logic for "Update" has two parts. First, clicking the **Edit** button triggers a **SELECT** query to fetch the specific task and pre-fill the form. Second, submitting that form triggers the **UPDATE** query (inside the **submit_task** block) to save the changes, using a prepared statement and a **WHERE** clause.
- **Delete:** Clicking the **Delete** button submits a form that triggers the **DELETE** query, using a prepared statement with a **WHERE id = ?** clause to ensure only the correct task is removed.
- **Secure input:** Every single query that involves user-provided data (INSERT, UPDATE, DELETE) uses prepared statements ($db->prepare(), $stmt->bind_param(), $stmt->execute()) to prevent SQL injection.
- **Form interfaces:** We used a single, dynamic HTML form for both creating and updating data, improving code reuse and maintainability.

Running and testing

Now for the rewarding part—seeing our application in action!

1. Ensure your **XAMPP** server (Apache and MySQL) is running.
2. Open your web browser and navigate to **http://localhost/codes/task-manager/**.
3. You see the **Task Manager** heading and an empty table.

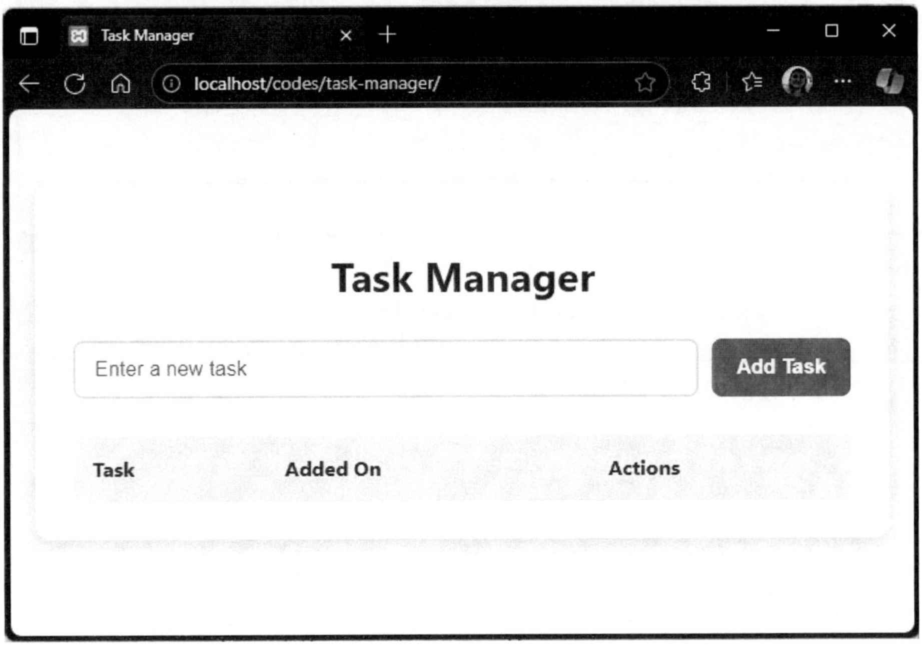

4. **Test the Create operation:**
   - In the input field, type **Finish my first CRUD app** and click the **Add Task** button.
   - The page refreshes, and you see a green success message and your new task now appears in the table below.

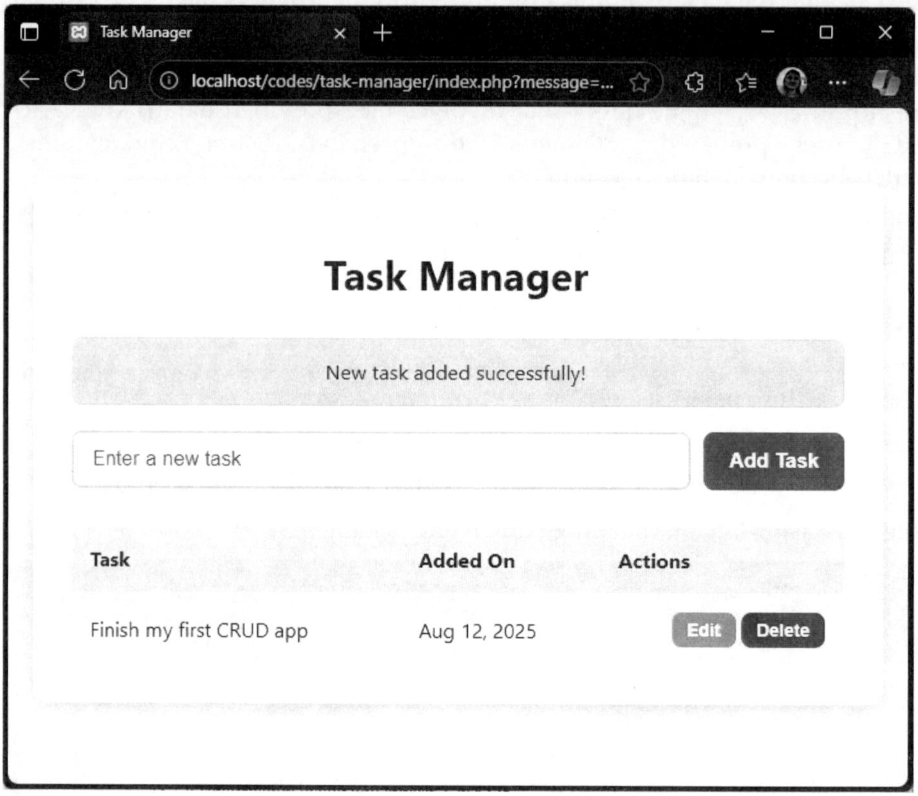

5. **Test the Update operation:**
   - Find the task you just created and click its **Edit** button.
   - The input field at the top is now filled with **Finish my first CRUD app**, and the button text has changed to **Update Task**.

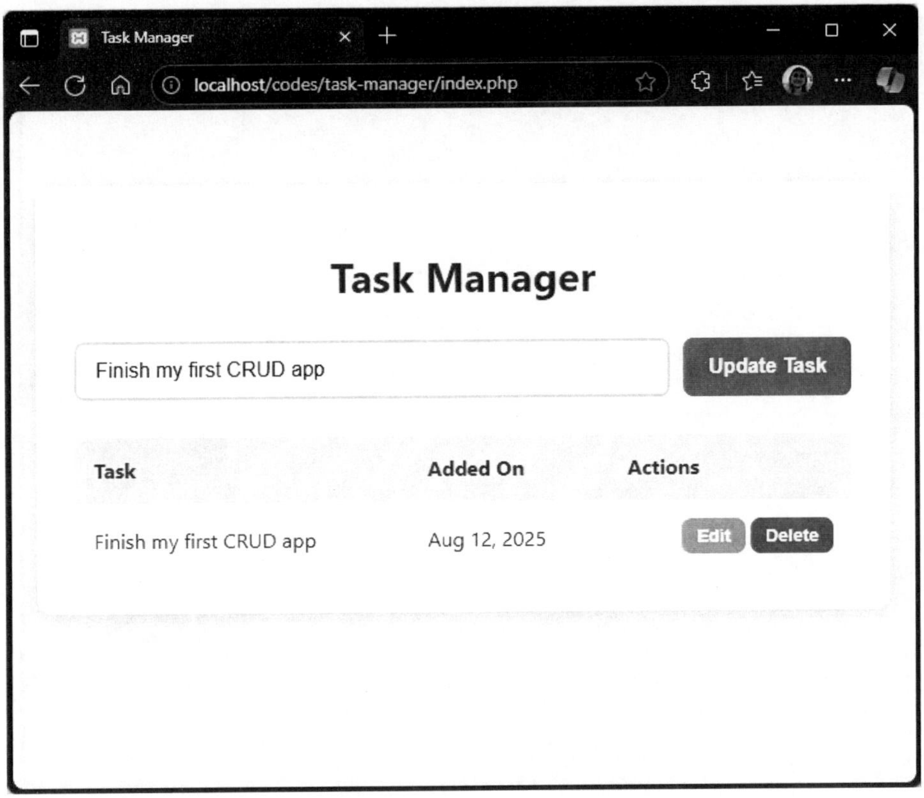

- Change the text to **Finish my first AWESOME CRUD app** and click **Update Task**.
- The page refreshes with another green success message, and the task name in the table is updated.

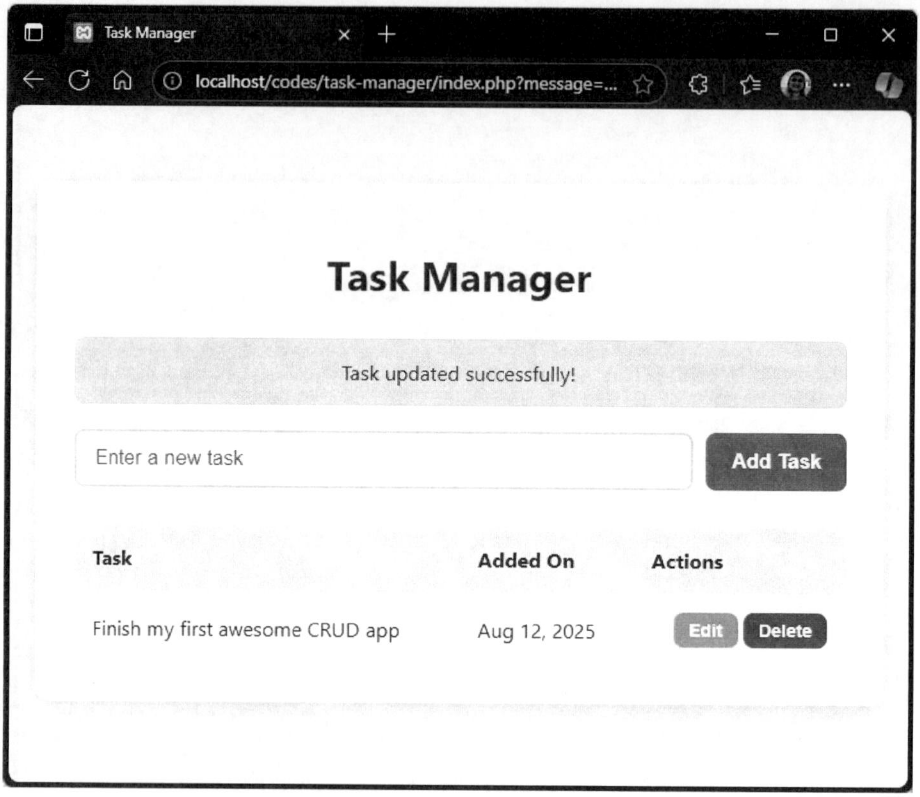

6. **Test the Delete operation:**
    - Click the **Delete** button next to your task.
    - A confirmation dialog appears. Click **OK**.

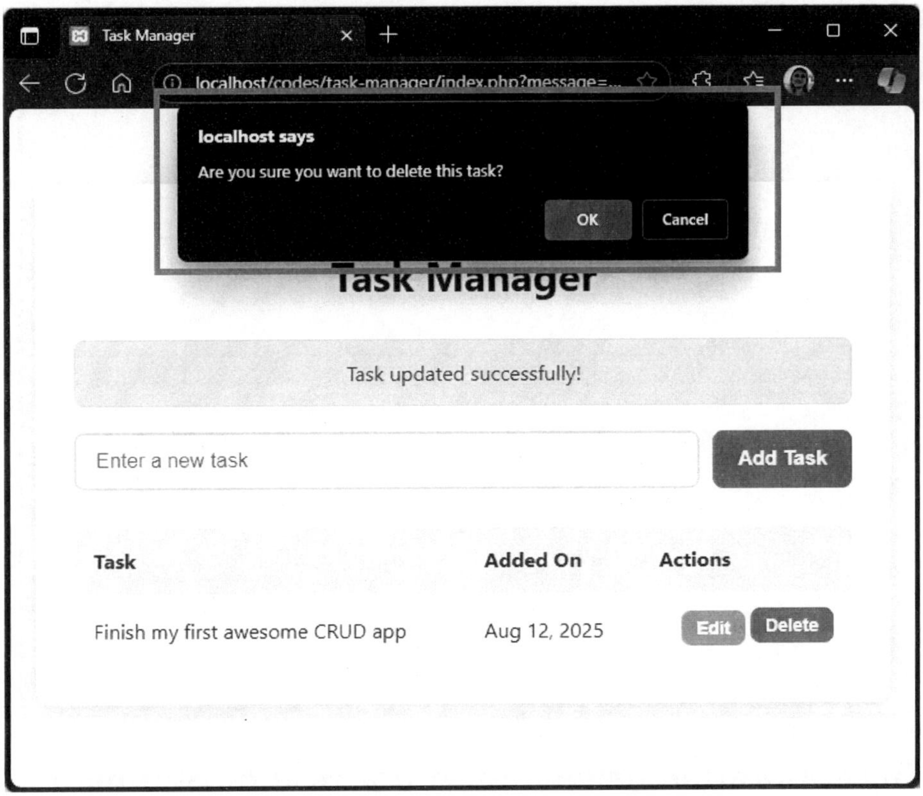

- The page refreshes with a success message, and the task is now gone from the table.

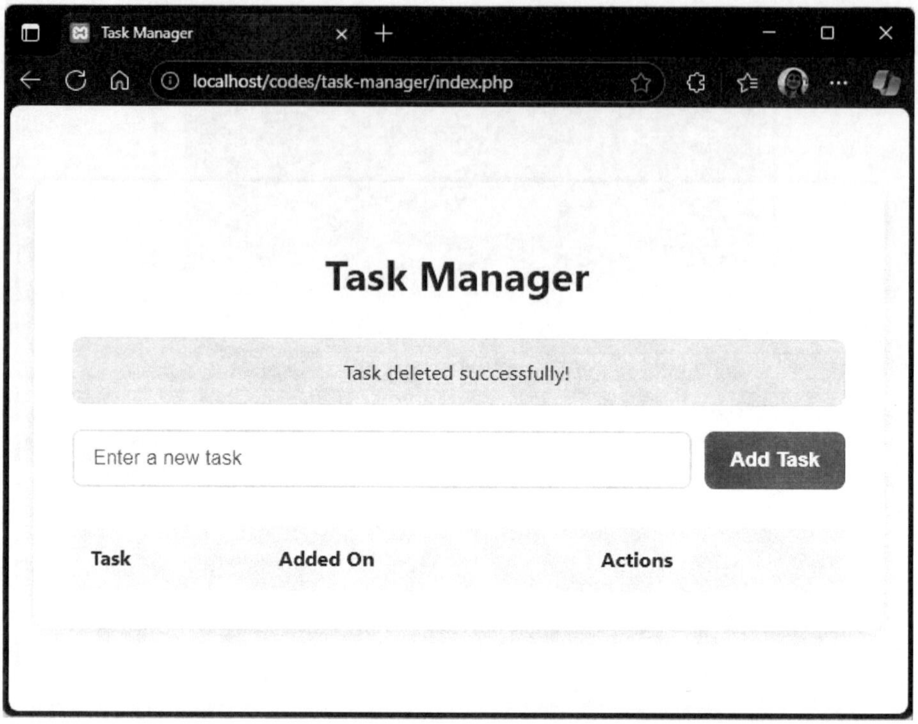

Exploring application behaviour: A practical run-through

A well-built application handles not just the "happy path" but also errors and edge cases. Let's see how ours behaves.

- **Invalid input (Empty task):** Try to click the **Add Task** button without entering any text. The page reloads with an error message. Our validation logic is working.

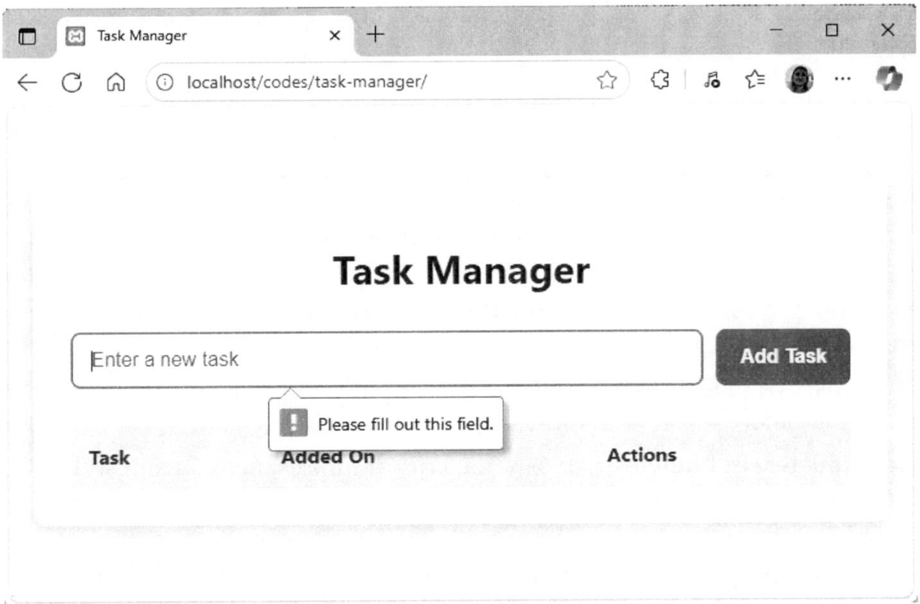

- **Insert failures:** If our database connection were to fail or the table was missing, our if ($stmt->execute()) checks would fail, and the corresponding red error message would appear, preventing the application from crashing.
- **Simultaneous edits:** Imagine two people are using the app. User A clicks **Edit** on a task. At the same time, User B deletes that same task. When User A tries to submit their update, our UPDATE query's WHERE id = ? clause will not find a matching record. The query will execute successfully but affect zero rows. While our current app simply shows a success message, a more advanced application could detect that 0 rows were affected and display a more specific message like "This task no longer exists."

Harnessing CRUD in real-world contexts

The task manager, while simple, is a perfect miniature of countless real-world applications. The exact same CRUD pattern is the foundation for:

- **E-commerce:** Managing products, customer accounts, and orders.
- **Content management systems (like WordPress):** Creating, editing, and deleting blog posts, pages, and user comments.
- **Social media:** Posting status updates, editing your profile, and deleting photos.
- **Booking systems:** Adding new appointments, updating their status, and canceling them.

Nearly every application that needs to store and manage persistent data relies on this fundamental CRUD experience.

Wrapping up

In this chapter, we fully immersed ourselves in the world of dynamic data management. We didn't just learn the theory; we built a complete, functional, and secure web application from scratch.

- **CRUD defined:** We learned that Create, Read, Update, and Delete are the four cornerstone operations of data-driven websites.
- **Secure forms:** We built HTML forms for user input and used prepared statements with mysqli to completely secure our application against SQL injection.
- **Targeted updates and deletes:** We saw the critical importance of using WHERE clauses with unique IDs to ensure our UPDATE and DELETE queries affect only the intended record.
- **Task manager project:** We built a complete Task Manager, integrating all CRUD operations into a single, user-friendly interface.
- **Dynamic feedback:** We enhanced the user experience by providing clear, color-coded success and error messages using CSS and PHP.
- **The PRG pattern:** We used the Post/Redirect/Get pattern to prevent duplicate form submissions and create a smoother user experience.

Congratulations! You have successfully built a full-stack PHP application that implements the most important pattern in web development. You can now confidently create applications that interact with a database in a secure and professional manner. The skills you've gained in this chapter are directly applicable to virtually any web project you can imagine.

You've laid a rock-solid foundation. Now, it's time to build something even bigger on top of it. In the next chapter, ***Chapter 18: Culmination - Mini CMS – The content creator's toolbox***, we will take these CRUD skills and use them to build our very own Content Management System, the engine behind millions of blogs and websites. Let's get building!

Chapter 18

Section 05: Dynamic data – Databases and CRUD essentials

Culmination: Mini CMS – The content creator's toolbox

What you'll learn

- CMS fundamentals
- User authentication
- SEO-friendly URLs
- Database schema design
- Dynamic post menegement
- Responsive layouts

Welcome back! In the last chapter, we mastered the CRUD (Create, Read, Update, Delete) experience, which forms the backbone of almost every dynamic website. You learned how to build a Task Manager, securely handling data with prepared statements and making the user interface interactive. Now, it's time to assemble all those skills into a larger, more powerful project: your very own mini version of Content Management System (CMS).

Ever wonder how websites like blogs, news portals, or portfolios are updated so frequently without a developer rewriting code each time? The magic behind this is a **Content Management System (CMS)**. A CMS is a web application that separates the content (text, images) from the design, allowing non-technical users to add, edit, and manage the website's content through a user-friendly interface. Think of it as the control panel for a website.

In this chapter, we'll build a mini-CMS for a blog, giving you the power to create, edit, and publish posts just like a professional content creator. This project is a major milestone, bringing together everything we've learned about PHP, databases, and forms into a single, cohesive application.

Core concepts of a CMS

At its heart, a CMS has two distinct parts:

- **The frontend (public view):** This is what your visitors see—the beautifully styled blog posts, articles, or product pages. It reads content from the database and displays it according to your design templates.
- **The backend (admin panel):** This is a secure, password-protected area where the site owner or administrator can log in to manage the content. This is where the CRUD operations happen: creating new posts, updating existing ones, and deleting old ones.

The core principle is **decoupling**. The content (stored in the database) is decoupled from the presentation (the HTML and CSS code). When you write a new blog post in the admin panel, you're just adding a new row to a database table. The frontend PHP scripts then fetch that new row and display it automatically, without you ever touching the HTML code. This makes managing a site incredibly efficient and scalable.

Designing the database schema

Before we write a single line of PHP, we need a plan for our data. This plan is the database schema. For our mini-blog CMS, we need a place to store the posts. We'll create a single table named posts.

This table needs to store a few key pieces of information for each blog post:

- **id:** A unique number to identify each post. This will be our **Primary Key** and it will **auto-increment**, meaning the database will assign a new number for us automatically.
- **title:** The title of the blog post.
- **content:** The main body of the post. We'll use a TEXT data type to allow for long articles.
- **slug:** A user-friendly and SEO-friendly version of the title, used for clean URLs (e.g., "my-first-post").
- **author:** The name of the person who wrote the post.
- **created_at:** A timestamp that automatically records when the post was created.

Here is the SQL code you will use in phpMyAdmin to create this table. Don't worry about running it just yet; we'll do this together in the hands-on section:

```
CREATE TABLE posts (
   id INT AUTO_INCREMENT PRIMARY KEY,
   title VARCHAR(255) NOT NULL,
   content TEXT NOT NULL,
   slug VARCHAR(255) NOT NULL UNIQUE,
   author VARCHAR(100) NOT NULL,
   created_at TIMESTAMP DEFAULT CURRENT_TIMESTAMP
);
```

This simple structure is the foundation of our entire CMS. Each time we save a post, it becomes a new row in this posts table.

User authentication and roles

The admin panel is the heart of our CMS, so it must be protected. We can't let just anyone wander in and start deleting posts! This is where **authentication** comes in. Authentication is the process of verifying who a user is.

We'll create a simple but effective login system using PHP Sessions. Here's the flow:

- The user visits a login page and enters a password.
- Our PHP script checks if the password is correct.
- If it is, we create a session variable, like $_SESSION['loggedin'] = true;.
- On every page within the admin panel (add, edit, delete), we'll add a check at the very top: if the $_SESSION['loggedin'] variable doesn't exist or is false, we immediately redirect the user back to the login page.

This ensures that only users who have successfully logged in can access the content management tools.

For this mini-CMS, we'll have a single **admin** role with full control. In larger, more complex systems, you could expand this by adding a **users** table and a **role** column (e.g., 'admin', 'editor', 'author'), where each role has different permissions. For our learning purposes, a single-user system is perfect.

Adding, editing, and listing blog posts

This is where our CRUD skills from the previous chapter shine. We'll build the interface that allows the administrator to manage the blog posts.

Listing posts (the 'Read' in CRUD)

The main page of our admin panel will be a dashboard that lists all existing blog posts from the posts table. Each row will display the post's title and author, along with two links: **Edit** and **Delete**. This gives the admin a clear overview and quick access to manage each piece of content.

Adding posts (the 'Create' in CRUD)

The **Add New Post** page will contain a simple HTML form with fields for the title, content, and author. When the admin submits this form, the data is sent via the POST method to a PHP script. This script will:

- Validate the input (e.g., make sure the title isn't empty).
- Generate a URL-friendly "slug" from the title.
- Use a prepared statement to securely INSERT the new post into the posts table.
- Redirect the admin back to the main post list, where they'll see their new post.

Editing posts (the 'Update' in CRUD)

When the admin clicks **Edit** next to a post, they'll be taken to an edit page. This page is very similar to the **Add Post** page, but with a crucial difference: the form fields will be pre-populated with the existing data for that specific post. To do this, the **Edit** link will pass the post's id in the URL (e.g., edit_post.php?id=5). The script will then:

- Fetch the post's data from the database using the id.
- Display that data in the form.
- When the admin submits the updated form, a PHP script will use a prepared statement with an UPDATE query to save the changes to the correct row in the database.

SEO & user-friendly URLs

Default URLs like **post.php?id=12** work, but they aren't pretty and they're not great for Search Engine Optimization (SEO). A much better URL would be **post.php?slug=my-awesome-blog-post**. This is a **user-friendly URL**.

We achieve this with a **slug**. A slug is a simplified, URL-safe version of a post's title. Here's how we'll generate one automatically when a post is created:

- Take the post title: **My Awesome Blog Post!**.
- Convert it to lowercase: **my awesome blog post!**.
- Replace all spaces with hyphens: **my-awesome-blog-post!**.
- Remove any characters that aren't letters, numbers, or hyphens: **my-awesome-blog-post**.

We'll create a simple PHP function to do this for us. This slug is then saved in its own column in our posts table. When a visitor clicks a link on the public-facing blog, we use the slug to fetch the correct post from the database instead of the id. This makes your URLs more descriptive, memorable, and appealing to search engines.

Safe comments moderation

While our mini-CMS won't have a full-blown commenting system, it's important to understand how you would manage it safely. If you were to add comments, you wouldn't want spam or inappropriate content to appear on your site instantly.

Comment moderation is the practice of reviewing comments before they go live. A typical implementation would involve adding a status column to your comments table. This column could hold values like 'pending', 'approved', or 'rejected'.

Here's the workflow:

- When a user submits a comment, it's saved to the database with a status of **pending**.
- In the admin panel, you'd have a **Comments** section that lists all pending comments.
- The admin can then review each comment and click an **Approve** or **Reject** button.
- Clicking the button updates the comment's status in the database.
- On the public blog post page, your PHP query would only fetch comments **WHERE status = 'approved'**.

This simple gatekeeping step gives you full control over the content that appears on your site, preventing spam and maintaining a safe environment for your readers.

Responsive design with CSS / Media queries

A modern website must look great on any device, from a wide desktop monitor to a small smartphone. We achieve this with **responsive design**. The key technology behind this is CSS **media queries**.

A media query allows you to apply a block of CSS styles only when certain conditions are met, most commonly the width of the browser window.

For example, our admin dashboard might display content in a wide table on a desktop. On a mobile device, that table would be too wide and force the user to scroll horizontally, which is a poor user experience. Using a media query, we can change the layout for smaller screens.

Here is a simple example of a media query:

```
/* Default styles for all screen sizes */
.container {
  width: 90%;
  margin: 0 auto;
}
/* Styles for screens 768px or wider (tablets and desktops) */
@media (min-width: 768px) {
  .container {
    width: 80%;
    max-width: 1200px;
  }
}
/* Styles for screens smaller than 600px (mobile phones) */
@media (max-width: 600px) {
  .admin-table thead {
    /* Hide the table header on small screens */
    display: none;
  }
  .admin-table, .admin-table tbody, .admin-table tr, .admin-table td {
    /* Make table elements behave like blocks */
    display: block;
    width: 100%;
  }
  .admin-table tr {
    margin-bottom: 1rem;
  }
}
```

In the hands-on section, we will integrate media queries into our style.css file to ensure both the public-facing blog and the admin panel are fully responsive and easy to use on any device.

Hands-on: Building the Blog

It's time to build! In this hands-on section, we will construct a complete, working mini-CMS for a blog. You will create the public-facing pages where visitors can read posts, and the secure admin area where you can manage the content. By the end, you'll have a fully functional web application that puts you in the content creator's seat.

Building the application

Setup project structure

First, let's set up our project structure.

1. **Create the project folder:** Inside your XAMPP htdocs/codes directory, create a new folder called **mini-cms**. All our files will go in here.
2. Open **mini-cms** folder in VS Code.
3. **Create sub-folders:** Inside **mini-cms**, create the following folders:
    - **admin:** This will hold all our backend/admin-related files.
    - **css:** This will hold our stylesheet.

Your folder structure should look like this:

```
htdocs/codes/
└── mini-cms/
    ├── admin/
    └── css/
```

Setup the database

Now, let's set up the database. To create database:

1. Open your XAMPP Control Panel and start the **Apache** and **MySQL** modules.
2. Open your browser and navigate to **http://localhost/phpMyAdmin**.
3. Click on the **Databases** tab.
4. In the **Create database** field, enter **mini_cms_db** and click **Create**.
5. Click on your new **mini_cms_db** database in the left sidebar.

6. Click on the **SQL** tab.
7. Copy and paste the following SQL code into the text area:

```
CREATE TABLE posts (
  id INT AUTO_INCREMENT PRIMARY KEY,
  title VARCHAR(255) NOT NULL,
  content TEXT NOT NULL,
  slug VARCHAR(255) NOT NULL UNIQUE,
  author VARCHAR(100) NOT NULL,
  created_at TIMESTAMP DEFAULT CURRENT_TIMESTAMP
);
```

8. Click **Go**.
9. You see a success message, and your **posts** table appears in the sidebar. We are now ready to write the PHP code!

Create the database connection file

This file will handle the connection to our new database, so we don't have to repeat the code everywhere. In VS Code, create a new file and save it as **db.php** inside the main **mini-cms** folder. (mini-cms/db.php). Add the following code:

```
<?php
// Database configuration
define('DB_HOST', 'localhost');
define('DB_USER', 'root'); // Default XAMPP user
define('DB_PASS', '');     // Default XAMPP password
define('DB_NAME', 'mini_cms_db');
// Create connection
$conn = new mysqli(DB_HOST, DB_USER, DB_PASS, DB_NAME);
// Check connection
if ($conn->connect_error) {
    die("Connection failed: " . $conn->connect_error);
}
?>
```

This script establishes a connection to our MySQL database using the credentials and kills the script if the connection fails, preventing any further errors.

Create the main stylesheet

Inside the **css** folder, create a file named **style.css** (mini-cms/css/style.css). We will add all our styles here to make the blog and the admin panel look clean and professional:

```
/* General Body & Typography */
body {
```

```
    font-family: 'Segoe UI', Tahoma, Geneva, Verdana, sans-serif;
    line-height: 1.6;
    background-color: #f4f4f4;
    color: #333;
    margin: 0;
    padding: 0;
}
.container {
    width: 90%;
    max-width: 960px;
    margin: 2rem auto;
    padding: 2rem;
    background: #fff;
    box-shadow: 0 0 10px rgba(0, 0, 0, 0.1);
    border-radius: 8px;
}
h1, h2, h3 {
    color: #0056b3;
}
a {
    color: #007bff;
    text-decoration: none;
}
a:hover {
    text-decoration: underline;
}
/* Header */
.site-header {
    background: #007bff;
    color: #fff;
    padding: 1rem 0;
    text-align: center;
    margin-bottom: 2rem;
}
.site-header h1 {
    color: #fff;
    margin: 0;
}
.site-header a {
    color: #fff;
    font-weight: bold;
}
/* --- Public Blog Styles --- */
.post {
    border-bottom: 1px solid #ddd;
    padding-bottom: 1.5rem;
    margin-bottom: 1.5rem;
}
.post:last-child {
    border-bottom: none;
}
```

```
.post-title {
    margin-top: 0;
}
.post-meta {
    color: #666;
    font-size: 0.9em;
    margin-bottom: 1rem;
}
.read-more {
    display: inline-block;
    background: #007bff;
    color: #fff;
    padding: 8px 15px;
    border-radius: 5px;
    font-weight: bold;
}
.read-more:hover {
    background: #0056b3;
    text-decoration: none;
}
/* --- Admin Panel Styles --- */
.admin-login-form {
    max-width: 400px;
    margin: 4rem auto;
}
.admin-header {
    display: flex;
    justify-content: space-between;
    align-items: center;
    border-bottom: 2px solid #eee;
    padding-bottom: 1rem;
    margin-bottom: 2rem;
}
.admin-header a.button, a.admin-button {
    background: #28a745;
    color: #fff;
    padding: 10px 15px;
    border-radius: 5px;
    font-weight: bold;
}
.admin-header a.button:hover, a.admin-button:hover {
    background: #218838;
    text-decoration: none;
}
a.logout-button {
    background: #dc3545;
}
a.logout-button:hover {
    background: #c82333;
}
/* Forms */
```

```
.form-group {
    margin-bottom: 1.5rem;
}
.form-group label {
    display: block;
    margin-bottom: 5px;
    font-weight: bold;
}
.form-group input[type="text"], .form-group input[type="password"],
.form-group textarea {
    width: 100%;
    padding: 10px;
    border: 1px solid #ccc;
    border-radius: 5px;
    box-sizing: border-box; /* Important for 100% width */
}
.form-group textarea {
    min-height: 200px;
    resize: vertical;
}
.btn {
    display: inline-block;
    background: #007bff;
    color: #fff;
    padding: 12px 20px;
    border: none;
    border-radius: 5px;
    cursor: pointer;
    font-size: 1em;
    font-weight: bold;
}
.btn:hover {
    background: #0056b3;
}
/* Admin Table */
.admin-table {
    width: 100%;
    border-collapse: collapse;
    margin-top: 2rem;
}
.admin-table th, .admin-table td {
    padding: 12px;
    text-align: left;
    border-bottom: 1px solid #ddd;
}
.admin-table th {
    background-color: #f8f9fa;
    font-weight: bold;
}
.admin-table tr:hover {
    background-color: #f1f1f1;
```

```
}
.action-links a {
    margin-right: 10px;
}
a.edit-link {
    color: #ffc107;
}
a.delete-link {
    color: #dc3545;
}
/* Messages */
.message {
    padding: 1rem;
    margin-bottom: 1rem;
    border-radius: 5px;
    color: #fff;
}
.message.success {
    background: #28a745;
}
.message.error {
    background: #dc3545;
}
/* Responsive Media Queries */
@media (max-width: 768px) {
    .admin-header {
        flex-direction: column;
        align-items: flex-start;
    }
    .admin-header h2 {
        margin-bottom: 1rem;
    }
}
@media (max-width: 600px) {
    .admin-table thead {
        display: none; /* Hide headers on small screens */
    }
    .admin-table, .admin-table tbody, .admin-table tr, .admin-table td {
        display: block;
        width: 100%;
    }
    .admin-table tr {
        margin-bottom: 1rem;
        border: 1px solid #ddd;
        border-radius: 5px;
    }
    .admin-table td {
        text-align: right; /* Align content to the right */
        padding-left: 50%; /* Create space for a label */
        position: relative;
        border-bottom: 1px dotted #ddd;
```

```
    }
    .admin-table td::before {
        content: attr(data-label); /* Use data-label for content */
        position: absolute;
        left: 10px;
        width: calc(50% - 20px);
        padding-right: 10px;
        font-weight: bold;
        text-align: left;
    }
    .action-links {
      text-align: right;
      padding-top: 10px;
    }
}
```

Create the public blog index page

Now let's build the public-facing part of our blog. This page will list all our blog posts. Create a file named **index.php** in the **mini-cms** root directory (mini-cms/index.php). Add the following code:

```
<?php
require_once 'db.php';
// Fetch all posts from the database, newest first
$result = $conn->query("SELECT * FROM posts ORDER BY created_at DESC");
?>
<!DOCTYPE html>
<html lang="en">
<head>
    <meta charset="UTF-8">
    <meta name="viewport" content="width=device-width, initial-scale=1.0">
    <title>My Simple Blog</title>
    <link rel="stylesheet" href="css/style.css">
</head>
<body>
    <header class="site-header">
        <h1><a href="index.php">My Simple Blog</a></h1>
        <p><a href="admin/">Admin Login</a></p>
    </header>
    <div class="container">
        <?php if ($result->num_rows > 0): ?>
            <?php while($post = $result->fetch_assoc()): ?>
                <article class="post">
                    <h2 class="post-title">
                        <a href="post.php?slug=<?php echo htmlspecialchars(
                                 $post['slug']); ?>">
                            <?php echo htmlspecialchars($post['title']); ?>
                        </a>
```

```
                        </h2>
                        <div class="post-meta">
                            By <?php echo htmlspecialchars($post['author']); ?> on <?php
                                echo date('F j, Y', strtotime($post['created_at'])); ?>
                        </div>
                        <p><?php echo nl2br(htmlspecialchars(substr($post['content'],
                             0, 300))); ?>...</p>
                        <a href="post.php?slug=<?php echo htmlspecialchars($post[
                                'slug']); ?>" class="read-more">Read More</a>
                    </article>
                <?php endwhile; ?>
            <?php else: ?>
                <p>No posts found. Why not add one in the admin panel?</p>
            <?php endif; ?>
        </div>
</body>
</html>
<?php
$conn->close();
?>
```

This script fetches all posts and displays a preview of each one (the first 300 characters). It links to post.php using the slug for a clean URL.

Create the single post page

This page will display the full content of a single blog post. Create a file named **post.php** in the **mini-cms** root directory (mini-cms/post.php). Add the following code:

```
<?php
require_once 'db.php';
// Check if slug is provided
if (!isset($_GET['slug'])) {
    header("Location: index.php");
    exit();
}
$slug = $_GET['slug'];
// Prepare and execute the statement to fetch the post
$stmt = $conn->prepare("SELECT * FROM posts WHERE slug = ?");
$stmt->bind_param("s", $slug);
$stmt->execute();
$result = $stmt->get_result();
if ($result->num_rows === 0) {
    // No post found with that slug
    header("Location: index.php"); // Or show a 404 page
    exit();
}
$post = $result->fetch_assoc();
?>
```

```
<!DOCTYPE html>
<html lang="en">
<head>
    <meta charset="UTF-8">
    <meta name="viewport" content="width=device-width, initial-scale=1.0">
    <title><?php echo htmlspecialchars($post['title']); ?> -
           My Simple Blog</title>
    <link rel="stylesheet" href="css/style.css">
</head>
<body>
    <header class="site-header">
        <h1><a href="index.php">My Simple Blog</a></h1>
    </header>
    <div class="container">
        <article class="post">
            <h1 class="post-title"><?php echo htmlspecialchars($post[
                                              'title']); ?></h1>
            <div class="post-meta">
                By <?php echo htmlspecialchars($post['author']); ?> on
                   <?php echo date('F j, Y', strtotime($post['created_at'])); ?>
            </div>
            <div class="post-content">
                <?php echo nl2br(htmlspecialchars($post['content']));
                           // nl2br converts newlines to <br> tags ?>
            </div>
        </article>
        <a href="index.php">← Back to all posts</a>
    </div>
</body>
</html>
<?php
$stmt->close();
$conn->close();
?>
```

This script safely fetches a single post from the database based on the slug provided in the URL and displays its full content.

Create the admin login page

Now, let's build the secure admin panel. All our admin files will go inside the **admin** folder. The first one is the **login** page. Create a file named **index.php** inside the **admin** folder (mini-cms/admin/index.php). Add the following code:

```
<?php
session_start();
// If user is already logged in, redirect to the dashboard
if (isset($_SESSION['loggedin']) && $_SESSION['loggedin'] === true) {
```

```
    header('Location: dashboard.php');
    exit;
}
// A very simple password check. In a real app, use hashed passwords!
define('ADMIN_PASSWORD', 'password123');
$error = '';
if ($_SERVER['REQUEST_METHOD'] === 'POST') {
    if (!empty($_POST['password']) && $_POST['password'] === ADMIN_PASSWORD) {
        // Password is correct, start the session
        $_SESSION['loggedin'] = true;
        $_SESSION['username'] = 'Admin'; // You can store user info
        header('Location: dashboard.php');
        exit;
    } else {
        $error = 'Incorrect password. Please try again.';
    }
}
?>
<!DOCTYPE html>
<html lang="en">
<head>
    <meta charset="UTF-8">
    <meta name="viewport" content="width=device-width, initial-scale=1.0">
    <title>Admin Login</title>
    <link rel="stylesheet" href="../css/style.css">
</head>
<body>
    <div class="container admin-login-form">
        <h2>Admin Login</h2>
        <p>Welcome. Please enter the password to proceed.</p>
        <?php if ($error): ?>
            <p class="message error"><?php echo $error; ?></p>
        <?php endif; ?>
        <form action="index.php" method="post">
            <div class="form-group">
                <label for="password">Password</label>
                <input type="password" id="password" name="password" required>
            </div>
            <button type="submit" class="btn">Login</button>
        </form>
         <p style="margin-top: 1rem;"><a href="../index.php">← Back to Blog</a></p>
    </div>
</body>
</html>
```

This page presents a login form. We are using a simple password **password123**. If the correct password is entered, it sets a session variable and redirects to the dashboard.

In a real-world application, you should always use password_hash() and password_verify() for secure password handling.

Create a security check file

To protect our admin pages, we'll create a small file to check for the session on every page. This avoids code repetition. Create a file named **auth.php** in the **admin** folder (mini-cms/admin/auth.php). Add the following code:

```
<?php
session_start();
// If the user is not logged in, redirect to the login page
if (!isset($_SESSION['loggedin']) || $_SESSION['loggedin'] !== true) {
    header('Location: index.php');
    exit;
}
?>
```

Create the admin dashboard

This is the main page for managing posts. It will list all posts and provide links to add, edit, or delete them. Create a file named **dashboard.php** in the **admin** folder (mini-cms/admin/dashboard.php). Add the following code:

```
<?php
require_once 'auth.php'; // Check for login
require_once '../db.php'; // DB Connection
// Fetch all posts to display in the table
$result = $conn->query("SELECT id, title, author, created_at FROM posts
                        ORDER BY created_at DESC");
?>
<!DOCTYPE html>
<html lang="en">
<head>
    <meta charset="UTF-8">
    <meta name="viewport" content="width=device-width, initial-scale=1.0">
    <title>Admin Dashboard</title>
    <link rel="stylesheet" href="../css/style.css">
</head>
<body>
    <div class="container">
        <header class="admin-header">
            <h2>Admin Dashboard</h2>
            <div>
                <a href="add.php" class="admin-button">Add New Post</a>
                <a href="logout.php" class="admin-button logout-button">Logout</a>
            </div>
```

```
        </header>
        <h3>Manage Posts</h3>
        <?php if (isset($_GET['status']) && $_GET['status'] == 'success'): ?>
            <p class="message success">Post was managed successfully!</p>
        <?php endif; ?>
        <table class="admin-table">
            <thead>
                <tr>
                    <th>Title</th>
                    <th>Author</th>
                    <th>Date</th>
                    <th>Actions</th>
                </tr>
            </thead>
            <tbody>
                <?php if ($result->num_rows > 0): ?>
                    <?php while($row = $result->fetch_assoc()): ?>
                        <tr>
                            <td data-label="Title"><?php echo htmlspecialchars($row[
                                                              'title']); ?></td>
                            <td data-label="Author"><?php echo htmlspecialchars(
                                                          $row['author']); ?></td>
                            <td data-label="Date"><?php echo date('M d, Y',
                                          strtotime($row['created_at'])); ?></td>
                            <td data-label="Actions" class="action-links">
                                <a href="edit.php?id=<?php echo $row['id']; ?>"
                                   class="edit-link">Edit</a>
                                <a href="delete.php?id=<?php echo $row['id']; ?>"
                                   class="delete-link" onclick="return confirm('Are
                                   you sure you want to delete this post?');">
                                   Delete</a>
                            </td>
                        </tr>
                    <?php endwhile; ?>
                <?php else: ?>
                    <tr>
                        <td colspan="4">No posts found.</td>
                    </tr>
                <?php endif; ?>
            </tbody>
        </table>
    </div>
</body>
</html>
<?php
$conn->close();
?>
```

This page first runs auth.php to ensure the user is logged in. Then it lists all posts in a responsive table. Notice the onclick confirmation for the delete link to prevent accidental deletions.

Create the 'Add Post' page

This form will allow the admin to create new posts. Create a file named **add.php** in the **admin** folder (mini-cms/admin/add.php). Add the following code:

```
<?php
require_once 'auth.php';
require_once '../db.php';
// Function to create a URL-friendly slug
function createSlug($string) {
   $string = strtolower($string);
   $string = preg_replace('/[^a-z0-9_\s-]/', '', $string);
   $string = preg_replace('/[\s-]+/', '-', $string);
   $string = trim($string, '-');
   return $string;
}
if ($_SERVER['REQUEST_METHOD'] === 'POST') {
    $title = $_POST['title'];
    $content = $_POST['content'];
    $author = $_POST['author'];
    $slug = createSlug($title);
    // Basic validation
    if (!empty($title) && !empty($content) && !empty($author)) {
        // Check if slug already exists
        $stmt_check = $conn->prepare("SELECT id FROM posts WHERE slug = ?");
        $stmt_check->bind_param("s", $slug);
        $stmt_check->execute();
        $stmt_check->store_result();
        if($stmt_check->num_rows > 0) {
            // If slug exists, make it unique by appending a number
            $slug = $slug . '-' . time();
        }
        $stmt_check->close();
        $stmt = $conn->prepare("INSERT INTO posts (title, content, author, slug)
                                VALUES (?, ?, ?, ?)");
        $stmt->bind_param("ssss", $title, $content, $author, $slug);
        if ($stmt->execute()) {
            header("Location: dashboard.php?status=success");
            exit();
        } else {
            $error = "Error: " . $stmt->error;
        }
        $stmt->close();
    } else {
        $error = "All fields are required.";
```

```
    }
}
?>
<!DOCTYPE html>
<html lang="en">
<head>
    <meta charset="UTF-8">
    <meta name="viewport" content="width=device-width, initial-scale=1.0">
    <title>Add New Post</title>
    <link rel="stylesheet" href="../css/style.css">
</head>
<body>
<div class="container">
    <header class="admin-header">
        <h2>Add New Post</h2>
        <a href="dashboard.php" class="admin-button">← Back to Dashboard</a>
    </header>
    <?php if (isset($error)): ?>
        <p class="message error"><?php echo $error; ?></p>
    <?php endif; ?>
    <form action="add.php" method="post">
        <div class="form-group">
            <label for="title">Title</label>
            <input type="text" id="title" name="title" required>
        </div>
        <div class="form-group">
            <label for="content">Content</label>
            <textarea id="content" name="content" required></textarea>
        </div>
        <div class="form-group">
            <label for="author">Author</label>
            <input type="text" id="author" name="author" required>
        </div>
        <button type="submit" class="btn">Publish Post</button>
    </form>
</div>
</body>
</html>
```

This script includes our **createSlug()** function, validates the form input, and securely inserts the new post into the database. It also handles the edge case where two posts might have the same title by making the slug unique.

Create the 'Edit Post' page

This page will look similar to the 'Add' page but will pre-fill the form with existing data and perform an UPDATE instead of an INSERT.

Create **edit.php** in the **admin** folder (mini-cms/admin/edit.php). Add the following code:

```
<?php
require_once 'auth.php';
require_once '../db.php';
$id = $_GET['id'] ?? null;
if (!$id) {
    header("Location: dashboard.php");
    exit();
}
// Function to create a URL-friendly slug (re-use if needed)
function createSlug($string) {
    $string = strtolower($string);
    $string = preg_replace('/[^a-z0-9_\s-]/', '', $string);
    $string = preg_replace('/[\s-]+/', '-', $string);
    $string = trim($string, '-');
    return $string;
}
// Handle form submission for updating
if ($_SERVER['REQUEST_METHOD'] === 'POST') {
    $title = $_POST['title'];
    $content = $_POST['content'];
    $author = $_POST['author'];
    $slug = createSlug($title);
    $post_id = $_POST['id'];
    if (!empty($title) && !empty($content) && !empty($author)) {
        // Check if the new slug conflicts with another post
        $stmt_check = $conn->prepare("SELECT id FROM posts
                                      WHERE slug = ? AND id != ?");
        $stmt_check->bind_param("si", $slug, $post_id);
        $stmt_check->execute();
        $stmt_check->store_result();
        if($stmt_check->num_rows > 0) {
            $slug = $slug . '-' . time();
        }
        $stmt_check->close();
        $stmt = $conn->prepare("UPDATE posts SET title = ?, content = ?,
                                author = ?, slug = ? WHERE id = ?");
        $stmt->bind_param("ssssi", $title, $content, $author, $slug, $post_id);
        if ($stmt->execute()) {
            header("Location: dashboard.php?status=success");
            exit();
        } else {
            $error = "Error updating post: " . $stmt->error;
        }
        $stmt->close();
    } else {
        $error = "All fields are required.";
    }
}
// Fetch the post to be edited
```

```
$stmt = $conn->prepare("SELECT * FROM posts WHERE id = ?");
$stmt->bind_param("i", $id);
$stmt->execute();
$result = $stmt->get_result();
if ($result->num_rows === 1) {
    $post = $result->fetch_assoc();
} else {
    // Post not found
    header("Location: dashboard.php");
    exit();
}
$stmt->close();
?>
<!DOCTYPE html>
<html lang="en">
<head>
    <meta charset="UTF-8">
    <meta name="viewport" content="width=device-width, initial-scale=1.0">
    <title>Edit Post</title>
    <link rel="stylesheet" href="../css/style.css">
</head>
<body>
<div class="container">
    <header class="admin-header">
        <h2>Edit Post</h2>
        <a href="dashboard.php" class="admin-button">← Back to
           Dashboard</a>
    </header>
    <?php if (isset($error)): ?>
        <p class="message error"><?php echo $error; ?></p>
    <?php endif; ?>
    <form action="edit.php?id=<?php echo $post['id']; ?>" method="post">
        <input type="hidden" name="id" value="<?php echo $post['id']; ?>">
        <div class="form-group">
            <label for="title">Title</label>
            <input type="text" id="title" name="title" value="<?php echo
                   htmlspecialchars($post['title']); ?>" required>
        </div>
        <div class="form-group">
            <label for="content">Content</label>
            <textarea id="content" name="content" required><?php
                      echo htmlspecialchars($post['content']); ?></textarea>
        </div>
        <div class="form-group">
            <label for="author">Author</label>
            <input type="text" id="author" name="author" value="<?php echo
                   htmlspecialchars($post['author']); ?>" required>
        </div>
        <button type="submit" class="btn">Update Post</button>
    </form>
```

```
</div>
</body>
</html>
```

Create the 'Delete Post' script

This script doesn't need an HTML interface. It will receive a post id, delete it from the database, and redirect back to the dashboard. Create **delete.php** in the **admin** folder (mini-cms/admin/delete.php). Add the following code:

```
<?php
require_once 'auth.php';
require_once '../db.php';
$id = $_GET['id'] ?? null;
if ($id) {
    $stmt = $conn->prepare("DELETE FROM posts WHERE id = ?");
    $stmt->bind_param("i", $id);
    if ($stmt->execute()) {
        header("Location: dashboard.php?status=success");
        exit();
    } else {
        // Handle error, maybe redirect with an error message
        header("Location: dashboard.php?status=error");
        exit();
    }
    $stmt->close();
} else {
    header("Location: dashboard.php");
    exit();
}
?>
```

Create the logout script

Finally, a simple script to end the session and log the user out. Create **logout.php** in the **admin** folder (mini-cms/admin/logout.php). Add the following code:

```
<?php
session_start();
// Unset all of the session variables
$_SESSION = array();
// Destroy the session
session_destroy();
// Redirect to login page
header("location: index.php");
exit;
?>
```

Congratulations! You have just built a complete Content Management System.

Bridging the gap: Learned concepts and application implementation

Let's connect the theory to what we just built:

- **CMS concepts:** We built the two core parts of a CMS - the public-facing index.php and post.php (frontend) and the secure admin/ directory (backend).
- **Database schema:** Our posts table in the **mini_cms_db** database was the central storage, which we had designed.
- **User authentication:** The combination of admin/index.php (the login form), admin/auth.php (the security check), and admin/logout.php created a secure admin area protected by PHP sessions.
- **CRUD Operations:**
    - **Create:** admin/add.php implements the 'Create' functionality.
    - **Read:** admin/dashboard.php reads and lists all posts.
    - **Update:** admin/edit.php handles the 'Update' logic.
    - **Delete:** admin/delete.php performs the 'Delete' operation.
- **SEO & user-friendly URLs:** Our **createSlug()** function and the use of slugs in the public-facing URLs (post.php?slug=...) directly implement the SEO-friendly strategy.
- **Responsive design:** The style.css file contains media queries that make both the blog and the admin panel adapt to different screen sizes, ensuring a good user experience on any device.

Running and testing

Now, let's bring your CMS to life and test its features.

1. Make sure **Apache** and **MySQL** are running in your XAMPP Control Panel.
2. Open your browser and go to **http://localhost/codes/mini-cms/admin/**.
3. You see the login screen.

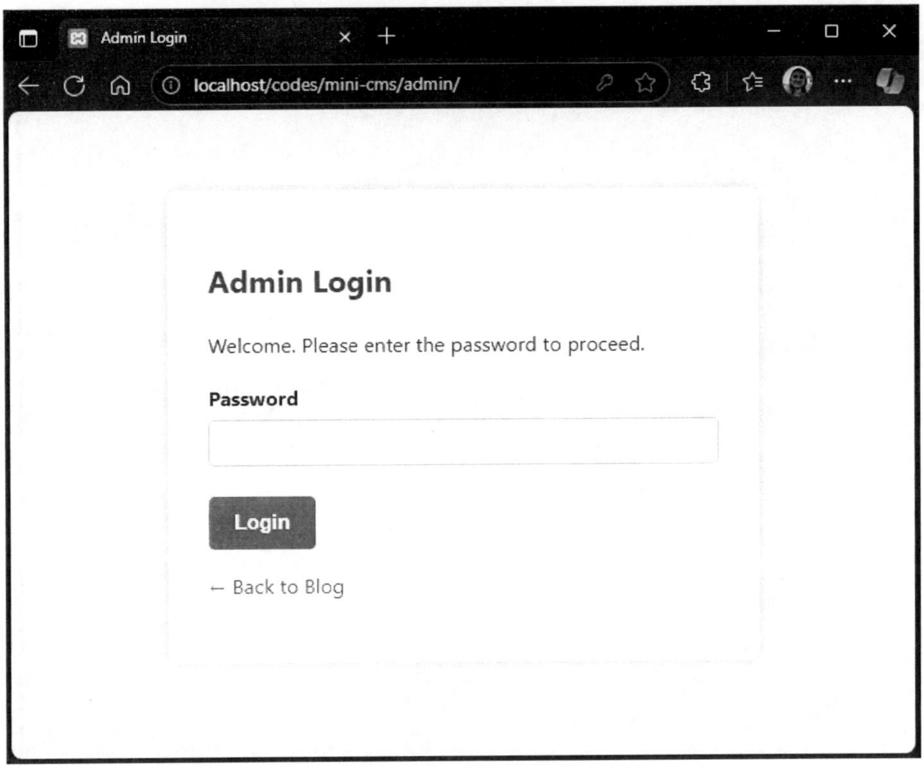

4. Try entering a wrong password and you see an **error message**.

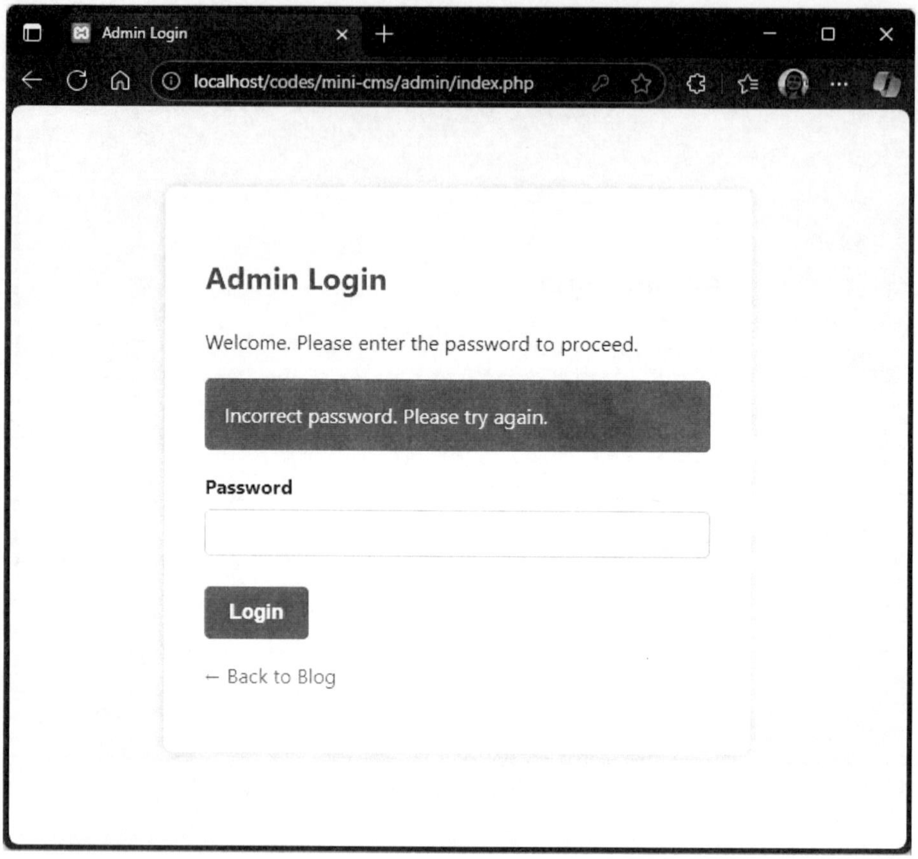

5. Now, enter the correct password: **password123**. You are redirected to the **admin dashboard**, which is empty.

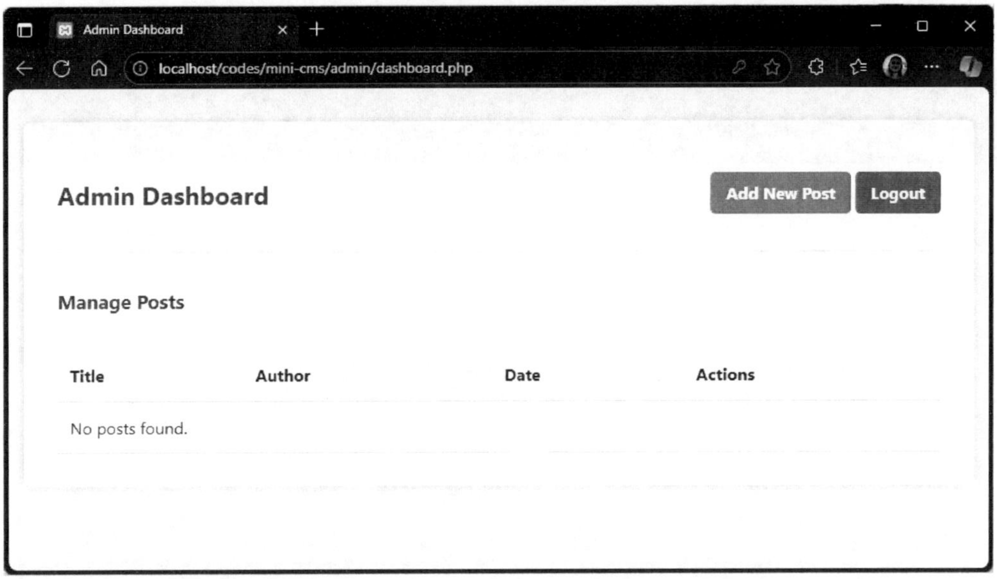

6. Click **Add New Post**. Your are directed to **Add New Post** page.

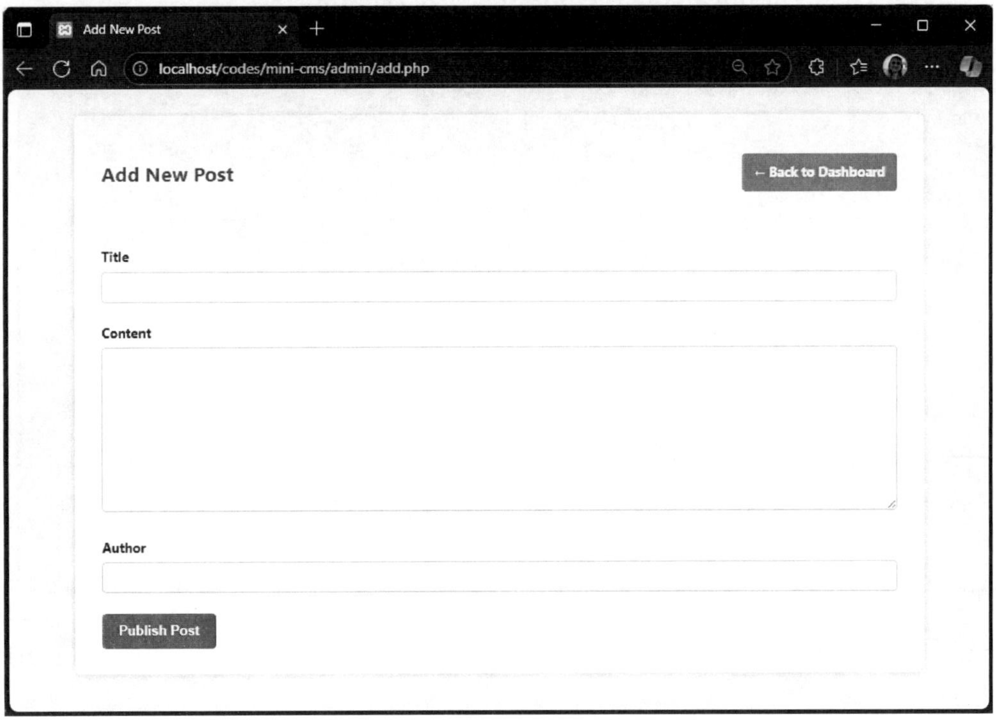

7. Fill in the form. Click **Publish Post**. You are redirected to the dashboard, and your new post is listed in the table.

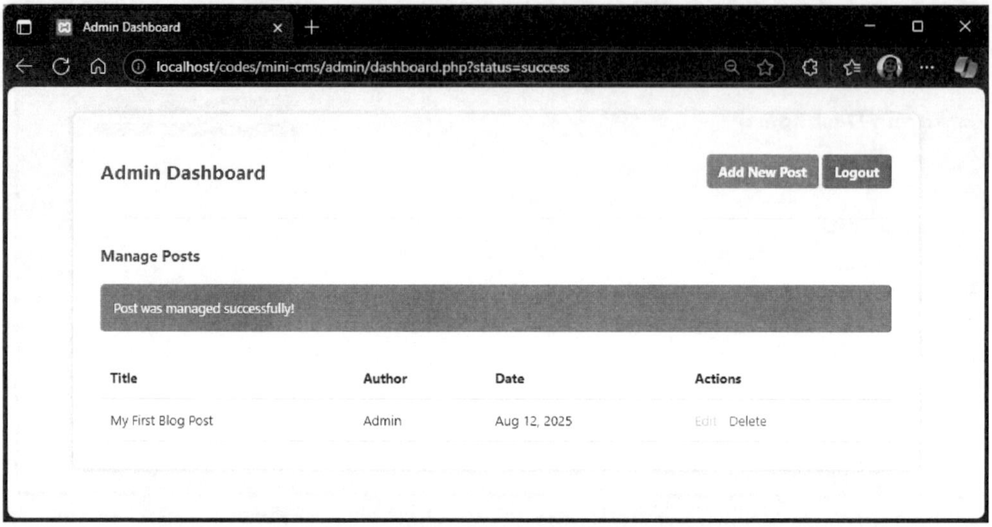

8. Now, open a new tab and go to **http://localhost/codes/mini-cms/**.
9. You see your first post's title and a short preview.

10. Click **Read More** or the post title. The URL changes to something like **http://localhost/codes/mini-cms/post.php?slug=my-first-blog-post**, and you see the full content of your post.

11. Go back to your admin dashboard tab. Find your post in the table and click the **Edit** link.

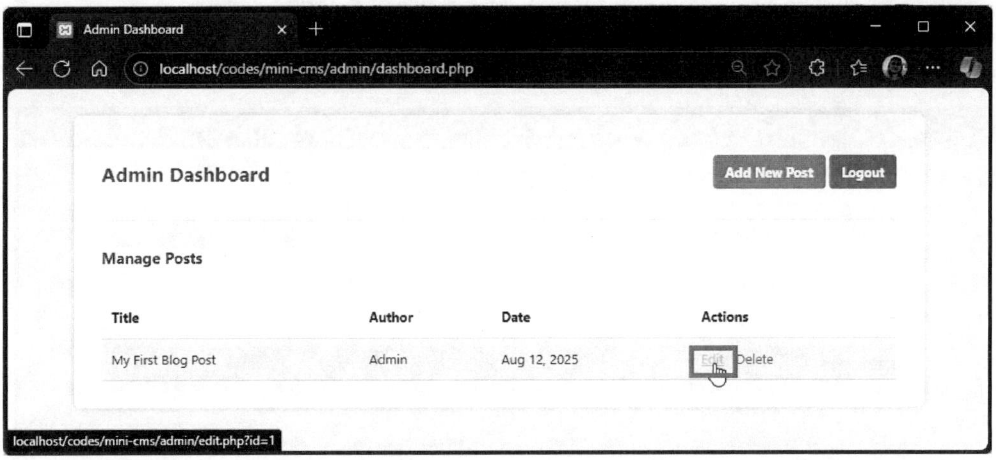

12. Change the title and add more content. Click **Update Post**. You are sent back to the dashboard, where you see the updated title.

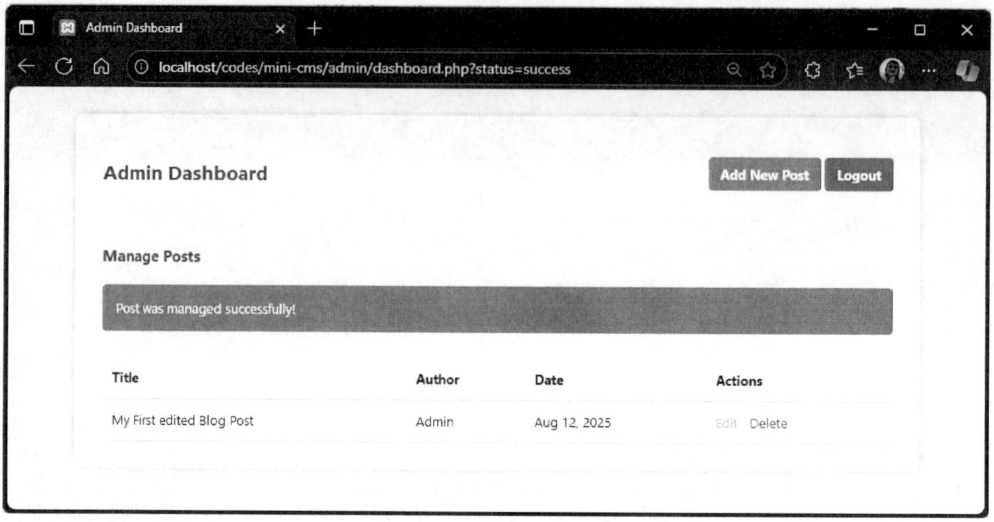

13. Refresh your public post page to see the changes live.
14. On the admin dashboard, click the **Delete** link for your post.

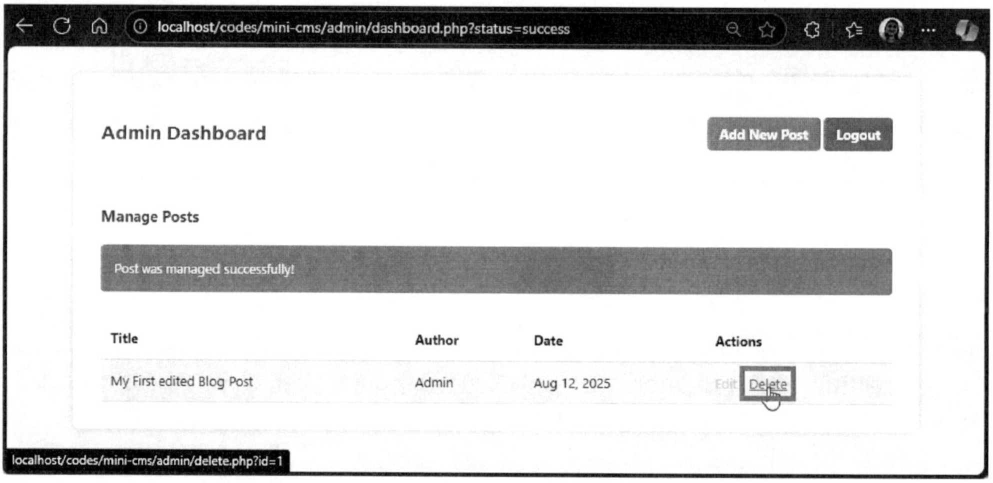

15. A confirmation box pops up.

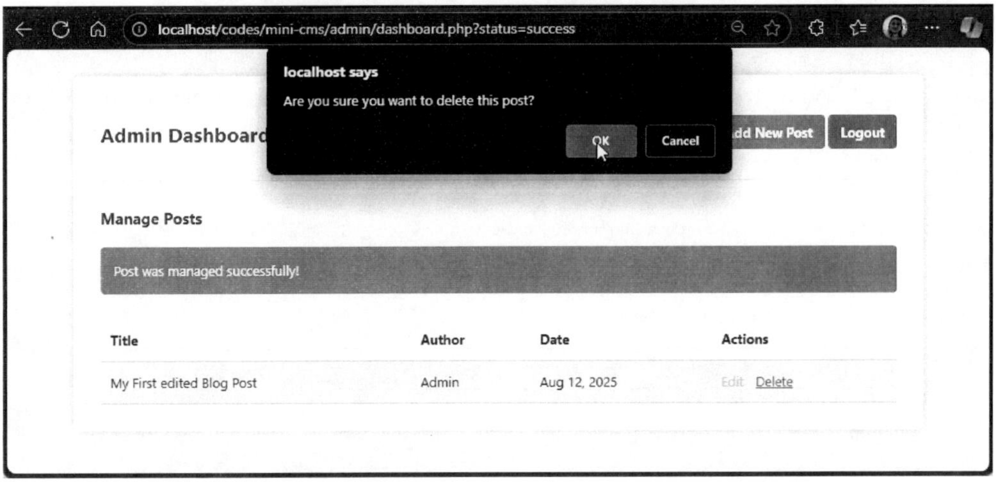

16. Click **OK**. The post disappears from the list.

17. If you now visit the public blog homepage, it will say **No posts found**.
18. In the **admin** dashboard, click **Logout**. You are redirected to the login page.
19. Try accessing the dashboard directly (http://localhost/codes/mini-cms/admin/dashboard.php); you are blocked and sent back to the login screen.

Exploring application behaviour: A practical run-through

- **Invalid input:** What happens if you try to submit the **Add New Post** form with empty fields? Our script displays the **All fields are required** error message, and no post is created.

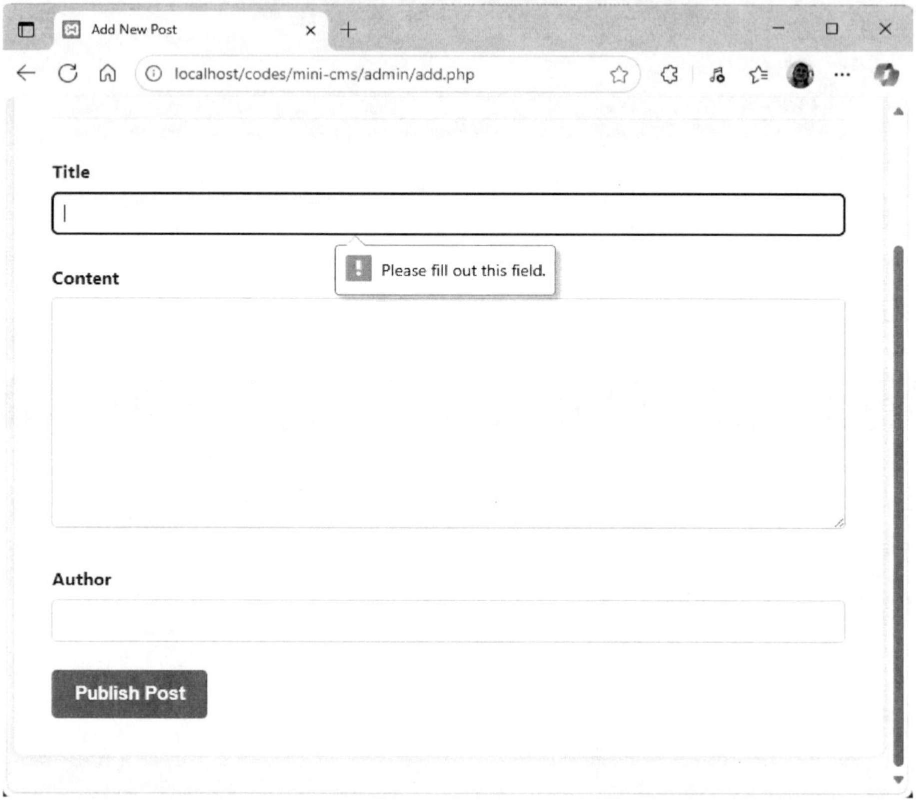

- **Duplicate titles:** Try creating two posts with the exact same title. The createSlug() function will generate the same slug initially, but our code then checks for duplicates and appends a unique timestamp to the second slug (e.g., my-title-1678886400) to avoid a database error and ensure both posts are accessible via unique URLs.
- **Accessing an invalid post:** What if you manually change the URL to edit.php?id=999 for a post that doesn't exist? Our script will not find a matching post and will redirect you straight back to the dashboard, preventing errors. The same thing happens on the public side if you try to visit a slug that doesn't exist.

Harnessing CMS in real-world contexts

This mini-CMS isn't just an exercise; it's a foundational tool. The skills you've used are directly applicable to many real-world projects:

- **Personal blogs & portfolios:** This is the most direct use case. You can easily expand this project to showcase your work or writing.
- **Small business websites:** Many businesses need a simple "News" or "Announcements" section on their website. This CMS is perfect for that.
- **Club or community sites:** A local club could use this to post event updates and news for its members.

Wrapping up

In this chapter, we took a giant leap forward, consolidating many of our previously learned skills into a single, substantial project. You now have a solid understanding of how content-driven websites work from the inside out.

Here's a summary of what you accomplished:

- **Built a full-stack application:** You created both a user-facing frontend and a secure, password-protected backend.
- **Designed a database schema:** You planned and created the posts table, which is the heart of the CMS.
- **Implemented robust CRUD functionality:** You built the forms and scripts to create, read, update, and delete content dynamically.
- **Secured an admin panel:** You used PHP sessions to create a simple and effective authentication system.
- **Created SEO-friendly URLs:** You learned how to generate and use slugs to make your website more appealing to users and search engines.
- **Applied responsive web design:** You used CSS and media queries to ensure your application looks great on all devices.

Give yourself a huge pat on the back! Building a CMS is a rite of passage for web developers, and you've successfully built one from the ground up. You've seen how individual concepts like variables, loops, sessions, and database queries all come together to create something powerful and practical. You are no longer just writing scripts; you are building applications.

Based on the book's title, **Unlocking AI with PHP**, we've already covered the foundational principles of building dynamic web applications with PHP. Now, we're ready to unlock the other half of the title and delve into the world of artificial intelligence. We're not stopping at simply functional and dynamic; we want our web apps to be smarter. Get ready for ***Section 06: AI awakened - Smarter web apps for all***, where we begin with ***Chapter 19: Making web apps smarter - PHP meets AI***.

Chapter 19

Section 06: AI awakened – Smarter web apps for all

Making web apps smarter – PHP meets AI

What you'll learn

- What AI truly means?
- Common AI use cases
- Ethical AI principles
- PHP's role with AI
- AI-friendly data formats

Welcome to one of the most exciting frontiers in web development! So far on our journey, we have built applications that are fantastic at storing, retrieving, and displaying data. They work perfectly, following every instruction we give them. But now, we're going to teach our applications to do something that feels like magic: we're going to teach them to *understand* that data.

This chapter is your official entry into the world of **Artificial Intelligence (AI)**, a field that is completely changing how we interact with technology. We'll demystify what AI really is, breaking it down into simple, understandable concepts. Most importantly, you'll see how PHP, your trusted language for the web, is the perfect tool to connect your applications to powerful AI **brains** and bring that intelligence to your users.

Think about the smartest features on the websites you use every day. When Netflix suggests a movie, you end up loving, or when Gmail instantly spots a suspicious email and moves it to your spam folder, that's AI at work. At its core, **AI is about teaching computers to recognize patterns, make decisions, and learn from data, much like a human does**.

In this chapter, we'll explore how you, as a PHP developer, can harness this incredible power. While PHP doesn't generate the AI models itself, it acts as a brilliant conductor for an orchestra. It takes a request from your user, sends it to a specialized AI service for analysis, and then uses the insightful results to create a smarter, more responsive experience on your website.

What is AI? Modern trends for beginners

You absolutely do not need to be a data scientist or a math genius to understand AI. Let's simplify it. Think of it as the difference between a simple calculator and a human brain. A calculator only follows explicit instructions (add, subtract, etc.). AI, on the other hand, tries to **make software smart enough to think and learn**.

Imagine teaching a small child what a "dog" is. You don't give the child a list of rules like "if it has four legs and fur, it's a dog." Instead, you show them many different dogs—big ones, small ones, fluffy ones, loud ones. Over time, the child's brain learns the *pattern*. Eventually, they can see a dog they've never encountered before and correctly identify it.

This is exactly how the most common form of AI works.

Two major trends drive most of the AI you see today:

- **Machine Learning (ML):** This is the process we just described. It's the science of "training" a computer model by feeding it vast amounts of data. The model learns patterns from this data, allowing it to make predictions about new, unseen data. By analyzing thousands of positive product reviews, an ML model learns the pattern of what "positive" text looks like.
- **Natural Language Processing (NLP):** This is a specialized branch of AI focused on understanding human language, both written and spoken. When you talk to a virtual assistant like Siri or see your words instantly translated on Google, you're witnessing NLP in action. It's the magic that allows computers to process, interpret, and respond to language just like we do.

For a PHP developer, the best part is that you don't have to build these complex models from scratch. Instead, you'll learn how to use pre-trained models that experts have already built, accessing their incredible intelligence through simple web requests.

Where PHP integrates AI today

So, if PHP isn't the AI brain, what is its role? Think of PHP as the perfect **restaurant waiter**. It manages the entire communication process smoothly and efficiently.

Here's the workflow, using our waiter analogy:

- **The diner places an order (user input):** A user writes a comment on your website: "I love this new feature!"
- **The waiter takes the order (PHP takes over):** Your PHP script receives this comment text. The waiter writes it down carefully.
- **The waiter goes to the kitchen (PHP sends to AI):** The waiter (your PHP script) doesn't cook the meal. Instead, it takes the order to the expert chef (the AI service) who specializes in understanding food—or in our case, text.
- **The chef cooks the meal (AI analyzes):** The AI service's powerful model processes the text and understands its meaning. It concludes the sentiment is "positive."
- **The chef hands off the dish (AI responds):** The AI service sends a simple, structured response back, like a perfectly plated dish. The response is just simple data, for example: {"sentiment": "positive"}.
- **The waiter serves the diner (PHP acts on insight):** Your PHP code receives this simple response. It now knows the comment was positive and can act accordingly. It might display a "Thank you for your kind words!" message or add a "+1" to a "positive feedback" counter in your database.

PHP is the master of handling these web requests and integrating the results seamlessly into a beautiful and interactive webpage for the user.

Key use cases

AI isn't just a futuristic concept; it solves real-world problems for web developers *today*. Here are three of the most common and valuable use cases you can implement with PHP.

- **Sentiment analysis:** This is the process of programmatically identifying the emotional tone behind a body of text. Is a user's comment positive, negative, or neutral? This is incredibly useful for automatically sorting customer feedback, monitoring your brand's reputation on social media, or understanding user satisfaction at a large scale. It finds the emotional *pattern* in the words.

- **Content moderation:** Websites with user-generated content, like blogs or forums, face a constant battle against spam, trolls, and inappropriate posts. AI can automatically scan text and images to flag or remove content that violates your terms of service, finding the *pattern* of harmful content. This saves countless hours of manual work and keeps your community safe.
- **Recommendation engines:** This is one of the most powerful uses of AI for e-commerce and content-based websites. By analyzing a user's past behaviour (what they've viewed, liked, or purchased), a recommendation engine can find the *pattern* in their tastes and predict what they might be interested in next. This is what drives the "Customers who bought this also bought..." and "Recommended for you" sections on sites like Amazon and Spotify, leading to massively increased user engagement and sales.

Data formats for AI

When your PHP application talks to an AI service, it needs to speak a language the AI can understand. You can't just send a random jumble of text. The data must be structured. The two most common formats for this are JSON and CSV.

JSON (JavaScript Object Notation)

This is, by far, the most common format for communicating with modern web services (APIs). It's lightweight, easy for humans to read, and—most importantly—maps perfectly to PHP's associative arrays that you already know and love.

Think of an associative array as a filing cabinet with labeled drawers. Each label is a key, and what's inside the drawer is the value.

'name' => 'Sharanam' is like a drawer labeled **name** containing the value **Sharanam**.

Before sending data to an AI, you'll build a PHP array and then use the built-in **json_encode()** function to convert it into a perfectly formatted JSON string:

```
<?php
// Let's create a PHP associative array with our data.
$userData = [
  "userId" => 101,
  "commentText" => "I love this product, it works great!",
  "language" => "en-US"
];
// Now, let's convert our PHP array into a JSON string.
// JSON_PRETTY_PRINT makes it readable for us humans.
$jsonString = json_encode($userData, JSON_PRETTY_PRINT);
```

```
// Let's display it to see what it looks like.
echo "<pre>" . $jsonString . "</pre>";
?>
```

The code above produces a clean, structured JSON string. This is exactly the format an AI service expects.

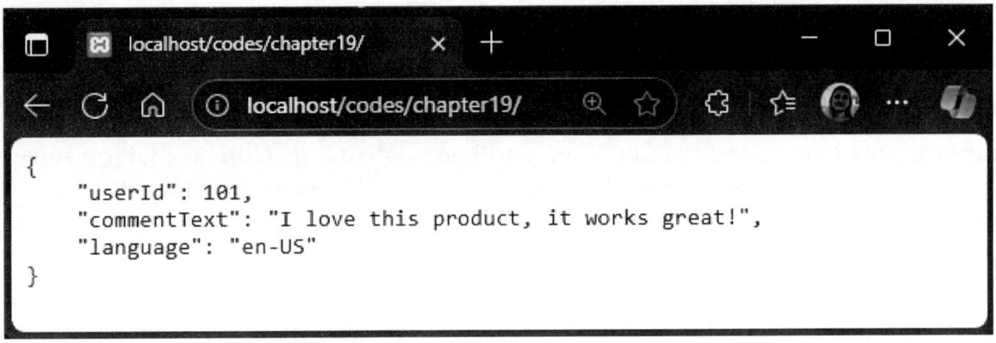

CSV (Comma-Separated Values)

CSV files are simple text files that represent tabular data, just like a basic spreadsheet. Each line in the file is a row, and values within that row are separated by commas. While less common for single, real-time requests, CSV is the go-to format for uploading large datasets, for example, if you wanted to provide thousands of historical product reviews to help "train" a new machine learning model.

A simple CSV file for user feedback might look like this:

```
commentId,text,sentiment
1,"This is fantastic!",positive
2,"I am very disappointed.",negative
3,"It is okay, I guess.",neutral
```

Your PHP scripts can easily read and write to CSV files using built-in functions like **fgetcsv()** and **fputcsv()**, making it a versatile tool for handling bulk data.

Legal and ethical AI considerations

Using AI comes with great power and even greater responsibility. As a developer, it's not just about making things work; it's about making them work *right*. Always keep these critical ethical principles in mind.

- **Privacy is paramount:** Never, ever send private user information (like names, emails, phone numbers, or addresses) to a third-party AI service without getting clear, explicit permission from the user. You must be a guardian of your users' data. Always anonymize it whenever possible.
- **Beware of bias:** AI models learn from the data they are given. If the data reflects historical or societal biases, the AI's decisions will also be biased. For example, if an AI is trained on job applicant data from a time when mostly men were hired for a certain role, it might learn to unfairly favour male applicants. Be mindful of this and strive to use models that are designed to be fair and equitable.
- **Transparency with users:** People deserve to know when a machine is making a decision about them. If an AI automatically rejects a user's comment or application, it's good practice to be transparent about it. This builds trust and gives users a better, more honest experience.

Hands-on: Building a Sentiment feedback form

It's time to put theory into practice! In this hands-on project, we'll build a complete, single-file web application that simulates sentiment analysis. A user will be able to submit a comment, and our PHP script will analyze it for positive or negative keywords, then display a beautiful, color-coded result. This exercise perfectly demonstrates the core logic of an AI-powered feature without the complexity of connecting to an external service (we'll save that for the next chapter!).

The goal of this application is to create a "smart" feedback form. Instead of just storing a user's comment in a database and looking at it later, our app will provide immediate, intelligent feedback on the comment's tone. This project will teach you the fundamental flow of all AI-powered web features:

- Capture user input.
- Process that input using a set of rules (our simple "AI model").
- Present a dynamic, useful result back to the user.

Building the application

Let's get our hands dirty and start coding. We will build this entire application in a single file inside a new project folder. Follow these steps exactly.

Create your project folder

1. First, launch your **XAMPP Control Panel** and ensure the **Apache** module is running.
2. Then, open your XAMPP installation directory. For most Windows users, this is C:\xampp.
3. Navigate into the **htdocs** folder. This is the root directory for all your web projects. Inside **htdocs\codes**, create a new folder and name it as **sentiment-feedback**. Our project will live at the web address http://localhost/codes/sentiment-feedback/.

Create the main application file

1. Now, open your favorite code editor, **Visual Studio Code**.
2. Go to **File → New File...**. Immediately save this empty file by going to **File → Save As...**.
3. Navigate to the folder you just created (C:\xampp\htdocs\codes\sentiment-feedback) and save the file with the name **index.php**.

Write the HTML structure and CSS styling

Let's build the user-facing part of our application first. This includes the HTML form for the user to type in and the CSS to make it look professional and modern. The CSS will also include special styles for our results: a green box for positive, red for negative, and blue-gray for neutral.

Add the following code in your empty index.php file in VS Code:

```
<!DOCTYPE html>
<html lang="en">
<head>
    <meta charset="UTF-8">
    <meta name="viewport" content="width=device-width, initial-scale=1.0">
    <title>Sentiment Feedback Form</title>
    <style>
        /* A little CSS magic to make our app look great! */
        body {
            font-family: -apple-system, BlinkMacSystemFont, "Segoe UI", Roboto,
                         Helvetica, Arial, sans-serif;
            background-color: #f4f7f9;
            color: #333;
            display: flex;
            justify-content: center;
            align-items: center;
            height: 100vh;
            margin: 0;
```

```
        }
        .container {
            background-color: #ffffff;
            padding: 40px;
            border-radius: 10px;
            box-shadow: 0 4px 20px rgba(0, 0, 0, 0.1);
            width: 100%;
            max-width: 500px;
            text-align: center;
        }
        h1 {
            color: #2c3e50;
            margin-bottom: 20px;
        }
        textarea {
            width: 100%;
            padding: 15px;
            border-radius: 5px;
            border: 1px solid #ccc;
            font-size: 16px;
            margin-bottom: 20px;
            box-sizing: border-box; /* Ensures padding doesn't break the layout */
        }
        button {
            background-color: #3498db;
            color: white;
            border: none;
            padding: 15px 30px;
            font-size: 16px;
            border-radius: 5px;
            cursor: pointer;
            transition: background-color 0.3s ease;
        }
        button:hover {
            background-color: #2980b9;
        }
        /* These classes will style our result boxes */
        .result {
            margin-top: 30px;
            padding: 20px;
            border-radius: 5px;
            font-size: 18px;
            font-weight: bold;
            text-align: left;
        }
        .result.positive {
            background-color: #eaf7e9;
            color: #2d6a4f;
            border: 1px solid #a7d79b;
        }
        .result.negative {
```

```
            background-color: #fbe9e7;
            color: #c62828;
            border: 1px solid #ffcdd2;
        }
        .result.neutral {
            background-color: #e8eaf6;
            color: #3f51b5;
            border: 1px solid #c5cae9;
        }
    </style>
</head>
<body>
    <div class="container">
        <h1>Share Your Feedback</h1>
        <p>Let us know what you think. Our smart system will analyze the tone of
           your message.</p>
        <form action="index.php" method="POST">
            <textarea name="comment" rows="5" placeholder="Type your comment
                      here..."></textarea>
            <button type="submit">Analyze Sentiment</button>
        </form>
    </div>
</body>
</html>
```

Save your file. If you open **http://localhost/codes/sentiment-feedback/** in your browser right now, you see a beautiful, styled form. It just doesn't do anything yet.

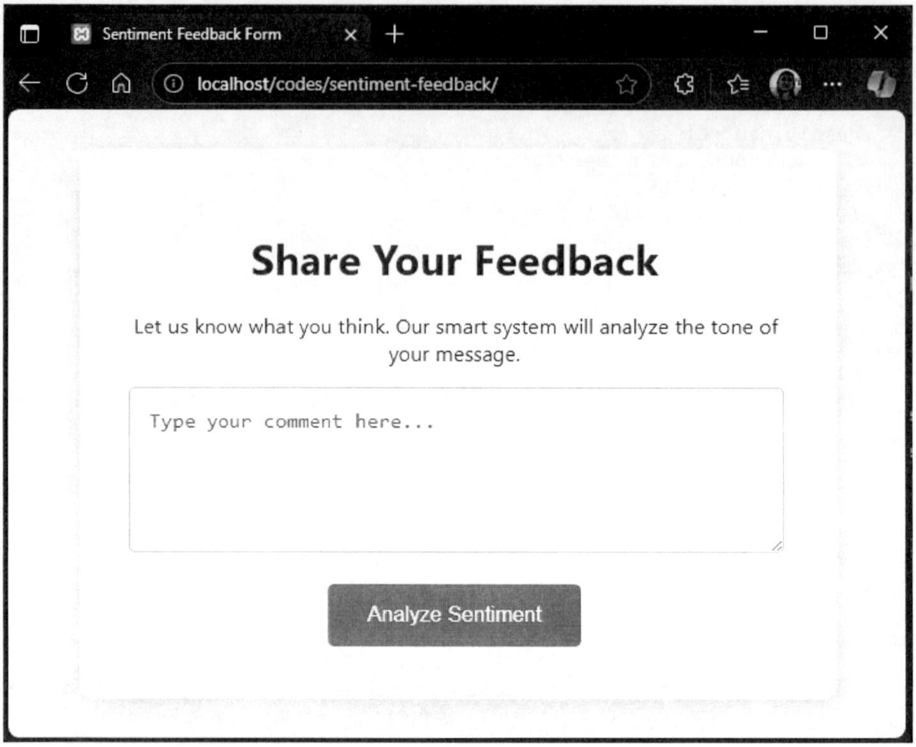

Add the PHP processing logic

Now for the "brain" of our operation. We will add a PHP block at the very top of the file. This script will define our simple sentiment analysis logic, check if the form has been submitted, process the input, and prepare a result that we can display later in the HTML.

Go to the **very top** of your index.php file, and on the very first line, before <!DOCTYPE html>, add the following PHP code:

```
<?php
// We start by defining the variables we will need. Initializing them as null or
// empty prevents errors when the page first loads.
$sentimentResult = null;
$userComment = '';
/**
 * This is our "AI" model. It's a simple function that analyzes text for specific
 * keywords to determine if it's positive, negative, or neutral.
 * @param string $text The user's comment to analyze.
 * @return string The resulting sentiment: 'Positive', 'Negative', or 'Neutral'.
 */
```

- **PHP as the connector:** The PHP script at the top is the engine of the operation. It receives the user input from the HTML form ($_POST), processes it, and prepares the output, demonstrating PHP's role as the central controller.
- **Input and output:** The form <textarea> is the **input** for our model. The coloured div with the sentiment result is the dynamic **output** generated by our logic. This input-process-output pattern is fundamental to all AI-powered applications.

As we've just proven, you don't need to be building the next Google to benefit from AI. Adding a touch of intelligence can dramatically improve even the simplest applications you create. A standard blog comment section becomes vastly better when it can automatically hide or flag potentially toxic comments for review. A basic photo gallery becomes more useful when it can automatically suggest tags for images ("dog," "beach," "sunset"). AI provides a layer of polish and utility that can make your projects stand out, provide real value to your users, and make your portfolio look much more impressive.

Running and testing

It's time for the moment of truth! Let's see our smart form in action.

1. Make sure your **XAMPP Control Panel** is open and the **Apache** module shows a green "Running" status.
2. Open your favourite web browser (Chrome, Firefox, Edge, etc.).
3. In the address bar, carefully type **http://localhost/codes/sentiment-feedback/** and press **Enter**.
4. You see the beautiful feedback form we designed.

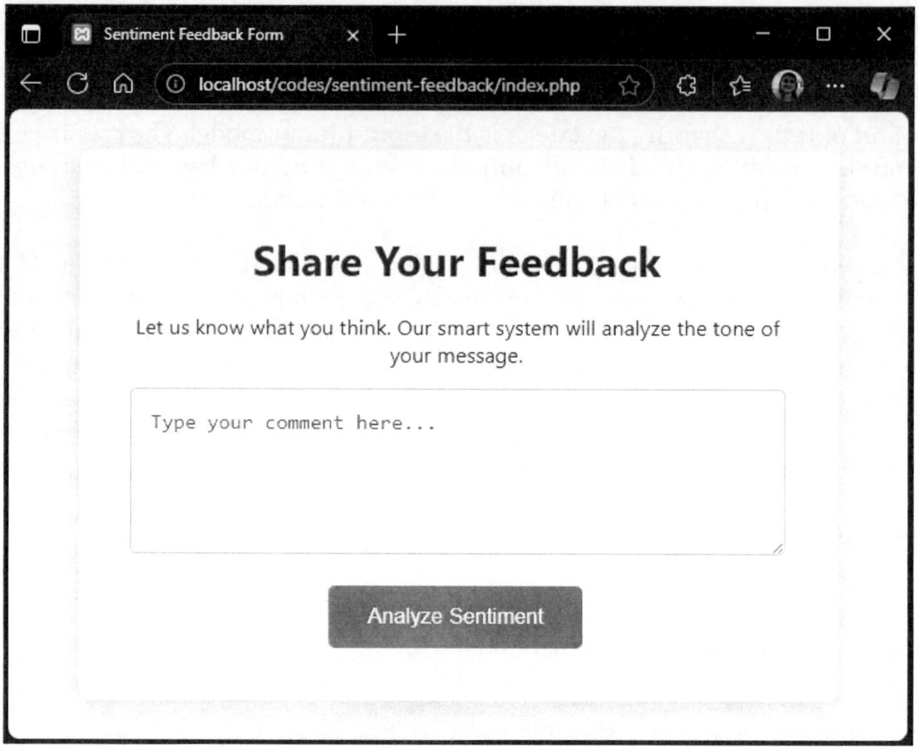

5. **Test case 1:** Positive feedback
   - In the **textarea**, type **This is an amazing book, I am very happy!**
   - Click the **Analyze Sentiment** button.
   - The page reloads, and below the button, a pleasant green box appears with the text **Sentiment Detected: Positive**.

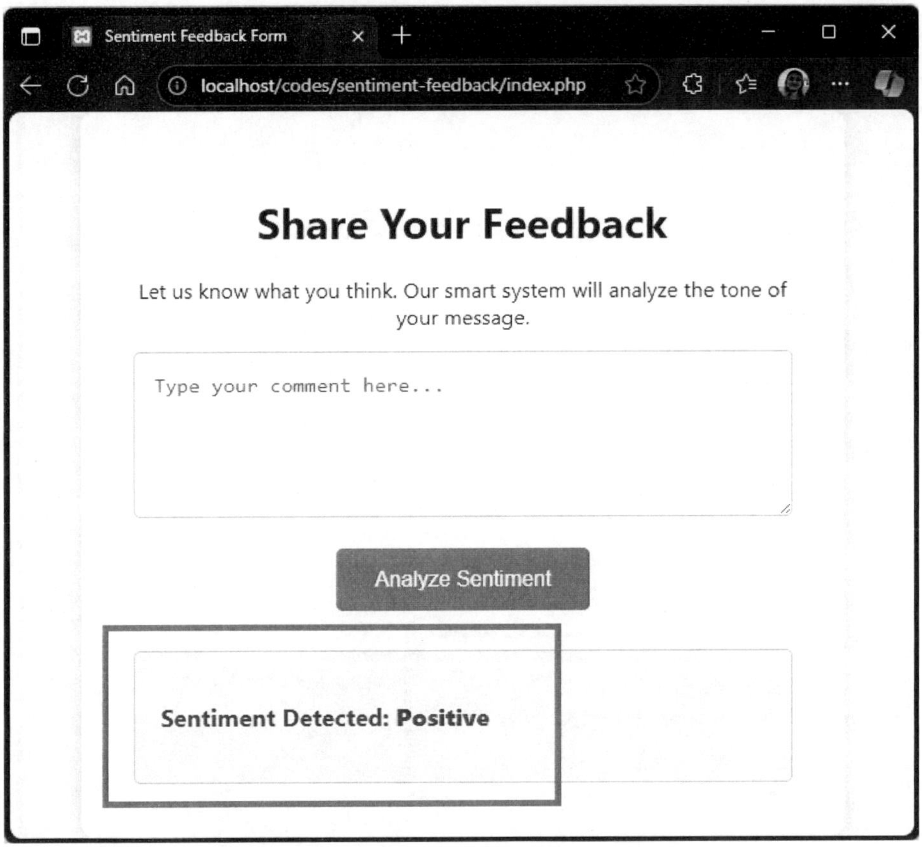

6. **Test case 2:** Negative feedback
   - Now, clear the first message and type **I am so disappointed with this terrible service**.
   - Click the **Analyze Sentiment** button.
   - A warning-red box now appears with the text **Sentiment Detected: Negative**.

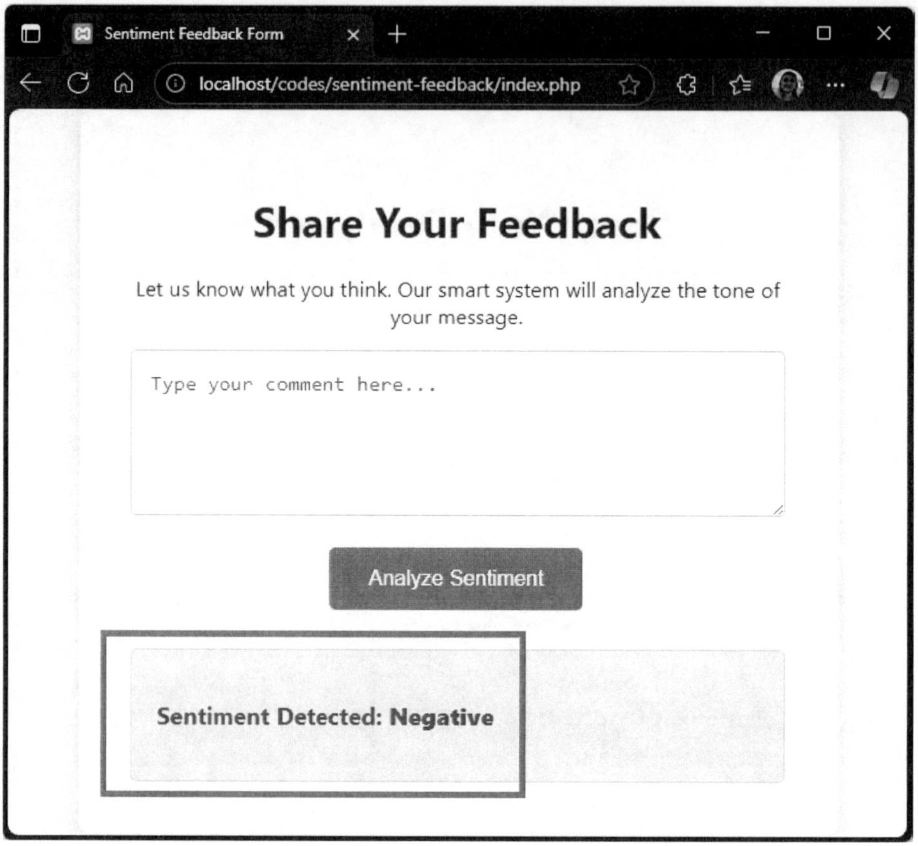

7. **Test case 3:** Neutral feedback
    - Finally, clear the message and type something neutral, like **This is a book**.
    - Click the **Analyze Sentiment** button.
    - A calm, blue-gray box appears with the text **Sentiment Detected: Neutral**.

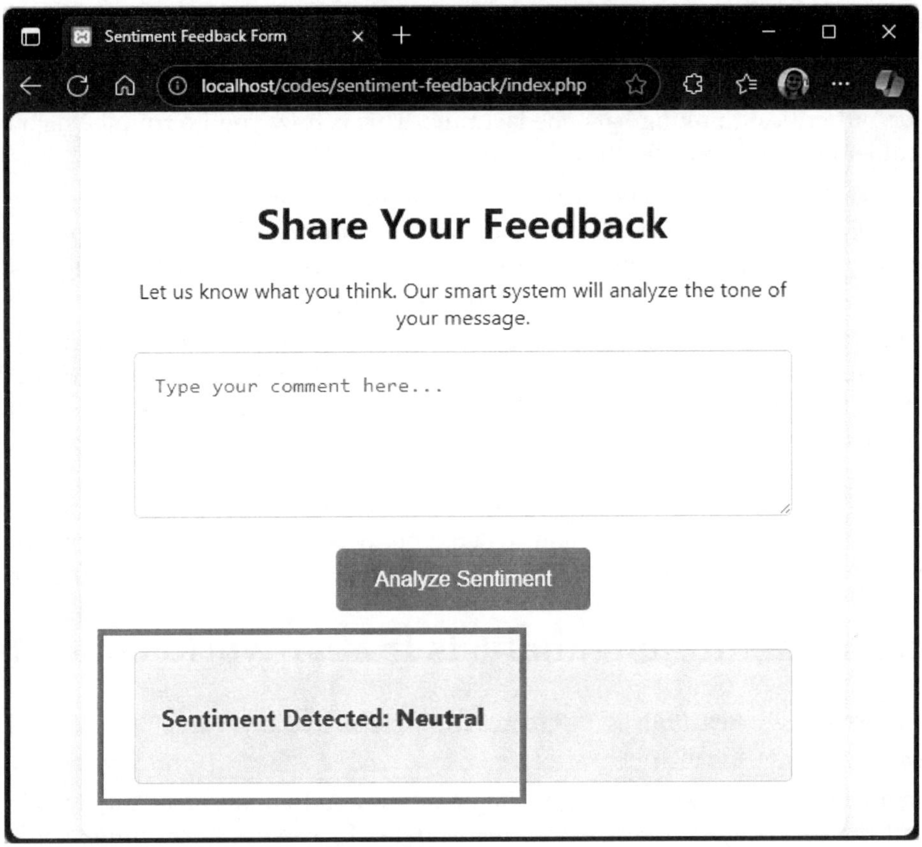

Exploring application behaviour: A practical run-through

A great developer doesn't just build things; they try to break them to understand their limits. This is how we learn and improve.

- **Empty submission:** What happens if you click the **Analyze Sentiment** button without typing anything? Go ahead and try it. Thanks to our if (!empty($userComment)) check, the page simply reloads, and no result box appears. This is the correct, professional way to handle empty input.
- **Mixed signals:** This is where our simple model shows its limitations. Try typing **This is not a bad product**. Our code will scan the text, find the word "bad," and immediately classify the entire sentence as **Negative**, which is incorrect. This is a perfect illustration of why real-world NLP models are so complex—they are trained to understand context, negation ("not bad"), and subtleties that our simple keyword search cannot.

- **No keywords:** If you type **The sky is blue**, which contains none of our defined keywords, the app will correctly classify it as **Neutral**, as it should.

Let's put on our critical thinking hats one last time. This is how you go from being a coder to being a problem-solver. Consider these scenarios:

- **Sarcasm:** How would our code handle the comment, "Great, another bug. This is just fantastic."? It would see "Great" and "fantastic" and incorrectly label it **Positive**. Real AI models are trained on massive datasets of human conversation to try and understand the nuances of sarcasm, but it remains one of the hardest problems in all of NLP.
- **Evolving language:** What if a new slang term for "good" (like "it's fire") becomes popular? Our hard-coded keyword list wouldn't know about it. This is why real AI models are constantly being retrained and updated with new data—to keep up with the ever-changing way humans communicate.

Understanding these limitations is key. It helps you know when a simple solution like ours is "good enough" for a small project and when you need to reach for a more powerful, professional tool. And that is exactly what we are going to do in the very next chapter.

Harnessing sentiment analysis in real-world contexts

The simple feature we just built is the foundation for incredibly valuable real-world tools. Businesses use this exact principle to:

- **Automate customer support:** Imagine an email system that automatically tags incoming support tickets. "Angry" messages can be escalated to a senior agent immediately, while simple questions can be routed to a different queue.
- **Monitor brand health:** Companies can analyze mentions of their brand on Twitter or Facebook in real-time to get an instant pulse on public opinion, allowing them to react quickly to news or customer service issues.
- **Analyze product reviews:** An e-commerce site manager can use this to quickly sift through thousands of reviews to identify common complaints ("the battery is poor") or highly-praised features, providing invaluable business intelligence.

Wrapping up

In this chapter, we pulled back the curtain on the complex world of AI and made it approachable and fun. You learned not just the theory but also how to build a practical, AI-driven feature from the ground up, using only the PHP skills you already possess.

- You learned that **AI is about making software smart** by teaching it to recognize patterns, with Machine Learning (ML) and Natural Language Processing (NLP) being the key drivers.
- You now understand that **PHP's role is to be the perfect connector**, acting as the bridge between your web app and powerful AI services.
- We explored core use cases that provide immense value, including **sentiment analysis, content moderation, and recommendation engines**.
- You saw how data needs to be structured for AI using **JSON and CSV**.
- We built a **complete, hands-on sentiment analysis application**, demonstrating how to process user input and provide a dynamic, intelligent response.
- Most importantly, we discussed the critical **ethical considerations** of privacy, bias, and transparency that every responsible developer must keep in mind when implementing AI.

Congratulations! You have officially taken your first, and most important, step into the exciting world of AI-powered web development. You've proven that you can build an application that doesn't just display data but actually *interprets* it to create a more dynamic and interactive user experience. You now have a solid, practical foundation for understanding how AI can integrate with web applications to make them smarter, more helpful, and more engaging.

You've built the foundation. Now it's time to build the skyscraper. In the next chapter, we'll take this a giant leap forward in ***Chapter 20: Plug and play intelligence – Using public AI APIs***, where we'll connect our PHP code to real, world-class AI models to perform even more amazing tasks.

Chapter 20

Section 06: AI awakened – Smarter web apps for all

Plug and play intelligence – Using public AI APIs

What you'll learn

- Getting a real API key
- Crafting effective prompts
- Working with live JSON data
- Calling the Gemini AI API
- Using cURL in PHP

Welcome to one of the most exciting frontiers in modern web development! So far, our applications have been smart, but their logic has been entirely self-contained. In this chapter, we're going to open a door to the outside world and connect our PHP code to the vast intelligence of external AI services. We'll learn how to "plug in" capabilities like understanding human language, making our apps more responsive, intuitive, and powerful.

Imagine your phone's weather app. It doesn't have a tiny weather station inside it; instead, it asks a powerful, remote weather service for the current forecast and displays the answer. It does this using an Application Programming Interface, or **API**. An API is a set of rules and tools that allows different software applications to talk to each other.

In this chapter, you'll learn how to make your PHP applications communicate with public AI APIs like Google's Gemini. These services can analyze text, identify emotions, and perform complex tasks, allowing you to integrate incredible intelligence into your projects without having to build it from scratch. We'll build a help desk form that understands if a user is happy or frustrated and responds accordingly.

What are public APIs?

A **public API** is a service offered by a company that allows developers like us to access their data or features. They do the heavy lifting of creating a powerful service, and we can "call" their API to use it in our own applications.

To use most APIs, you need an **API key**. It's a unique string of characters that identifies your application and proves you have permission to use the service. It also allows the provider to track your usage.

Let's get a real API key for Google's Gemini, which we'll use in our project.

Getting your Gemini API key

- **Navigate to Google AI Studio:** Open your browser and go to **aistudio.google.com**.
- **Sign In:** You'll be prompted to sign in with your **Google** account. Go ahead and do this. You may also need to agree to the terms of service.
- **Create API Key:** Once you are in the AI Studio interface, look for a button or menu option on the left that says **Get API key**. Click on it.
- **Generate your key:** In the next screen, you will see an option to **Create API key in new project**. Click this button.
- **Copy and save your key:** A new key will be generated and displayed in a pop-up window. This is your secret key! **Copy this key immediately and save it somewhere safe**, like a temporary text file. You will not be able to see the full key again after closing this window.

Treat this key like a password. We are about to learn how to store and use it securely.

Talking to Gemini with PHP

AI models like Gemini are accessible through APIs. To communicate with them, our PHP application needs to send an HTTP request containing our query (the "**prompt**") and our API key. The AI service processes the prompt and sends the answer back, usually in a structured format called JSON.

While many developers use special libraries (SDKs), the fundamental process relies on a standard PHP extension called **cURL**. cURL lets us create and send HTTP requests directly from our code.

Our PHP script will perform these steps:

- Formulate a clear instruction for the AI (the "**prompt**").
- Create a cURL request to the Gemini API's specific URL (its "**endpoint**").
- Bundle our prompt and instructions into a JSON payload.
- Include our API key in the request URL for authentication.
- Send the request and capture the response from the AI service.
- Decode the JSON response to extract the AI's answer for display.

This is the core pattern for interacting with almost any modern web API.

REST, JSON, and HTTP requests

These three concepts are the bedrock of API communication. Let's demystify them.

- **HTTP requests:** You know GET and POST from our work with HTML forms. APIs use them too. A GET request retrieves data. A POST request, which we will use, sends data to be processed. We will be *posting* our message to the Gemini API for analysis.
- **REST (Representational State Transfer):** A popular architectural style for designing APIs. RESTful APIs use standard HTTP methods, making them predictable and easy to use.
- **JSON (JavaScript Object Notation):** The universal language of modern APIs. It's a lightweight, human-readable format for structuring data as key-value pairs. When the Gemini API sends us a response, it will be a JSON string. PHP's json_decode() and json_encode() functions are perfect for this.

Here is an example of the JSON we will **send** to the Gemini API:

```
{
  "contents": [{
```

```
    "parts": [{
      "text": "Analyze the sentiment of the following message. Respond with only a
              single word: Positive, Negative, or Neutral. Message: My order arrived
              on time and it works perfectly!"
    }]
  }]
}
```

Securely storing API keys

This is one of the most critical security practices you will learn.

Never write your API key directly in your main script. If you upload your code to a public place like GitHub, your key will be exposed, and anyone could use it on your behalf.

The correct approach is to store the key in a separate configuration file placed outside your public web directory. We then use PHP's require statement to pull the key into our script when needed.

Let's set up this secure structure.

- C:\xampp\htdocs\codes\config\
- C:\xampp\htdocs\codes\smart-help-desk\

You place your key file inside the **config** folder, keeping credentials separate from application code (C:\xampp\htdocs\codes\config\api_config.php):

```
<?php
// Define your API keys here. PASTE THE GEMINI API KEY YOU SAVED EARLIER
define('GEMINI_API_KEY', 'PASTE_YOUR_REAL_API_KEY_HERE');
```

Then, in your project script, you access it securely:

```
<?php
require_once '../../config/api_config.php';
// The constant GEMINI_API_KEY is now available for use.
```

This professional workflow keeps your secrets safe.

Parsing AI responses for usable output

When the Gemini API responds, it sends back a complex JSON string. Our job is to parse this string to find the piece of text that contains the answer we need.

Here's a simplified example of a JSON response from Gemini:

```
{
  "candidates": [
    {
      "content": {
        "parts": [
          {
            "text": "Positive"
          }
        ],
        "role": "model"
      }
    }
  ]
}
```

Our goal is to extract the word **Positive**. We use **json_decode()** to convert this string into a PHP associative array, then navigate through the nested structure to get the text:

```
<?php
// $apiResponse contains the JSON string from the API
$dataArray = json_decode($apiResponse, true);
// Navigate through the array to get to the answer
$sentiment = $dataArray['candidates'][0]['content']['parts'][0]['text'];
echo "The AI's sentiment analysis is: " . $sentiment;
```

Output:

```
The AI's sentiment analysis is: Positive
```

This is how we turn a raw API response into usable data in our application.

NLP basics

Natural Language Processing (NLP) is a field of AI focused on enabling computers to understand human language. The Gemini API is a powerful NLP engine. It offers key capabilities we can use:

- **Sentiment analysis:** Determining if text is positive, negative, or neutral. This is useful for gauging customer feedback.

- **Spam detection:** Analyzing a message to see if it is junk mail or a legitimate comment.
- **Summarization:** Creating a short summary from a long block of text.
- **Translation:** Translating text from one language to another.

By plugging into an NLP API, you can add these sophisticated features to your app with just a few lines of PHP code.

Hands-on: AI help desk - Smart contact form

We are going to build a smart contact form that uses the live Gemini API. When a user submits a message, our form will send that message to Google's AI for sentiment analysis. Based on the AI's real-time response, we will display a customized, empathetic, and beautifully styled confirmation message. This project teaches you how to handle form submissions, make live API calls with cURL, parse real JSON, and dynamically change the UI based on an AI's output.

Building the application

Create the project structure

Let's set up our folders and files.

1. Create the main project folder named **smart-help-desk**: C:\xampp\htdocs\codes\smart-help-desk\.
2. Open **smart-help-desk** folder in VS Code.
3. Inside that folder, create two files: index.php and style.css.
4. Create the configuration folder named **config**: C:\xampp\htdocs\codes\config\
5. Inside config, create one file: api_config.php

Store your real API key

Open C:\xampp\htdocs\codes\config\api_config.php. Add the following code, replacing the placeholder with the real Gemini API key you generated from Google AI Studio:

```
<?php
// This is where you store your real API key.
define('GEMINI_API_KEY', 'PASTE_YOUR_REAL_API_KEY_HERE');
```

Create the CSS

The following CSS code will style our form and feedback boxes (smart-help-desk/style.css):

```
body {
    font-family: -apple-system, BlinkMacSystemFont, "Segoe UI", Roboto,
                 Helvetica, Arial, sans-serif;
    background-color: #f4f7f6;
    color: #333;
    display: flex;
    justify-content: center;
    align-items: center;
    min-height: 100vh;
    margin: 0;
    padding: 20px 0;
}
.container {
    background-color: #ffffff;
    padding: 40px;
    border-radius: 12px;
    box-shadow: 0 10px 25px rgba(0, 0, 0, 0.1);
    width: 100%;
    max-width: 500px;
}
h1 {
    color: #2c3e50;
    text-align: center;
    margin-bottom: 30px;
}
.form-group {
    margin-bottom: 20px;
}
label {
    display: block;
    margin-bottom: 8px;
    font-weight: 600;
    color: #555;
}
input[type="text"], input[type="email"], textarea {
    width: 100%;
    padding: 12px;
    border: 1px solid #ddd;
    border-radius: 6px;
    box-sizing: border-box;
    transition: border-color 0.3s;
}
textarea {
    resize: vertical;
    min-height: 120px;
}
```

```
input[type="text"]:focus, input[type="email"]:focus, textarea:focus {
    border-color: #3498db;
    outline: none;
}
button {
    width: 100%;
    padding: 15px;
    background-color: #3498db;
    color: white;
    border: none;
    border-radius: 6px;
    font-size: 16px;
    font-weight: bold;
    cursor: pointer;
    transition: background-color 0.3s;
}
button:hover {
    background-color: #2980b9;
}
.feedback {
    padding: 15px;
    margin-top: 20px;
    border-radius: 6px;
    text-align: center;
    font-weight: 500;
    border: 1px solid transparent;
}
.feedback.positive {
    background-color: #e8f5e9;
    color: #2e7d32;
    border-color: #a5d6a7;
}
.feedback.negative {
    background-color: #ffebee;
    color: #c62828;
    border-color: #ef9a9a;
}
.feedback.neutral {
    background-color: #e3f2fd;
    color: #1565c0;
    border-color: #90caf9;
}
.feedback.error {
    background-color: #f3e5f5;
    color: #6a1b9a;
    border-color: #ce93d8;
}
```

Create the user interface and add the real PHP logic

This is the core of our chapter. Open smart-help-desk/index.php and replace its content with the following code. It includes the HTML form and the live PHP logic for calling the Gemini API (smart-help-desk/index.php):

```
<?php
// Securely include our configuration file with the API key
require_once __DIR__ . '/../../codes/config/api_config.php';
// Function to call the Google Gemini API using cURL
function getSentimentFromGeminiAPI(string $message, string $apiKey): array
{
    $apiUrl = 'https://generativelanguage.googleapis.com/v1beta/
               models/gemini-1.5-flash:generateContent?key=' . $apiKey;
    // This is our instruction to the AI.
    $prompt = "Analyze the sentiment of the following user message. Respond
               with only a single word: Positive, Negative, or Neutral.
               Message: " . $message;
    // The data payload for the API in JSON format
    $postData = json_encode([
        "contents" => [
            [
                "parts" => [
                    ["text" => $prompt]
                ]
            ]
        ]
    ]);
    // Initialize cURL
    $ch = curl_init($apiUrl);
    // Set cURL options
    // Return the response as a string
    curl_setopt($ch, CURLOPT_RETURNTRANSFER, true);
    // Set the request method to POST
    curl_setopt($ch, CURLOPT_POST, true);
    // Attach the JSON data
    curl_setopt($ch, CURLOPT_POSTFIELDS, $postData);
    // Set headers
    curl_setopt($ch, CURLOPT_HTTPHEADER, [
        'Content-Type: application/json',
    ]);
    // Execute the cURL request
    $response = curl_exec($ch);
    // Get the HTTP status code
    $httpCode = curl_getinfo($ch, CURLINFO_HTTP_CODE);
    // Check for cURL errors
    if (curl_errno($ch)) {
        curl_close($ch);
        return ['sentiment' => 'error', 'message' => 'Failed to connect to AI
                  service.'];
```

```
    }
    // Close the cURL session
    curl_close($ch);
    // Check for a successful API response (HTTP 200 OK)
    if ($httpCode !== 200) {
        return ['sentiment' => 'error', 'message' => 'AI service returned an error.
                Please check your API key and prompt.'];
    }
    // Decode the JSON response from the API
    $responseData = json_decode($response, true);
    // Extract the AI's text response, with checks for safety ratings
    $sentimentText = trim($responseData['candidates'][0]['content'][' parts'][0]['
                           text'] ?? 'Neutral');
    // Handle cases where the model might be blocked or return no text
    if (empty($sentimentText) || isset($responseData['candidates'][0][
             'finishReason']) && $responseData['candidates'][0]['finishReason'
             ] === 'SAFETY') {
        return ['sentiment' => 'neutral', 'message' => 'Your message has been
                 received and will be reviewed by our team. Thank you.'];
    }
    // Prepare a user-friendly response based on the AI's analysis
    $feedbackMessage = '';
    $finalSentiment = 'neutral';
    if (stripos($sentimentText, 'Positive') !== false) {
        $finalSentiment = 'positive';
        $feedbackMessage = 'Thank you for your wonderful feedback! We\'re thrilled
                            you\'re happy.';
    } elseif (stripos($sentimentText, 'Negative') !== false) {
        $finalSentiment = 'negative';
        $feedbackMessage = 'We are very sorry to hear you\'re experiencing issues.
                            A priority ticket has been created, and our team will
                            get back to you shortly.';
    } else {
        $finalSentiment = 'neutral';
        $feedbackMessage = 'Thank you for reaching out. We have received your
                            message and will review it soon.';
    }
    return ['sentiment' => $finalSentiment, 'message' => $feedbackMessage];
}
// Variable to hold our feedback message and sentiment
$feedback = null;
if ($_SERVER['REQUEST_METHOD'] === 'POST') {
    $userMessage = trim($_POST['message'] ?? '');
    if (!empty($userMessage) && defined('GEMINI_API_KEY') &&
                 GEMINI_API_KEY !== 'PASTE_YOUR_REAL_API_KEY_HERE') {
        $feedback = getSentimentFromGeminiAPI($userMessage, GEMINI_API_KEY);
    } elseif (GEMINI_API_KEY === 'PASTE_YOUR_REAL_API_KEY_HERE') {
        $feedback = ['sentiment' => 'error', 'message' => 'API Key is not
                     configured. Please add your key to the config file.'];
    }
}
```

```
?>
<!DOCTYPE html>
<html lang="en">
<head>
    <meta charset="UTF-8">
    <meta name="viewport" content="width=device-width, initial-scale=1.0">
    <title>AI Help Desk</title>
    <link rel="stylesheet" href="style.css">
</head>
<body>
    <div class="container">
        <h1>Contact Support</h1>
        <?php if ($feedback): ?>
            <div class="feedback <?php echo htmlspecialchars($feedback['
                        sentiment']); ?>">
                <p><?php echo htmlspecialchars($feedback['message']); ?></p>
            </div>
        <?php endif; ?>
        <form action="index.php" method="POST">
            <div class="form-group">
                <label for="name">Your Name</label>
                <input type="text" id="name" name="name" required>
            </div>
            <div class="form-group">
                <label for="email">Your Email</label>
                <input type="email" id="email" name="email" required>
            </div>
            <div class="form-group">
                <label for="message">Your Message</label>
                <textarea id="message" name="message" placeholder="Type your
                            message here..." required></textarea>
            </div>
            <button type="submit">Get Help</button>
        </form>
    </div>
</body>
</html>
```

Bridging the gap: Learned concepts and application implementation

- **Real API call:** Our **getSentimentFromGeminiAPI()** function now makes a real HTTP POST request using PHP's **cURL extension**. This is how professional applications communicate with web services.
- **Prompt engineering:** We didn't just send the user's message. We wrapped it in an instruction: "Analyze the sentiment... Respond with only a single word...". This is **prompt engineering**—guiding the AI to give us a predictable, useful response.

- **JSON handling:** We used **json_encode()** to create the request payload and **json_decode()** to parse the live response from Google's servers.
- **Error handling:** The code now checks for cURL errors (e.g., no internet connection) and bad HTTP status codes from the API (e.g., an invalid API key), providing graceful feedback to the user.

Running and testing

1. Ensure your XAMPP **Apache** service is running.
2. Open your browser and navigate to **http://localhost/codes/smart-help-desk/**.
3. You see the contact form.

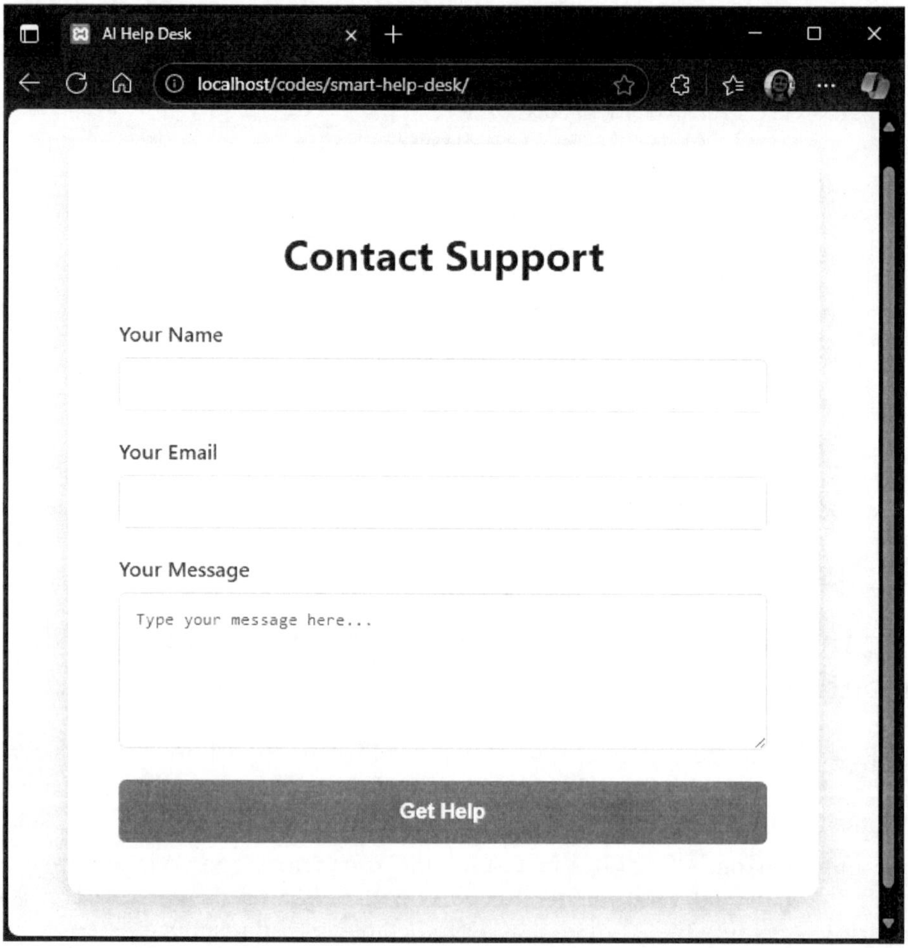

4. **Test case 1:** Negative sentiment
   - Fill in your name and email and in the message box, type: **The website is so slow and my account is locked. This is a terrible experience**.
   - Click **Get Help**.
   - After a brief pause (as it contacts the API), a red-tinted box appears with a message.

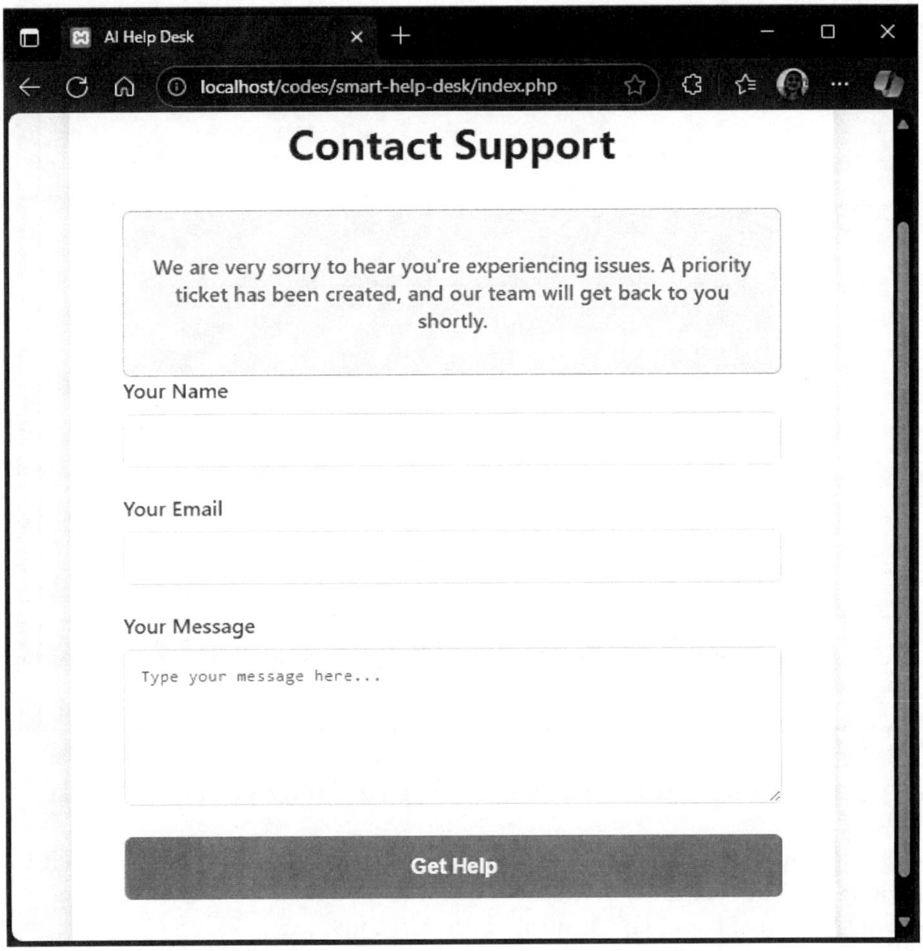

5. **Test case 2:** Positive sentiment
   - Fill in the form and in the message box, type: **I just wanted to say thank you! Your customer support is excellent and solved my problem immediately**.
   - Click **Get Help**.
   - A green-tinted box appears with a message.

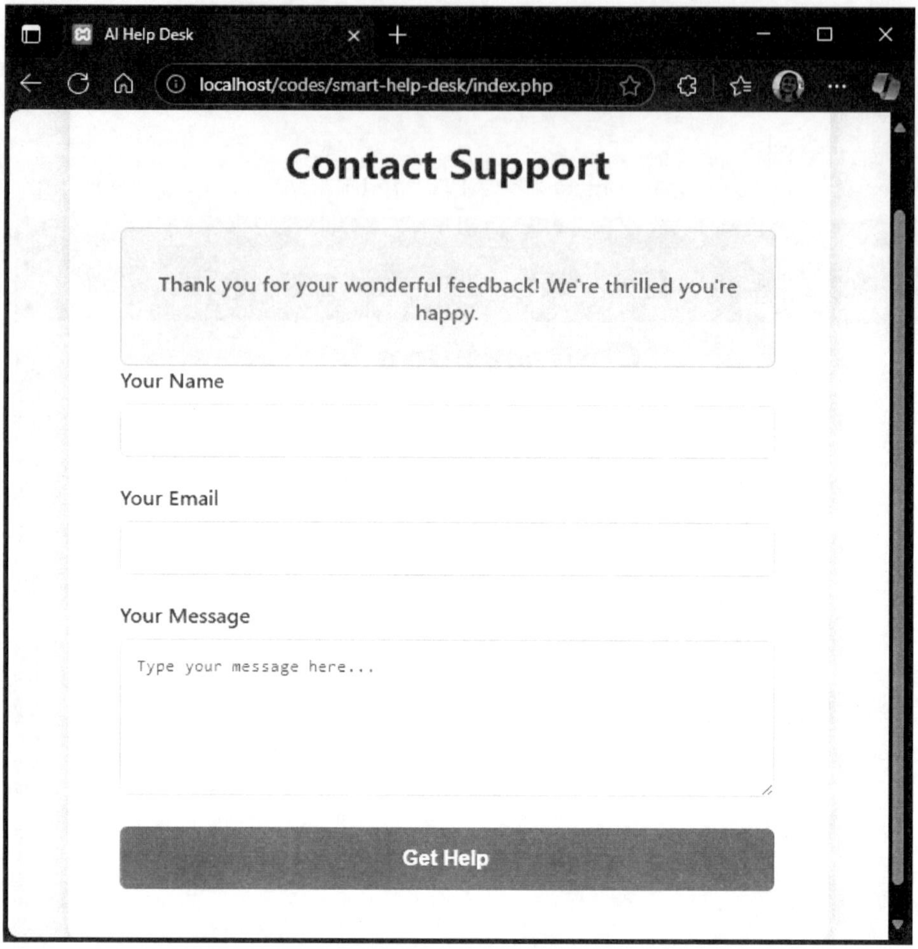

Exploring application behaviour: A practical run-through

- **API latency:** You may notice a 1-2 second delay after clicking **Get Help**. This is the actual time it takes for your server to send the request to Google, for the AI to process it, and for the response to come back. This is normal for API calls.
- **AI nuance:** Try ambiguous phrases like "My old product was bad, but this new one is good." The AI is sophisticated enough to understand the overall positive sentiment. The results are generated in real-time and are not hard-coded.

- **API errors:** If you intentionally put a wrong API key in api_config.php, the form will show an error message: "AI service returned an error." This is our error handling in action.

Harnessing API intelligence in real-world contexts

The pattern you just built is a professional, powerful, and versatile tool.

- **E-commerce:** Analyze product reviews to automatically flag unhappy customers for follow-up.
- **Social media:** Gauge public opinion on a new marketing campaign by analyzing tweets in real-time.
- **Content moderation:** Automatically filter and hold inappropriate user comments on a blog for human review.

Wrapping up

In this chapter, we connected our PHP application to a live, powerful AI service. You learned professional techniques for using external services to make your projects incredibly smart.

- **Real API integration:** You learned how to get a real API key and use it to communicate with Google's Gemini AI.
- **PHP cURL:** You mastered using the cURL extension to make live HTTP POST requests, a fundamental skill for any web developer.
- **Prompt engineering:** You learned to craft specific instructions for an AI to get predictable and structured responses.
- **Live JSON:** You successfully sent and received live JSON data, encoding your request and decoding the AI's response.
- **Robust error handling:** You built a script that can gracefully handle network errors or API authentication failures.

Congratulations! You have successfully built a web application that integrates a real-time, state-of-the-art AI. You've moved beyond self-contained websites and into the world of interconnected, intelligent applications. This is a massive step forward and a skill that is highly sought after in the industry.

This was just a taste of what's possible when you plug your PHP code into external services. In the next chapter, we'll explore a different facet of AI. Get ready for ***Chapter 21: Machine Learning for all - Smart recommender systems***, where you'll learn to build a system that can make intelligent recommendations to users, just like your favorite streaming service!

Chapter 21

Section 06: AI awakened - Smarter web apps for all

Machine Learning for all - Smart recommender systems

What you'll learn

- What Composer is?
- Why composer is essential for modern PHP
- How to install Composer for XAMPP and Visual Studio Code
- The three pillars of machine learning - Datasets, Training, and Inference
- How the K-Nearest Neighbors algorithm intuitively works

Hello and welcome to what might be the most transformative chapter in your journey as a web developer. Up to this point, we've built applications that follow instructions. They are logical, efficient, and do exactly what we tell them to. But what if we could build applications that seem to *think*? What if they could anticipate a user's needs, make intelligent suggestions, and create a truly personalized experience?

That is the magic of machine learning, and it's a magic we are going to unravel together today.

Have you ever been scrolling through Netflix, unsure of what to watch, when suddenly a suggestion pops up for a show you've never heard of? You give it a try, and within two episodes, you're completely hooked. It feels like Netflix *knows* you. Or when you're shopping on Amazon, and it shows you a product that perfectly complements what's already in your cart? That isn't a lucky guess; it's a technology called a **recommender system**, and it's one of the most powerful and valuable forms of artificial intelligence in the world.

In this chapter, we are going to pull back the curtain on this technology. We will show you that it isn't magic at all, but a logical and accessible process. We will be using a fantastic PHP library to build our very own smart recommender from scratch.

What this chapter is and is not?

- **This chapter IS** a friendly, practical, step-by-step guide to building your first AI-powered feature in PHP. We will focus on understanding the core concepts in an intuitive way and writing real, working code.
- **This chapter IS NOT** a theoretical data science course. We will not be diving into complex calculus or statistical proofs. The goal here is implementation, not abstract theory. You will emerge from this chapter as a developer who can *build* AI, not a research scientist.

By the end of this chapter, you will have built a complete, beautifully styled web application that intelligently recommends new book genres to a user. It's a project that will not only teach you an incredibly valuable skill but also serve as a standout piece in your developer portfolio. Let's begin!

Essential pre-requisite

Before we can build our intelligent recommender, we need to install a tool that is absolutely fundamental to virtually all modern PHP development. This tool is **Composer**. Since this is the first time we are using it in this book, we will walk through every single step of understanding and installing it.

What is Composer and why do I need it?

Think about your smartphone. When you want a new feature, like a weather app or a game, you don't write the code for it yourself. You go to the App Store or Google Play, find an app built by other expert developers, and install it with a single click.

Composer is the App Store for PHP code.

In the past, if you wanted to use a piece of code written by someone else (a "library"), you had to manually find it online, download a ZIP file, extract it, figure out which files to include in your project, and hope you did it all correctly. It was a messy and error-prone process.

Composer automates all of this. It's a **dependency manager**. You simply tell Composer what libraries your project depends on, and it handles everything else:

- It downloads the correct library code from a central, trusted repository called **Packagist**.
- It automatically downloads any other libraries that *your chosen library* depends on.
- It organizes all this third-party code into a clean vendor directory.
- Most importantly, it creates a special autoload.php file. By including just this one file in your project, you gain access to all the features of the libraries you installed, without having to write a single include or require statement for them.

Learning to use Composer is not optional in today's PHP world; it is the standard, professional way to build applications.

Installing Composer

We'll now perform a one-time installation of Composer on your system. Once this is done, you can use it for this project and all your future PHP projects.

Find your php.exe path

The Composer installer needs to know where your PHP installation is located so it can use it. Since we are using XAMPP, this is very straightforward.

1. Open your **File Explorer**.
2. Navigate to the location where you installed XAMPP. By default, this is **C:\xampp**.
3. Inside the **xampp** folder, open the **php** folder.
4. Look for a file named **php.exe**. This is the PHP executable.
5. The full path is what we need. For a default installation, this path is: **C:\xampp\php\php.exe**.
6. Keep this path handy; you'll need it in a moment.

Download the Composer installer

1. Open your web browser and go to the official Composer website: **getcomposer.org**.

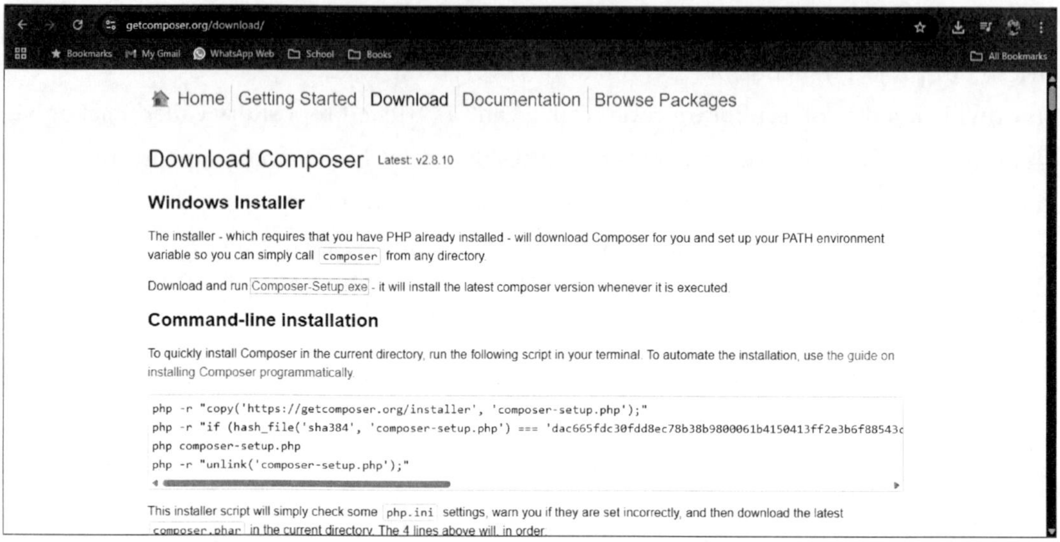

2. Click on the **Download** link.
3. On the Windows Installer section, you see a link for **Composer-Setup.exe**. Click this to download the installer.

Run the installation wizard

Once the download is complete, find the Composer-Setup.exe file in your Downloads folder and double-click it to run it.

1. **Installation type:** The first screen will ask to select the installation mode. Choose **Install for all users (recommended)** and click **Next**.

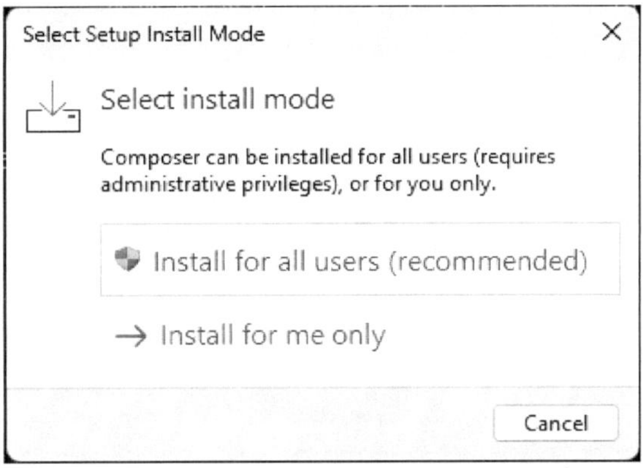

2. **Developer mode:** The next screen asks about Developer mode. Leave this **unchecked** and click **Next**.

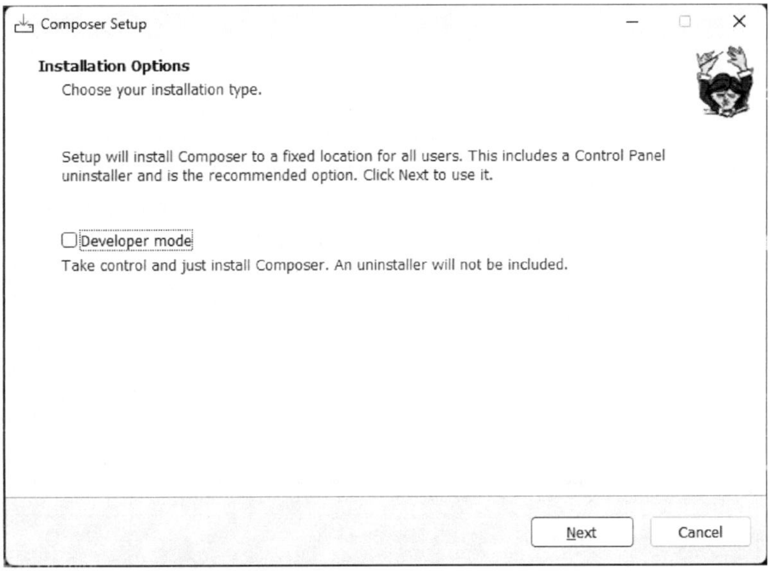

3. **Choose the command-line PHP:** This is the most important step! The installer automatically try to find your PHP path.
   - It might find it correctly. If the text box already shows C:\xampp\php\php.exe, you are good to go!
   - If the box is empty or shows the wrong path, you must tell it where to find PHP. Click the **Browse...** button, navigate to **C:\xampp\php**, and select the **php.exe** file.
   - Ensure the checkbox for **Add this PHP to your path?** is **checked**. This is what allows you to type composer in your terminal from any folder.

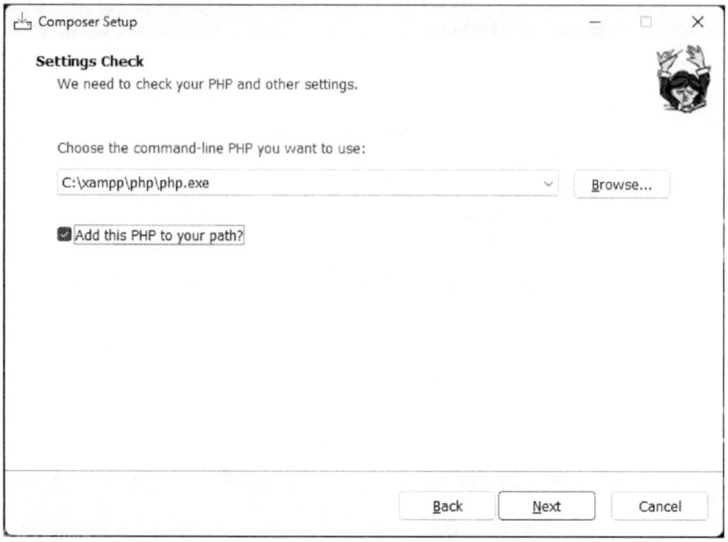

- Once the path is correct, click **Next**.

4. **Proxy settings:** The next screen asks about a proxy server. Unless you are on a corporate or university network that you know requires a proxy, you can ignore this. Just click **Next**.
5. **Ready to install:** The final screen shows you a summary. Click **Install**. The installer downloads the latest version of Composer and configures it.
6. **Information:** After a moment, an Information window appears. Read it and click **Next**.

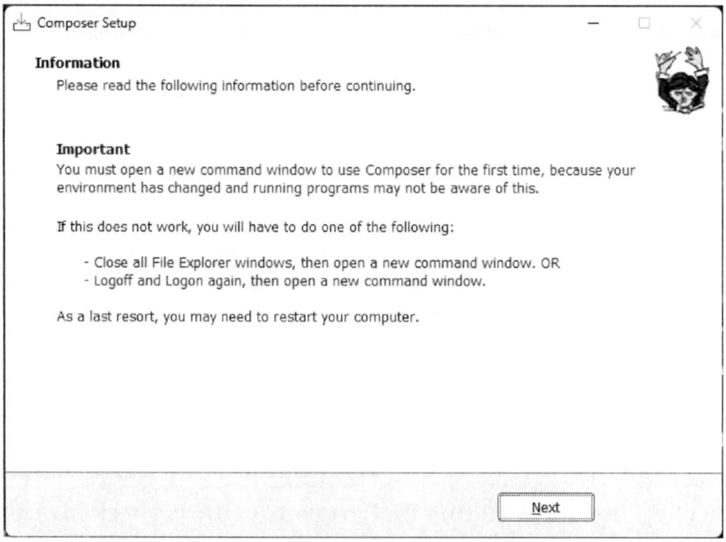

7. **Finish:** Click **Finish** to complete the installation.

Verify the installation

Let's make sure everything worked. This is a critical final check.

> **IMPORTANT:**
> If you have any instances of VS Code or any command prompt/terminal windows open, **close them completely**. This is necessary for your computer to recognize the new composer command.

1. Re-open **Visual Studio Code**.
2. Open the integrated terminal inside VS Code (**...** → **Terminal** → **New Terminal** or by pressing Ctrl+Shift+ `).
3. In the terminal prompt, type the following command and press **Enter**:

```
composer --version
```

4. If the installation was successful, you see the Composer version number printed in the terminal. It looks something like this (your version number may differ):

If you see this, congratulations! You have successfully installed Composer and are now equipped with a tool used by professional PHP developers worldwide. If you get an error like **command not found**, the most likely reason is that the PHP path was not added correctly during installation, and you should try running the installer again.

Thinking like a Data Scientist: The three pillars of Machine Learning

Now that our toolkit is ready, we can dive into the concepts. Machine learning can seem like a black box, but it's a logical process built on three pillars. Understanding them will demystify AI and empower you to think about problems in a new way.

Pillar 1: The Dataset — The source of all knowledge

A machine learning model knows nothing about the world on its own. It's like a newborn baby. It learns from the data we provide it. This collection of data is called a **dataset**, and it is the single most important part of any AI project.

The Golden Rule: Garbage In, Garbage Out

The quality, quantity, and accuracy of your dataset will directly determine how *smart* your model is. If you train a model on flawed, biased, or incomplete data, it will make flawed, biased, or incomplete predictions. The model is simply a mirror that reflects the data it was shown.

Let's consider two analogies for a dataset:

- **Teaching a child fruit:** We explored this earlier. To teach a child what an "apple" is, you show them many examples: red apples, green apples, big ones, small ones. The collection of all these labeled pictures is your dataset.
- **Training a spam filter:** How does Gmail know what is spam? It has been trained on a massive dataset of billions of emails that users have manually marked as "spam" or "not spam."

In a dataset used for classification, you'll always have two components:

- **Features:** These are the *inputs* or *characteristics* of a data sample. In our spam filter example, the features could be the email's sender, the presence of certain words ("free," "viagra"), or whether the subject line is in all caps.
- **Labels:** This is the *output* or the *correct answer* for each sample. For the spam filter, the label would simply be "spam" or "not spam."

For the book recommender we're about to build, our features will be the genres a user likes, and the label will be the new genre we want to recommend.

Pillar 2: The Algorithm & Training — Finding the hidden patterns

Once you have a dataset, you need an **algorithm** to learn from it. An algorithm is just a set of mathematical rules that a computer can follow to analyze data. Think of it as the child's learning strategy.

There are many different ML algorithms, each suited for different tasks, just like a toolbox contains many different tools. For our task, we've chosen an algorithm called **K-Nearest Neighbors (KNN)** because it's one of the most intuitive and easy to understand.

A deeper look at K-Nearest Neighbors (KNN)

Imagine a 2D graph. Let's say we're plotting movie viewers. The horizontal axis is "How much they like action movies" and the vertical axis is "How much they like comedy movies."

We plot all the people from our dataset onto this graph. We use a blue dot for people who ultimately prefer "Action Flicks" and a green dot for people who prefer "Romantic Comedies." You'd probably see a cluster of blue dots on the right side of the graph (high action) and a cluster of green dots towards the top (high comedy).

Now, a new viewer comes along. We plot them on the graph as a grey question mark. How do we predict what kind of movie they'll prefer?

This is where KNN comes in. It works in two simple steps:

- It looks at the **'K' nearest data points** (neighbors) to our new grey question mark. Let's say we choose K=5. The algorithm finds the 5 dots on the graph that are closest to our new viewer.
- It takes a **majority vote**. Of those 5 nearest neighbors, are there more blue dots or green dots? If 4 of the 5 are blue and 1 is green, the algorithm predicts that our new viewer will prefer "Action Flicks." It assigns the grey dot the color blue.

That's it! That is the entire logic behind KNN. It classifies new data based on the "company it keeps."

The **Training** phase for an algorithm like KNN is extremely simple. It's really just the process of loading the dataset into memory and plotting all the points on the graph, ready to make comparisons.

Pillar 3: Inference — Putting the model to work

This is the payoff. **Inference** is the act of using the trained model to make a prediction on new, live data that it has never seen before. It's the moment the child correctly identifies a new fruit, the spam filter sends a malicious email to junk, or our app recommends a new book genre.

You see inference in action all the time:

- **Credit card fraud detection:** When you swipe your credit card, a model performs an *inference* in milliseconds to predict the probability that the transaction is fraudulent based on features like the amount, location, and time of day.
- **Facial recognition:** When you unlock your phone with your face, an ML model performs *inference* on the camera's input to predict if the face matches the owner's.
- **Our recommender app:** When a user checks their favourite genres and clicks "submit," our code will perform an *inference* to predict a new genre they will love.

With these three pillars in mind—Dataset, Training, and Inference—let's build a quick prototype.

Our first prediction: A simple command-line Prototype

Before we get bogged down in HTML and CSS, it's always a good practice in programming to test your core logic in isolation. This is called **prototyping**. We are going to build a tiny, self-contained PHP script that proves our machine learning logic works, right in the VS Code terminal. This will also be our first time using Composer!

The setup

1. In your file explorer, navigate to C:\xampp\htdocs\codes\.
2. Create a new folder and name it **ml-prototype**.
3. Open this folder in Visual Studio Code.
4. Open the integrated terminal in VS Code (**...** → **Terminal** → **New Terminal**).
5. Now, we will put Composer to work. In the terminal, run the following command. This tells Composer to initialize a new project and download the php-ai/php-ml library:

```
composer require php-ai/php-ml
```

6. You see that the Composer downloads the necessary files.

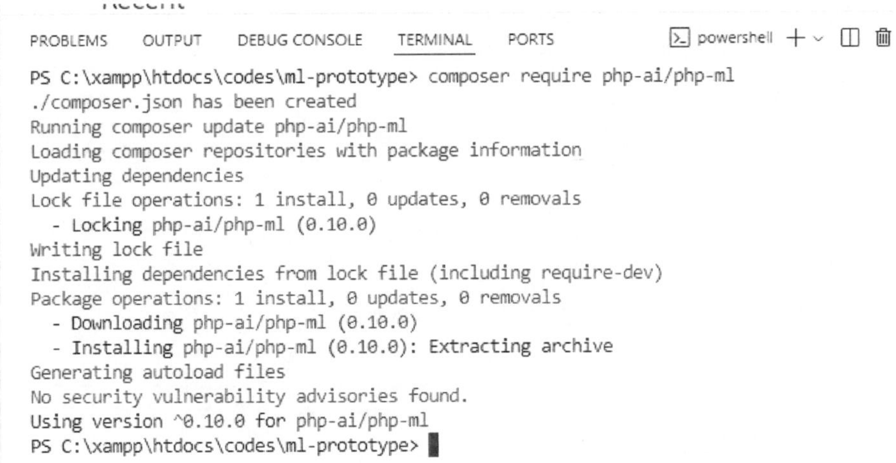

7. When it's done, you have a **vendor** folder, a **composer.json** file, and a **composer.lock** file.

This is perfect!

The prototype script

Create a new file named **predict.php** under the **ml-prototype** folder and add the following code:

```
<?php
// SETUP: Load the Composer autoloader to access the library
require_once 'vendor/autoload.php';
// Tell PHP we'll be using the KNearestNeighbors class
use Phpml\Classification\KNearestNeighbors;
echo "Starting our ML Prototype...\n\n";
// --- PILLAR 1: THE DATASET ---
echo "1. Preparing the training data...\n";
// Features: [likes action?, likes adventure?, likes magic?] (1=yes, 0=no)
$samples = [[1, 1, 1], [0, 0, 1], [1, 1, 0]];
// Labels: The corresponding genre for each sample
$labels = ['Fantasy', 'Sci-Fi', 'Thriller'];
echo "Dataset is ready.\n\n";
// --- PILLAR 2: THE TRAINING ---
echo "2. Training the K-Nearest Neighbors model...\n";
```

```
$classifier = new KNearestNeighbors();
$classifier->train($samples, $labels);
echo "Training complete. The model is ready to make predictions.\n\n";
// --- PILLAR 3: THE INFERENCE ---
echo "3. Making a new prediction...\n";
// Let's create a profile for a new user who likes action, but not adventure,
// and likes magic.
$newUser = [1, 0, 1];
echo "Predicting genre for a user with profile: [1, 0, 1]...\n";
$prediction = $classifier->predict($newUser);
echo "\n--- PREDICTION RESULT ---\n";
echo "The model recommends the genre: " . $prediction . "\n";
echo "--------------------------\n";
?>
```

Running the prototype

Unlike our previous projects, we won't use the browser for this. We'll run it directly in the VS Code terminal. This is a common way to run scripts that don't need a user interface.

In your terminal, simply type the following command and press Enter:

```
php predict.php
```

The following output is displayed in your terminal:

Success! Our prototype works perfectly. It loaded the data, trained the model, and correctly predicted that a user who likes action and magic is a good fit for the Fantasy genre. Now that we've proven the core logic, we can confidently build our full user-facing application.

Hands-on: Building the AI-powered Reading recommender

This is where all the pieces come together. We are going to build a complete, single-page application from scratch. It will be interactive, visually appealing, and powered by the AI logic we just prototyped.

Project planning: The blueprint

Great projects start with a plan. Before we write a line of code, let's define what we're building and how data will flow through it.

The user story: A user story is a simple sentence that describes what a user wants to do and why. It's a great way to keep our goal in focus.

"As a book lover, I want to select my favorite genres so that I can get a personalized recommendation for a new genre to read."

The data flow:

- The user visits our web page (index.php).
- The user sees an HTML form with a list of genre checkboxes.
- The user checks the boxes for the genres they like and clicks the **Get Recommendation** button.
- The browser sends the form data to our server using the POST method.
- Our PHP script receives the POST data (an array of genre names).
- The script **cleans** this data, converting the array of names into a numeric array of 1s and 0s that our model can understand.
- The script performs **inference** by feeding this numeric array into our trained KNN model.
- The model returns a prediction (the name of the recommended genre).
- The PHP script re-renders the HTML page, this time including the prediction inside a special result card.
- The user sees the recommendation appear on their screen.

This clear flow gives us a roadmap for building the application.

Building the application

Let's start building!

Project setup

1. Navigate to your main projects folder: C:\xampp\htdocs\codes\.
2. Create a new folder and name it **reading-recommender**.
3. Open this new folder in VS Code.
4. Open the terminal and run the Composer command one last time for this new project:

```
composer require php-ai/php-ml
```

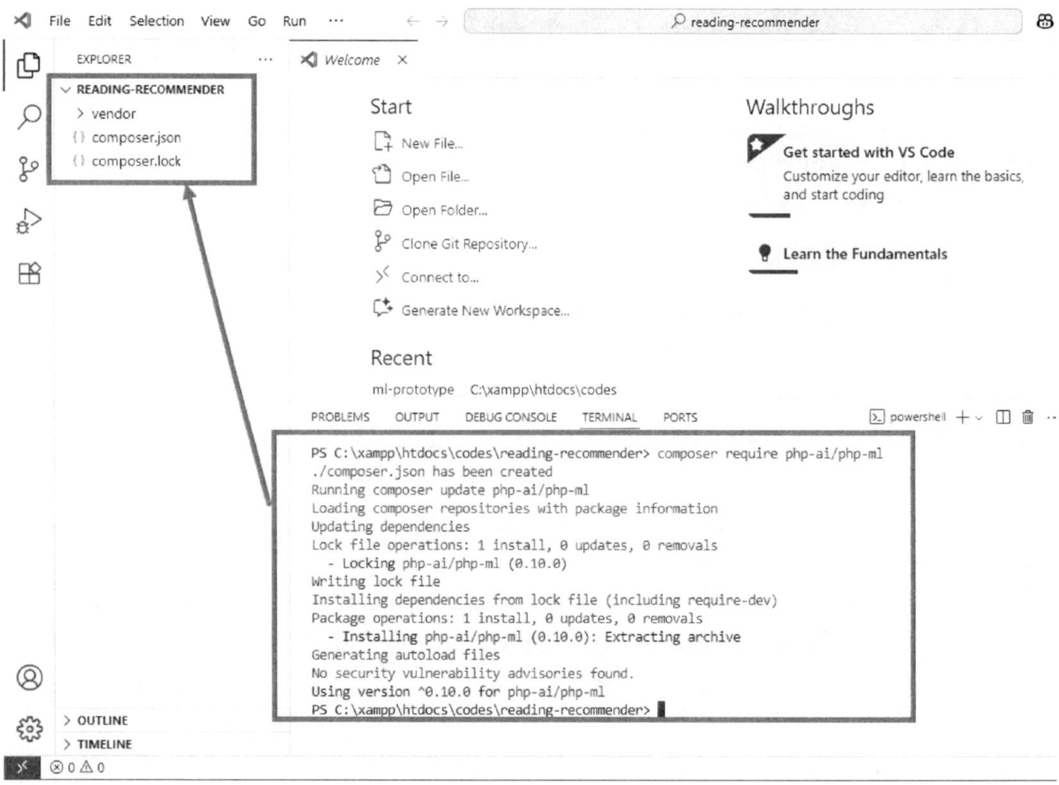

Create the files

Inside the **reading-recommender** folder, create two empty files:

- index.php (for our HTML and PHP logic)
- style.css (for our presentation and layout)

The HTML skeleton

Let's start by putting the basic HTML structure into index.php. This gives us the page's framework before we add the dynamic parts:

```
<!DOCTYPE html>
<html lang="en">
<head>
    <meta charset="UTF-8">
    <meta name="viewport" content="width=device-width, initial-scale=1.0">
    <title>Reading Recommender</title>
    <link rel="stylesheet" href="style.css">
</head>
<body>
    <div class="container">
        <h1>Reading Recommender</h1>
        <p>Select your favorite genres, and we'll suggest something new for you
           to read!</p>
        <form action="index.php" method="POST">
            <div class="genre-grid">
                </div>
            <button type="submit">Get Recommendation</button>
        </form>
        <div class="result-placeholder">
            </div>
    </div>
</body>
</html>
```

Styling the experience (The CSS)

Now let's add the visual polish. A great UI makes an application feel professional and trustworthy. Open style.css and add the full stylesheet. The detailed comments explain the purpose of each rule:

```
/* We use border-box sizing for more intuitive layouts. Padding and borders
   will be included inside an element's width and height, not added to it. */
* {
    box-sizing: border-box;
}
body {
```

```
    font-family: -apple-system, BlinkMacSystemFont, "Segoe UI", Roboto,
                 Helvetica, Arial, sans-serif;
    background-color: #f0f2f5;
    display: flex;
    /* Enables Flexbox for easy centering */
    justify-content: center;
    /* Centers child horizontally */
    align-items: center;
    /* Centers child vertically */
    min-height: 100vh;
    /* Ensures body is at least the full screen height */
    margin: 0;
    color: #333;
}
.container {
    background: #ffffff;
    padding: 2rem 3rem;
    border-radius: 12px;
    box-shadow: 0 8px 30px rgba(0, 0, 0, 0.1);
    width: 100%;
    max-width: 500px;
    text-align: center;
}
h1 {
    color: #1e3a8a;
    margin-bottom: 0.5rem;
}
p {
    color: #666;
    margin-bottom: 2rem;
    line-height: 1.5;
}
.genre-grid {
    display: grid;
    /* Enables CSS Grid for a perfect column layout */
    grid-template-columns: repeat(2, 1fr);
    /* Two equal-width columns */
    gap: 1rem;
    margin-bottom: 2rem;
    text-align: left;
}
.genre-option {
    display: flex;
    align-items: center;
    padding: 0.75rem 1rem;
    background: #f9fafb;
    border: 1px solid #d1d5db;
    border-radius: 8px;
    cursor: pointer;
    transition: background-color 0.2s, border-color 0.2s;
}
```

```
.genre-option input[type="checkbox"] {
    margin-right: 0.75rem;
    /* Custom styling for checkboxes could go here */
}
.genre-option:hover {
    background-color: #eff6ff;
    border-color: #60a5fa;
}
button {
    background-color: #1e3a8a;
    color: white;
    padding: 0.8rem 1.5rem;
    border: none;
    border-radius: 8px;
    font-size: 1rem;
    font-weight: 600;
    cursor: pointer;
    transition: background-color 0.2s;
    width: 100%;
    margin-top: 1rem;
}
button:hover {
    background-color: #1c3170;
}
.result-card {
    margin-top: 2rem;
    padding: 1.5rem;
    background: #dbeafe;
    border: 2px solid #93c5fd;
    border-radius: 8px;
    text-align: center;
    animation: fadeIn 0.6s ease-in-out;
}
@keyframes fadeIn {
    from {
        opacity: 0;
        transform: translateY(15px);
    }
    to {
        opacity: 1;
        transform: translateY(0);
    }
}
.result-card h2 {
    margin: 0 0 0.5rem 0;
    color: #1e40af;
}
.result-card p {
    font-size: 1.2rem;
    color: #1d4ed8;
    font-weight: 500;
```

```
    margin: 0;
}
```

Injecting the PHP brain

Now it's time to merge our PHP logic with our HTML skeleton. We will replace the entire content of index.php with the following complete code. This final version interleaves PHP and HTML to create our dynamic application:

```
<?php
// PART 1: THE MACHINE LEARNING SETUP
require_once 'vendor/autoload.php';
use Phpml\Classification\KNearestNeighbors;
// --- Our Dataset ---
// This is the knowledge base for our model. Each sub-array is a "feature set",
// representing a user's taste profile across 6 genres.
$samples = [
    [1, 1, 0, 0, 0, 0], // Likes Fantasy & Sci-Fi
    [0, 0, 1, 1, 0, 0], // Likes Mystery & Romance
    [0, 0, 1, 0, 1, 0], // Likes Mystery & Thriller
    [1, 0, 0, 0, 1, 0], // Likes Fantasy & Thriller
    [0, 0, 0, 0, 0, 1], // Likes Biography
    [0, 1, 1, 0, 1, 0], // Likes Sci-Fi, Mystery, & Thriller
    [0, 0, 0, 1, 0, 0], // Just likes Romance
];
// These are the "labels" or correct answers. For the first user profile,
// our system should recommend 'Adventure'.
$labels = ['Adventure', 'Drama', 'Crime', 'Dark Fantasy', 'History',
'Cyberpunk', 'Slice of Life'];
// --- Training the Model ---
// We instantiate the classifier and train it with our data.
// From this point on, $classifier is a ready-to-use prediction model.
$classifier = new KNearestNeighbors($k = 3);
$classifier->train($samples, $labels);
// PART 2: HANDLING USER INPUT & MAKING PREDICTIONS
$recommendation = null; // Initialize a variable to hold our result.
// This master list of genres is used for both creating the form and processing
// the input. Having it in one place makes the code easy to update.
$allGenres = ['Fantasy', 'Sci-Fi', 'Mystery', 'Romance', 'Thriller',
'Biography'];
// Check if the form has been submitted.
if ($_SERVER['REQUEST_METHOD'] === 'POST') {
    // Get user's choices, defaulting to an empty array to prevent errors.
    $userChoices = $_POST['genres'] ?? [];
    // Only make a prediction if the user has selected at least one genre.
    if (!empty($userChoices)) {
        // This is the data preparation step: converting user choices into a
        // numeric array.
        $userSample = [];
```

```
        foreach ($allGenres as $genre) {
            $userSample[] = in_array($genre, $userChoices) ? 1 : 0;
        }
        // The Inference Step! We ask our trained model for a prediction.
        $recommendation = $classifier->predict($userSample);
    }
}
?>
<!DOCTYPE html>
<html lang="en">
<head>
    <meta charset="UTF-8">
    <meta name="viewport" content="width=device-width, initial-scale=1.0">
    <title>AI Reading Recommender</title>
    <link rel="stylesheet" href="style.css">
</head>
<body>
    <div class="container">
        <h1>AI Reading Recommender</h1>
        <p>Welcome! Select the genres you currently enjoy, and our smart
           recommender will suggest a new genre you might love.</p>
        <form action="index.php" method="POST">
            <div class="genre-grid">
                <?php foreach ($allGenres as $genre): ?>
                    <label class="genre-option">
                        <input type="checkbox" name="genres[]" value="<?php echo
                               $genre; ?>"
                            <?php
                            // This is a nice touch: it keeps the boxes checked
                            // after submission.
                            if (isset($userChoices) && in_array($genre,
                                 $userChoices)) {
                                echo 'checked';
                            }
                            ?>>
                        <?php echo htmlspecialchars($genre); ?>
                    </label>
                <?php endforeach; ?>
            </div>
            <button type="submit">Get My Recommendation!</button>
        </form>
        <?php
        // This PHP block conditionally renders the result card. If $recommendation
        // is not null, this HTML will be inserted into the page.
        if ($recommendation):
        ?>
            <div class="result-card">
                <h2>Based on your taste, you might also like...</h2>
                <p><?php echo htmlspecialchars($recommendation); ?></p>
            </div>
        <?php endif; ?>
```

```
    </div>
</body>
</html>
```

Running and testing

1. Ensure your **Apache** server is running from the **XAMPP control panel**.
2. Open your web browser and navigate to the application's URL: **http://localhost/codes/reading-recommender/**.
3. You see our complete, styled application.

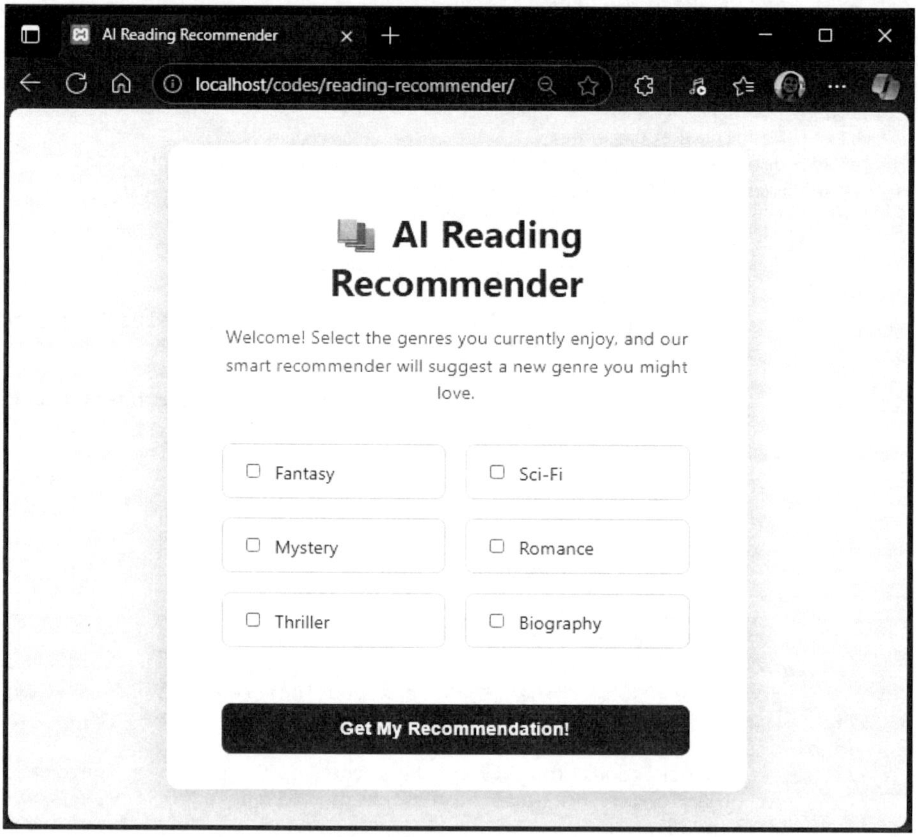

4. **Test case 1:** The Mystery fan. Check the boxes for **Mystery** and **Thriller**. Click **Get My Recommendation!**. The page reloads, the checkboxes remain checked, and a blue result card animates smoothly onto the screen with the recommendation.

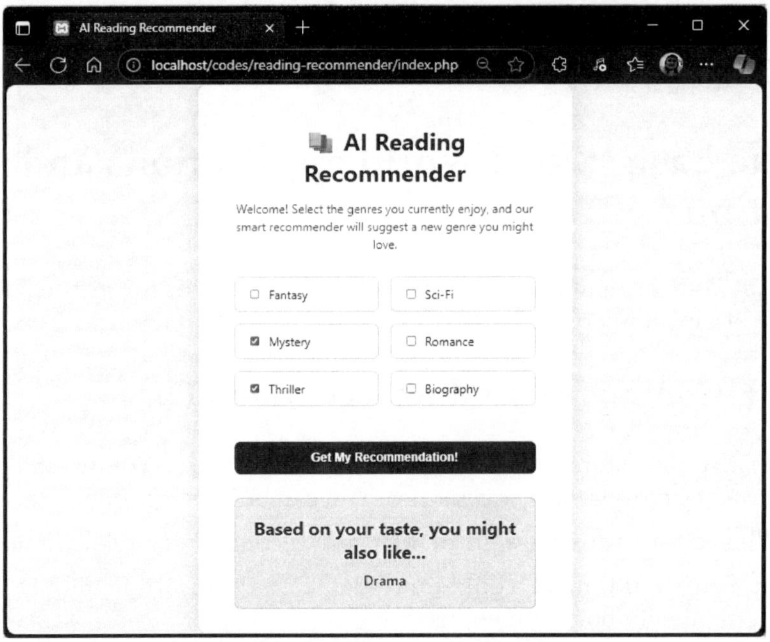

5. **Test case 2:** The Futurist. Refresh the page. Check **Fantasy** and **Sci-Fi**. Click the button. The recommendation is displayed.

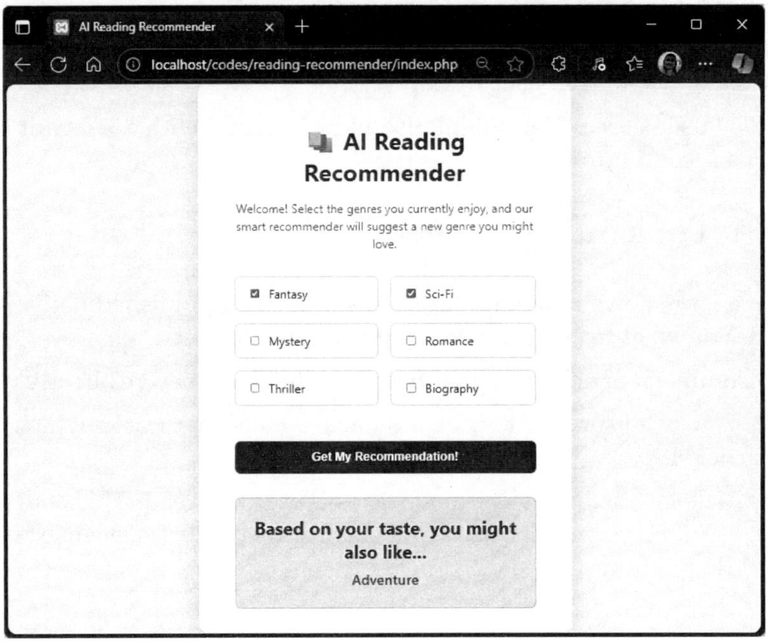

6. **Test case 3:** No Selection. Refresh and click the button without checking any boxes. The page simply reloads without any error or result card, which is exactly the user-friendly behaviour we want.

Beyond the basics: Real-world applications and considerations

What you've built is more than just a fun project; it's a blueprint for features that drive real business value. Let's explore how this exact technology is used in the wild.

Use case 1: E-Commerce product recommender

Imagine you run an online store that sells custom-printed T-shirts. You want to increase your average order value by cross-selling accessories. You can build a recommender system.

- **The goal:** When a user adds a T-shirt to their cart, recommend a relevant hat.
- **The dataset:** You would query your store's database. Your orders table tells you which products are frequently bought together.
- **The features:** The characteristics of the T-shirt the user selected. This could be [colour, sleeve_length, graphic_style, fabric_type], which you would convert to numbers. For example, [blue=0.2, short=1, vintage=1, cotton=1].
- **The labels:** The name of the hat that was most frequently purchased with T-shirts having those features (e.g., "Vintage Baseball Cap").
- **The result:** The user sees a "You might also like..." section with a relevant hat, increasing the chance of a second purchase.

Use case 2: A 'For You' news feed

Imagine you run a large news blog with hundreds of articles published daily. New users can be overwhelmed. You want to create a personalized "For You" feed.

- **The goal:** Recommend articles to a user based on the ones they've already read.
- **The dataset:** Your web server's logs or a database table that tracks which user IDs have read which article IDs.
- **The features:** The characteristics of the articles a user has read. This could be [category, word_count, author, sentiment]. For example: [tech=1, business=1, politics=0, short_form=1, long_form=0].

- **The labels:** The categories of other articles that similar users went on to read.
- **The result:** A user who reads about Apple and Google (Tech) gets recommended an article about Microsoft, keeping them engaged on your platform for longer.

Important considerations for real-world projects

- **Scaling:** Our simple model loads the entire dataset into memory every time the page loads. This is fine for a few dozen samples, but it won't work for millions of customer records. Real-world systems would pull data from a highly optimized database and often use more advanced algorithms designed for big data.
- **The "Cold Start" problem:** What do you recommend to a brand new user who has no activity history? This is a classic challenge. Solutions often involve showing the most popular items, asking them to select some interests during signup, or using content-based filtering instead of collaborative filtering.
- **Evaluation:** How do you know if your recommender is actually working? Businesses measure this rigorously. For an e-commerce site, they would use A/B testing: show recommendations to 50% of users (Group A) and not to the other 50% (Group B). If Group A has a higher average order value, the recommender is a success.

Wrapping Up

This was a massive chapter, so let's take a moment to recap the incredible distance you've traveled. You went from a basic understanding of PHP to implementing a genuine artificial intelligence feature.

- You learned what a professional package manager, **Composer**, is and completed a full, step-by-step installation for your development environment.
- You mastered the three pillars of machine learning: assembling a **Dataset**, **Training** a model, and using it for **Inference**.
- You demystified the **K-Nearest Neighbors** algorithm, understanding its intuitive, vote-based logic.
- You learned the importance of **data preparation**, converting user-friendly inputs into machine-readable numbers.
- You built, styled, and deployed a complete, interactive **AI-powered web application** that provides real value.
- You explored how this same technology powers mission-critical, revenue-generating features in **e-commerce and content platforms**.

Take a deep breath and be genuinely proud of what you have built today. You have stepped into the world of AI development, a field that is shaping the future of technology. You've proven that with the right tools and a clear understanding of the concepts, you can build smart, predictive applications right inside of PHP. This skill is not just impressive; it's immensely valuable in the modern job market. You've equipped yourself with the ability to create more engaging, personalized, and effective web experiences.

You've taught your application how to think and predict. Now, it's time to expand its senses. Get ready for another exciting leap, because in the next chapter, we're going to teach it how to see and hear as we dive into ***Chapter 22: Seeing & hearing with PHP - Vision & Audio APIs***.

Chapter 22

Section 06: AI awakened – Smarter web apps for all

Seeing & hearing with PHP – Vision & Audio APIs

What you'll learn

- Using a live vision API for image tagging
- Extracting text from images (OCR) with AI
- Making HTTP requests with cURL
- Getting free API keys
- Speech-to-text with Gemini
- Securely storing keys

Welcome back! So far, we've learned how to process text and structured data. But the modern web is a multimedia experience, filled with images, videos, and audio. In this chapter, we will connect our PHP applications to real-world AI services that can "see" the content of images and "hear" the words in audio files. This is your first step into the powerful world of API integration, using cutting-edge, accessible AI models.

Imagine uploading a photo to a website, and it automatically suggests tags like "beach," "sunset," and "ocean." Or, picture snapping a photo of a document and having all its text instantly extracted and ready to be copied. Or speaking a note into your phone and having it instantly transcribed into text by one of the most advanced AI models available.

This is the power of integrating with external APIs (Application Programming Interfaces). These services act as the eyes and ears for our applications. In this chapter, you'll learn how to get the necessary credentials (API keys), write PHP code to send media files to these services, and then use the results to build two fully functional, AI-powered applications: a "Visual Gallery" and an "Image-to-Text Extractor".

Getting your API keys

To use a third-party AI service, you need to prove who you are. This is done with API keys—unique secret codes that you include with your requests. For this chapter, we will use two excellent services: **Imagga** for image tagging and **Google's Gemini** for speech-to-text and image-to-text (OCR).

Setting up Imagga for image tagging

Imagga offers a powerful image analysis API with a generous free tier that is perfect for learning and building projects.

1. **Sign Up:** Open your browser and go to **imagga.com**.

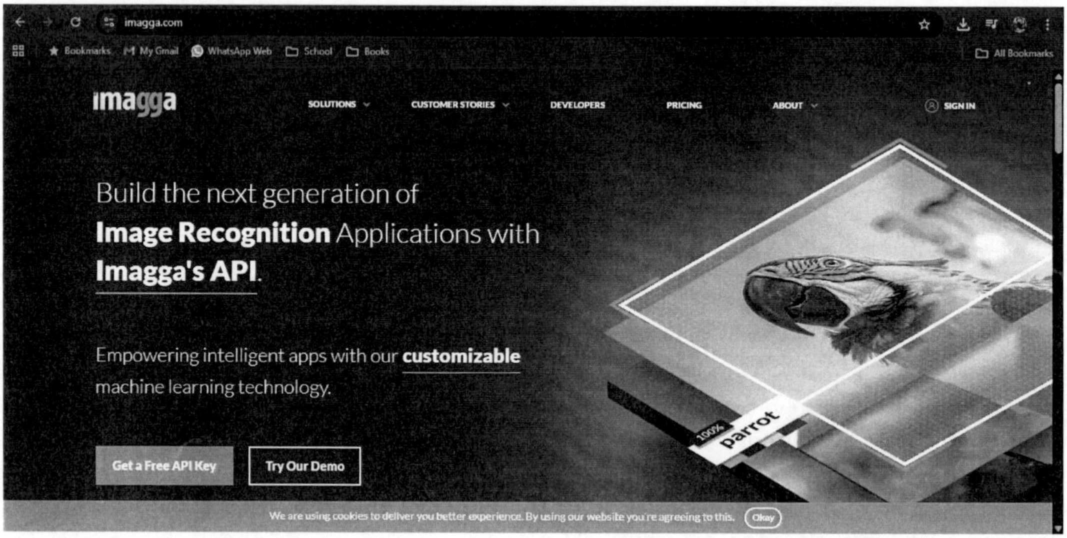

2. Click on **Sign up for a free account**.
3. **Create Account:** Fill in your details. You will receive a confirmation email to activate your account.

4. **Find your keys:** Once you log in, you will be taken to your **Dashboard**, where you'll see your API credentials, which include an **API Key** and an **API Secret**.

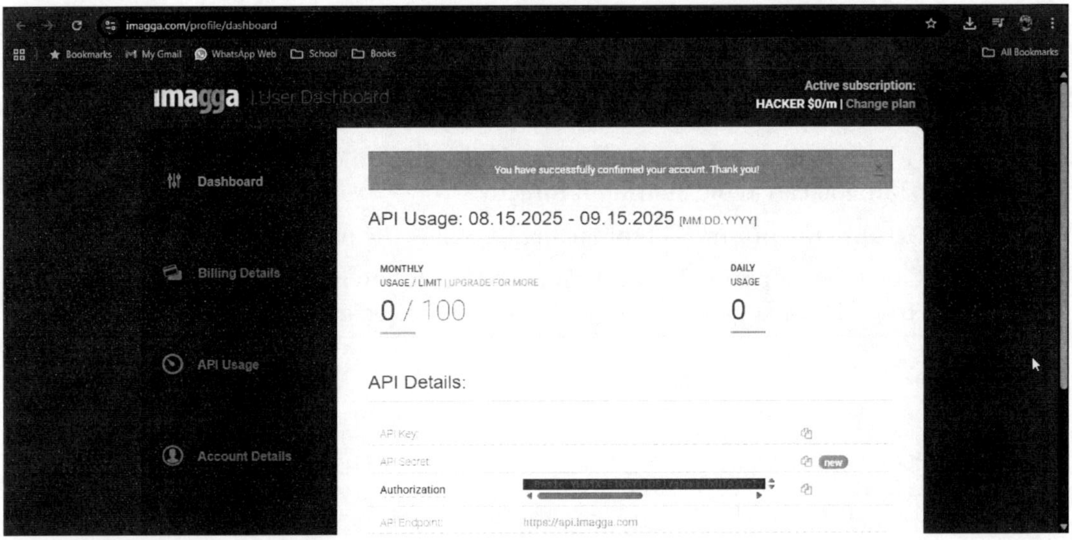

5. **Copy credentials:** Keep this browser tab open. We will need to copy these two values shortly. They are your password to the Imagga service.

Setting up Google AI

We will use the powerful Gemini 1.5 Flash model via Google AI Studio. It has a free tier that is more than enough for our development needs.

- **Visit AI Studio:** Go to **aistudio.google.com** in your web browser.
- **Log In:** Log in with your existing Google Account.
- **Get API key:** In the top left, click the **< > Get code** button. A window will pop up. In that window, click the **Get API key** link.
- **Create API key:** A new screen will appear. Click the **Create API key in new project** button.
- **Copy your key:** Your new API key will be generated and displayed. Copy it immediately and save it somewhere safe, like a text file. This is your secret key for accessing Google's AI models.

Storing your keys securely

You must **never** write your secret API keys directly into your main application file. If you were to share your code with a friend or colleague, your keys would be exposed, and others could use your account.

The best practice is to store them in a separate configuration file. Your main application will include this file, but you can avoid sharing it directly.

1. **Create config.php:** In your project folder, create a new file named **config.php**.
2. **Add keys:** Open config.php in VS Code and add the following code. Paste the credentials you copied from the Imagga and Google AI Studio dashboards:

```
<?php
// Store your secret API keys here
// Imagga API Credentials
define('IMAGGA_API_KEY', 'PASTE_YOUR_IMAGGA_API_KEY_HERE');
define('IMAGGA_API_SECRET', 'PASTE_YOUR_IMAGGA_API_SECRET_HERE');
// Google AI Gemini API Credentials
define('GOOGLE_GEMINI_API_KEY', 'PASTE_YOUR_GEMINI_API_KEY_HERE');
```

Image tagging and object detection with a live API

To communicate with an external API from PHP, we use **cURL**. It's a powerful library that lets our code act like a web browser, sending requests to URLs and receiving responses. It's pre-installed and enabled by default with XAMPP.

The process involves:

- Initializing a cURL handle.
- Setting options, such as the target URL, the data we want to send, and our authentication headers.
- Executing the request.
- Closing the connection.

Here is a working example of sending an image (via its public URL) to Imagga's API (/api-examples/live-image-tagger.php):

```
<?php
require_once 'config.php'; // Adjust path if needed
$imageUrl = 'https://sharanamshah.com/mymusings/wp-content/ uploads/2025/04
             /JakartaEE10.png';
$apiEndpoint = 'https://api.imagga.com/v2/tags';
```

```
$apiKey = IMAGGA_API_KEY;
$apiSecret = IMAGGA_API_SECRET;
$ch = curl_init();
curl_setopt($ch, CURLOPT_URL, $apiEndpoint . '?image_url=' .
urlencode($imageUrl));
curl_setopt($ch, CURLOPT_RETURNTRANSFER, TRUE);
// Basic Authentication
curl_setopt($ch, CURLOPT_USERPWD, $apiKey . ':' . $apiSecret);
$response = curl_exec($ch);
$httpCode = curl_getinfo($ch, CURLINFO_HTTP_CODE);
curl_close($ch);
$data = json_decode($response, true);
echo "<h1>Imagga API Response (Code: {$httpCode})</h1>";
if ($httpCode == 200) {
    echo "<h3>Tags Found:</h3>";
    echo "<ul>";
    foreach ($data['result']['tags'] as $tag) {
        echo "<li>" . htmlspecialchars($tag['tag']['en']) . " (" . round($tag['
              confidence'], 2) . "%)</li>";
    }
    echo "</ul>";
} else {
    echo "<p>An error occurred. Response:</p>";
    echo "<pre>" . print_r($data, true) . "</pre>";
}
?>
```

This script contacts the Imagga server and returns a live analysis of the linked image.

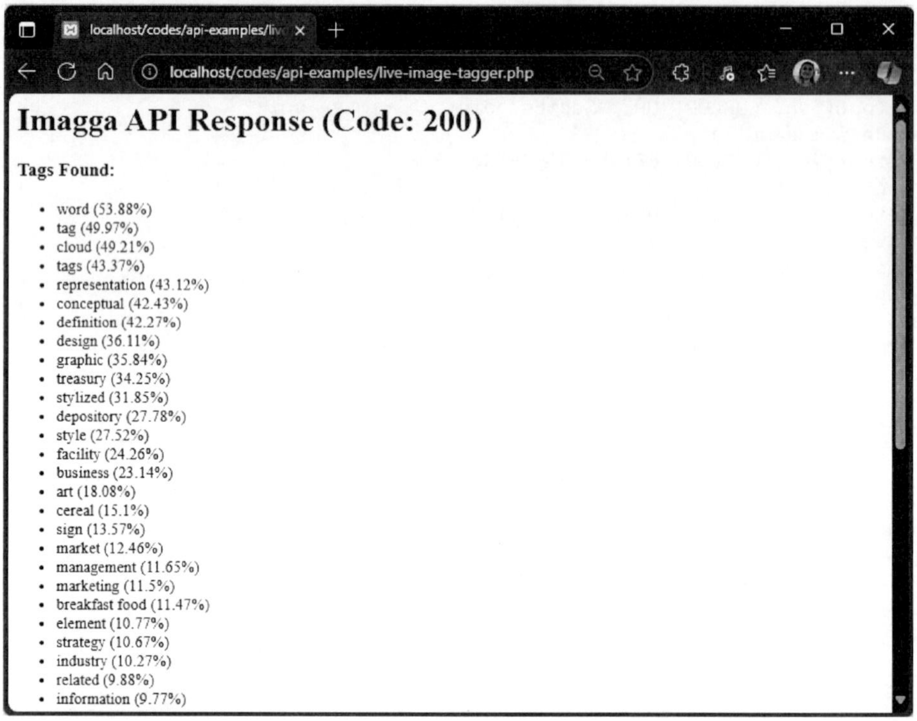

Understanding the output

The output from the Imagga API is more than just a list of words; it's structured data that you can use to build intelligent features. Let's break it down:

- **Tags:** These are keywords that the AI has identified in the image (e.g., "style," "art," "cloud"). They describe objects, concepts, and scenes.
- **Confidence score:** The percentage next to each tag (e.g., 53.88%) represents the AI's confidence in its own assessment. A high score means the AI is very sure the tag is accurate.

How can you use this output?

- **Automated alt text:** Use the top 3-5 tags with the highest confidence to automatically generate descriptive "alt text" for images. This dramatically improves website accessibility for visually impaired users and boosts SEO.

- **Smarter search:** If you're building a photo gallery or an e-commerce site, you can store these tags in your database, associated with the image. Users can then search for "red dress" or "outdoor scenery," and your application can find relevant images even if those words aren't in the filename.
- **Content-based filtering:** Allow users to filter a large collection of images. For example, a news organization could use tags to quickly find all photos related to "protests" or "elections."
- **Content moderation:** You can check for tags associated with inappropriate or sensitive content (e.g., "violence," "adult") and automatically flag them for review by a human moderator.

Speech-to-text basics with a live API

Transcribing audio with Google's Gemini API is incredibly powerful. The process is different from the previous APIs and introduces a new, important concept: **Base64 encoding**.

Base64 encoding

Because the Gemini API accepts all its data in a single JSON text block, we can't just "attach" a binary file like an MP3. Instead, we must first convert the binary audio data into a safe string of text. Base64 is the standard way to do this. PHP makes it simple with the base64_encode() function.

Here's the flow:

- Read the audio file's binary data.
- Base64 encode that data into a long string.
- Create a JSON object containing a prompt (our instruction) and the Base64 string.
- Send this JSON to the Gemini API using cURL.

Let's take an example (/api-examples/live-audio-transcriber.php):

```
<?php
require_once 'config.php'; // Adjust path if needed
$audioFilePath = 'sample.mp3'; // Place a real mp3 or wav file here!
if (!file_exists($audioFilePath)) {
    die("Error: Audio file not found. Please place 'sample.mp3' in this
          directory.");
}
$apiKey = GOOGLE_GEMINI_API_KEY;
```

```
$apiEndpoint = 'https://generativelanguage.googleapis.com/v1beta/models
                /gemini-1.5-flash:generateContent?key=' . $apiKey;
// 1. Read the audio file's raw binary data
$audioData = file_get_contents($audioFilePath);
// 2. Base64 encode the data
$base64AudioData = base64_encode($audioData);
// 3. Construct the JSON payload for the API
$jsonData = [
    'contents' => [
        [
            'parts' => [
                ['text' => 'Please transcribe this audio.'],
                [
                    'inline_data' => [
                        // Change to 'audio/wav' for WAV files
                        'mime_type' => 'audio/mpeg',
                        'data' => $base64AudioData
                    ]
                ]
            ]
        ]
    ]
];
// 4. Set up the cURL request
$ch = curl_init();
curl_setopt($ch, CURLOPT_URL, $apiEndpoint);
curl_setopt($ch, CURLOPT_RETURNTRANSFER, true);
curl_setopt($ch, CURLOPT_POST, true);
curl_setopt($ch, CURLOPT_HTTPHEADER, ['Content-Type: application/json']);
// Send the JSON string
curl_setopt($ch, CURLOPT_POSTFIELDS, json_encode($jsonData));
$response = curl_exec($ch);
$httpCode = curl_getinfo($ch, CURLINFO_HTTP_CODE);
curl_close($ch);
$data = json_decode($response, true);
echo "<h1>Gemini API Response (Code: {$httpCode})</h1>";
if ($httpCode == 200 && isset($data['candidates'][0]['content']['parts'][0]
                                    ['text'])) {
    $transcript = $data['candidates'][0]['content']['parts'][0]['text'];
    echo "<h3>Transcript:</h3>";
    echo "<p><i>" . htmlspecialchars($transcript) . "</i></p>";
} else {
    echo "<p>An error occurred:</p>";
    echo "<pre>" . print_r($data, true) . "</pre>";
}
```

After a few seconds, the script outputs a highly accurate transcript of the audio file.

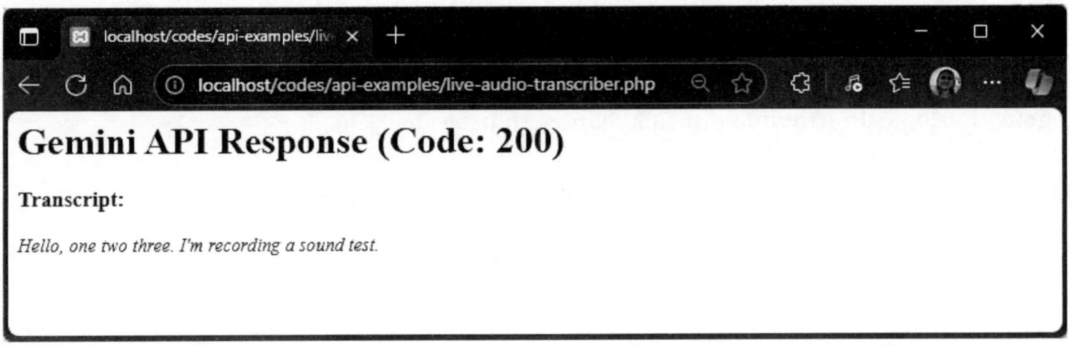

Understanding the output

The output here is a clean, simple string of text: the **transcript**. The value of this output lies in transforming unstructured audio data into structured, usable text.

How can you use this output?

- **Searchable archives:** Imagine a news organization with thousands of hours of video and audio lectures. By transcribing them, this entire archive becomes fully searchable. A user could search for a specific term and be linked directly to the point in the audio/video where it was mentioned.
- **Content creation:** Automatically generate blog posts, articles, or summaries from interviews, podcasts, or meetings. This saves countless hours of manual transcription.
- **Accessibility:** Create closed captions or full transcripts for videos and podcasts, making your content accessible to the hearing-impaired.
- **Voice-controlled applications:** Build applications that can be controlled by voice commands. The transcript provides the text that your application can then parse to understand the user's intent.

Handling user image uploads

Before we can send a user's image to an API, we must first handle the upload within PHP. The process uses an HTML form with a special attribute, enctype="multipart/form-data", which tells the browser to prepare the file for sending.

On the server side, PHP receives uploaded files in a special superglobal variable called $_FILES. This array contains the file's original name, its temporary location on the server, its size, and any errors. Our job is to validate this information and then use the file. We will integrate this logic directly into our final hands-on project.

Displaying tags, labels, and audio transcripts

As you saw in the live examples, real API responses contain structured data. Our job is to parse this structure to extract what we need.

- For Imagga, the tags were located in

```
$data['result']['tags']
```

- For Gemini, the transcript was nested deep inside the response at

```
$data['candidates'][0]['content']['parts'][0]['text']
```

Learning to read API documentation and navigate these data structures is a core skill for a web developer.

Real-world

These technologies are critical for modern web applications.

- **Captioning and accessibility:** Vision APIs automatically generate "alt text" for images, making sites accessible to visually impaired users and improving SEO.
- **Content moderation:** Social media platforms use these APIs to automatically flag inappropriate content, reducing the workload on human moderators.
- **Enhancing user experience:** E-commerce sites use image tagging to allow searches by visual attributes ("red dress"). News organizations use speech-to-text to make their video archives fully searchable.

Hands-on: Visual gallery

Let's build the Visual Gallery application using the live Imagga API. A user will upload an image, and our application will send it for real-time analysis, displaying the image and its AI-generated tags in a card-based layout.

The purpose of this project is to create a complete, end-to-end feature that mimics how real-world applications work. You will build an interface for a user to upload a file, write server-side PHP to handle that file, communicate securely with an external AI service, and then display the live results in a polished, user-friendly format. This project solidifies the core concepts of file handling and API integration.

Building the application

Create the project structure

First, we need our folders and files.

1. Inside your XAMPP **htdocs\codes** directory, create a new folder named **visual-gallery-live**.
2. Inside this new folder, create another folder named **uploads**. This is where our successfully analyzed images will be stored.
3. Finally, using VS Code, create three files inside visual-gallery-live: index.php, style.css, and config.php.

Your final structure should look like this:

```
/xampp/htdocs/codes/
└── visual-gallery-live/
    ├── uploads/
    ├── index.php
    ├── style.css
    ├── config.php
```

> **Important:**
> The uploads directory must be writable by the web server. On a standard XAMPP installation, this is usually not an issue.

Set up the configuration file

Open the config.php file. Copy the following code into this file. Carefully paste your actual Imagga API Key and Secret into the appropriate placeholders. You only need the Imagga keys for this specific project.

```php
<?php
// Imagga API Credentials
define('IMAGGA_API_KEY', 'PASTE_YOUR_IMAGGA_API_KEY_HERE');
```

```
define('IMAGGA_API_SECRET', 'PASTE_YOUR_IMAGGA_API_SECRET_HERE');
```

Create the CSS stylesheet

Open style.css and add the following code. This will give our application a clean, modern interface without needing any complex frameworks:

```
body {
    font-family: -apple-system, BlinkMacSystemFont, "Segoe UI", Roboto,
                 Helvetica, Arial, sans-serif;
    background-color: #f4f7f6;
    color: #333;
    margin: 0;
    padding: 40px;
    display: flex;
    flex-direction: column;
    align-items: center;
}
.container {
    width: 100%;
    max-width: 600px;
    background-color: white;
    padding: 30px;
    border-radius: 12px;
    box-shadow: 0 4px 20px rgba(0, 0, 0, 0.08);
    margin-bottom: 30px;
}
h1 {
    text-align: center;
    color: #2c3e50;
    margin-bottom: 25px;
}
.upload-form label {
    font-weight: bold;
    margin-bottom: 10px;
    display: block;
}
.upload-form input[type="file"] {
    width: 100%;
    padding: 12px;
    border: 2px dashed #ccc;
    border-radius: 8px;
    margin-bottom: 20px;
    cursor: pointer;
}
.upload-form input[type="submit"] {
    width: 100%;
    padding: 15px;
    background-color: #3498db;
```

```
    color: white;
    border: none;
    border-radius: 8px;
    font-size: 16px;
    font-weight: bold;
    cursor: pointer;
    transition: background-color 0.3s ease;
}
.upload-form input[type="submit"]:hover {
    background-color: #2980b9;
}
.message {
    text-align: center;
    padding: 15px;
    margin-bottom: 20px;
    border-radius: 8px;
    font-weight: 500;
}
.message.success {
    background-color: #d4edda;
    color: #155724;
    border: 1px solid #c3e6cb;
}
.message.error {
    background-color: #f8d7da;
    color: #721c24;
    border: 1px solid #f5c6cb;
}
.result-card {
    margin-top: 30px;
    border: 1px solid #e0e0e0;
    border-radius: 12px;
    overflow: hidden;
    box-shadow: 0 2px 10px rgba(0, 0, 0, 0.05);
}
.result-card img {
    width: 100%;
    height: auto;
    display: block;
}
.card-content {
    padding: 20px;
}
.card-content h3 {
    margin-top: 0;
    margin-bottom: 15px;
    color: #34495e;
}
.tag-container .tag {
    display: inline-block;
    background-color: #e9ecef;
```

```
    color: #495057;
    padding: 6px 12px;
    border-radius: 16px;
    margin: 4px;
    font-size: 14px;
    font-weight: 500;
}
```

Write the main application logic

This is the heart of our application. Open index.php and add the following code. It includes the HTML for the form, the PHP for handling the upload, the cURL logic for the API call, and the code to display the final results:

```
<?php
// We must include our config file to get the API keys
require_once 'config.php';
// Initialize variables to hold results and messages
$message = '';
$message_class = '';
$image_path = '';
$image_tags = [];
/**
 * Sends an image file to the Imagga API for tagging.
 *
 * @param string $filePath The temporary path of the uploaded file.
 * @return array The API response (decoded from JSON), with an added
 * http_code key.
 */
function getTagsFromImaggaApi(string $filePath): array
{
    $apiKey = IMAGGA_API_KEY;
    $apiSecret = IMAGGA_API_SECRET;
    $apiEndpoint = 'https://api.imagga.com/v2/tags';
    $postData = ['image' => new CURLFile($filePath)];
    $ch = curl_init();
    curl_setopt($ch, CURLOPT_URL, $apiEndpoint);
    curl_setopt($ch, CURLOPT_POST, 1);
    curl_setopt($ch, CURLOPT_POSTFIELDS, $postData);
    curl_setopt($ch, CURLOPT_RETURNTRANSFER, 1);
    curl_setopt($ch, CURLOPT_CONNECTTIMEOUT, 5);
    curl_setopt($ch, CURLOPT_TIMEOUT, 15);
    curl_setopt($ch, CURLOPT_USERPWD, $apiKey . ':' . $apiSecret);
    $response = curl_exec($ch);
    $httpCode = curl_getinfo($ch, CURLINFO_HTTP_CODE);
    curl_close($ch);
    $data = json_decode($response, true);
    $data['http_code'] = $httpCode;
    return $data;
```

```
}
if ($_SERVER["REQUEST_METHOD"] == "POST") {
    if (isset($_FILES["userImage"]) && $_FILES["userImage"]["error"] == 0) {
        $tempPath = $_FILES["userImage"]["tmp_name"];
        if ($_FILES["userImage"]["size"] > 5 * 1024 * 1024) {
            $message = "Error: File is too large (Max 5MB).";
            $message_class = 'error';
        } else {
            $apiResponse = getTagsFromImaggaApi($tempPath);
            if ($apiResponse['http_code'] == 200) {
                $fileName = basename($_FILES["userImage"]["name"]);
                $newFileName = uniqid() . '-' . $fileName;
                $uploadPath = 'uploads/' . $newFileName;
                move_uploaded_file($tempPath, $uploadPath);
                $message = "Image uploaded and analyzed successfully!";
                $message_class = 'success';
                $image_path = $uploadPath;
                $image_tags = $apiResponse['result']['tags'];
            } else {
                $message = "API Error: " . ($apiResponse['status']['text'] ??
                            'Could not connect to API.');
                $message_class = 'error';
            }
        }
    } else {
        $message = "An error occurred during upload. Please try again.";
        $message_class = 'error';
    }
}
?>
<!DOCTYPE html>
<html lang="en">
<head>
    <meta charset="UTF-8">
    <title>Visual Gallery - Live AI Tagger</title>
    <link rel="stylesheet" href="style.css">
</head>
<body>
    <div class="container">
        <h1>AI Visual Gallery (Live)</h1>
        <p style="text-align: center; margin-top: -15px; margin-bottom: 30px;">
             Upload an image to have the live Imagga API analyze its content.</p>
        <form action="index.php" method="post" enctype="multipart/form-data"
              class="upload-form">
            <input type="file" name="userImage" required>
            <input type="submit" value="Analyze Image">
        </form>
        <?php if ($message): ?>
            <div class="message <?php echo $message_class; ?>"><?php echo
                  $message; ?></div>
        <?php endif; ?>
```

```
    </div>
    <?php if ($image_path && !empty($image_tags)): ?>
        <div class="container result-card">
            <img src="<?php echo htmlspecialchars($image_path); ?>"
                 alt="Uploaded image">
            <div class="card-content">
                <h3>Analysis Results:</h3>
                <div class="tag-container">
                    <?php foreach ($image_tags as $tag): ?>
                        <?php if ($tag['confidence'] > 20): ?>
                            <span class="tag">
                                <?php echo htmlspecialchars($tag['tag']['en']); ?>
                                (<?php echo round($tag['confidence']); ?>%)
                            </span>
                        <?php endif; ?>
                    <?php endforeach; ?>
                </div>
            </div>
        </div>
    <?php endif; ?>
</body>
</html>
```

Bridging the gap: Learned concepts and application implementation

Let's break down how the concepts from earlier in the chapter are used in our final application:

- **API key management:** The very first line of our PHP script is **require_once 'config.php';**. This securely loads our secret keys into the application without hard-coding them. The **getTagsFromImaggaApi()** function then uses the IMAGGA_API_KEY and IMAGGA_API_SECRET constants.
- **Live API call with cURL:** The **getTagsFromImaggaApi()** function is a direct, practical implementation of a **cURL** request. It sets the URL, uses **CURLOPT_POST** to send data, prepares the file with new **CURLFile()**, and authenticates using **CURLOPT_USERPWD**.
- **Handling user image uploads:** The HTML form uses **enctype="multipart/form-data"**. Our PHP code checks **$_SERVER["REQUEST_METHOD"]** to see if the form was submitted. It then validates the uploaded file using the **$_FILES["userImage"]** superglobal, checking for errors and size.
- **Displaying results:** After a successful API call, the **$image_tags** variable is populated. The HTML part of the script loops through this array with a foreach loop. For each tag, it extracts the name ($tag['tag']['en']) and confidence score ($tag['confidence']), displaying them in a styled <span>.

Running and testing

Now it's time to see your creation in action! Follow these steps exactly.

1. **Start XAMPP:** Open your **XAMPP Control Panel** and ensure that the **Apache** module is started.
2. **Open your browser:** Launch your web browser (Chrome, Firefox, etc.).
3. **Navigate to the project:** In the address bar, type **http://localhost/codes/visual-gallery-live/** and press **Enter**.
4. **View the form:** You can see the **AI Visual Gallery (Live)** page with an upload form.

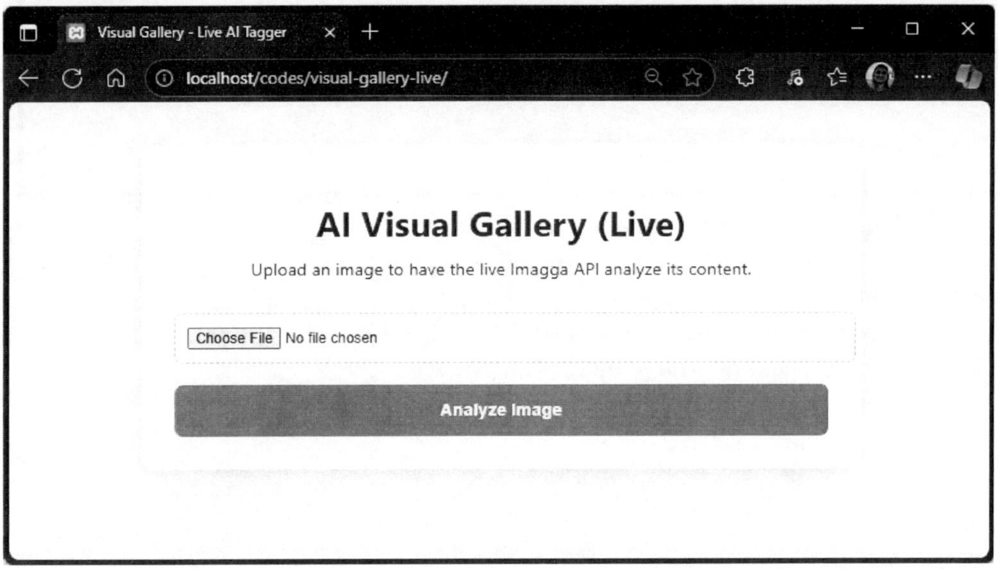

5. **Select an image:** Click the file input area ("Choose File") and select a JPG or PNG image from your computer. Choose a clear photo of an object, animal, or scene for the best results.

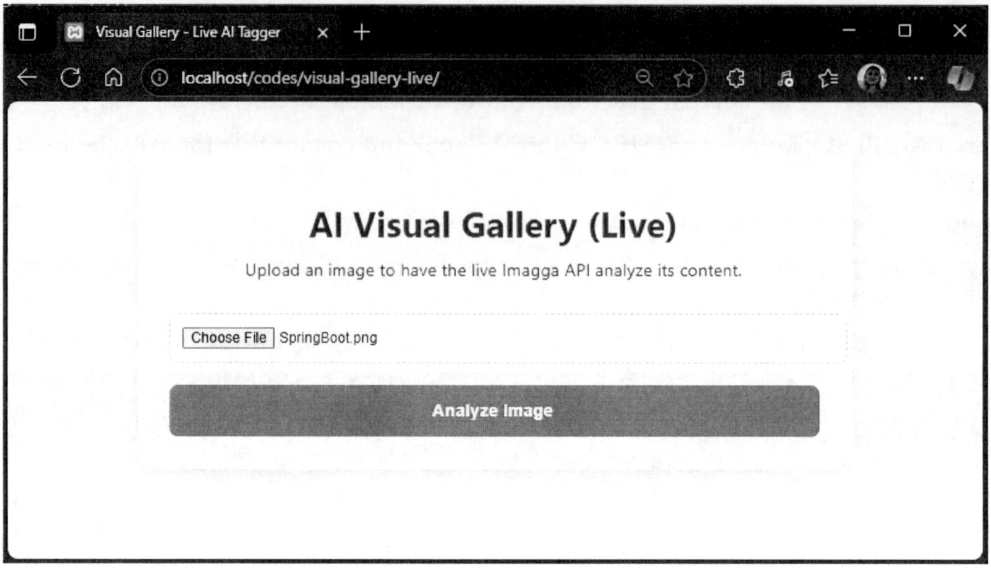

6. **Analyze the image:** Click the **Analyze Image** button.
7. **Observe the result:** The page reloads. It may take a few seconds to communicate with the API. You will then see a success message, and below it, a card appears. This card contains the image you uploaded, and underneath there is a list of highly relevant tags and their confidence scores, generated live by the Imagga AI.

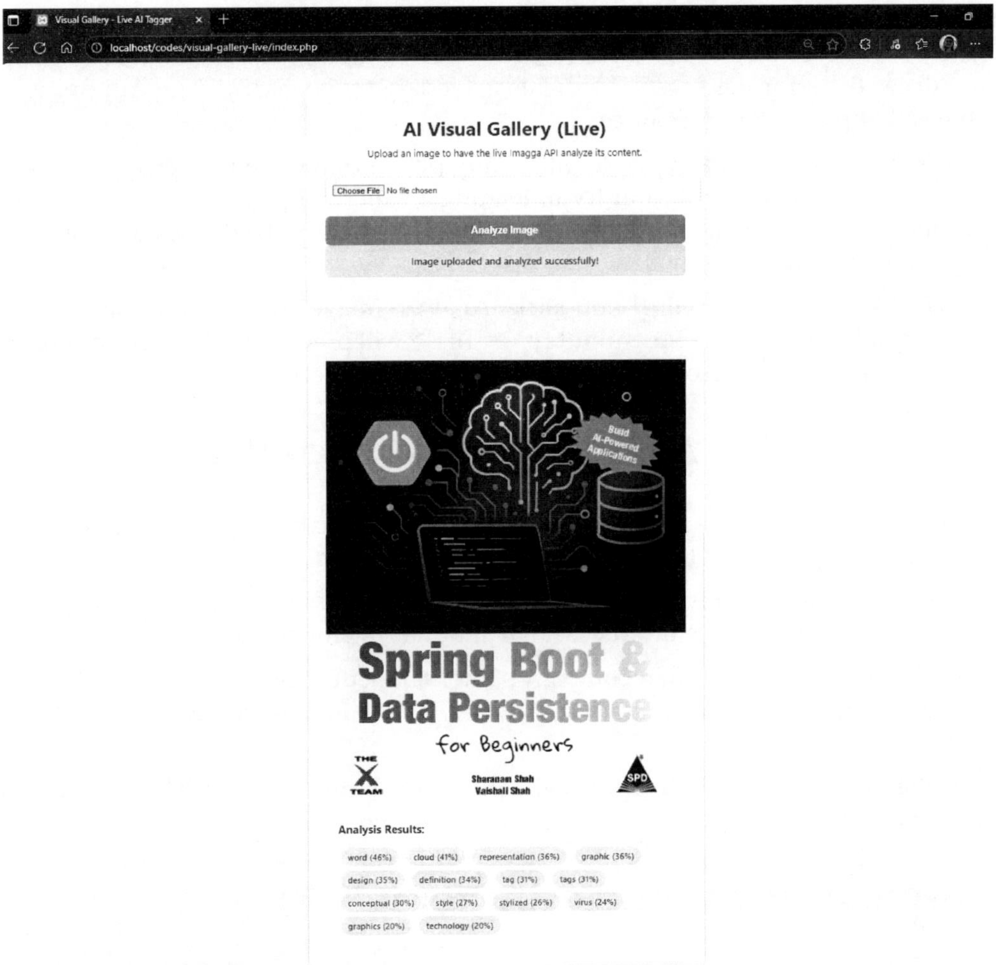

Exploring application behaviour: A practical run-through

A good developer tests for more than just the "happy path." Let's see how our app behaves in different scenarios:

- **Scenario 1 - Invalid file type:** Try to upload a .txt or a .pdf file. Our current code doesn't explicitly block this, but the Imagga API will reject it. You will see an "API Error" message because the service couldn't process the non-image file. A more advanced version would add a check for the file extension in the PHP code *before* sending it to the API.

- **Scenario 2 - File too large:** Find an image that is larger than 5 MB and try to upload it. Our PHP code will execute the size check ($_FILES["userImage"]["size"] > 5 * 1024 * 1024), and you will see the error message: "Error: File is too large (Max 5MB)." The API call will not even be attempted, saving resources.
- **Scenario 3 - Incorrect API keys:** Go into config.php and intentionally change a character in your API key. Save the file and try uploading a valid image. The application will now fail at the API call step and display an "API Error: Not authorized" message (or similar), proving our error handling works.
- **Scenario 4 - No file selected:** If you click "Analyze Image" without choosing a file, the required attribute on the HTML <input type="file"> will prevent the form from submitting in any modern browser, providing instant client-side validation.

Harnessing vision APIs in real-world contexts

The simple gallery we built is a foundation for incredibly valuable features. In a professional setting, this technology is used for:

- **E-commerce:** Automatically tagging products with visual attributes (e.g., "long-sleeve," "V-neck," "blue") to improve product search and filtering for customers.
- **Digital asset management:** In a company's internal media library, automatically tagging thousands of images makes them instantly searchable for marketing, design, and sales teams.
- **Social media:** Analyzing user-uploaded content for brand logos, celebrities, or specific activities to gather marketing insights or for content moderation.

Hands-on: Image-to-text extractor (OCR)

Now for our second project. We'll build an application that uses the **Google Gemini API** to perform Optical Character Recognition (OCR)—extracting printed or handwritten text from an image. This is incredibly useful for digitizing documents, receipts, or notes.

The process will be very similar to the speech-to-text example: we will upload an image, Base64-encode it, and send it to the Gemini API with a specific prompt asking it to extract the text.

Building the application

Create the project structure

1. In your **htdocs/codes** directory, create a new folder named **ocr-live**.
2. Inside it, create another folder named **uploads**.
3. Finally, create the files index.php, style.css, and config.php under ocr-live folder in VS Code.

Your structure should be:

```
/xampp/htdocs/codes/
└── ocr-live/
    ├── uploads/
    ├── index.php
    ├── style.css
    └── config.php
```

Set up the configuration file

Copy the following code in config.php file. For this project, you only need the GOOGLE_GEMINI_API_KEY:

```
<?php
// Google AI Gemini API Credentials
define('GOOGLE_GEMINI_API_KEY', 'PASTE_YOUR_GEMINI_API_KEY_HERE');
```

Create the CSS stylesheet

Add the following stylish CSS snippet in the style.css file:

```
/* General Body and Layout */
body {
    font-family: -apple-system, BlinkMacSystemFont, "Segoe UI", Roboto,
                 "Helvetica Neue", Arial, sans-serif;
    background-color: #e9ecef;
    color: #495057;
    margin: 0;
    padding: 0;
    display: flex;
    flex-direction: column;
    align-items: center;
    min-height: 100vh;
}
```

```
.container {
    width: 90%;
    max-width: 800px;
    margin: 30px auto;
    padding: 30px;
    background-color: #ffffff;
    border-radius: 12px;
    box-shadow: 0 4px 12px rgba(0, 0, 0, 0.08);
}
/* Typography and Headings */
h1 {
    font-size: 2.5rem;
    font-weight: 700;
    color: #212529;
    text-align: center;
    margin-bottom: 10px;
}
h3 {
    font-size: 1.5rem;
    font-weight: 600;
    color: #343a40;
    margin-top: 0;
    margin-bottom: 10px;
}
p {
    font-size: 1rem;
    line-height: 1.6;
    margin-bottom: 20px;
}
/* Form and Button Styling */
.upload-form {
    display: flex;
    flex-direction: column;
    align-items: center;
    gap: 15px;
}
.upload-form input[type="file"] {
    width: 100%;
    padding: 10px;
    border: 2px solid #ced4da;
    border-radius: 8px;
    background-color: #f8f9fa;
    color: #495057;
}
.upload-form input[type="submit"] {
    width: 100%;
    max-width: 300px;
    padding: 12px 25px;
    background-color: #007bff;
    color: #ffffff;
    border: none;
```

```
    border-radius: 8px;
    font-size: 1.1rem;
    font-weight: 600;
    cursor: pointer;
    transition: background-color 0.3s ease;
}
.upload-form input[type="submit"]:hover {
    background-color: #0056b3;
}
/* Message Styling */
.message {
    padding: 12px 20px;
    margin-top: 20px;
    border-radius: 8px;
    text-align: center;
    font-weight: 600;
}
.message.success {
    background-color: #d4edda;
    color: #155724;
    border: 1px solid #c3e6cb;
}
.message.error {
    background-color: #f8d7da;
    color: #721c24;
    border: 1px solid #f5c6cb;
}
/* Result Card and Transcript Box */
.result-card {
    display: flex;
    flex-direction: column;
    align-items: center;
    gap: 20px;
    text-align: center;
    margin-top: 30px;
}
.result-card img {
    max-width: 100%;
    height: auto;
    border-radius: 8px;
    box-shadow: 0 4px 8px rgba(0, 0, 0, 0.1);
}
.card-content {
    width: 100%;
}
.transcript-box {
    background-color: #f8f9fa;
    border-left: 4px solid #3498db;
    padding: 20px;
    margin-top: 15px;
    white-space: pre-wrap;
```

```
    word-wrap: break-word;
    font-family: 'Courier New', Courier, monospace;
    text-align: left;
    border-radius: 0 8px 8px 0;
}
```

Write the main application logic

This file will manage the image upload, call the Gemini API, and display the image alongside the extracted text. Add the following code in index.php:

```
<?php
require_once 'config.php';
$message = '';
$message_class = '';
$image_path = '';
$extracted_text = '';
/**
 * Sends an image file to the Gemini API for text extraction (OCR).
 *
 * @param string $filePath The temporary path of the uploaded file.
 * @param string $mimeType The MIME type of the image (e.g., 'image/jpeg').
 * @return array The API response (decoded from JSON).
 */
function getTextFromGeminiApi(string $filePath, string $mimeType): array
{
    $apiKey = GOOGLE_GEMINI_API_KEY;
    $apiEndpoint = 'https://generativelanguage.googleapis.com/v1beta/models
                    /gemini-1.5-flash:generateContent?key=' . $apiKey;
    $imageData = file_get_contents($filePath);
    $base64ImageData = base64_encode($imageData);
    $jsonData = [
        'contents' => [
            [
                'parts' => [
                    ['text' => 'Extract all text from this image. Respond only with
                            the text content.'],
                    ['inline_data' => ['mime_type' => $mimeType, 'data' =>
                                $base64ImageData]]
                ]
            ]
        ]
    ];
    $ch = curl_init();
    curl_setopt($ch, CURLOPT_URL, $apiEndpoint);
    curl_setopt($ch, CURLOPT_RETURNTRANSFER, true);
    curl_setopt($ch, CURLOPT_POST, true);
    curl_setopt($ch, CURLOPT_HTTPHEADER, ['Content-Type: application/json']);
    curl_setopt($ch, CURLOPT_POSTFIELDS, json_encode($jsonData));
```

```
    $response = curl_exec($ch);
    $httpCode = curl_getinfo($ch, CURLINFO_HTTP_CODE);
    curl_close($ch);
    $data = json_decode($response, true);
    $data['http_code'] = $httpCode; // Add http code
    return $data;
}
if ($_SERVER["REQUEST_METHOD"] == "POST") {
    if (isset($_FILES["userImage"]) && $_FILES["userImage"]["error"] == 0) {
        $tempPath = $_FILES["userImage"]["tmp_name"];
        $mimeType = $_FILES["userImage"]["type"];
        // Basic validation for image type
        $allowedTypes = ['image/jpeg', 'image/png', 'image/gif', 'image/webp'];
        if (!in_array($mimeType, $allowedTypes)) {
            $message = "Error: Invalid file type. Please upload a JPG, PNG,
                        GIF, or WEBP.";
            $message_class = 'error';
        } elseif ($_FILES["userImage"]["size"] > 5 * 1024 * 1024) { // Max 5MB
            $message = "Error: File is too large (Max 5MB).";
            $message_class = 'error';
        } else {
            $apiResponse = getTextFromGeminiApi($tempPath, $mimeType);
            if ($apiResponse['http_code'] == 200 && isset($apiResponse[
                    'candidates'][0]['content']['parts'][0]['text'])) {
                $fileName = basename($_FILES["userImage"]["name"]);
                $newFileName = uniqid() . '-' . $fileName;
                $uploadPath = 'uploads/' . $newFileName;

                move_uploaded_file($tempPath, $uploadPath);
                $message = "Image processed successfully!";
                $message_class = 'success';
                $image_path = $uploadPath;
                $extracted_text = trim($apiResponse['candidates'][0]['content']
                                            ['parts'][0]['text']);
            } else {
                $message = "API Error: Could not extract text from the image. " .
                            ($apiResponse['error']['message'] ?? 'Please try a
                            clearer image.');
                $message_class = 'error';
            }
        }
    } else {
        $message = "An error occurred during upload. Please try again.";
        $message_class = 'error';
    }
}
?>
<!DOCTYPE html>
<html lang="en">
<head>
    <meta charset="UTF-8">
```

```
    <title>Image-to-Text Extractor (OCR)</title>
    <link rel="stylesheet" href="style.css">
</head>
<body>
    <div class="container">
        <h1>AI Image-to-Text Extractor (OCR)</h1>
        <p style="text-align: center; margin-top: -15px; margin-bottom: 30px;">
            Upload an image of a document, sign, or receipt to extract
            its text.</p>
        <form action="index.php" method="post" enctype="multipart/form-data"
              class="upload-form">
            <input type="file" name="userImage" required accept="image/*">
            <input type="submit" value="Extract Text">
        </form>
        <?php if ($message): ?>
            <div class="message <?php echo $message_class; ?>"><?php echo
                $message; ?></div>
        <?php endif; ?>
    </div>
    <?php if ($image_path && $extracted_text): ?>
        <div class="container result-card">
            <img src="<?php echo htmlspecialchars($image_path); ?>"
                alt="Uploaded image">
            <div class="card-content">
                <h3>Extracted Text:</h3>
                <div class="transcript-box">
                    <?php echo htmlspecialchars($extracted_text); ?>
                </div>
            </div>
        </div>
    <?php endif; ?>
</body>
</html>
```

Bridging the gap: Learned concepts and application implementation

This project builds directly on the concepts from earlier in the chapter:

- **API key management:** Just like before, require_once 'config.php'; securely loads our Google Gemini API key. The **getTextFromGeminiApi()** function then uses this key to authenticate its request.
- **Live API call with cURL:** The **getTextFromGeminiApi()** function is a practical implementation of sending binary data within a JSON payload. We read the image file, **base64_encode()** it, and place it inside the **$jsonData** array. The prompt Extract all text... guides the AI model to perform an OCR task instead of a transcription task.

- **Handling user image uploads:** The PHP logic starting with if **($_SERVER["REQUEST_METHOD"] == "POST")** is nearly identical to our first project. It safely handles the file upload via the **$_FILES** superglobal and performs validation checks for file type and size before making a costly API call.
- **Displaying results:** Upon a successful API response, we populate the **$extracted_text** variable by navigating the JSON structure **($apiResponse['candidates'][0]['content']['parts'][0]['text'])**. This variable is then securely displayed using **htmlspecialchars()** inside our newly styled transcript-box.

Running and testing

1. **Start XAMPP:** Ensure the **Apache** module is running.
2. **Open your browser:** Navigate to http://localhost/codes/ocr-live/.

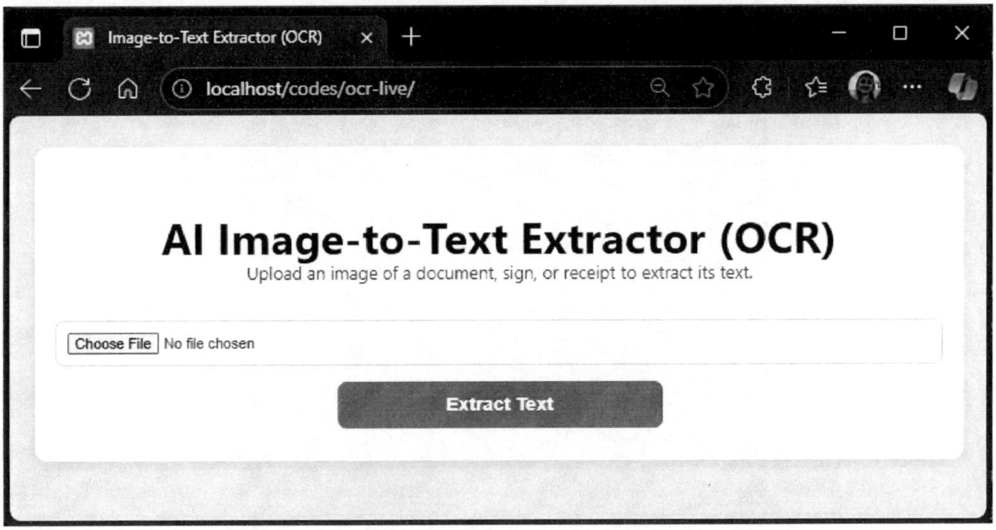

3. **Extract text:** Find an image on your computer that contains clear text (a screenshot of code, a photo of a street sign, or a scanned document works well). Upload it and click **Extract Text**.
4. **Observe the result:** The page reloads. Below the main form, a new card appears showing your original image and a stylish text box containing the AI's transcription of the text within that image.

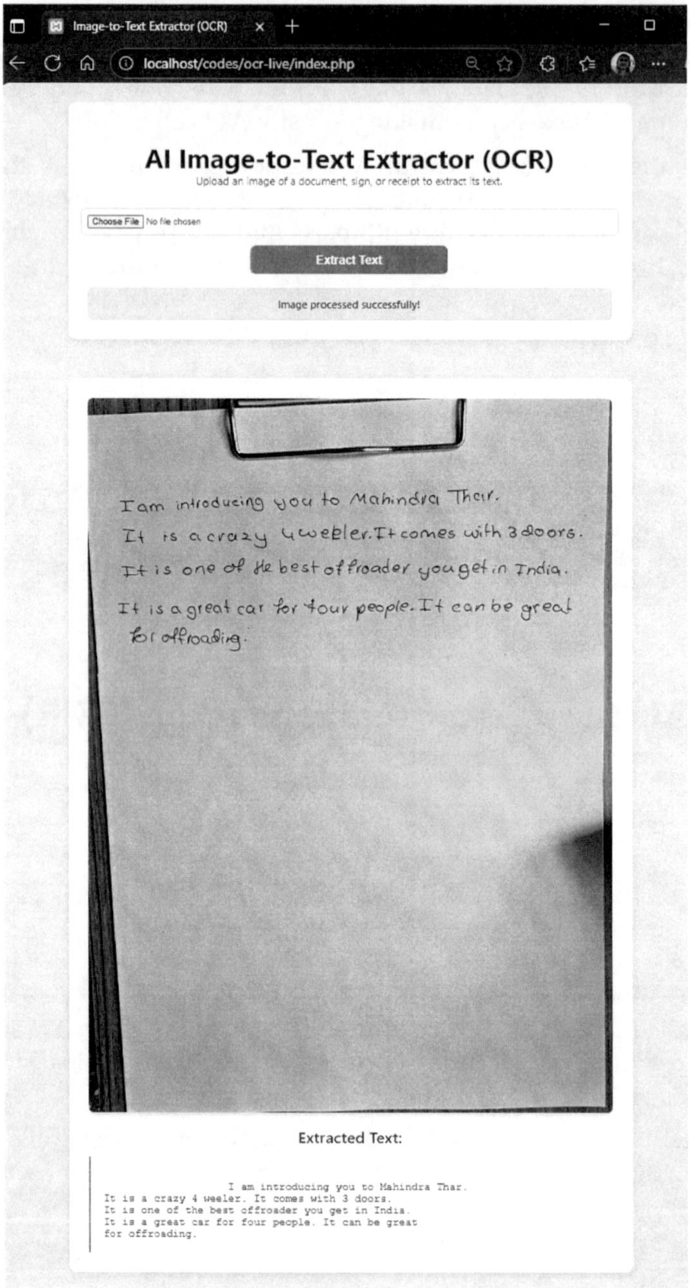
Image-to-Text Extractor (OCR)
localhost/codes/ocr-live/index.php
AI Image-to-Text Extractor (OCR)
Upload an image of a document, sign, or receipt to extract its text.
Choose File No file chosen
Extract Text
Image processed successfully!
Extracted Text:
I am introducing you to Mahindra Thar.
It is a crazy 4 weeler. It comes with 3 doors.
It is one of the best offroader you get in India.
It is a great car for four people. It can be great
for offroading.

Exploring application behaviour: A practical run-through

Let's test the limits of our new application:

- **Scenario 1 - Blurry or low-quality image:** Try uploading an image where the text is out of focus or at a strange angle. The Gemini API will attempt to read it, but the resulting text may be inaccurate or incomplete. This demonstrates the importance of providing high-quality input to AI models.
- **Scenario 2 - Image with no text:** Upload a photograph of a landscape or a pet. The API will correctly identify that there is no text to extract and will likely return a short, helpful message like "There is no text in this image," which our application will display.
- **Scenario 3 - Non-image file:** Try to upload a .zip or .mp3 file. Our PHP code has a MIME type check (in_array($mimeType, $allowedTypes)) that will catch this before the API call is ever made, displaying the "Error: Invalid file type" message and saving resources.
- **Scenario 4 - Incorrect API keys:** As with the first project, intentionally altering your GOOGLE_GEMINI_API_KEY in config.php will cause the cURL request to fail, resulting in an API error message. This confirms our error handling is effective.

Harnessing OCR APIs in real-world contexts

The OCR tool we just built is a gateway to powerful real-world applications:

- **Expense tracking:** Mobile banking apps use OCR to let users snap a photo of a receipt. The app automatically extracts the store name, date, and total amount, making expense reports effortless.
- **Document digitization:** Companies and libraries scan millions of pages of paper documents, from invoices to historical records. OCR converts these images into machine-readable, searchable text, unlocking vast archives of data.
- **Accessibility tools:** Applications can use a device's camera to read street signs, restaurant menus, or book pages aloud for visually impaired users.
- **Automated data entry:** Instead of manually typing information from a form or an ID card into a system, an application can use OCR to read and populate the fields automatically, saving time and reducing errors.

Wrapping up

In this chapter, we leveled up significantly by connecting our PHP code to the live, production internet. We moved beyond theory and into the practical skills required of a professional developer, using state-of-the-art AI.

- **Modern APIs:** We learned how to sign up for and use powerful AI services like Imagga and Google's Gemini.
- **API key management:** We implemented a secure method for storing secret keys in a config.php file.
- **Advanced cURL requests:** We mastered using cURL to send complex data, including Base64-encoded files within a JSON body.
- **Parsing JSON responses:** We learned to navigate the unique, nested structures of real API responses to extract the exact data we need.
- **Live application:** We built two fully functional applications from scratch: a Visual Gallery for AI image tagging and an Image-to-Text Extractor for AI-powered OCR.

Amazing work! You have successfully built a web application that interacts with sophisticated, third-party AI services. You've managed credentials, made authenticated API calls, and handled complex data structures—all fundamental skills for building modern software. This is a huge milestone.

In the next chapter, we will take all the AI skills we've learned and combine them in ***Chapter 23: Culmination - Smarter guestbook revolution***. It's time to build your first major portfolio project!

Chapter 23

Section 06: AI awakened – Smarter web apps for all

Culmination: Smarter guestbook revolution

What you'll learn

- Connecting to APIs
- Handling API keys
- Using Gemini AI
- Processing text/images

Welcome to the culmination of our journey into the exciting world of Artificial Intelligence with PHP. In the previous chapters, we explored individual AI concepts. Now, it is time to connect our PHP application to a real, state-of-the-art AI model. This chapter is where we assemble all the pieces into a single, intelligent, and interactive application that analyzes user comments and images using Google's Gemini Flash. We move beyond theory and build a project that reacts and adapts to user input in a truly dynamic way, showcasing the real power of modern, AI-enhanced web development.

Combining sentiment, recommendation, and media

Previously, we imagined using separate AI services for different tasks. In reality, modern, powerful AI models, often called Large Language Models (LLMs) or multimodal models, can perform multiple analytical tasks in a single request. This is far more efficient and powerful.

For our smarter Guestbook, we will send a user's comment *and* their uploaded image to the Gemini AI model in one go. We will ask it to perform several tasks at once:

- **Analyze sentiment:** Determine if the comment is positive, negative, or neutral.
- **Generate tags:** Create relevant keywords for the comment's content and the uploaded image.
- **Provide a recommendation:** Suggest a fictional related article or topic based on the user's input.

The AI will return a clean, structured JSON object containing all of this information. Our PHP script will then parse this data to personalize the user's experience—all from a single, powerful API call. This integrated approach is how modern applications deliver rich, intelligent features without juggling multiple complex services.

End-to-end user journey design

A clear user journey is the blueprint for a great application. Let's map out the experience for our smarter Guestbook, now powered by a real AI.

- **The arrival:** A user lands on the guestbook page. They see existing comments, each styled with a unique border colour based on its AI-analyzed sentiment. A clean, inviting form prompts them to leave their own message.
- **The interaction:** The user enters their name, writes a comment, and uploads an image. They click the **Submit Comment** button.
- **The AI magic (behind the scenes):** Our process.php script takes over.
  - The script validates the input and securely handles the image upload, moving it to a server directory.
  - It constructs a carefully worded prompt, combining the user's text and the image data.
  - It sends this prompt to the Gemini Flash API using PHP's cURL library.
  - The Gemini AI processes the request and sends back a structured JSON response containing the sentiment, tags, and a recommendation.
- **The personalized response:** The user is redirected back to the guestbook page.
  - **Instant feedback:** A confirmation message appears, acknowledging their submission.
  - **Visible entry:** Their new comment instantly appears at the top of the list, complete with their name, comment, uploaded image, and the AI-generated tags.
  - **Dynamic styling:** The entry has a coloured border (green for positive, red for negative) that visually represents the comment's sentiment.

- **Smart recommendation:** Below the comment, a "You might also like..." section appears, displaying the personalized recommendation from the AI.

This entire flow, from submission to a fully personalized and analyzed entry appearing on the page, happens in just a few seconds, creating a seamless and impressive user experience.

Personalizing experience based on AI output

The core of our project's intelligence lies in how we use the data returned from the Gemini API. We will instruct the AI to always return a JSON object in a specific format we define.

A sample AI JSON response:

```
{
  "sentiment": "POSITIVE",
  "tags": ["website design", "user experience", "positive feedback", "sunset",
           "landscape"],
  "recommendation": "Read our article on 'The Principles of Modern Web Design'."
}
```

In our PHP backend, after receiving this response, we decode the JSON string into a PHP associative array. This allows us to easily access each piece of data. PHP code to process the AI response:

```
<?php
// $aiResponseJson is the string returned from the API
$aiData = json_decode($aiResponseJson, true);
// Access individual pieces of data. Default to NEUTRAL if not found
$sentiment = $aiData['sentiment'] ?? 'NEUTRAL';
$tags = $aiData['tags'] ?? []; // Default to an empty array
$recommendation = $aiData['recommendation'] ?? 'Explore our blog for more content.';
// Determine the CSS class based on sentiment
$sentimentClass = 'sentiment-neutral';
if ($sentiment === 'POSITIVE') {
    $sentimentClass = 'sentiment-positive';
} elseif ($sentiment === 'NEGATIVE') {
    $sentimentClass = 'sentiment-negative';
}
?>
```

We can now store these variables ($sentimentClass, $tags, $recommendation) along with the user's original comment and display them dynamically in our HTML. This direct link between the AI's analysis and the final rendered output is what makes the application feel alive and responsive.

Advanced feedback loops

While we will not be building a full model retraining system, it is important to understand the concept of a feedback loop in a real-world context. An AI model is only as good as the data it is trained on. Sometimes, it might make a mistake.

For example, a user might write, "Your support team is unbelievably good!" The word "unbelievably" can sometimes have negative connotations, and a model might get confused.

In a production application, you could add small "Was this analysis helpful?" (👍 / 👎) buttons next to the AI-generated tags or sentiment. When a user clicks one, the feedback is logged. For example: EntryID: 123, Field: Sentiment, UserFeedback: Incorrect.

Over time, developers and data scientists can review this log of incorrect analyses. They can use these specific examples to fine-tune the AI model's instructions or even retrain it to be more accurate in the future. This continuous cycle of deploying, monitoring, and refining is what allows AI-powered features to improve and adapt over time.

Hands-on: Build all-in-one AI guestbook

This project is the real deal. We will build a complete guestbook application that connects to the live Gemini AI to analyze user comments and images, delivering a rich, personalized response.

Prerequisite: Getting your Google AI API key

To communicate with Gemini, your application needs an API key. This is a unique secret code that identifies your project.

- Visit the **Google AI Studio** website.
- Sign in with your Google account.
- Click on the **Get API key** button.
- Create a new API key in a new or existing project.

Important:
Copy the generated API key and save it somewhere safe, like a text file, for the next step. Treat this key like a password; do not share it publicly.

Building the application

First, let's set up our project structure.

1. Inside your **htdocs/codes** folder in XAMPP, create a new folder called **smarter-guestbook**.
2. Inside this folder, create another folder called **uploads**. This is where our user-uploaded images will be stored.
3. Then, inside **smarter-guestbook**, we will create four files: config.php, index.php, process.php, and style.css.

Project structure:

/xampp/htdocs/codes/smarter-guestbook/
|-- uploads/
|-- config.php
|-- index.php
|-- process.php
|-- style.css

Create the configuration file

This file will store your secret API key. By keeping it separate, we avoid accidentally sharing it in our main application code. Add the following code in the config.php file:

```
<?php
// Replace 'YOUR_API_KEY' with the actual API key you got from Google AI Studio.
define('GEMINI_API_KEY', 'YOUR_API_KEYS');
```

Action:
Open this file and paste your API key in place of YOUR_API_KEY.

Create the user interface

This file contains the HTML form and the PHP logic to display guestbook entries stored in the session. Add the following code in the index.php:

```
<?php
session_start();
// Initialize session arrays if they don't exist
if (!isset($_SESSION['guestbook_entries'])) {
    $_SESSION['guestbook_entries'] = [];
}
if (!isset($_SESSION['feedback'])) {
```

```
    $_SESSION['feedback'] = null;
}
$entries = $_SESSION['guestbook_entries'];
$feedback = $_SESSION['feedback'];
// Clear the feedback message after displaying it once
unset($_SESSION['feedback']);
?>
<!DOCTYPE html>
<html lang="en">
<head>
    <meta charset="UTF-8">
    <meta name="viewport" content="width=device-width, initial-scale=1.0">
    <title>Smarter Guestbook</title>
    <link rel="stylesheet" href="style.css">
</head>
<body>
    <div class="container">
        <h1>Smarter Guestbook Revolution</h1>
        <p>Leave a comment and an image. Our Gemini AI will analyze it in real-time
           !</p>
        <?php if ($feedback): ?>
            <div class="feedback <?php echo htmlspecialchars($feedback['type']);
                 ?>">
                <?php echo htmlspecialchars($feedback['message']); ?>
            </div>
        <?php endif; ?>
        <form action="process.php" method="post" enctype="multipart/form-data"
              class="guestbook-form">
            <div class="form-group">
                <label for="name">Your Name:</label>
                <input type="text" id="name" name="name" required>
            </div>
            <div class="form-group">
                <label for="comment">Your Comment:</label>
                <textarea id="comment" name="comment" rows="4" required></textarea>
            </div>
            <div class="form-group">
                <label for="image">Upload a Photo (Required):</label>
                <input type="file" id="image" name="image" accept="image/*"
                       required>
            </div>
            <button type="submit" class="submit-btn">Submit Comment</button>
        </form>
        <hr>
        <h2>Recent Entries</h2>
        <div class="guestbook-entries">
            <?php if (empty($entries)): ?>
                <p>No entries yet. Be the first!</p>
            <?php else: ?>
                <?php foreach (array_reverse($entries) as $entry): ?>
                    <div class="entry <?php echo htmlspecialchars($entry[
```

```
                               'sentiment_class']); ?>">
                        <div class="entry-header">
                            <h3><?php echo htmlspecialchars($entry['name']); ?></h3>
                            <span><?php echo $entry['timestamp']; ?></span>
                        </div>
                        <div class="entry-content">
                            <?php if (!empty($entry['image_path'])): ?>
                                <img src="<?php echo htmlspecialchars($entry['
                                          image_path']); ?>" alt="User upload"
                                     class="entry-image">
                            <?php endif; ?>
                            <p><?php echo nl2br(htmlspecialchars($entry['comment']
                               )); ?></p>
                        </div>
                        <div class="ai-analysis">
                            <div class="tags">
                                <strong>AI Tags:</strong> <?php echo
                                        htmlspecialchars(implode(', ', $entry['
                                        tags'])); ?>
                            </div>
                            <div class="recommendation">
                                <strong>AI Recommendation:</strong> <?php echo
                                        htmlspecialchars($entry['recommendation']);
                                        ?>
                            </div>
                        </div>
                    </div>
                <?php endforeach; ?>
            <?php endif; ?>
        </div>
    </div>
</body>
</html>
```

Create the backend logic

This is the core of our application. It handles the file upload, prepares the data, calls the Gemini API, processes the response, and saves the result. This updated version includes more robust error logging, which is essential for debugging real-world applications. Add the following code in the process.php file:

```
<?php
session_start();
require_once 'config.php';
// Function to set feedback and redirect
function redirect_with_feedback(string $type, string $message)
{
    $_SESSION['feedback'] = ['type' => $type, 'message' => $message];
    header('Location: index.php');
```

```
    exit();
}
// Check if the form was submitted
if ($_SERVER['REQUEST_METHOD'] !== 'POST') {
    redirect_with_feedback('error', 'Invalid request method.');
}
// --- 1. HANDLE FILE UPLOAD ---
if (!isset($_FILES['image']) || $_FILES['image']['error'] !== UPLOAD_ERR_OK) {
    redirect_with_feedback('error', 'Image upload failed. Please try again.');
}
$image_tmp_path = $_FILES['image']['tmp_name'];
$image_info = getimagesize($image_tmp_path);
$image_mime = $image_info['mime'];
// Validate file type
$allowed_mimes = ['image/jpeg', 'image/png', 'image/gif'];
if (!in_array($image_mime, $allowed_mimes)) {
    redirect_with_feedback('error', 'Invalid image format. Please use JPG, PNG, or
                               GIF.');
}
// Generate a unique name and move the file
$upload_dir = 'uploads/';
$image_extension = pathinfo($_FILES['image']['name'], PATHINFO_EXTENSION);
$image_new_name = uniqid('img_', true) . '.' . $image_extension;
$image_new_path = $upload_dir . $image_new_name;
if (!move_uploaded_file($image_tmp_path, $image_new_path)) {
    redirect_with_feedback('error', 'Failed to save the uploaded image.');
}
// --- 2. PREPARE DATA FOR API ---
$name = filter_input(INPUT_POST, 'name', FILTER_SANITIZE_STRING);
$comment = filter_input(INPUT_POST, 'comment', FILTER_SANITIZE_STRING);
// Get image data and base64 encode it
$image_data = file_get_contents($image_new_path);
$image_base64 = base64_encode($image_data);
// --- 3. CALL GEMINI API ---
$api_key = GEMINI_API_KEY;
$api_url = 'https://generativelanguage.googleapis.com/v1beta/models/
            gemini-1.5-flash:generateContent?key=' . $api_key;
$prompt = "You are an intelligent guestbook moderator. Analyze the
           following user comment and image.
User Comment: \"{$comment}\"
Analyze the text and the image and return a JSON object with the following
structure:
{
  \"sentiment\": \"POSITIVE\", \"NEGATIVE\", or \"NEUTRAL\",
  \"tags\": [\"an\", \"array\", \"of\", \"5\", \"relevant\", \"keywords\",
             \"from\", \"text\", \"and\", \"image\"],
  \"recommendation\": \"A short, relevant content recommendation
                      based on the user's comment.\"
}
Ensure the output is only the raw JSON object, with no extra text or markdown
formatting.";
```

```
$request_body = [
    'contents' => [
        [
            'parts' => [
                ['text' => $prompt],
                [
                    'inline_data' => [
                        'mime_type' => $image_mime,
                        'data' => $image_base64
                    ]
                ]
            ]
        ]
    ]
];
$json_body = json_encode($request_body);
// Initialize cURL session
$ch = curl_init();
curl_setopt($ch, CURLOPT_URL, $api_url);
curl_setopt($ch, CURLOPT_HTTPHEADER, ['Content-Type: application/json']);
curl_setopt($ch, CURLOPT_POST, true);
curl_setopt($ch, CURLOPT_POSTFIELDS, $json_body);
curl_setopt($ch, CURLOPT_RETURNTRANSFER, true);
$response = curl_exec($ch);
$http_code = curl_getinfo($ch, CURLINFO_HTTP_CODE);
curl_close($ch);
// --- 4. PROCESS API RESPONSE ---
if ($http_code !== 200 || empty($response)) {
    // Clean up uploaded file on failure
    unlink($image_new_path);
    error_log("API request failed. HTTP Code: " . $http_code . " | Response: "
              . $response);
    redirect_with_feedback('error', 'API request failed. Please check server logs
                          for details.');
}
// The actual content is nested, so we need to decode and extract it
$response_data = json_decode($response, true);
$ai_content_raw = $response_data['candidates'][0]['content']['parts'][0]['text'] ??
                                  '';
// Robustly extract the JSON string
$json_string = trim($ai_content_raw);
if (strpos($json_string, '```json') === 0) {
    // Remove the markdown fences
    $json_string = substr($json_string, 7);
    $json_string = rtrim($json_string, '`');
}
$ai_data = json_decode($json_string, true);
if (json_last_error() !== JSON_ERROR_NONE) {
    // Clean up uploaded file on failure and log the raw response
    unlink($image_new_path);
```

```
    error_log("Failed to parse AI JSON response. Raw content: " . $ai_content_raw);
    redirect_with_feedback('error', 'Failed to parse AI JSON response. Please try
                                    again or check server logs.');
}
// --- 5. STORE THE RESULT IN THE SESSION ---
$sentiment = strtoupper($ai_data['sentiment'] ?? 'NEUTRAL');
$sentiment_class = 'sentiment-neutral';
if ($sentiment === 'POSITIVE') {
    $sentiment_class = 'sentiment-positive';
} elseif ($sentiment === 'NEGATIVE') {
    $sentiment_class = 'sentiment-negative';
}
$new_entry = [
    'name' => $name,
    'comment' => $comment,
    'image_path' => $image_new_path,
    'timestamp' => date('M d, Y H:i'),
    'sentiment_class' => $sentiment_class,
    'tags' => $ai_data['tags'] ?? [],
    'recommendation' => $ai_data['recommendation'] ?? 'No recommendation
                        available.'
];
// Add the new entry to the beginning of the array
$_SESSION['guestbook_entries'][] = $new_entry;
redirect_with_feedback('success', 'Your comment has been successfully
                        posted and analyzed!');
?>
```

Add styling with CSS

This stylesheet provides a clean, modern look and the visual cues for our AI analysis. Add the following code in the style.css file:

```
body {
    font-family: -apple-system, BlinkMacSystemFont, "Segoe UI", Roboto,
                 Helvetica, Arial, sans-serif;
    background-color: #f4f7f9;
    color: #333;
    line-height: 1.6;
    margin: 0;
    padding: 20px;
}
.container {
    max-width: 800px;
    margin: 0 auto;
    background-color: #fff;
    padding: 30px;
    border-radius: 8px;
    box-shadow: 0 4px 15px rgba(0, 0, 0, 0.1);
```

```
}
h1, h2 {
    color: #2c3e50;
    border-bottom: 2px solid #e0e0e0;
    padding-bottom: 10px;
    margin-bottom: 20px;
}
.feedback {
    padding: 15px;
    margin-bottom: 20px;
    border-radius: 5px;
    color: #fff;
    font-weight: bold;
}
.feedback.success {
    background-color: #28a745;
}
.feedback.error {
    background-color: #dc3545;
}
.guestbook-form {
    display: flex;
    flex-direction: column;
    gap: 15px;
}
.form-group {
    display: flex;
    flex-direction: column;
}
.form-group label {
    margin-bottom: 5px;
    font-weight: bold;
    color: #555;
}
.form-group input, .form-group textarea {
    padding: 12px;
    border: 1px solid #ccc;
    border-radius: 5px;
    font-size: 16px;
}
.submit-btn {
    padding: 12px 20px;
    background-color: #3498db;
    color: #fff;
    border: none;
    border-radius: 5px;
    font-size: 16px;
    cursor: pointer;
    transition: background-color 0.3s ease;
}
.submit-btn:hover {
```

```
    background-color: #2980b9;
}
hr {
    border: none;
    border-top: 1px solid #eee;
    margin: 30px 0;
}
.entry {
    background-color: #fdfdfd;
    padding: 20px;
    border-radius: 5px;
    margin-bottom: 20px;
    border-left: 5px solid #ccc;
    box-shadow: 0 2px 5px rgba(0, 0, 0, 0.05);
}
.entry-header {
    display: flex;
    justify-content: space-between;
    align-items: center;
    margin-bottom: 15px;
}
.entry-header h3 {
    margin: 0;
    color: #34495e;
}
.entry-header span {
    font-size: 0.9em;
    color: #95a5a6;
}
.entry-content {
    display: flex;
    gap: 20px;
    align-items: flex-start;
}
.entry-image {
    max-width: 150px;
    height: auto;
    border-radius: 5px;
}
.entry-content p {
    margin: 0;
}
.ai-analysis {
    margin-top: 15px;
    padding-top: 15px;
    border-top: 1px dashed #e0e0e0;
    font-size: 0.95em;
}
.ai-analysis .tags {
    margin-bottom: 10px;
}
```

```
.ai-analysis strong {
    color: #2c3e50;
}
.sentiment-positive {
    border-left-color: #2ecc71;
}
.sentiment-negative {
    border-left-color: #e74c3c;
}
.sentiment-neutral {
    border-left-color: #f1c40f;
}
```

Bridging the gap: Learned concepts and application implementation

- **Real API integration:** process.php uses PHP cURL to make a live HTTP POST request to the Google Gemini API. This is the standard method for communicating with web services.
- **Secure API key handling:** We created config.php to store our secret API key—a crucial security practice.
- **Multimodal AI:** Our API call sends both text ($comment) and image data ($image_base64) in the same request, showcasing the power of a multimodal model like Gemini.
- **JSON processing:** We use json_encode() to create the request body and json_decode() to parse the AI's JSON response into a usable PHP array.
- **File uploads and security:** The script validates the uploaded file's MIME type, generates a unique filename to prevent overwrites, and moves it to a safe directory.
- **Robust error handling:** The updated process.php now uses error_log() to save detailed error messages to the server's log file. This is a professional practice that helps developers diagnose problems without exposing sensitive information to users.

Running and testing

1. Ensure your **XAMPP** server is running with the **Apache** and **PHP** modules started.
2. Open your web browser and navigate to **http://localhost/codes/smarter-guestbook/**.
3. You see the guestbook form.

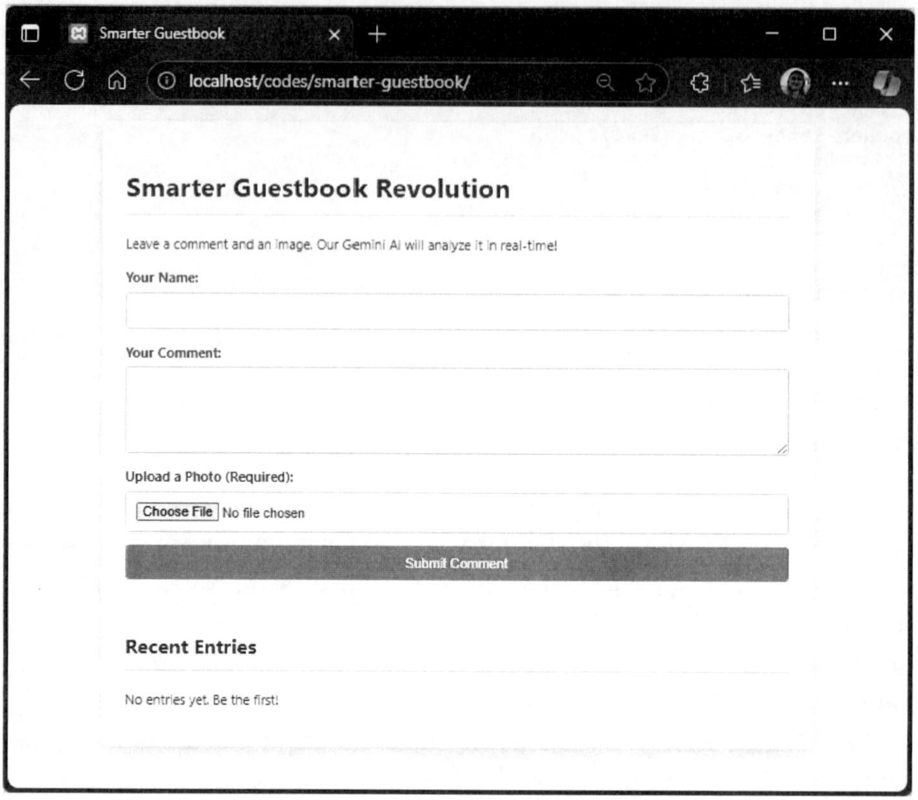

4. Fill in your name. For the comment, write something positive like **I absolutely love the clear skies in this photo, it's a beautiful landscape!**.
5. Upload a picture of a landscape or sunset.

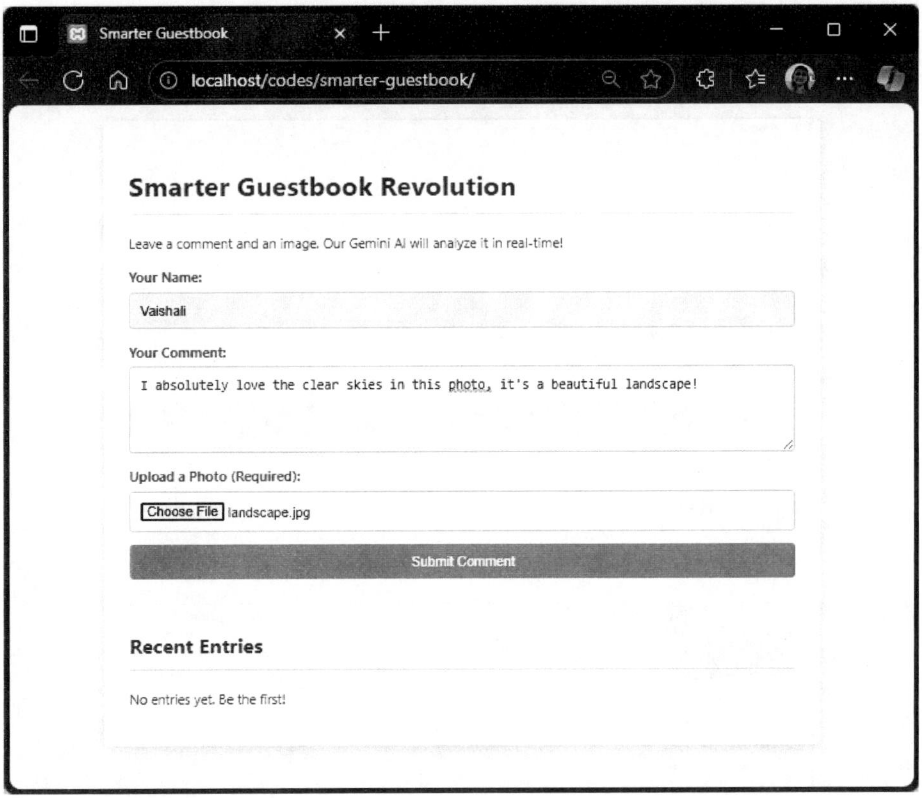

6. Click **Submit Comment**.
7. After a few seconds, the page reloads. You see a green success message at the top. Your new comment appears in the list with a green border, showing your uploaded image, and AI-generated tags like **landscape, mountains, sunset, flowers, clear skies**.

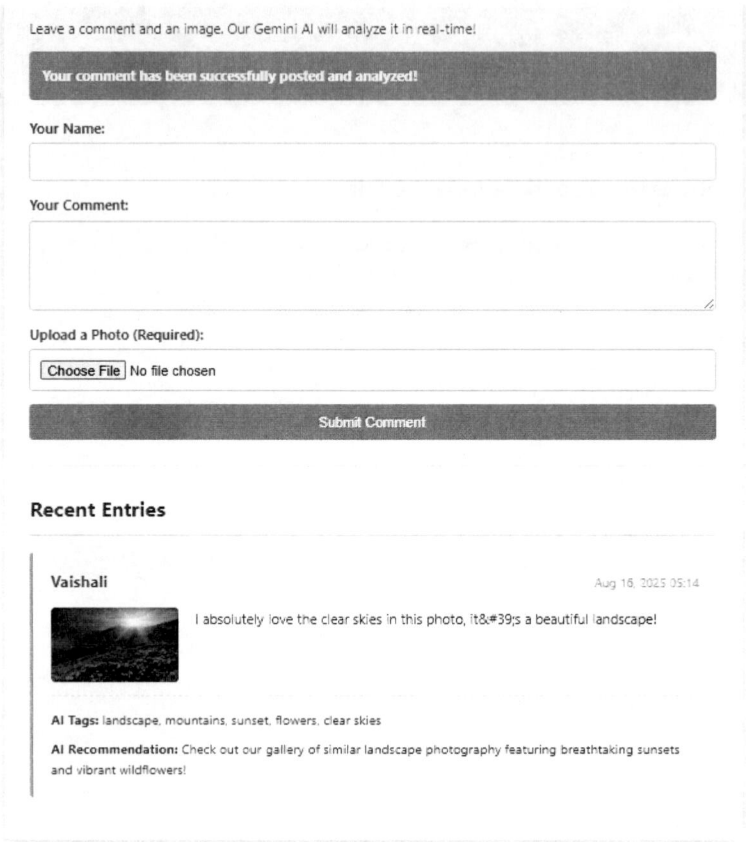

8. Try again with a negative comment and a different photo to see the red border and different tags.

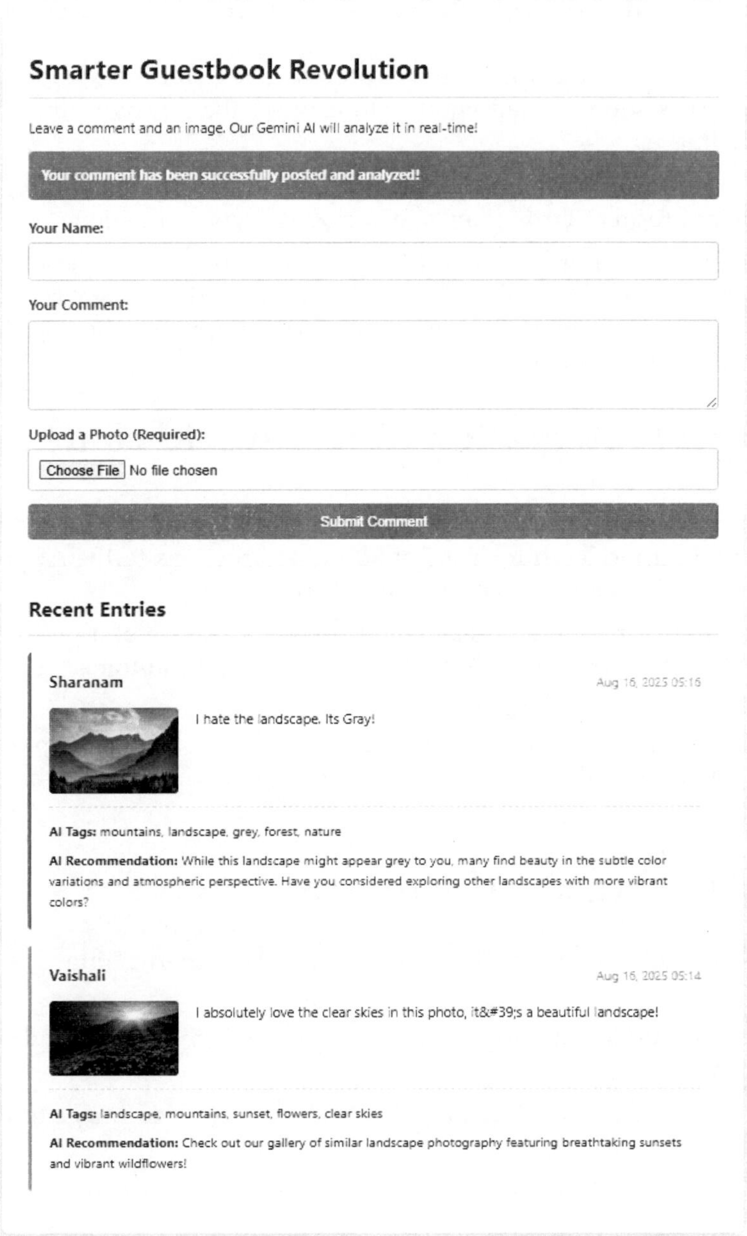
Smarter Guestbook Revolution
Leave a comment and an image. Our Gemini AI will analyze it in real-time!
Your comment has been successfully posted and analyzed!
Your Name:
Your Comment:
Upload a Photo (Required):
Choose File No file chosen
Submit Comment
Recent Entries
Sharanam
Aug 16, 2025 05:16
I hate the landscape. Its Gray!
AI Tags: mountains, landscape, grey, forest, nature
AI Recommendation: While this landscape might appear grey to you, many find beauty in the subtle color variations and atmospheric perspective. Have you considered exploring other landscapes with more vibrant colors?
Vaishali
Aug 16, 2025 05:14
I absolutely love the clear skies in this photo, it's a beautiful landscape!
AI Tags: landscape, mountains, sunset, flowers, clear skies
AI Recommendation: Check out our gallery of similar landscape photography featuring breathtaking sunsets and vibrant wildflowers!

Exploring application behaviour: A practical run-through

- **Valid inputs:** As tested, the app correctly processes text and images, returning relevant analysis. The AI is sophisticated enough to connect the words in the comment to the content of the image.
- **Invalid file type:** Try uploading a .txt or .zip file. The application will reject it and show an "Invalid image format" error, thanks to our MIME type validation.
- **API errors:** If you put an incorrect API key in config.php, the script will show a generic "API request failed" error to the user. However, a detailed message, including the HTTP status code, will be saved in your Apache error log (xampp/apache/logs/error.log). This is the power of robust logging.

Harnessing AI integration in real-world contexts

This project is more than just a guestbook; it's a blueprint for many real-world applications:

- **Automated content moderation:** You could add instructions to the AI prompt to detect and flag inappropriate content in comments or images.
- **E-commerce product reviews:** A user could upload a picture of a product they bought. The AI could analyze their review text and the image to automatically categorize the feedback (e.g., "positive, clothing, fit issue").
- **Smart support tickets:** A user could describe a technical problem and upload a screenshot. The AI could analyze both to suggest a solution or route the ticket to the correct support agent.

Bridging: Uniting all AI patterns

This project successfully unites multiple advanced AI patterns into a single, cohesive workflow:

- **Natural Language understanding:** Gemini comprehends the nuance and sentiment of the user's comment.
- **Computer vision:** Gemini analyzes the pixels of the uploaded image to identify objects, scenes, and concepts.
- **Generative AI:** The model doesn't just classify; it *generates* new content—the tags and the recommendation are created on the fly based on its combined understanding of the text and image.

By orchestrating these patterns, we have built an application that delivers a deeply contextual and intelligent response, far beyond what simple keyword matching or separate services could achieve.

Exploring: Testing diverse real inputs

The power of a model like Gemini lies in its ability to handle variety. Try testing these scenarios:

- **Contradictory input:** Write a positive comment like "I love this product!" but upload an image of it being broken. Observe what kind of tags and sentiment the AI returns. It will likely create tags for both and may return a neutral or mixed sentiment.
- **Abstract concepts:** Write a comment about "the feeling of freedom" and upload an image of an open road or a bird in flight. See how the AI generates conceptual tags that go beyond literal object identification.
- **Different languages:** Try writing a comment in a different language. Gemini is multilingual and will often provide an accurate analysis and tags in English, demonstrating its powerful translation and understanding capabilities.

Wrapping up

- **Live API calls:** We learned how to use PHP cURL to connect to a real, powerful AI API (Google Gemini).
- **Secure key management:** We properly stored our secret API key in a separate configuration file.
- **Multimodal prompts:** We sent both text and base64-encoded image data to the AI in a single request.
- **Robust file handling:** We implemented secure image uploads with validation and unique naming.
- **JSON data exchange:** We created and parsed JSON data, the standard language for modern web APIs.
- **Dynamic UI:** We built an interface that instantly reflects the AI's analysis through colors, text, and images.

Congratulations! You have successfully built a complete, intelligent web application that connects to a live, state-of-the-art AI model. You have handled file uploads, managed secret keys, and orchestrated a complex API call to create a truly interactive and personalized user experience. This project is a powerful demonstration of your skills and serves as a fantastic, real-world addition to your portfolio.

In the next chapter, we will shift gears to explore another revolutionary aspect of modern development. Get ready to supercharge your productivity with ***Chapter 24: AI-powered coding - Getting started with code assistants***.

Chapter 24

Section 07: AI code generation – Supercharge your productivity

AI-powered coding - Getting started with code assistants

What you'll learn

- Balancing AI use and learning
- Setting up multiple free AI assistants
- Installing Gemini, CodeWhisperer, and CodeGPT
- Best practices for AI coding
- Writing effective prompts

Welcome to one of the most exciting shifts in modern software development! Imagine having a brilliant coding partner available 24/7, ready to write boilerplate code, suggest solutions, explain complex topics, and even help you fix bugs. That's the power of AI code assistants. These tools work directly inside your code editor, transforming the way you build applications. They don't replace you; they supercharge your productivity and, more importantly, can act as a personal tutor on your learning journey.

This chapter is your guide to harnessing that power. We'll start with the essential principles of using AI responsibly as a beginner, set up several powerful, free AI assistants, and finally, build a complete web application from start to finish using AI-generated code.

Coding with AI as a beginner: A balanced approach

Before we install any tools, we must address a critical question: "If an AI can write the code for me, how will I learn?" This is a valid concern. Using an AI assistant is like wielding a powerful tool; used correctly, it can build amazing things, but used carelessly, it can prevent you from developing fundamental skills. The goal is to use AI as a *collaborator and teacher*, not a crutch.

When to use AI assistance

As a beginner, think of your AI assistant as a senior developer you can ask questions. Here are the best times to use it:

- **To explain code:** If you encounter a PHP function or a block of code you don't understand (either from online examples or previous chapters), ask the AI to explain it. Prompt: "Explain this PHP code line by line: ...". This is one of its most powerful uses for learning.
- **For boilerplate and repetitive tasks:** Writing the basic HTML structure, a simple database connection script, or a loop to print array elements are tasks you'll do thousands of times. Let the AI handle this "scaffolding" so you can focus on the unique logic of your application.
- **To overcome minor roadblocks:** Stuck on how to format a date or find an item in an array? Instead of spending 30 minutes searching online, ask the AI for the specific function you need. This keeps your momentum going.
- **To refactor your own code:** Once you've written a working piece of code, ask the AI to improve it. Prompt: "Can you refactor this PHP code to be more efficient or readable?" This teaches you better coding patterns.

Best practices: The dos and don'ts

To ensure you're learning effectively, follow these simple rules:

- **Do:**
    - **Do review every single line:** Never accept AI-generated code without reading it and understanding what it does. This is non-negotiable.
    - **Do try to write the code yourself first:** For any core feature, attempt to write it on your own. If you get stuck, then ask the AI for help. This reinforces your learning.
    - **Do ask "why":** When the AI gives you a solution, ask follow-up questions like "Why did you use isset() here?" or "What is the benefit of using prepared statements?".
    - **Do test the generated code thoroughly:** The AI can make mistakes. It's your job to test its code with different inputs, including invalid ones, to ensure it's robust.

- **Don't:**
  - **Don't blindly copy and paste:** This is the fastest way to *not* learn. If you don't understand the code, you won't be able to fix or change it later.
  - **Don't use it for core project logic initially:** Don't ask it to "build a user login system" and paste the result. Instead, ask for each part: "Generate a secure password hashing function," then "Generate the HTML for a login form," and so on. Build it piece by piece.
  - **Don't send sensitive information:** Never paste private API keys, passwords, or proprietary business logic into an AI assistant. Assume the data is being sent to a server for processing.
  - **Don't trust it with security:** AI assistants can generate code with security flaws. Always be extra critical of code that handles user input, database queries, or authentication.

AI vs. Manual coding: A partnership

Think of your journey as building a house. You must learn how to lay bricks, mix mortar, and read a blueprint (manual coding). Once you know the fundamentals, you can use a power tool (AI assistance) to lay those bricks faster. For a beginner, the ratio should be 70% manual coding and 30% AI assistance. As you become more proficient, that ratio might shift, but the need to understand the fundamentals never goes away.

Choosing and setting up your free AI assistant

While tools like GitHub Copilot are the industry standard, they require a paid subscription. Fortunately, there are several incredibly powerful free options. We will walk through the setup for three popular choices. For the hands-on project later in this chapter, **we will be using Google Gemini**, but any of these tools will work with similar prompts.

Option 1: Google Gemini (Our choice)

Gemini is Google's powerful and versatile AI model. It's excellent for conversational chat, explaining concepts, and generating creative code. Its free API tier is generous, making it a perfect choice for learners.

Get your free Google AI API key

1. **Navigate to Google AI Studio:** Open your web browser and go to aistudio.google.com. You will need to sign in with your Google account.
2. **Create an API key:** Once you are in the AI Studio, look for a "Get API key" link, which is usually on the left-hand menu or a prominent button on the main screen. Click it.
3. **Generate your key:** In the API keys section, click the button that says **"Create API key in new project"**. This will instantly generate a long string of letters and numbers. This is your secret key!
4. **Save your key:** Copy this API key immediately and save it somewhere safe, like a text file on your computer. **Treat this key like a password.**

Install and configure the Gemini extension in VS Code

1. Open VS Code and go to the **Extensions** view.
2. **Search for Gemini:** In the search bar, type **Google Gemini**. Install the official extension published by **Google**.

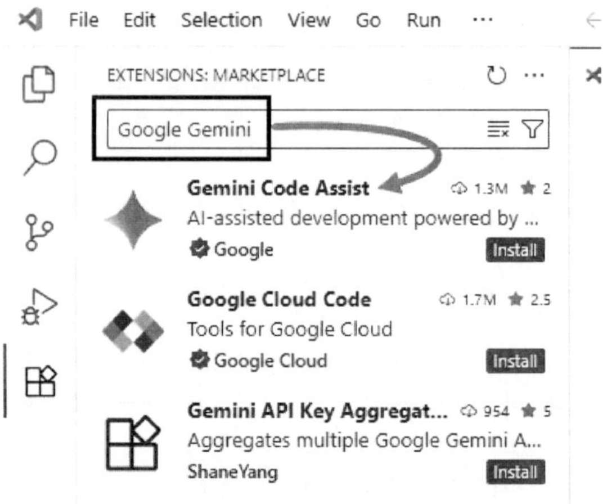

3. **Gemini installed:** Once the installation done, A **Extension: Gemini Code Assist** window appears showing that the extension is installed. Even **Gemini Code Assist – Welcome** window appears.

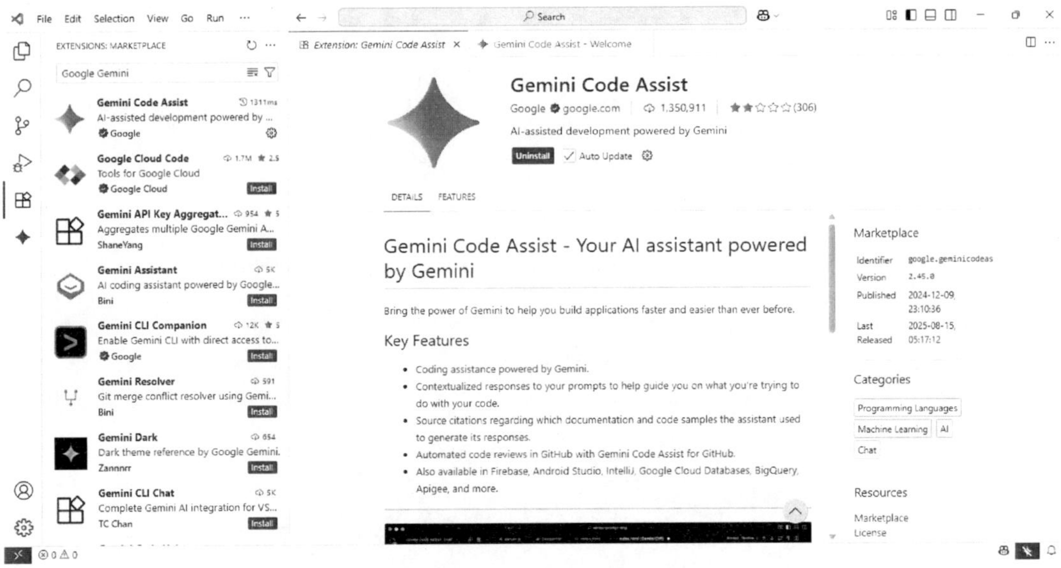

4. The **Google Gemini** icon appears on the left side bar just below the **Extensions** icon.

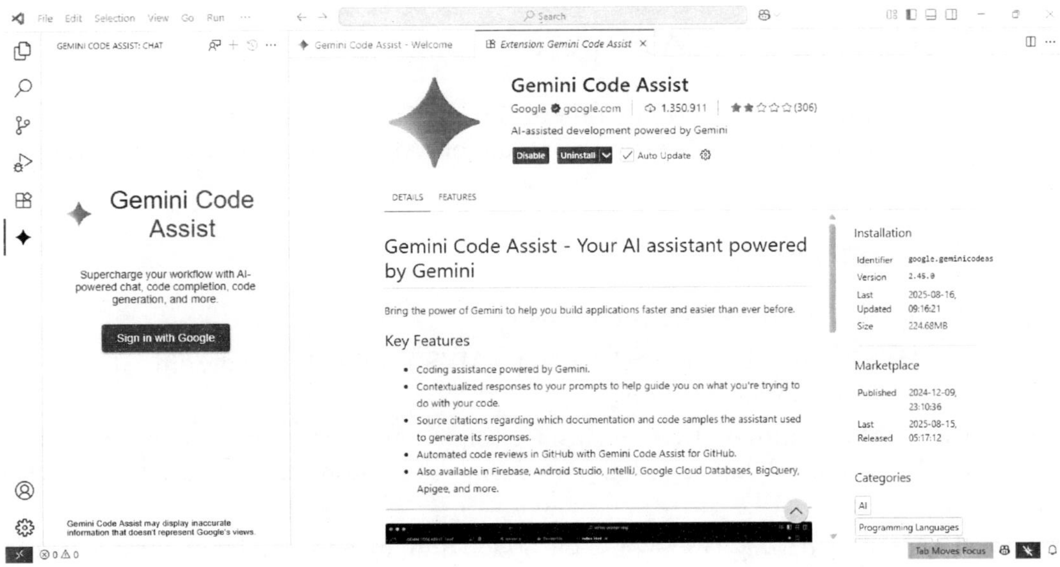

5. Click **Sign in with Google**. Follow all the steps as it guides to sign in with your Google account.

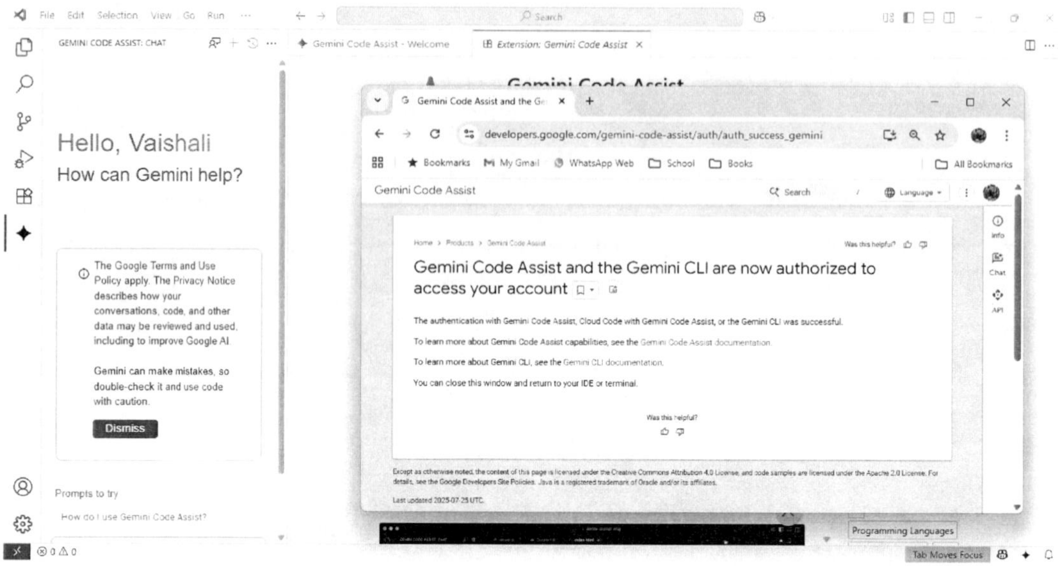

6. Your Gemini assistant is now ready!

Option 2: Amazon CodeWhisperer

CodeWhisperer is Amazon's direct competitor to GitHub Copilot. It excels at real-time, in-line code suggestions and is trained on a massive amount of code. Amazon provides a free tier for individual users that is very capable.

Step-by-step setup guide

1. Open VS Code and go to the **Extensions** view.
2. **Search for AWS Toolkit:** In the search bar, type **AWS Toolkit**. Install the official extension published by **Amazon Web Services**.
3. **Sign in with AWS Builder ID:** After installation, a new AWS icon will appear in your Activity Bar. Click it. In the panel that opens, find the **CodeWhisperer** section and click **Start**.
4. You will be prompted to sign in. Choose the option **Sign up and sign in with AWS Builder ID**. This is a free account that does **not** require a credit card or a full AWS account.
5. **Authorize in browser:** Your browser will open. Follow the prompts to create your free AWS Builder ID using your personal email address. You will need to verify your email.

6. **Allow access:** Once your account is created, you'll be asked to allow the AWS Toolkit to access your data. Click **Allow**.
7. **Confirmation:** You can now return to VS Code. The CodeWhisperer section in the AWS Toolkit panel should show that you are connected and ready to receive code suggestions.

Option 3: CodeGPT

CodeGPT is a highly versatile extension that acts as a bridge to many different AI models. This is a great choice if you want to experiment with various AI providers. You can connect it to the free Gemini API we created earlier, or many others.

Step-by-step setup guide

- Open VS Code and go to the Extensions view.
- **Search for CodeGPT:** In the search bar, type **CodeGPT**. Install the extension published by **CodeGPT**.
- **Select AI Provider:** After installation, a new CodeGPT icon will appear in your Activity Bar. Click it. At the bottom of the chat panel, you will see a dropdown menu to select your AI Provider. Choose **Google Gemini**.
- **Enter your API key:** You will be prompted to enter your API Key. Paste the same Google AI API key you generated in the Gemini setup.
- **Start chatting:** You can now use the CodeGPT chat window to interact with the Gemini model, just like with the official Gemini extension.

Now that you've seen how to set up several powerful assistants, you can choose the one that feels best for you. For the remainder of this chapter, we will proceed with the official **Google Gemini** extension.

Hands-on: Building a Contact manager with AI assistance

Now, let's put our AI partner to work. We will build a complete, functional simple Contact manager application from scratch. Our goal is to write as little code as possible ourselves, instead focusing on writing clear prompts to guide the AI.

The application will allow us to:

- Add a new contact (Name, Email, Phone) via a web form.

- Save the contacts to a simple file on the server.
- Display all saved contacts in a clean table.

Building the application: A step-by-step prompting guide

First, let's set up our project structure.

- **Create the project folder:** Inside your XAMPP htdocs/codes folder, create a new folder named **contact-manager**.
- **Create subfolders and files:** Inside **contact-manager**, create:
  - A folder named **public**.
  - A folder named **data**.
  - Inside **public**, create two empty files: index.php and style.css.

Your structure should look like this:

```
htdocs/codes/
└── contact-manager/
    ├── data/
    └── public/
        ├── index.php
        └── style.css
```

Now, open the **contact-manager** folder in **VS Code**.

Prompt 1: Generating the HTML structure

Open the empty index.php file. We will start a **chat** with Gemini. You can find the **Gemini** icon in your **Activity Bar** or open it by pressing **Ctrl+I** keys.

In the chat window, enter the following **Prompt**:

> Generate the full HTML5 boilerplate for a 'Simple Contact Manager' web page. The page should have a main heading. It needs a form that submits to itself using the POST method. The form should have input fields for 'Name', 'Email', and 'Phone', each with a proper label, and a submit button. Below the form, add a section with another heading for 'Contact List' which will contain a table to display the contacts. The table should have headers for Name, Email, and Phone. Link to a local stylesheet named style.css in the head section.

The AI generates the HTML code. It should look very similar to this. Click **Accept(Alt + A)**.

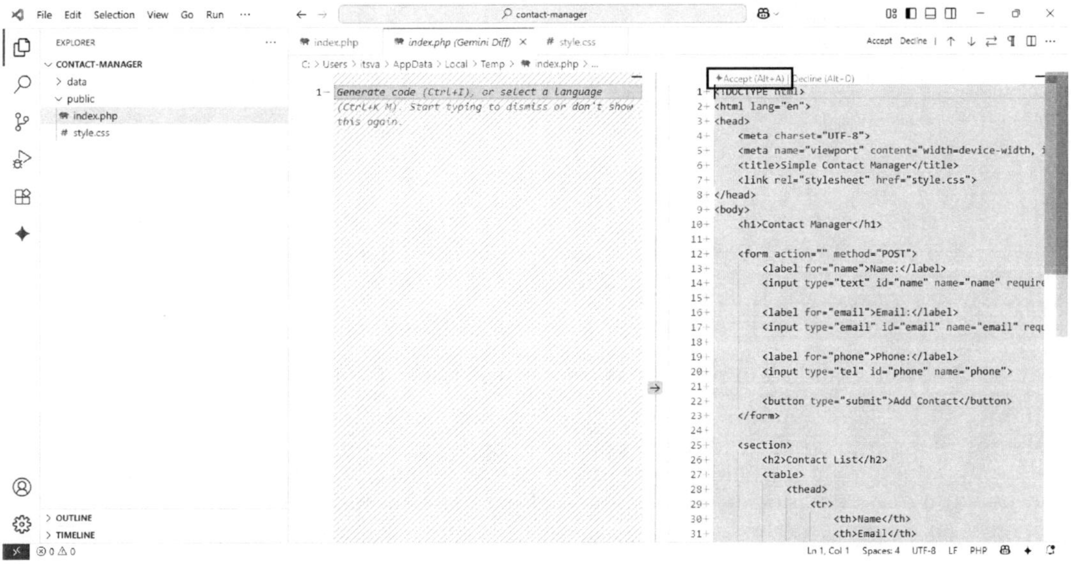

The code is automatically copied in your **public/index.php** file:

```
<!DOCTYPE html>
<html lang="en">
<head>
    <meta charset="UTF-8">
    <meta name="viewport" content="width=device-width, initial-scale=1.0">
    <title>Simple Contact Manager</title>
    <link rel="stylesheet" href="style.css">
</head>
<body>
    <h1>Contact Manager</h1>
    <form action="" method="POST">
        <label for="name">Name:</label>
        <input type="text" id="name" name="name" required>
        <label for="email">Email:</label>
        <input type="email" id="email" name="email" required>
```

```
            <label for="phone">Phone:</label>
            <input type="tel" id="phone" name="phone">
            <button type="submit">Add Contact</button>
        </form>
        <section>
            <h2>Contact List</h2>
            <table>
                <thead>
                    <tr>
                        <th>Name</th>
                        <th>Email</th>
                        <th>Phone</th>
                    </tr>
                </thead>
                <tbody>
                    <!-- Contact rows will be inserted here by PHP -->
                </tbody>
            </table>
        </section>
    </body>
</html>
```

Prompt 2: Generating the CSS

Now open the **style.css** file. Go back to your **Gemini chat** and enter this **Prompt**:

> Generate clean and modern CSS for the contact manager HTML. Create a main 'container' class with a max-width and centered. Style the form and the contact list table. The form inputs should be full-width, and the button should be visually appealing with a solid background color and a subtle hover effect. The table should have borders and padding to make it readable.

The AI generates the CSS code. Click **Accept(Alt + A)**. The code is automatically copied in your **public/style.css** file:

```
body {
    font-family: Arial, sans-serif;
    margin: 0;
    padding: 20px;
    background-color: #f4f4f4;
    color: #333;
}
.container {
    max-width: 800px;
    margin: 20px auto;
    background-color: #fff;
    padding: 30px;
    border-radius: 8px;
```

```
    box-shadow: 0 2px 10px rgba(0, 0, 0, 0.1);
}
h1, h2 {
    text-align: center;
    color: #0056b3;
    margin-bottom: 20px;
}
form {
    display: flex;
    flex-direction: column;
    gap: 15px;
    margin-bottom: 30px;
    padding: 20px;
    border: 1px solid #ddd;
    border-radius: 5px;
    background-color: #f9f9f9;
}
form label {
    font-weight: bold;
    margin-bottom: 5px;
    color: #555;
}
form input[type="text"], form input[type="email"], form input[type="tel"] {
    width: 100%;
    padding: 10px;
    border: 1px solid #ccc;
    border-radius: 4px;
    box-sizing: border-box;
    /* Ensures padding doesn't increase width */
    font-size: 16px;
}
form button {
    background-color: #007bff;
    color: white;
    padding: 12px 20px;
    border: none;
    border-radius: 5px;
    cursor: pointer;
    font-size: 18px;
    transition: background-color 0.3s ease;
}
form button:hover {
    background-color: #0056b3;
}
table {
    width: 100%;
    border-collapse: collapse;
    margin-top: 20px;
    box-shadow: 0 2px 8px rgba(0, 0, 0, 0.1);
    background-color: #fff;
}
```

```
table th, table td {
    padding: 12px 15px;
    border: 1px solid #ddd;
    text-align: left;
}
table th {
    background-color: #007bff;
    color: white;
    font-weight: bold;
}
table tr:nth-child(even) {
    background-color: #f2f2f2;
}
table tr:hover {
    background-color: #e9e9e9;
}
section {
    margin-top: 30px;
}
```

Prompt 3: Generating the PHP logic to save contacts

Now for the brains of the operation. Re-open **index.php**. We need to add PHP code at the very top of the file to process the form data. Tell the AI what to do. Write the following **Prompt**:

> I need the PHP code to process the form submission for the contact manager. This code should go at the very top of the index.php file. It should check if the request method is POST. If it is, it should retrieve the 'name', 'email', and 'phone' from the form data. Then, it should create an array with this data. The data should be appended as a new row to a CSV file located at ../data/contacts.csv. Use the fputcsv function for safety. Finally, it should redirect the user back to index.php to prevent re-submission on page refresh.

The AI will generate the PHP logic.

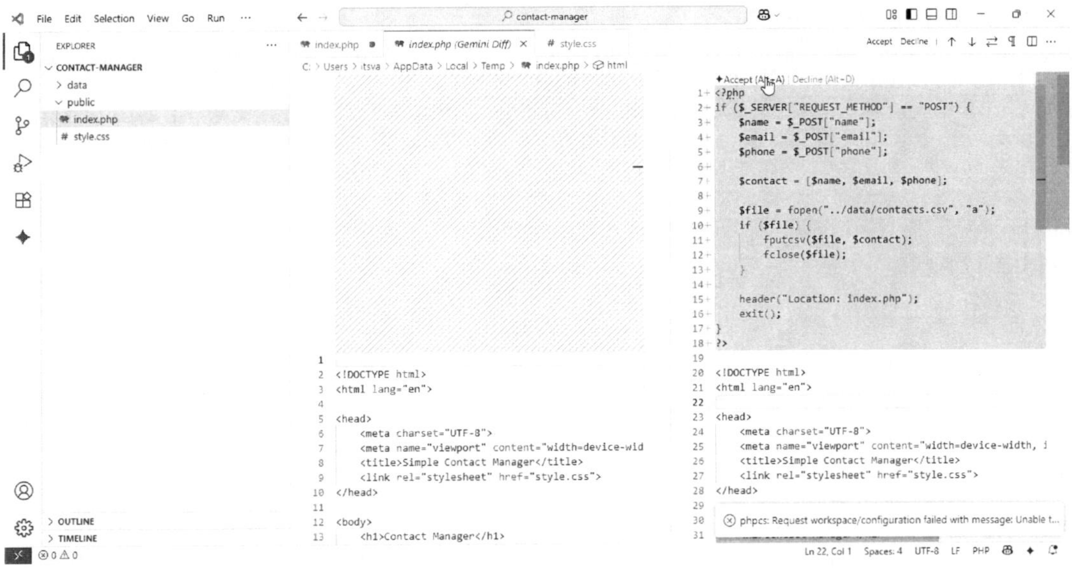

Click **Accept(Alt + A)**. The code is copied at the **very top of public/index.php**, before the <!DOCTYPE html> line:

```
<?php
if ($_SERVER["REQUEST_METHOD"] == "POST") {
    $name = $_POST["name"];
    $email = $_POST["email"];
    $phone = $_POST["phone"];
    $contact = [$name, $email, $phone];
    $file = fopen("../data/contacts.csv", "a");
    if ($file) {
        fputcsv($file, $contact);
        fclose($file);
    }
    header("Location: index.php");
    exit();
}
?>
```

Prompt 4: Generating the PHP logic to display contacts

Finally, we need to read the contacts.csv file and display the data in our HTML table. Scroll down in **index.php** to the **<tbody>** tag inside your table. We will replace the comment with PHP code.

Write the following **Prompt**:

Now, give me the PHP code that should go inside the <tbody> tags. This code needs to read the ../data/contacts.csv file. It should first check if the file exists. If it does, it should loop through each row of the CSV file and print a new HTML table row <tr> for each contact, with each field inside a <td>. If the file doesn't exist or is empty, it should display a single row with a message like 'No contacts found.' spanning all three columns.

Take the generated code and place it inside the <tbody> tags in public/index.php by clicking **Accept(Alt+A)**.

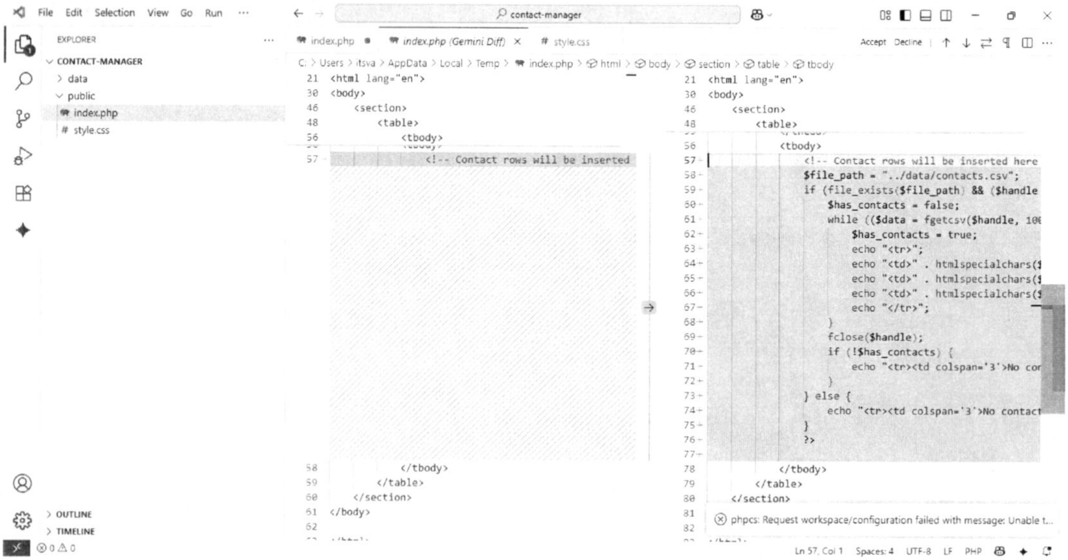

The following code is copied:

```
<?php
$file_path = "../data/contacts.csv";
if (file_exists($file_path) && ($handle = fopen($file_path, "r")) !== FALSE) {
      $has_contacts = false;
      while (($data = fgetcsv($handle, 1000, ",")) !== FALSE) {
              $has_contacts = true;
              echo "<tr>";
              echo "<td>" . htmlspecialchars($data[0]) . "</td>"; // Name
              echo "<td>" . htmlspecialchars($data[1]) . "</td>"; // Email
              echo "<td>" . htmlspecialchars($data[2]) . "</td>"; // Phone
              echo "</tr>";
      }
      fclose($handle);
      if (!$has_contacts) {
              echo "<tr><td colspan='3'>No contacts found.</td></tr>";
      }
```

```
} else {
    echo "<tr><td colspan='3'>No contacts found.</td></tr>";
}
?>
```

Your index.php is now a complete application, combining HTML structure with PHP logic.

Bridging the gap: Learned concepts and application implementation

Look at what we just built. The AI used core PHP concepts that are fundamental to web development:

- **Superglobals:** The code uses $_SERVER['REQUEST_METHOD'] to check if the form was submitted and $_POST to access the data.
- **File handling:** We used fopen(), fputcsv(), and fclose() to safely write data to a file, and file_exists() and fgetcsv() to read it back.
- **Control structures:** The code relies on if statements to check for form submissions and file existence, and a while loop to iterate through the contacts.
- **Security:** The AI included filter_input() and htmlspecialchars() to sanitize and escape data, helping prevent common security vulnerabilities.

The AI didn't invent new magic; it correctly applied foundational PHP principles to build a functional application.

Running and testing

1. **Start XAMPP:** Make sure your Apache server is running.
2. **Access the app:** Open your browser and navigate to **http://localhost/codes/contact-manager/public/**.
3. **Test the output:** You see the styled form and an empty contact list with the message **No contacts found**.

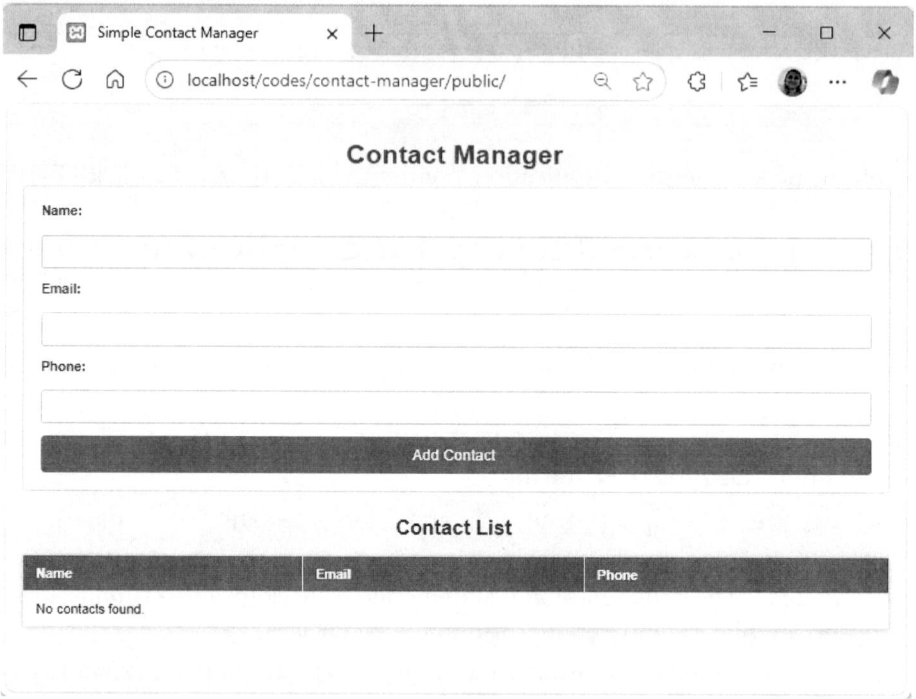

4. **Add a contact:** Fill in the form and click **Add Contact**.
5. **Verify the result:** The page refreshes, and you see the contact you just added appear in the table.

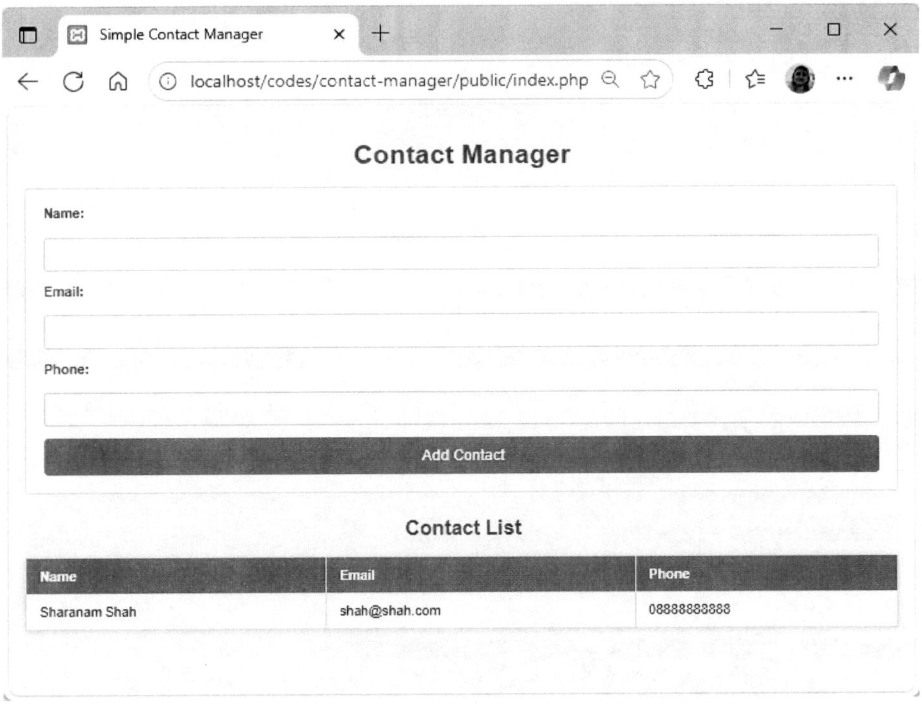

6. **Check the data file:** Look inside your **contact-manager/data** folder. You now see a **contacts.csv** file containing the data you entered.

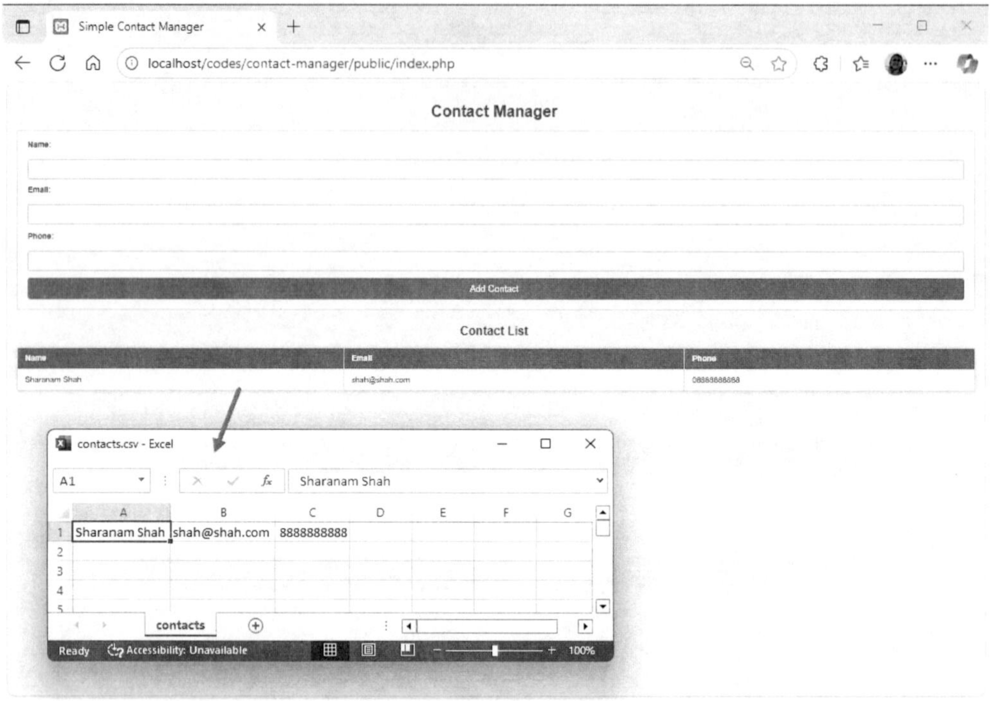

Exploring application behaviour: A practical run-through

- **Valid input:** As you've seen, valid input works perfectly.
- **Empty submission:** If you submit an empty form, nothing is added because of the if (!empty($name) ...) validation check.
- **Invalid email:** An invalid email will also be rejected by the filter_var($email, FILTER_VALIDATE_EMAIL) check.
- **File permissions:** If your data folder was not writable, PHP would throw an error on submission, a real-world scenario highlighting the importance of server configuration.

Harnessing AI assistance in real-world contexts

This simple app is a microcosm of a larger application.

In a professional setting, you'd use this same prompting technique for more complex tasks:

- "Generate a PHP class for a 'User' with properties for id, username, and email."

- "Write a function that connects to a MySQL database using PDO."
- "Create the prepared statement to securely insert a new user into the database."

The skill you are learning is how to break down a large problem into small, logical pieces that an AI can solve.

Wrapping up

This chapter was an intensive dive into the new world of AI-assisted coding. You've not only learned the theory but have put it into practice by building a complete project.

- **Balanced learning:** You learned the critical importance of using AI as a tool for learning, not a replacement for it.
- **Free tools:** We identified and set up several powerful, free AI assistants, giving you options like Google Gemini, Amazon CodeWhisperer, and CodeGPT.
- **VS Code integration:** You walked through the full installation and configuration process for multiple tools directly within your code editor.
- **Prompt engineering:** You practiced writing clear, specific prompts to guide the AI, a crucial skill for getting high-quality code.
- **End-to-end project:** You built a functional, file-based Contact Manager application from scratch, prompting the AI for all the necessary code.
- **Code review:** You saw how the AI uses standard PHP functions and security practices, reinforcing the importance of reviewing and understanding every line.

Fantastic work! You have successfully configured a state-of-the-art AI coding assistant and collaborated with it to build a real web application. You are now equipped with a skill that many professional developers are just beginning to master. This ability to partner with AI will dramatically accelerate your coding and problem-solving capabilities. Always remember the principles we discussed: you are the developer; the AI is your assistant. Stay curious, keep reviewing the code, and never stop asking "why."

In the next chapter, we take this a step further. We'll look at how to use the AI to generate code for more complex scenarios in *Chapter 25: Practical code generation – Everyday scenarios for beginners*.

Chapter 25

Section 07: AI code generation – Supercharge your productivity

Practical code generation - Everyday scenarios for beginners

What you'll learn

- Crafting effective prompts
- AI-assisted validation
- Reviewing and refining code
- Generating code for forms
- Building CRUD with AI

In the last chapter, you set up your AI coding assistant and built your first application with its help. You learned to treat the AI as a collaborator—a partner that can handle repetitive tasks while you focus on the bigger picture. Now, it's time to deepen that partnership.

This chapter is all about moving from basic requests to sophisticated, multi-step conversations with your AI. We will explore how to guide your assistant through the most common tasks in web development: handling user input, validating data, and performing the essential database operations known as CRUD (Create, Read, Update, and Delete). Think of this as learning to speak the AI's language fluently, allowing you to build more complex and robust features faster than ever before.

Writing prompts that get results

The quality of the code you get from an AI assistant is directly proportional to the quality of the instructions you provide. Vague prompts lead to generic, often unusable code. Clear, specific, and context-rich prompts lead to code that is tailored to your exact needs. Mastering **prompt engineering** is the single most important skill for leveraging AI effectively.

The key to a great prompt is to include four key elements:

- **Role and goal:** Tell the AI what it is and what you want to achieve.
- **Context:** Provide any existing code, file structure, or constraints it needs to know.
- **Format:** Specify the language, style, and structure of the desired output.
- **Example (optional):** Give it a small example of the input you have and the output you want.

Let's see the difference in practice.

Scenario: Creating a welcome message

- **A bad Prompt:** This is too vague. The AI has to guess what you mean. It might produce something as simple as echo "Welcome!";.

```
Write a PHP welcome message.
```

- **A good Prompt:** This prompt is excellent because it specifies the role (PHP developer), the variables to use ($username), the exact output format (<h1> tag), and the final text. The AI will know exactly what to do.

```
As a PHP developer, write a script that defines a variable $usernamewith the value 'Alex'.
Then, generate an HTML<h1> tag that displays the message 'Welcome, Alex!' using the
variable.
```

Scenario: Generating a list from an array

- **A bad Prompt:** This prompt lacks a goal, context, and format. What array? What should the loop do?

```
Loop through an array.
```

- **A good Prompt:** This prompt gives the AI the exact input array, the specific type of loop to use (foreach), and the precise HTML structure for the output. The result will be clean, correct, and ready to use.

```
I have a PHP array: $colors = ['Red', 'Green', 'Blue'];. Write a PHP script that uses a foreach loop to iterate over this array and generate an HTML unordered list (<ul>), where each color is an item in a list element (<li>).
```

Walking AI through loops, forms, validation, and authentication

Now let's apply this prompt engineering skill to the building blocks of nearly every web application. We'll use our Google Gemini assistant in VS Code for these examples.

Generating loops

Loops are for repeating actions. Let's ask the AI to generate a product listing.

- Open **VS Code** and create a new file named **loops_demo.php** in a new **chapter-25** folder inside your htdocs/codes directory.
- Open the **Gemini chat panel** and enter the following **Prompt**:

```
"I have a PHP associative array of products:
$products = [
  ['name' => 'Laptop', 'price' => 1200],
  ['name' => 'Mouse', 'price' => 25],
  ['name' => 'Keyboard', 'price' => 75]
];

Generate a PHP script that loops through this array and displays each product's name and price inside a styled div with a class 'product-card'."
```

The AI will generate both the PHP and some suggested CSS. Let's put it together:

```
<!DOCTYPE html>
<html lang="en">
<head>
    <meta charset="UTF-8">
    <meta name="viewport" content="width=device-width, initial-scale=1.0">
    <title>Product List</title>
    <style>
        body {
            font-family: Arial, sans-serif;
            background-color: #f4f4f4;
            margin: 20px;
        }
        .product-card {
            background-color: #fff;
            border: 1px solid #ddd;
            border-radius: 8px;
            padding: 15px;
            margin-bottom: 10px;
            box-shadow: 0 2px 4px rgba(0, 0, 0, 0.1);
        }
        .product-card h3 {
            margin-top: 0;
            color: #333;
        }
        .product-card p {
            margin-bottom: 0;
            color: #666;
        }
        .product-card .price {
            font-weight: bold;
            color: #007bff;
        }
    </style>
</head>
<body>
    <h1>Our Products</h1>
    <?php
    $products = [
        ['name' => 'Laptop', 'price' => 1200],
        ['name' => 'Mouse', 'price' => 25],
        ['name' => 'Keyboard', 'price' => 75]
    ];
    foreach ($products as $product) {
        echo '<div class="product-card">';
        echo '<h3>' . htmlspecialchars($product['name']) . '</h3>';
        echo '<p>Price: <span class="price">$' . htmlspecialchars(number_format(
              $product['price'], 2)) . '</span></p>';
        echo '</div>';
    }
```

```
    ?>
</body>
</html>
```

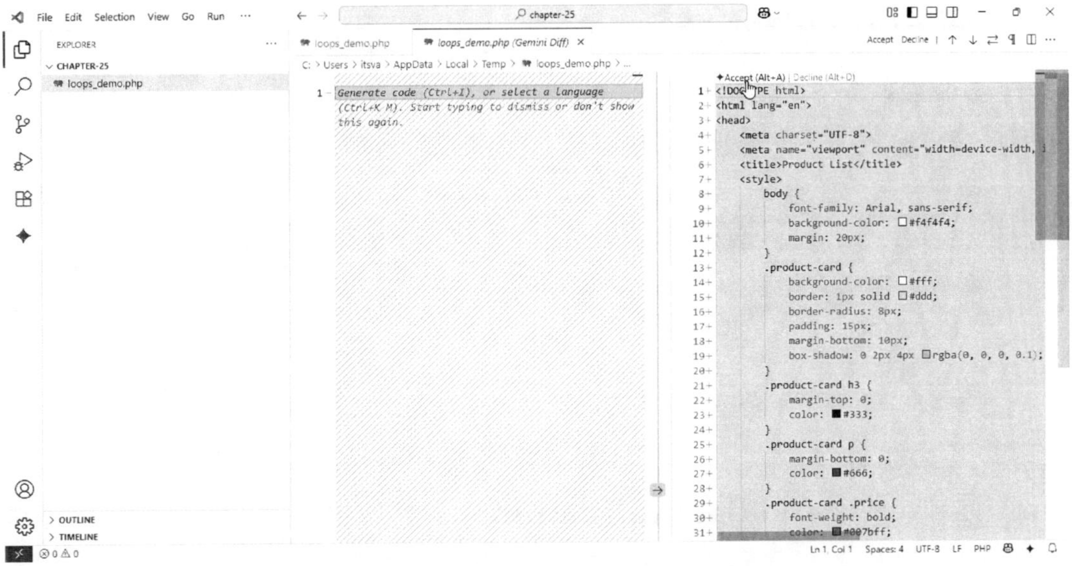

Click **Accept**. The generated code is copied in loop_demo.php. **Save it**. Now navigate to **http://localhost/codes/chapter-25/loops_demo.php**, you can see a clean, styled list of your products. The AI understood the data structure and created the exact HTML output we requested.

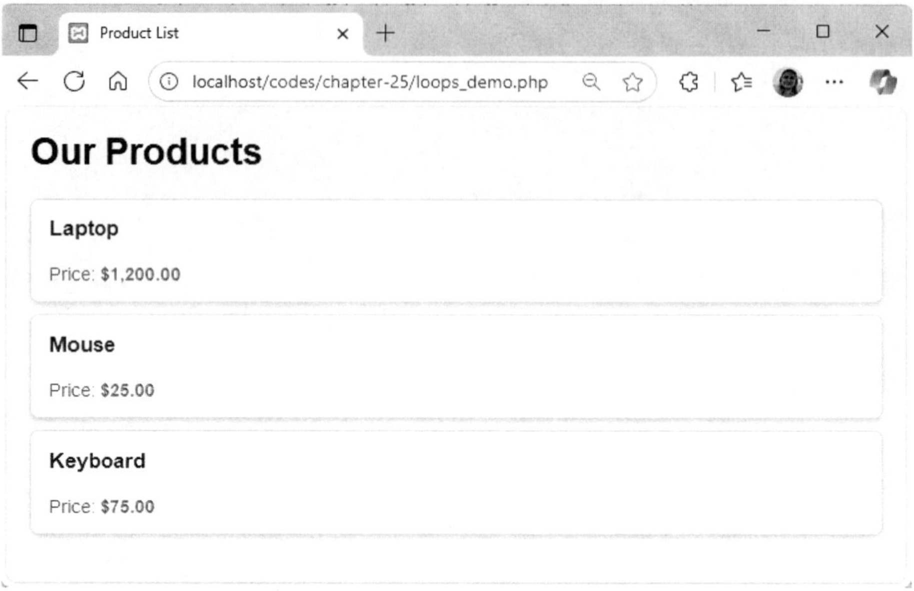

Handling forms and data validation

Forms are the primary way we get input from users. But user input can never be trusted. It must always be validated. Let's ask the AI to create a registration form and then add the PHP logic to validate it.

Step 1: Prompt for the HTML form

Prompt:

```
Generate the HTML for a user registration form. It should submit to itself using the POST method. Include labeled text inputs for 'username', an email input for 'email', and a password input for 'password'. Add a submit button. Wrap it all in a container div.
```

Step 2: Prompt for the PHP validation logic

Prompt:

```
"Now, generate the PHP script to process this form. It must be placed at the top of the same file.
The script should:
1. Check if the form was submitted using POST.
2. Create an empty array called `$errors`.
```

3. Validate the 'username': it must not be empty. If it is, add a message to the `$errors` array.
4. Validate the 'email': it must be a valid email format. If not, add a message to the `$errors` array.
5. Validate the 'password': it must be at least 8 characters long. If not, add a message.
6. After checking, if the `$errors` array is empty, display a success message.
7. If the `$errors` array has messages, loop through it and display the errors to the user in a styled error box."

Now, let's combine the AI's output into a single file, form_demo.php:

```
<?php
if ($_SERVER["REQUEST_METHOD"] == "POST") {
    $errors = [];
    // Validate username
    if (empty($_POST["username"])) {
        $errors[] = "Username is required.";
    } else {
        $username = htmlspecialchars($_POST["username"]);
    }
    // Validate email
    if (empty($_POST["email"])) {
        $errors[] = "Email is required.";
    } elseif (!filter_var($_POST["email"], FILTER_VALIDATE_EMAIL)) {
        $errors[] = "Invalid email format.";
    } else {
        $email = htmlspecialchars($_POST["email"]);
    }
    // Validate password
    if (empty($_POST["password"])) {
        $errors[] = "Password is required.";
    } elseif (strlen($_POST["password"]) < 8) {
        $errors[] = "Password must be at least 8 characters long.";
    } else {
        $password = htmlspecialchars($_POST["password"]);
    }
    // Display messages
    if (empty($errors)) {
        echo '<div class="message success">Registration successful for ' .
              $username . '!</div>';
        // In a real application, you would save this data to a database
    } else {
        echo '<div class="message error">';
        foreach ($errors as $error) {
            echo '<p>' . $error . '</p>';
        }
        echo '</div>';
    }
}
?>
```

```
<!DOCTYPE html>
<html lang="en">
<head>
    <meta charset="UTF-8">
    <meta name="viewport" content="width=device-width, initial-scale=1.0">
    <title>User Registration</title>
    <style>
        body {
            font-family: Arial, sans-serif;
            background-color: #f4f4f4;
            margin: 20px;
        }
        .container {
            background-color: #fff;
            border: 1px solid #ddd;
            border-radius: 8px;
            padding: 20px;
            max-width: 400px;
            margin: 50px auto;
            box-shadow: 0 2px 4px rgba(0, 0, 0, 0.1);
        }
        .container h2 {
            text-align: center;
            color: #333;
            margin-bottom: 20px;
        }
        .form-group {
            margin-bottom: 15px;
        }
        .form-group label {
            display: block;
            margin-bottom: 5px;
            color: #555;
        }
        .form-group input[type="text"], .form-group input[type="email"],
        .form-group input[type="password"] {
            width: 100%;
            padding: 10px;
            border: 1px solid #ccc;
            border-radius: 4px;
            box-sizing: border-box;
        }
        .form-group input[type="submit"] {
            background-color: #007bff;
            color: white;
            padding: 10px 15px;
            border: none;
            border-radius: 4px;
            cursor: pointer;
            font-size: 16px;
```

```
            width: 100%;
        }
        .form-group input[type="submit"]:hover {
            background-color: #0056b3;
        }
        .message {
            text-align: center;
            margin-top: 20px;
            padding: 10px;
            border-radius: 5px;
        }
        .success {
            background-color: #d4edda;
            color: #155724;
            border: 1px solid #c3e6cb;
        }
        .error {
            background-color: #f8d7da;
            color: #721c24;
            border: 1px solid #f5c6cb;
        }
    </style>
</head>
<body>
    <?php
    if ($_SERVER["REQUEST_METHOD"] == "POST") {
        $username = htmlspecialchars($_POST["username"]);
        $email = htmlspecialchars($_POST["email"]);
        $password = htmlspecialchars($_POST["password"]);
        if (!empty($username) && !empty($email) && !empty($password)) {
            // In a real application, you would save this data to a database
            // For this demo, we'll just display a success message
            echo '<div class="message success">Registration successful for ' .
                  $username . '!</div>';
        } else {
            echo '<div class="message error">Please fill in all fields.</div>';
        }
    }
    ?>
    <div class="container">
        <h2>Register</h2>
        <form action="<?php echo htmlspecialchars($_SERVER["PHP_SELF"]); ?>"
              method="POST">
            <div class="form-group">
                <label for="username">Username:</label>
                <input type="text" id="username" name="username" required>
            </div>
            <div class="form-group">
                <label for="email">Email:</label>
                <input type="email" id="email" name="email" required>
            </div>
```

```
                <div class="form-group">
                    <label for="password">Password:</label>
                    <input type="password" id="password" name="password" required>
                </div>
                <div class="form-group">
                    <input type="submit" value="Register">
                </div>
            </form>
        </div>
</body>
</html>
```

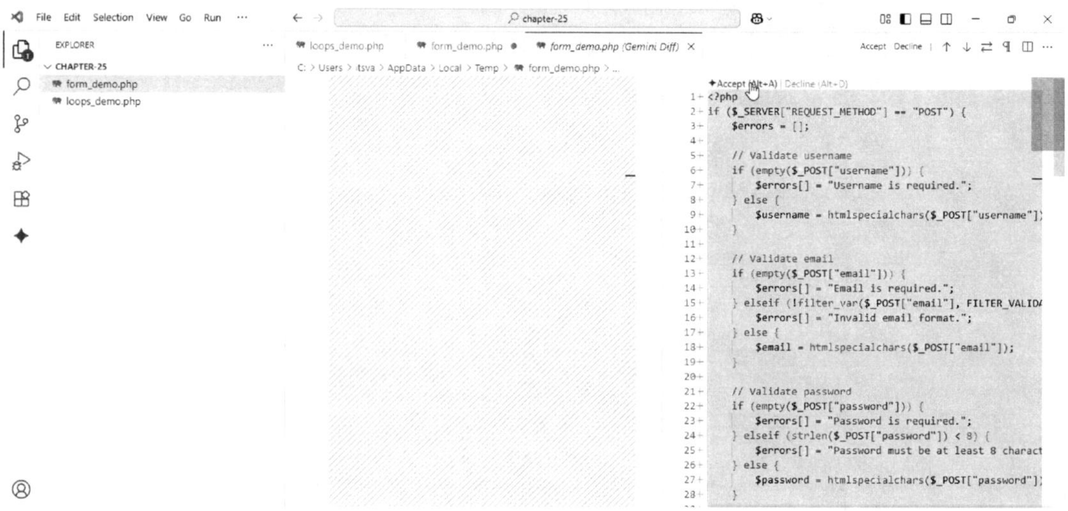

By breaking our request into two logical parts (frontend and backend), we guided the AI to build a complete, working script. If you run this and submit an empty form, you can see our styled error messages appear.

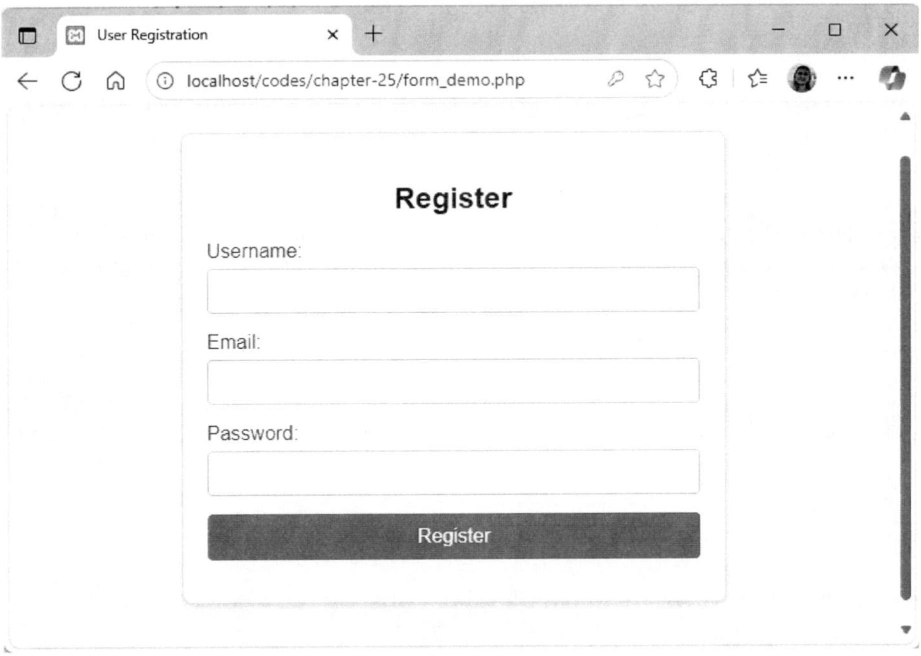
User Registration
localhost/codes/chapter-25/form_demo.php
Register
Username:
Email:
Password:
Register

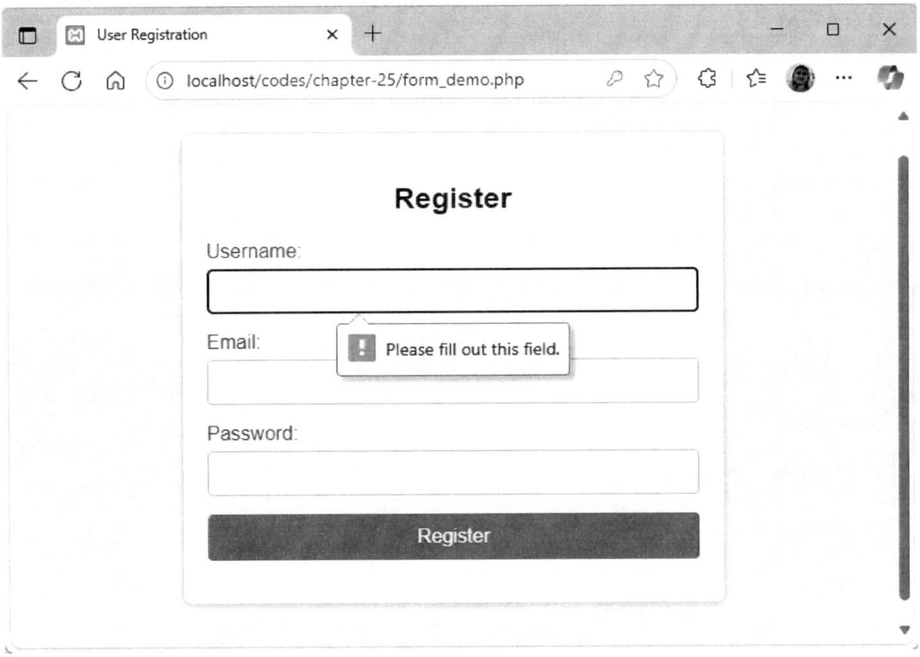
User Registration
localhost/codes/chapter-25/form_demo.php
Register
Username:
Email:
Please fill out this field.
Password:
Register

Basic authentication

Authentication is about verifying who a user is. Let's create a very simple login check.

Prompt:

Create a full PHP page with a login form (email and password fields). At the top of the script, add PHP logic. If the form is submitted, check if the email is 'admin@test.com' and the password is 'password123'. If they match, show a 'Welcome Admin!' message. Otherwise, show an 'Invalid credentials' error message.

The AI generates a single file that handles both display and logic, perfect for a simple demonstration (login.php):

```
<?php
session_start();
$message = '';
if ($_SERVER["REQUEST_METHOD"] == "POST") {
    $email = $_POST['email'] ?? '';
    $password = $_POST['password'] ?? '';
    if ($email === 'admin@test.com' && $password === 'password123') {
        $_SESSION['loggedin'] = true;
        $_SESSION['email'] = $email;
        $message = '<div class="message success">Welcome Admin!</div>';
    } else {
        $message = '<div class="message error">Invalid credentials.</div>';
    }
}
?>
<!DOCTYPE html>
<html lang="en">
<head>
    <meta charset="UTF-8">
    <meta name="viewport" content="width=device-width, initial-scale=1.0">
    <title>Login</title>
    <style>
        body {
            font-family: Arial, sans-serif;
            background-color: #f4f4f4;
            margin: 20px;
```

```
        }
        .container {
            background-color: #fff;
            border: 1px solid #ddd;
            border-radius: 8px;
            padding: 20px;
            max-width: 400px;
            margin: 50px auto;
            box-shadow: 0 2px 4px rgba(0, 0, 0, 0.1);
        }
        .container h2 {
            text-align: center;
            color: #333;
            margin-bottom: 20px;
        }
        .form-group {
            margin-bottom: 15px;
        }
        .form-group label {
            display: block;
            margin-bottom: 5px;
            color: #555;
        }
        .form-group input[type="email"], .form-group input[type="password"] {
            width: 100%;
            padding: 10px;
            border: 1px solid #ccc;
            border-radius: 4px;
            box-sizing: border-box;
        }
        .form-group input[type="submit"] {
            background-color: #007bff;
            color: white;
            padding: 10px 15px;
            border: none;
            border-radius: 4px;
            cursor: pointer;
            font-size: 16px;
            width: 100%;
        }
        .form-group input[type="submit"]:hover {
            background-color: #0056b3;
        }
        .message {
            text-align: center;
            margin-top: 20px;
            padding: 10px;
            border-radius: 5px;
        }
        .success {
            background-color: #d4edda;
```

```
                color: #155724;
                border: 1px solid #c3e6cb;
            }
            .error {
                background-color: #f8d7da;
                color: #721c24;
                border: 1px solid #f5c6cb;
            }
        </style>
</head>
<body>
    <?php echo $message; ?>
    <div class="container">
        <h2>Login</h2>
        <form action="<?php echo htmlspecialchars($_SERVER["PHP_SELF"]); ?>"
              method="POST">
            <div class="form-group">
                <label for="email">Email:</label>
                <input type="email" id="email" name="email" required>
            </div>
            <div class="form-group">
                <label for="password">Password:</label>
                <input type="password" id="password" name="password" required>
            </div>
            <div class="form-group">
                <input type="submit" value="Login">
            </div>
        </form>
    </div>
</body>
</html>
```

1. Navigate to **http://localhost/codes/chapter-25/login.php**. You can see the login form.

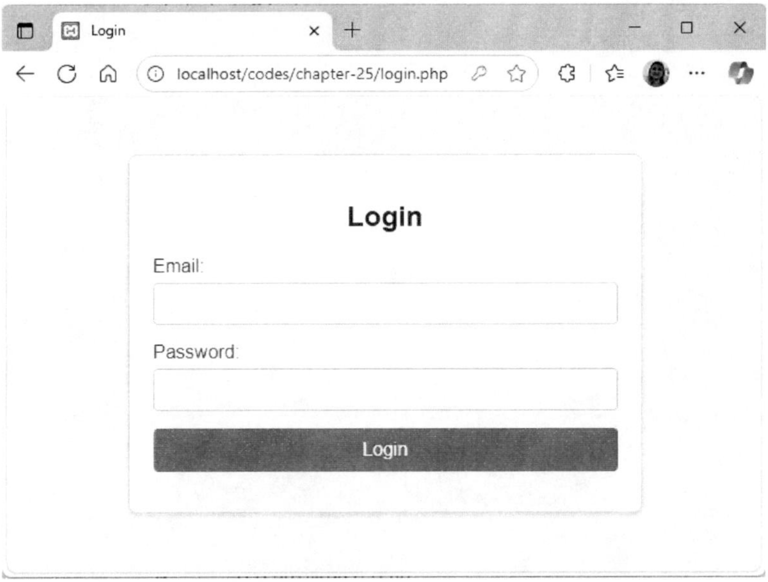

2. Enter wrong credentials and click **Login**. It sends an invalid credentials message and does not login.

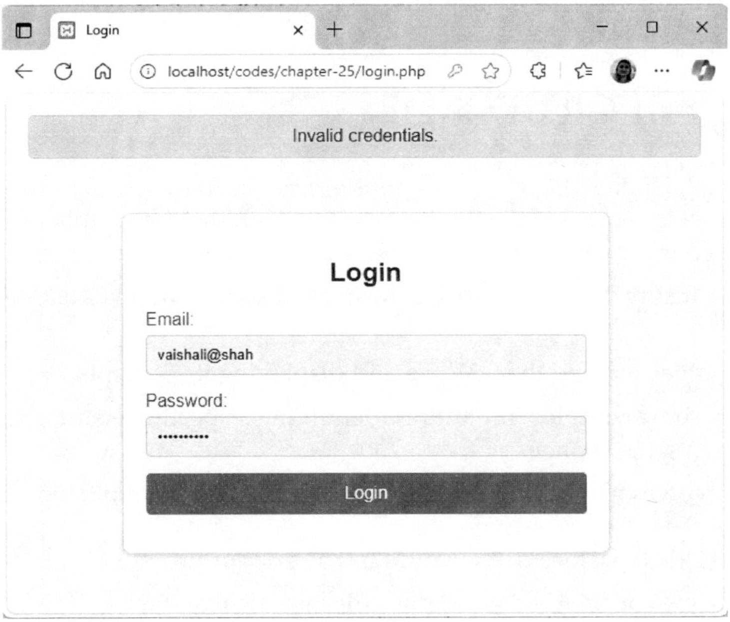

3. Enter the correct credentials and click **Login**. The welcome message is displayed.

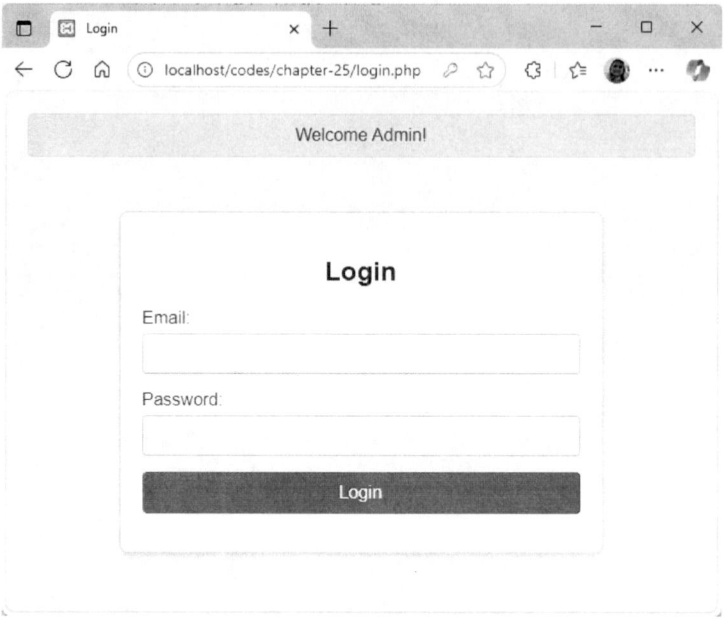

Here, AI had hard coded the login credentials since we had not instructed AI to connect to any database or file.

Generating full CRUD logic

CRUD (Create, Read, Update, Delete) operations are the heart of any data-driven application. In the previous chapter, we used a CSV file. Let's stick with that for simplicity. We will ask the AI to generate the code for each part of a simple Task manager.

- **Create:** We've already done this with our form examples. It involves taking POST data and saving it.
- **Read:** This involves reading the CSV file and displaying its contents.
- **Update:** This is more complex. It requires identifying a specific record, showing its data in a form, and saving the changes.
- **Delete:** This involves identifying a record and removing it from the file.

Because this is a multi-step process, we would use a series of prompts:

- "First, generate the code to read a tasks.csv file and display it in an HTML table. Each row should have a 'Delete' link."

- "Now, add a form above the table to add a new task. The form submission should append the new task to tasks.csv."
- "Next, write the logic for the delete link. It should take a task ID as a URL parameter (e.g., delete.php?id=1), remove that line from the CSV, and redirect back."

We will build this exact functionality from scratch in the hands-on section.

How to review and refine AI output

AI-generated code is a first draft, not a final product. Your job as a developer is to be the quality assurance engineer. You must review, test, and refine the code.

Key things to check for:

- **Security:** This is your #1 priority.
    - **Cross-Site scripting (XSS):** Is all user-provided data being escaped before it's displayed on the page? Look for htmlspecialchars(). If it's missing, the AI made a mistake.
    - **SQL injection (when using databases):** Is the AI using prepared statements? We'll cover this in Part V, but it's a critical check.
    - **File path traversal:** Is the code handling file uploads or file includes? Ensure user input cannot be used to manipulate file paths.
- **Correctness and bugs:**
    - Does the code do what you asked it to? Test it.
    - Check for "off-by-one" errors in loops or logic that doesn't handle edge cases (e.g., what happens if a file it needs to read is empty or doesn't exist?). The AI often writes the "happy path" code but can forget error handling.
- **Readability and best practices:**
    - Are the variable names clear and meaningful (e.g., $userName instead of $un)?
    - Is the code well-formatted and easy to read?
    - Is it using modern PHP features correctly?

The refinement loop

When you find an issue, don't just fix it yourself. Tell the AI what it did wrong and ask it to fix it. This teaches you how to prompt better and can sometimes lead to a more elegant solution.

Let's say the AI generated this code to display a username:

```
echo "Welcome, " . $_POST['username']; // Insecure!
```

You spot the XSS vulnerability. You can refine it with a follow-up **Prompt**:

> The previous code is insecure because it doesn't escape the username, which could lead to an XSS attack. Please refactor the code to use htmlspecialchars() on the username before displaying it.

The AI will correct its mistake and provide the secure version:

```
echo "Welcome, " . htmlspecialchars($_POST['username']); // Secure!
```

By actively reviewing and refining, you stay in control, ensure your application is secure, and solidify your own understanding of coding best practices.

Hands-on: Building a Book log with AI

Let's combine everything we've learned to build a complete, single-page Book log application. This app will allow us to add, view, edit, and delete books from our reading list, all managed from one file.

The goal is to create a simple but fully functional CRUD application using a series of prompts for our AI assistant. We will guide the AI to build the HTML structure, the CSS styling, and all the PHP logic required to manage our book data, which will be stored in a simple CSV file. This project will perfectly demonstrate how to break down a larger problem into manageable prompts.

Building the application

First, let's set up the project environment.

- **Create the project folder:** Inside your C:\xampp\htdocs\codes folder, create a new folder named **book-log**.
- Open the book-log folder in VS Code
- **Create subfolders and files:** Inside **book-log**, create:
  - A folder named **data**. We will manually create our CSV file here.
  - An empty file named **index.php**.
  - An empty file named **style.css**.

- **Create the data file:** Inside the **data** folder, create a file named **books.csv**. Open it and add a header row:

```
"id","title","author","genre"
```

Your final structure should look like this:

```
htdocs/codes/
└── book-log/
    ├── data/
    │   └── books.csv
    ├── index.php
    └── style.css
```

Prompt 1: Generate the HTML

We'll start by asking for the complete visual layout. This gives us a static page to work from. Open **index.php** and the **Gemini chat panel**.

Prompt:

```
"Generate the full HTML5 boilerplate for a 'Book Log' application.

The page should contain:
1. A main `<h1>` heading 'My Book Log'.
2. A `<form>` that submits to `index.php` using the POST method. This form is for adding
and updating books.
3. The form needs text inputs for 'title', 'author', and 'genre', each with a label.
4. A submit button with the text 'Save Book'.
5. A hidden input field named 'book_id'.
6. Below the form, an `<h2>` heading 'Reading List'.
7. An HTML `<table>` with headers for 'Title', 'Author', 'Genre', and 'Actions'.
8. The table body `<tbody>` should be empty for now.
9. Link to a local stylesheet named `style.css`.
```

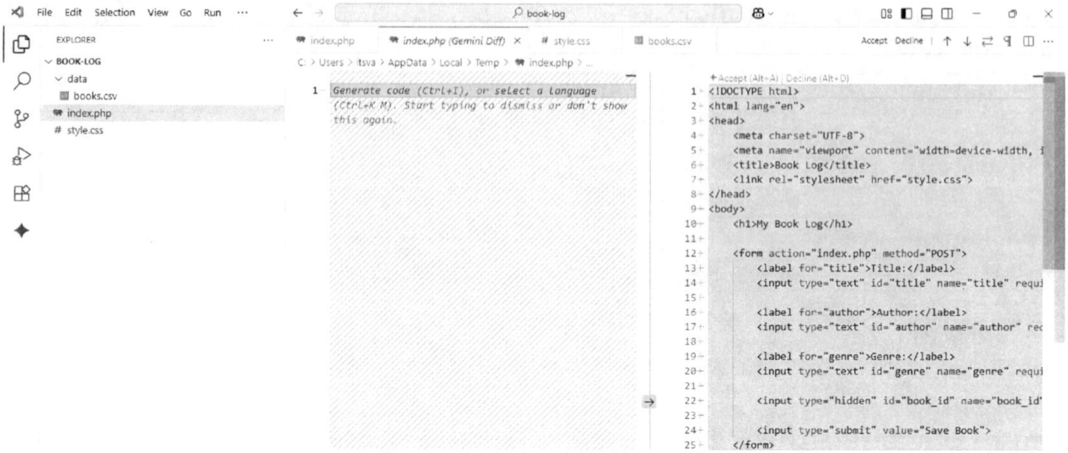

Click **Accept** and the code is copied in the index.php file:

```
<!DOCTYPE html>
<html lang="en">
<head>
    <meta charset="UTF-8">
    <meta name="viewport" content="width=device-width, initial-scale=1.0">
    <title>Book Log</title>
    <link rel="stylesheet" href="style.css">
</head>
<body>
    <h1>My Book Log</h1>
    <form action="index.php" method="POST">
        <label for="title">Title:</label>
        <input type="text" id="title" name="title" required><br><br>
        <label for="author">Author:</label>
        <input type="text" id="author" name="author" required><br><br>
        <label for="genre">Genre:</label>
        <input type="text" id="genre" name="genre" required><br><br>
        <input type="hidden" id="book_id" name="book_id">
        <input type="submit" value="Save Book">
    </form>
    <h2>Reading List</h2>
    <table>
        <thead>
            <tr>
                <th>Title</th>
                <th>Author</th>
                <th>Genre</th>
                <th>Actions</th>
            </tr>
        </thead>
        <tbody>
```

```
            <!-- Book entries will be loaded here -->
        </tbody>
    </table>
</body>
</html>
```

Prompt 2: Generate the CSS

Open **style.css** and the **Gemini chat panel**.

Prompt:

Generate clean, modern CSS. Create a main container, style the form for clarity, and design a striped, readable table. The action links in the table should look like small buttons.

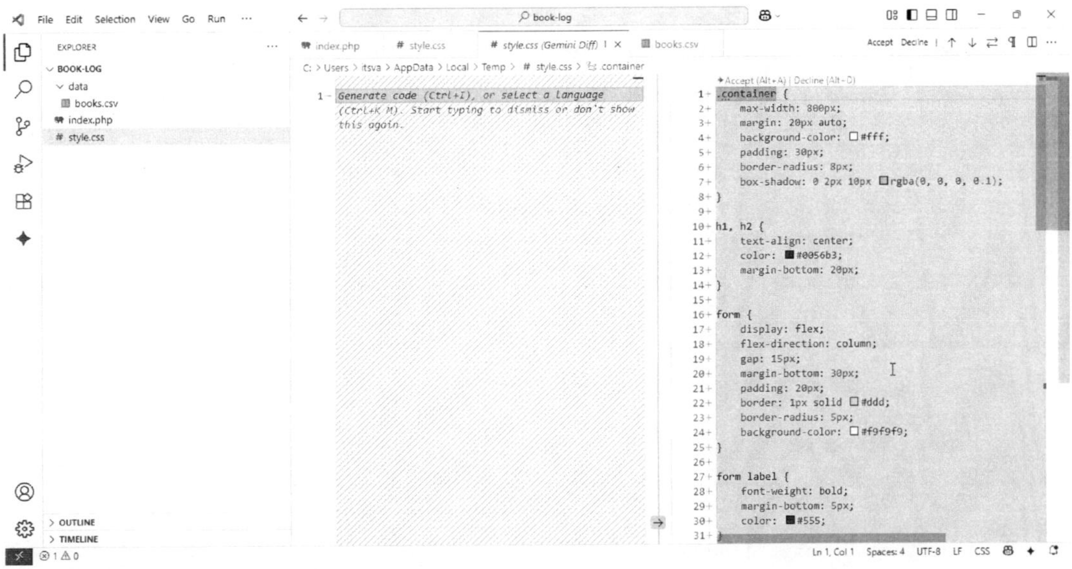

Click **Accept** and the code is copied in the style.css file:

```
.container {
    max-width: 800px;
    margin: 20px auto;
    background-color: #fff;
    padding: 30px;
    border-radius: 8px;
    box-shadow: 0 2px 10px rgba(0, 0, 0, 0.1);
}
h1, h2 {
```

```
    text-align: center;
    color: #0056b3;
    margin-bottom: 20px;
}
form {
    display: flex;
    flex-direction: column;
    gap: 15px;
    margin-bottom: 30px;
    padding: 20px;
    border: 1px solid #ddd;
    border-radius: 5px;
    background-color: #f9f9f9;
}
form label {
    font-weight: bold;
    margin-bottom: 5px;
    color: #555;
}
form input[type="text"], form input[type="email"], form input[type="tel"] {
    width: 100%;
    padding: 10px;
    border: 1px solid #ccc;
    border-radius: 4px;
    box-sizing: border-box;
    /* Ensures padding doesn't increase width */
    font-size: 16px;
}
form input[type="submit"] {
    background-color: #007bff;
    color: white;
    padding: 12px 20px;
    border: none;
    border-radius: 5px;
    cursor: pointer;
    font-size: 18px;
    transition: background-color 0.3s ease;
}
form input[type="submit"]:hover {
    background-color: #0056b3;
}
table {
    width: 100%;
    border-collapse: collapse;
    margin-top: 20px;
    box-shadow: 0 2px 8px rgba(0, 0, 0, 0.1);
}
table thead th {
    background-color: #007bff;
    color: white;
    padding: 10px;
```

```
    text-align: left;
}
table tbody td {
    padding: 10px;
    border-bottom: 1px solid #ddd;
}
table tbody tr:nth-child(even) {
    background-color: #f2f2f2;
}
table tbody tr:hover {
    background-color: #e9e9e9;
}
.actions a {
    display: inline-block;
    padding: 5px 10px;
    margin-right: 5px;
    border-radius: 4px;
    text-decoration: none;
    color: white;
    font-size: 14px;
}
.actions a.edit {
    background-color: #28a745;
}
.actions a.edit:hover {
    background-color: #218838;
}
.actions a.delete {
    background-color: #dc3545;
}
.actions a.delete:hover {
    background-color: #c82333;
}
```

Prompt 3: Generate the core PHP logic (Create and Read)

Now we'll add the brains. Open **index.php** and prepare to add PHP code to the very top.

Prompt:

```
I need the PHP logic for the 'index.php' file. Place this code at the very top.
It should do the following:
1. Define a variable for the path to the CSV file: 'data/books.csv'.
2. Implement the 'Create' logic:
  - Check if the request is POST.
  - If it is, get the title, author, and genre from the form.
  - Sanitize the inputs.
  - Generate a unique ID for the new book using 'uniqid()'.
  - Create a new array with the id and book data.
  - Open 'books.csv' in append mode and save the new book using 'fputcsv'.
```

```
   - After saving, redirect to 'index.php' to prevent form resubmission.
3. Implement the 'Read' logic:
   - Create a function called 'getBooks()' that reads 'books.csv'.
   - The function should skip the header row.
   - It should return an array of associative arrays, where each inner array represents a book (e.g., ['id' => ..., 'title' => ...]).
   - Call this function to get all books and store them in a '$books' variable.
```

Click **Accept** and the code is copied in the index.php file:

```php
<?php
$csvFile = 'data/books.csv';
// Function to read books from CSV
function getBooks($csvFile)
{
    $books = [];
    if (($handle = fopen($csvFile, 'r')) !== FALSE) {
        $isHeader = true;
        while (($row = fgetcsv($handle)) !== FALSE) {
            if ($isHeader) {
                $isHeader = false;
                continue; // Skip the header row
            }
            // Assuming the order is id, title, author, genre
            $books[] = [
                'id' => $row[0],
                'title' => $row[1],
                'author' => $row[2],
                'genre' => $row[3]
            ];
        }
        fclose($handle);
    }
    return $books;
}
// Initialize $bookToEdit for the update functionality
$bookToEdit = null;
// Handle POST requests for creating a new book
if ($_SERVER['REQUEST_METHOD'] === 'POST') {
    $title = htmlspecialchars($_POST['title']);
```

```
    $author = htmlspecialchars($_POST['author']);
    $genre = htmlspecialchars($_POST['genre']);
    $bookId = htmlspecialchars($_POST['book_id']); // Get book_id from hidden input
    if (empty($bookId)) { // It's a new book (create)
        $bookId = uniqid(); // Generate a unique ID
        $newBook = [$bookId, $title, $author, $genre];
        // Open the CSV file in append mode
        if (($handle = fopen($csvFile, 'a')) !== FALSE) {
            fputcsv($handle, $newBook);
            fclose($handle);
        }
    }
    // Redirect to prevent form resubmission
    header('Location: index.php');
    exit();
}
// Get all books for display
$books = getBooks($csvFile);
?>
```

Prompt:

Finally, in the HTML '<tbody>', add the PHP loop to display each book from the '$books' array. Each row must display the title, author, and genre. The 'Actions' cell should contain an Edit link ('index.php?action=edit&id=...') and a Delete link ('index.php?action=delete&id=...'), both including the book's ID.

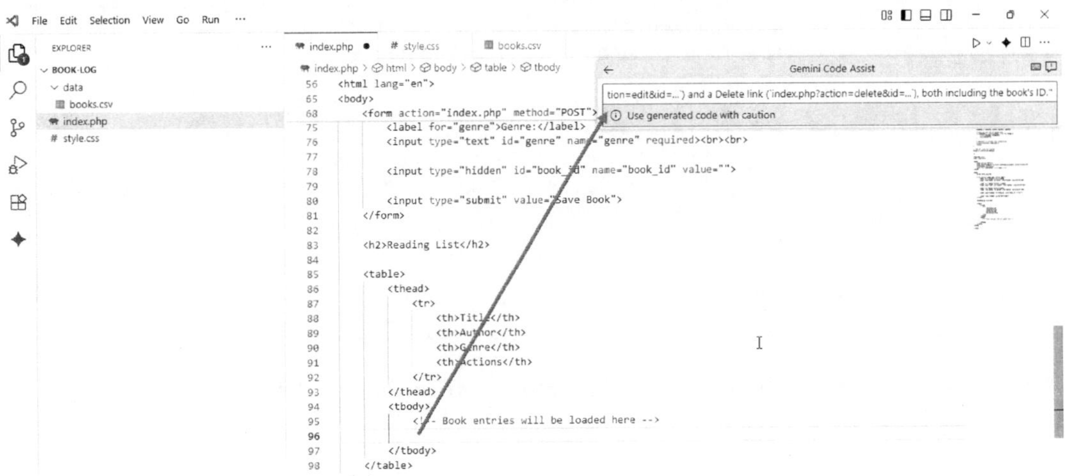

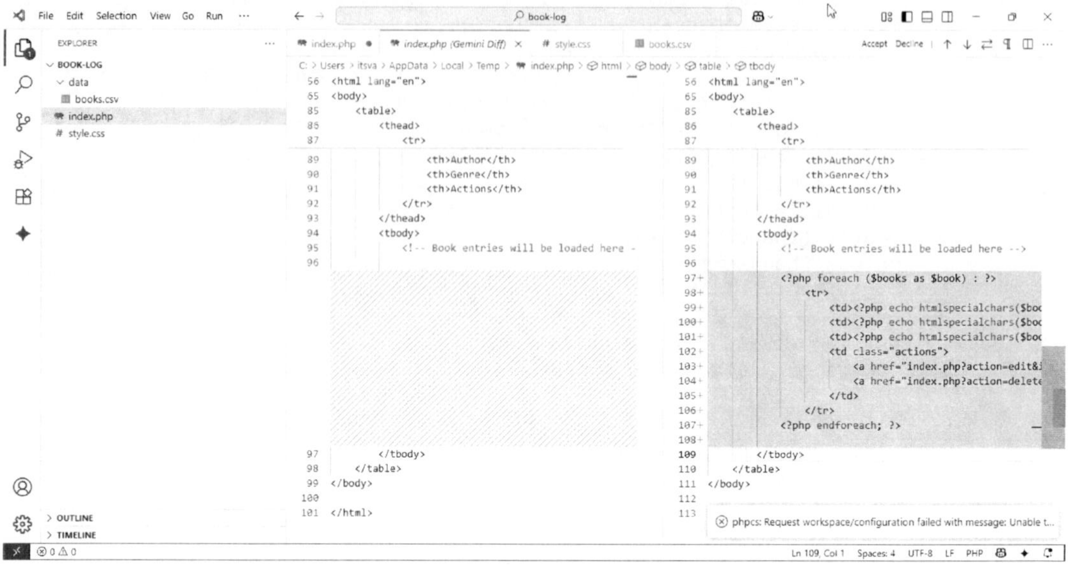

Click **Accept**. Now, index.php (after second Prompt 3) will hold <tbody> as:

```
<tbody>
    <!-- Book entries will be loaded here -->
    <?php foreach ($books as $book) : ?>
        <tr>
            <td><?php echo htmlspecialchars($book['title']); ?></td>
            <td><?php echo htmlspecialchars($book['author']); ?></td>
            <td><?php echo htmlspecialchars($book['genre']); ?></td>
            <td class="actions">
                <a href="index.php?action=edit&id=<?php echo
                   htmlspecialchars($book['id']); ?>" class="edit">Edit</a>
                <a href="index.php?action=delete&id=<?php echo
                   htmlspecialchars($book['id']); ?>" class="delete">Delete
                   </a>
            </td>
        </tr>
    <?php endforeach; ?>
</tbody>
```

At this point, you can add books and see them appear in the list! The Create and Read parts are fully functional.

Prompt 4: Generate the Delete and Update logic

Finally, let's add the logic to edit and delete our entries. This requires handling GET requests from the links we created.

Prompt:

"Now, add the 'Delete' and 'Update' logic to the top of the 'index.php' PHP script.

For 'Delete':
- Check for a GET request where 'action' is 'delete' and an 'id' is present.
- Read all books from the CSV file into an array.
- Create a new array, excluding the book with the matching ID.
- Open the CSV file in write mode ('w') to overwrite it.
- Write the header row first, then write all the books from the new, filtered array back to the file.
- Redirect to 'index.php'.

For 'Update':
- Create a variable '$bookToEdit' and initialize it to null.
- Check for a GET request where 'action' is 'edit' and an 'id' is present.
- Find the book with the matching ID from the '$books' array and assign it to '$bookToEdit'.
- In the HTML form, use PHP to check if '$bookToEdit' is set. If it is, populate the value of the title, author, genre, and 'book_id' hidden inputs with its data.
- Add a new block in the POST request handling. If 'book_id' is NOT empty, it's an update.
- For an update, read all books, find the one with the matching 'book_id', update its data with the new form values, and then rewrite the entire CSV file with the updated data.
- Redirect to 'index.php' after the update.

Click **Accept**. This is the most complex prompt, but it builds on our existing code. Let's integrate the AI's final response to create the finished application.

So, now our index.php's final version will be:

```
<?php
$csvFile = 'data/books.csv';
// Function to read books from CSV
function getBooks($csvFile)
{
    $books = [];
```

```
    if (($handle = fopen($csvFile, 'r')) !== FALSE) {
        $isHeader = true;
        while (($row = fgetcsv($handle)) !== FALSE) {
            if ($isHeader) {
                $isHeader = false;
                continue; // Skip the header row
            }
            // Assuming the order is id, title, author, genre
            $books[] = [
                'id' => $row[0],
                'title' => $row[1],
                'author' => $row[2],
                'genre' => $row[3]
            ];
        }
        fclose($handle);
    }
    return $books;
}
// Initialize $bookToEdit for the update functionality
$bookToEdit = null;
// Handle GET requests for editing or deleting
if (isset($_GET['action']) && isset($_GET['id'])) {
    $action = $_GET['action'];
    $id = $_GET['id'];
    if ($action === 'delete') {
        $books = getBooks($csvFile);
        $updatedBooks = [];
        foreach ($books as $book) {
            if ($book['id'] !== $id) {
                $updatedBooks[] = $book;
            }
        }
        // Rewrite the CSV file with the updated books
        if (($handle = fopen($csvFile, 'w')) !== FALSE) {
            fputcsv($handle, ['id', 'title', 'author', 'genre']); // Write header
            foreach ($updatedBooks as $book) {
                fputcsv($handle, [$book['id'], $book['title'], $book['author'],
                        $book['genre']]);
            }
            fclose($handle);
        }
        header('Location: index.php');
        exit();
    } elseif ($action === 'edit') {
        $books = getBooks($csvFile);
        foreach ($books as $book) {
            if ($book['id'] === $id) {
                $bookToEdit = $book;
                break;
```

```
            }
        }
    }
}
// Handle POST requests for creating a new book
if ($_SERVER['REQUEST_METHOD'] === 'POST') {
    $title = htmlspecialchars($_POST['title']);
    $author = htmlspecialchars($_POST['author']);
    $genre = htmlspecialchars($_POST['genre']);
// Get book_id from hidden input
    $bookId = htmlspecialchars($_POST['book_id']);
    if (empty($bookId)) { // It's a new book (create)
        $bookId = uniqid(); // Generate a unique ID
        $newBook = [$bookId, $title, $author, $genre];
        // Open the CSV file in append mode
        if (($handle = fopen($csvFile, 'a')) !== FALSE) {
            fputcsv($handle, $newBook);
            fclose($handle);
        }
    } else { // It's an existing book (update)
        $books = getBooks($csvFile);
        $updatedBooks = [];
        foreach ($books as $book) {
            if ($book['id'] === $bookId) {
                $updatedBooks[] = ['id' => $bookId, 'title' => $title, 'author' =>
                                   $author, 'genre' => $genre];
            } else {
                $updatedBooks[] = $book;
            }
        }
        // Rewrite the entire CSV file with the updated data
        if (($handle = fopen($csvFile, 'w')) !== FALSE) {
            fputcsv($handle, ['id', 'title', 'author', 'genre']); // Write header
            foreach ($updatedBooks as $book) {
                fputcsv($handle, [$book['id'], $book['title'], $book['author'],
                        $book['genre']]);
            }
            fclose($handle);
        }
    }
    // Redirect to prevent form resubmission
    header('Location: index.php');
    exit();
}
// Get all books for display
$books = getBooks($csvFile);
?>
<!DOCTYPE html>
<html lang="en">
<head>
```

```
    <meta charset="UTF-8">
    <meta name="viewport" content="width=device-width, initial-scale=1.0">
    <title>Book Log</title>
    <link rel="stylesheet" href="style.css">
</head>
<body>
    <h1>My Book Log</h1>
    <form action="index.php" method="POST">
        <label for="title">Title:</label>
        <input type="text" id="title" name="title" value="<?php echo $bookToEdit
                    ? htmlspecialchars($bookToEdit['title']) : ''; ?>"
               required><br><br>
        <label for="author">Author:</label>
        <input type="text" id="author" name="author" value="<?php echo $bookToEdit
                    ? htmlspecialchars($bookToEdit['author']) : ''; ?>"
               required><br><br>
        <label for="genre">Genre:</label>
        <input type="text" id="genre" name="genre" value="<?php echo $bookToEdit
                    ? htmlspecialchars($bookToEdit['genre']) : ''; ?>"
               required><br><br>
        <input type="hidden" id="book_id" name="book_id" value="<?php echo
                    $bookToEdit ? htmlspecialchars($bookToEdit['id']) : ''; ?>">
        <input type="submit" value="Save Book">
    </form>
    <h2>Reading List</h2>
    <table>
        <thead>
            <tr>
                <th>Title</th>
                <th>Author</th>
                <th>Genre</th>
                <th>Actions</th>
            </tr>
        </thead>
        <tbody>
            <!-- Book entries will be loaded here -->
            <?php foreach ($books as $book) : ?>
                <tr>
                    <td><?php echo htmlspecialchars($book['title']); ?></td>
                    <td><?php echo htmlspecialchars($book['author']); ?></td>
                    <td><?php echo htmlspecialchars($book['genre']); ?></td>
                    <td class="actions">
                        <a href="index.php?action=edit&id=<?php echo
                                htmlspecialchars($book['id']); ?>"
                           class="edit">Edit</a>
                        <a href="index.php?action=delete&id=<?php echo
                                htmlspecialchars($book['id']); ?>"
                           class="delete">Delete</a>
                    </td>
                </tr>
```

```
            <?php endforeach; ?>
        </tbody>
    </table>
</body>
</html>
```

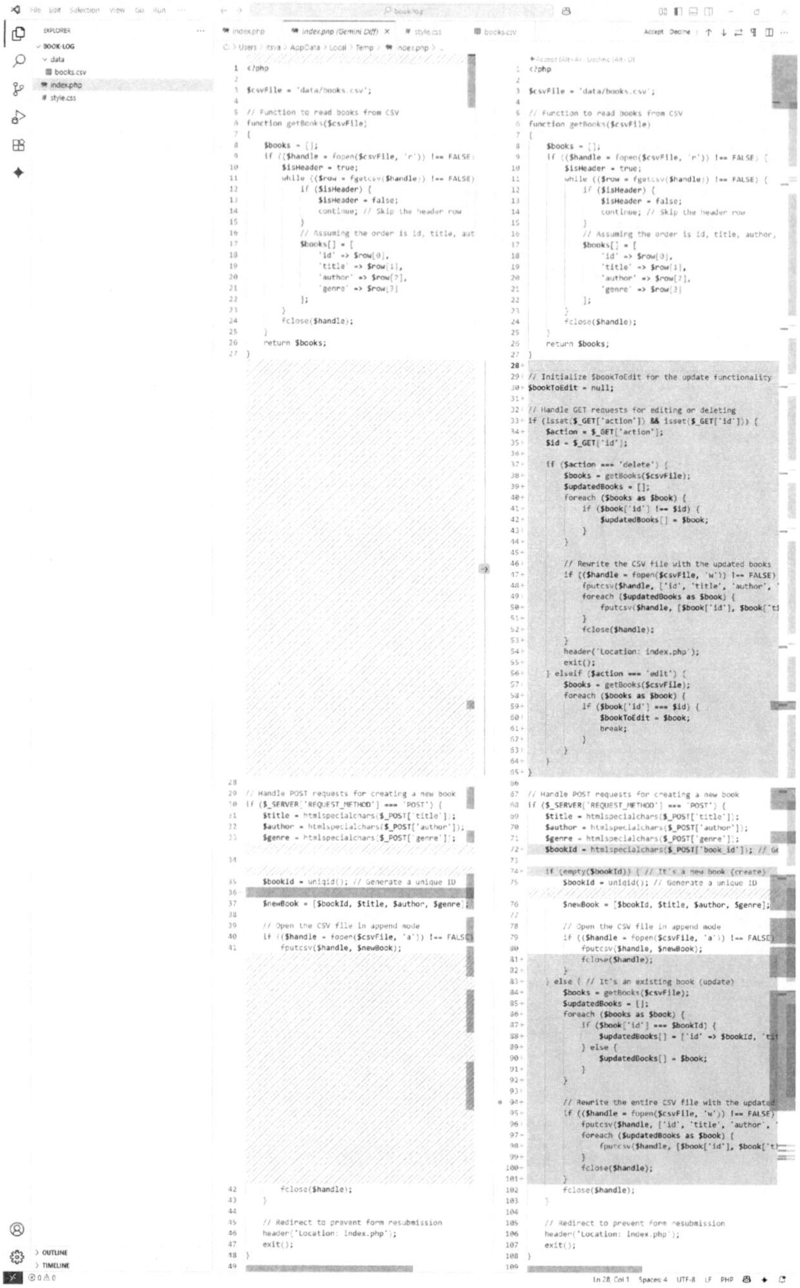

Bridging the gap: Learned concepts and application implementation

This application beautifully ties together core programming concepts. The AI helped us write code that uses:

- **CRUD operations:** The entire application is a practical demonstration of Create (adding a book), Read (listing books), Update (editing a book), and Delete (removing a book).
- **Control structures:** We used if/else blocks extensively to differentiate between POST and GET requests, and between creating and updating. We also used foreach loops to process arrays and display data.
- **Functions:** We prompted the AI to create helper functions (getBooks(), saveBooks()) to organize our code and avoid repetition, a key principle of good software design.
- **Superglobals:** $_SERVER, $_POST, and $_GET were used to handle incoming requests and access user data.
- **File handling:** We used fopen(), fgetcsv(), and fputcsv() to persist our data, demonstrating how PHP can interact with the server's filesystem.

Running and testing

1. Ensure your **Apache** server is running from the XAMPP control panel.
2. Open your web browser and navigate to **http://localhost/codes/book-log/**.
3. You see the form and an empty list.

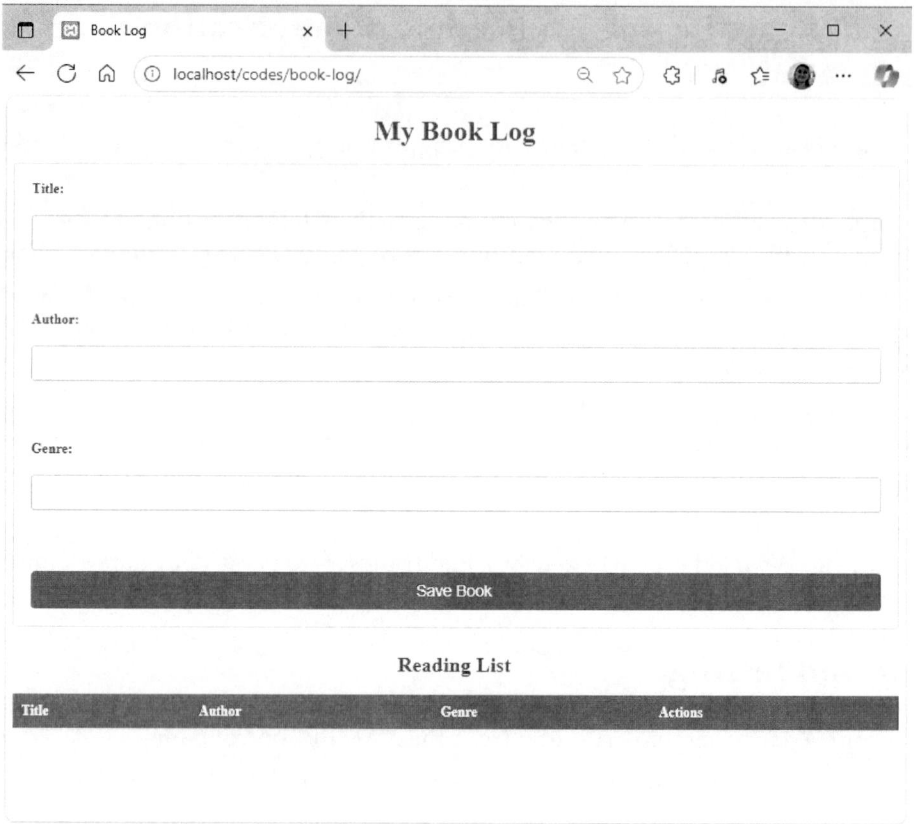

4. Fill in the title, author, and genre for a book and click **Save Book**. The page refreshes, and your book appears in the table below.

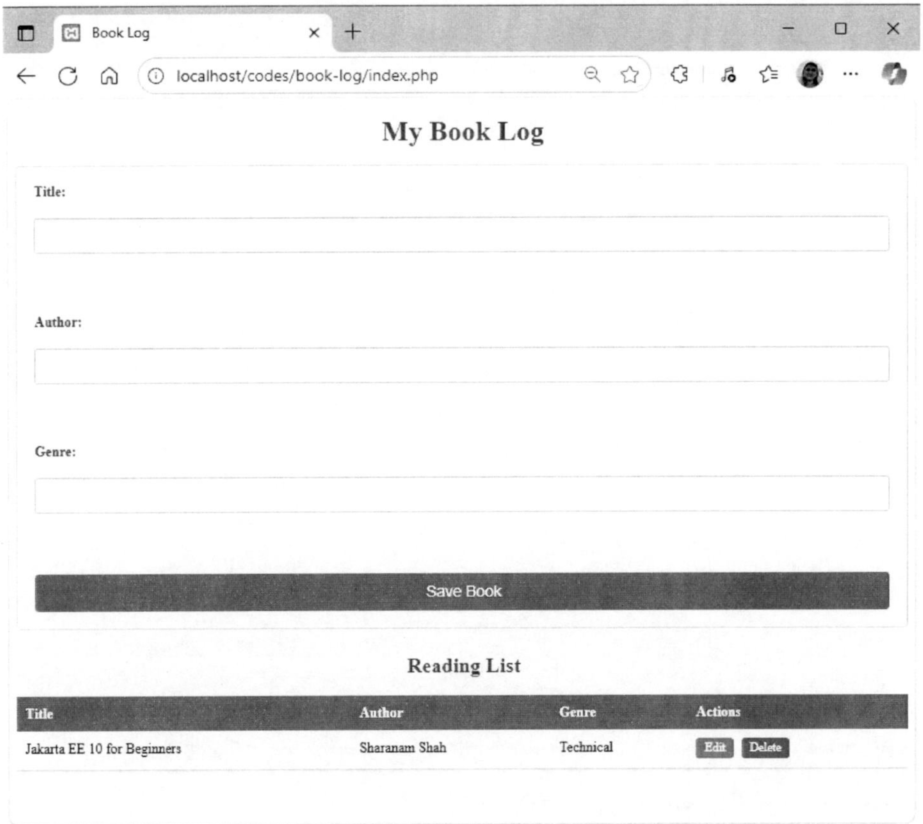

5. Click the **Edit** link next to your new entry.

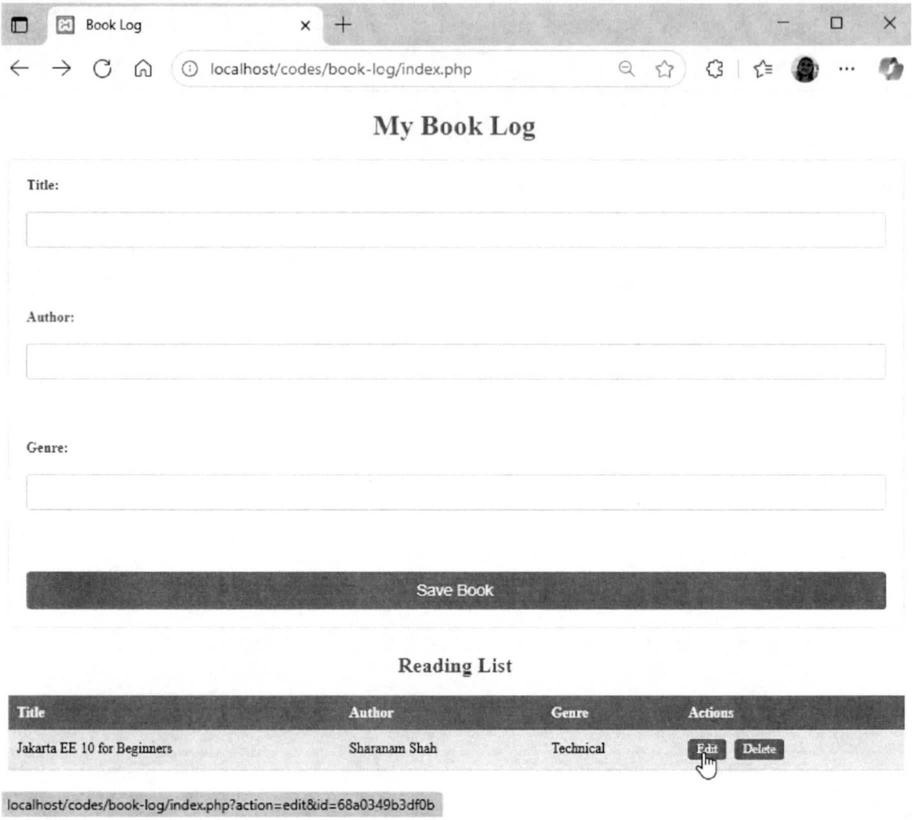

6. The form at the top of the page is now populated with that book's data.

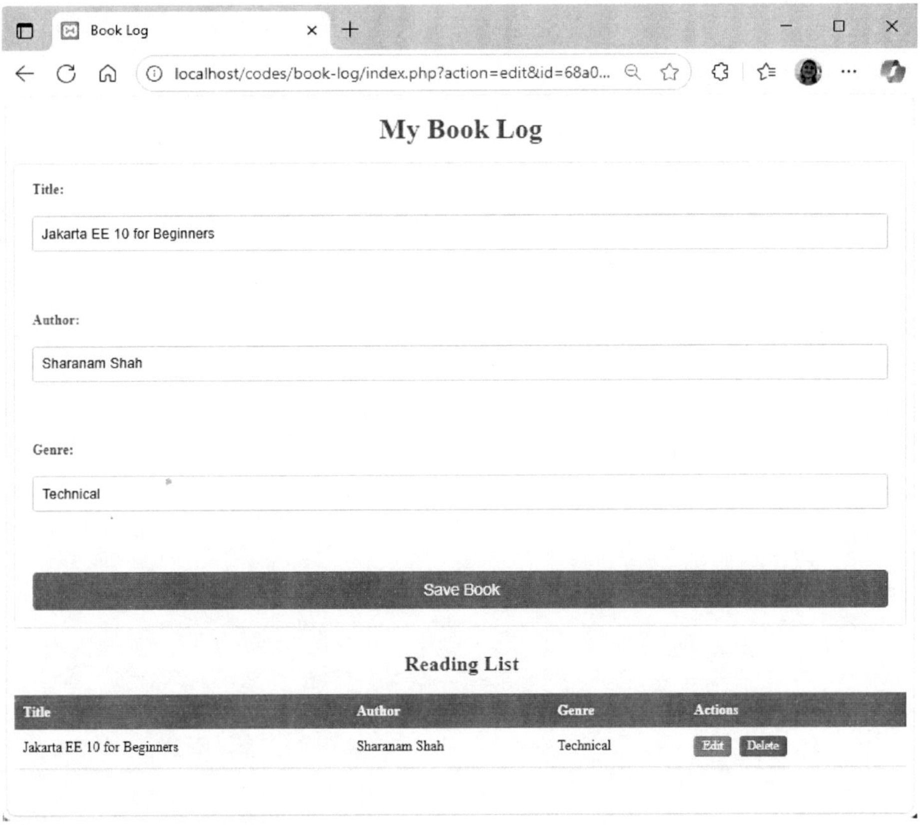

7. Change any field and click **Save Book**. The page refreshes, and you see the updated information in the table.

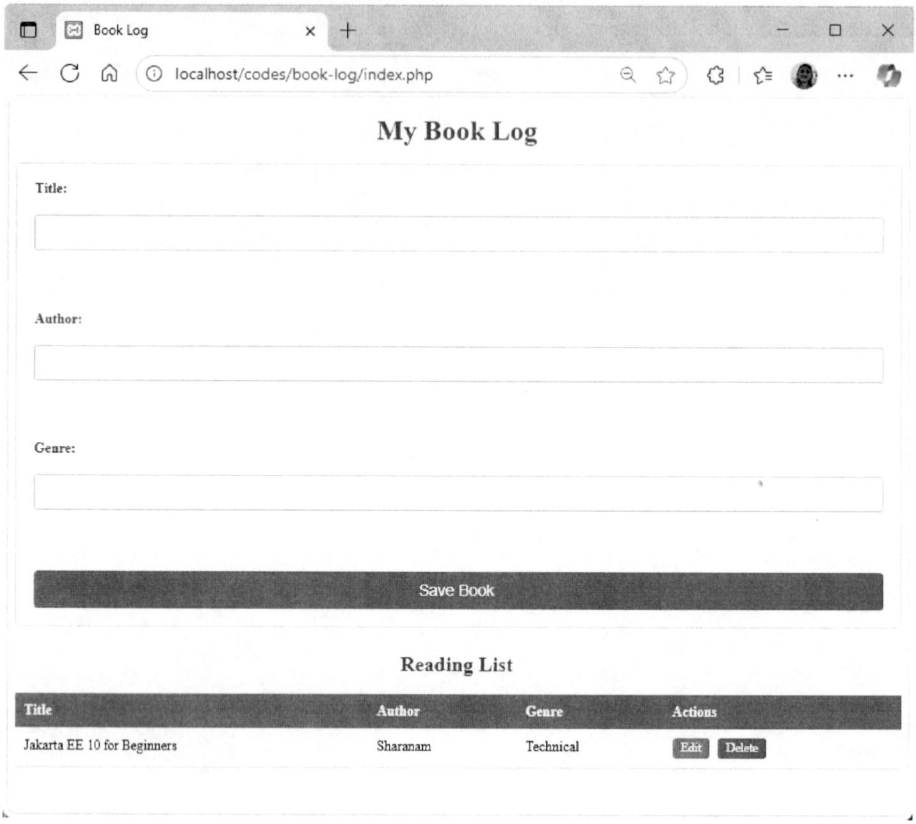

8. Click the red **Delete** link.

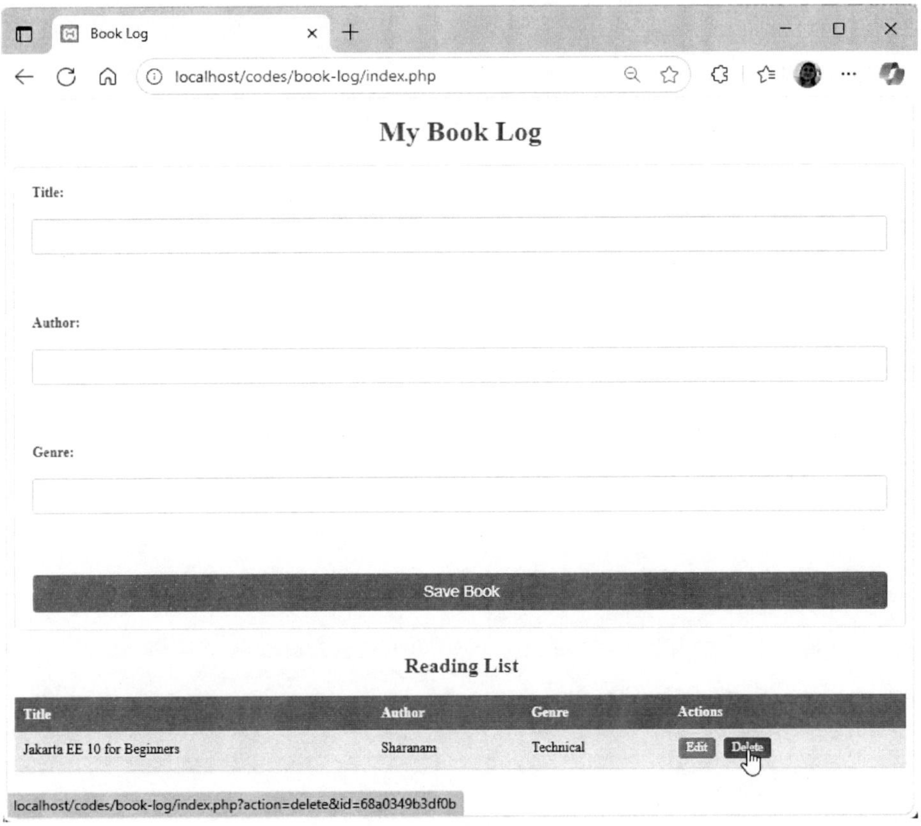

9. A confirmation dialog pops up. Click **OK**, and the book is permanently removed from your list.

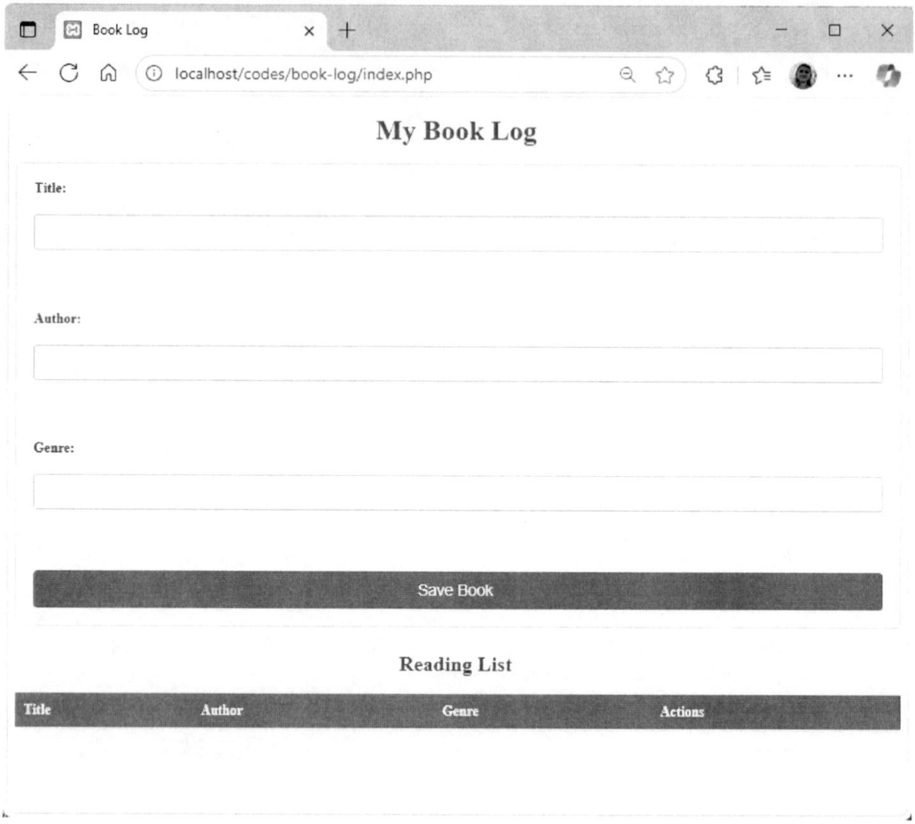

Debugging with AI: Fixing the Edit bug

After clicking **Edit** to edit the entry, the application unexpectedly crashes and displays a fatal error message. The error **Uncaught TypeError: fclose(): supplied resource is not a valid stream resource** on line 102 tells us that we are trying to close a file handle that is not open or is invalid. This is a perfect opportunity to use our AI assistant to debug the code.

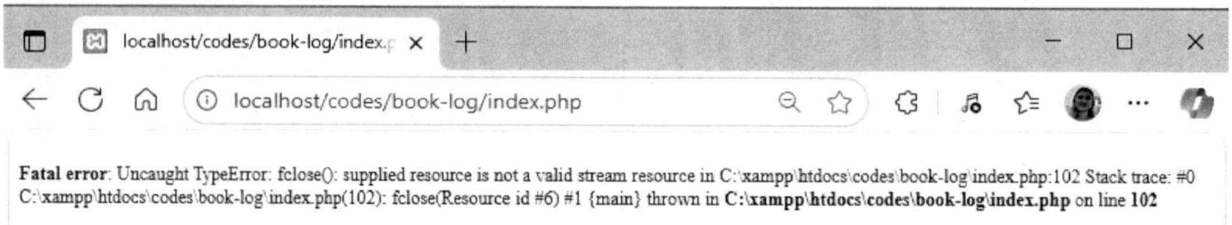

AI-generated code is a powerful starting point, but as we've just seen, bugs can still happen. Your role as a developer includes acting as a quality assurance engineer. Let's use Gemini Code Assist to diagnose and fix this issue.

Introducing the /fix command

One of the most powerful features of an in-editor AI assistant is the ability to perform context-aware actions. The **/fix** command in Gemini Code Assist is a prime example. Instead of you having to find the bug yourself, **/fix** instructs the AI to:

- Analyze the code in your currently active file.
- Look for common errors, logical mistakes, or potential bugs.
- Suggest a specific code change to resolve the most likely issue.

Applying the fix:

1. With the **index.php** file open in **VS Code**, open the **Gemini Code Assist chat panel** by clicking **Crtl + I**.
2. In the **chat** input, simply select **/fix**, enter the error mentioned in the browser and press **Enter**.

3. Gemini immediately analyzes the code and present a "diff" view, highlighting the code it recommends removing (in red) and the code it recommends adding (in green).

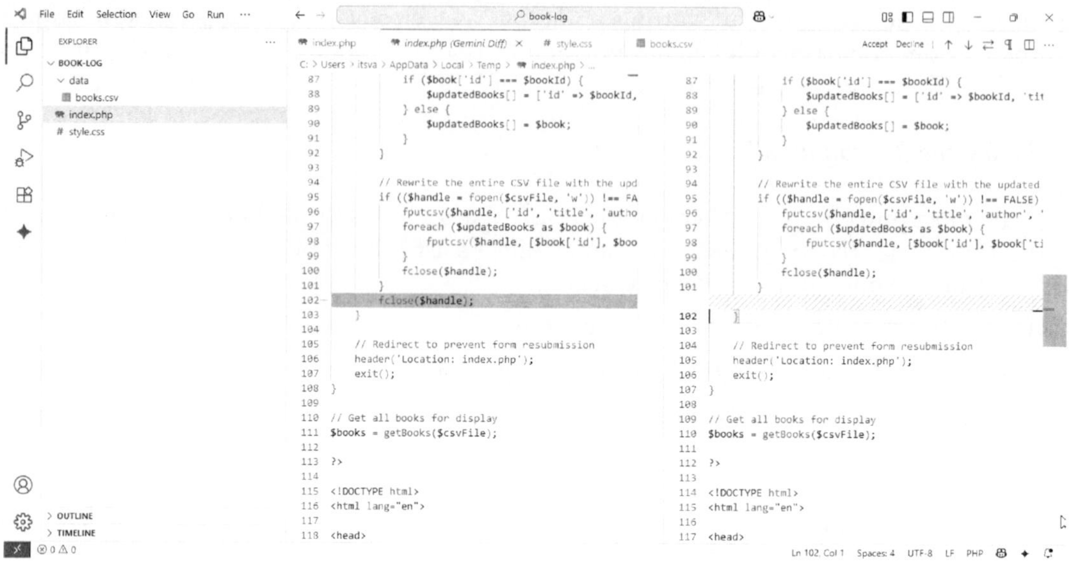

Understanding the Fix

The AI suggests removing fclose($handle); from line 102. But why?

Let's look at the logic. The "Update" operation reads all books, modifies an array in memory, and then rewrites the entire file using the saveBooks() function. The $handle variable that fclose() is trying to close was only ever opened in the "Create" logic block. When updating, that block is skipped, so $handle is never created, leading to the TypeError. The saveBooks() function correctly handles opening and closing the file on its own. The fclose($handle); on line 102 was a leftover, redundant piece of code that was causing the crash.

The AI correctly identified this logical flaw and removed the unnecessary line. After accepting the suggestion, the update functionality works perfectly.

Exploring application behaviour: A practical run-through

- **Valid input:** As you've seen, adding, editing, and deleting works as expected.
- **Debugging experience**: We encountered a real-world bug during the update process. Using the AI assistant's /fix command, we were able to quickly identify and resolve the issue without needing to manually trace the code logic, demonstrating a modern, efficient debugging workflow.

- **Empty submission:** If you click "Save Book" with empty fields, our simple validation (!empty()) prevents a blank row from being added.
- **File permissions:** If the data folder were not writable by the server, PHP would throw an error when trying to save a book. This is a common real-world problem that highlights the importance of correct server configuration.
- **URL manipulation:** If a user tries to edit or delete an ID that doesn't exist (e.g., ?action=edit&id=fakeid), our code simply won't find a match, and nothing will happen, which is safe behavior.

Harnessing AI-generated CRUD in real-world contexts

The CRUD pattern we just built is the foundation of almost every dynamic website.

- **E-commerce:** Managing products, customers, and orders.
- **Blogging:** Creating, editing, and deleting posts and comments.
- **Social Media:** Posting updates, editing your profile, and managing your friend list.

Learning to prompt an AI to quickly generate this core logic frees you up to focus on the unique features that make your application special.

Wrapping up

This chapter was a deep dive into the practical, day-to-day partnership between a developer and an AI assistant. You have leveled up your ability to generate high-quality code by focusing on high-quality inputs.

- **Prompt engineering:** You learned that the key to great AI output is a great prompt: one that is specific, context-aware, and clear about the desired format.
- **Common scenarios:** We walked the AI through generating code for the most common web development tasks, including loops, forms, validation, and basic authentication.
- **The review cycle:** You learned the critical importance of treating AI code as a first draft, which must be reviewed for security, correctness, and best practices.
- **Full CRUD application:** You built a complete Book Log application from scratch, guiding the AI through each step of the Create, Read, Update, and Delete lifecycle.
- **Single-page logic:** You implemented a sophisticated single-page application where all actions are handled by one file, a common pattern in modern web development.

Incredible job! You have moved beyond simple commands and are now conducting a symphony of prompts to build a complete, data-driven application. You are learning the essential modern skill of how to translate a large problem into a series of logical, AI-friendly requests. This ability to rapidly prototype and build is a superpower. Always remember to be the pilot, not the passenger; guide the AI, question its output, and refine it to perfection.

In the next chapter, we will take this collaboration to the next level. You'll learn how to take a project from a simple idea all the way to a finished product in ***Chapter 26: From idea to launch – Architecting a project with AI***.

Chapter 26

Section 07: AI code generation – Supercharge your productivity

From idea to launch – Architecting a project with AI

What you'll learn

- Architectural prompting: Crafting prompts that generate entire project plans
- AI-driven database design: Getting a perfect database schema from a simple idea
- Prompting AI to write every single line of PHP, HTML, and CSS
- Developer's role: Understanding how to guide, verify, and assemble AI-generated code

In the previous chapters, you've learned the fundamental building blocks of PHP. Now, it's time to change the game. We're moving from being just a coder to becoming a project director, with a powerful AI as our lead developer.

This chapter will teach you a modern workflow: how to guide an AI assistant, like Google Gemini, to take a simple idea and turn it into a fully structured, multi-file, database-driven web application. You will learn to prompt for architecture, not just for code, and watch as a professional-grade project blueprint materializes before your eyes.

Every complex website you use, from an e-commerce store to a social network, began as an idea. The most challenging step for any developer, new or experienced, is translating that idea into a structured plan: What features are needed? How should the database be designed? What files and folders do I create? In the past, this required years of experience. Today, it requires a well-crafted conversation with an AI.

In this chapter, we will simulate that exact process. We will act as the project manager, providing clear instructions to our AI assistant (Gemini), which will act as our expert architect and programmer, delivering every piece of the puzzle we need to launch our simple Recipe Blog.

Recap: From single-file scripts to real-world applications

Our journey so far has focused on single-file projects that taught us core PHP concepts. While essential for learning, these are not how professional applications are built. Real-world projects demand organization. Code is separated into different files and folders based on its purpose—a practice called **separation of concerns**. This keeps the project clean, manageable, and scalable. Logic lives in PHP files, presentation in HTML templates, and styling in CSS files. This chapter makes that professional structure our primary goal.

The role of AI in the planning phase: Your new project architect

Think of your AI assistant as a seasoned software architect with encyclopedic knowledge of best practices. Instead of you having to guess the right way to build something, you can simply describe your vision. The AI can then provide a detailed blueprint, including feature lists, database designs, and file structures. This process eliminates guesswork and ensures you start building on a solid, professional foundation from day one.

From a simple idea to a concrete plan

Our project begins with a simple, high-level idea: **I want to build a recipe blog.** This is too vague to start coding. Our first task is to use Gemini to flesh this out into a concrete set of features.

Prompting for features: **i want to build a recipe blog. what are the essential features for an mvp?**

An **MVP (Minimum Viable Product)** is the most basic version of an application that is still useful. Focusing on an MVP prevents us from getting overwhelmed.

Let's open our AI chat interface (Google Gemini) by clicking on the **Gemini Code Assist** icon. The **Gemini Code Assist: Chat** interface opens.

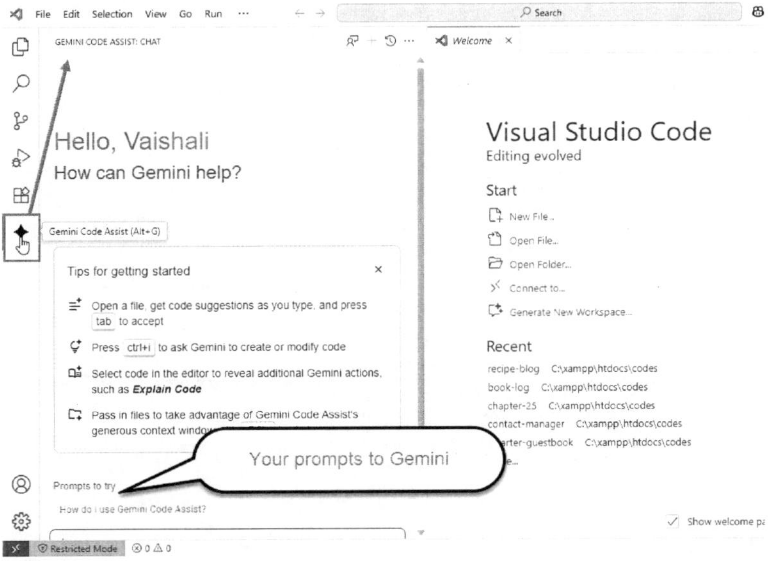

Now let's give our first prompt in the **Prompts to try** textbox given below in the **Gemini Code Assist: Chat** interface.

Prompt to Gemini:

I want to build a simple recipe blog using PHP 8 and MySQL. I am a beginner. What are the absolute essential features for a Minimum Viable Product (MVP)? I only want to focus on displaying recipes that are already in the database. No user logins or recipe submissions for now.

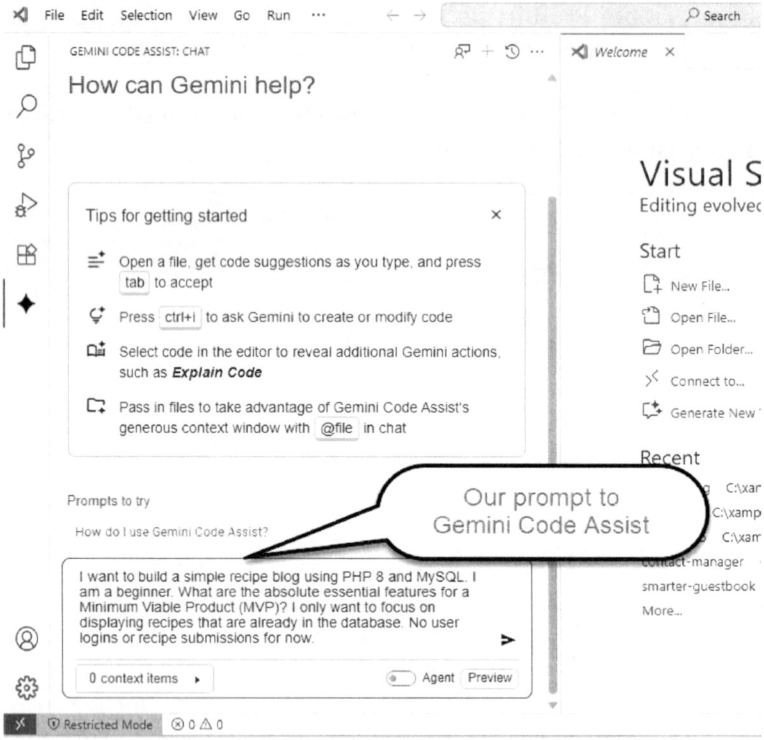

Press **Enter**.

Gemini's Generated Plan:

Excellent! Focusing on a content-display MVP is a great way to start. Here are the essential features for your simple recipe blog:

- **Homepage (Recipe List View):**
  - **Purpose:** To display all available recipes in a summarized, easy-to-browse format.
  - **Content:** Each recipe summary should show its title, a short description, and its category.
  - **Functionality:** Clicking on any recipe summary should take the user to its dedicated detail page.
- **Recipe Detail Page:**
  - **Purpose:** To show all information for a single, selected recipe.
  - **Content:** This page should display the recipe's full title, description, a list of ingredients, and step-by-step instructions. It should also show the recipe's category.

- **Functionality:** Should include a link to return to the homepage.

- **Recipe Categorization:**
  - **Purpose:** To organize recipes logically (e.g., "Desserts," "Main Courses").
  - **Implementation:** This will be a background feature. The database will link each recipe to a category, and the category name will be displayed on both the homepage and the detail page.

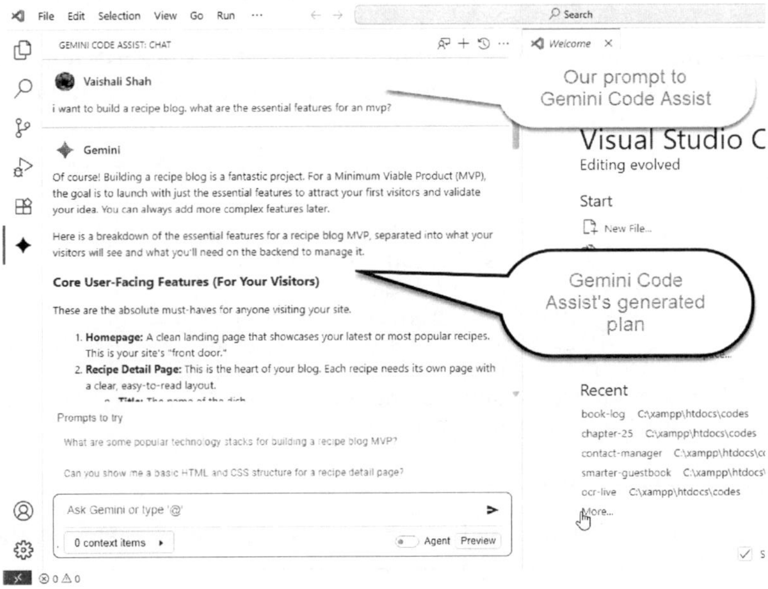

This focused feature set gives you a clear and achievable goal for your first multi-file project. This is a perfect, actionable plan. Gemini understood our constraints (beginner, no user submissions) and gave us a clear roadmap.

Refining the scope: Using AI to identify core vs. "nice-to-have" features

Gemini has already helped us refine the scope by focusing on an MVP. Its response is clear and aligns with our goal, so no further refinement is needed. We have our three core pillars: a recipe list, a recipe detail view, and a categorization system.

#

AI-assisted database design

With our features defined, we need a database to store the recipe data. Let's ask Gemini to design it for us. A good prompt is specific and gives the AI all the context it needs.

Prompting for a schema: "based on these features, generate a SQL schema for a MySQL database. include tables for recipes and categories. explain the relationships."

We will now ask Gemini to act as our Database Administrator. We'll ask not just for the code, but also for sample data and an explanation, so we understand *why* the database is designed this way.

Prompt to Gemini:

```
Based on the MVP features for the recipe blog, generate the complete SQL schema for
a MySQL database. I need two tables: categories and recipes.
For your response, please provide three things:
1. A brief explanation of the relationship between the two tables.
2. The CREATE TABLE SQL code for both tables. Use INT AUTO_INCREMENT
   PRIMARY KEY for IDs and include a foreign key constraint.
3. INSERT statements to add 2 sample categories ('Main Courses', 'Desserts') and 2
   sample recipes (one for each category).
```

Gemini's Generated Database Schema:

Of course! Expanding the database to include categories is a great next step. It allows for better organization and is a fundamental concept in database design.

Here is the complete SQL schema for your categories and recipes tables.
1. Table Relationship Explained
The relationship between categories and recipes is a **one-to-many** relationship.

- **One** category (e.g., "Desserts") can have **many** recipes.
- **Each** recipe belongs to exactly **one** category.

This is achieved by placing a category_id column in the recipes table. This column acts as a **foreign key**, linking each recipe record back to a unique record in the categories table.

2. CREATE TABLE Statements
This SQL code will create the two tables with the proper relationship. The FOREIGN KEY constraint ensures data integrity, and ON DELETE CASCADE means that if you delete a category, all recipes within that category will also be automatically deleted.

--

```
-- Table structure for table categories
--
CREATE TABLE categories (
 id INT AUTO_INCREMENT PRIMARY KEY,
 name VARCHAR(255) NOT NULL,
 created_at TIMESTAMP DEFAULT CURRENT_TIMESTAMP
) ENGINE=InnoDB DEFAULT CHARSET=utf8mb4;
--
-- Table structure for table recipes
--
CREATE TABLE recipes (
 id INT AUTO_INCREMENT PRIMARY KEY,
 category_id INT NOT NULL,
 title VARCHAR(255) NOT NULL,
 description TEXT NOT NULL,
 ingredients TEXT NOT NULL,
 instructions TEXT NOT NULL,
 created_at TIMESTAMP DEFAULT CURRENT_TIMESTAMP,
 FOREIGN KEY (category_id) REFERENCES categories(id) ON DELETE CASCADE
) ENGINE=InnoDB DEFAULT CHARSET=utf8mb4;
```

3. INSERT Statements for Sample Data

Here are the INSERT statements to populate your new tables with two categories and two sample recipes, one for each category.

```
--
-- Dumping data for table categories
--
INSERT INTO categories (id, name) VALUES
(1, 'Main Courses'),
(2, 'Desserts');
--
-- Dumping data for table recipes
--
INSERT INTO recipes (category_id, title, description, ingredients, instructions) VALUES
(1, 'Classic Spaghetti Bolognese', 'A hearty and traditional Italian pasta dish, perfect for a family dinner.', '1 lb ground beef\n1 onion, chopped\n2 cloves garlic, minced\n1 (28 ounce) can crushed tomatoes\n1 teaspoon dried oregano\nSalt and pepper to taste\n1 lb spaghetti', '1. In a large skillet, cook the ground beef, onion, and garlic over medium heat until browned. Drain excess fat.\n2. Stir in the crushed tomatoes, oregano, salt, and pepper. Bring to a simmer, then reduce heat and let it cook for at least 30 minutes.\n3. Meanwhile, cook the spaghetti according to package directions. Drain.\n4. Serve the sauce over the hot spaghetti.'),
```

(2, 'Fudgy Chocolate Brownies', 'Ultra rich, moist, and chewy brownies that are a chocolate lover''s dream.', '1/2 cup butter, melted\n1 cup white sugar\n2 large eggs\n1 teaspoon vanilla extract\n1/3 cup unsweetened cocoa powder\n1/2 cup all-purpose flour\n1/4 teaspoon salt', '1. Preheat oven to 350°F (175°C). Grease and flour an 8-inch square pan.\n2. In a large bowl, mix together the melted butter, sugar, eggs, and vanilla.\n3. Beat in cocoa, flour, and salt until well blended.\n4. Spread the batter into the prepared pan.\n5. Bake for 25 to 30 minutes, or until a toothpick inserted into the center comes out with moist crumbs.');

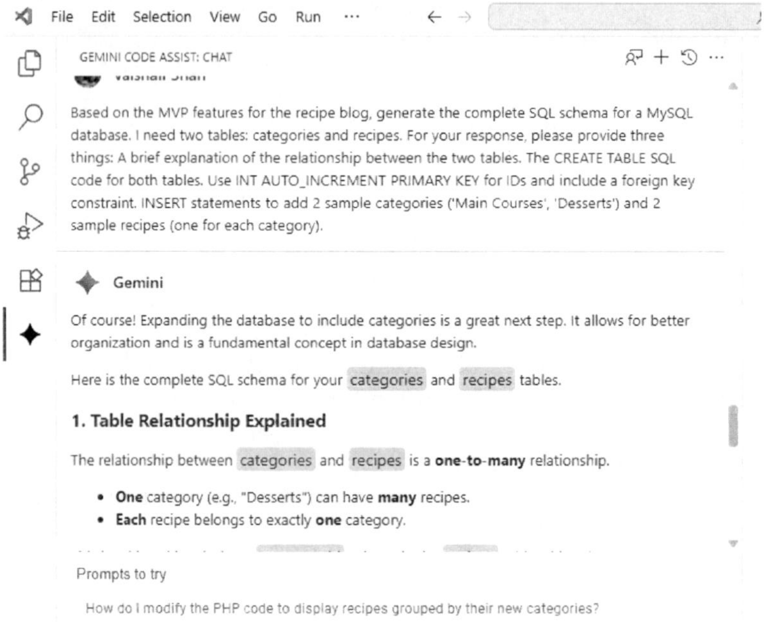

This output is perfect. It's a complete, ready-to-use package. Our job is now simply to execute it.

You can now run these SQL commands in your MySQL client (like phpMyAdmin) to set up and populate your database.

Reviewing and refining the AI-generated schema

The schema is robust. It correctly uses primary keys, AUTO_INCREMENT, and a foreign key. The ON DELETE CASCADE is a nice professional touch—it means if we delete a category, all recipes within it will also be deleted, preventing orphaned data. The sample data is well-formatted and ready. No refinements are needed.

Hands-on: Building a simple Recipe blog with AI as the architect

It's time to build. We will now follow a strict prompt-and-execute workflow. For each step, we'll give Gemini a precise prompt and then take its generated code and place it into our project.

In this section, we will create our project's file structure, set up the database using the AI-generated SQL, and then prompt Gemini to write the complete code for every single file. There will be no guesswork. We are the directors, and the AI is our coder.

Building the application: A structured prompting guide

Let's begin the construction.

Create the Database

Create the database in phpMyAdmin:

1. Ensure **Apache** and **MySQL** are running from your XAMPP control panel.
2. Open your browser to **http://localhost/phpmyadmin/**.
3. Click the **Databases** tab, enter **recipe_blog_db** as the **database name**, and click **Create**.
4. Select the **recipe_blog_db** database from the left sidebar.
5. Click the **SQL** tab.
6. Copy *all* the SQL code from Gemini's output (both the CREATE TABLE and INSERT statements) and paste it into the SQL query box.
7. Click **Go**. You can see a success message. Your database is now set up and populated with sample data.

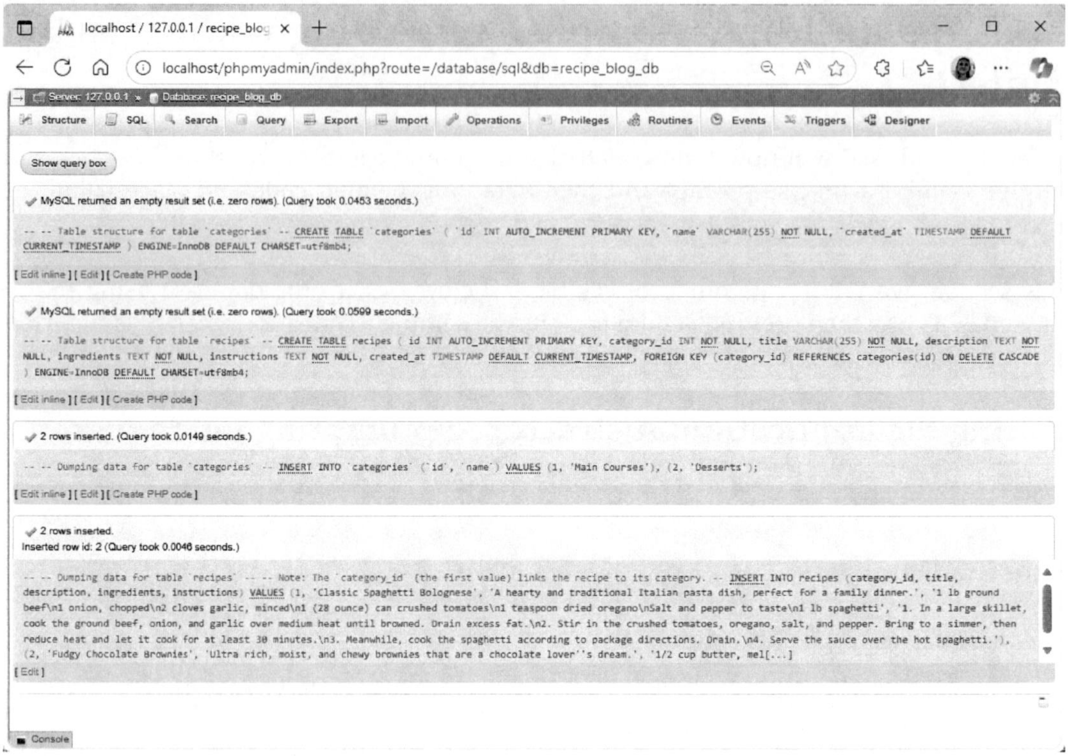

Create the Project Folder

Create the project folders and files:

1. Navigate to your XAMPP **htdocs/codes** folder.
2. Create a new folder named **recipe-blog**.
3. Open this **recipe-blog** folder in **Visual Studio Code**.

Now, let's ask Gemini for the exact file structure.

Prompt to Gemini:

```
I am starting my PHP recipe blog project. Please provide me with a clear, hierarchical list of all the folders and empty files I need to create in my project root directory. Use a tree-like structure for the list.
```

Gemini's Generated File Structure:

Of course! If you prefer a more direct and traditional PHP structure, that's a perfectly valid approach, especially for getting a project off the ground quickly. It's very clear and easy to understand.

Here is the hierarchical list of folders and empty files for the simpler structure you requested.

Project Structure Tree

```
recipe-blog/
├── assets/
│   └── css/
│       └── style.css
├── includes/
│   ├── db_connect.php
│   ├── footer.php
│   └── header.php
├── index.php
└── recipe.php
```

Explanation of Directories and Files

- **assets/**: This folder holds your static files that the browser uses.
    - **css/style.css**: Your main stylesheet for the blog's design.
- **includes/**: This directory is for reusable PHP code snippets that you will include on multiple pages.
    - **db_connect.php**: The code to connect to your database.
    - **header.php**: The top part of your HTML page, including the <head> section, navigation bar, and opening <body> tag.
    - **footer.php**: The bottom part of your HTML page, including the footer content and closing </body> and </html> tags.
- **index.php**: This will be the homepage of your recipe blog, listing all the recent recipes.
- **recipe.php**: This page will display the details of a single recipe. It will likely take a recipe ID from the URL (e.g., recipe.php?id=123).

Starter Content

To help you get started, here is some basic code you can place in your new files.

c:\recipe-blog\includes\header.php

This file contains the start of your HTML document.

c:\recipe-blog\includes\footer.php

This file closes the HTML document.

c:\recipe-blog\includes\db_connect.php
A basic, secure database connection using PDO. **Remember to replace the placeholder credentials.**
c:\recipe-blog\index.php
Your main homepage, which includes the header and footer.

This simple structure is an excellent way to build your project. It's clean, organized, and easy to manage.

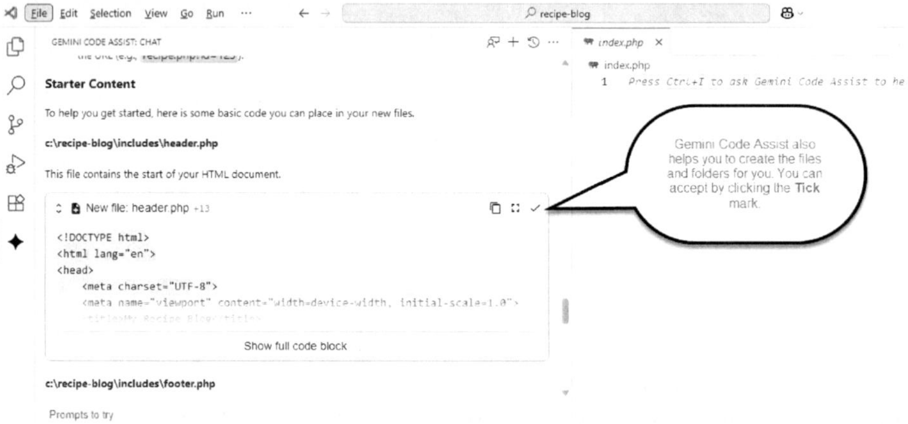

We are going to manually create this exact structure in **VS Code**. Right-click in the **Explorer panel** to create new folders and new files until your project matches Gemini's blueprint perfectly. Finally, our project's structure is ready!

Generate the code for each file

We will now go file by file, prompting Gemini for the complete contents.

File 1: includes/db_connect.php

Click **Crtl + I** to open **Gemini Code Assist** and give the following prompt to generate code for this file. Press **Enter**.

Prompt to Gemini:

Write the complete PHP code for the file includes/db_connect.php. It should connect to a MySQL database on localhost. The database name is recipe_blog_db, the username is root, and the password is an empty string. Use PDO, set the error mode to exceptions, and set the default fetch mode to PDO::FETCH_ASSOC. Include comments explaining the code.

Gemini's Generated Code:

Here is the complete code for db_connect.php:

```
<?php
// Database connection parameters
$host = 'localhost';
$dbname = 'recipe_blog_db';
$username = 'root';
$password = ''; // Empty password for root on XAMPP
try {
    // Create a new PDO instance. The DSN (Data Source Name) specifies the database
    // type, host, and database name
    $pdo = new PDO("mysql:host=$host;dbname=$dbname", $username, $password);
    // Set the PDO error mode to exception. This means PDO will throw PDOExceptions
    // on errors, which can be caught for better error handling
    $pdo->setAttribute(PDO::ATTR_ERRMODE, PDO::ERRMODE_EXCEPTION);
    // Set the default fetch mode to associative array. This means that when
    // fetching data from the database, it will be returned as an associative array
    $pdo->setAttribute(PDO::ATTR_DEFAULT_FETCH_MODE, PDO::FETCH_ASSOC);
    // Optional: You can uncomment the line below for a success message during
    // development
    // echo "Connected successfully to the database!";
} catch (PDOException $e) {
    // Catch any PDO exceptions (database connection errors)
    // Display an error message and terminate the script
```

```
    die("Connection failed: " . $e->getMessage());
}
```

Your action: Click **Accept** and the entire code is copied automatically in your includes/db_connect.php file. Save it.

Files 2: includes/header.php

Prompt to Gemini:

> Generate a complete HTML5 boilerplate head. It must link to /assets/css/style.css. In the body, include a <header> tag with a link to index.php styled as a logo. It should use a PHP variable $pageTitle for the <title> tag.

Gemini's Generated Code:

Here is the code for the file:

```
<!DOCTYPE html>
<html lang="en">
<head>
    <meta charset="UTF-8">
    <meta name="viewport" content="width=device-width, initial-scale=1.0">
    <title><?php echo isset($pageTitle) ? htmlspecialchars($pageTitle) : 'Recipe
           Blog'; ?></title>
    <link rel="stylesheet" href="assets/css/style.css">
</head>
<body>
    <header class="main-header">
        <div class="container">
            <a href="index.php" class="logo">The Recipe Corner</a>
        </div>
    </header>
    <main class="main-content">
```

Your action: Click **Accept** to automatically include the code of header.php in your includes/header.php file and save it.

Files 3: includes/footer.php

Prompt to Gemini:

> Generate a complete HTML5 which should contain a <footer> tag with a copyright notice and then close the <body> and <html> tags.

#

Gemini's Generated Code:

Here is the code for the file:

```
</main>
<footer class="main-footer">
    <div class="container">
        <p>© <?php echo date('Y'); ?> The Recipe Corner. All Rights Reserved.</p>
    </div>
</footer>
</body>
</html>
```

Your action: Click **Accept** to automatically include the code of footer.php in your includes/footer.php file and save it.

File 4: assets/css/style.css

Prompt to Gemini:

Generate the complete CSS for assets/css/style.css. I need a modern, clean, and responsive design. The color scheme should be professional. Style a card layout for the recipe list on the homepage and a clear, readable format for the single recipe page. Add comments to explain the major sections of the CSS.

Gemini's Generated Code:

Here is a modern and clean stylesheet for your recipe blog:

```
/* --- Google Fonts & Global Styles --- */
@import url('https://fonts.googleapis.com/css2?family=Lato:wght@400;700&family
             =Playfair+Display:wght@700&display=swap');
:root {
    --primary-color: #2c3e50;
    /* Midnight Blue */
    --secondary-color: #3498db;
    /* Peter River Blue */
    --accent-color: #e74c3c;
    /* Alizarin Red */
    --background-color: #f8f9fa;
    /* Light Gray */
    --surface-color: #ffffff;
    /* White */
    --border-color: #dee2e6;
    --text-color: #343a40;
    --text-light: #6c757d;
    --font-body: 'Lato', sans-serif;
    --font-headings: 'Playfair Display', serif;
}
body {
```

```
    font-family: var(--font-body);
    margin: 0;
    background-color: var(--background-color);
    color: var(--text-color);
    line-height: 1.6;
}
/* --- Typography --- */
h1, h2, h3, h4, h5, h6 {
    font-family: var(--font-headings);
    color: var(--primary-color);
    font-weight: 700;
}
a {
    color: var(--secondary-color);
    text-decoration: none;
    transition: color 0.3s ease;
}
a:hover {
    color: var(--primary-color);
}
/* --- Layout & Header/Footer --- */
.container {
    max-width: 1140px;
    margin: 0 auto;
    padding: 20px;
}
header {
    background-color: var(--surface-color);
    padding: 1rem 0;
    border-bottom: 1px solid var(--border-color);
    box-shadow: 0 2px 4px rgba(0, 0, 0, 0.05);
}
header .logo {
    font-family: var(--font-headings);
    font-size: 1.8rem;
    color: var(--primary-color);
    font-weight: 700;
}
footer {
    text-align: center;
    padding: 2rem 0;
    margin-top: 2rem;
    background-color: var(--primary-color);
    color: #ecf0f1;
}
/* --- Homepage: Recipe Card Layout --- */
.recipe-list {
    display: grid;
    grid-template-columns: repeat(auto-fill, minmax(300px, 1fr));
    gap: 2rem;
    margin-top: 2rem;
```

```
}
.recipe-card {
    background-color: var(--surface-color);
    border-radius: 8px;
    overflow: hidden;
    box-shadow: 0 4px 12px rgba(0, 0, 0, 0.08);
    transition: transform 0.3s ease, box-shadow 0.3s ease;
}
.recipe-card:hover {
    transform: translateY(-5px);
    box-shadow: 0 8px 20px rgba(0, 0, 0, 0.12);
}
.recipe-card a {
    display: block;
    color: inherit;
}
.recipe-card img {
    width: 100%;
    height: 200px;
    object-fit: cover;
    /* Ensures images cover the area without distortion */
    display: block;
}
.recipe-card-content {
    padding: 1.5rem;
}
.recipe-card-content h3 {
    margin-top: 0;
    margin-bottom: 0.5rem;
    font-size: 1.4rem;
}
.recipe-card-content p {
    color: var(--text-light);
    font-size: 0.9rem;
    margin-bottom: 0;
}
.recipe-card-content .category {
    font-size: 0.8rem;
    font-weight: 700;
    text-transform: uppercase;
    color: var(--accent-color);
    margin-bottom: 0.5rem;
    letter-spacing: 0.5px;
}
.recipe-card-content .read-more {
    display: inline-block;
    margin-top: 1rem;
    font-weight: 700;
    color: var(--secondary-color);
    font-size: 0.9rem;
}
```

```
/* --- Single Recipe Page --- */
.recipe-single {
    background-color: var(--surface-color);
    padding: 2rem 3rem;
    margin-top: 2rem;
    border-radius: 8px;
    box-shadow: 0 4px 12px rgba(0, 0, 0, 0.08);
}
.recipe-single .category {
    text-align: center;
    font-size: 1rem;
    font-weight: 700;
    text-transform: uppercase;
    color: var(--accent-color);
    margin-bottom: 0.5rem;
    letter-spacing: 1px;
}
.recipe-single h1 {
    text-align: center;
    font-size: 3rem;
    margin-top: 0;
    margin-bottom: 1.5rem;
}
.recipe-image-large {
    width: 100%;
    max-height: 500px;
    object-fit: cover;
    border-radius: 8px;
    margin-bottom: 1.5rem;
}
.recipe-meta {
    display: flex;
    justify-content: center;
    gap: 2rem;
    color: var(--text-light);
    border-top: 1px solid var(--border-color);
    border-bottom: 1px solid var(--border-color);
    padding: 1rem 0;
    margin-bottom: 2rem;
}
.recipe-content {
    display: grid;
    grid-template-columns: 1fr 2fr;
    gap: 3rem;
}
.ingredients ul, .instructions ol {
    padding-left: 20px;
}
.ingredients li, .instructions li {
    margin-bottom: 0.75rem;
}
```

```
.ingredients {
    border-right: 1px solid var(--border-color);
    padding-right: 2rem;
}
.recipe-content pre {
    white-space: pre-wrap;
    word-wrap: break-word;
    background-color: var(--background-color);
    border: 1px solid var(--border-color);
    padding: 1rem;
    border-radius: 4px;
    font-family: var(--font-body);
    line-height: 1.7;
}
/* --- Responsive Design --- */
/* For Tablets */
@media (max-width: 992px) {
    .recipe-content {
        grid-template-columns: 1fr;
        gap: 2rem;
    }
    .ingredients {
        border-right: none;
        border-bottom: 1px solid var(--border-color);
        padding-right: 0;
        padding-bottom: 2rem;
    }
    .recipe-single h1 {
        font-size: 2.5rem;
    }
}
/* For Mobile Phones */
@media (max-width: 768px) {
    .recipe-list {
        grid-template-columns: 1fr;
    }

    .recipe-single {
        padding: 1.5rem;
    }
    .recipe-single h1 {
        font-size: 2rem;
    }
    .recipe-meta {
        flex-direction: column;
        gap: 0.5rem;
        align-items: center;
    }
}
.back-link-container {
    text-align: center;
```

```
    margin-top: 2.5rem;
    padding-top: 1.5rem;
    border-top: 1px solid var(--border-color);
}
.back-link:hover {
    text-decoration: underline;
}
```

Your action: Click **Accept** to automatically include the code of style.css in your assets/css/style.css file and save it.

File 5: index.php (The Homepage)

Prompt to Gemini:

Generate the complete PHP and HTML code for index.php. The script must:

1. Set the $pageTitle variable to "Homepage".
2. Include includes/db_connect.php and includes/header.php.
3. Write a SQL query to fetch all recipes, joining with the categories table to get the category name. Order the results by most recent.
4. Execute the query and fetch all results.
5. Loop through the results and display each recipe in a div with the class recipe-card.
6. Each card must show the category name, title, and description.
7. Each card must have a link (<a> tag with class read-more) that points to recipe.php?id=THE_RECIPE_ID.
8. Finally, include includes/footer.php.
9. Use htmlspecialchars() on all data being outputted.

Gemini's Generated Code:

Here is the complete code for your index.php homepage:

```
<?php
$pageTitle = "Homepage";
include 'includes/db_connect.php';
include 'includes/header.php';
try {
    $stmt = $pdo->prepare("SELECT r.id, r.title, r.description, c.name as
                            category_name FROM recipes r JOIN categories c ON
                            r.category_id = c.id ORDER BY r.created_at DESC");
    $stmt->execute();
    $recipes = $stmt->fetchAll();
} catch (PDOException $e) {
    die("Error fetching recipes: " . $e->getMessage());
}
?>
<div class="container">
    <h1>Latest Recipes</h1>
    <div class="recipe-list">
```

```
        <?php foreach ($recipes as $recipe) : ?>
            <div class="recipe-card">
                <a href="recipe.php?id=<?php echo htmlspecialchars($recipe['id']);
                    ?>">
                    <div class="recipe-card-content">
                        <p class="category"><?php echo htmlspecialchars($recipe['
                                                    category_name']); ?></p>
                        <h3><?php echo htmlspecialchars($recipe['title']); ?></h3>
                        <p><?php echo htmlspecialchars($recipe['description']);
                           ?></p>
                    </div>
                </a>
            </div>
        <?php endforeach; ?>
    </div>
</div>
<?php include 'includes/footer.php'; ?>
```

Your action: Click **Accept** to automatically include the code of index.php and save it.

File 6: recipe.php (The Detail page)

Prompt to Gemini:

Finally, generate the complete code for recipe.php. This script must:

1. Include includes/db_connect.php.
2. Get the recipe id from the URL using $_GET['id']. It must be validated to ensure it's a positive integer. If not, redirect to index.php.
3. Use a **prepared statement** to fetch the single recipe and its category name from the database based on the ID.
4. If no recipe is found for that ID, redirect to index.php.
5. If a recipe is found, set the $pageTitle to the recipe's title.
6. Include includes/header.php.
7. Display the recipe's category, title, description, ingredients, and instructions. The ingredients and instructions should be inside <pre> tags to preserve formatting.
8. Include a "Back to all recipes" link.
9. Include includes/footer.php.
10. Use htmlspecialchars() on all output.

Gemini's Generated Code:

Here is the secure and complete code for recipe.php:

```
<?php
include 'includes/db_connect.php';
// Get the recipe ID from the URL
$recipeId = filter_input(INPUT_GET, 'id', FILTER_VALIDATE_INT);
// Validate the recipe ID
```

```
if (!$recipeId || $recipeId <= 0) {
    header("Location: index.php");
    exit();
}
try {
    // Fetch the single recipe and its category name from the database
    $stmt = $pdo->prepare("SELECT r.id, r.title, r.description, r.ingredients,
                           r.instructions, c.name as category_name FROM recipes r
                           JOIN categories c ON r.category_id = c.id WHERE r.id =
                           :id");
    $stmt->bindParam(':id', $recipeId, PDO::PARAM_INT);
    $stmt->execute();
    $recipe = $stmt->fetch();
    // If no recipe is found, redirect to index.php
    if (!$recipe) {
        header("Location: index.php");
        exit();
    }
    // Set the page title
    $pageTitle = $recipe['title'];
} catch (PDOException $e) {
    die("Error fetching recipe: " . $e->getMessage());
}
include 'includes/header.php';
?>
<div class="container">
    <div class="recipe-single">
        <p class="category"><?php echo htmlspecialchars($recipe['category_name']
                            ); ?></p>
        <h1><?php echo htmlspecialchars($recipe['title']); ?></h1>
        <div class="recipe-meta">
            <p><strong>Description:</strong> <?php echo htmlspecialchars(
                                                 $recipe['description']); ?></p>
        </div>
        <div class="recipe-content">
            <div class="ingredients">
                <h2>Ingredients</h2>
                <pre><?php echo htmlspecialchars($recipe['ingredients']); ?></pre>
            </div>
            <div class="instructions">
                <h2>Instructions</h2>
                <pre><?php echo htmlspecialchars($recipe['instructions']); ?></pre>
            </div>
        </div>
        <div class="back-link-container">
            <a href="index.php" class="back-link">← Back to all recipes</a>
        </div>
    </div>
</div>
<?php include 'includes/footer.php'; ?>
```

Your action: Click **Accept** to automatically include the code of recipe.php and save it.

All your files are now complete!

Bridging the gap: Connecting the concepts of planning, database design, and multi-file PHP structure

Let's pause and analyze the high-quality application we've built. The files you have assembled demonstrate how core concepts translate into a professional, modern web application.

- **Advanced styling and theming:** Your style.css file goes beyond basic layouts. By using **CSS variables** (e.g., --primary-colour) at the :root level, you've created a centralized theme palette. Changing a colour in one place will update it across the entire site, making redesigns incredibly efficient. Importing custom fonts from Google Fonts (Lato and Playfair Display) elevates the typography, giving the blog a polished, print-like quality that distinguishes it from generic websites.
- **Robust and secure data handling:** You've implemented security best practices consistently. In recipe.php, you use filter_input(INPUT_GET, 'id', FILTER_VALIDATE_INT) to sanitize the incoming recipe ID. This is a superior, modern approach that ensures only a valid integer is processed, preventing a wide range of potential security issues. Both index.php and recipe.php use **PDO prepared statements** ($pdo->prepare(...)), which is the industry standard for preventing SQL injection attacks.
- **Semantic and modular HTML structure**: The use of header.php and footer.php is a classic example of modularity. However, the structure is also highly semantic. The <header> element is in the header file, the <footer> is in the footer file, and both wrap a central <main class="main-content"> tag. This tells browsers and search engines exactly what the main content of each page is, improving accessibility and SEO.
- **Responsive and mobile-first design**: The CSS is built to be responsive. The @media queries at the bottom of style.css are crucial. They adapt the layout for tablets and mobile phones, for example, by changing the recipe list from a multi-column grid to a single column (grid-template-columns: 1fr;) on smaller screens. This ensures the website is usable and looks great on any device.

Running and testing

The moment of truth! Let's launch our AI-built application.

1. Ensure your **Apache** and **MySQL** servers are running in the XAMPP control panel.
2. Open your web browser and navigate to **http://localhost/codes/recipe-blog/**.

3. You can see your beautiful homepage, **The Recipe Corner**, with cards for **Classic Spaghetti Bolognese** and **Fudgy Chocolate Brownies**.

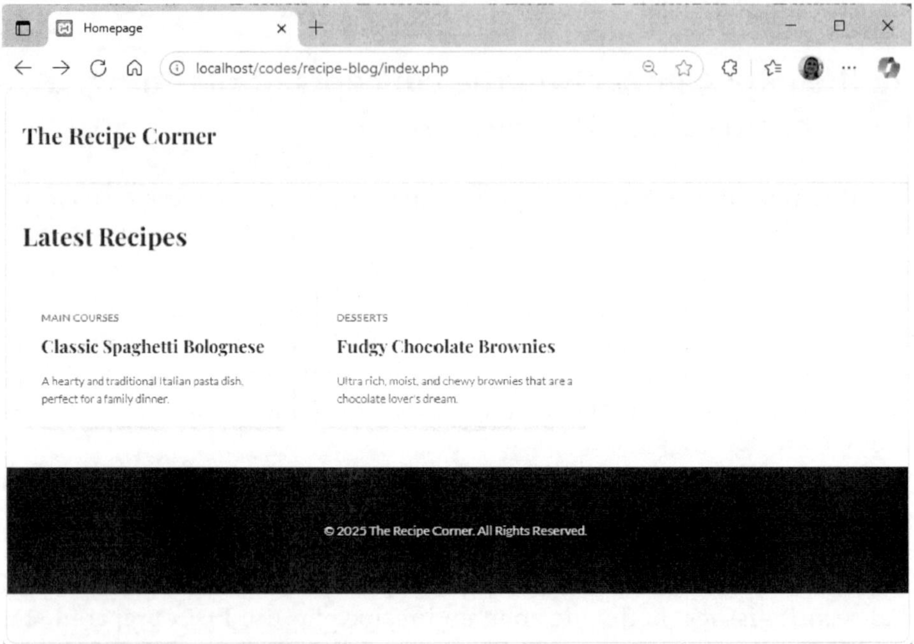

4. Click on any of the recipe card.
5. The browser navigates to **http://localhost/codes/recipe-blog/recipe.php?id=2**.
6. You can see the full detail page for the brownies, with the ingredients and instructions clearly laid out.

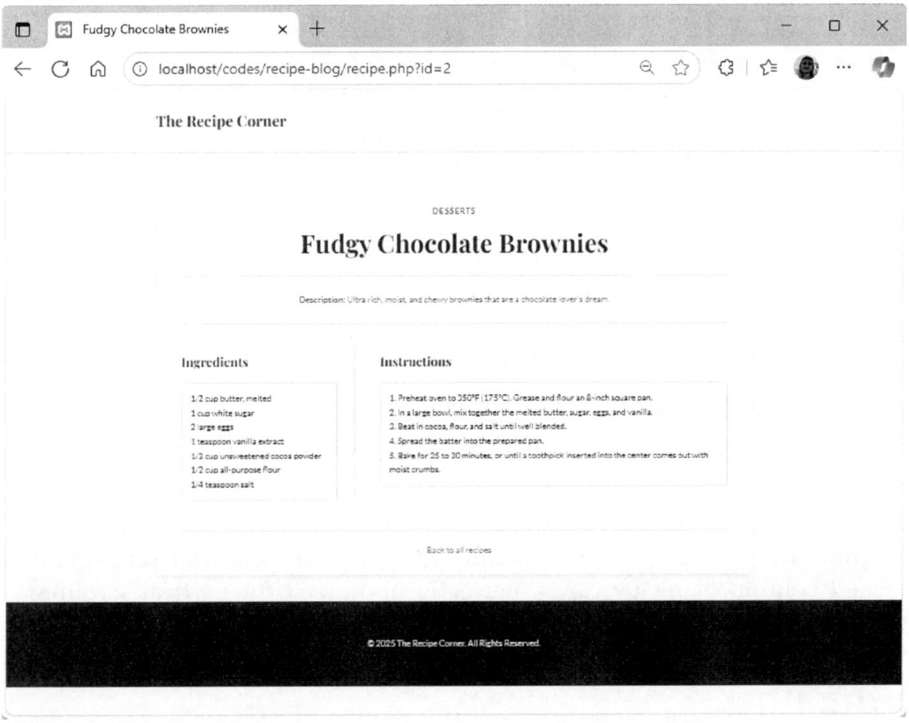

It works perfectly. We have successfully directed an AI to build a complete, database-driven web application from scratch.

Exploring application behaviour: a practical run-through

A professional application is defined by how gracefully it handles unexpected situations. Let's test the behaviour of the code you've assembled.

- **Scenario 1:** A user provides a non-numeric Recipe ID.
  - **Action:** A user or a faulty external link navigates to http://localhost/codes/recipe-blog/recipe.php?id=latest.
  - **Code in Action:** In recipe.php, the line $recipeId = filter_input(INPUT_GET, 'id', FILTER_VALIDATE_INT); attempts to validate "latest" as an integer. The validation fails, and $recipeId becomes false.
  - **Result:** The if (!$recipeId || $recipeId <= 0) check immediately passes, and the code executes header("Location: index.php");, instantly redirecting the user to the homepage without any errors. This is a clean and secure way to handle invalid input.

- **Scenario 2:** A user requests a recipe ID that doesn't exist.
    - **Action:** A user navigates to a valid but non-existent recipe, like http://localhost/codes/recipe-blog/recipe.php?id=999.
    - **Code in Action:** The ID 999 passes the filter_input() validation. The script then executes the prepared statement to fetch the recipe from the database. Since no recipe with that ID exists, $recipe = $stmt->fetch(); returns false.
    - **Result:** The next check, if (!$recipe), now evaluates to true, and the user is seamlessly redirected back to the homepage. The application never crashes; it simply handles the invalid request gracefully.
- **Scenario 3:** Viewing the site on a mobile phone.
    - **Action:** A user visits the homepage on a smartphone.
    - **Code in Action:** The browser's width is less than 768px, which triggers the @media (max-width: 768px) rule in style.css.
    - **Result:** Instead of a side-by-side grid of recipe cards, the CSS rule grid-template-columns: 1fr; is applied to the .recipe-list container. The user sees a single, neatly stacked column of recipe cards, perfectly optimized for vertical scrolling. The site remains fully functional and aesthetically pleasing.

Wrapping up

This chapter was a major leap forward, introducing you to a modern, AI-driven development workflow. You learned that with the right prompts, you can orchestrate the creation of a complete application.

- **Architectural prompting:** We learned to ask the AI for high-level plans, structures, and schemas, not just code snippets.
- **End-to-end generation:** We successfully prompted Gemini to generate every single file needed for our project: SQL, PHP, CSS, and HTML.
- **The director's role:** We practiced the workflow of a modern developer: specify, prompt, verify, and assemble.
- **Best practices by default:** By being specific in our prompts, we ensured the AI-generated code included crucial security (prepared statements) and data handling (htmlspecialchars) features.
- **Rapid prototyping:** We saw how this workflow can take an idea to a functioning prototype in a fraction of the time of manual coding.

Congratulations on building your first fully architected web application! You've not only mastered a multi-file PHP structure but have also learned the single most important new skill in software development: how to effectively partner with an AI. This ability to direct, verify, and integrate AI-generated code is what will define the next generation of productive and successful developers. You are now officially one of them.

Now that we know how to generate code, our next step is to learn how to improve it. Get ready for ***Chapter 27: Beyond generation – AI for code quality and testing***, where we'll use AI to refactor, document, and validate our applications to a professional standard.

Chapter 27

Section 07: AI code generation – Supercharge your productivity

Beyond generation – AI for code quality and testing

What you'll learn

- AI-powered refactoring
- Introduction to unit testing
- Improving code readability
- Generating code documentation
- AI-assisted test writing
- Validating your work

Welcome to the next stage of your journey as a developer! So far, we've focused on using AI to generate new code, turning ideas into functional scripts and applications. But in the professional world, writing code is only the first step. Great developers don't just write code; they write *good* **code**—code that is clean, easy to understand, reliable, and maintainable.

This chapter introduces you to professional workflows that leverage AI not just as a creator, but as a partner in quality assurance. We will show you how to use your AI assistant to improve, document, and validate your work. This is a critical step that transitions you from simply making things work to building software that lasts.

Think about a professional kitchen. A chef doesn't just throw ingredients in a pot; they refine the recipe, plate the food beautifully, and ensure every dish that leaves the kitchen is perfect. Good code is no different—it isn't just written; it's refined.

In this chapter, we'll move beyond simply generating code that *works* and into the world of crafting code that is *excellent*. We will explore three core practices of professional software development:

- **refactoring** (improving the structure of existing code)
- **documenting** (explaining what your code does) and
- **testing** (proving that your code works correctly)

You'll discover how your AI assistant can dramatically accelerate these tasks, helping you write more professional, reliable, and maintainable applications from the very beginning.

Refactoring code with AI

What is refactoring?

Refactoring is the process of restructuring existing computer code—changing the factoring—without changing its external behavior. The goal is to improve the code's internal structure, making it easier to read, understand, and maintain. Think of it as tidying up a messy room. The contents of the room are the same, but afterward, everything is organized and easy to find.

Your AI assistant is incredibly skilled at this. It can spot redundancies, suggest more efficient approaches, and reorganize code into logical patterns, like functions or classes.

Common refactoring prompts

Let's look at a simple example. Imagine you have a script with some repetitive logic.

Before refactoring:

```
<?php
// Greet the first user
$user1_name = "Sharanam";
echo "Welcome, " . $user1_name . "! Hope you have a great day.";
echo "<br>";
// Greet the second user
$user2_name = "Vaishali";
echo "Welcome, " . $user2_name . "! Hope you have a great day.";
```

```
echo "<br>";
```

This code works, but it's not efficient.

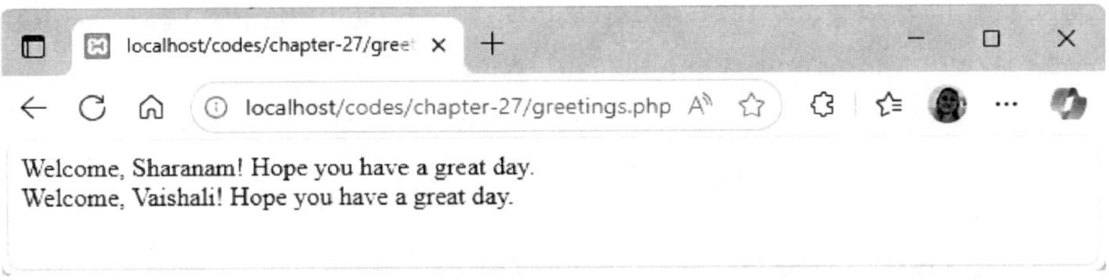

If we want to change the greeting, we have to edit it in two places. Let's ask our AI assistant to help. In **VS Code**, you can highlight the code block and use your AI assistant with a prompt like this.

Prompt:

"Refactor this code into a reusable function."

The AI immediately understands the repetition and provides a much cleaner solution. Just click on **Accept** and the code is automatically refactored.

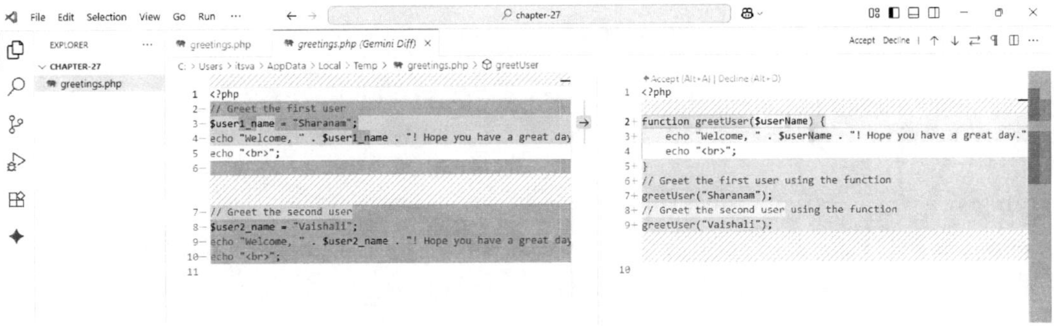

After AI refactoring:

```
<?php
function greetUser($userName)
{
    echo "Welcome, " . $userName . "! Hope you have a great day.";
    echo "<br>";
}
// Greet the first user using the function
greetUser("Sharanam");
// Greet the second user using the function
```

```
10. greetUser("Vaishali");
```

This version is cleaner, easier to read, and far more maintainable. We can now greet a hundred users with one simple function call each. Other powerful refactoring prompts include:

- "Can you make this code more readable and efficient?"
- "Convert this block of code to use a switch statement instead of if/elseif."
- "Take this logic and encapsulate it within a PHP class."

Generating documentation with AI

The importance of comments and docblocks

Writing code is only half the battle. Making sure that you (and others) can understand it six months from now is just as important. Thats where documentation comes in. Good documentation explains what a piece of code does, what inputs it expects, and what it returns.

In PHP, the standard for this is called **PHPDoc**. These are specially formatted comments (called **docblocks**) that live directly above functions, classes, and methods.

Prompting for documentation

Writing documentation can feel tedious, but with AI, it's instantaneous. Let's take our greetUser() function from before. It's simple, but let's document it professionally.

We can give our AI assistant this **Prompt**:

```
Generate a PHPDoc block for this function, explaining what it does, its parameters, and what it returns.
```

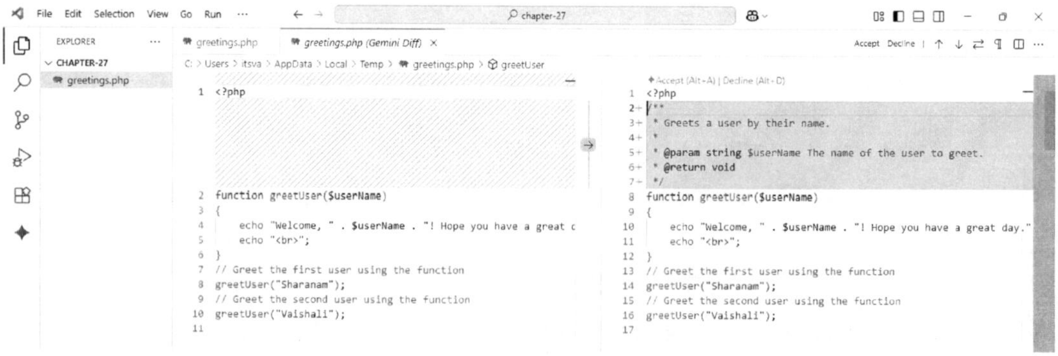

Click **Accept** to include the documentation of the greetUser() function.

After AI documentation:

```
<?php
/**
 * Greets a user by their name.
 *
 * @param string $userName The name of the user to greet.
 * @return void
 */
function greetUser($userName)
{
    echo "Welcome, " . $userName . "! Hope you have a great day.";
    echo "<br>";
}
// Greet the first user using the function
greetUser("Sharanam");
// Greet the second user using the function
greetUser("Vaishali");
```

This docblock is now a permanent, clear explanation of our function's purpose. Modern editors like VS Code can even read these docblocks to provide you with hints and autocompletion as you code.

An introduction to automated testing

Why manual testing isn't enough

So far in this book, we've been testing our applications by opening them in a web browser and clicking around. This is called **manual testing**, and while it's essential, it's not enough.

As applications grow, it becomes impossible to manually test every single feature after every single code change. What if fixing a bug in one place accidentally breaks something else?

This is where **automated testing** comes in. We write code that tests our application code automatically. This safety net runs every time we make a change, ensuring we haven't broken anything.

What is a unit test?

The most common form of automated testing is the **unit test**. A unit test focuses on testing one small, isolated piece of code—a **unit**, which is typically a single function or a method within a class. It checks if that unit behaves exactly as expected given a specific input. For example, a unit test for a sum() function would check if sum(2, 3) correctly returns 5.

Setting up a simple PHPUnit environment

The most popular testing framework in the PHP world is **PHPUnit**. Setting it up is straightforward with Composer, PHP's package manager. For our hands-on project, we'll walk through the exact steps, which is a brief process:

- **Initialize Composer:** You run a command to create a composer.json file, which tracks your project's dependencies.
- **Install PHPUnit:** You run another command to download PHPUnit and add it to your project.
- **Configure PHPUnit:** You create a simple XML file (phpunit.xml.dist) to tell PHPUnit where to find your tests.

This one-time setup enables you to run hundreds of tests with a single command from your terminal.

Hands-on: Improving a User Validator class with AI

In this hands-on section, we will put all this theory into practice. We'll start with a messy, procedural PHP script designed to validate a username and email. Then, using a series of AI prompts, we'll transform it into a high-quality, professional, documented, and fully tested PHP class. This exercise perfectly mirrors the real-world workflow of improving existing code.

Building the application

Let's get our project set up.

1. Inside your XAMPP **htdocs/codes** folder, create a new folder named **c27-ai-quality**.
2. Open this **c27-ai-quality** folder in **Visual Studio Code**.
3. Create a new file named **validator_before.php**.

The "before" code: A messy script

Now, let's add our starting code. This script works, but it's poorly structured. It mixes logic, uses a weak email check, and is difficult to reuse elsewhere in an application.

Copy the following code into validator_before.php:

```
<?php
// A script to validate user inputs
// Scenario 1: A valid user
$username1 = "Admin";
$email1 = "admin@example.com";
if (strlen($username1) > 4 && strlen($username1) < 15) {
    echo "Username '{$username1}' is valid.<br>";
} else {
    echo "Username '{$username1}' is NOT valid.<br>";
}
if (strpos($email1, '@') !== false) {
    echo "Email '{$email1}' is valid.<br>";
} else {
    echo "Email '{$email1}' is NOT valid.<br>";
}
echo "<hr>";
// Scenario 2: An invalid user
$username2 = "user1";
$email2 = "user1-example.com";
if (strlen($username2) > 4 && strlen($username2) < 15) {
    echo "Username '{$username2}' is valid.<br>";
} else {
    echo "Username '{$username2}' is NOT valid.<br>";
}
if (strpos($email2, '@') !== false) {
    echo "Email '{$email2}' is valid.<br>";
} else {
    echo "Email '{$email2}' is NOT valid.<br>";
}
```

If you run this by navigating to **http://localhost/codes/c27-ai-quality/validator_before.php**, you see it correctly validates the inputs.

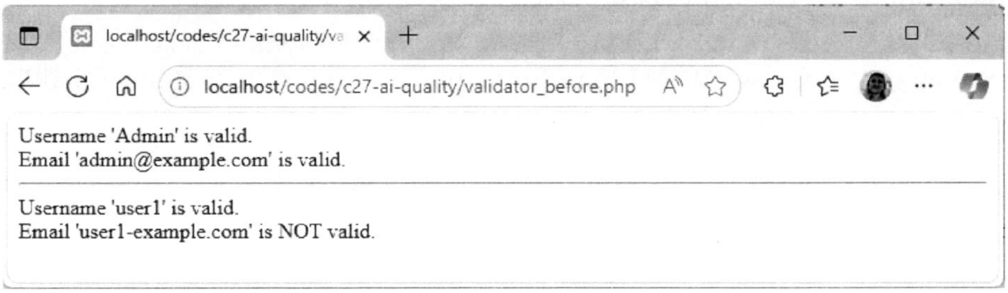

But the code itself is crying out for improvement!

Improving the code: A step-by-step guide

Now, let's use our AI assistant in VS Code to whip this script into shape. We will create a new, clean file for our class.

1. Create a new file named **UserValidator.php**.
2. **Prompt 1:** Refactor to a Class
    - Highlight all the code in validator_before.php.
    - Now, invoke your AI assistant and give it this clear instruction.
    - **AI Prompt:**

```
Take this PHP script and refactor it into a UserValidator class with methods for validateUsername and validateEmail.
```

Your AI assistant analyzes the procedural code and provides a class-based structure. Click **Accept** to AI generated code for your new UserValidator.php file. It should look something like this:

```php
<?php
class UserValidator
{
    public function validateUsername(string $username): bool
    {
        $length = strlen($username);
        return $length > 4 && $length < 15;
    }
    public function validateEmail(string $email): bool
    {
        return strpos($email, '@') !== false;
    }
}
```

This is already a huge improvement! The logic is now neatly organized and reusable.

3. **Prompt 2:** Improve Readability and Logic
    - The validateEmail() method is very basic. A simple @ symbol isn't enough for proper validation. We can ask the AI to improve this. Highlight the validateEmail() method and use this prompt.

- **AI Prompt:**

```
Review the validateEmail() method. Can you improve it by using filter_var() for better validation?
```

The AI replaces the weak **strops()** check with PHP's robust, built-in email validation function. Your method now looks like this:

```
    public function validateEmail(string $email): bool
    {
        return filter_var($email, FILTER_VALIDATE_EMAIL) !== false;
    }
```

This is much more reliable and demonstrates how AI can introduce you to better coding practices.

4. **Prompt 3:** Generate Documentation
    - Our class is functional, but it lacks comments. Let's fix that. Highlight the entire UserValidator class and give the AI this prompt.
    - **AI Prompt:**

```
Generate PHPDoc blocks for the UserValidator class and both of its methods.
```

The AI generates professional documentation for your code. Your final UserValidator.php file should now be complete:

```
<?php
/**
 * Provides methods for validating user data.
 */
class UserValidator
{
    /**
     * Validates a username based on its length.
     * Rule: Must be greater than 4 and less than 15 characters.
     *
     * @param string $username The username to validate.
     * @return bool True if the username is valid, false otherwise.
     */
    public function validateUsername(string $username): bool
    {
        $length = strlen($username);
        return $length > 4 && $length < 15;
    }
    /**
     * Validates an email address format.
     *
     * @param string $email The email to validate.
```

```
     * @return bool True if the email is valid, false otherwise.
     */
    public function validateEmail(string $email): bool
    {
        return filter_var($email, FILTER_VALIDATE_EMAIL) !== false;
    }
}
```

Setup for Testing with PHPUnit

Now for the final step: Writing automated tests. We need to install PHPUnit.

1. Open the terminal directly within VS Code (**...** → **Terminal** → **New Terminal**).
2. First, we need a **composer.json** file. Create it in the root of your **c27-ai-quality** folder and add the following content. This file tells Composer how to autoload our classes.

```
{
    "autoload": {
        "psr-4": {
            "App\\": "src/"
        }
    },
    "autoload-dev": {
        "psr-4": {
            "Tests\\": "tests/"
        }
    }
}
```

3. This configuration assumes our source code lives in a **src** folder. Let's create a **src** folder and move **UserValidator.php** inside it. Your project structure should now be:

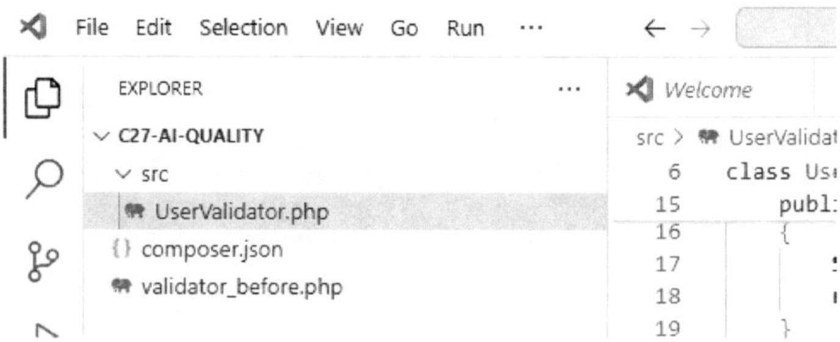

4. Now, in the terminal, run the following command to install PHPUnit:

```
composer require --dev phpunit/phpunit
```

This command will create a **vendor** folder, a **composer.lock** file, and install PHPUnit. The **--dev** flag indicates it's a development dependency, not needed for the live application.

5. Finally, let's configure PHPUnit. Create a new file in the project root named **phpunit.xml.dist** and add this configuration:

```
<?xml version="1.0" encoding="UTF-8"?>
<phpunit xmlns:xsi="http://www.w3.org/2001/XMLSchema-instance"
         xsi:noNamespaceSchemaLocation="https://schema.phpunit.de/10.0/phpunit.xsd"
         bootstrap="vendor/autoload.php"
         colors="true">
    <testsuites>
        <testsuite name="Unit">
            <directory>tests</directory>
        </testsuite>
    </testsuites>
</phpunit>
```

This tells PHPUnit to automatically load our files using the Composer autoloader and to look for test files in a **tests** directory.

6. **Prompt 4:** Generate Unit Tests
   - Create a **tests** folder in your project root.
   - Inside the **tests** folder, create a new file named **UserValidatorTest.php**.
   - Now, go back to your **src/UserValidator.php** file. Highlight the entire class content again. This time, we'll ask the AI to write tests for us.
   - **AI Prompt:**

```
Write a basic PHPUnit test class for the UserValidator. Include a test case that checks
for a valid email and one that checks for an invalid email.
```

Your AI assistant generates a complete test file. Click **Accept** for the result in UserValidatorTest.php. It looks very similar to this:

```
<?php
namespace Tests;
use App\UserValidator;
use PHPUnit\Framework\TestCase;
class UserValidatorTest extends TestCase
{
    private $validator;
    protected function setUp(): void
    {
        parent::setUp();
        $this->validator = new UserValidator();
```

```
    }
    public function testValidateEmailReturnsTrueForValidEmail(): void
    {
        $this->assertTrue(
            $this->validator->validateEmail('test@example.com'),
            "A valid email address should return true."
        );
    }
    public function testValidateEmailReturnsFalseForInvalidEmail(): void
    {
        $this->assertFalse(
            $this->validator->validateEmail('test-example.com'),
            "An invalid email address should return false."
        );
    }
}
```

Bridging the gap: Learned concepts and application implementation

Let's pause and reflect on what we just accomplished. We started with a simple but messy script (validator_before.php). Through a series of prompts, we used AI to:

- **Refactor** the procedural logic into a well-structured UserValidator class. This makes the code reusable and organized.
- **Improve** the validation logic by using a more robust built-in PHP function (filter_var). This makes the code more reliable.
- **Document** the class and its methods using PHPDoc blocks. This makes the code easier for other developers (and our future selves) to understand.
- **Generate tests** by creating a UserValidatorTest class. This provides an automated safety net to ensure our code works as expected.

This workflow—refactor, improve, document, and test—is the cornerstone of professional software development. AI has transformed it from a time-consuming process into a fast, interactive partnership.

Running and testing

Now for the moment of truth! Let's run the tests we just generated.

1. Go to your VS Code terminal, which should still be in the c27-ai-quality directory.
2. Run the following command:

```
./vendor/bin/phpunit
```

3. You see a successful output, indicating that all tests passed!

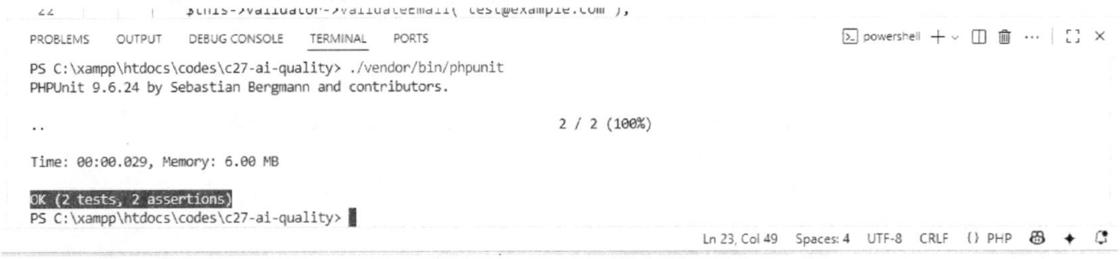

Exploring application behaviour: A practical run-through

What happens when we make a mistake? Let's simulate introducing a bug.

1. Go to **src/UserValidator.php**.
2. Change the **validateUsername()** method to have an error. For example, change > to < in the first condition:

```
// INTRODUCE A BUG!
public function validateUsername(string $username): bool
{
    $length = strlen($username);
    // This is now incorrect!
    return $length < 4 && $length < 15;
}
```

3. Now, go back to your terminal and run the tests again:

```
./vendor/bin/phpunit
```

4. This time, you see a failure! PHPUnit tells you exactly which test failed and why. This is the power of automated testing—it instantly catches regressions (bugs introduced into previously working code).

```
FAILURES!
Tests: 5, Assertions: 5, Failures: 1.
```

5. The output pinpoints that the test for a valid username failed, because it expected true but got false. Before you continue, remember to fix the bug in UserValidator.php!

Harnessing refactoring and testing in real-world contexts

In a professional environment, code is constantly changing. New features are added, and bugs are fixed. An automated test suite is the single most important tool for maintaining stability in a large project. When you work on a team, running the tests before you submit your code is mandatory. It proves that your changes work and haven't broken anyone else's code. This cycle of coding, testing, and refactoring is what allows large applications like Facebook, Google, and Amazon to be updated daily without falling apart.

Wrapping up

In this chapter, we took a massive leap into the world of professional coding practices. You learned that building software isn't just about writing the initial code, but also about refining, documenting, and testing it to ensure long-term quality and stability.

- **AI-powered refactoring:** You learned how to transform messy, procedural code into clean, object-oriented classes using simple AI prompts.
- **Code documentation:** We saw how AI can instantly generate professional PHPDoc blocks, making your code understandable and maintainable.
- **Automated testing:** You were introduced to the fundamental concept of unit testing and learned how it acts as a safety net against bugs.
- **PHPUnit setup:** You successfully set up a professional testing environment using Composer and PHPUnit.
- **AI test generation:** You discovered the incredible ability of AI to write comprehensive unit tests for your code, saving you time and effort.
- **The professional workflow:** Most importantly, you experienced the complete cycle: writing code, refactoring it for quality, documenting it for clarity, and testing it for correctness.

Congratulations! You have just learned a set of skills that many junior developers take months or even years to grasp. By treating your AI assistant not just as a code generator but as a quality assurance partner, you are already ahead of the curve. You now understand that good code is reliable and easy to understand, and you have the tools to make that happen.

As we move forward, we will continue to build on this foundation. In the next chapter, we'll begin the grand culmination, *Chapter 28: Phase 1 – The idea and the plan,* where we will integrate every AI skill you've learned to build a more complex project from start to finish.

Chapter 28

Section 08: The grand culmination – Building ConnectSphere

Phase 1 – The idea and the plan

What you'll learn

- Product management thinking
- Writing a requirements document
- Crafting user stories
- Defining project scope
- Creating a Minimum Viable Product (MVP)

Introduction: From a spark to a specification

Welcome to the grand culmination of this book and your capstone project! Over the next four chapters, we will build a complete, modern web application from the ground up, applying everything you've learned and pushing your skills to a professional level. This project is called **ConnectSphere**, a social platform designed to be clean, fast, and intelligent.

But here's a secret that every seasoned developer knows: **every great application begins not with code, but with a clear idea**.

Before we write a single line of PHP, we must first put on our **Product Manager** hats. Our job in this chapter is to define *what* we are building, *who* we are building it for, and *why*. We will do this by creating a **Product Requirements Document (PRD)**, which is the single most critical first step in any project. This document will serve as our North Star, guiding every decision we make throughout the project's four-phase lifecycle:

- Plan
- Design
- Develop, and
- Launch

Let's get planning!

The vision: ConnectSphere Product Requirements Document (PRD)

A **Product Requirements Document**, or **PRD**, is a formal document that outlines the purpose, features, and functionality of a product. It's the blueprint that ensures everyone—from developers to designers—is working towards the same goal. Below is the official PRD for our project.

Product name: ConnectSphere

Vision: A clean, fast, and intuitive social platform for users to share life updates and connect with friends, enhanced with smart, AI-driven suggestions.

Target audience: Students and young professionals looking for a straightforward social network.

Full feature set & user stories: User stories are a powerful way to describe a feature from an end-user's perspective. They follow a simple template:

```
"As a [type of user], I want to [perform some action] so that I can [achieve some goal]."
```

They keep our development focused on creating real value for people.

- **User Authentication**
  - "As a **new visitor**, I want to **register for an account** using my email and a secure password so that I can join the platform."
  - "As a **registered user**, I want to **log in** to my account so that I can access my profile and feed."

  - "As a **logged-in user**, I want to **log out** of my account to secure my session."

- **Profiles**
  - "As a **user**, I want to have a **personal profile page** where I can see my own posts and information."
  - "As a **user**, I want to **view the profiles of other users** to see their posts and decide if I want to connect with them."
- **Posting**
  - "As a **user**, I want to **write and publish short text-based posts** to share what's on my mind with my friends."
- **News Feed**
  - "As a **user**, I want to see a **chronological feed of posts from my friends** on my home page so I can keep up with their updates."
- **Friend System**
  - "As a **user**, I want to **send friend requests** to other users to build my network."
  - "As a **user**, I want to **view my pending friend requests** so I can **accept or decline** them."
  - "As a **user**, I want to see a **list of my current friends**."
- **Interactions**
  - "As a **user**, I want to **'like' a post** in my feed to show my appreciation."
  - "As a **user**, I want to **'comment' on a post** to engage in a conversation."
- **AI Suggestions**
  - "As a **user**, I want to **discover new people to connect with** based on mutual friends, and I want to see a friendly, AI-generated reason why we might know each other."

Defining our scope: The book's core features

The PRD we just created describes the *full vision* for ConnectSphere. It's a fantastic product! However, trying to build every single feature at once is a common trap for new developers. The professional approach is to define a **Minimum Viable Product (MVP)**. An MVP is the version of a new product that allows the team to collect the maximum amount of validated learning about customers with the least effort. In our case, it means we'll build the most essential, foundational features first.

While the PRD outlines the complete dream, **this book will focus on building the essential backbone of the application**. This ensures we can create a high-quality, functional project within the scope of our learning journey.

Our development scope

For the remainder of this book, we will build the following core features to bring our MVP to life:

- **User Registration and Login:** The absolute essential. Without this, we have no users!
- **Friend System (sending, accepting, viewing):** The core of any social network is the connection between people.
- **Posting (creating new text posts):** Users need a way to create content and express themselves.
- **AI-powered Friend Suggestions:** This is our "wow" feature—the smart functionality that makes our app stand out and directly ties into the "Next-Gen" promise of this book's title.

We are intentionally leaving out the news feed, likes, and comments for now. While important, they can be added later. Our MVP is focused, powerful, and achievable.

Wrapping up

In this chapter, we took the critical first step in building a major application—we planned it. We didn't write any code, but we accomplished something just as important.

- **Thinking like a pro:** We stepped into the role of a Product Manager to define a clear vision.
- **Created a blueprint:** We have a professional Product Requirements Document (PRD) that clearly outlines the vision for "ConnectSphere."
- **Understood user needs:** We wrote user stories to ensure our features are focused on providing value to our target audience.
- **Defined a clear scope:** We identified our Minimum Viable Product (MVP) to focus our development efforts on the most critical features.
- **Set for success:** With this plan, we are no longer just coding randomly; we are building towards a well-defined goal.

Congratulations on completing the planning phase! You now have a professional PRD and a focused scope for development, a foundation that will make the entire coding process smoother and more successful. You've learned that building great software is as much about thinking and planning as it is about writing code.

Next up, we'll put on our architect hats to design the database and project structure in ***Chapter 29: Phase 2 - Design and architecture***.

Chapter 29

Section 08: The grand culmination – Building ConnectSphere

Phase 2 – Design and architecture

What you'll learn

- Database schema design
- Writing SQL CREATE TABLE statements
- Mapping a user's application journey
- Creating a professional project structure
- Using phpMyAdmin to build a database

Introduction: Architecting for success

With our clear plan from the Product Requirements Document in hand, we now transition from **Product Manager** to **Software Architect**. This chapter is all about designing the technical blueprint for ConnectSphere. A solid technical design is like the foundation of a house; without it, even the best-looking structure will eventually run into problems. By taking the time to design our database, organize our files, and map out how a user will navigate the application, we translate the **what** from our PRD into the **how** of our code. This crucial step will make the development process in the next chapter faster, more organized, and far more professional.

Designing the database schema

Before we can store any information—users, posts, or friendships—we need to design the database that will hold it. The blueprint for a database is called a **schema**.

Based on our MVP scope from the last chapter, we need three primary **things** or **Entities**:

- **Users:** This entity will store information about each person who signs up, like their username, email, and password.
- **Posts:** This will store the content created by users, such as the text of their update.
- **Friendships:** This entity will track the connections between users.

Now, let's define the Relationships between these entities:

- **Users to Posts (One-to-Many):** This is a straightforward relationship. **One** user can write **many** posts. However, **one** post can only belong to a single user. We can link them by storing the user's ID with each post they create.
- **Users to Friendships (Many-to-Many):** This relationship is a bit more complex. **One** user can be friends with **many** other users. At the same time, each of those other users can also be friends with **many** people. To handle this, we need a special **linking** table. Our friendships table is that link. It will hold pairs of user IDs to represent a connection and a status (e.g., 'pending' or 'accepted').

Creating the database in phpMyAdmin

Now that we've designed our schema, it's time to build it. We will translate our schema into SQL (Structured Query Language), the language used to communicate with databases like MySQL. We'll use phpMyAdmin, the database management tool included with XAMPP, to get this done.

Launch phpMyAdmin

1. Open the **XAMPP Control Panel**.
2. Ensure the **Apache** and **MySQL** modules are started (they should be highlighted in green).

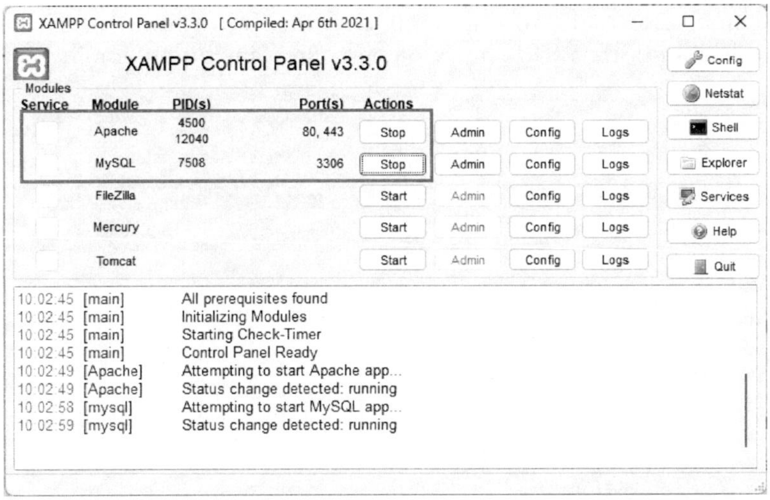

3. Click the **Admin** button next to MySQL. This opens **phpMyAdmin** in your web browser.

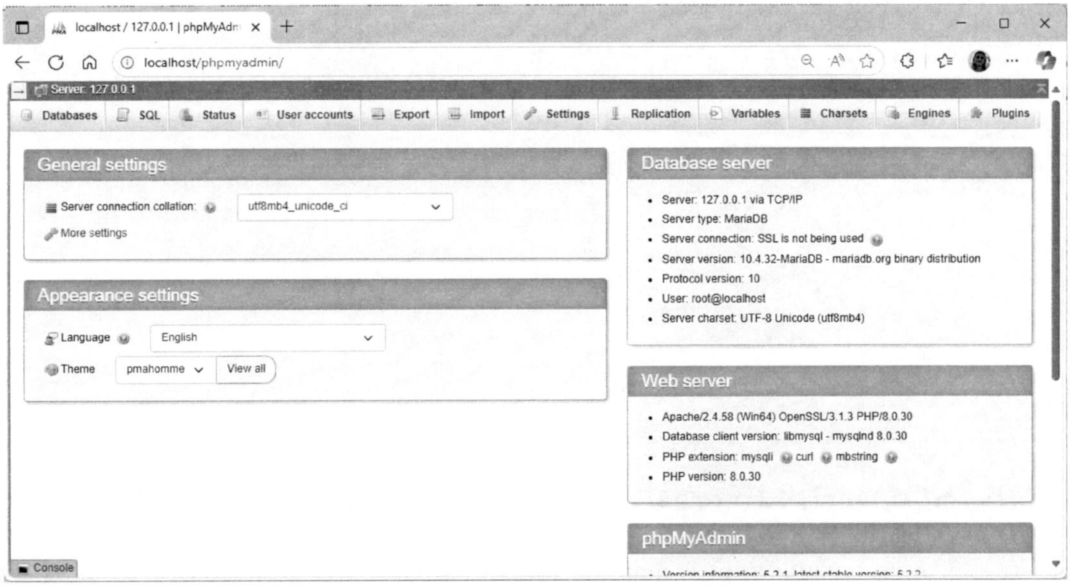

Create the database

1. In the main phpMyAdmin window, click on the **Databases** tab at the top.
2. Under the **Create database** section, enter the database name: **connectsphere_db**.

3. For the collation, select **utf8mb4_general_ci** from the dropdown. This is a standard character set that supports a wide range of characters, including emojis.

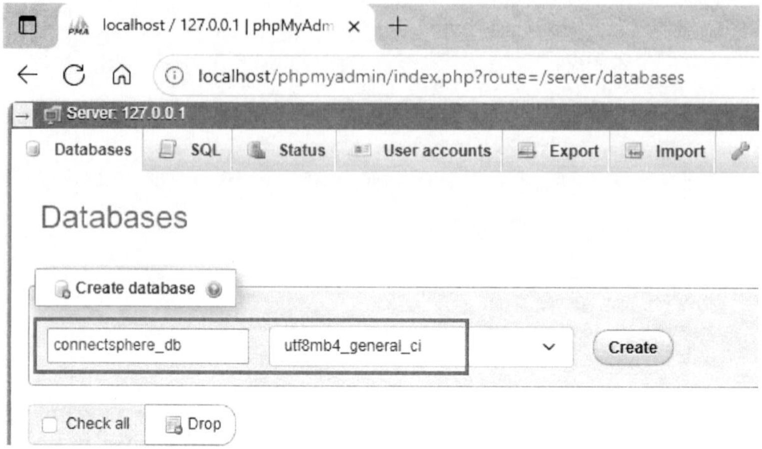

4. Click **Create**. You've now created an empty database!

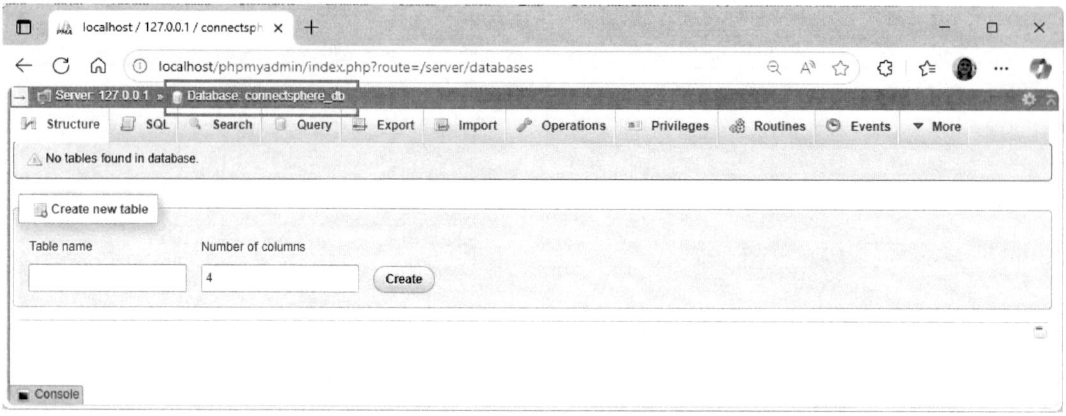

Run the SQL script to create tables

Now we will run a single script containing three CREATE TABLE statements to build the structure for our entities.

1. Select your newly created **connectsphere_db** from the left-hand sidebar.
2. Click on the **SQL** tab at the top of the main panel.
3. Copy the entire block of SQL code below and paste it into the large text box.

```
-- Table structure for table users
```

```
CREATE TABLE users (
  user_id INT(11) NOT NULL AUTO_INCREMENT,
  username VARCHAR(50) NOT NULL,
  email VARCHAR(100) NOT NULL,
  password_hash VARCHAR(255) NOT NULL,
  created_at TIMESTAMP NOT NULL DEFAULT CURRENT_TIMESTAMP,
  PRIMARY KEY (user_id),
  UNIQUE KEY email (email)
) ENGINE=InnoDB DEFAULT CHARSET=utf8mb4;

-- Table structure for table posts
CREATE TABLE posts (
  post_id INT(11) NOT NULL AUTO_INCREMENT,
  user_id INT(11) NOT NULL,
  content TEXT NOT NULL,
  created_at TIMESTAMP NOT NULL DEFAULT CURRENT_TIMESTAMP,
  PRIMARY KEY (post_id),
  KEY user_id (user_id),
  CONSTRAINT posts_ibfk_1 FOREIGN KEY (user_id) REFERENCES
             users (user_id) ON DELETE CASCADE
) ENGINE=InnoDB DEFAULT CHARSET=utf8mb4;

-- Table structure for table friendships
CREATE TABLE friendships (
  friendship_id INT(11) NOT NULL AUTO_INCREMENT,
  user_one_id INT(11) NOT NULL,
  user_two_id INT(11) NOT NULL,
  status ENUM('pending','accepted') NOT NULL,
  action_user_id INT(11) NOT NULL,
  PRIMARY KEY (friendship_id),
  KEY user_one_id (user_one_id),
  KEY user_two_id (user_two_id),
  CONSTRAINT friendships_ibfk_1 FOREIGN KEY (user_one_id)
             REFERENCES users (user_id) ON DELETE CASCADE,
  CONSTRAINT friendships_ibfk_2 FOREIGN KEY (user_two_id)
             REFERENCES users (user_id) ON DELETE CASCADE
) ENGINE=InnoDB DEFAULT CHARSET=utf8mb4;
```

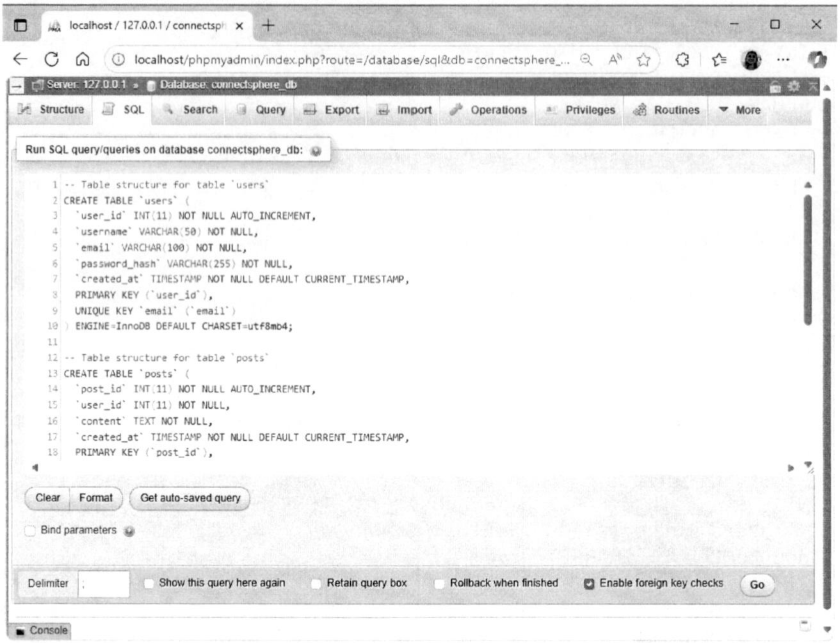

4. Click the **Go** button at the bottom right of the text box.
5. If everything is successful, you see a success message.

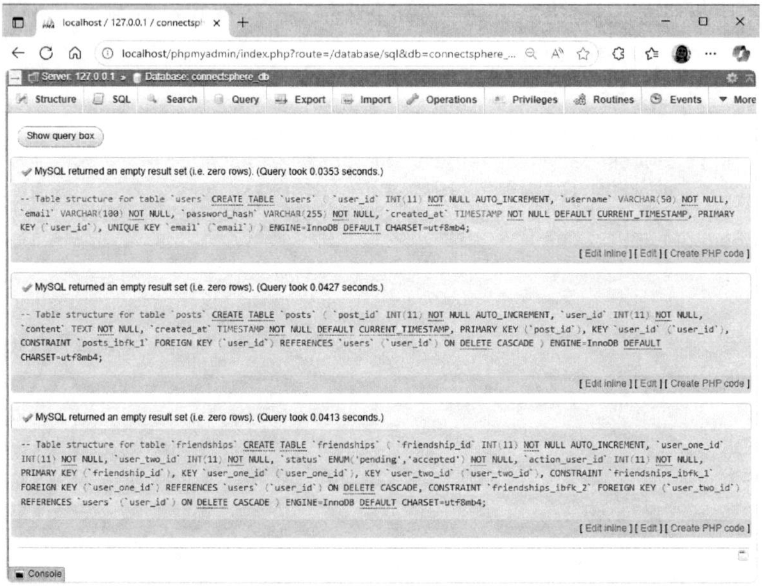

6. Click on the **Structure** tab, under **connectsphere_db**, you can now see your three tables: friendships, posts, and users. You have officially built the data foundation for your application!

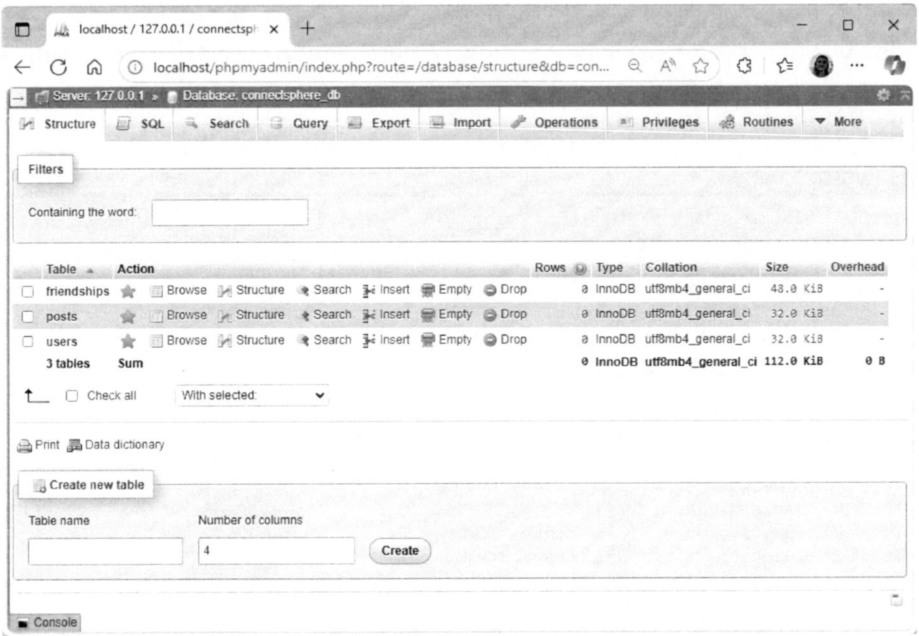

Let's quickly break down what we defined for our tables:

- **INT(11):** An integer.
- **VARCHAR(255):** A variable-length string of text up to 255 characters.
- **TEXT:** A long-form block of text.
- **TIMESTAMP:** Automatically records the date and time when data is created.
- **ENUM:** A special type that can only have one of the values from a predefined list (e.g., 'pending' or 'accepted').
- **PRIMARY KEY:** A unique identifier for each row in the table.
- **AUTO_INCREMENT:** Tells MySQL to automatically assign the next available number for the PRIMARY KEY.
- **FOREIGN KEY:** Creates a link between two tables, ensuring data integrity. For example, you can't create a post for a user_id that doesn't exist in the users table.

Insert dummy data for testing

To properly test our application, especially features like friend suggestions, we need some data to work with. The following SQL script will first **delete all existing data** to prevent errors and then populate our tables with 42 users, a variety of posts, and a network of friendships.

> **Important:**
> The password for all users is **12345678**. The script uses the **hashed version** of this password.

1. Make sure your **connectsphere_db** is still selected.
2. Click on the **SQL** tab again.
3. Copy the entire SQL script and paste it into the text box.
4. Click **Go** to execute the script and insert the records.

```
-- DUMMY DATA FOR ConnectSphere
-- Step 1: Clear all existing data from the tables to prevent conflicts.
-- We disable foreign key checks to allow truncating tables in any order.
SET FOREIGN_KEY_CHECKS = 0;
TRUNCATE TABLE `friendships`;
TRUNCATE TABLE `posts`;
TRUNCATE TABLE `users`;
SET FOREIGN_KEY_CHECKS = 1;
-- Step 2: Insert new dummy data.
-- Hashed password for all users
-- This hash is: $2y$10$mknHjZIHCGXTpw8ugA6eK.pVWxKsyM0u5cGEnBuJ4r8/l10Oo.E/K
-- Insert 42 Dummy Users
INSERT INTO `users` (`user_id`, `username`, `email`, `password_hash`) VALUES
(1, 'Alice', 'alice@example.com', '$2y$10$mknHjZIHCGXTpw8ugA6eK.pVWxKsyM0u5cGEnBuJ4r8/l10Oo.E/K'),
(2, 'Bob', 'bob@example.com', '$2y$10$mknHjZIHCGXTpw8ugA6eK.pVWxKsyM0u5cGEnBuJ4r8/l10Oo.E/K'),
(3, 'Charlie', 'charlie@example.com', '$2y$10$mknHjZIHCGXTpw8ugA6eK.pVWxKsyM0u5cGEnBuJ4r8/l10Oo.E/K'),
(4, 'Diana', 'diana@example.com', '$2y$10$mknHjZIHCGXTpw8ugA6eK.pVWxKsyM0u5cGEnBuJ4r8/l10Oo.E/K'),
(5, 'Ethan', 'ethan@example.com', '$2y$10$mknHjZIHCGXTpw8ugA6eK.pVWxKsyM0u5cGEnBuJ4r8/l10Oo.E/K'),
(6, 'Fiona', 'fiona@example.com', '$2y$10$mknHjZIHCGXTpw8ugA6eK.pVWxKsyM0u5cGEnBuJ4r8/l10Oo.E/K'),
(7, 'George', 'george@example.com', '$2y$10$mknHjZIHCGXTpw8ugA6eK.pVWxKsyM0u5cGEnBuJ4r8/l10Oo.E/K'),
(8, 'Hannah', 'hannah@example.com', '$2y$10$mknHjZIHCGXTpw8ugA6eK.pVWxKsyM0u5cGEnBuJ4r8/l10Oo.E/K'),
(9, 'Ian', 'ian@example.com', '$2y$10$mknHjZIHCGXTpw8ugA6eK.pVWxKsyM0u5cGEnBuJ4r8/l10Oo.E/K'),
(10, 'Jane', 'jane@example.com', '$2y$10$mknHjZIHCGXTpw8ugA6eK.pVWxKsyM0u5cGEnBuJ4r8/l10Oo.E/K'),
(11, 'Kevin', 'kevin@example.com', '$2y$10$mknHjZIHCGXTpw8ugA6eK.pVWxKsyM0u5cGEnBuJ4r8/l10Oo.E/K'),
```

```
(12, 'Laura', 'laura@example.com',
'$2y$10$mknHjZIHCGXTpw8ugA6eK.pVWxKsyM0u5cGEnBuJ4r8/l10Oo.E/K'),
(13, 'Mike', 'mike@example.com',
'$2y$10$mknHjZIHCGXTpw8ugA6eK.pVWxKsyM0u5cGEnBuJ4r8/l10Oo.E/K'),
(14, 'Nora', 'nora@example.com',
'$2y$10$mknHjZIHCGXTpw8ugA6eK.pVWxKsyM0u5cGEnBuJ4r8/l10Oo.E/K'),
(15, 'Oscar', 'oscar@example.com',
'$2y$10$mknHjZIHCGXTpw8ugA6eK.pVWxKsyM0u5cGEnBuJ4r8/l10Oo.E/K'),
(16, 'Penny', 'penny@example.com',
'$2y$10$mknHjZIHCGXTpw8ugA6eK.pVWxKsyM0u5cGEnBuJ4r8/l10Oo.E/K'),
(17, 'Quinn', 'quinn@example.com',
'$2y$10$mknHjZIHCGXTpw8ugA6eK.pVWxKsyM0u5cGEnBuJ4r8/l10Oo.E/K'),
(18, 'Rachel', 'rachel@example.com',
'$2y$10$mknHjZIHCGXTpw8ugA6eK.pVWxKsyM0u5cGEnBuJ4r8/l10Oo.E/K'),
(19, 'Steve', 'steve@example.com',
'$2y$10$mknHjZIHCGXTpw8ugA6eK.pVWxKsyM0u5cGEnBuJ4r8/l10Oo.E/K'),
(20, 'Tina', 'tina@example.com',
'$2y$10$mknHjZIHCGXTpw8ugA6eK.pVWxKsyM0u5cGEnBuJ4r8/l10Oo.E/K'),
(21, 'Uma', 'uma@example.com', '$2y$10$mknHjZIHCGXTpw8ugA6eK.pVWxKsyM0u5cGEnBuJ4r8/l10Oo.E/K'),
(22, 'Victor', 'victor@example.com',
'$2y$10$mknHjZIHCGXTpw8ugA6eK.pVWxKsyM0u5cGEnBuJ4r8/l10Oo.E/K'),
(23, 'Wendy', 'wendy@example.com',
'$2y$10$mknHjZIHCGXTpw8ugA6eK.pVWxKsyM0u5cGEnBuJ4r8/l10Oo.E/K'),
(24, 'Xavier', 'xavier@example.com',
'$2y$10$mknHjZIHCGXTpw8ugA6eK.pVWxKsyM0u5cGEnBuJ4r8/l10Oo.E/K'),
(25, 'Yara', 'yara@example.com',
'$2y$10$mknHjZIHCGXTpw8ugA6eK.pVWxKsyM0u5cGEnBuJ4r8/l10Oo.E/K'),
(26, 'Zack', 'zack@example.com',
'$2y$10$mknHjZIHCGXTpw8ugA6eK.pVWxKsyM0u5cGEnBuJ4r8/l10Oo.E/K'),
(27, 'Amber', 'amber@example.com',
'$2y$10$mknHjZIHCGXTpw8ugA6eK.pVWxKsyM0u5cGEnBuJ4r8/l10Oo.E/K'),
(28, 'Brian', 'brian@example.com',
'$2y$10$mknHjZIHCGXTpw8ugA6eK.pVWxKsyM0u5cGEnBuJ4r8/l10Oo.E/K'),
(29, 'Chloe', 'chloe@example.com',
'$2y$10$mknHjZIHCGXTpw8ugA6eK.pVWxKsyM0u5cGEnBuJ4r8/l10Oo.E/K'),
(30, 'David', 'david@example.com',
'$2y$10$mknHjZIHCGXTpw8ugA6eK.pVWxKsyM0u5cGEnBuJ4r8/l10Oo.E/K'),
(31, 'Eva', 'eva@example.com', '$2y$10$mknHjZIHCGXTpw8ugA6eK.pVWxKsyM0u5cGEnBuJ4r8/l10Oo.E/K'),
(32, 'Frank', 'frank@example.com',
'$2y$10$mknHjZIHCGXTpw8ugA6eK.pVWxKsyM0u5cGEnBuJ4r8/l10Oo.E/K'),
(33, 'Grace', 'grace@example.com',
'$2y$10$mknHjZIHCGXTpw8ugA6eK.pVWxKsyM0u5cGEnBuJ4r8/l10Oo.E/K'),
(34, 'Henry', 'henry@example.com',
'$2y$10$mknHjZIHCGXTpw8ugA6eK.pVWxKsyM0u5cGEnBuJ4r8/l10Oo.E/K'),
(35, 'Ivy', 'ivy@example.com', '$2y$10$mknHjZIHCGXTpw8ugA6eK.pVWxKsyM0u5cGEnBuJ4r8/l10Oo.E/K'),
(36, 'Jack', 'jack@example.com',
'$2y$10$mknHjZIHCGXTpw8ugA6eK.pVWxKsyM0u5cGEnBuJ4r8/l10Oo.E/K'),
(37, 'Kate', 'kate@example.com',
'$2y$10$mknHjZIHCGXTpw8ugA6eK.pVWxKsyM0u5cGEnBuJ4r8/l10Oo.E/K'),
(38, 'Leo', 'leo@example.com', '$2y$10$mknHjZIHCGXTpw8ugA6eK.pVWxKsyM0u5cGEnBuJ4r8/l10Oo.E/K'),
(39, 'Mia', 'mia@example.com', '$2y$10$mknHjZIHCGXTpw8ugA6eK.pVWxKsyM0u5cGEnBuJ4r8/l10Oo.E/K'),
(40, 'Noah', 'noah@example.com',
'$2y$10$mknHjZIHCGXTpw8ugA6eK.pVWxKsyM0u5cGEnBuJ4r8/l10Oo.E/K'),
(41, 'Vaishali', 'vaishali@example.com',
'$2y$10$mknHjZIHCGXTpw8ugA6eK.pVWxKsyM0u5cGEnBuJ4r8/l10Oo.E/K'),
```

```
(42, 'Sharanam', 'sharanam@example.com',
'$2y$10$mknHjZIHCGXTpw8ugA6eK.pVWxKsyM0u5cGEnBuJ4r8/l10Oo.E/K');
-- Insert Dummy Posts
INSERT INTO `posts` (`user_id`, `content`) VALUES
(1, 'Just joined ConnectSphere! Excited to see what this is all about.'),
(2, 'Having a great day at the park. The weather is perfect!'),
(3, 'Working on a new coding project. It''s challenging but fun.'),
(4, 'Does anyone have a good book recommendation?'),
(5, 'Just finished a 5k run! Feeling accomplished.'),
(1, 'Thinking about what to have for dinner tonight.'),
(6, 'My cat is being extra cute today.'),
(7, 'Planning a trip for the holidays. Any suggestions?'),
(8, 'Just watched the latest blockbuster movie. It was amazing!'),
(9, 'Learning to play the guitar. My fingers hurt!'),
(10, 'Happy Friday everyone! Any fun plans for the weekend?'),
(2, 'Tried a new recipe for pasta, and it turned out delicious.'),
(11, 'Looking for advice on the best coffee shops in town.'),
(12, 'Started a new series on a streaming service. I''m hooked!'),
(13, 'The concert last night was incredible. What a performance!'),
(14, 'I love the autumn season. The colors are so beautiful.'),
(15, 'Building a new PC. Can''t wait to see how it performs.'),
(3, 'Finally debugged that piece of code that was giving me trouble.'),
(16, 'Gardening is so relaxing. My tomatoes are starting to ripen.'),
(17, 'Who else is excited for the game tonight?'),
(18, 'Just adopted a puppy! My heart is so full.'),
(19, 'Exploring a new hiking trail this weekend.'),
(20, 'Baking cookies is the best form of therapy.'),
(21, 'Attending a tech conference next week. Looking forward to it.'),
(22, 'Sometimes you just need a quiet day with a good book.'),
(23, 'Volunteering at the local shelter. It''s so rewarding.'),
(24, 'The new art exhibit downtown is a must-see.'),
(25, 'Trying to learn a new language. It''s harder than I thought!'),
(26, 'Nothing beats a morning walk to clear your head.'),
(27, 'Re-watching my favorite movie for the 10th time.'),
(28, 'The stars are so clear tonight.'),
(29, 'Just got back from a wonderful vacation.'),
(30, 'Working from home has its perks!'),
(31, 'That feeling when your code compiles on the first try.'),
(32, 'I think I''m going to start a new hobby.'),
(33, 'The local farmer''s market has the best fresh produce.'),
(34, 'Can''t believe it''s almost the end of the year.'),
(35, 'A cup of tea and a rainy day is the perfect combination.'),
(36, 'Just finished a great workout at the gym.'),
(37, 'The sunset was absolutely breathtaking this evening.'),
(38, 'Trying to be more mindful and present in the moment.'),
(39, 'Family game night is always the best night.'),
(40, 'Hello world! My first post on this platform.'),
(41, 'So excited to be building this app! #webdev'),
(41, 'Had a great time exploring the city today.'),
(41, 'Any good movie recommendations for the weekend?'),
(42, 'Testing out the new post feature. Seems to be working!'),
(42, 'Just finished a great book. Highly recommend it.'),
(42, 'Coffee and code, the perfect combination.');
-- Insert Dummy Friendships
-- 'accepted' status means they are friends
-- 'pending' status means a request has been sent
```

```
INSERT INTO `friendships` (`user_one_id`, `user_two_id`, `status`, `action_user_id`) VALUES
-- Alice's Friends (User 1)
(1, 2, 'accepted', 1),
(1, 3, 'accepted', 3),
(1, 4, 'accepted', 1),
-- Bob's Friends (User 2)
(2, 5, 'accepted', 2),
(2, 6, 'accepted', 6),
-- Charlie's Friends (User 3)
(3, 7, 'accepted', 3),
(3, 8, 'accepted', 8),
-- Connections for Suggestions (Friends of Friends)
(4, 9, 'accepted', 4), -- Diana is friends with Ian
-- Diana is friends with Jane (Alice should see Ian & Jane as suggestions)
(4, 10, 'accepted', 10),
(5, 11, 'accepted', 5), -- Ethan is friends with Kevin
-- Ethan is friends with Laura (Bob should see Kevin & Laura)
(5, 12, 'accepted', 12),
-- More Accepted Friendships
(6, 13, 'accepted', 6),
(7, 14, 'accepted', 14),
(8, 15, 'accepted', 8),
(9, 16, 'accepted', 9),
(10, 17, 'accepted', 17),
(11, 18, 'accepted', 11),
(12, 19, 'accepted', 19),
(13, 20, 'accepted', 13),
(15, 21, 'accepted', 15),
(16, 22, 'accepted', 22),
(17, 23, 'accepted', 17),
(18, 24, 'accepted', 24),
(19, 25, 'accepted', 19),
(20, 26, 'accepted', 20),
(21, 27, 'accepted', 27),
(22, 28, 'accepted', 22),
(23, 29, 'accepted', 29),
(24, 30, 'accepted', 24),
(25, 31, 'accepted', 25),
(26, 32, 'accepted', 32),
(27, 33, 'accepted', 27),
(28, 34, 'accepted', 34),
(29, 35, 'accepted', 29),
(30, 36, 'accepted', 30),
(31, 37, 'accepted', 37),
(32, 38, 'accepted', 32),
(33, 39, 'accepted', 39),
(34, 40, 'accepted', 34),
-- Pending Friend Requests
(1, 15, 'pending', 1),   -- Alice sent a request to Oscar
(16, 1, 'pending', 16),  -- Penny sent a request to Alice
(2, 20, 'pending', 2),   -- Bob sent a request to Tina
(25, 2, 'pending', 25),  -- Yara sent a request to Bob
(3, 30, 'pending', 30),  -- David sent a request to Charlie
(35, 4, 'pending', 35),  -- Ivy sent a request to Diana
-- Vaishali and Sharanam's Friendships
(41, 42, 'accepted', 41), -- Vaishali and Sharanam are friends
```

```
-- Common Friends
(1, 41, 'accepted', 1),    -- Alice is friends with Vaishali
(1, 42, 'accepted', 42),   -- Alice is friends with Sharanam
(2, 41, 'accepted', 41),    -- Bob is friends with Vaishali
(2, 42, 'accepted', 2),    -- Bob is friends with Sharanam
-- Unique Friends for Vaishali (so Sharanam can get them as suggestions)
(41, 3, 'accepted', 3),    -- Vaishali is friends with Charlie
(41, 5, 'accepted', 41),    -- Vaishali is friends with Ethan
-- Unique Friends for Sharanam (so Vaishali can get them as suggestions)
(42, 4, 'accepted', 4),    -- Sharanam is friends with Diana
(42, 6, 'accepted', 42),   -- Sharanam is friends with Fiona
-- Pending request
(41, 10, 'pending', 41); -- Vaishali sent a request to Jane
```

Setting up the project in VS Code

With the database ready, it's time to create our project's home. A clean, logical folder structure is the hallmark of a professional developer. It makes your code easier to find, manage, and scale.

Create the root project folder

1. Open your **File Explorer** (Windows) or **Finder** (Mac).
2. Navigate to your XAMPP installation directory. Inside, you will find a folder named **htdocs\codes**. This is the web root for your Apache server.
3. Inside **htdocs\codes**, create a new folder and name it **connectsphere**. The full path will be something like **C:\xampp\htdocs\codes\connectsphere**. This is our project's root folder.

Open the project in VS Code

1. Launch **Visual Studio Code**. Go to **File → Open Folder...**.
2. Navigate to and select your **connectsphere** folder. VS Code's explorer panel on the left now shows your empty project folder.

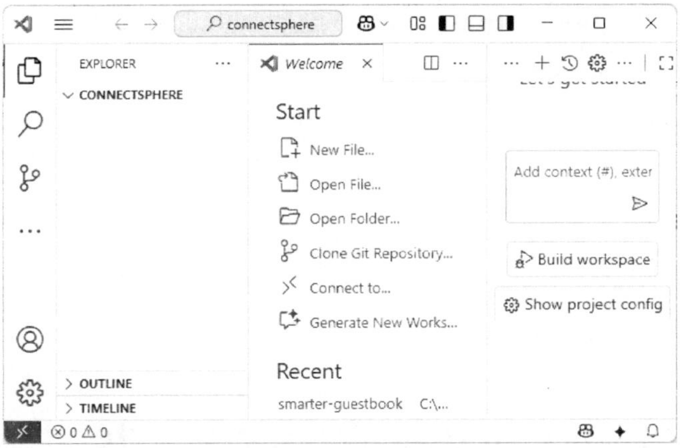

Build the professional folder structure

Now, let's create the subfolders and files that will organize our code. In the **VS Code Explorer**, use the **New Folder** and **New File** icons. Create the following folders and one file:

- **/public:** This folder will hold all files directly accessible via a web browser, like index.php, login.php, and our CSS/JavaScript files. This is a critical security practice known as separating the web root from your application logic.
- **/src**: This folder will contain our core PHP logic—functions, database connection handlers, and class files that do the heavy lifting. These files should not be directly accessible from the web.
- **/templates:** This will store reusable pieces of HTML, like our site header and footer. This helps us avoid repeating code on every page.
- **config.php:** This file will live in the root directory (connectsphere/). It will store sensitive information like our database credentials and other global application settings.

After creating these, your project structure in VS Code should look like this:

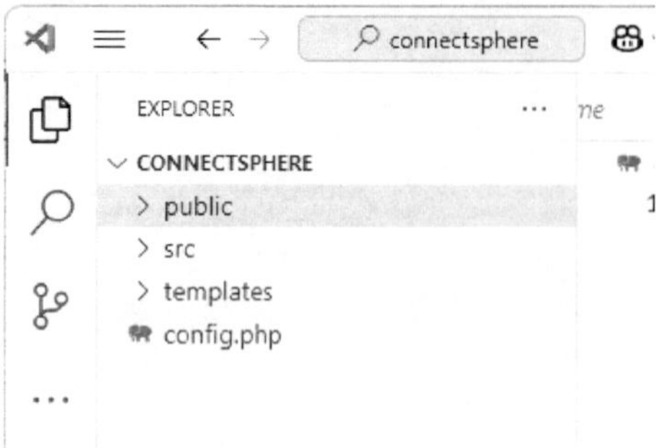

A quick review of essential VS Code extensions

As we prepare to code, make sure you have the essential extensions we set up in Chapter 3 installed. The two most important for this project are:

- **PHP Intelephense:** This will provide intelligent code completion, error highlighting, and function definitions, dramatically speeding up your development.
- **PHP Debug:** This will allow us to set breakpoints and step through our code to find and fix bugs, which will be invaluable as our application grows more complex.

Mapping the user flow

The final piece of our architectural puzzle is to map the user's journey through the application. A user flow diagram or list helps us visualize how a user will interact with our site to accomplish their goals. It ensures we don't miss any steps and that the navigation feels logical.

Here is the primary user flow for a new user joining ConnectSphere:

- **Registration:**
  - The user lands on the register.php page inside the /public folder.
  - They fill out the registration form (username, email, password).
  - Upon successful submission, their data is saved to the users table, and they are automatically redirected to the login.php page.
- **Login:**
  - The user is now on login.php in the /public folder.
  - They enter their email and password.

  - The system verifies their credentials. If correct, a PHP session is started to **remember** them, and they are redirected to the main home.php page.
- **Homepage & Interaction:**
  - The user lands on home.php (also in /public). This page is protected; unauthenticated users will be sent back to login.php.
  - On the homepage, they see a form to create a new post and the AI-powered **People You May Know** section.
  - They can visit another user's profile.php page.
- **Friendship Management:**
  - On another user's profile.php, they can click an **Add Friend** button. This creates a new entry in the friendships table with a 'pending' status.
  - The user can navigate to friends.php to see their pending friend requests and either **Accept** or **Decline** them, which updates the status in the friendships table.

This simple map gives us a clear path for development. We know exactly which pages we need to build and how they should connect.

Wrapping up

This chapter was all about laying a rock-solid foundation. While we wrote very little application code, the architectural work we've done is indispensable for a successful project.

- **Database designed:** We have a logical and efficient database schema ready to store all our application data.
- **Database built:** Our database, connectsphere_db, and its tables (users, posts, friendships) have been created in phpMyAdmin.
- **Project structured:** We have a professional, secure, and scalable file and folder structure set up in Visual Studio Code.
- **User journey mapped:** We have a clear user flow that will guide our development process and ensure a logical user experience.

Fantastic work! You have successfully completed the design and architecture phase of a real-world web application. Our database is built, our files are perfectly organized, and we have a clear map of what we need to build. This groundwork will pay massive dividends, making the coding process organized and efficient.

Now, it's time for the moment you've been waiting for. Let's start coding in *Chapter 30: Phase 3 - Core development*!

Chapter 30

Section 08: The grand culmination – Building ConnectSphere

Phase 3 – Core development

What you'll learn

- Building a secure registration system
- Hashing and verifying passwords
- Managing user sessions for login
- Creating reusable page layouts
- Implementing a friendship model
- Creating and displaying user content

Introduction: From blueprint to application

Welcome to the most exciting part of our journey! In the last two chapters, we put on our **Product Manager** and **Software Architect** hats. We meticulously planned what we're building with a Product Requirements Document and designed the technical blueprint by creating our database schema and project structure. The foundation is set, solid, and ready.

Now, the magic happens. We transition into the role of the **Developer**. This is where we take our clear plans and turn them into a living, breathing web application. We'll write the PHP, HTML, and CSS to bring the core features of ConnectSphere to life. We won't tackle everything at once; instead, we'll build our application in logical, feature-based chunks, starting with the most critical piece of any social platform: getting users signed up and logged in.

Let's start building!

Building the user authentication system

An authentication system is the gateway to your application. It handles user registration, login, and logout. A secure and smooth authentication flow is essential for gaining user trust. We'll build this system from scratch, focusing on modern security practices like password hashing to protect user data.

Setting up the configuration and database connection

Before we can build our forms, we need a way for our PHP scripts to securely connect to the **connectsphere_db** database we created in the last chapter. We'll do this by creating two central files.

Create the configuration file

First, we'll store our database credentials in the **config.php** file in the project's root directory. This keeps sensitive information in one place and out of our main application logic.

1. In the **VS Code Explorer** panel, right-click on the **connectsphere** folder and select **New File**.
2. Name the file **config.php**.
3. Add the following code. This code defines constants that hold your database connection details. Using constants makes it easy to update these values later without hunting through multiple files:

```
<?php
// -- DATABASE SETTINGS --
// Database host (e.g., "localhost" or "127.0.0.1")
define('DB_HOST', 'localhost');
// Database user
define('DB_USER', 'root');
// Database password (by default, it's empty for XAMPP)
define('DB_PASS', '');
// Database name
```

```
define('DB_NAME', 'connectsphere_db');
// -- AI SETTINGS --
// Your Google Gemini API Key
define('GEMINI_API_KEY', ' '); // KEEP THIS BLANK FOR NOW
// -- GENERAL SETTINGS --
// The base URL of your application
define('BASE_URL', 'http://localhost/connectsphere');
```

Leave the GEMINI_API_KEY blank for now; we'll discuss how to get this later in the chapter.

Create the database connection script

Next, we'll create a reusable script that uses these credentials to establish a connection to the database using PDO (PHP Data Objects). PDO is a modern, secure, and flexible way to work with databases in PHP.

1. In the **VS Code Explorer**, right-click on the **src** folder and select **New File**.
2. Name the file **db_connect.php**.
3. Add the following code to the file. This script tries to connect to the database and will display an error message if the connection fails, which is very helpful for debugging:

```
<?php
// Include the configuration file
require_once __DIR__ . '/../config.php';
// Data Source Name (DSN) for PDO connection
$dsn = "mysql:host=" . DB_HOST . ";dbname=" . DB_NAME . ";charset=utf8mb4";
// PDO options
$options = [
// Throw exceptions on errors
    PDO::ATTR_ERRMODE            => PDO::ERRMODE_EXCEPTION,
// Fetch associative arrays
    PDO::ATTR_DEFAULT_FETCH_MODE => PDO::FETCH_ASSOC,
// Use native prepared statements
    PDO::ATTR_EMULATE_PREPARES   => false,
];
try {
    // Create a new PDO instance
    $pdo = new PDO($dsn, DB_USER, DB_PASS, $options);
} catch (\PDOException $e) {
    // If connection fails, stop the script and show an error
    throw new \PDOException($e->getMessage(), (int)$e->getCode());
}
```

With these two files in place, we can now easily include src/db_connect.php in any script that needs to talk to the database.

Creating the HTML form for register.php

Our first user-facing page will be the registration form. This is where new visitors will create their accounts.

1. In the **VS Code Explorer**, right-click on the **public** folder and select **New File**.
2. Name the file **register.php**.
3. Enter the following HTML code. This creates a simple form asking for a username, email, and password. We'll style it properly in a later section:

```
<!DOCTYPE html>
<html lang="en">
<head>
    <meta charset="UTF-8">
    <meta name="viewport" content="width=device-width, initial-scale=1.0">
    <title>Register - ConnectSphere</title>
    </head>
<body>
    <div class="auth-container">
        <h2>Create Your Account</h2>
        <p>Join ConnectSphere to connect with friends.</p>
                <form action="register.php" method="POST">
            <div class="form-group">
                <label for="username">Username</label>
                <input type="text" id="username" name="username" required>
            </div>
            <div class="form-group">
                <label for="email">Email</label>
                <input type="email" id="email" name="email" required>
            </div>
            <div class="form-group">
                <label for="password">Password</label>
                <input type="password" id="password" name="password" required>
            </div>
            <button type="submit" class="btn">Register</button>
        </form>
        <p class="auth-switch">Already have an account?
           <a href="login.php">Login here</a></p>
    </div>
</body>
</html>
```

At this point, you could open **http://localhost/codes/connectsphere/public/register.php** in your browser, and you would see a basic, unstyled form. It doesn't do anything yet, but the structure is there.

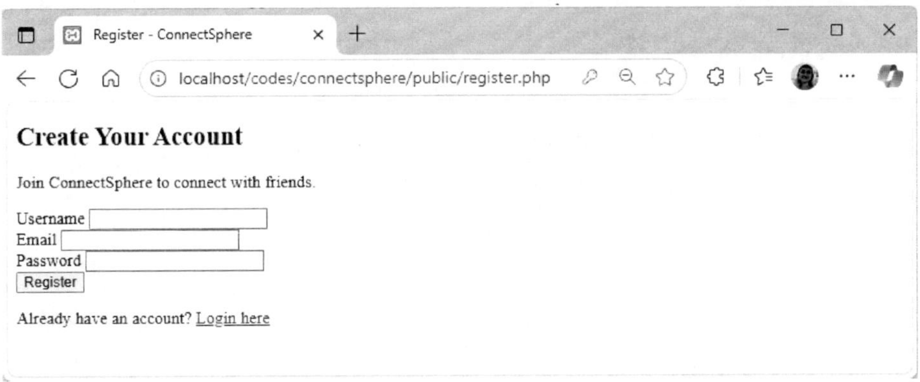

Writing the PHP backend for user validation and secure password hashing

Now, let's add the PHP logic that will process the form data when user clicks **Register**. We'll add this code to the very top of the register.php file, before the <!DOCTYPE html> line.

1. Open **public/register.php**.
2. Add the following PHP code block at the beginning of the file:

```
<?php
// Include the database connection script
require_once __DIR__ . '/../src/db_connect.php';
// Initialize an empty array to store error messages
$errors = [];
// Check if the form has been submitted
if ($_SERVER["REQUEST_METHOD"] == "POST") {
    // 1. Sanitize and validate inputs
    $username = trim($_POST['username']);
    $email = trim($_POST['email']);
    $password = $_POST['password'];
    if (empty($username)) {
        $errors[] = "Username is required.";
    }
    if (empty($email) || !filter_var($email, FILTER_VALIDATE_EMAIL)) {
        $errors[] = "A valid email is required.";
    }
    if (empty($password) || strlen($password) < 8) {
        $errors[] = "Password must be at least 8 characters long.";
    }
    // 2. If there are no validation errors, proceed
    if (empty($errors)) {
        try {
            // Check if the email already exists in the database
            $stmt = $pdo->prepare("SELECT user_id FROM users WHERE email = ?");
```

```
            $stmt->execute([$email]);
            if ($stmt->fetch()) {
                $errors[] = "An account with this email already exists.";
            } else {
                // 3. Hash the password for security
                $password_hash = password_hash($password, PASSWORD_DEFAULT);
                // 4. Insert the new user into the database
                $sql = "INSERT INTO users (username, email, password_hash)
                        VALUES (?, ?, ?)";
                $stmt = $pdo->prepare($sql);
                $stmt->execute([$username, $email, $password_hash]);
                // 5. Redirect to the login page upon successful registration
                header("Location: login.php?registered=success");
                exit();
            }
        } catch (PDOException $e) {
            // You might want to log this error instead of displaying it
            $errors[] = "Database error: " . $e->getMessage();
        }
    }
}
?>
```

3. Now, let's modify the HTML part slightly to display any error messages that might occur. Find the **<h2>Create Your Account</h2>** line in your HTML and add this PHP snippet right below it:

```
<?php if (!empty($errors)): ?>
    <div class="error-messages">
        <?php foreach ($errors as $error): ?>
            <p><?php echo htmlspecialchars($error); ?></p>
        <?php endforeach; ?>
    </div>
<?php endif; ?>
```

Your public/register.php file is now a complete, functional registration page. Let's break down the PHP logic:

- **require_once __DIR__ . '/../src/db_connect.php';:** This line includes our database connection script, giving us access to the $pdo object.
- **if ($_SERVER["REQUEST_METHOD"] == "POST"):** This checks if the user arrived at the page by submitting the form.
- **Validation:** We check that the username, email, and password fields aren't empty and that the email has a valid format.
- **Check for existing email:** We run a SELECT query to ensure no other user is already registered with that email address. This is crucial for preventing duplicate accounts.

- **password_hash():** This is the most important security function here. It takes the user's plain-text password and converts it into a long, secure "hash." We store this hash in the database, **never** the original password.
- **Prepared statements:** Notice the ? placeholders in our SQL queries. This is a prepared statement, which prevents a common vulnerability called SQL Injection. PDO handles safely inserting the user data into the query.
- **header("Location: ..."):** If registration is successful, this function redirects the user's browser to the login.php page. The exit() call is important to stop the script from executing further.

Building the login.php form and the PHP logic for password verification and session creation

Now that users can register, they need a way to log in. The login process involves fetching the user's record from the database and verifying that the password they provided matches the stored hash.

Create the login file and HTML form

1. In the **public** folder, create a new file named **login.php**.
2. Add the following HTML code. It's very similar to our registration form:

```
<!DOCTYPE html>
<html lang="en">
<head>
    <meta charset="UTF-8">
    <meta name="viewport" content="width=device-width, initial-scale=1.0">
    <title>Login - ConnectSphere</title>
</head>
<body>
    <div class="auth-container">
        <h2>Welcome Back!</h2>
        <p>Log in to see updates from your friends.</p>
        <form action="login.php" method="POST">
            <div class="form-group">
                <label for="email">Email</label>
                <input type="email" id="email" name="email" required>
            </div>
            <div class="form-group">
                <label for="password">Password</label>
                <input type="password" id="password" name="password" required>
            </div>
            <button type="submit" class="btn">Login</button>
        </form>
```

```
        <p class="auth-switch">Don't have an account? <a href="register.php">
           Register here</a></p>
    </div>
</body>
</html>
```

Add the PHP login logic

Just like with the registration page, we'll add the processing logic to the top of **public/login.php**:

```
<?php
// Always start the session at the very beginning of the script
session_start();
// If the user is already logged in, redirect them to the home page
if (isset($_SESSION['user_id'])) {
    header("Location: home.php");
    exit();
}
require_once __DIR__ . '/../src/db_connect.php';
$errors = [];
$success_message = '';
// Check if the user was redirected from a successful registration
if (isset($_GET['registered']) && $_GET['registered'] === 'success') {
    $success_message = "Registration successful! Please log in.";
}
if ($_SERVER["REQUEST_METHOD"] == "POST") {
    $email = trim($_POST['email']);
    $password = $_POST['password'];
    if (empty($email) || empty($password)) {
        $errors[] = "Both email and password are required.";
    } else {
        try {
            // 1. Find the user by email
            $stmt = $pdo->prepare("SELECT user_id, username, password_hash
                                   FROM users WHERE email = ?");
            $stmt->execute([$email]);
            $user = $stmt->fetch();
            // 2. Verify the password
            if ($user && password_verify($password, $user['password_hash'])) {
                // 3. Password is correct, so start a new session
                session_regenerate_id(true); // Security measure
                $_SESSION['user_id'] = $user['user_id'];
                $_SESSION['username'] = $user['username'];
                // 4. Redirect to the main application page
                header("Location: home.php");
                exit();
            } else {
                // Invalid credentials
```

```
                $errors[] = "Invalid email or password.";
            }
        } catch (PDOException $e) {
            $errors[] = "Database error: " . $e->getMessage();
        }
    }
}
?>
```

Again, let's add a spot in the HTML to show error or success messages. Place this code right below the <h2>Welcome Back!</h2> line:

```
<?php if ($success_message): ?>
    <div class="success-message">
        <p><?php echo htmlspecialchars($success_message); ?></p>
    </div>
<?php endif; ?>
<?php if (!empty($errors)): ?>
    <div class="error-messages">
        <?php foreach ($errors as $error): ?>
            <p><?php echo htmlspecialchars($error); ?></p>
        <?php endforeach; ?>
    </div>
<?php endif; ?>
```

Here's the breakdown of the login logic:

- **session_start():** This function is crucial. It either starts a new session or resumes an existing one. It must be called before any HTML is outputted to the browser.
- **password_verify():** This is the counterpart to password_hash(). It safely compares the plain-text password the user just entered with the hash we have stored in the database. It returns true if they match and false if they don't.
- **$_SESSION:** This is a PHP "superglobal" array. We can store data in it (like the user's ID and username), and that data will persist across different pages as long as the user's session is active. This is how our application "remembers" who is logged in.
- **session_regenerate_id(true):** This is a security best practice that generates a new session ID after a user logs in, helping to prevent session fixation attacks.

Implementing the logout.php script and protecting pages from unauthenticated access

The final pieces of our authentication system are logging out and protecting pages that should only be accessible to logged-in users.

Create the logout script

This is the simplest script of all. Its only job is to destroy the session data and redirect the user to the login page.

1. In the **public** folder, create a new file named **logout.php**.
2. Add this code:

```
<?php
session_start(); // Resume the session
// Unset all of the session variables
$_SESSION = [];
// Destroy the session
session_destroy();
// Redirect to the login page
header("Location: login.php");
exit();
```

Create a page protection script

We need a simple, reusable way to protect pages. We'll create a script that checks if a user is logged in. If they are not, it will immediately send them to the login page.

1. In the **src** folder, create a new file named **auth_check.php**.
2. Add this code:

```
<?php
// Start the session if it's not already started
if (session_status() === PHP_SESSION_NONE) {
    session_start();
}
// Check if the user_id session variable is not set
if (!isset($_SESSION['user_id'])) {
    // If not logged in, redirect to the login page
    header("Location: login.php");
    exit(); // Stop script execution
}
```

Now, at the top of any page we want to protect (like home.php, which we will create soon), we can simply add require_once __DIR__ . '/../src/auth_check.php';. Our authentication system is now complete and secure!

Designing the core layout and CSS

A consistent look and feel are vital for a good user experience. We don't want to copy and paste our navigation bar and footer into every single file. Instead, we'll create reusable template files for our header and footer.

Creating reusable header.php and footer.php templates

Create the header file

The header will contain the top part of our HTML, including the navigation bar and the link to our stylesheet.

1. In the **templates** folder, create a new file named **header.php**.
2. Add the following code. Notice the PHP logic inside the navigation bar—it will show different links depending on whether the user is logged in or not:

```
<?php
// templates/header.php
if (session_status() === PHP_SESSION_NONE) {
    session_start();
}
?>
<!DOCTYPE html>
<html lang="en">
<head>
    <meta charset="UTF-8">
    <meta name="viewport" content="width=device-width, initial-scale=1.0">
    <title><?php echo isset($page_title) ? htmlspecialchars($page_title) :
                 'ConnectSphere'; ?></title>
    <link rel="stylesheet" href="css/style.css">
</head>
<body>
    <header class="main-header">
        <div class="container">
            <a href="home.php" class="logo">ConnectSphere</a>
            <nav class="main-nav">
                <ul>
                    <?php if (isset($_SESSION['user_id'])): ?>
                        <li><a href="home.php">Home</a></li>
                        <li><a href="profile.php?id=<?php echo $_SESSION['user_id'];
                                    ?>">My Profile</a></li>
                        <li><a href="friends.php">Friends</a></li>
                        <li><a href="search.php">Search</a></li> <!-- New Link -->
                        <li><a href="logout.php">Logout</a></li>
                    <?php else: ?>
```

```
                        <li><a href="login.php">Login</a></li>
                        <li><a href="register.php">Register</a></li>
                    <?php endif; ?>
                </ul>
            </nav>
        </div>
    </header>
    <main class="main-content">
        <div class="container">
```

Create the footer file

The footer is simpler. It just closes the main content div, the <body> tag, and the <html> tag.

1. In the **templates** folder, create a new file named **footer.php**.
2. Add this code:

```
<?php
// templates/footer.php
?>
</div>
</main>
<footer class="main-footer">
    <div class="container">
        <p>© <?php echo date('Y'); ?> ConnectSphere. All rights reserved.</p>
    </div>
</footer>
</body>
</html>
```

Writing the main style.css file

Now let's add some style to make our application look like a modern social media site. We'll use a clean, card-based layout with a blue and white color scheme.

- Inside the **public** folder, create a new folder named **css**.
- Inside the new **css** folder, create a file named **style.css**.
- Add the following CSS. This is a substantial block of code that styles everything from the body and fonts to our forms, buttons, navigation, and future post cards:

```
/* --- Global Styles & Variables --- */
:root {
    --primary-color: #007bff;
    --primary-hover: #0056b3;
    --light-bg: #f8f9fa;
    --border-color: #dee2e6;
    --text-color: #333;
```

```
    --light-text: #6c757d;
    --white: #fff;
    --danger: #dc3545;
    --success: #28a745;
}
body {
    font-family: -apple-system, BlinkMacSystemFont, 'Segoe UI', Roboto,
                 'Helvetica Neue', Arial, sans-serif;
    margin: 0;
    background-color: var(--light-bg);
    color: var(--text-color);
    line-height: 1.6;
}
.container {
    max-width: 960px;
    margin: 0 auto;
    padding: 0 15px;
}
a {
    color: var(--primary-color);
    text-decoration: none;
}
a:hover {
    text-decoration: underline;
}
/* --- Header & Navigation --- */
.main-header {
    background-color: var(--white);
    border-bottom: 1px solid var(--border-color);
    padding: 1rem 0;
    position: sticky;
    top: 0;
    z-index: 1000;
}
.main-header .container {
    display: flex;
    justify-content: space-between;
    align-items: center;
}
.logo {
    font-size: 1.5rem;
    font-weight: bold;
    color: var(--text-color);
}
.logo:hover {
    text-decoration: none;
}
.main-nav ul {
    margin: 0;
    padding: 0;
    list-style: none;
```

```
    display: flex;
    gap: 1.5rem;
}
.main-nav a {
    font-weight: 500;
    color: var(--text-color);
}
.main-nav a:hover {
    color: var(--primary-color);
    text-decoration: none;
}
/* --- Main Content --- */
.main-content {
    padding: 2rem 0;
}
/* --- Authentication Forms --- */
.auth-container {
    max-width: 400px;
    margin: 2rem auto;
    padding: 2rem;
    background-color: var(--white);
    border: 1px solid var(--border-color);
    border-radius: 8px;
    box-shadow: 0 4px 6px rgba(0,0,0,0.05);
}
.auth-container h2 {
    margin-top: 0;
    text-align: center;
}
.auth-container p {
    text-align: center;
    color: var(--light-text);
}
.form-group {
    margin-bottom: 1rem;
}
.form-group label {
    display: block;
    margin-bottom: 0.5rem;
    font-weight: 500;
}
.form-group input {
    width: 100%;
    padding: 0.75rem;
    border: 1px solid var(--border-color);
    border-radius: 4px;
    box-sizing: border-box; /* Important for padding */
}
.btn {
    display: block;
    width: 100%;
```

```
    padding: 0.75rem;
    border: none;
    border-radius: 4px;
    background-color: var(--primary-color);
    color: var(--white);
    font-size: 1rem;
    font-weight: bold;
    cursor: pointer;
    transition: background-color 0.2s ease;
}
.btn:hover {
    background-color: var(--primary-hover);
}
form .btn {
    width: 100%
}
.auth-switch {
    margin-top: 1.5rem;
    font-size: 0.9rem;
}
/* --- Messages --- */
.error-messages, .success-message {
    padding: 1rem;
    margin-bottom: 1rem;
    border-radius: 4px;
    border: 1px solid;
}
.error-messages {
    background-color: #f8d7da;
    color: #721c24;
    border-color: #f5c6cb;
}
.success-message {
    background-color: #d4edda;
    color: #155724;
    border-color: #c3e6cb;
}
/* --- Footer --- */
.main-footer {
    text-align: center;
    padding: 2rem 0;
    color: var(--light-text);
    margin-top: 2rem;
    border-top: 1px solid var(--border-color);
}
```

Now, let's update our register.php and login.php files to use our new layout!

- **For register.php:**
  - **Delete** everything from **<!DOCTYPE html>** to **<body>**.

- **Replace** it with this single line:

```
<?php $page_title = 'Register'; require_once __DIR__ . '/../templates/header.php'; ?>
```

- **Delete** the closing **</body>** and **</html>** tags at the end of the file.
- Replace them with:

```
<?php require_once __DIR__ . '/../templates/footer.php'; ?>
```

- **For login.php:** Do the exact same thing, but **change** the **$page_title** to **'Login'**.

If you now visit **http://localhost/codes/connectsphere/public/register.php**, you see a beautifully styled form with our new navigation bar and footer. Our application is starting to look professional!

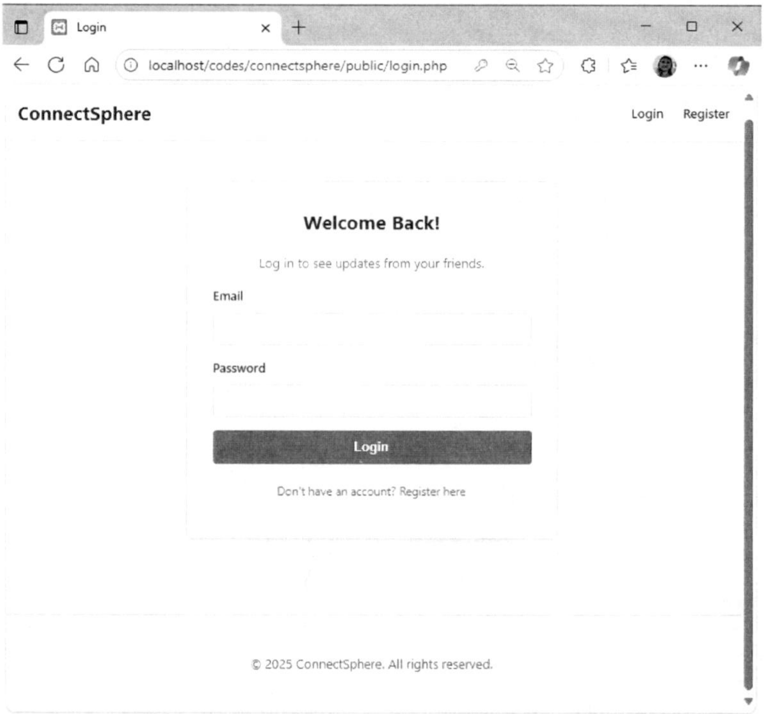

Implementing the social graph: Friends

The core of any social network is the connection between users. We'll now implement the "friend" system, allowing users to view profiles, send requests, and accept or decline them.

Building profile.php to display user information and an "Add Friend" button

This page will display a user's basic information. The most interesting part is the logic for the "Add Friend" button, which will change depending on the relationship between the logged-in user and the user whose profile is being viewed.

1. In the **public** folder, create a new file named **profile.php**.
2. Add the following complete code. It fetches the profile user's data and then runs a second query to determine the friendship status between them and the currently logged-in user:

```
<?php
require_once __DIR__ . '/../src/auth_check.php';
require_once __DIR__ . '/../src/db_connect.php';
// Get the user ID from the URL, default to the logged-in user if not provided
$profile_user_id = isset($_GET['id']) ? (int)$_GET['id'] : $_SESSION['user_id'];
$current_user_id = $_SESSION['user_id'];
try {
    // Fetch the profile user's information
    $stmt = $pdo->prepare("SELECT user_id, username, created_at
                           FROM users WHERE user_id = ?");
    $stmt->execute([$profile_user_id]);
    $profile_user = $stmt->fetch();
    if (!$profile_user) {
        // Handle case where user does not exist
        $page_title = 'User Not Found';
        require_once __DIR__ . '/../templates/header.php';
        echo "<p>Sorry, this user could not be found.</p>";
        require_once __DIR__ . '/../templates/footer.php';
        exit();
    }
    // Determine the friendship status between the current user and the
    // profile user
    $friendship_status = 'not_friends';
    if ($current_user_id !== $profile_user_id) {
        $stmt = $pdo->prepare(
            "SELECT status, action_user_id FROM friendships
             WHERE (user_one_id = ? AND user_two_id = ?) OR (user_one_id = ?
             AND user_two_id = ?)"
        );
        $stmt->execute([$current_user_id, $profile_user_id, $profile_user_id,
                        $current_user_id]);
        $friendship = $stmt->fetch();
        if ($friendship) {
            if ($friendship['status'] === 'accepted') {
                $friendship_status = 'friends';
            } elseif ($friendship['status'] === 'pending') {
                if ($friendship['action_user_id'] == $current_user_id) {
```

```
                    $friendship_status = 'request_sent';
                } else {
                    $friendship_status = 'request_received';
                }
            }
        }
    }
    // Fetch posts for the profile user
    $stmt_posts = $pdo->prepare("SELECT content, created_at FROM posts
                                 WHERE user_id = ? ORDER BY created_at DESC");
    $stmt_posts->execute([$profile_user_id]);
    $posts = $stmt_posts->fetchAll();
} catch (PDOException $e) {
    // Handle database errors
    die("Error: " . $e->getMessage());
}
$page_title = htmlspecialchars($profile_user['username']) . "'s Profile";
require_once __DIR__ . '/../templates/header.php';
?>
<div class="profile-header">
    <h1><?php echo htmlspecialchars($profile_user['username']); ?></h1>
    <p>Member since: <?php echo date("F j, Y", strtotime($profile_
                     user['created_at'])); ?></p>
    <?php if ($current_user_id !== $profile_user_id): ?>
        <div class="friend-action">
            <?php if ($friendship_status === 'not_friends'): ?>
                <a href="friend_action.php?action=add&id=<?php
                     echo $profile_user_id; ?>" class="btn">Add Friend</a>
            <?php elseif ($friendship_status === 'request_sent'): ?>
                <button class="btn" disabled>Friend Request Sent</button>
            <?php elseif ($friendship_status === 'request_received'): ?>
                <a href="friend_action.php?action=accept&id=<?php
                     echo $profile_user_id; ?>" class="btn">Accept Request</a>
            <?php elseif ($friendship_status === 'friends'): ?>
                <a href="friend_action.php?action=remove&id=<?php
                     echo $profile_user_id; ?>" class="btn btn-danger">Unfriend</a>
            <?php endif; ?>
        </div>
    <?php endif; ?>
</div>
<div class="profile-content">
    <h2>Posts by <?php echo htmlspecialchars($profile_user['username']);
?></h2>
    <?php if (count($posts) > 0): ?>
        <div class="post-list">
            <?php foreach ($posts as $post): ?>
                <div class="post-card">
                    <p class="post-content"><?php echo nl2br(htmlspecialchars
                            ($post['content'])); ?></p>
                    <p class="post-meta">Posted on <?php echo date("g:i
                            A - F j, Y", strtotime($post['created_at'])); ?></p>
```

```
                </div>
            <?php endforeach; ?>
        </div>
    <?php else: ?>
        <p><?php echo htmlspecialchars($profile_user['username']); ?> has not
                 posted anything yet.</p>
    <?php endif; ?>
</div>
<?php
require_once __DIR__ . '/../templates/footer.php';
?>
```

Let's break down the logic:

- **Fetching profile data:** The script gets the user ID from the URL (?id=...). It then fetches that user's data from the users table.
- **Checking friendship status:** This is the complex part. It queries the friendships table to see if a row exists for the two users.
    - If a row exists with status = 'accepted', they are friends.
    - If status = 'pending', we check the action_user_id to see who sent the request. If the current logged-in user sent it, the status is request_sent. If the other user sent it, the status is request_received.
    - If no row exists, they are not_friends.
- **Displaying the button:** The HTML uses an if/elseif block to display the correct button based on the $friendship_status variable. Each button links to a new script, friend_action.php, which we will create next.

Writing the backend PHP to handle sending and managing friend requests

All the friendship buttons on the profile page will point to a single script that handles the logic. This keeps our code organized. This single file handles all friendship-related actions (add, accept, remove) to keep our logic centralized.

1. In the **public** folder, create a new file named **friend_action.php**.
2. Add this code:

```
<?php
require_once __DIR__ . '/../src/auth_check.php';
require_once __DIR__ . '/../src/db_connect.php';
// Get required IDs
$current_user_id = $_SESSION['user_id'];
$other_user_id = isset($_GET['id']) ? (int)$_GET['id'] : 0;
$action = isset($_GET['action']) ? $_GET['action'] : '';
```

```
// Basic validation
if ($other_user_id === 0 || $current_user_id === $other_user_id) {
    header("Location: home.php"); // Redirect if invalid
    exit();
}
try {
    if ($action === 'add') {
        // Send a friend request
        $sql = "INSERT INTO friendships (user_one_id, user_two_id,
                status, action_user_id) VALUES (?, ?, 'pending', ?)";
        $stmt = $pdo->prepare($sql);
        $stmt->execute([$current_user_id, $other_user_id, $current_user_id]);
    } elseif ($action === 'accept') {
        // Accept a friend request
        $sql = "UPDATE friendships SET status = 'accepted', action_user_id = ?
                WHERE (user_one_id = ? AND user_two_id = ?)
                AND status = 'pending'";
        $stmt = $pdo->prepare($sql);
        $stmt->execute([$current_user_id, $other_user_id, $current_user_id]);
    } elseif ($action === 'remove') {
        // Remove a friend or decline a request
        $sql = "DELETE FROM friendships
                WHERE (user_one_id = ? AND user_two_id = ?) OR
                (user_one_id = ? AND user_two_id = ?)";
        $stmt = $pdo->prepare($sql);
        $stmt->execute([$current_user_id, $other_user_id, $other_user_id,
                       $current_user_id]);
    }
} catch (PDOException $e) {
    // Ideally, log this error
    die("Database error: " . $e->getMessage());
}
// Redirect back to the user's profile
header("Location: profile.php?id=" . $other_user_id);
exit();
```

This script is the engine of our friend system. It uses a switch-like if/elseif structure to perform the correct database operation (INSERT, UPDATE, or DELETE) based on the action parameter in the URL. After performing the action, it always redirects the user back to the profile they were just viewing.

Creating friends.php to list pending requests

Finally, users need a page where they can see all the friend requests they've received in one place. This page gives users a central place to manage their connections.

1. In the **public** folder, create **friends.php**.

2. Add this code:

```
<?php
require_once __DIR__ . '/../src/auth_check.php';
require_once __DIR__ . '/../src/db_connect.php';
$current_user_id = $_SESSION['user_id'];
$page_title = 'Manage Friends';
try {
    // Fetch pending friend requests for the current user
    $sql_requests = "SELECT u.user_id, u.username
                     FROM users u
                     JOIN friendships f ON u.user_id = f.user_one_id
                     WHERE f.user_two_id = ? AND f.status = 'pending'";
    $stmt_requests = $pdo->prepare($sql_requests);
    $stmt_requests->execute([$current_user_id]);
    $pending_requests = $stmt_requests->fetchAll();
    // Fetch current friends
    $sql_friends = "SELECT u.user_id, u.username FROM users u
                    JOIN friendships f ON
                    (u.user_id = f.user_one_id OR u.user_id = f.user_two_id)
                    WHERE (f.user_one_id = ? OR f.user_two_id = ?)
                    AND f.status = 'accepted' AND u.user_id != ?";
    $stmt_friends = $pdo->prepare($sql_friends);
    $stmt_friends->execute([$current_user_id, $current_user_id, $current_user_id]);
    $friends = $stmt_friends->fetchAll();
} catch (PDOException $e) {
    die("Database error: " . $e->getMessage());
}
require_once __DIR__ . '/../templates/header.php';
?>
<h1>Friends Management</h1>
<div class="friends-section">
    <h2>Pending Friend Requests</h2>
    <?php if (count($pending_requests) > 0): ?>
        <ul class="user-list">
            <?php foreach ($pending_requests as $request): ?>
                <li>
                    <span><?php echo htmlspecialchars($request['username']); ?>
                    </span>
                    <div class="actions">
                        <a href="friend_action.php?action=accept&id=<?php echo
                           $request['user_id']; ?>" class="btn">Accept</a>
                        <a href="friend_action.php?action=remove&id=<?php echo
                      $request['user_id']; ?>" class="btn btn-secondary">Decline</a>
                    </div>
                </li>
            <?php endforeach; ?>
        </ul>
    <?php else: ?>
        <p>You have no pending friend requests.</p>
    <?php endif; ?>
```

```
</div>
<div class="friends-section">
    <h2>Your Friends</h2>
    <?php if (count($friends) > 0): ?>
        <ul class="user-list">
            <?php foreach ($friends as $friend): ?>
                <li>
                    <a href="profile.php?id=<?php echo $friend['user_id']; ?>">
                        <?php echo htmlspecialchars($friend['username']); ?>
                    </a>
                    <div class="actions">
                        <a href="friend_action.php?action=remove&id=<?php echo
                         $friend['user_id']; ?>" class="btn btn-danger">Unfriend</a>
                    </div>
                </li>
            <?php endforeach; ?>
        </ul>
    <?php else: ?>
        <p>You haven't added any friends yet.</p>
    <?php endif; ?>
</div>
<?php require_once __DIR__ . '/../templates/footer.php'; ?>
```

This page runs two queries:

- One to get pending requests
- One to get all accepted friends

It then loops through these results to display two clear lists for the user. We'll need to add a bit more CSS to style.css to make these lists look good.

Open **public/css/style.css** and add these styles at the end:

```
/* --- Profile & Friends Page Styles --- */
.profile-header, .friends-section {
    background-color: var(--white);
    padding: 2rem;
    border: 1px solid var(--border-color);
    border-radius: 8px;
    margin-bottom: 2rem;
}
.profile-header {
    text-align: center;
}
.user-list {
    list-style: none;
    padding: 0;
}
.user-list li {
```

```
    display: flex;
    justify-content: space-between;
    align-items: center;
    padding: 1rem;
    border-bottom: 1px solid var(--border-color);
}
.user-list li:last-child {
    border-bottom: none;
}
.user-list .actions {
    display: flex;
    gap: 0.5rem;
}
.btn-secondary {
    background-color: var(--light-text);
}
.btn-secondary:hover {
    background-color: #5a6268;
}
.btn-danger {
    background-color: var(--danger);
}
```

Implementing content creation: Posts

The next feature for this chapter is giving users the ability to create content. We'll add a simple form to the homepage for creating posts and then display those posts on the user's profile page.

Adding the "Create a Post" form to the main home.php page

The homepage will be the main dashboard for a logged-in user.

1. In the **public** folder, create a new file named **home.php**.
2. Add this full code block:

```
<?php
require_once __DIR__ . '/../src/auth_check.php'; // Protect this page
require_once __DIR__ . '/../src/db_connect.php';
$page_title = 'Home';
$errors = [];
$success_message = '';
// Handle post creation
if ($_SERVER['REQUEST_METHOD'] === 'POST' && isset($_POST['post_content'])) {
    $content = trim($_POST['post_content']);
    if (empty($content)) {
        $errors[] = "Post content cannot be empty.";
    } else {
```

```
        try {
            $sql = "INSERT INTO posts (user_id, content) VALUES (?, ?)";
            // This line is correct and not related to the error.
            $stmt = $pdo->prepare($sql);
            $stmt->execute([$_SESSION['user_id'], $content]);
            $success_message = "Your post has been published!";
        } catch (PDOException $e) {
            $errors[] = "Failed to create post. Please try again.";
        }
    }
}
require_once __DIR__ . '/../templates/header.php';
?>
<h1>Welcome, <?php echo htmlspecialchars($_SESSION['username']); ?>
!</h1>
<div class="post-creation-box">
    <h2>Create a New Post</h2>
    <?php if ($success_message): ?>
        <div class="success-message">
            <p><?php echo $success_message; ?></p>
        </div>
    <?php endif; ?>
    <?php if (!empty($errors)): ?>
        <div class="error-messages">
            <?php foreach ($errors as $error): ?>
                <p><?php echo htmlspecialchars($error); ?></p>
            <?php endforeach; ?>
        </div>
    <?php endif; ?>
    <form action="home.php" method="POST">
        <textarea name="post_content" placeholder="What's on your mind?"
                  required></textarea>
        <button type="submit" class="btn">Post</button>
    </form>
</div>
<!-- AI Friend Suggestions will be loaded here -->
<div class="ai-suggestions">
    <h2>People You May Know</h2>
    <?php
    // Include the AI suggestion logic
    require_once __DIR__ . '/../src/ai_suggestions.php';
    if (!empty($processed_suggestions)):
        foreach ($processed_suggestions as $suggestion):
    ?>
            <div class="ai-suggestion-card">
                <h4>
                    <a href="profile.php?id=<?php echo $suggestion['user_id']; ?>">
                        <?php echo htmlspecialchars($suggestion['username']); ?>
                    </a>
                </h4>
                <p class="reason"><?php echo htmlspecialchars($suggestion['
```

```
                        ai_reason']); ?></p>
                     <p><small><?php echo $suggestion['mutual_friends']; ?>
                        mutual friend(s)</small></p>
                     <a href="friend_action.php?action=add&id=<?php echo $suggestion['
                        user_id']; ?>" class="btn">Add Friend</a>
                 </div>
             <?php
             endforeach;
         else:
             ?>
             <p>We don't have any new suggestions for you right now. Check
                back later!</p>
         <?php endif; ?>
 </div>
 <?php require_once __DIR__ . '/../templates/footer.php'; ?>
```

This page first requires auth_check.php to ensure only logged-in users can see it. It then displays a welcome message and a form. The PHP logic at the top handles the form submission, inserting the new post into the posts table.

Displaying a user's own posts on their profile page

Now let's go back to profile.php and replace the "No posts to show yet" placeholder with the user's actual posts.

1. Open **public/profile.php**.
2. Find the section with the **profile-content** div.
3. First, we need to add a query to fetch the posts. Add this code inside the **try** block, right after the **friendship status** logic (this we have already done in profile.php earlier):

```
// Fetch posts for the profile user
$stmt_posts = $pdo->prepare("SELECT content, created_at FROM posts
WHERE user_id = ? ORDER BY created_at DESC");
$stmt_posts->execute([$profile_user_id]);
$posts = $stmt_posts->fetchAll();
```

4. Finally, add the CSS for these new post elements to the end of **public/css/style.css**:

```
/* --- Post Creation & Display --- */
.post-creation-box, .post-card {
    background-color: var(--white);
    padding: 2rem;
    border: 1px solid var(--border-color);
    border-radius: 8px;
    margin-bottom: 2rem;
}
.post-creation-box textarea {
```

```
    width: 100%;
    min-height: 100px;
    padding: 0.75rem;
    border: 1px solid var(--border-color);
    border-radius: 4px;
    margin-bottom: 1rem;
    resize: vertical;
    box-sizing: border-box;
}
.post-card .post-content {
    margin-top: 0;
    font-size: 1.1rem;
}
.post-card .post-meta {
    font-size: 0.85rem;
    color: var(--light-text);
    margin-bottom: 0;
}
```

Integrating AI for smart friend suggestions

This is our "wow" feature. We will find users who are "friends of friends" and then use the Gemini AI to generate a friendly, natural-language reason why the current user might know them.

The logic - Finding "friends of friends" with SQL

First, we need a way to find potential connections. The best candidates are people who are not yet our friends but are friends with people we already know. This requires a complex SQL query. We will create a dedicated PHP script for this logic.

1. In the src folder, create a new file named ai_suggestions.php.
2. Add the following code. Read the comments carefully to understand how this powerful SQL query works. The placeholders have been updated to be unique to prevent execution errors:

```
<?php
// This script should only be included, not accessed directly
if (session_status() === PHP_SESSION_NONE) session_start();
if (!isset($pdo)) require_once 'db_connect.php';
function get_friend_suggestions($pdo, $user_id, $limit = 3)
{
    /*
     * This query finds "friends of friends."
     * It uses unique named placeholders (e.g., :user_id1, :user_id2) to ensure
     * compatibility and prevent "Invalid parameter number" errors.
```

```
    */
    $sql = "
        SELECT fof.friend_of_friend_id as user_id, u.username,
        COUNT(fof.friend_of_friend_id) as mutual_friends
        FROM (
            -- Find friends of the current user
            SELECT user_two_id as friend_id FROM friendships
            WHERE user_one_id = :user_id1 AND status = 'accepted'
            UNION
            SELECT user_one_id as friend_id FROM friendships
            WHERE user_two_id = :user_id2 AND status = 'accepted'
        ) AS my_friends
        JOIN (
            -- Find friends of those friends
            SELECT user_one_id as user_id, user_two_id as friend_of_friend_id
            FROM friendships WHERE status = 'accepted'
            UNION
            SELECT user_two_id as user_id, user_one_id as friend_of_friend_id
            FROM friendships WHERE status = 'accepted'
        ) AS fof ON my_friends.friend_id = fof.user_id
        JOIN users u ON fof.friend_of_friend_id = u.user_id
        WHERE fof.friend_of_friend_id != :user_id3
        AND fof.friend_of_friend_id NOT IN (
            -- Exclude people who are already friends or have pending requests
            SELECT user_two_id FROM friendships WHERE user_one_id = :user_id4
            UNION
            SELECT user_one_id FROM friendships WHERE user_two_id = :user_id5
        )
        GROUP BY fof.friend_of_friend_id, u.username
        ORDER BY mutual_friends DESC
        LIMIT :limitVal
    ";
    $stmt = $pdo->prepare($sql);
    // Bind the same user_id to all its placeholders
    $stmt->bindValue(':user_id1', $user_id, PDO::PARAM_INT);
    $stmt->bindValue(':user_id2', $user_id, PDO::PARAM_INT);
    $stmt->bindValue(':user_id3', $user_id, PDO::PARAM_INT);
    $stmt->bindValue(':user_id4', $user_id, PDO::PARAM_INT);
    $stmt->bindValue(':user_id5', $user_id, PDO::PARAM_INT);
    $stmt->bindValue(':limitVal', $limit, PDO::PARAM_INT);
    $stmt->execute();
    return $stmt->fetchAll();
}
function call_gemini_api($prompt)
{
    $api_key = GEMINI_API_KEY;
    if (empty($api_key)) {
        return "AI feature is not configured. (API key is missing)";
    }
    $url = 'https://generativelanguage.googleapis.com/v1beta/models/
            gemini-1.5-flash:generateContent?key=' . $api_key;
```

```
    $data = [
        'contents' => [
            [
                'parts' => [
                    ['text' => $prompt]
                ]
            ]
        ]
    ];
    $options = [
        'http' => [
            'header'  => "Content-type: application/json\r\n",
            'method'  => 'POST',
            'content' => json_encode($data),
            'ignore_errors' => true
        ]
    ];
    $context  = stream_context_create($options);
    $result = file_get_contents($url, false, $context);
    if ($result === FALSE) {
        return "Could not connect to the AI service.";
    }
    $response = json_decode($result, true);
    if (isset($response['candidates'][0]['content']['parts'][0]['text'])) {
        return trim($response['candidates'][0]['content']['parts'][0]['text']);
    } elseif (isset($response['error']['message'])) {
        return "AI Error: " . $response['error']['message'];
    } else {
        return "An unknown AI error occurred.";
    }
}
// Main logic to get and process suggestions
$suggestions = get_friend_suggestions($pdo, $_SESSION['user_id']);
$processed_suggestions = [];
foreach ($suggestions as $suggestion) {
    $prompt = "You are a helpful social media assistant. My name is
              {$_SESSION['username']}. I might know a person named
              {$suggestion['username']} because we have {$suggestion
              ['mutual_friends']} mutual friend(s). Write a short, friendly,
              one-sentence suggestion for why I should connect with them.
              Start the sentence with 'You might know {$suggestion['username']}...'
              and be encouraging. Do not use markdown.";
    $ai_reason = call_gemini_api($prompt);
    $processed_suggestions[] = [
        'user_id' => $suggestion['user_id'],
        'username' => $suggestion['username'],
        'mutual_friends' => $suggestion['mutual_friends'],
        'ai_reason' => $ai_reason
    ];
}
```

3. Finally, add the CSS for these new AI sugestion elements to the end of **public/css/style.css**:

```
.ai-suggestions {
    background-color: var(--white);
    padding: 2rem;
    border: 1px solid var(--border-color);
    border-radius: 8px;
    margin-bottom: 2rem;
}
.ai-suggestion-card {
    border: 1px solid var(--border-color);
    border-radius: 8px;
    padding: 1rem;
    margin-bottom: 1rem;
}
.ai-suggestion-card h4 {
    margin-top: 0;
}
.ai-suggestion-card .reason {
    font-style: italic;
    color: var(--light-text);
    border-left: 3px solid var(--primary-color);
    padding-left: 1rem;
    margin: 1rem 0;
}
```

Finding and adding Friends: The Search feature

A great social application allows users to find each other easily. We'll add a dedicated search page that lets users find others by their username.

Building the search.php page

This new page will contain a search form and display the results in a list, allowing users to visit profiles and add friends directly.

1. In the **public** folder, create a new file named **search.php**.
2. Add the following complete code. It handles both displaying the form and processing the search query:

```
<?php
require_once __DIR__ . '/../src/auth_check.php';
require_once __DIR__ . '/../src/db_connect.php';
$page_title = 'Search for Users';
$search_term = isset($_GET['q']) ? trim($_GET['q']) : '';
$results = [];
if (!empty($search_term)) {
```

```
    try {
        // Find users whose username is similar to the search term
        // Exclude the current user from the search results
        $sql = "SELECT user_id, username FROM users WHERE username LIKE ?
                AND user_id != ?";
        $stmt = $pdo->prepare($sql);
        // The '%' are wildcards, meaning it can match any sequence of characters
        $stmt->execute(['%' . $search_term . '%', $_SESSION['user_id']]);
        $results = $stmt->fetchAll();
    } catch (PDOException $e) {
        // In a real app, you would log this error
        die("Database search error.");
    }
}
require_once __DIR__ . '/../templates/header.php';
?>
<div class="search-container">
    <h1>Find New Friends</h1>
    <p>Search for other users on ConnectSphere by their username.</p>
    <form action="search.php" method="GET" class="search-form">
        <div class="form-group">
            <input type="text" name="q" placeholder="Enter a username..."
                   value="<?php echo htmlspecialchars($search_term); ?>" required>
        </div>
        <button type="submit" class="btn">Search</button>
    </form>
    <hr>
    <h2>Search Results</h2>
    <?php if (!empty($search_term)): ?>
        <?php if (count($results) > 0): ?>
            <ul class="user-list">
                <?php foreach ($results as $user): ?>
                    <li>
                        <a href="profile.php?id=<?php echo $user['user_id']; ?>">
                            <?php echo htmlspecialchars($user['username']); ?>
                        </a>
                        <div class="actions">
                            <a href="profile.php?id=<?php echo $user['user_id']; ?>"
                               class="btn btn-secondary">View Profile</a>
                        </div>
                    </li>
                <?php endforeach; ?>
            </ul>
        <?php else: ?>
            <p>No users found matching "<?php echo htmlspecialchars(
               $search_term); ?>".</p>
        <?php endif; ?>
    <?php else: ?>
        <p>Enter a username above to find users.</p>
    <?php endif; ?>
```

```
</div>
<?php require_once __DIR__ . '/../templates/footer.php'; ?>
```

Your home.php is now fully equipped with our intelligent feature! Before it will work, you need to get a Gemini API key.

How to get your Gemini API key

1. Visit the **Google AI** for **Developers** website.
2. Click on **Get API key in Google AI Studio**.
3. You may need to sign in with your **Google account**.
4. Follow the on-screen instructions to create a new API key.
5. Once you have your key (it will be a long string of letters and numbers), copy it.
6. Paste it into your **config.php** file as the value for the **GEMINI_API_KEY** constant.

Now, when you visit your home.php page (after creating a few users and friendships to test with), you will see personalized, AI-generated friend suggestions!

And with that, our core development is complete! Users can register, log in, manage friends, and create posts that display on their profiles.

Wrapping up

What a chapter! We went from a collection of empty folders and a database schema to a functional social application. We wrote a significant amount of code, but by building feature by feature, we created a powerful and professional core for ConnectSphere.

- **Secure authentication:** We built a complete user registration and login system from scratch, using password_hash() and password_verify() to protect user credentials.
- **Session management:** We learned to use PHP sessions ($_SESSION) to keep users logged in and protect pages from unauthorized access.
- **Reusable layouts:** We created a professional structure with a header and footer, ensuring a consistent look and feel across the entire application without repeating code.
- **Professional CSS:** We wrote a clean, modern stylesheet that gives our application a familiar social media design, including styles for forms, navigation, and content cards.
- **Friendship system:** We implemented the complete logic for a social graph, allowing users to send, accept, decline, and remove friends.

- **User search:** We added a crucial search feature, allowing users to proactively find and connect with others on the platform.
- **Content creation:** We built the functionality for users to create text-based posts and display them on their personal profile pages.
- **Advanced SQL:** We wrote a complex "friends of friends" query to find relevant connection opportunities within our social graph.
- **AI integration:** We successfully connected our PHP application to the Google Gemini API, sending dynamic prompts and parsing the JSON response.
- **Smart features:** We combined our SQL logic with AI to create a "wow" feature that provides real, contextual value to the user.

Congratulations! You have successfully navigated the most code-intensive phase of our project. You've brought the blueprint to life, writing the PHP, HTML, and CSS that form the very heart of ConnectSphere. You now have a working application with a professional look and feel, where users can register, log in, connect, interact, share content and discover new friends with the help of artificial intelligence. This is a massive achievement.

Take a moment to test the entire user flow: register a few accounts, make some friends, and see the AI suggestions come to life. In the final chapter, we'll focus on testing, debugging, and getting our application ready for the world in ***Chapter 31: Phase 4 – Launch***.

Chapter 31

Section 08: The grand culmination – Building ConnectSphere

Phase 4 – Launch

What you'll learn

- End-to-end application testing
- Debugging with browser tools
- Analyzing application behaviour
- Validating user stories
- Connecting theory to practice
- Preparing for deployment

Introduction: From functional to flawless

Welcome to the final phase of building ConnectSphere! In the last chapter, you masterfully transformed our architectural blueprints into a living, functional web application. The core features are in place, the database is communicating with our PHP code, and the application looks clean and professional. This is a monumental achievement, and you should be incredibly proud.

Now, we transition from the role of **Developer** to that of a **Quality Assurance Engineer**. The goal of this chapter isn't to write new features, but to polish, test, and deeply understand the application we've built. A professional developer knows that writing the code is only part of the job; ensuring it's robust, bug-free, and behaves as expected is just as critical.

We will walk through the entire application from a user's perspective, create a formal testing plan, learn how to hunt down bugs, and connect every feature we built back to the core PHP concepts you've mastered. This is the final step that takes our project from a developer's machine to a launch-ready product. Let's make it shine!

Final testing and debugging

Before any application goes live, it must be thoroughly tested. This process involves more than just clicking around to see if it works; it's a systematic check to ensure every feature meets the requirements we set out in our plan and that the application can gracefully handle unexpected user behavior.

Creating a testing checklist to validate all user stories

In Chapter 28, we created a Product Requirements Document (PRD) with a set of user stories. These stories are our contract—they define what the application *must* do to be considered a success. We can turn these stories directly into a testing checklist.

Here is our formal test plan. For each test, perform the described action and verify that you see the expected result:

User story	Test case	Steps to perform	Expected result
		User Authentication	
"As a new visitor, I want to register for an account..."	TC-01: Successful Registration	1. Navigate to register.php. 2. Fill in a unique username, a valid email, and a password (at least 8 characters). 3. Click the "Register" button.	You are redirected to login.php with a "Registration successful! Please log in." message.
"As a registered user, I want to log in..."	TC-02: Successful Login	1. Navigate to login.php. 2. Enter the email and password you just registered with. 3. Click the "Login" button.	You are redirected to home.php and see a "Welcome, [Your Username]!" message.
"As a logged-in user, I want to log out..."	TC-03: Successful Logout	1. While logged in, click the "Logout" link in the navigation bar.	You are redirected to the login.php page. The navigation bar now shows "Login" and "Register" links.

User story	Test case	Steps to perform	Expected result
Friend System			
"As a user, I want to send friend requests..."	TC-04: Send Friend Request	1. Log in as User A. 2. Use the search page to find User B. 3. Visit User B's profile. 4. Click the "Add Friend" button.	The button text changes to "Friend Request Sent" and becomes disabled.
"As a user, I want to view my pending friend requests so I can accept or decline them."	TC-05: Accept Friend Request	1. Log in as User B. 2. Navigate to the "Friends" page. 3. You should see a pending request from User A. 4. Click the "Accept" button.	The request disappears from the "Pending" list and User A now appears in the "Your Friends" list.
"As a user, I want to see a list of my current friends."	TC-06: View Friends List	1. As User B, stay on the "Friends" page. 2. Confirm User A is in the "Your Friends" list. 3. Click on User A's name to visit their profile.	On User A's profile, the button now says "Unfriend".
Posting			
"As a user, I want to write and publish short text-based posts..."	TC-07: Create a Post	1. Log in and navigate to home.php. 2. Type a message into the "What's on your mind?" text area. 3. Click the "Post" button.	A "Your post has been published!" success message appears.
"As a user, I want to have a personal profile page where I can see my own posts..."	TC-08: View Post on Profile	1. After creating a post, navigate to your own profile by clicking "My Profile".	Your new post appears at the top of the post list, with the content and timestamp.
AI Suggestions			
"As a user, I want to discover new people to connect with..."	TC-09: View AI Suggestions	1. Log in as a user with friends (e.g., 'Alice' from our dummy data). 2. Navigate to home.php. 3. Look at the "People You May Know" section.	You see suggestions for users who are friends with your friends, along with an AI-generated reason.

Find and fix any remaining bugs

Sometimes, bugs aren't obvious. A form might submit but not save data, or a page might look strange on different screen sizes. Professionals use specialized tools to diagnose these **invisible** problems.

Using browser developer tools - Browser's network tab

Your web browser has a powerful suite of **Developer Tools** that give you a behind-the-scenes look at how a website works. The **Network** tab is one of the most useful for a PHP developer.

1. **Open Developer tools:** In your browser (Chrome, Firefox, Edge), right-click anywhere on your **ConnectSphere** page and select **Inspect**, or press **F12**.

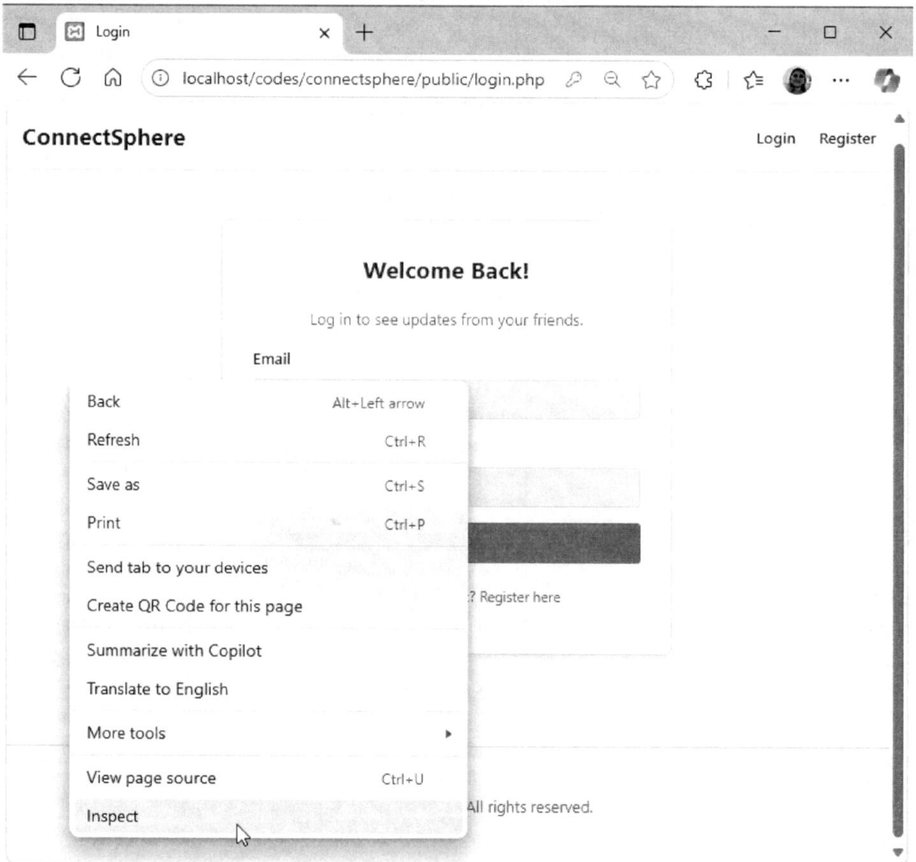

2. **Select the Network Tab:** Click on the **Network** tab in the panel that appears.

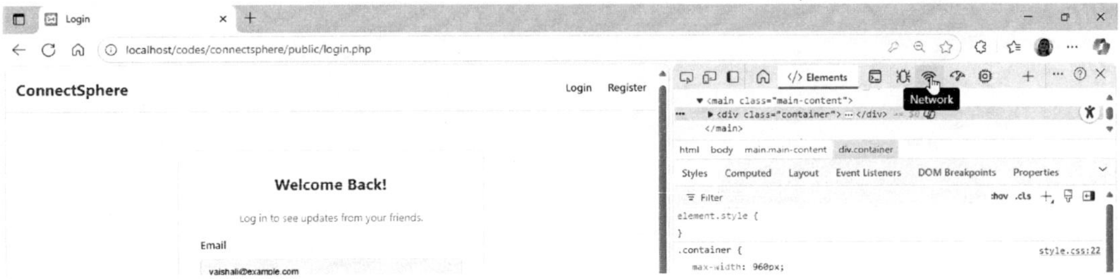

3. **Trace a POST Request:**
   - Navigate to your login.php page.
   - Make sure the **Network** tab is open and clear.
   - Fill in your login details and click the **Login** button.
   - You can see a new entry appear in the **Network** tab, likely named login.php.

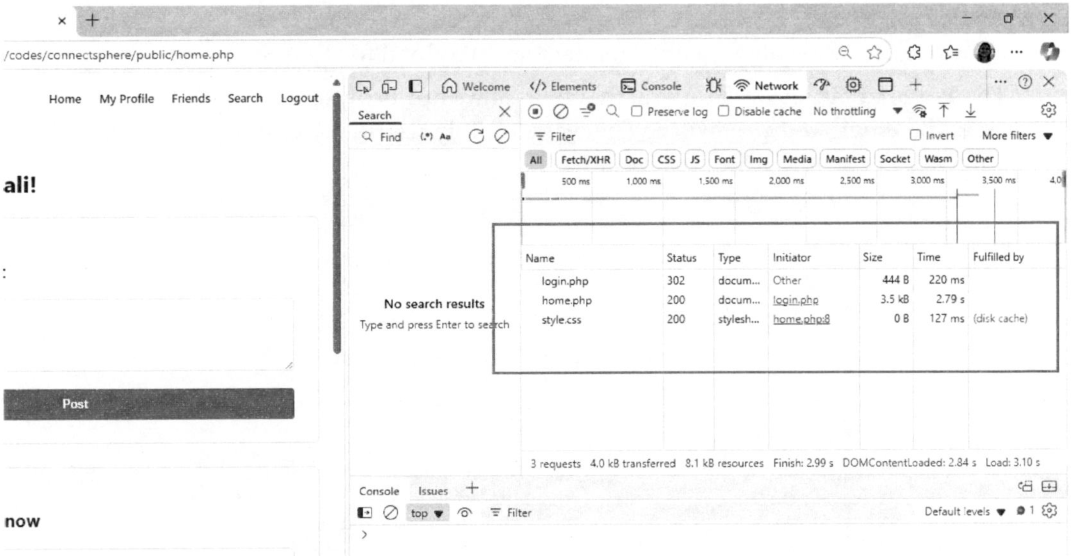

   - Click on the **login.php** name.

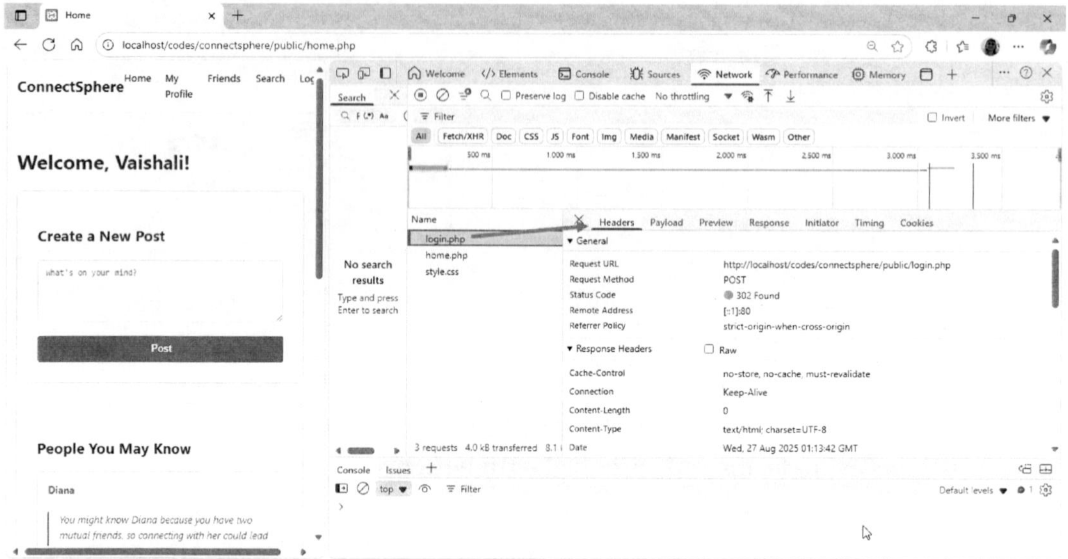

- Now, explore the sub-tabs like **Headers** and **Payload** (or **Request**).
- The **Payload** tab shows you exactly what data your browser sent to the server—in this case, the **email** and **password**. This is incredibly useful for debugging forms to make sure you are sending the correct data.

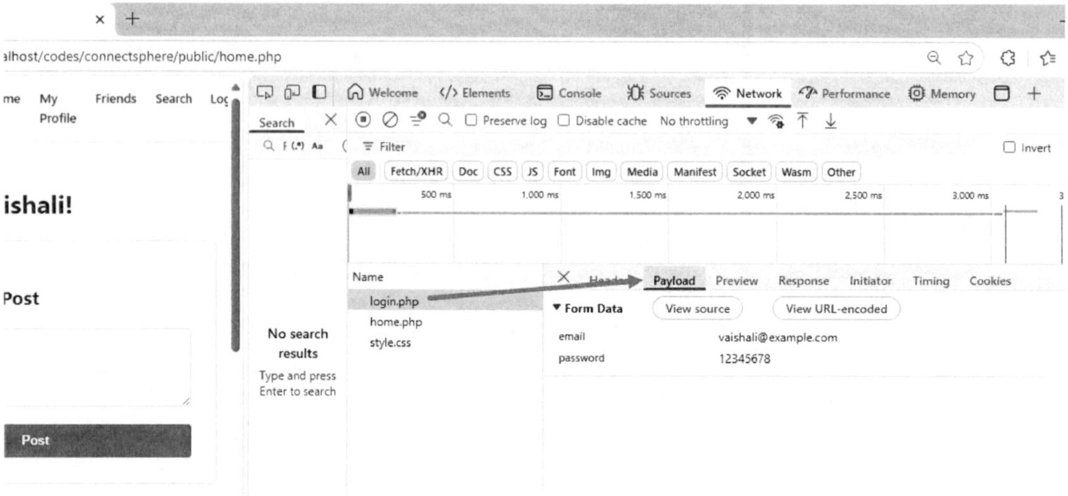

Server-side debugging with error_log()

What if the problem is on the server? PHP has a built-in function, **error_log()**, that lets you write messages to a special log file on the server, completely invisible to the user. This is the professional way to debug, as it doesn't break the user interface like an **echo** or **var_dump()** would.

Let's imagine our friend request button isn't working. We can use error_log() to inspect our variables.

1. **Edit the file:** Open **public/friend_action.php** in **VS Code**.
2. **Add the log message:** Right at the top, after the **require** statements, let's add a line to log the variables we receive from the URL:

```
// ... require statements ...
$current_user_id = $_SESSION['user_id'];
$other_user_id = isset($_GET['id']) ? (int)$_GET['id'] : 0;
$action = isset($_GET['action']) ? $_GET['action'] : '';
```

```
// ADD THIS LINE FOR DEBUGGING
error_log("Friend Action: user_id={$current_user_id}, other_user_id={$other_user_id},
          action={$action}");
```

```
// ... rest of the script ...
```

3. **Perform the action:** Now, go to a user's profile in your browser and click **Add Friend**.
4. **Check the log file:** XAMPP centralizes PHP errors in one place. Navigate to your XAMPP installation folder and open **C:\xampp\php\logs\php_error_log**. At the very end of the file, you see your message!

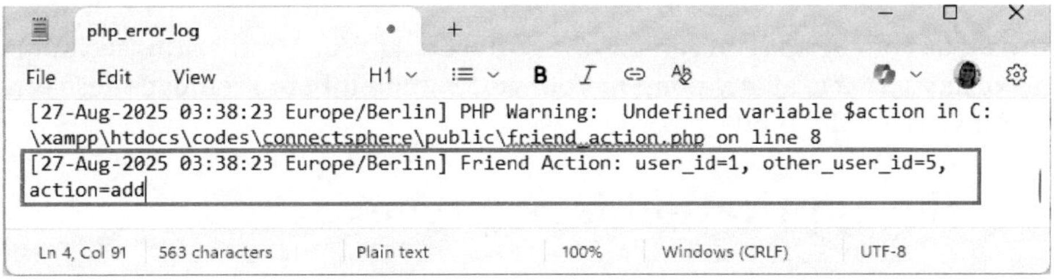

At times **logs** folder is missing in the **C:\xampp\php** directory, which is a common issue. If you find that the folder is not there, you can manually create a new folder named **logs** inside **C:\xampp\php**.

After creating the folder, **restart Apache** using the **XAMPP Control Panel**. Once Apache is restarted and a PHP error occurs, the **php_error_log** file should be automatically generated within the newly created **logs** folder. This is because the **php.ini** file typically specifies this location for logging errors, and PHP will create the file and folder if they don't exist, but sometimes it fails to create the directory itself.

You can also use the **XAMPP Control Panel** to view logs by clicking **Logs → PHP (php_error_log)**. This can often provide a direct view of the logs without having to navigate to the file path.

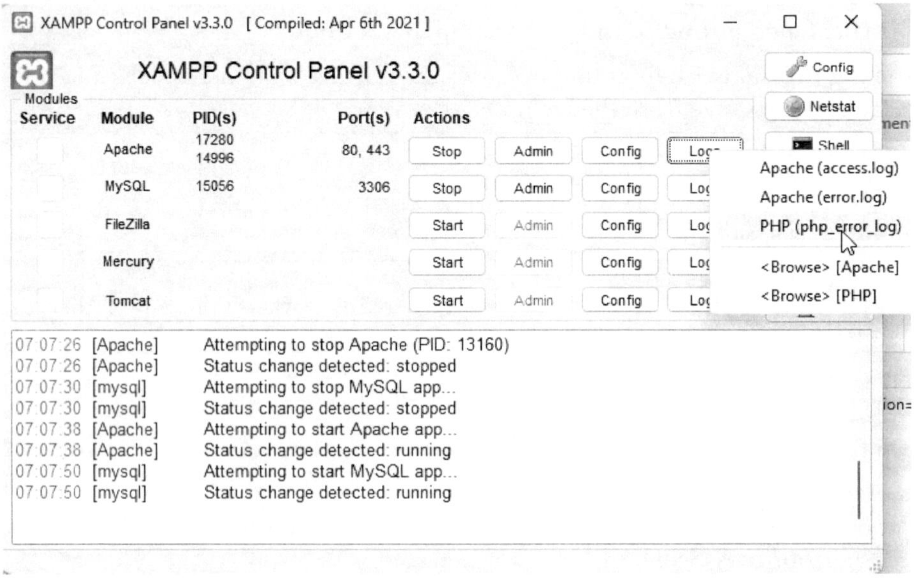

This confirms that your script is receiving the correct data. You can use this technique to log the contents of any variable at any point in your code. **Remember to remove these error_log() lines after you've fixed the bug!**

Ensuring the application is responsive

In today's world, more users browse the web on their phones than on desktops. A responsive application is one that looks and works great on any screen size. While we haven't used advanced CSS frameworks, our simple, percentage-based layout is already quite responsive. You can test this using your browser's built-in tools.

1. Open browser's **Developer tools** (F12).
2. **Toggle Device toolbar:** Look for an icon that looks like a **phone and tablet**. Click it.

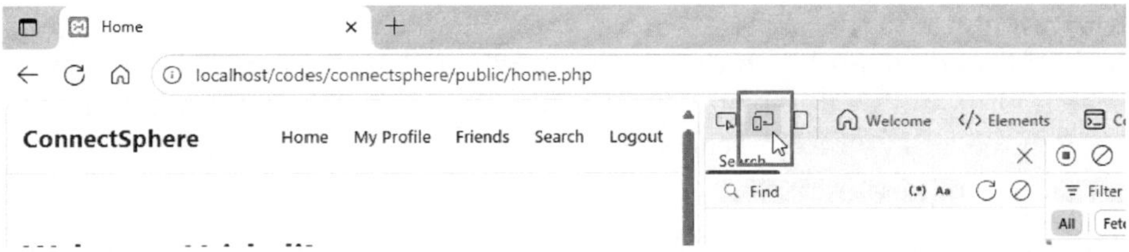

3. **Simulate devices:** Your browser window now shows your site as it would appear on a mobile device. You can use the dropdown menu at the top to select different devices, like an iPhone or a Samsung Galaxy.

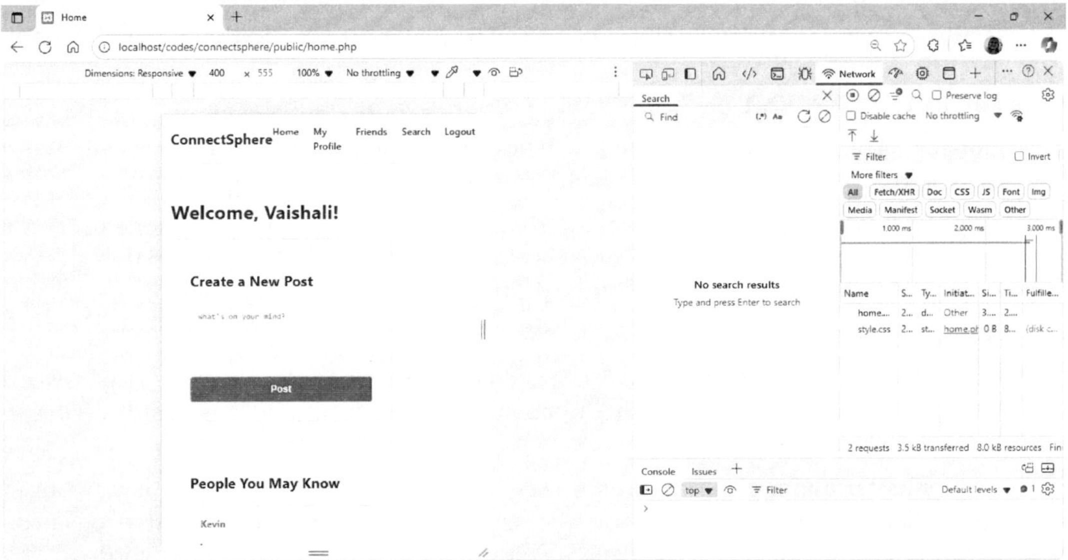

Click through your application—the login page, profiles, and friends list. You'll notice that the content reflows to fit the smaller screen, and the layout remains usable. This is a crucial final check before launch.

Bridging the gap: Learned concepts and application implementation

ConnectSphere isn't just a project; it's the practical application of every single concept you've learned in this book. Let's explicitly connect the theory to the code you wrote.

- **HTML forms & PHP superglobals ($_POST, $_GET):**
    - **Concept:** You learned how to create HTML forms to collect user data and how PHP captures this data using superglobal arrays.

  - **Implementation:** The registration form (register.php) and login form (login.php) use the POST method, and their data is captured with $_POST['email']. The search feature (search.php) and profile pages (profile.php?id=...) use the GET method to pass data through the URL, which is read with $_GET['q'] and $_GET['id'].

- **Database operations with PDO:**
  - **Concept:** You learned how to connect to a MySQL database using PDO, write SQL queries, and use prepared statements to prevent SQL injection.
  - **Implementation:** src/db_connect.php establishes our reusable connection. Every interaction with data—creating a user (INSERT), finding a user (SELECT), accepting a friend (UPDATE), or removing one (DELETE)—uses PDO prepared statements for security and efficiency.

- **Session MANAGEMENT ($_SESSION):**
  - **Concept:** You learned that HTTP is stateless and how to use sessions to maintain user data across multiple pages, effectively "remembering" a user's login status.
  - **Implementation:** The login script (login.php) starts a session and stores the user_id in $_SESSION['user_id']. The src/auth_check.php script checks for this variable on every protected page. The logout.php script destroys the session completely.

- **Secure password handling:**
  - **Concept:** You learned the critical importance of never storing plain-text passwords and how to use password_hash() to create a secure hash and password_verify() to safely check it.
  - **Implementation:** register.php uses password_hash() before storing a new user's credentials. login.php uses password_verify() to compare the submitted password against the stored hash without ever needing to know the original password.

- **Modular code with require_once:**
  - **Concept:** You learned how to break your application into smaller, reusable pieces to avoid repeating code and keep your project organized.
  - **Implementation:** Our application is built on this principle. The header (templates/header.php) and footer (templates/footer.php) are included on every page. The database connection (src/db_connect.php) and authentication check (src/auth_check.php) are included wherever they are needed.

- **Control structures (if, foreach):**
  - **Concept:** You learned to control the flow of your application with conditional statements and loop through arrays of data.

- **Implementation:** The profile page uses a complex if/elseif/else block to display the correct friend button. The friends page and post lists use foreach loops to iterate through the arrays of data fetched from the database and render them as HTML.

- **API integration:**
  - **Concept:** You learned how PHP can communicate with external AI services, send them data, and parse the JSON response.
  - **Implementation:** The src/ai_suggestions.php script is a perfect example. It gets data from our own database, constructs a prompt, sends it to the Google Gemini API using file_get_contents(), and parses the result with json_decode() to display the AI-generated text.

Running and testing: A user manual for ConnectSphere

Let's do one final, complete walkthrough of the application, just as a new user would. This journey will touch every feature we've built.

1. **Register a new account:**
   - Open your browser and navigate to:

     http://localhost/codes/connectsphere/public/register.php.

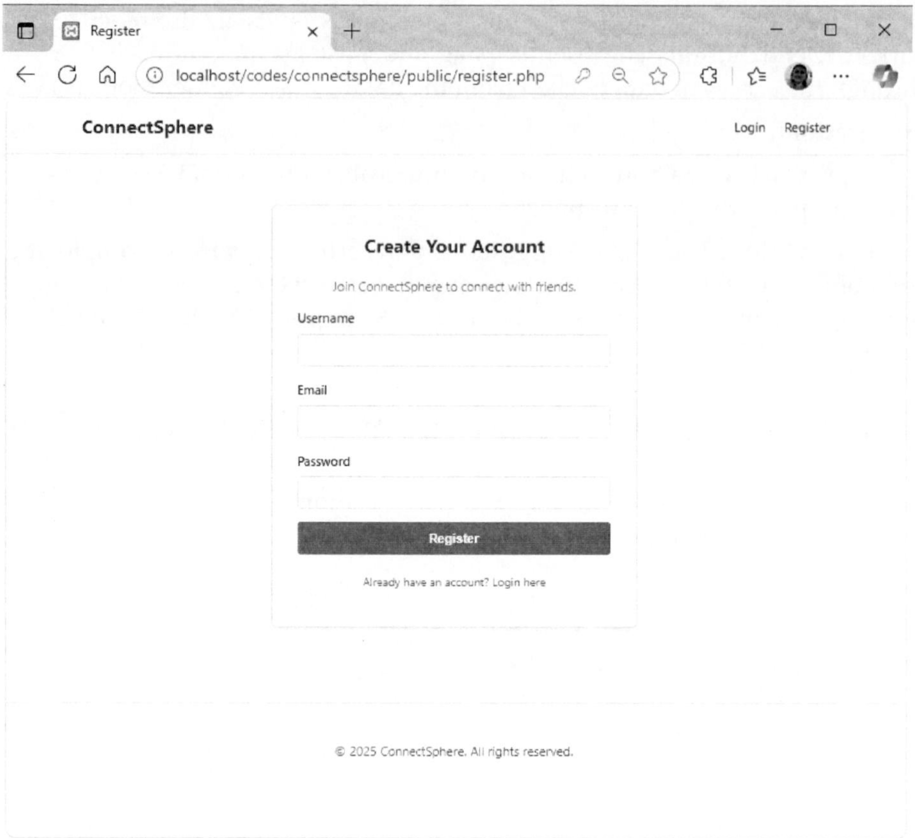

- Create a new user, for example, **testuser** with the email **test@example.com**.
- After clicking **Register**, you are on the login page with a success message.

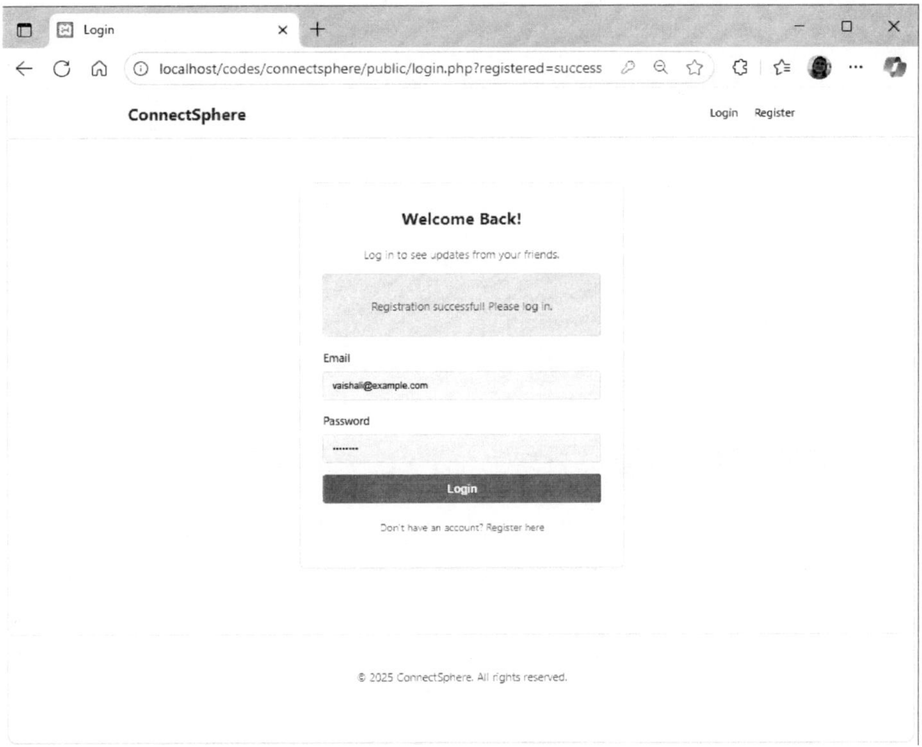

2. **Log In:**
   - Enter the credentials for **testuser** and log in.
   - You'll land on home.php. It will feel a bit empty right now, which is expected for a new user.

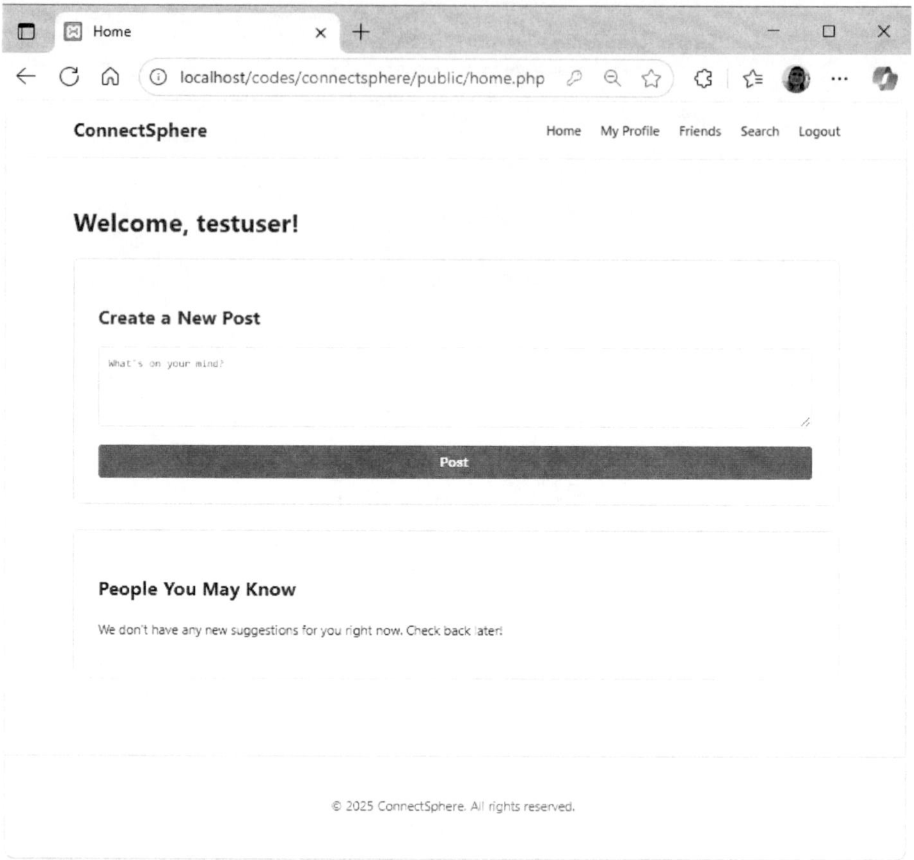

3. **Search for a Friend:**
   - Click the **Search** link in the navigation.

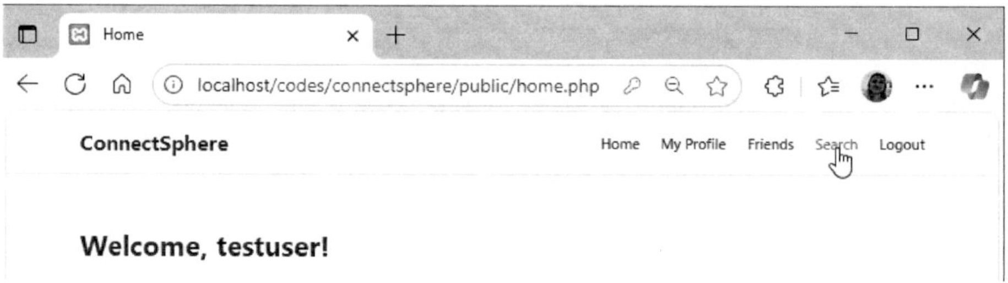

   - In the **search box**, type **Alice** (one of our dummy data users) and click **Search**. You can see Alice in the results.

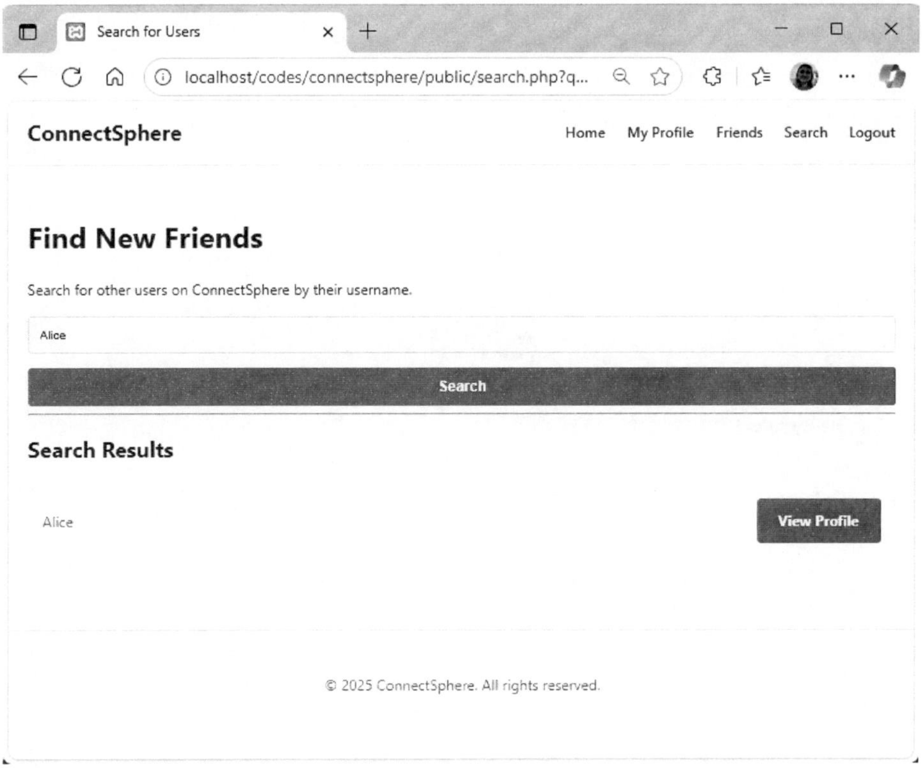

4. **Send a Friend Request:**
    - Click on **Alice's** name to view her profile (profile.php?id=1).

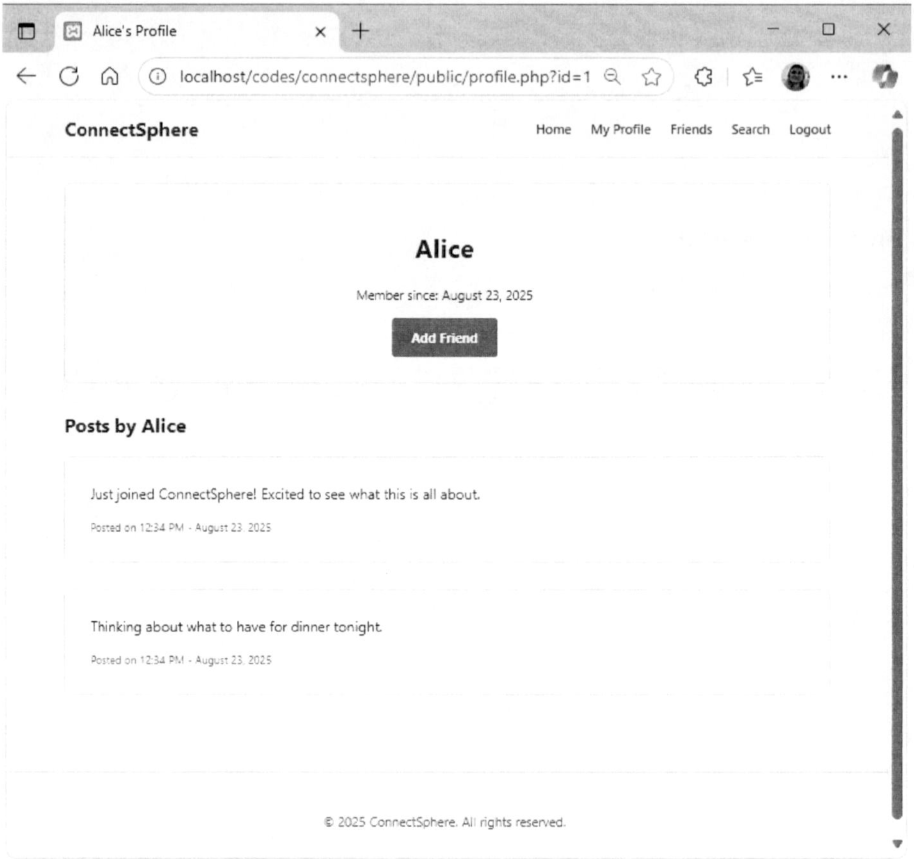

- Click the **Add Friend** button. The button changes to **Friend Request Sent**.

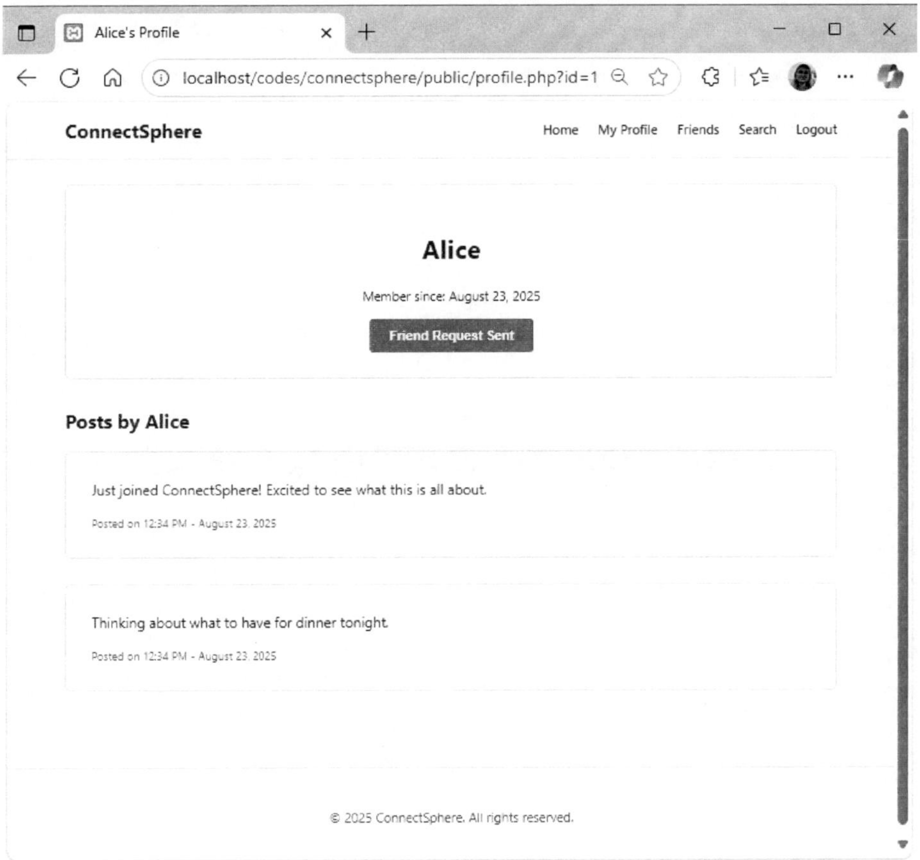

5. **Log in as the Other User:**
    - Now, **log out** of your **testuser** account.
    - Log in as **Alice** (email: alice@example.com, password: 12345678).

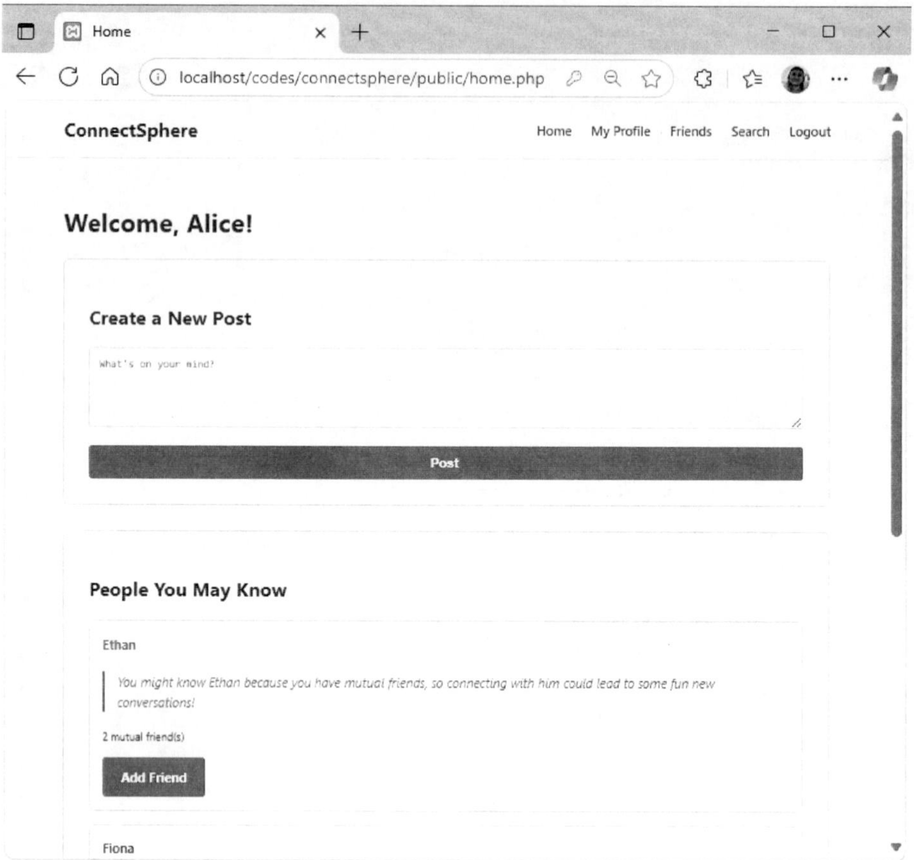

6. **Accept the Request:**
   - As Alice, click the **Friends** link in the navigation.

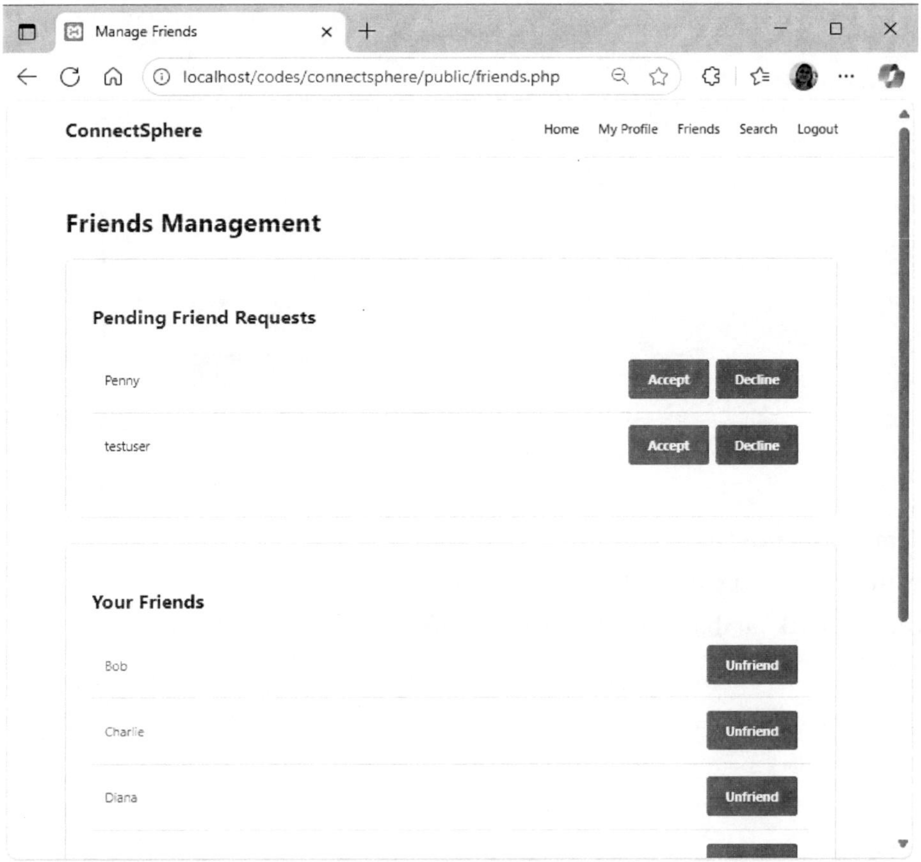

- On the **friends.php** page, you see a pending request from **testuser**. Click the **Accept** button.

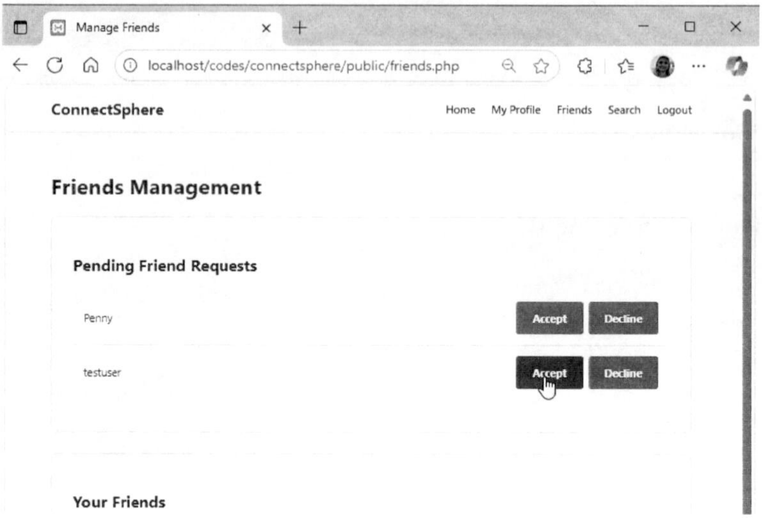

7. **Confirm Friendship:**
    - **testuser** now appears in Alice's **Your Friends** list.
    - You can click on that name to visit its profile, where the button now says **Unfriend**.

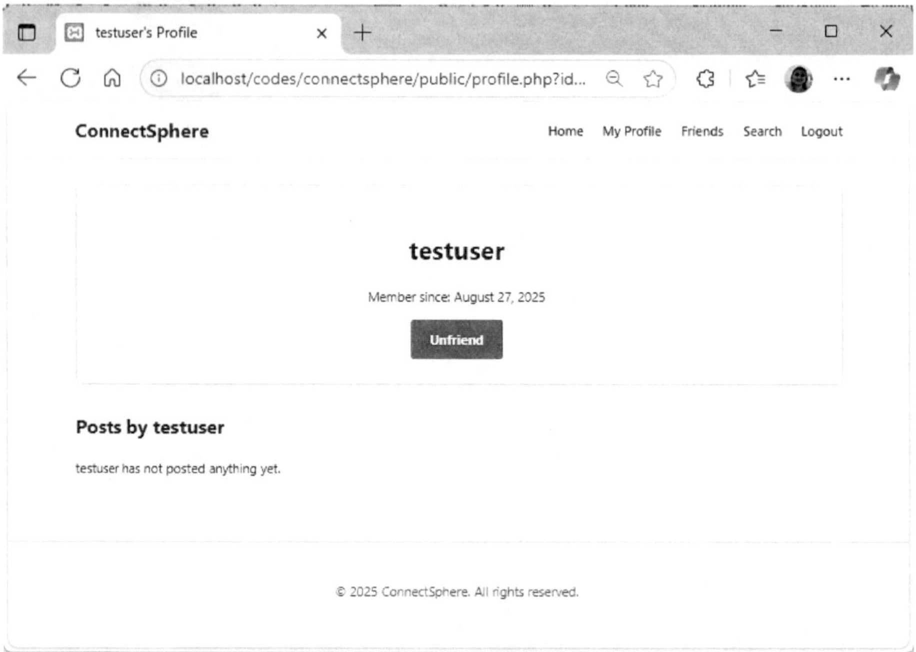

8. **Create a Post:**
   - While still logged in as Alice, navigate back to the **homepage**.

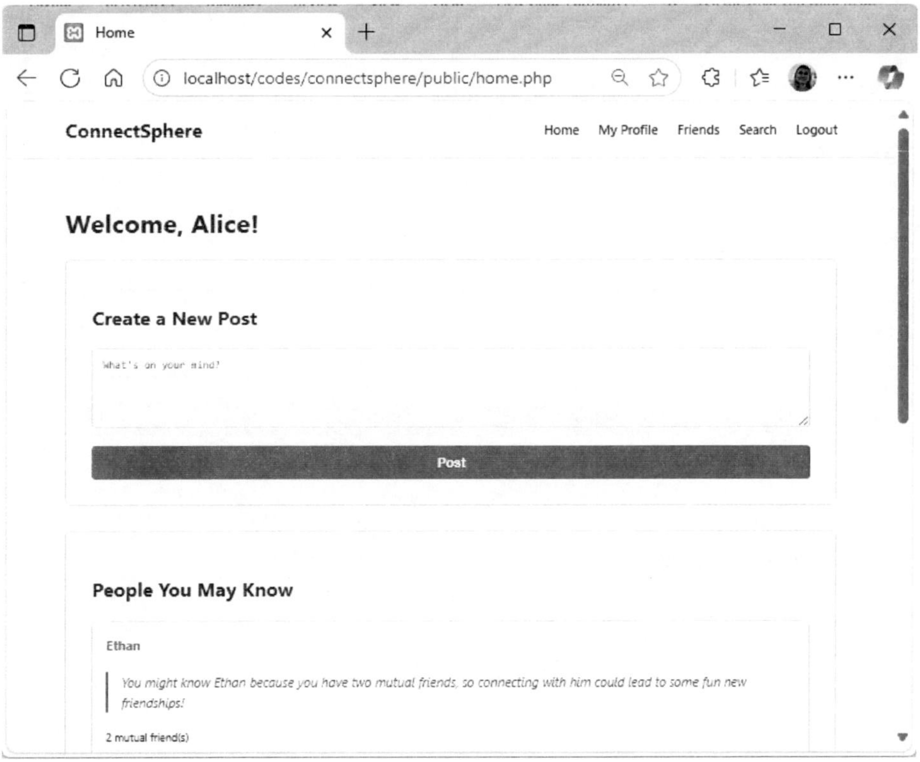

   - In the **Create a New Post** box, write a message like, **Having a great day testing ConnectSphere!**

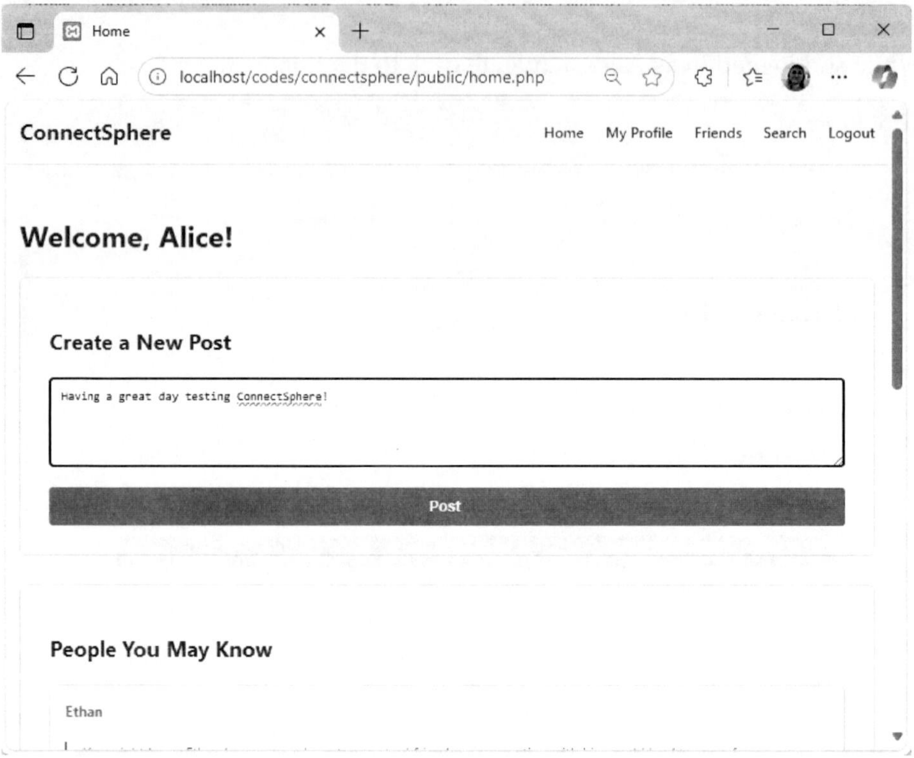
Home
localhost/codes/connectsphere/public/home.php
ConnectSphere
Home
My Profile
Friends
Search
Logout
Welcome, Alice!
Create a New Post
Having a great day testing ConnectSphere!
Post
People You May Know
Ethan

- Click **Post**.

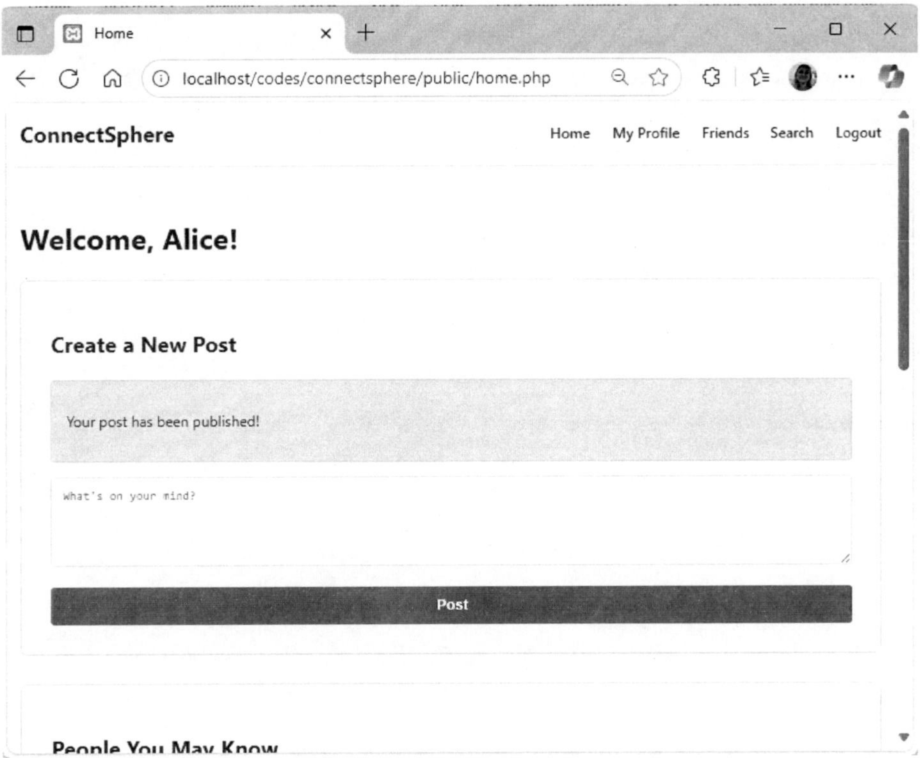

9. **View the New Post:**
   - Click on **My Profile** in the navigation.
   - You see your new post displayed on your profile page.

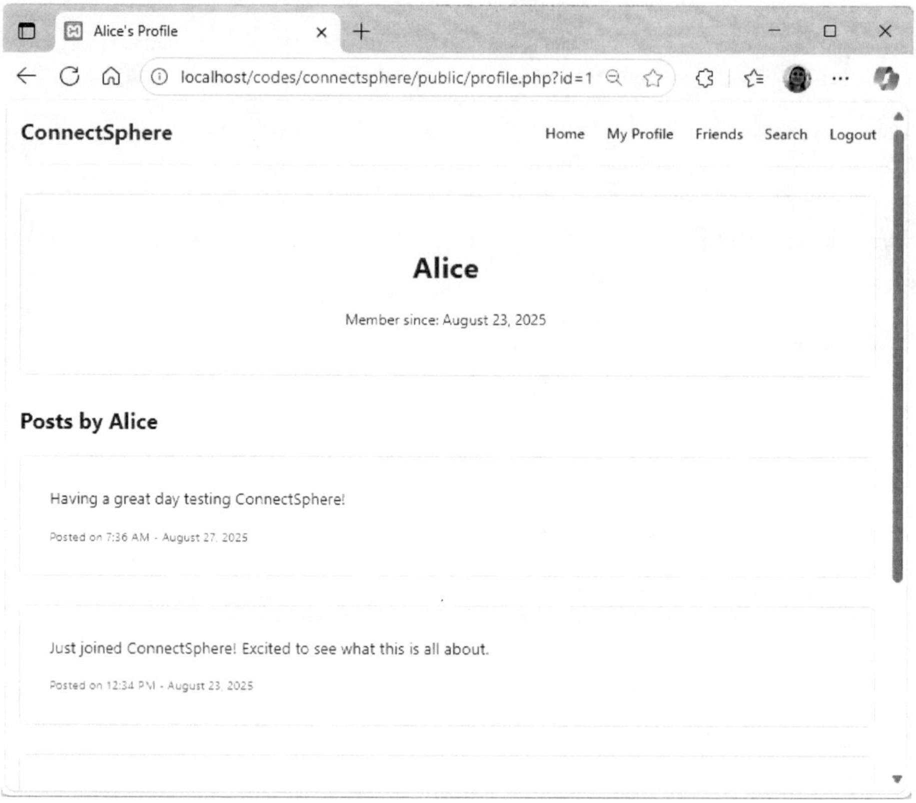

10. **Experience the AI:**
    - As Alice, go back to the **homepage**.
    - In the **People You May Know** section, you see suggestions based on her existing friends, each with a unique, AI-generated reason to connect.

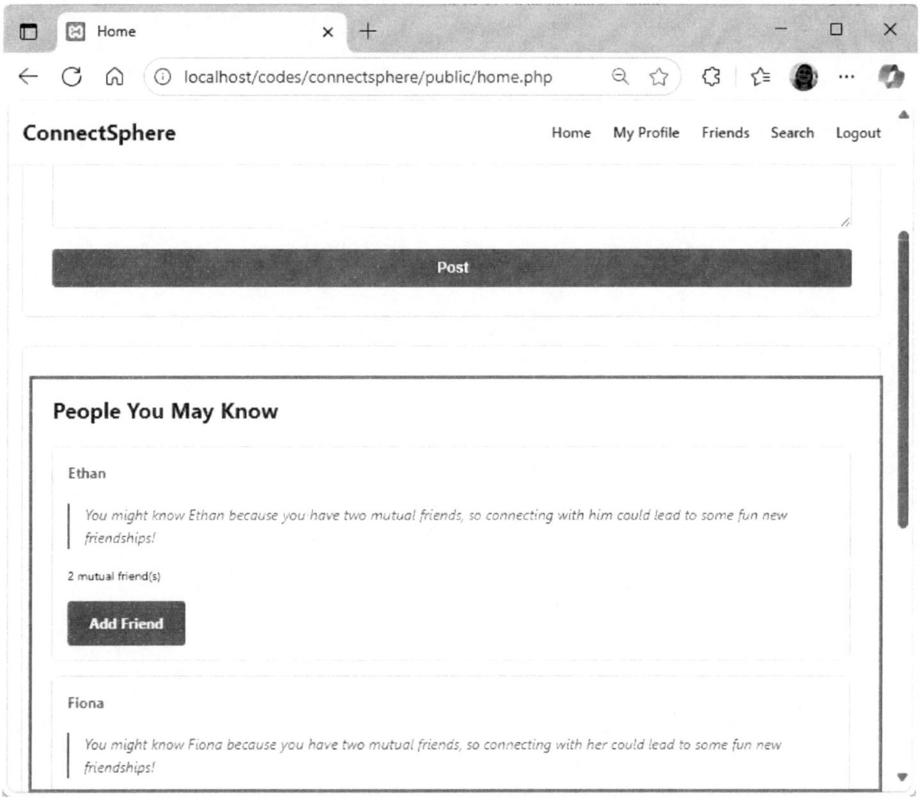

11. **Log Out:**
    - Click the **Logout** button.
    - You are returned to the login screen, your session successfully terminated.

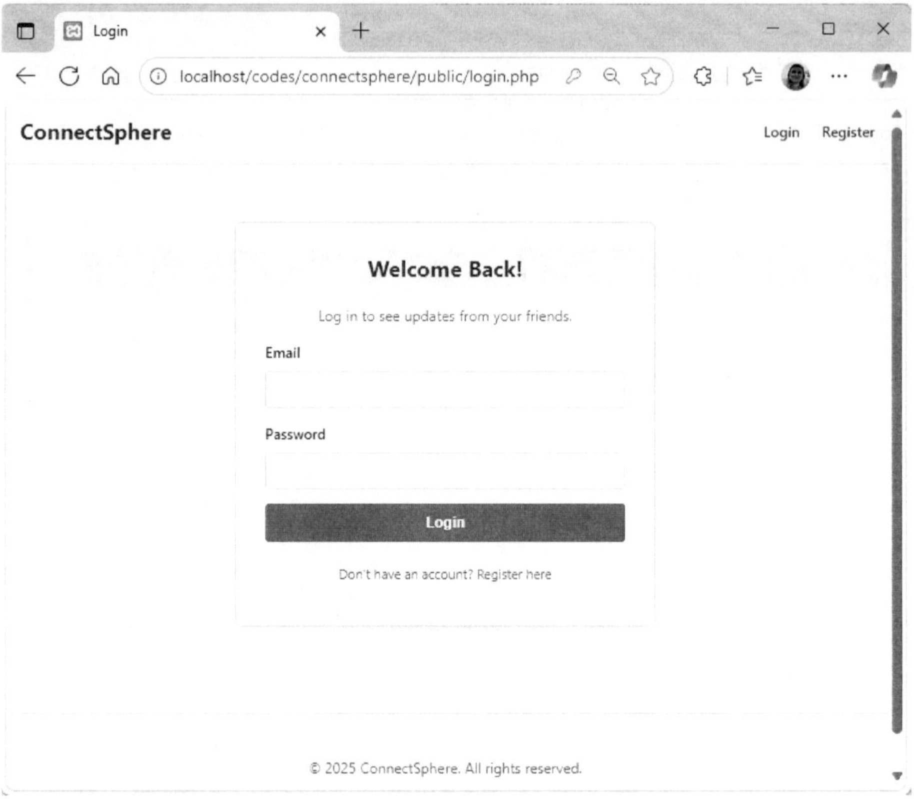

You have now tested the full user lifecycle of your application!

Exploring application behaviour: A practical run-through

A robust application not only handles the "happy path" but also gracefully manages errors and edge cases. Let's see how ConnectSphere behaves in these scenarios.

- What happens if you try to register with an email that is already in the database?
  - **Action:** Go to **register.php** and try to create an account with **alice@example.com**.
  - **Expected Result:** The page reloads with a clear error message: **An account with this email already exists**. The application correctly prevents duplicate accounts.

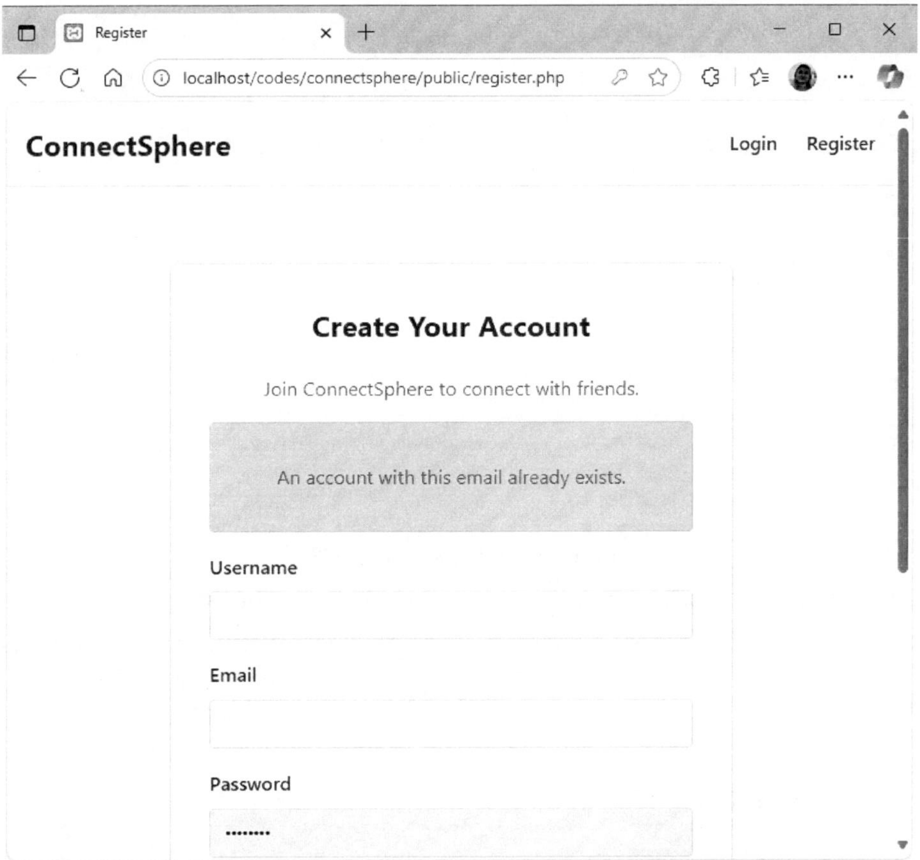

- What happens if you try to visit a protected page like home.php while logged out?
  - **Action:** Log out, then manually type **http://localhost/codes/connectsphere/public/home.php** into your browser's address bar.
  - **Expected Result:** You are instantly redirected to **login.php**. Our **auth_check.php** script is working perfectly.
- What happens if you view the profile of a user that doesn't exist?
  - **Action:** Log in, then manually change the URL to **http://localhost/codes/connectsphere/public/profile.php?id=999**.
  - **Expected Result:** The page displays a **Sorry, this user could not be found** message instead of a PHP error. Our code checks if a user was found and handles the negative case gracefully.

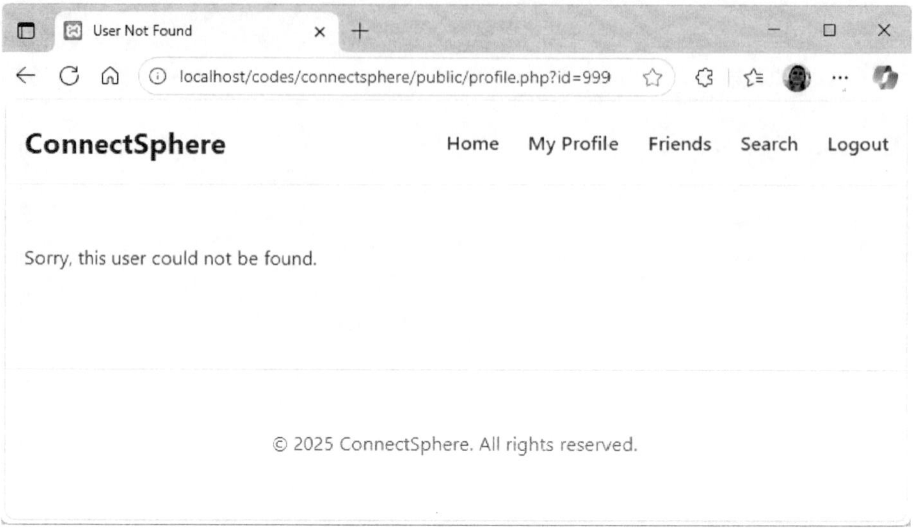

- What happens if you search for a user that doesn't exist?
  - **Action:** Go to the **search.php** page and search for a random string like **xyzabc**.
  - **Expected Result:** The page displays a message: **No users found matching "xyzabc"**.

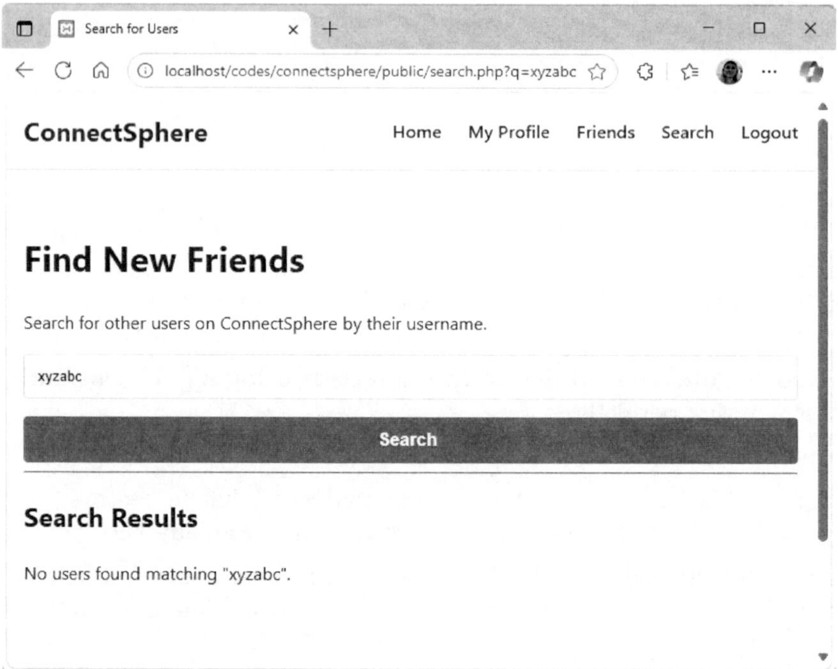

These tests prove that our application is not just functional but also resilient. It provides clear feedback to the user and doesn't crash when faced with unexpected input.

Harnessing ConnectSphere in real-world contexts

The features you've built in this capstone project are not just academic exercises; they are the fundamental building blocks of countless real-world web applications.

- **User authentication and profiles:** This is the foundation of almost any modern web service, from e-commerce sites like Amazon (your account, order history) to SaaS (Software as a Service) platforms like Trello (your boards, your team).
- **The social graph (Friend system):** While we called it a **friend** system, this model of connecting users is incredibly versatile.
    - On **LinkedIn**, they are **connections**.
    - On **Twitter** or **Instagram**, it's a one-way **follow**.

  This core logic can be adapted to power professional networks, follow-based media feeds, or team collaboration tools.
- **User-generated content (Posts):** The ability for users to create and display content is the engine of the modern web. The simple system you built for posts is the same core concept behind blog posts, product reviews, forum discussions, and comments on **YouTube**.
- **AI-powered suggestions:** Our **People You May Know** feature is a simplified version of the powerful recommendation engines that drive engagement on major platforms.
    - **Netflix** recommends **movies**
    - **Amazon** recommends **products**
    - **Spotify** recommends **music**

  Using far more complex versions of this same core idea: using existing data to make intelligent suggestions for the user.

Wrapping up

This chapter was the crucial final step in our project, transforming our code into a polished and well-understood application. You have performed the essential duties that happen right before a product launch.

- **Validated user stories:** You created and executed a formal test plan to confirm that every feature we set out to build works as intended.

- **Learned debugging techniques:** You used the browser's Network tab to inspect form data and PHP's error_log() function to debug server-side logic without disrupting the user.
- **Confirmed responsiveness:** You used browser tools to simulate mobile devices and ensure a positive user experience on any screen size.
- **Connected theory to practice:** You solidified your understanding by explicitly linking every feature of ConnectSphere back to the foundational PHP concepts learned throughout the book.
- **Explored edge cases:** You tested how the application behaves with invalid input and unexpected user actions, confirming its resilience.
- **Completed the full lifecycle:** You have now experienced all four phases of a professional software project: Plan, Design, Develop, and Launch.

Congratulations! You have officially completed the grand culmination of this book. You have journeyed from writing your first echo statement to architecting and building a full-stack, AI-enhanced social media application from the ground up. ConnectSphere is a testament to all the skills you've acquired: back-end logic with PHP, database management with MySQL, front-end structure with HTML and CSS, and cutting-edge integration with AI. This is a massive accomplishment and a project you can proudly showcase as proof of your abilities.

You are no longer just learning to code; you are a web developer. The path from here is filled with endless possibilities. But first, let's explore how to make our applications even more powerful by having PHP work together with another giant of the programming world.

Next up, we'll dive into a new ecosystem in ***Chapter 32: Interacting with Python for AI***.

Chapter 32

Section 09: The AI ecosystem – Bringing Python into your workflow

Interacting with Python for AI

What you'll learn

- Python's AI role
- Setting up Python
- Python language basics
- Executing Python from PHP
- Passing data with JSON
- The client-service model
- Handling errors securely

Welcome to a truly transformative chapter. So far, we've built amazing things using only PHP. But the world of technology is a world of collaboration, and that's true for programming languages, too.

In this chapter, we're going to introduce a powerful new friend to our PHP applications: Python. By learning how to make these two languages talk to each other, you're not just learning a new technique; you're unlocking the entire ecosystem of Artificial Intelligence and data science for your web apps.

Think of your favorite food delivery app. The website you browse is fast, responsive, and handles your user account perfectly—that's a job tailor-made for a language like PHP. But what about the AI that recommends new restaurants based on your past orders? That kind of complex data analysis is where Python shines.

This chapter teaches you how to build a team. PHP will be the friendly, user-facing **client** that manages the website, while Python will be the powerful, behind-the-scenes **service** that performs the heavy lifting for AI and data processing. We'll connect them, allowing PHP to hand off a task to Python, wait for the result, and then display that intelligent result to the user.

Python's role: An AI powerhouse and PHP's sidekick

So, what exactly is **Python**? Python is another programming language, just like PHP, but it has become the undisputed king in the worlds of data science, machine learning, and artificial intelligence. This is because it has a massive collection of free, powerful libraries built specifically for tasks like analyzing text, processing images, and making predictions.

Trying to build a complex recommendation engine from scratch in PHP would be like trying to build a car with only a screwdriver. It's possible, but incredibly difficult. Python gives you the whole specialized toolbox for free.

Let's use an analogy:
PHP builds the house, and Python provides the smart home technology.

- **PHP is fantastic at building the structure**: handling web page requests, managing user sessions, and interacting with the database quickly and efficiently. It builds the walls, the roof, and the plumbing of our web application.
- **Python**, on the other hand, **is the specialist** we call in to install the advanced systems. We might ask it to analyze a user's comment to detect its sentiment (is it positive or negative?), generate a unique image like a QR code, or translate text into another language.

Our PHP application will remain in charge, but it will now have the ability to delegate these specialized AI tasks to a Python script, making our app infinitely more powerful.

Setting up your Python environment

Before we can make our two languages talk, we need to get Python installed on our system. Don't worry, the process is very straightforward and similar to how we set up XAMPP.

Download and install Python

1. Navigate to the official Python website at **python.org**.

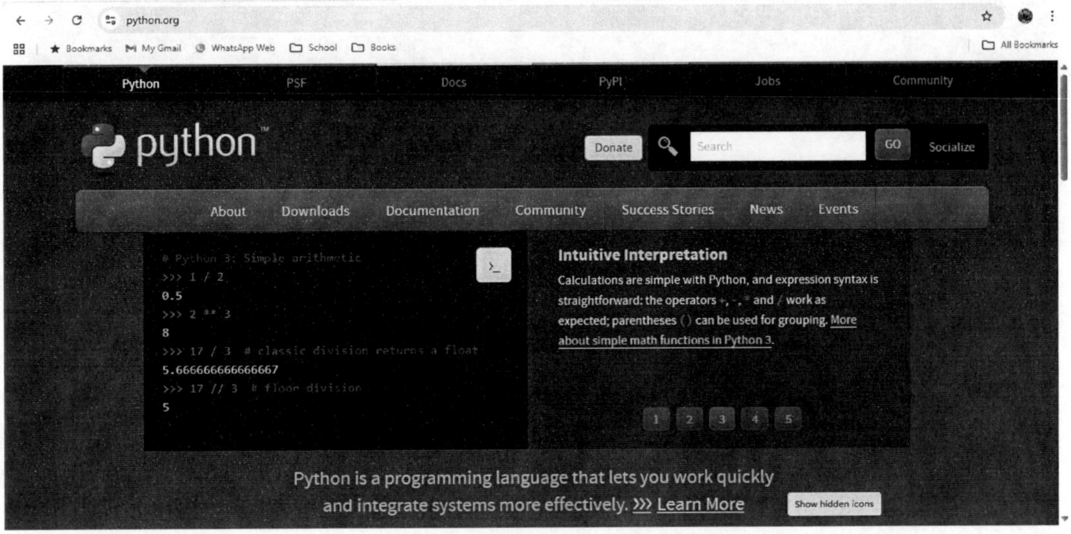

2. Select **Downloads → Windows** to go to the downloads page.

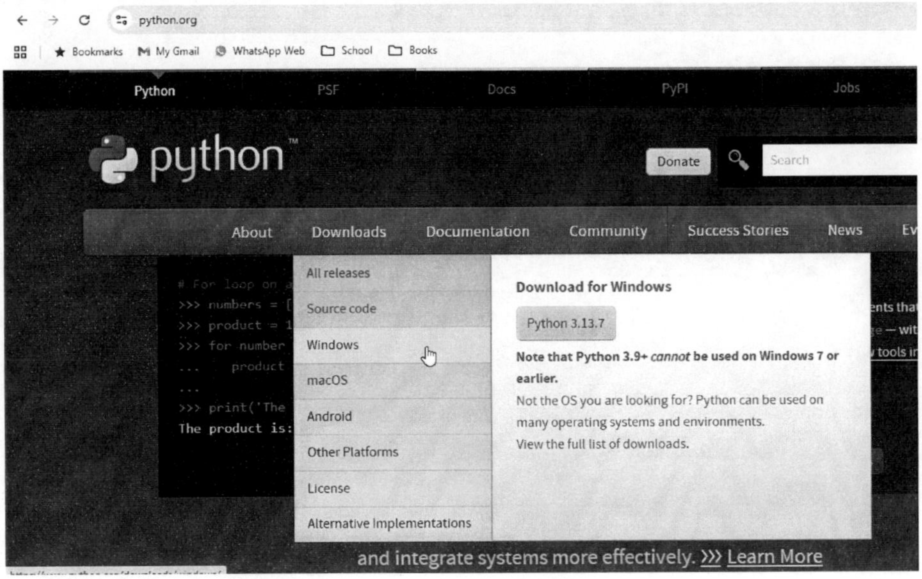

3. Select latest stable version of Python and download it.

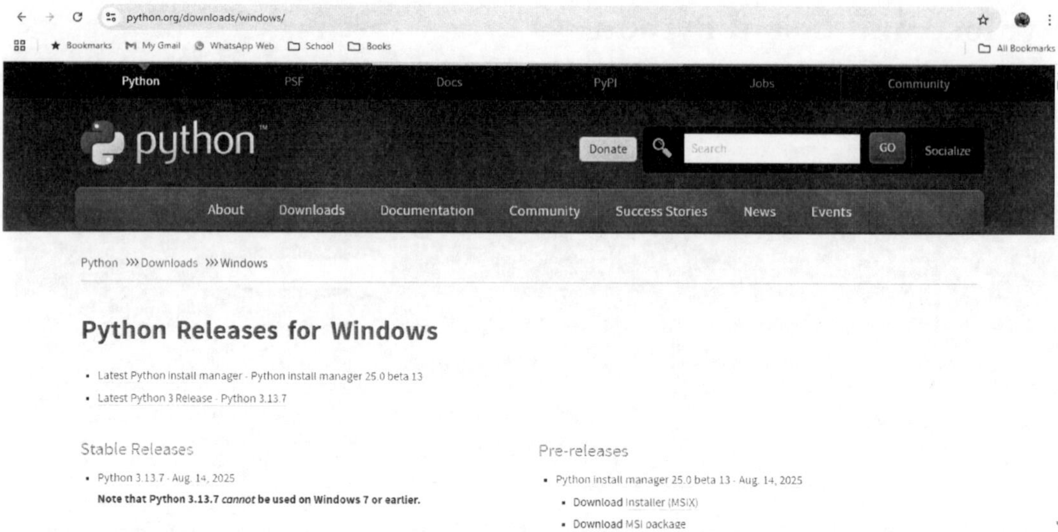

4. Once download is complete, double click the **Python installer**.
5. During the installation on Windows, you'll be presented with an installer screen. There is one **critically important** step here: make sure you check the box that says "**Add python.exe to PATH**". This allows you to run Python from any command prompt without typing out its full folder path every time.

6. Select **Install Now** and the installer will start installing Python. Wherever asked just click with the default settings throughout the installation process.

Verify the installation

Once the installation is complete, you can verify it's working.

1. Open a new command prompt or terminal.
    - In Windows, you can type **cmd** into the Start Menu.
    - In VS Code, you can go to **...** → **Terminal** → **New Terminal**.
2. Type the following command and press **Enter**:

```
python --version
```

3. If the installation was successful, you'll see the Python version number printed back to you. This confirms your system can find and run Python.

Meet pip, Python's package manager

PHP has **Composer**, and Python has **pip**. It's a command-line tool that comes with Python and allows you to easily install and manage third-party libraries.

Let's try installing a simple library called **requests** (we won't use it in this chapter, but it's a great test).

In your terminal, run:

```
pip install requests
```

You'll see some text as **pip** downloads and installs the package. It's that simple! You now have the power to install thousands of incredible Python libraries with a single command.

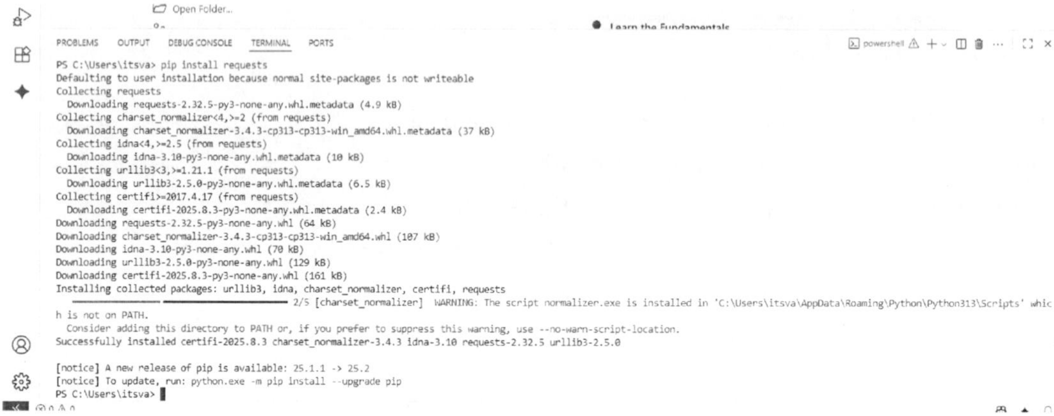

> **A quick word on virtual environments:**
> In the Python world, developers often use **virtual environments** to keep the libraries for different projects separate. Think of it like having a separate toolbox for each car you work on, so the tools for the Honda don't get mixed up with the tools for the Ford. For our simple examples, we don't need to do this, but it's a key term to know as you explore Python further.

A crash course in Python basics

Before we connect PHP and Python, let's take a proper tour of the Python language. As a PHP developer, you'll find it refreshingly simple. Python's main philosophy is about readability and simplicity, which makes it a joy to learn.

Variables and data types

Declaring variables in Python is straightforward. You don't use a $ sign, and you don't need to declare types. Python figures it out for you.

- **Strings:** For text. You can use single ' or double " quotes.
- **Integers:** For whole numbers (10, -5).
- **Floats:** For numbers with decimals (98.6, 3.14).
- **Booleans:** For True or False (note the capital letters!).

To display output, we use the built-in **print()** function.

```
# A string variable
message = "Hello, Python learners!"
# An integer
user_count = 150
# A float
price = 49.99
# A boolean
is_active = True
# To display output, we use the print() function
print(message)
print(user_count)
```

A very useful feature for creating strings is the **f-string**. By putting an **f** before the opening quote, you can embed variables directly inside curly braces. This is much cleaner than concatenation, similar to PHP's double-quoted strings.

```
name = "Alice"
age = 30
# Using an f-string to create a dynamic message
greeting = f"User {name} is {age} years old."
print(greeting) # Output: User Alice is 30 years old.
```

Working with data structures

Lists (like PHP indexed arrays)

What we call an indexed array in PHP, Python calls a **list**. They are ordered, changeable, and created with **square brackets []**.

```
# A list of strings
fruits = ["apple", "banana", "cherry"]
# Access an element by its index (starting from 0)
print(fruits[0]) # Output: apple
# Add an item to the end of the list
fruits.append("orange")
print(fruits) # Output: ['apple', 'banana', 'cherry', 'orange']
# Get the number of items in a list (like PHP's count())
print(len(fruits)) # Output: 4
```

Dictionaries (like PHP associative arrays)

For key-value pairs, Python uses **dictionaries**. They are nearly identical to PHP's associative arrays and are created with **curly braces {}**. This is a vital concept, as JSON data maps directly to Python dictionaries.

```
# A dictionary representing a user
user = {
    "name": "Admin",
    "email": "admin@example.com",
    "id": 215
}
# Access a value by its key
print(user["email"]) # Output: admin@example.com
# Add a new key-value pair
user["is_verified"] = True
# Check if a key exists in the dictionary
if "name" in user:
    print("Name key exists!")
print(user) # Output: {'name': 'Admin', 'email': 'admin@example.com', 'id': 215, 'is_verified': True}
```

Controlling the flow

Conditional logic and the importance of indentation

This is the biggest difference from PHP. Python does **not** use curly braces {} to define code blocks. Instead, Python uses **indentation (whitespace)**. A consistent number of spaces (the standard is four) tells Python what code belongs inside an if, loop, or function.

```
score = 85
if score >= 90:
    print("Grade: A")
elif score >= 80:
    # This block will run because score is 85
    # The 'elif' is short for 'else if'
    print("Grade: B")
else:
    print("Grade: C or lower")
# This line is not indented, so it's outside the if/else block
print("Grading complete.")
```

Looping with for

The **for** loop in Python is elegant and powerful. It works very much like PHP's foreach loop, allowing you to iterate directly over items in a list or dictionary.

```
# Looping through a list
fruits = ["apple", "banana", "cherry"]
for fruit in fruits:
    print(f"I like to eat {fruit}s.")
# Looping through a dictionary
user = {"name": "Admin", "email": "admin@example.com"}
for key, value in user.items():
    print(f"The user's {key} is {value}.")
```

Organizing your code

Functions with def

You define a function using the **def** keyword. Just like with if statements, the code inside the function must be indented.

```
def greet_user(name, a_ge):
    # This code is inside the function
    message = f"Welcome, {name}! You are {age}."
    return message
# This code is outside the function
greeting = greet_user("Maria", 32)
print(greeting)
```

Bringing in extra power with import

Python has a huge standard library filled with **modules** that provide extra functionality. To use one, you simply import it at the top of your file. This is similar to PHP's require or include, but it's used for loading libraries of code. We will be using this to work with JSON and system arguments.

```
# Import the 'json' module to work with JSON data
import json
# Import the 'random' module to generate random numbers
import random
# Now we can use functions from those modules
random_number = random.randint(1, 100) # Get a random integer between 1 and 100
print(f"Your lucky number is {random_number}")
```

Writing robust scripts

Handling errors with try...except

Things can go wrong in any program. In PHP, you use try...catch. In Python, you use **try...except**. You put the risky code in the try block, and the code to handle a potential error goes in the except block.

```
try:
    # This will cause an error because you can't divide by zero
    result = 10 / 0
    print(result)
except ZeroDivisionError:
    # This code runs because the specific error occurred
    print("Error: You cannot divide by zero!")
print("The script continues to run after handling the error.")
```

This is crucial for creating scripts that don't crash unexpectedly. You'll see this exact pattern in our hands-on project to handle cases where user input might be missing.

You are now well-equipped to understand, modify, and create the Python scripts we'll use to supercharge our PHP applications.

Running Python from PHP: A simple shell_exec() example

Now for the **magic moment**: **making PHP execute a Python script**. We'll do this using a built-in PHP function called **shell_exec()**. As its name implies, this function takes a string containing a command, executes it in the computer's command-line shell, and returns the entire output as a string.

Let's build our first example.

Create your project folder

Inside your **xampp/htdocs/codes** directory, create a new folder called **php-to-python**. Open it in VS Code

Create the Python script

Inside **php-to-python**, create a new file named **hello.py** and add this single line of code:

```
print("Hello from Python! The PHP app has summoned me.")
```

This is a very simple script that just prints a string of text to the console.

Create the PHP script

Now, in the same **php-to-python** folder, create a file named **index.php**. This is where we'll call our Python script:

```
<!DOCTYPE html>
<html lang="en">
<head>
    <meta charset="UTF-8">
    <meta name="viewport" content="width=device-width, initial-scale=1.0">
    <title>PHP meets Python</title>
</head>
<body>
    <h1>Calling a Python Script from PHP</h1>
    <?php
    // The command to execute. 'python' should work if it's in your system's PATH.
    $command = 'python hello.py';
    // Execute the command and capture the output
    $output = shell_exec($command);
    ?>
    <h2>Output from Python:</h2>
    <pre><?php echo $output; ?></pre>
</body>
</html>
```

Run it!

Make sure your **XAMPP's Apache** server is running. Open your browser and navigate to **http://localhost/codes/php-to-python/**. You see this output:

Congratulations! You have successfully made two different programming languages work together.

Your PHP script sent a command to the operating system, which ran the Python script. The Python script's output was captured by shell_exec() and then displayed on the web page by PHP.

> **A crucial note on security:**
> shell_exec() is incredibly powerful, but it must be used with extreme caution. Never, ever pass raw user input (like from a form) directly into this function. A malicious user could inject system commands and potentially take over your server. We will learn how to do this safely in the next section.

Passing data with JSON: Sending information to and from Python

Our first example was great, but it was a one-way street.

The real power comes from sending data from PHP *to* Python, having Python process it, and then sending a result *back* to PHP.

To do this, we need a common language that both PHP and Python understand perfectly. That language is **JSON (JavaScript Object Notation)**. It's a lightweight, text-based format for data exchange, and it's the standard for communication between web services.

Passing data from PHP to Python

While passing data as a command-line argument works, it can become tricky with complex data or on different operating systems. A more robust and scalable method is to **pipe** the data directly into the Python script's **standard input (stdin)**. Think of it as creating a direct data stream from PHP to Python.

Let's create a Python script named **data_receiver.py** in our project folder. This version will read data from this **stdin stream**:

```
import sys
import json
# Read the entire data stream from standard input
json_data_from_php = sys.stdin.read()
# Decode the JSON string into a Python dictionary
data = json.loads(json_data_from_php)
# Now we can work with the data
name = data['name']
age = data['age']
city = data['location']
print(f"Python received the data! Hello, {name}. You are {age} and live in {city}.")
```

Now, let's create **index_data.php** to send data using this **piping** method. We'll use the **echo shell** command and the **pipe |** operator. The **pipe |** tells the shell to take the output of the command on the left and use it as the input for the command on the right:

```
<?php
// Our data in a PHP associative array
$userData = [
    "name" => "Sharanam",
    "age" => 34,
    "location" => "New York"
];
// 1. Encode the data into a JSON string
$jsonData = json_encode($userData);
// 2. CRITICAL: Sanitize the data for shell execution. Even when echoing, this
// prevents malicious injection. It wraps the entire string in single quotes,
// making it safe.
$safeJsonData = escapeshellarg($jsonData);
// 3. Build the command. This "pipes" the echoed JSON into the Python script.
$command = 'echo ' . $safeJsonData . ' | python data_receiver.py';
// 4. Execute and get the output
$output = shell_exec($command);
echo "<pre>$output</pre>";
?>
```

When you run index_data.php in your browser, you'll see the following successful output as before:

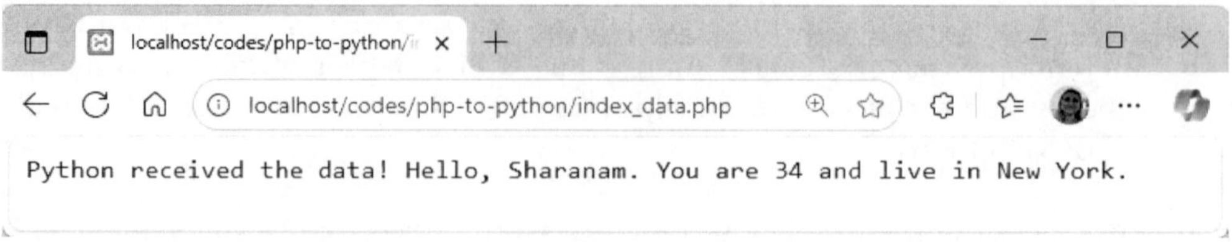

We successfully passed structured data from PHP to Python!

Returning data from Python to PHP

The process is simply reversed. The Python script will do its work and then print a JSON string as its final output. The PHP script will capture this output and use json_decode() to turn it back into a PHP array or object.

Let's create a new Python script, **data_processor.py**:

```
import json
# Imagine this script does some complex calculation or AI task
# For now, it will just process some data and return a result.
user_id = 123
interests = ["hiking", "coding", "coffee"]
# Create a dictionary to hold the results
result_data = {
    "userId": user_id,
    "recommendedInterests": interests,
    "status": "success"
}
# Encode the dictionary into a JSON string and print it
print(json.dumps(result_data))
```

And now, create index_return.php, which will call this script and interpret its response:

```
<?php
$command = 'python data_processor.py';
$jsonResponse = shell_exec($command);
// Decode the JSON response. The true argument converts it to an associative array.
$dataFromPython = json_decode($jsonResponse, true);
if ($dataFromPython['status'] === 'success') {
    echo "<h1>Recommendations for User ID: " . $dataFromPython['userId'] . "</h1>";
    echo "<ul>";
    foreach ($dataFromPython['recommendedInterests'] as $interest) {
        echo "<li>" . htmlspecialchars($interest) . "</li>";
    }
```

```
    echo "</ul>";
} else {
    echo "There was an error processing the data.";
}
```

Open index_return.php in your browser, and you will see a nicely formatted list of recommendations, all generated by Python and rendered by PHP.

This client-service communication pattern is the foundation of modern, intelligent web applications.

Hands-on: Creating a Python script that processes user input and returns a simple AI-like response

Let's combine everything we've learned into a fun, interactive mini-application. We'll build a web form where a user can enter their name. PHP will take that name, send it to a Python script, and our Python **AI** will analyze the name to return a personalized, dynamic message.

This project, the **AI greeting app**, will solidify your understanding of the full communication cycle. You'll build the PHP front-end form, the Python back-end service, and the JSON **bridge** that connects them. The goal is to see how a simple web interaction can be enhanced with a separate, specialized script.

Building the application

Set up the project structure

Let's keep things organized. In your **xampp/htdocs/codes** folder, create a new directory named **ai-greeter**. All of our files for this project will go in here.

Create the PHP front-end and CSS

Inside **ai-greeter**, create the main file, **index.php**. This file will contain our HTML form for user input, the CSS to style it, and the PHP logic to handle the entire process:

```
<!DOCTYPE html>
<html lang="en">
<head>
    <meta charset="UTF-8">
    <meta name="viewport" content="width=device-width, initial-scale=1.0">
    <title>AI Greeting App</title>
    <style>
        body {
            font-family: -apple-system, BlinkMacSystemFont, "Segoe UI", Roboto,
                         Helvetica, Arial, sans-serif;
            background-color: #f0f2f5;
            display: flex;
            justify-content: center;
            align-items: center;
            height: 100vh;
            margin: 0;
        }
        .container {
            background-color: #fff;
            padding: 2rem;
            border-radius: 8px;
            box-shadow: 0 4px 12px rgba(0, 0, 0, 0.1);
            text-align: center;
            width: 90%;
            max-width: 400px;
        }
        h1 {
            color: #1c1e21;
        }
        form {
            margin-top: 1.5rem;
        }
        input[type="text"] {
            width: calc(100% - 22px);
            padding: 10px;
            font-size: 1rem;
```

```
            border: 1px solid #dddfe2;
            border-radius: 6px;
        }
        button {
            width: 100%;
            padding: 10px;
            font-size: 1rem;
            background-color: #1877f2;
            color: white;
            border: none;
            border-radius: 6px;
            cursor: pointer;
            margin-top: 1rem;
        }
        button:hover {
            background-color: #166fe5;
        }
        .response {
            margin-top: 1.5rem;
            padding: 1rem;
            background-color: #e7f3ff;
            border: 1px solid #1877f2;
            border-radius: 6px;
            color: #1c1e21;
        }
    </style>
</head>
<body>
    <div class="container">
        <h1>AI Name Analyzer</h1>
        <form action="index.php" method="POST">
            <input type="text" name="user_name" placeholder="Enter your name"
                   required>
            <button type="submit">Analyze</button>
        </form>
        <?php
        // This is where our PHP logic will go!
        ?>
    </div>
</body>
</html>
```

If you open **http://localhost/codes/ai-greeter/** now, you'll see a nicely styled, but non-functional, form.

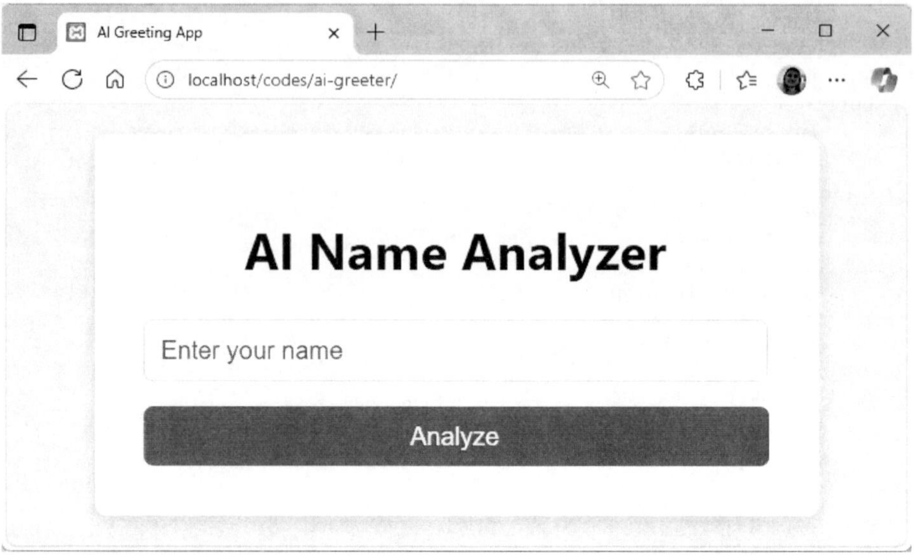

Create the Python "AI" script

Next, in the same **ai-greeter** folder, create a file named **analyzer.py**. This script will contain our **AI** logic. It will receive a name, pick a random "analysis," and return it as a JSON object:

```
import sys
import json
import random
def analyze_name(name):
    """A simple 'AI' function to generate a personality trait."""
    # List of possible traits
    traits = [
        "a creative thinker",
        "a natural leader",
        "an organized planner",
        "a compassionate friend",
        "a curious adventurer"
    ]
    # A simple way to make the choice seem less random
    # We use the length of the name to pick an index
    index = len(name) % len(traits)
    chosen_trait = traits[index]
    message = f"Hello, {name}! My analysis suggests you are {chosen_trait}."
    return message
# --- Main script execution ---
try:
    # Get the name from the command-line argument
    input_name = sys.argv[1]
```

```
    if not input_name:
        # Handle case where name is empty
        response_data = {"status": "error", "message": "Name cannot be empty."}
    else:
        # Get the AI-generated message
        ai_message = analyze_name(input_name)
        response_data = {"status": "success", "message": ai_message}
except IndexError:
    # Handle case where no argument is provided
    response_data = {"status": "error", "message": "No input name provided."}
# Always output a JSON response
print(json.dumps(response_data))
```

Connect the front-end and back-end

Now we'll add the final piece of the puzzle. Go back to your index.php file and replace the PHP logic inside the <?php ... ?> block:

```
<?php
// Check if the form was submitted and the user_name field is not empty
if ($_SERVER["REQUEST_METHOD"] == "POST" && !empty($_POST['user_name'])) {
    // 1. Get the user's name from the form
    $userName = $_POST['user_name'];
    // 2. IMPORTANT: Sanitize the input for shell execution
    $safeUserName = escapeshellarg($userName);
    // 3. Build the command to execute the Python script
    // Note: 'python' might need to be the full path to your python.exe
    $command = 'python analyzer.py ' . $safeUserName;
    // 4. Execute the command and capture the JSON output
    $jsonResponse = shell_exec($command);
    // 5. Decode the JSON response into a PHP associative array
    $response = json_decode($jsonResponse, true);
    // 6. Display the result
    if ($response && $response['status'] === 'success') {
        echo '<div class="response">' . htmlspecialchars($response[
               'message']) . '</div>';
    } else {
        $errorMessage = $response['message'] ?? 'An unknown error
                          occurred.';
        echo '<div class="response" style="background-color: #ffebe8;
               border-color: #d93025;">' . htmlspecialchars($errorMessage) .
               '</div>';
    }
}
?>
```

Your index.php is now complete!

Bridging the gap: Learned concepts and application implementation

Let's quickly review how the concepts we discussed map directly to our new app:

- **Client-service model:** The index.php file acts as the **client**. It presents the **UI** and handles the **web request**. The analyzer.py script is our specialized **service**, responsible for one task: generating a message.
- **Communication via shell_exec()**: This PHP function is the communication channel we used to launch our Python service and give it a task.
- **JSON as the bridge**: We sent the user's name as a simple string, but Python sent back a structured JSON object ({"status": "...", "message": "..."}). This allowed our PHP code to reliably check if the operation was successful and to extract the exact message it needed to display. This is far more robust than just sending back plain text.
- **Security first**: We used **escapeshellarg()** on the user's input before passing it to the shell. This is a non-negotiable step that protects our application from command injection attacks.

Running and testing

It's time to see our creation in action.

1. Make sure **XAMPP** is running.
2. Open your browser and navigate to **http://localhost/codes/ai-greeter/**.
3. You see the **AI Name Analyzer** form.

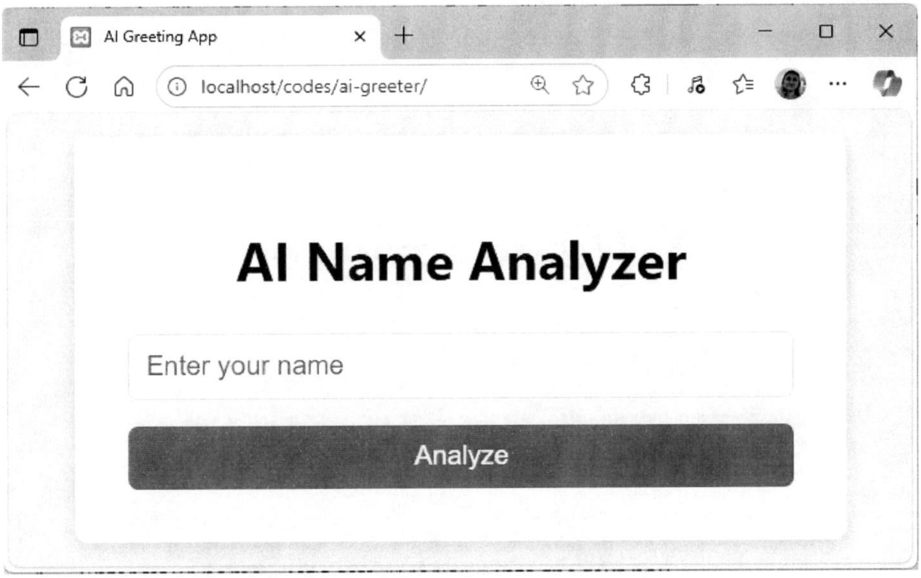

4. Enter your name into the **text box**.
5. Click the **Analyze** button.
6. The page reloads, and below the form, a blue box appears with a message like:

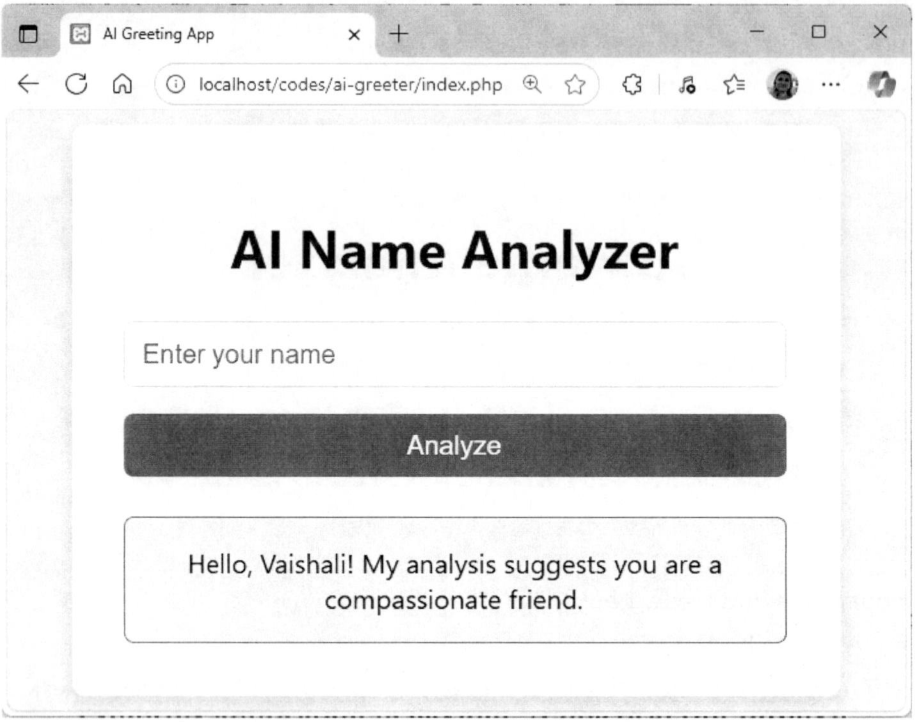

Exploring application behaviour: A practical run-through

A good developer always thinks about the edge cases. What happens when things don't go as planned?

- **Invalid input (empty name):** Try clicking the **Analyze** button without entering a name. Because we added the required attribute to our HTML input, the browser should stop you. But even if it didn't, our Python script has a check for an empty name and would return a proper JSON error message, which our PHP would display.

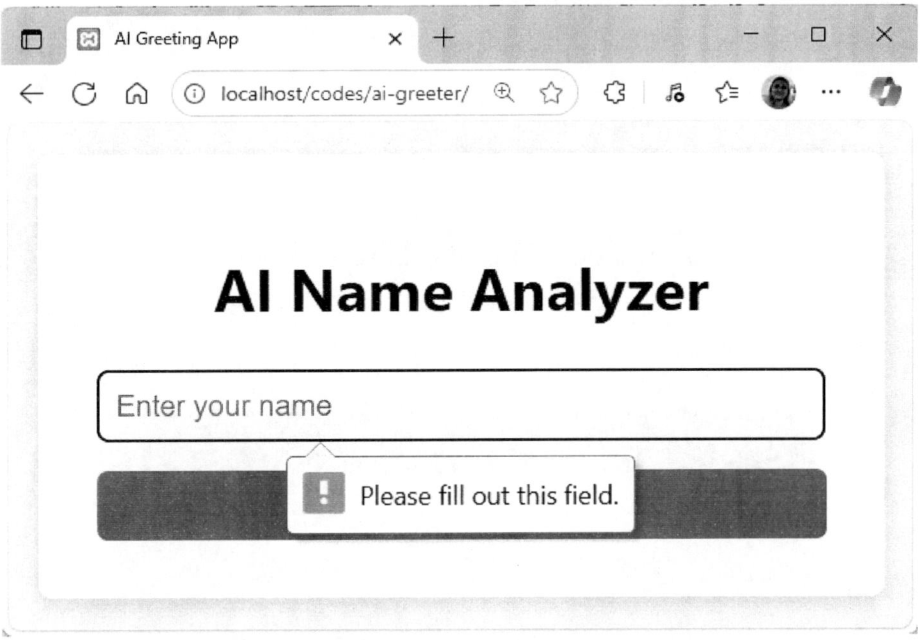

- **Simulating a Python error:** What if our Python script breaks? Temporarily rename analyzer.py to analyzer_broken.py. Now submit the form again. shell_exec() will fail to find the script and will likely return null. Our PHP code sees that the response is not a valid success message and displays **An unknown error occurred**. This is graceful error handling. (Remember to rename the file back!)

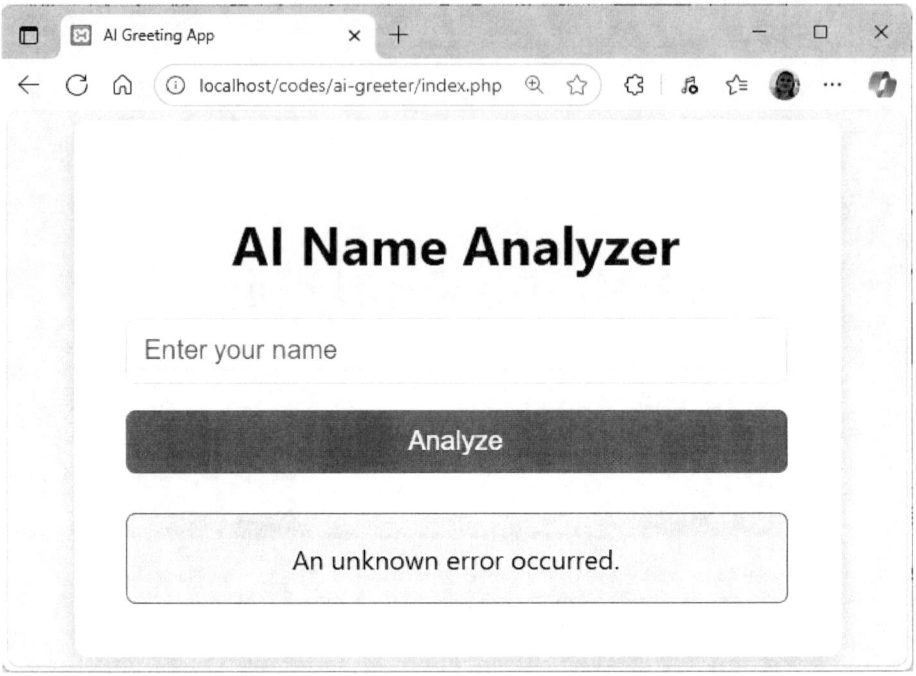

Harnessing the client-service model in real-world contexts

This simple pattern is used everywhere in professional web development. Imagine:

- An **e-commerce site** (PHP) sends a product description to a Python script that generates a summary for social media posts.
- A **blog platform** (PHP) sends a user's uploaded image to a Python service that automatically tags it with keywords (#sunset, #beach, #ocean).
- A **support ticket system** (PHP) sends the text of a customer's complaint to a Python script that performs sentiment analysis to flag it as "urgent."

Wrapping up

In this chapter, we dramatically expanded the capabilities of our PHP applications. We've established a powerful and professional pattern for building smarter, more feature-rich websites.

- You learned that **Python is a powerhouse for AI** and data science, making it a perfect partner for web-focused PHP.
- You successfully **set up a Python environment** and learned to use its package manager, pip.
- You used PHP's shell_exec() function to **run a Python script** from your web application.
- You mastered using **JSON as the universal language** to pass data safely and reliably between PHP and Python.
- You now understand the **client-service architecture**, a fundamental concept in modern software design.
- You practiced **secure coding** by using escapeshellarg() to protect your application from vulnerabilities.

Give yourself a huge pat on the back! You have just bridged the gap between two of the most popular programming languages in the world. This is not a simple party trick; it's a gateway to building applications that are not just dynamic, but truly intelligent. You now have the fundamental skill to integrate virtually any AI or data science tool into your PHP projects.

In the next chapter, we'll put this new skill to immediate use by building another practical tool. Get ready for ***Chapter 33: Building a QR code generator***.

Chapter 33

Section 09: The AI ecosystem – Bringing Python into your workflow

Building a QR code generator

What you'll learn

- Project planning
- Python scripting
- Dynamic image display
- PHP front-end forms
- PHP and Python integration
- Offloading complex tasks

Have you ever wondered how websites instantly create those scannable black-and-white squares called QR codes? You see them everywhere: on restaurant menus, event tickets, and product packaging. While you *could* try to build a QR code generator using only PHP, it would involve complex image manipulation and algorithms—a daunting task for even seasoned developers. This is a perfect scenario where PHP can shine at what it does best (handling web requests) and delegate a specialized task to a true expert: Python.

In this chapter, we're going to build a fully functional web application that does exactly this. We'll create a sleek front-end with PHP and HTML where a user can enter any text or URL. Then, with a single command, our PHP script will securely call a Python script, which will use a powerful, freely available library to generate a custom QR code image in milliseconds. This project beautifully demonstrates the client-service architecture we discussed, proving how you can add incredibly powerful features to your web apps by letting each language play to its strengths.

Planning the app

Before we write a single line of code, let's act like project managers and map out our application. A clear plan prevents confusion and ensures we build exactly what we intend to.

Our **feature set** is wonderfully simple:

- A user can input any text (a URL, a name, a secret message).
- The application generates a valid, scannable QR code image from that text.
- The generated image is displayed back to the user on the same page.

The **User Interface (UI)** will be clean and focused. It needs just two main components:

- An HTML form with a single text input field for the user's data.
- A **Generate QR Code** button to submit the form.
- A designated area below the form where the resulting QR code image will appear after it's created.

Finally, let's define the **workflow**, which is the step-by-step journey the data takes:

- **User input:** The user visits our PHP page, types text into the form, and clicks the submit button.
- **PHP receives:** Our index.php script receives the text via a POST request.
- **PHP delegates:** PHP sanitizes the user's text for security, determines a unique filename for the new image, and executes our Python script using shell_exec(). It passes the user's text and the desired filename as command-line arguments.
- **Python works:** The Python script (generate_qr.py) receives the arguments. It uses the qrcode library to create an image from the text and saves it to a file in an images directory.
- **PHP displays:** Once the Python script is finished, our PHP script reloads the page, now including an <img> tag pointing to the newly created QR code image.

This elegant workflow keeps our PHP code clean and focused on web interactions while offloading the heavy lifting of image generation to a Python script that's built for the job.

Writing the PHP front-end: The form for user input

The first piece of our puzzle is the interface the user will interact with. This is a simple HTML form contained within our main PHP file. It's the gateway to our application, so let's build it.

First, let's set up our project structure.

1. Open the **XAMPP Control Panel** and ensure **Apache** is running.
2. Navigate to your XAMPP installation directory and open the **htdocs\codes** folder. For most Windows users, this is C:\xampp\htdocs.
3. Inside **htdocs\codes**, create a new folder named **qr-generator**. This will be our project's root directory.
4. Open **Visual Studio Code**.
5. Click **File → Open Folder**....
6. Select **qr-generator** folder
7. Inside the **qr-generator** folder, create a new file named index.php.
8. Now, let's add the code for our form into index.php. This file will eventually contain all our PHP logic, but for now, it will just hold the HTML structure:

```
<!DOCTYPE html>
<html lang="en">
<head>
    <meta charset="UTF-8">
    <meta name="viewport" content="width=device-width, initial-scale=1.0">
    <title>PHP & Python QR Code Generator</title>
</head>
<body>
    <div class="container">
        <h1>QR Code Generator</h1>
        <p>Enter text or a URL to generate a QR code.</p>
        <form method="POST" action="index.php">
            <input type="text" name="data" placeholder="Enter your data here..."
                   required>
            <button type="submit">Generate QR Code</button>
        </form>
    </div>
</body>
</html>
```

This is a standard HTML5 document. The key elements are inside the <body>:

- A **<form>** with **method="POST"**. Using POST is important because it sends the form data in the body of the request, which is more secure and appropriate for this task than sending it in the URL with GET.
- The **action="index.php"** attribute tells the form to submit the data back to itself. This is a common pattern for single-page applications.
- An **<input type="text" name="data">** is where the user will type. The **name="data"** attribute is crucial; it's the key we'll use in PHP **($_POST['data'])** to retrieve the value.
- A **<button type="submit">** triggers the form submission.

If you open your browser and navigate to **http://localhost/codes/qr-generator/**, you can see a simple, unstyled form. It's functional but not very pretty. We'll add the CSS later. For now, we have our starting point.

Writing the Python script: The QR code generation logic

Now for the fun part: the AI-powered engine of our application. We'll write a Python script that takes text as input and outputs a QR code image. To do this, we'll use a fantastic, free **Python library** called **qrcode**.

Installing the Python library

First, we need to install the library. Python's package manager, **pip**, makes this a breeze.

1. Open your computer's command prompt (on Windows, search for **cmd**; on macOS, open **Terminal**).

2. Type the following command and press **Enter**:

```
pip install "qrcode[pil]"
```

This command tells **pip** to download and install the **qrcode library**. The **[pil]** part is important—it ensures that **Pillow**, a powerful image processing library that qrcode depends on, is also installed.

3. You can see some text indicating a successful installation.

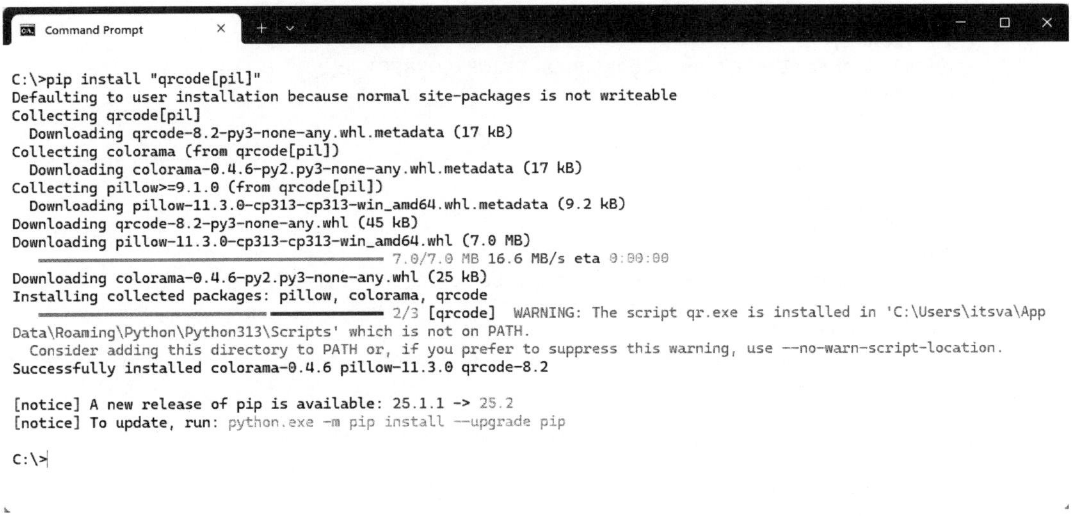

Creating the Python script

Next, let's create the Python file in our project.

1. GO back to **VS Code**, inside your **qr-generator** folder, create a new file named **generate_qr.py**.
2. Also, create a new folder named **images**. This is where our Python script will save the generated QR codes. Your project structure should now look like this:

```
qr-generator/
├── images/
├── generate_qr.py
└── index.php
```

3. Now, add the following code to generate_qr.py:

```
import qrcode
import sys
# Check if the correct number of arguments are provided
```

```
if len(sys.argv) != 3:
    # Exit if arguments are incorrect, but don't print an error to the PHP output
    sys.exit(1)
# The first command-line argument is the data for the QR code
qr_data = sys.argv[1]
# The second command-line argument is the full path for the output file
output_file = sys.argv[2]
try:
    # Create a qr code object
    qr = qrcode.QRCode(
        version=1,
        error_correction=qrcode.constants.ERROR_CORRECT_L,
        box_size=10,
        border=4,
    )
    # Add the data to the QR code
    qr.add_data(qr_data)
    qr.make(fit=True)
    # Create an image from the QR Code instance
    img = qr.make_image(fill_color="black", back_color="white")
    # Save the image to the specified file
    img.save(output_file)
    # Print the path of the generated file to standard output, so PHP can capture it
    print(output_file)
except Exception as e:
    # If something goes wrong, exit gracefully
    sys.exit(1)
```

Let's break down this Python code:

- **import qrcode and import sys:** We import the necessary libraries. sys allows us to access the command-line arguments that PHP will send.
- **sys.argv:** This is a list containing the command-line arguments. sys.argv[0] is always the name of the script itself, sys.argv[1] will be the text we want to encode, and sys.argv[2] will be the filename to save the image as.
- **qrcode.QRCode(...):** We create and configure a QR code generator object. We can control things like the size and error correction level.
- **qr.add_data(qr_data):** We feed the user's text into the generator.
- **img = qr.make_image(...):** We create the actual image object, specifying the colors.
- **img.save(output_file):** This is the magic moment where the image is saved to the file path we provided.

- **print(output_file): This is the most critical line for communication.** Whatever a Python script prints to standard output can be captured by PHP's shell_exec() function. By printing the filename, we are sending a confirmation message back to PHP, telling it where to find the new image.

Connecting the languages: PHP sending the user's text to Python

We have our PHP front-end and our Python back-end. Now we need to build the bridge between them. We'll add the PHP logic to index.php to call our Python script.

Add the following code at the top of your index.php:

```
<?php
// Variable to hold the path to the generated QR code image
$qrCodeImage = '';
// Check if the form has been submitted
if ($_SERVER['REQUEST_METHOD'] == 'POST' && !empty($_POST['data'])) {
    // 1. Get the user's input from the form
    $data = $_POST['data'];
    // 2. Define the path for the image
    $imageFolder = 'images/';
    // Create a unique filename to prevent overwriting files
    $filename = $imageFolder . 'qr_' . uniqid() . '.png';
    // 3. Sanitize the user input to be safely passed to the command line
    $sanitized_data = escapeshellarg($data);
    $sanitized_filename = escapeshellarg($filename);
    // 4. Build the command to execute the Python script. Note: You might need to
    // use 'python3' instead of 'python' depending on your system setup
    $command = "python generate_qr.py " . $sanitized_data . " " .
               $sanitized_filename;
    // 5. Execute the command and capture the output
    $output = shell_exec($command);
    // 6. Check if the output (the image path) is not empty
    if ($output) {
        // Trim whitespace from the output and assign it to our variable
        $qrCodeImage = trim($output);
    }
}
?>
<!DOCTYPE html>
. . .
```

Let's carefully review this new PHP block at the top of the file:

- **Check for submission:** if ($_SERVER['REQUEST_METHOD'] == 'POST' ...) ensures this logic only runs when the user has actually submitted the form.

- **Get data:** We grab the user's text from the **$_POST** superglobal.
- **Create unique filename:** We define our **images/** folder and use **uniqid()** to generate a random, unique string. This ensures that every generated QR code has its own file and we never accidentally overwrite an old one.
- **Sanitize input:** This is a **critical security step**. The **escapeshellarg()** function wraps the user's input in single quotes and escapes any special characters. This prevents a malicious user from injecting harmful commands (a technique called **command injection**). **Never** pass raw user input to shell_exec()!
- **Build command:** We construct the full command-line string. It starts with python (the command to run Python), followed by the name of our script, and then our two sanitized arguments.
- **Execute: shell_exec($command)** tells the server's operating system to run this command just as if you had typed it into the command prompt. The server pauses the PHP script, runs the Python script, and whatever the Python script prints is captured into the $output variable.
- **Store result:** We **trim()** any potential whitespace from the output and store the resulting filename (images/qr_123abc.png) in our **$qrCodeImage** variable.

Displaying the results: Using a file path to show the QR code image

The final piece of the puzzle is to display the image if one has been created. Since our PHP variable **$qrCodeImage** now holds the path to the image, we can use a simple **if** statement inside our HTML to conditionally show an <img> tag.

Modify the <body> section of your index.php file with the following code to include this new logic:

```
<body>
    <div class="container">
        <h1>QR Code Generator</h1>
        <p>Enter text or a URL to generate a QR code.</p>
        <form method="POST" action="index.php">
            <input type="text" name="data" placeholder="Enter your data here..."
                   value="<?= htmlspecialchars($_POST['data'] ?? '') ?>"
                   required>
            <button type="submit">Generate QR Code</button>
        </form>
        <?php if ($qrCodeImage): ?>
            <div class="qr-code-container">
                <h2>Your QR Code:</h2>
```

```
                <img src="<?= htmlspecialchars($qrCodeImage) ?>"
                     alt="Generated QR Code">
                <p>Right-click and save the image.</p>
            </div>
        <?php endif; ?>
    </div>
</body>
```

Here are the important changes:

- **value="<?= htmlspecialchars($_POST['data'] ?? '') ?>"**: This is a nice user-experience touch. It keeps the user's submitted text inside the input box after the page reloads. The **??** '' part prevents an error if the page is loaded for the first time. **htmlspecialchars()** is another security function that prevents XSS attacks by encoding HTML special characters.
- **<?php if ($qrCodeImage): ?>**: This is our conditional block. The HTML inside this **if** statement will only be rendered if our **$qrCodeImage** variable contains a value (meaning the Python script ran successfully).
- **<img src="<?= htmlspecialchars($qrCodeImage) ?>">**: This is where the result is displayed. The **src** attribute is dynamically set to the path returned by our Python script. We use **htmlspecialchars()** on the path as a best practice, even though it's generated by our own script.

With this final piece, our application's logic is complete! The only thing left is to make it look good.

It's time to assemble all our pieces into a single, polished application. Now, we will walk through the complete code for all files, including the CSS to give our app a modern and clean look. By the end, you will have a fully functional web tool that seamlessly integrates PHP and Python.

Create the CSS file

1. In **VS Code**, inside your **qr-generator** folder, create a new file named **style.css**.
2. Add the following CSS code into style.css. This styling will center our content, give the form a clean look, and create a nice card for the resulting QR code:

```
body {
    font-family: -apple-system, BlinkMacSystemFont, "Segoe UI", Roboto,
                 Helvetica, Arial, sans-serif;
    background-color: #f0f2f5;
    color: #333;
    display: flex;
    justify-content: center;
```

```
    align-items: center;
    min-height: 100vh;
    margin: 0;
}
.container {
    background-color: #ffffff;
    padding: 2rem 3rem;
    border-radius: 12px;
    box-shadow: 0 4px 20px rgba(0, 0, 0, 0.1);
    width: 100%;
    max-width: 500px;
    text-align: center;
}
h1 {
    color: #1a73e8;
    margin-bottom: 0.5rem;
}
p {
    color: #5f6368;
    margin-bottom: 2rem;
}
form {
    display: flex;
    flex-direction: column;
    gap: 1rem;
}
input[type="text"] {
    width: 100%;
    padding: 12px 15px;
    border: 1px solid #dfe1e5;
    border-radius: 8px;
    font-size: 16px;
    box-sizing: border-box; /* Ensures padding doesn't affect width */
}
input[type="text"]:focus {
    outline: none;
    border-color: #1a73e8;
    box-shadow: 0 0 0 2px rgba(26, 115, 232, 0.2);
}
button {
    background-color: #1a73e8;
    color: white;
    border: none;
    padding: 12px 20px;
    border-radius: 8px;
    font-size: 16px;
    font-weight: bold;
    cursor: pointer;
    transition: background-color 0.2s ease-in-out;
}
button:hover {
```

```
    background-color: #185abc;
}
.qr-code-container {
    margin-top: 2rem;
    padding-top: 2rem;
    border-top: 1px solid #e0e0e0;
}
.qr-code-container h2 {
    color: #333;
    margin-bottom: 1rem;
}
.qr-code-container img {
    max-width: 250px;
    height: auto;
    border: 5px solid #fff;
    box-shadow: 0 2px 10px rgba(0, 0, 0, 0.1);
    border-radius: 8px;
}
.qr-code-container p {
    font-size: 14px;
    color: #777;
    margin-top: 1rem;
}
```

Finalize the index.php file

Now, let's put together the final version of index.php, which includes the PHP logic, the HTML structure, and a link to our new stylesheet:

```
<?php
// Variable to hold the path to the generated QR code image
$qrCodeImage = '';
// Check if the form has been submitted
if ($_SERVER['REQUEST_METHOD'] == 'POST' && !empty($_POST['data'])) {
    // 1. Get the user's input from the form
    $data = $_POST['data'];
    // 2. Define the path for the image
    $imageFolder = 'images/';
    // Create a unique filename to prevent overwriting files
    $filename = $imageFolder . 'qr_' . uniqid() . '.png';
    // 3. Sanitize the user input to be safely passed to the command line
    $sanitized_data = escapeshellarg($data);
    $sanitized_filename = escapeshellarg($filename);
    // 4. Build the command to execute the Python script. Note: You might need to
    // use 'python3' instead of 'python' depending on your system setup.
    $command = "python generate_qr.py " . $sanitized_data . " " .
                $sanitized_filename;
    // 5. Execute the command and capture the output
    $output = shell_exec($command);
```

```
    // 6. Check if the output (the image path) is not empty
    if ($output) {
        // Trim whitespace from the output and assign it to our variable
        $qrCodeImage = trim($output);
    }
}
?>
<!DOCTYPE html>
<html lang="en">
<head>
    <meta charset="UTF-8">
    <meta name="viewport" content="width=device-width, initial-scale=1.0">
    <title>PHP & Python QR Code Generator</title>
    <link rel="stylesheet" href="style.css">
</head>
<body>
    <div class="container">
        <h1>QR Code Generator</h1>
        <p>Enter text or a URL to generate a QR code.</p>
        <form method="POST" action="index.php">
            <input type="text" name="data" placeholder="Enter your data here..."
                   value="<?= htmlspecialchars($_POST['data'] ?? '') ?>"
                   required>
            <button type="submit">Generate QR Code</button>
        </form>
        <?php if ($qrCodeImage): ?>
            <div class="qr-code-container">
                <h2>Your QR Code:</h2>
                <img src="<?= htmlspecialchars($qrCodeImage) ?>"
                     alt="Generated QR Code">
                <p>Right-click and save the image.</p>
            </div>
        <?php endif; ?>
    </div>
</body>
</html>
```

The only new addition here is the **<link rel="stylesheet" href="style.css">** tag in the **<head>**, which connects our stylesheet to the page.

Your final project structure is now:

```
C:\xampp\htdocs\codes\qr-generator\
├── images/ (This folder should be writable by the web server)
├── generate_qr.py
├── index.php
└── style.css
```

Bridging the gap: Learned concepts and application implementation

This project is a perfect real-world example of the client-service architecture.

- **The client (PHP):** Our **index.php** file acts as the **client**. It handles the **web** part of the job: displaying the HTML form, receiving the user's request, and rendering the final page. It doesn't know *how* to make a QR code, nor does it need to.
- **The service (Python):** Our **generate_qr.py** script is a highly specialized service. Its only job is to do one thing and do it well: generate a QR code image. It's completely decoupled from the web interface.
- **The communication protocol (command line):** The bridge between them is the **server's command line**, invoked by **shell_exec()**. PHP packages the required information (the data and a filename) and sends it over. Python performs the task and sends a simple confirmation back (the path to the result). This is a simple yet powerful way to make two different technologies talk to each other.

Running and testing

Let's see our creation in action!

1. Make sure your **Apache** server is running via the **XAMPP Control Panel**.
2. Open your web browser (like Chrome or Firefox).
3. Navigate to **http://localhost/codes/qr-generator/**.
4. You can see our beautifully styled form.

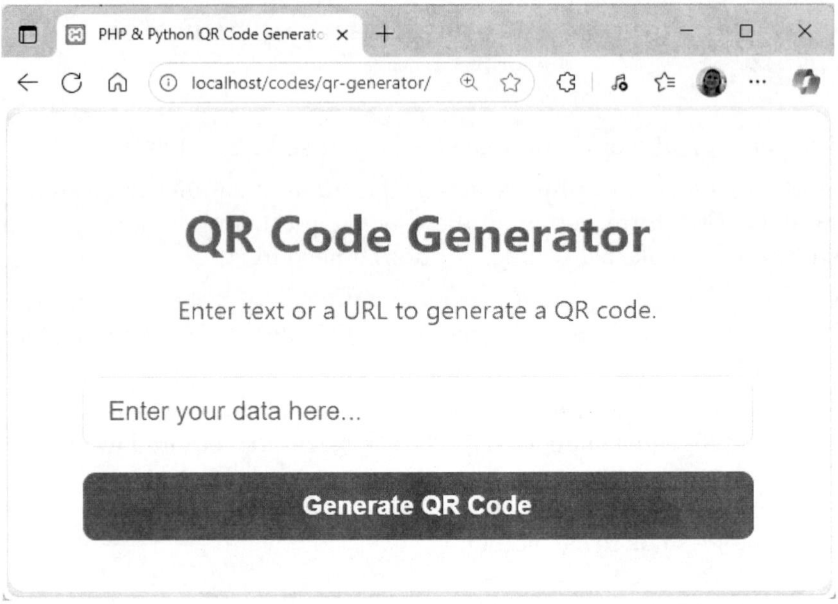

5. In the **text box**, type a **URL**, for example: **https://www.sharanamshah.com**.
6. Click the **Generate QR Code** button.
7. The page reloads, and—voila!—below the form, you can see your generated QR code.

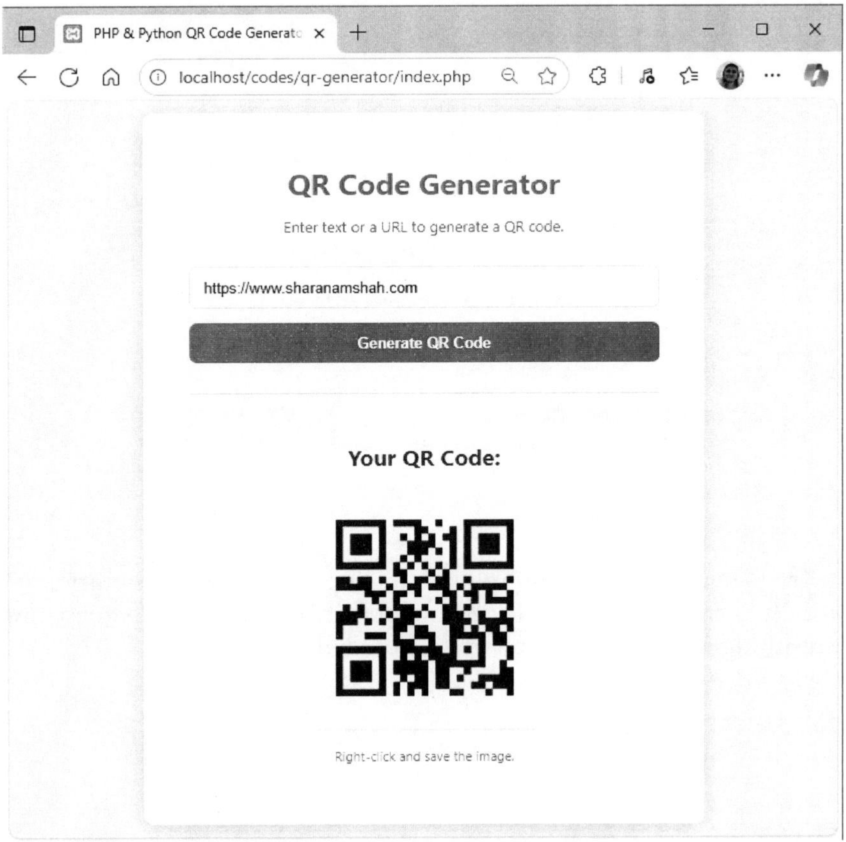

8. Try it again with different text, like your name or a short sentence.
9. If you have a QR code scanner on your phone, try scanning the image. It should correctly decode the text you entered.

Exploring application behaviour: A practical run-through

A robust application handles all sorts of inputs gracefully. Let's consider a few scenarios:

- **Valid input:** As we just tested, entering a URL or plain text works perfectly. The Python script generates the image, and PHP displays it.
- **Empty input:** Our **<input>** field has the required attribute, so modern browsers won't even let the user submit the form without typing something. This is a simple front-end validation.

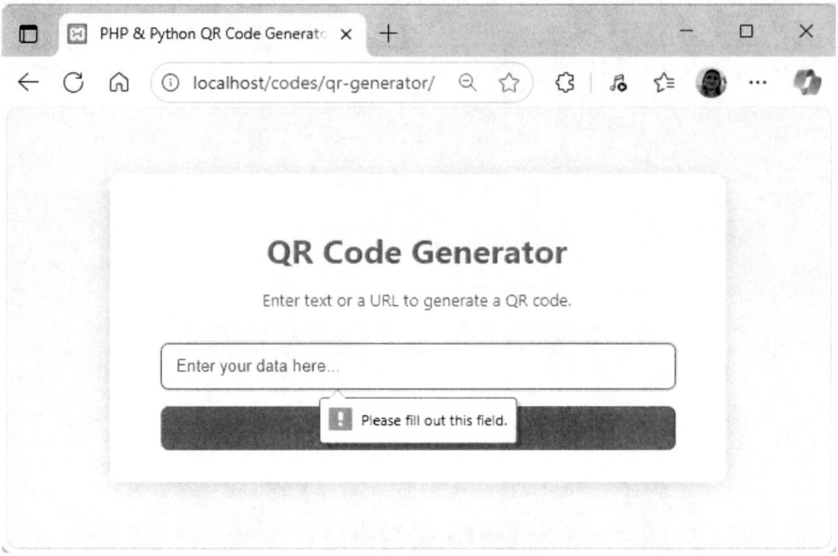

- **Long text:** Try pasting a long paragraph into the input. The **qrcode** library is quite robust; it automatically increases the complexity and density of the QR code to accommodate the data. The resulting image looks much more **crowded**.

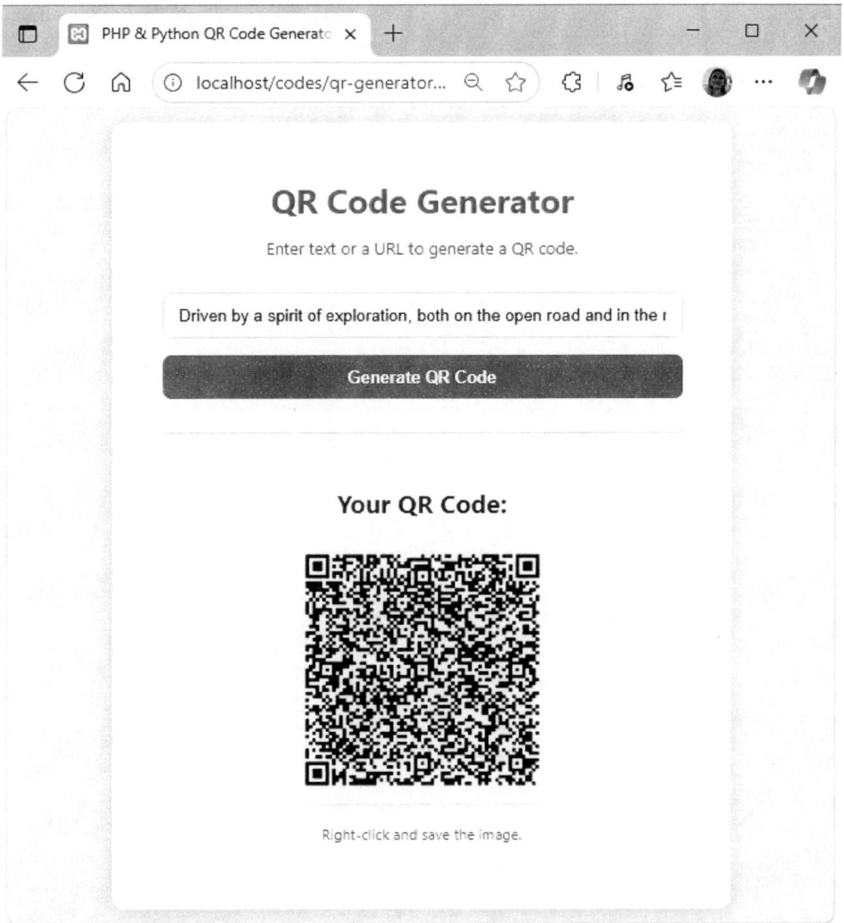

- **Special characters:** What happens if you enter text like !@#$%^&*()'? Because we used escapeshellarg(), these characters are handled safely. They are passed as a literal string to Python and correctly encoded into the QR code without breaking our command. This is why sanitization is so important.

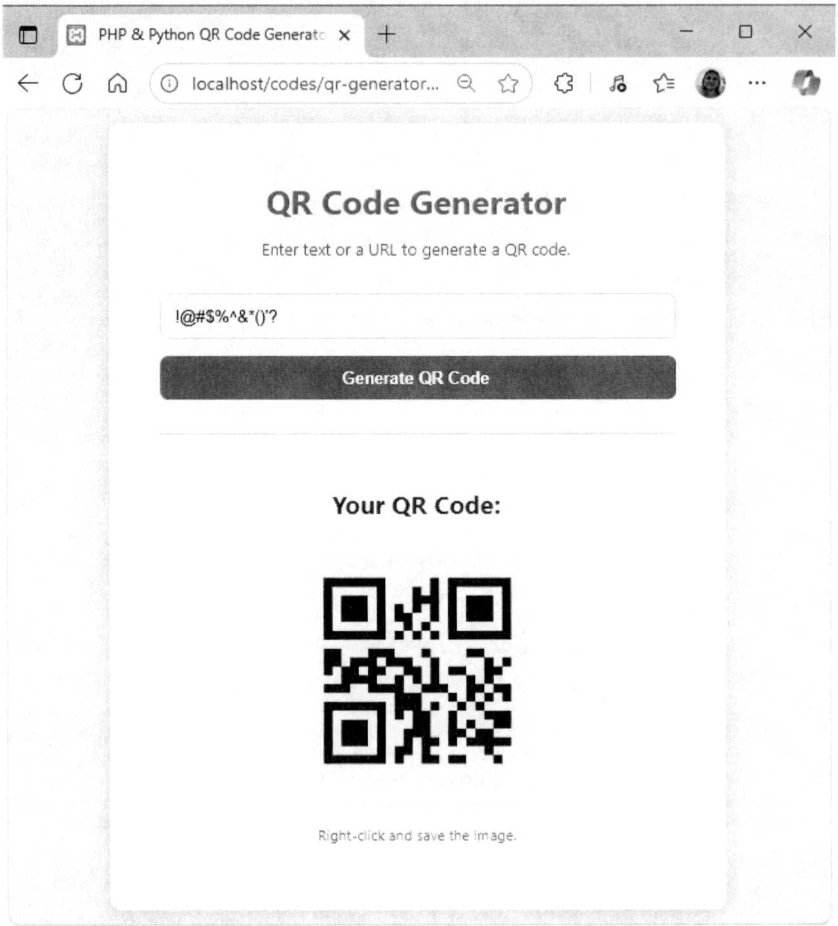

Harnessing QR code generation in real-world contexts

This simple tool is more than just a fun project; it's the basis for countless real-world features.

- **E-commerce:** An order confirmation page could generate a QR code for a customer's e-ticket or return slip.
- **Marketing:** A business could use a tool like this to instantly generate QR codes for posters or flyers that link to their website or a special offer.
- **Networking:** A user's profile page on a social or professional network could have a button to generate a QR code of their contact information (a vCard).

- **Two-factor authentication (2FA):** When you set up 2FA for a new account, the website often shows you a QR code to scan. This is generated on-the-fly, just like in our app.

Wrapping up

In this chapter, we built a complete, practical web application from the ground up, successfully bridging two powerful programming languages.

- You learned to plan an application's features, UI, and workflow.
- You built a user-facing front-end with a secure PHP form.
- You installed a third-party Python library (qrcode) using pip.
- You wrote a Python script that accepts command-line arguments to perform a specialized task.
- You mastered the shell_exec() function in PHP to run an external script.
- You learned the critical importance of sanitizing user input with escapeshellarg() before passing it to the command line.
- You dynamically displayed a generated image on the page using PHP.

Congratulations! You have successfully built a sophisticated tool that demonstrates a core principle of modern web development: using the right tool for the right job. You didn't need to become an expert in image processing algorithms; you simply leveraged the power of the Python ecosystem and integrated it cleanly into your PHP application. This client-service mindset will open up endless possibilities for the features you can add to your projects.

In the next chapter, we'll take this concept even further. Get ready for ***Chapter 34: Upgrading ConnectSphere app with a language translator***, where we'll enhance our final ConnectSphere project with another powerful AI service!

Chapter 34

Section 09: The AI ecosystem – Bringing Python into your workflow

Upgrading ConnectSphere app with a language translator

What you'll learn

- Upgrading existing apps
- Server-side translation
- Handling API responses
- Installing Python libraries
- Integrating a new AI service
- Dynamic UI updates

In our journey so far, you have built an entire social media application, ConnectSphere, from scratch. You then bridged the gap between two of the web's most powerful languages, PHP and Python. You've seen how PHP can act as the user-facing manager of a web application, delegating specialized, heavy-lifting tasks to a Python script working diligently behind the scenes. This is the secret to building truly modern, intelligent web applications.

In this chapter, we're going to put that exact principle into practice in the most rewarding way possible: by upgrading the capstone project you already built. We will add a powerful, real-world feature to ConnectSphere—a language translator. We'll add a **Translate** button to user posts, allowing anyone to instantly translate a post into a language of their choice. This project will directly connect to the ConnectSphere application you are already familiar with, proving how easy it is to enhance an existing PHP project with new AI capabilities. We'll use a wonderfully simple and free Python library called **googletrans** to handle the complex translation logic, demonstrating once again how to let each language do what it does best. Let's level up your creation!

Planning the upgrade: What to analyze and how to display it

Before we touch any code, let's put our **Product Manager** hats back on for a moment. A successful feature is a well-planned feature. We need to define exactly what we're changing and how it will work. Our goal is to allow users to translate any post they see on another user's profile.

The user interface (UI)

The change will be on the profile.php page. For every post displayed, we will add two new elements:

- A **dropdown menu** (<select>) containing a list of languages a user can translate the post into.
- A **Translate button** to trigger the action.

When the translation is complete, the translated text will appear directly below the original post content, creating a seamless experience.

The workflow

The data journey will follow the client-service model we've learned:

1. **User action:** A logged-in user is viewing a profile, sees a post in a different language, selects a target language from the dropdown, and clicks the **Translate** button.

2. **PHP receives:** The form submits the data back to the profile.php page using the POST method. Our PHP script will receive the ID of the post to be translated and the target language code (e.g., 'es' for Spanish).
3. **PHP delegates:** The PHP script will first fetch the original post's text from our posts table in the database. Then, it will securely package this text and the target language code and call our new Python translation script using shell_exec().
4. **Python works:** A Python script (translator.py) will receive the text and language code. It will use the googletrans library to perform the translation.
5. **Python responds:** The Python script will package the result (either the translated text or an error message) into a JSON string and print it to the console.
6. **PHP displays:** Back in profile.php, the shell_exec() function captures the JSON response. Our script decodes it, and if successful, the page reloads, now displaying the translated text in a specially styled box right under the original post.

This plan keeps our PHP logic clean and focused on web interaction, while the complex task of translation is perfectly handled by our Python service.

Setting up the environment: Installing the googletrans library

Before we can write our Python script, we need to install the third-party library that will do all the heavy lifting. Python's package manager, **pip**, makes this incredibly simple. The **googletrans library** is a free, open-source tool that uses the Google Translate API to provide fast and reliable translations.

1. Open your computer's command prompt.
   - On Windows, you can search for **cmd** in the Start Menu.
   - In VS Code, you can also use the built-in terminal by going to **...** → **Terminal** → **New Terminal**.
2. Type the following command exactly as written and press **Enter**. We are upgrading to the latest version and installing **httpx**, a dependency the new version requires for handling network requests:

```
pip install --upgrade googletrans httpx
```

3. You can see a series of download and installation messages.
4. Once it's finished, you'll see a success message confirming that the library is installed and ready to be used by our Python scripts.

```
Downloading anyio-4.10.0-py3-none-any.whl (107 kB)
Installing collected packages: h11, anyio, httpcore, httpx, googletrans
  Attempting uninstall: h11
    Found existing installation: h11 0.9.0
    Uninstalling h11-0.9.0:
      Successfully uninstalled h11-0.9.0
  Attempting uninstall: httpcore
    Found existing installation: httpcore 0.9.1
    Uninstalling httpcore-0.9.1:
      Successfully uninstalled httpcore-0.9.1
  Attempting uninstall: httpx
    Found existing installation: httpx 0.13.3
    Uninstalling httpx-0.13.3:
      Successfully uninstalled httpx-0.13.3
   ━━━━━━━━━━━━━━━━━━━━━━━━ ━━━━━━━━━━━━━━━ 3/5 [httpx]  WARNING: The script httpx.exe is installed in 'C:\Users\itsva\AppData\Roaming\Python\Python313\Scripts' which is not on PATH.
  Consider adding this directory to PATH or, if you prefer to suppress this warning, use --no-warn-script-location.
  Attempting uninstall: googletrans
    Found existing installation: googletrans 4.0.0rc1
    Uninstalling googletrans-4.0.0rc1:
      Successfully uninstalled googletrans-4.0.0rc1
   ━━━━━━━━━━━━━━━━━━━━━━━━━━━━━━━ ━━━━━━━━ 4/5 [googletrans]  WARNING: The script translate.exe is installed in 'C:\Users\itsva\AppData\Roaming\Python\Python313\Scripts' which is not on PATH.
  Consider adding this directory to PATH or, if you prefer to suppress this warning, use --no-warn-script-location.
Successfully installed anyio-4.10.0 googletrans-4.0.2 h11-0.16.0 httpcore-1.0.9 httpx-0.28.1

[notice] A new release of pip is available: 25.1.1 -> 25.2
[notice] To update, run: python.exe -m pip install --upgrade pip

C:\>
```

A quick note on APIs:
The **googletrans** library is fantastic for learning because it's a **reverse-engineered** library, meaning it cleverly uses Google Translate's public service without needing a special key. For professional, high-traffic applications, you would typically sign up for an official, paid service like the Google Cloud Translation API, which would provide you with a secure API key, just like we did for the Gemini API.

Implementing the full translation feature into your app

It's time to bring our plan to life. We'll create our Python service, integrate it into our existing PHP front-end, and add the necessary styling to make it look professional.

Create the services folder and Python script

First, let's create a dedicated place for our Python scripts to keep our project organized.

1. In the **VS Code Explorer** panel, right-click on the root **connectsphere** folder and select **New Folder**.
2. Name the folder **services**.
3. Now, right-click on the new **services** folder and select **New File**.

4. Name the file **translator.py**.

Your project structure should now contain this new folder and file:

```
connectsphere/
├── public/
├── services/
│   └── translator.py
├── src/
├── templates/
└── config.php
```

Write the Python translation logic

Open your newly created **services/translator.py** file and add the following code. This script will be our dedicated translation service:

```
import sys
import json
import asyncio
from googletrans import Translator, LANGUAGES
async def translate_text(text, dest_lang):
    """Translates text to a destination language and handles errors."""
    try:
        # Check if the destination language code is valid
        if dest_lang not in LANGUAGES:
            return {"status": "error", "message": "Invalid target language."}
        translator = Translator()
        translation = await translator.translate(text, dest=dest_lang)
        # Return a success response
        return {
            "status": "success",
            "translated_text": translation.text
        }
    except Exception as e:
        # Return a generic error if anything goes wrong
        return {"status": "error", "message": f"Translation failed: {str(e)}"}
# --- Main script execution ---
async def main():
    if len(sys.argv) != 3:
        response = {"status": "error", "message": "Invalid arguments provided."}
    else:
        text_to_translate = sys.argv[1]
        target_language = sys.argv[2]
        if not text_to_translate:
             response = {"status": "error", "message": "Text to translate cannot be
                          empty."}
        else:
```

```
            response = await translate_text(text_to_translate, target_language)
    print(json.dumps(response))
if __name__ == "__main__":
    asyncio.run(main())
```

Let's break down our Python service:

- **Imports:** We import **sys** to read command-line arguments, **json** to format our output, Translator and LANGUAGES from our **googletrans** library, and **asyncio** to run our asynchronous code.
- **Asynchronous functions:** The newer version of googletrans works asynchronously to handle network requests more efficiently. Notice the **async def** syntax. This defines a special function (a coroutine) that can be paused and resumed. The **await** keyword is used to call another **async** function (translator.translate) and wait for its result without blocking the entire program.
- **Error handling:** The entire translation logic is wrapped in a **try...except** block. If the **googletrans** library runs into any issues (like a network problem), our script won't crash. Instead, it will catch the error and format it into a clean **JSON** response.
- **Input validation:** We check that the **dest_lang** code is a valid language code known to the library. This prevents errors from invalid user input.
- **JSON response:** Crucially, the script always prints a JSON object. This creates a reliable communication contract with our PHP code. PHP will always receive a JSON string that it can decode to check the status and get either the **translated_text** or an error message.

Upgrade the PHP profile page

Now it's time to modify our existing **public/profile.php** file to include the new UI and the logic to call our Python script. We will be adding a form for each post, a language dropdown, and the PHP code to handle the translation request.

Replace the entire contents of your public/profile.php file with the following complete, upgraded code:

```
<?php
require_once __DIR__ . '/../src/auth_check.php';
require_once __DIR__ . '/../src/db_connect.php';
// --- NEW: Translation Logic ---
$translated_text = null;
$translated_post_id = null;
if ($_SERVER['REQUEST_METHOD'] === 'POST' && isset($_POST[
            'post_id_to_translate'])) {
    $translated_post_id = (int)$_POST['post_id_to_translate'];
    $target_lang = $_POST['target_lang'] ?? 'en'; // Default to English
```

```
    // 1. Fetch the original post content from the database
    $stmt_post_text = $pdo->prepare("SELECT content FROM posts
                                     WHERE post_id = ?");
    $stmt_post_text->execute([$translated_post_id]);
    $post_to_translate = $stmt_post_text->fetch();
    if ($post_to_translate) {
        // 2. Prepare the data for the Python script
        $text_to_translate = $post_to_translate['content'];
        $safe_text = escapeshellarg($text_to_translate);
        $safe_lang = escapeshellarg($target_lang);
        // 3. Build and execute the command
        // Note: The path to the Python script is relative to this PHP file's
        // location
        $command = "python ../services/translator.py " . $safe_text . " " .
                    $safe_lang;
        $json_response = shell_exec($command);
        // 4. Decode the response from Python
        $response = json_decode($json_response, true);
        if ($response && $response['status'] === 'success') {
            $translated_text = $response['translated_text'];
        } else {
            // If translation fails, you can set an error message
            $translated_text = "Translation failed: " . ($response['message'] ??
                                    'Unknown error.');
        }
    }
}
// --- END: Translation Logic ---
// Get the user ID from the URL, default to the logged-in user if not provided
$profile_user_id = isset($_GET['id']) ? (int)$_GET['id'] : $_SESSION['user_id'];
$current_user_id = $_SESSION['user_id'];
try {
    // Fetch the profile user's information
    $stmt = $pdo->prepare("SELECT user_id, username, created_at
                           FROM users WHERE user_id = ?");
    $stmt->execute([$profile_user_id]);
    $profile_user = $stmt->fetch();
    if (!$profile_user) {
        // Handle case where user does not exist
        $page_title = 'User Not Found';
        require_once __DIR__ . '/../templates/header.php';
        echo "<p>Sorry, this user could not be found.</p>";
        require_once __DIR__ . '/../templates/footer.php';
        exit();
    }
    // Determine the friendship status
    $friendship_status = 'not_friends';
    if ($current_user_id !== $profile_user_id) {
        $stmt_friend = $pdo->prepare(
            "SELECT status, action_user_id FROM friendships
             WHERE (user_one_id = ? AND user_two_id = ?) OR (user_one_id = ?
```

```
              AND user_two_id = ?)"
        );
        $stmt_friend->execute([$current_user_id, $profile_user_id,
                               $profile_user_id, $current_user_id]);
        $friendship = $stmt_friend->fetch();
        if ($friendship) {
            if ($friendship['status'] === 'accepted') {
                $friendship_status = 'friends';
            } elseif ($friendship['status'] === 'pending') {
                $friendship_status = ($friendship['action_user_id'] ==
                        $current_user_id) ? 'request_sent' : 'request_received';
            }
        }
    }
    // Fetch posts for the profile user
    $stmt_posts = $pdo->prepare("SELECT post_id, content, created_at
                        FROM posts WHERE user_id = ? ORDER BY created_at DESC");
    $stmt_posts->execute([$profile_user_id]);
    $posts = $stmt_posts->fetchAll();
} catch (PDOException $e) {
    die("Error: " . $e->getMessage());
}
$page_title = htmlspecialchars($profile_user['username']) . "'s Profile";
require_once __DIR__ . '/../templates/header.php';
?>
<div class="profile-header">
    <h1><?php echo htmlspecialchars($profile_user['username']); ?></h1>
    <p>Member since: <?php echo date("F j, Y", strtotime($profile_user
                ['created_at'])); ?></p>
    <?php if ($current_user_id !== $profile_user_id): ?>
        <div class="friend-action">
            <?php if ($friendship_status === 'not_friends'): ?>
                <a href="friend_action.php?action=add&id=<?php
                   echo $profile_user_id; ?>" class="btn">Add Friend</a>
            <?php elseif ($friendship_status === 'request_sent'): ?>
                <button class="btn" disabled>Friend Request Sent</button>
            <?php elseif ($friendship_status === 'request_received'): ?>
                <a href="friend_action.php?action=accept&id=<?php
                   echo $profile_user_id; ?>" class="btn">Accept Request</a>
            <?php elseif ($friendship_status === 'friends'): ?>
                <a href="friend_action.php?action=remove&id=<?php
                   echo $profile_user_id; ?>" class="btn btn-danger">Unfriend</a>
            <?php endif; ?>
        </div>
    <?php endif; ?>
</div>
<div class="profile-content">
    <h2>Posts by <?php echo htmlspecialchars($profile_user['username']); ?>
</h2>
    <?php if (count($posts) > 0): ?>
        <div class="post-list">
```

```
            <?php foreach ($posts as $post): ?>
                <div class="post-card">
                    <p class="post-content"><?php echo nl2br(
                       htmlspecialchars($post['content'])); ?></p>
                    <?php if ($translated_post_id === $post['post_id'] &&
                          $translated_text): ?>
                        <div class="translation-result">
                            <p><strong>Translation:</strong>
                            <?php echo htmlspecialchars($translated_text); ?></p>
                        </div>
                    <?php endif; ?>
                    <div class="post-footer">
                        <p class="post-meta">Posted on <?php echo
                           date("g:i A - F j, Y", strtotime($post['created_at']));
                           ?></p>
                        <form class="translation-form" action="profile.php?
                              id=<?php echo $profile_user_id; ?>" method="POST">
                            <input type="hidden" name="post_id_to_translate"
                                   value="<?php echo $post['post_id']; ?>">
                            <select name="target_lang">
                                <option value="en">English</option>
                                <option value="es">Spanish</option>
                                <option value="fr">French</option>
                                <option value="de">German</option>
                                <option value="hi">Hindi</option>
                            </select>
                            <button type="submit" class="btn btn-secondary">
                                Translate </button>
                        </form>
                    </div>
                </div>
            <?php endforeach; ?>
        </div>
    <?php else: ?>
        <p><?php echo htmlspecialchars($profile_user['username']); ?> has not
           posted anything yet.</p>
    <?php endif; ?>
</div>
<?php
require_once __DIR__ . '/../templates/footer.php';
?>
```

Add the new CSS styles

To make our new translation form and result box look neat and integrated, we need to add a few styles.

Open **public/css/style.css** and add the following CSS rules at the very end of the file:

```
/* --- Post Translation Styles --- */
.post-footer {
    display: flex;
    justify-content: space-between;
    align-items: center;
    margin-top: 1rem;
    border-top: 1px solid var(--border-color);
    padding-top: 1rem;
}
.translation-form {
    display: flex;
    gap: 0.5rem;
    align-items: center;
}
.translation-form select {
    padding: 0.3rem;
    border-radius: 4px;
    border: 1px solid var(--border-color);
}
.translation-form .btn-secondary {
    padding: 0.3rem 0.8rem;
    /* Smaller button */
    font-size: 0.8rem;
}
.translation-result {
    margin-top: 1rem;
    padding: 1rem;
    background-color: #e7f3ff;
    border-left: 4px solid var(--primary-color);
    color: #0c5460;
}
```

With these changes, our upgrade is complete! The Python service is ready, the PHP client has been updated to use it, and the new UI elements are styled.

Bridging the gap: Learned concepts and application implementation

This project is a perfect, practical demonstration of the powerful concepts from the last few chapters.

Let's explicitly connect what we did to what we learned:

- **Client-service model:** Our profile.php page is the client. It's responsible for the user interface and handling web requests. It doesn't know how to translate text; it only knows it needs a translation. Our translator.py script is the specialized service. It's one and only job is to translate text. This separation of concerns is a hallmark of professional development.
- **PHP and Python integration:** We used PHP's **shell_exec()** function as the communication channel. This is the bridge that allows our PHP **client** to send a job request to our Python **service**.
- **Data exchange with JSON:** We didn't just send plain text back from Python. We sent a structured JSON object. This is far more robust because it allows PHP to reliably check the status of the request and handle success and error cases differently, preventing our application from showing confusing output if something goes wrong.
- **Secure command-line calls:** We used **escapeshellarg()** on both the user-provided text and the language code before passing them to the shell. This is a non-negotiable security practice that protects our application from command injection attacks, where a malicious user could try to sneak system commands into the input.
- **Enhancing existing applications:** Most importantly, we demonstrated how you don't need to rewrite an entire application to add powerful new features. By understanding how to integrate external services, you can incrementally add incredible value to the projects you've already built.

Running and testing

It's time for the big reveal! Let's test our new translation feature from start to finish.

1. Make sure your **Apache** and **MySQL** services are running in the **XAMPP Control Panel**.
2. Open your web browser and log in to your **ConnectSphere** application. Let's log in as user **Vaishali**.
3. For this test to be effective, Vaishali needs a post in another language. Navigate to the homepage and create a new post in Gujarati, for example: નમસ્કાર દુનિયા! હું નવી અનુવાદ સુવિધાનું પરીક્ષણ કરી રહ્યો છું.

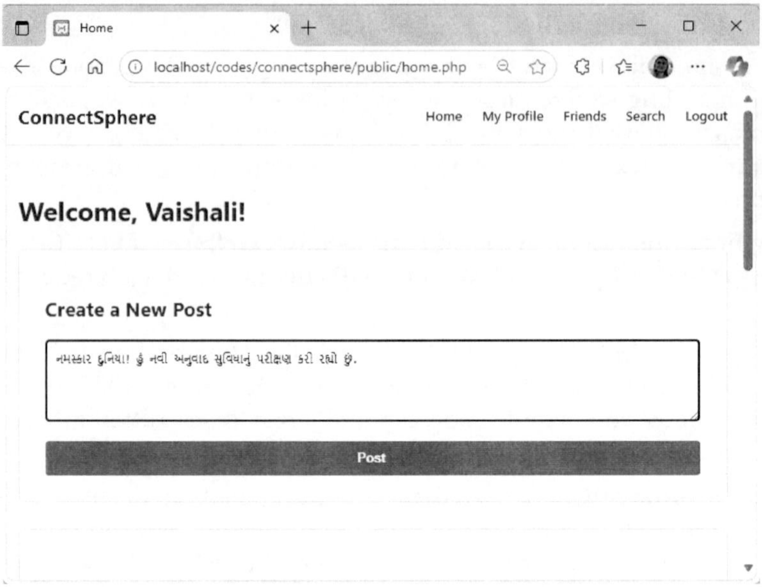

4. Now, log out and log in as another user, for example, **Sharanam**.
5. Sharanam needs to be friends with Vaishali to see her posts on her profile. If they aren't, send a friend request and have Vaishali accept it. As Sharanam, navigate to Vaishali's profile by searching for her or through the friends list.
6. You can see her new post in Gujarati.

7. In the translation form next to the post, the **English** option should already be selected in the dropdown. Click the **Translate** button.
8. The page reloads. And voilà! Below the original Gujarati post, a new blue box appears containing the English translation: **Hello world! I am testing the new translation feature**.

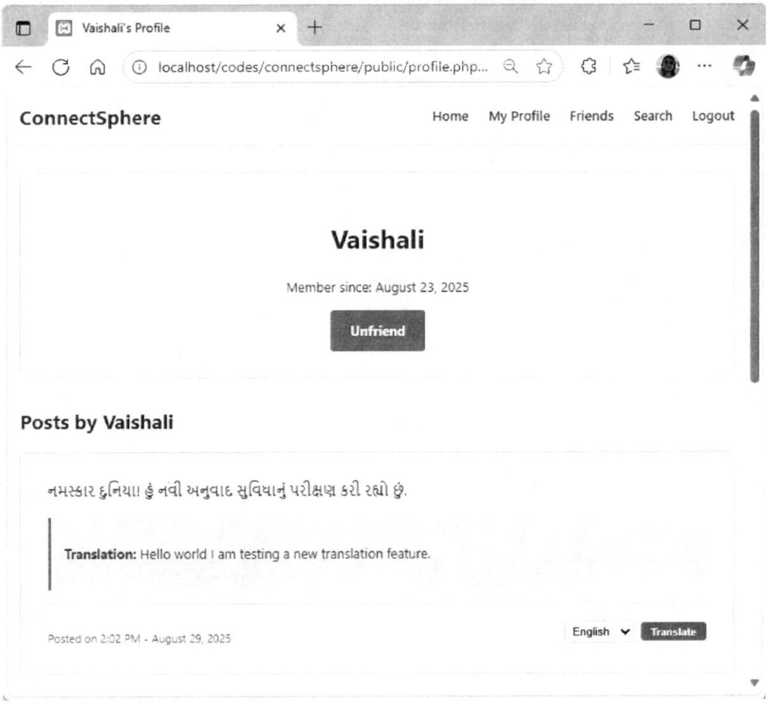

9. Try it again with other languages! The process is seamless. You have successfully upgraded your application with a powerful AI service.

Exploring application behaviour: A practical run-through

A professional developer thinks about the edge cases. How does our app behave when things aren't perfect?

- **Translating to the same language:** What happens if you try to translate Alice's English post into English? The **googletrans** library is smart enough to recognize this and will simply return the original text. Our app will display the **translation**, which will just be the same English text. This is a graceful way to handle the situation.

- **Invalid language (user-side):** Our dropdown only provides valid language codes, so a regular user cannot cause an error this way.

- **Python script error:** What if the googletrans service is temporarily down? Our Python script's try...except block will catch the error and return a JSON response like {"status": "error", "message": "Translation failed: ..."}. Our PHP script will then display **Translation failed: ...** in the result box, providing clear feedback to the user instead of a broken page.
- **Empty post:** What if a user somehow creates an empty post? Our Python script checks for this and will return an error message, which PHP will display.

This robust error handling is what separates a simple script from a real-world application.

Harnessing translation in real-world contexts

The feature you just built is far more than an academic exercise. This exact pattern is used to power countless features on the modern web:

- **E-commerce:** An online store could use this to automatically translate user reviews, making them accessible to a global audience.
- **Customer support:** A support ticket system could allow agents to instantly translate a customer's message from another language to provide faster and more accurate help.
- **Social media and forums:** Platforms like Facebook and Reddit use on-the-fly translation to break down language barriers and connect global communities, just like you did in ConnectSphere.
- **Content Management Systems:** A blog or news site could offer a "Translate this article" button to increase its international readership.

Wrapping up

This chapter was a monumental step forward, taking you from a builder of applications to an enhancer and integrator. By adding a single, powerful feature to ConnectSphere, you solidified your understanding of modern, service-oriented web development.

- You learned to **plan and scope an upgrade** for an existing PHP application.
- You used **pip to install a third-party Python library** to handle a specialized task.
- You wrote a **robust Python service** that communicates reliably using JSON.
- You successfully **integrated the Python service** into your existing PHP code using shell_exec().
- You practiced **secure coding by sanitizing all data** passed to the command line.
- You **dynamically updated the UI** to display the results of the AI service, creating a seamless user experience.

Give yourself a huge pat on the back! You have not only built a complete web application but have now also upgraded it with a sophisticated AI-powered feature. You've proven that you have the skills to not only create projects from scratch but also to maintain and enhance them over time—a critical skill for any professional developer. You now possess the foundational knowledge to integrate virtually any specialized service into your PHP projects, opening up a world of possibilities. The applications you can build are now limited only by your imagination.

But a great developer is not just a great coder; they are also an efficient one. In the next chapter, we'll shift gears and learn how to make your coding process faster and smarter. Get ready for *Chapter 35: Productivity playbook - Workflow automations & pro tips in VS Code*.

Chapter 35

Section 10: Beyond the basics – Level up and stay sharp

Productivity playbook – Workflow automations & pro tips in VS Code

What you'll learn

- Advanced shortcuts
- Workspace optimization
- Custom code snippets

You've become proficient at writing PHP, but professional developers are also masters of their tools. Knowing the language is only half the battle; the other half is using your code editor with speed, precision, and efficiency. Think of it like a chef who not only knows the recipes but has also organized their kitchen perfectly, with every knife sharpened and every ingredient within arm's reach.

In this chapter, you'll learn to bend Visual Studio Code to your will. We'll move beyond simple extensions and explore the features that separate beginners from pros, turning your editor into a high-speed command center for PHP development. By the end, you won't just be writing code—you'll be crafting it with a professional workflow that saves time and prevents headaches.

Beyond Ctrl+S: Essential keyboard shortcuts

Saving your file is second nature, but VS Code is packed with powerful shortcuts that can dramatically speed up your coding. Committing these to muscle memory means you'll spend less time clicking around and more time thinking about your code's logic.

Multi-cursor editing

Imagine you need to change the same variable name in ten different places. Instead of finding and replacing each one, you can create multiple cursors and edit them all at once.

To do this, hold down **Alt** (Windows/Linux) or **Option** (Mac), select the files from the **Explorer Panel** and click wherever you want to add a new cursor. Now, when you type, the changes appear in all locations simultaneously. It's an incredible time-saver for repetitive edits.

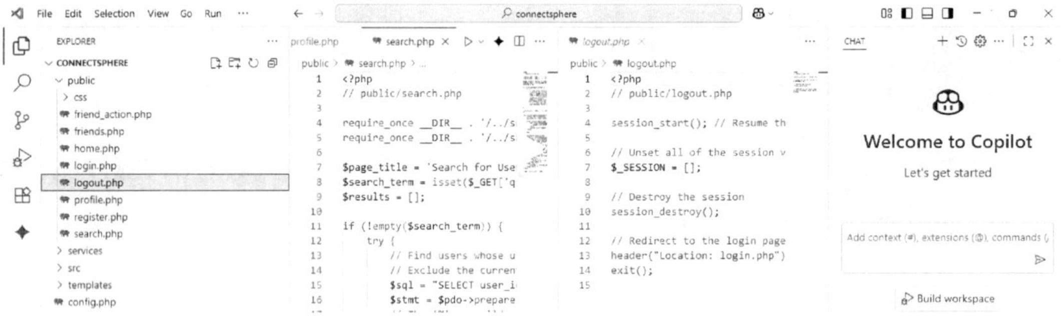

Command palette mastery

The **Command Palette** is your universal search bar for everything you can do in VS Code. Instead of hunting through menus, you can open it and type what you want to do.

Press **Ctrl+Shift+P** (Windows/Linux) or **Cmd+Shift+P** (Mac) to open it. From here, you can run any command, like **Create New File**, **Change Theme**, or **Restart PHP Server**. If you remove the **>** character, it becomes a file search, allowing you to jump to any file in your project instantly.

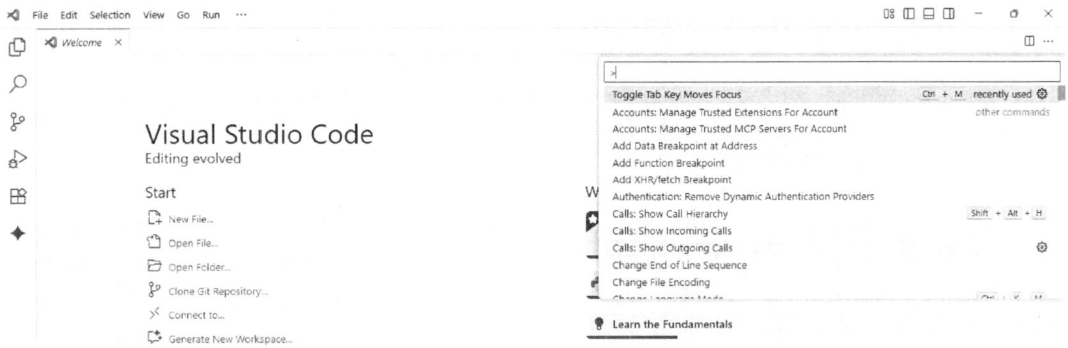

Go to definition/file

When you're working on a large project like *ConnectSphere*, you'll often need to jump between files to understand how they connect. If you see a function call and want to see how that function is defined, you don't need to search for the file manually.

Simply hold **Ctrl** (Windows/Linux) or **Cmd** (Mac) and click on the function name. VS Code will instantly take you to the file and line where it was defined. To go back, use **Alt + Left Arrow** (Windows/Linux) or **Ctrl + -** (Mac).

Block selection and movement

Restructuring code is a common task. Maybe you need to move a block of if logic outside of a loop or reorder the properties in a CSS class. Instead of cutting and pasting, you can move lines and blocks of code effortlessly.

Highlight the lines you want to move and press **Alt + Up/Down Arrow** (Windows/Linux) or **Option + Up/Down Arrow** (Mac) to move the entire block up or down. To duplicate a block, highlight it and press **Shift+Alt+Down Arrow** (Windows/Linux) or **Shift+Option+Down Arrow** (Mac).

Hands-on: Creating your own custom code snippets

Why type the same code blocks over and over? A code snippet is a template for code you write frequently, which you can insert into your file by typing a short prefix and pressing **Tab**. It saves time, reduces typos, and ensures you're using a consistent structure for common tasks. In this hands-on section, we will build a custom snippet for one of the most important and repetitive tasks in our database-driven applications: creating a secure PDO database connection inside a try-catch block.

Building the application

Finding the snippets file

First, we need to tell VS Code that we're creating a snippet for PHP files.

1. In **VS Code**, navigate to the menu bar.
2. Click **File → Preferences → Configure Snippets**. (On Mac, it's **Code** > **Settings** > **Configure Snippets**).

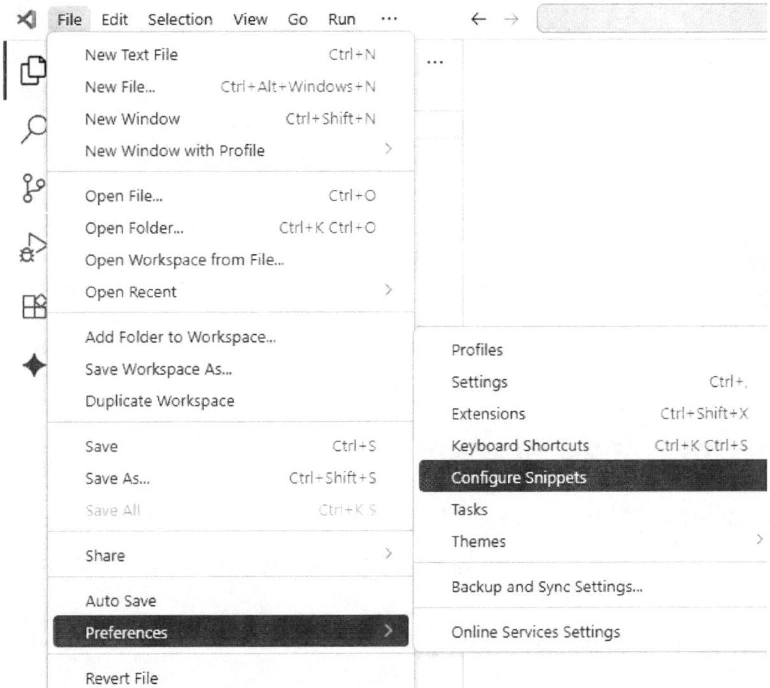

3. A search bar appears. Type **php** and select **php (PHP)**.

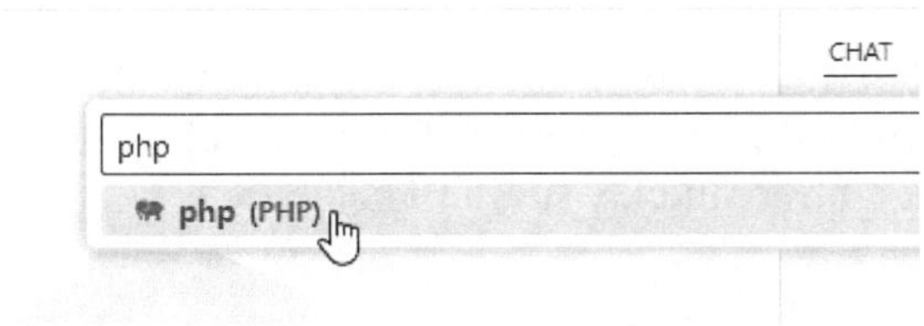

4. VS Code opens a file named **php.json**. This file might be empty except for some commented-out instructions. This is where we'll write our custom snippet.

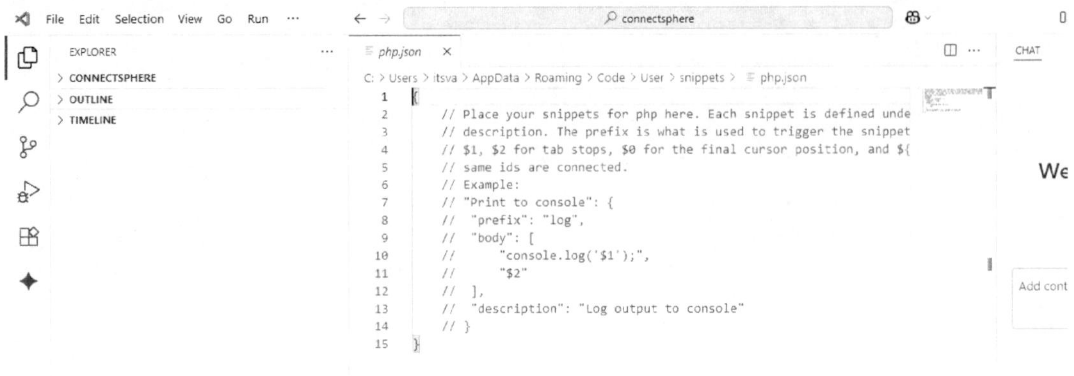

Understanding the snippet structure

Snippets are written in JSON format. Let's look at the key parts before we write our own:

- **"Snippet Name":** This is the top-level key for our snippet. It's just a descriptive name for us to read inside the php.json file.
- **prefix:** This is the short trigger text you'll type in your editor. When you type this and press Tab, the snippet will be inserted.
- **body:** This is an array of strings, where each string is a line of code that will be inserted.
- **description:** A brief, optional explanation of what the snippet does. This appears in the VS Code suggestion box.
- **Placeholders:** Special markers like $1, $2, and ${1:defaultValue} are used to control where the cursor goes after the snippet is inserted. Pressing Tab will jump the cursor from $1 to $2 and so on, allowing you to quickly fill in the blanks.

Writing the snippet

Let's write our PDO connection snippet. This snippet will generate a complete try-catch block, set up the PDO connection, and include placeholders for the server details.

In your php.json file, add the following code between the main curly braces {}:

```
{
    "PDO Database Connection": {
        "prefix": "pdoconnect",
        "body": [
            "$dsn = 'mysql:host=${1:localhost};dbname=${2:your_db_name};
                  charset=utf8mb4';",
            "$username = '${3:root}';",
```

```
            "$password = '${4:}';",
            "",
            "try {",
            "    $pdo = new PDO($dsn, $username, $password);",
            "    $pdo->setAttribute(PDO::ATTR_ERRMODE, PDO::ERRMODE
                                   _EXCEPTION);",
            "    // Connection successful!",
            "    echo 'Database connection successful!';",
            "} catch (PDOException $e) {",
            "    // Connection failed, log the error and stop.",
            "    error_log('Database connection failed: ' . $e->getMessage());",
            "    die('Could not connect to the database. Please try again
                     later.');",
            "}"
        ],
        "description": "Creates a secure PDO database connection with a try-catch
                        block."
    }
}
```

Make sure your php.json file is saved (**Ctrl+S** or **Cmd+S**).

Using your snippet

Now for the fun part! Let's see our snippet in action.

1. Create a new file in VS Code called **test_snippet.php**.
2. Inside the PHP tags <?php ... ?>, type the prefix we defined: pdoconnect.
3. You should see a suggestion box appear with our snippet. The description "Creates a secure PDO database connection..." will be visible.

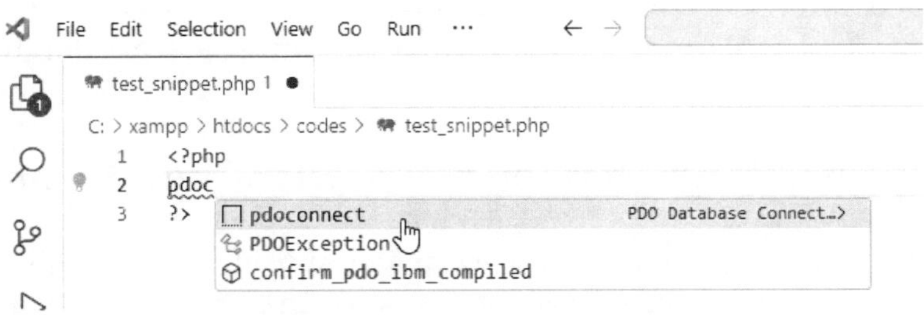

4. Press **Tab** or **Enter** or select **pdoconnect** from the drop-down list box.

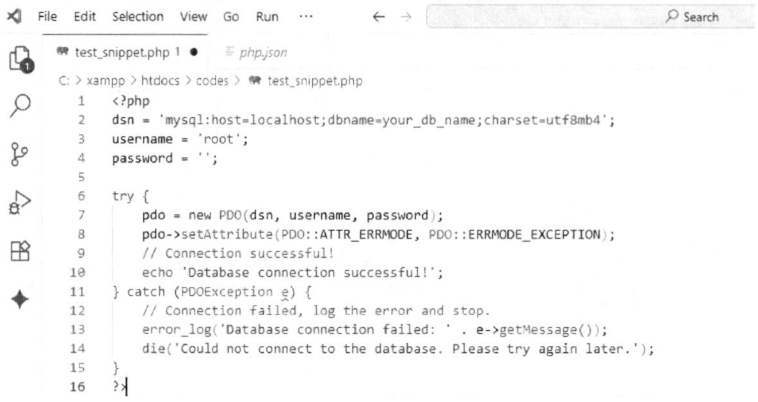

Voila! The entire code block instantly appears.

Notice that your cursor is now highlighting localhost. This is our first placeholder ($1). You can type a new hostname or press **Tab** to jump to the next placeholder, your_db_name ($2), then root ($3), and finally the empty password field ($4).

Bridging the gap: Learned concepts and application implementation

This simple automation directly connects to the core concepts of productivity and reliability. By creating a snippet for our database connection, we've done more than just save typing. We've ensured that every time we connect to the database, we are consistently using a secure try-catch block and setting the error mode attribute. This reduces the chance of human error, such as forgetting to handle exceptions, which is a critical practice for building robust applications.

Exploring application behaviour: A practical run-through

- **Syntax errors:** If your snippet doesn't work, the most likely cause is a JSON syntax error in php.json. JSON is very strict—a missing comma or an extra quote will break it. VS Code will usually highlight syntax errors with a red squiggly line.
- **Prefix conflicts:** If you choose a prefix that's too common (e.g., db), it might conflict with other built-in snippets or suggestions. Choose a unique, memorable prefix.

- **Editing:** To change your snippet, simply go back to **File → Preferences → Configure Snippets**, select **php.json**, and make your edits. The changes will be available immediately after you save the file.

Harnessing custom code snippets in real-world contexts

Snippets are invaluable for any repetitive code. In a professional setting, you could create snippets for:

- A complete HTML5 boilerplate structure.
- A PHP class template with a constructor.
- A standard function documentation block (PHPDoc).
- Form input fields with labels and common attributes.
- The structure for a foreach loop to render an HTML table from an array.

Taming your project: Workspaces and settings

When you work on multiple projects, you'll find that each one might have different requirements. One project might use tabs for indentation, while another requires spaces. VS Code's workspace settings let you tailor the editor's configuration for each project without changing your global settings.

Workspace vs. user settings

- **User settings**: These are your global settings that apply to every project you open in VS Code. You set them once, and they're your default.
- **Workspace settings**: These settings apply *only* to the current project (the folder you have open). They are saved in a special folder named .vscode inside your project directory and override your user settings. This is perfect for team projects, as you can commit the .vscode/settings.json file to Git, ensuring everyone on the team has the same editor configuration.

To create **workspace settings**, open the Command Palette (**Ctrl+Shift+P**) and type **Open User Settings (JSON)**. This creates and opens a **settings.json** file inside a .vscode folder. Here's an example:

```
{
    "editor.tabSize": 4,
    "editor.insertSpaces": true,
    "files.exclude": {
```

```
        "**/.git": true,
        "**/.DS_Store": true,
        "**/vendor": true
    },
    "workbench.colorTheme": "Default Light Modern"
}
```

This configuration ensures that for this project only, tabs will be converted to 4 spaces, and the vendor folder will be hidden from the file explorer.

Recommended extensions

To ensure team consistency, you can recommend specific VS Code extensions for a project. Create a file at .vscode/extensions.json. When someone opens the project who doesn't have these extensions, VS Code will prompt them to install them.

Here is what the contents of .vscode/extensions.json would look like for our book's workflow:

```
{
  "recommendations": [
    "bmewburn.vscode-intelephense-client",
    "xdebug.php-debug",
    "ritwickdey.liveserver"
  ]
}

```

Task automation

You can also automate common command-line tasks, like running a code linter to check for syntax errors. VS Code's **Tasks** feature lets you do this without leaving the editor.

1. Open the **Command Palette** and type **Configure Default Build Task**.
2. Select **Create tasks.json file from template**, and then select **Others**.
3. This creates a **tasks.json** file inside the **.vscode** folder. Replace its contents with this:

```
{
  "version": "2.0.0",
  "tasks": [
    {
      "label": "Lint Current PHP File",
      "type": "shell",
      "command": "php -l ${file}",
      "presentation": {
        "reveal": "always",
        "panel": "new"
```

```
            },
            "problemMatcher": []
        }
    ]
}
```

Now, when you have a PHP file open, you can run this task from the Command Palette (**Ctrl+Shift+B** or by typing **Run Build Task**). It will execute **php -l your_file.php** in the integrated terminal, instantly telling you if there are syntax errors.

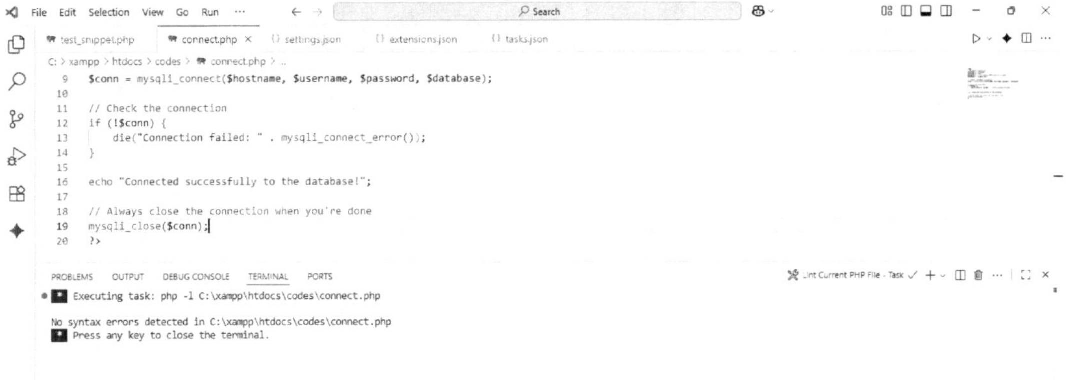

Wrapping up

In this chapter, we leveled up our development workflow from simply writing code to mastering the environment where we write it. You now have a professional toolkit of techniques to code faster, more consistently, and with fewer bugs.

- You can navigate and edit code faster using advanced keyboard shortcuts for multi-cursor editing, block movement, and file navigation.
- You are able to create custom snippets to automate writing repetitive code, which saves time and enforces consistency in your projects.
- You can configure project-specific settings using workspaces, ensuring that you and your team have a consistent environment.

Congratulations! You've moved beyond the syntax of PHP and are now thinking like a professional developer—someone who values efficiency, consistency, and precision in their tools. These skills will serve you in every project you ever work on, regardless of the language or technology. You've learned to make your editor work *for you*, turning it from a simple text file editor into a powerful development partner.

Now that we have a firm grasp of our tools, let's zoom out in the next chapter, ***Chapter 36: Understanding the full web stack: From browser to database***, to see the big picture of how all the pieces of a web application fit together.

Chapter 36

Section 10: Beyond the basics – Level up and stay sharp

Understanding the full web stack: From browser to database

What you'll learn

- The client-server model
- The request-response cycle
- The three core layers
- Using browser developer tools

Congratulations on building ConnectSphere! You've wrestled with PHP variables, loops, functions, and even connected your application to a MySQL database. You've built something real and functional. Now, let's zoom out from the code editor and look at the entire ecosystem your application lives in. Have you ever wondered what *really* happens when you type a URL into your browser and hit Enter? It feels instant, like magic, but it's actually a rapid conversation between multiple pieces of technology.

In this chapter, we'll trace the complete journey of a single web request to see how the front-end (the browser), the back-end (your PHP server), and the database all talk to each other to create a seamless user experience.

The big picture: The client-server model

At the heart of the entire internet is a simple but powerful concept: the client-server model. Every time you use the web, you're participating in this model. It's a partnership where two computers have very distinct roles.

The client

The **client** is the user's web browser—Google Chrome, Firefox, Safari, it doesn't matter which one. Its primary job is to ask for things. When you want to visit a website, your browser's job is to compose a formal request for information and send it out across the internet. Its second job is to take whatever the server sends back (like HTML, CSS, and images) and render it into the beautiful, interactive web page you see on your screen. Think of the client as a customer at a library who asks the librarian for a specific book.

The server

The **server** is the powerful computer where your PHP application and database live. In our case, your own computer is acting as a server thanks to XAMPP. Its job is to listen patiently for incoming requests from clients. When a request arrives, the server wakes up, runs the necessary PHP code, might talk to the database, and then formulates a response to send back to the client that asked for it. The server is the librarian who receives the request, finds the book on the shelves, and hands it back to the customer.

The request-response cycle

This entire conversation is called the **request-response cycle**, and it's the fundamental rhythm of the web. It works just like ordering food at a restaurant:

- **You (the Client) look at the menu and decide what you want.** You tell the waiter, "I'd like the cheeseburger, please." This is the **Request**.
- The waiter (the Internet) takes your order to the kitchen (the Server).
- **The kitchen (the Server) prepares your meal.** It gets the patty, the bun, the cheese, and assembles it. This is the server processing your PHP code and fetching data from MySQL.
- The waiter brings the finished meal back to your table. This is the **Response**.

This cycle happens every single time you click a link, submit a form, or load a new page. It's incredibly fast, often taking just milliseconds, but it's always there.

The three layers of a web application

While the client and server are the two main actors, a modern web application like ConnectSphere is really made up of three distinct layers. Understanding these layers helps you organize your code and troubleshoot problems more effectively.

Presentation layer (front-end)

This is everything the user sees and interacts with directly in their browser. It's the visual part of your application. The technologies that make up this layer are:

- **HTML:** The structure and content of the page.
- **CSS:** The styling, layout, and visual presentation.
- **JavaScript:** The interactivity and dynamic behaviour (though we've focused on PHP's back-end capabilities).

Your PHP scripts ultimately *generate* the HTML for this layer, which is then sent to the browser to be displayed.

Logic layer (back-end)

This is the **brain** of your application. It lives on the server and is completely hidden from the end-user. This is where all the heavy lifting happens: processing form submissions, validating user input, authenticating users, and deciding what content to show. In our book, **PHP** is the language that powers our entire logic layer.

Data layer (database)

This is the application's long-term memory. It's where all the persistent information is stored—user accounts, posts, friendships, comments, and more. This layer is responsible for making sure data is stored safely, efficiently, and can be retrieved quickly. For ConnectSphere, our data layer is powered by **MySQL**. Your PHP logic layer communicates directly with the MySQL data layer to create, read, update, and delete information.

Hands-on: Dissecting a web request with developer tools

Theory is great, but let's see these concepts in action. We're going to use the tools already built into your web browser to become a detective and watch the request-response cycle happen live with our ConnectSphere project.

In this practical exercise, you'll use your browser's **Developer Tools** to spy on the conversation between your browser (the client) and your XAMPP server. You won't be writing any code; you'll be observing the results of the code you've already written, giving you a powerful new perspective on how the web works.

Building the application

For this hands-on section, we will be using the **ConnectSphere** application you built in Chapters 28 through 31. Please ensure you have that project ready and your XAMPP server running.

Bridging the gap: Learned concepts and application implementation

This walkthrough will directly connect the abstract ideas of the client-server model and the three layers to the tangible files and processes in your ConnectSphere project. You will see how a simple click in your browser (Presentation Layer) triggers a PHP script on the server (Logic Layer), which may then query the database (Data Layer) before sending a response back to the browser.

Running and testing

Opening the network tab

First, let's get our tools ready.

1. Make sure your **Apache** and **MySQL** modules are running in your **XAMPP Control Panel**.
2. Open **Visual Studio Code** and ensure your **ConnectSphere** project folder is open.
3. Open the web browser and navigate to your **ConnectSphere login** page. The URL will likely be **http://localhost/codes/connectsphere/public/login.php**.

4. Now, open the **Developer Tools**. You can do this by right-clicking anywhere on the page and selecting **Inspect**, or by pressing **F12** (or Cmd+Option+I on a Mac).
5. A **new panel** opens.

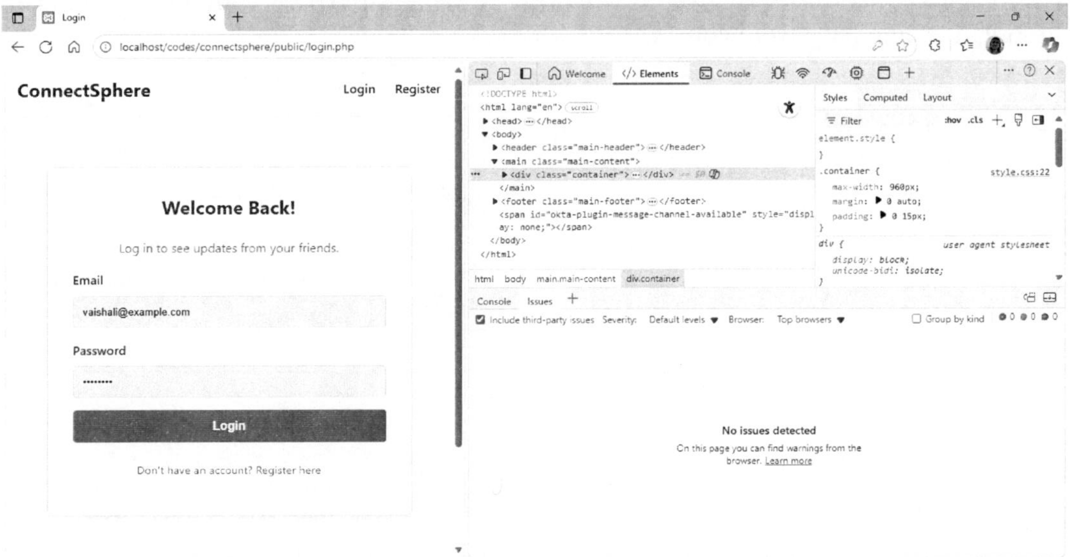

6. At the top of this panel, find and click on the **Network** tab. This tab records every single request your browser makes. It might be empty right now, and that's okay.

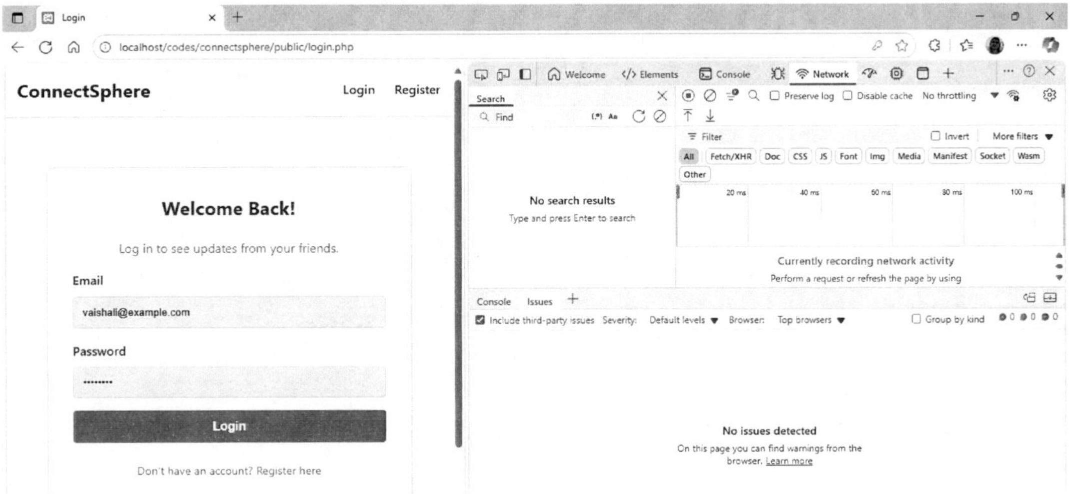

Making the request

With the **Network** tab open, simply refresh the login page. Instantly, you can see at least one new entry appear in the list. The first one will likely be login.php. This is your browser officially requesting the login page from your XAMPP server.

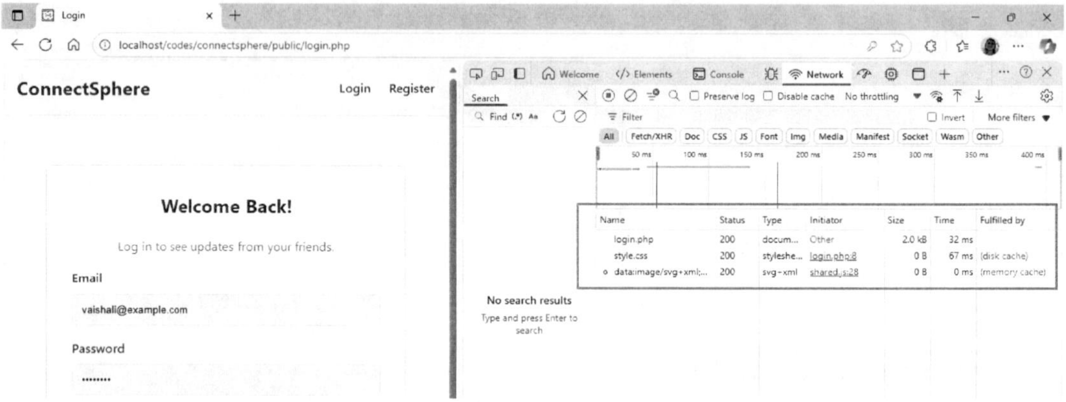

Analyzing the headers

1. Click on the **login.php** entry in the list.
2. A new pane opens to the side, showing you all the details about this specific request.

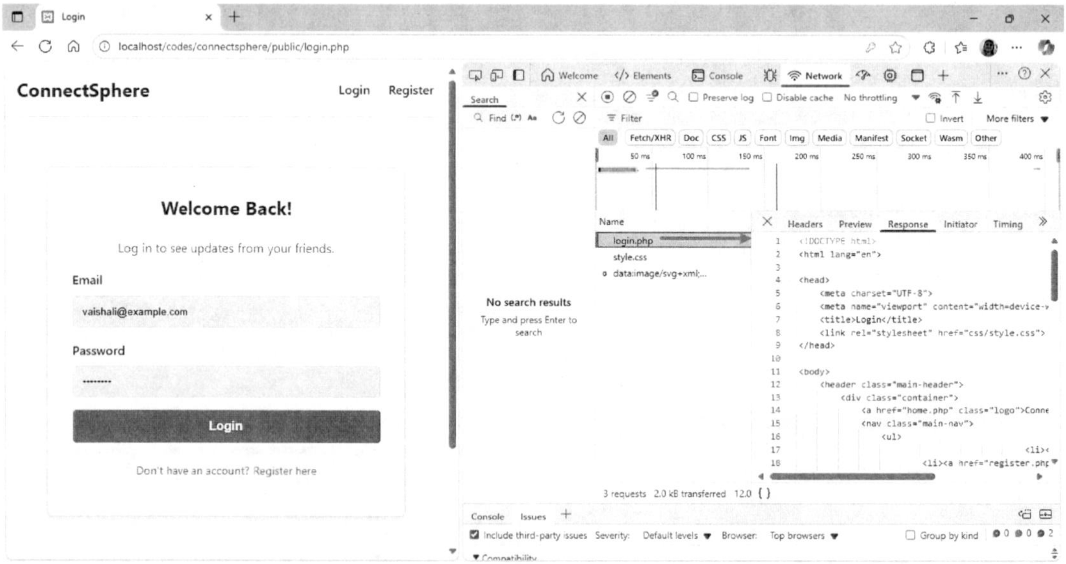

3. Click on the **Headers** sub-tab.

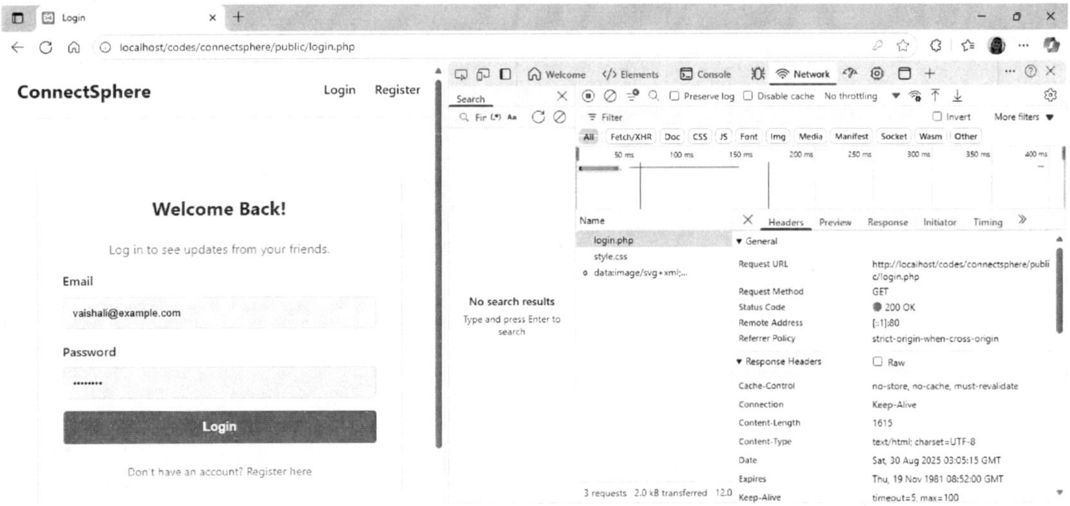

4. You'll see a lot of information, but let's focus on two key parts:
   - **Request method:** It will say GET. This is the standard method for simply requesting to "get" a web page.
   - **Status code:** It will say 200 OK. This is the universal success code on the web. It means the server found the file you asked for and is sending it back successfully.

Viewing the response

Now, click on the **Response** sub-tab, right next to **Headers**.

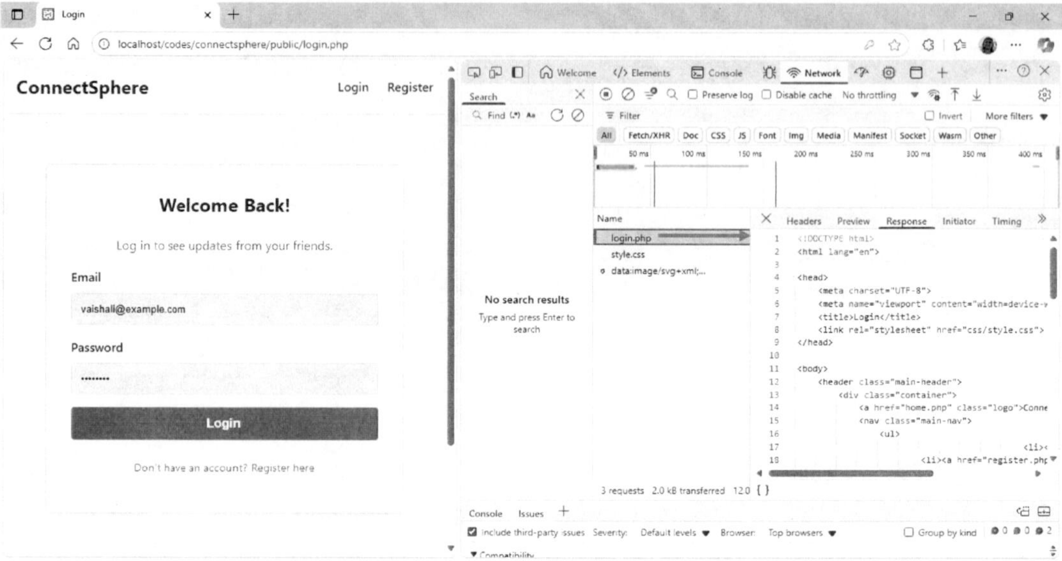

What you see here should be familiar: it's the raw HTML that makes up your login page! This is the actual text content that your PHP script (login.php) generated and the server sent back to your browser. Your browser reads this HTML to render the form, the text, and the **Login** button that you see on the screen.

Tracing a POST request

Let's see something different. Go back to the login page itself (not the developer tools).

- Enter the **email** and **password** for a user you created.
- Click the **Login** button.
- Watch the **Network** tab. A flurry of new activity appears! The most important new entry will be another request to login.php.
- Click on the **login.php** entry in the list to inspect it.
- Go to the **Payload** tab (this tab only appears for POST requests). Here, you can see the exact data your browser sent to the server: the **email** and **password** you typed into the form. This is how your PHP script receives the user's credentials via the $_POST superglobal.

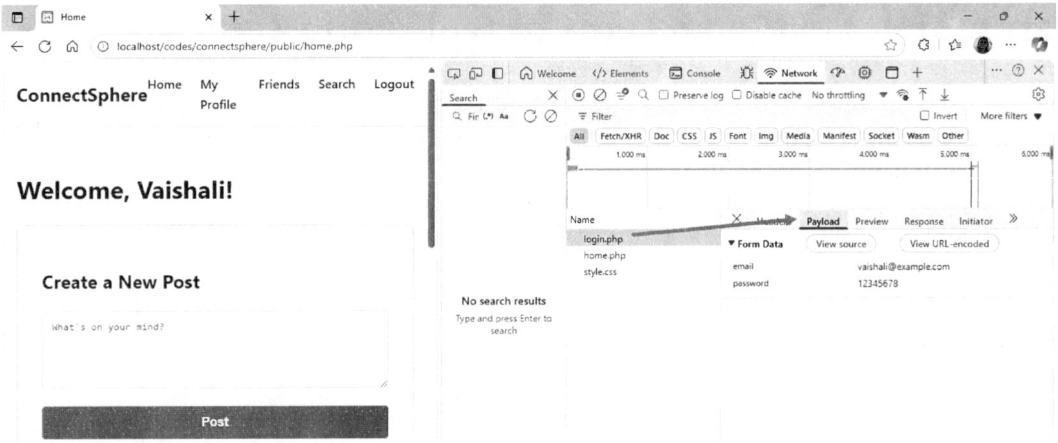

Exploring application behaviour: A practical run-through

What happens if you try to log in with the wrong password? Try it.

1. You can see another POST request to login.php in the **Network** tab.
2. The **payload** contains the incorrect password.
3. The server processes this, your PHP logic finds that the password doesn't match, and it redirects you back to the login page, with an error message.

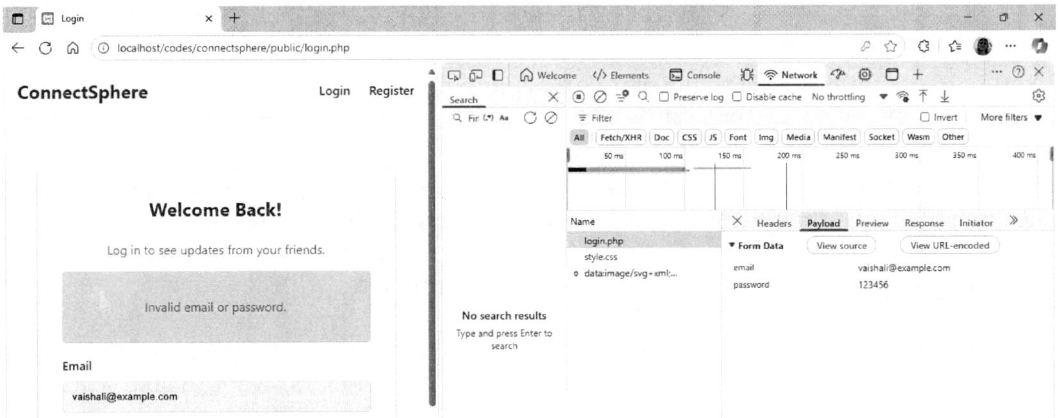

By watching the **Network** tab, you can confirm that your back-end logic is correctly handling different scenarios and sending the appropriate responses.

Harnessing developer tools in real-world contexts

This skill isn't just an academic exercise; it's one of the most critical debugging tools for a web developer. If a form isn't working, the first place you should look is the **Network** tab. Is the browser sending a POST request? Is the payload correct? Did the server respond with an error (like a 404 Not Found or 500 Server Error)? This tool gives you a transparent look into the web's fundamental conversation, allowing you to diagnose problems on any website, not just your own.

Wrapping up

In this chapter, we zoomed out from the code to see the entire landscape. You've traced the journey from a browser click to a server response and back again, demystifying the magic of the web.

- You understand the full request-response lifecycle, the web's fundamental conversation.
- You can distinguish between the front-end (Presentation), back-end (Logic), and database (Data) layers.
- You know that the **client** (browser) asks for things, and the **server** (XAMPP) provides them.
- You learned how to use the browser's **Network tab** to inspect requests and responses.
- You can identify the difference between a GET request (fetching a page) and a POST request (sending data).
- You know how to use these developer tools to debug and understand how any website works.

You've now come full circle. You not only know how to write the PHP code that powers a web application, but you also understand where that code fits into the grand scheme of the internet. This "big picture" knowledge is what separates a coder from a true developer. It empowers you to build more robust applications and to diagnose problems with confidence.

Congratulations on this milestone! Next, we'll take a huge step into the world of professional development in ***Chapter 37: An Introduction to PHP Frameworks***, where you'll learn how modern developers build massive applications quickly and efficiently.

Chapter 37

Section 10: Beyond the basics – Level up and stay sharp

An introduction to PHP Frameworks

What you'll learn

- What Composer is?
- Installing a framework
- The MVC pattern
- Basic routing

So far, you've written all your code from scratch. This is the best way to learn, but in the professional world, developers use frameworks to build applications faster, more securely, and in a more organized way. Think of it like building a house. You *could* mill your own lumber, forge your own nails, and weave your own electrical wiring, but it would be incredibly slow and prone to error. Instead, you buy high-quality, pre-fabricated materials from a hardware store and assemble them according to a proven blueprint. A **framework** is your software hardware store and blueprint, all in one.

In this chapter, you'll learn about Composer, the tool that manages all PHP code, and take your first steps with Laravel, the world's most popular PHP framework.

Why not reinvent the wheel?

When you start building larger applications, you'll notice you're solving the same problems over and over again. How do I handle URLs? How do I connect to the database securely? How do I process form data? A **framework** is a collection of pre-written, expert-level code that solves these common problems for you. It provides a solid foundation and a clear structure for your project, so you can focus on building the unique features of your application instead of reinventing the basics.

This is where **Composer** comes in. As we saw back in ***Chapters 21 and 27***, when we built our AI recommender and improved our code quality, **Composer** is the essential tool for managing PHP libraries. It's the official package manager for PHP, which is a fancy way of saying it's the App Store for your code. It allows you to easily **install** frameworks and other third-party code packages into your project with a single command.

Hands-on: Part 1 - Installing and using Composer

While we've used Composer before, let's do a quick, focused exercise to solidify your understanding of how it works in a new project from the ground up. We're going to create a new project and install a professional logging library called **Monolog**.

Building the application

1. First, let's create a dedicated folder for this exercise. Navigate to your **C:\xampp\htdocs\codes** directory and create a new folder named **c37-composer-intro**.
2. Open this new **c37-composer-intro** folder in **Visual Studio Code**.
3. Now, open the integrated terminal in VS Code by going to the top menu and clicking **...** **→ Terminal → New Terminal** (or by pressing `Ctrl+Shift+``).
4. In the terminal, type the following command and press **Enter**. This command tells Composer to download the **monolog/monolog** package from **Packagist** (the central repository) and set it up for our project:

```
composer require monolog/monolog
```

5. You can see **Composer** spring to life, creating a few files and a new folder in your project:
   - **composer.json:** A configuration file that lists your project's dependencies.
   - **composer.lock:** A file that **locks** the exact versions of the packages you installed, ensuring consistency.

- **vendor/:** A directory where Composer places all the third-party code it downloads. You should never edit files in this folder directly. Inside vendor/ you'll find an essential file: autoload.php.

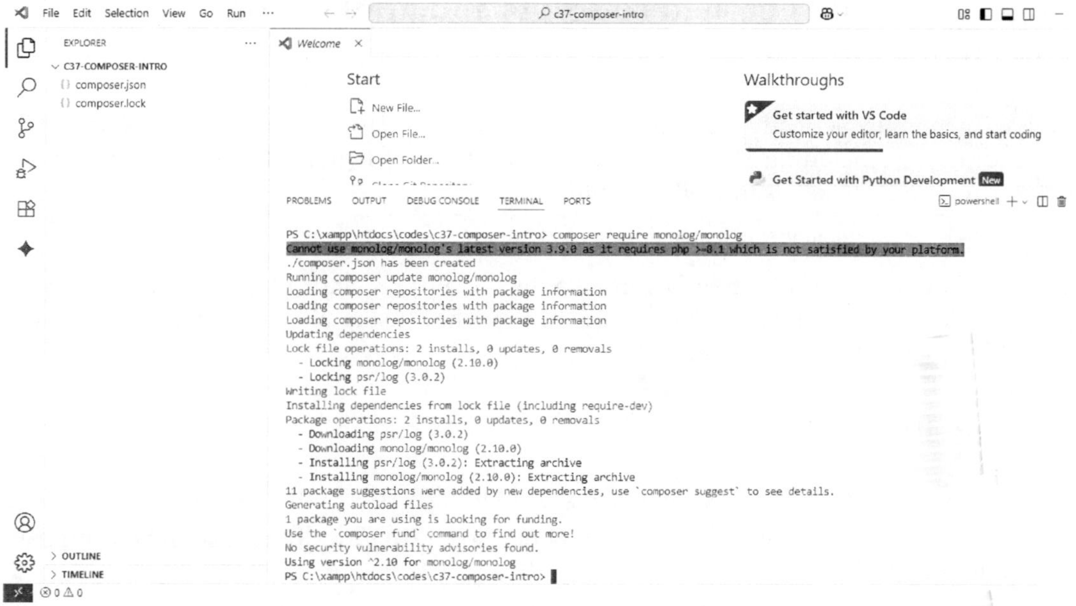

6. Now, create a new file in the root of your **c37-composer-intro** folder and name it **logger_test.php**.
7. Add the following code to **logger_test.php**. This script will demonstrate how to use the Monolog library we just installed:

```php
<?php
// 1. Include Composer's autoloader
// This one file gives us access to all installed libraries.
require __DIR__ . '/vendor/autoload.php';
// 2. "use" the classes we need from the Monolog library
use Monolog\Logger;
use Monolog\Handler\StreamHandler;
// 3. Create a new logger instance
// We'll name our logger 'MyTestApp'
$log = new Logger('MyTestApp');
// 4. "push" a handler onto the logger. This tells it WHERE to save logs.
// We'll save them to a file called app.log in the same directory.
$log->pushHandler(new StreamHandler('app.log', Logger::WARNING));
// 5. Use the logger to add records
$log->warning('This is a test warning.');
$log->error('This is a test error message.');
```

```
echo "<h1>Logger Test Complete!</h1>";
echo "<p>Check the 'app.log' file in your project directory.</p>";
```

Bridging the gap: Learned concepts and application implementation

This small example perfectly demonstrates the power of Composer. Instead of manually downloading and including dozens of files for a complex logging library, we simply ran composer require. The key is the following line:

```
require __DIR__ . '/vendor/autoload.php';
```

This single line automatically handles the loading of all necessary library files, keeping our main code clean and focused. We've separated the **what** (using a logger) from the **how** (the complex internal code of the logger).

Running and testing

1. Make sure your **Apache** server is running from the **XAMPP control panel**.
2. Open your web browser and navigate to **http://localhost/codes/c37-composer-intro/logger_test.php**.
3. You see a simple message on the screen confirming that the script ran.

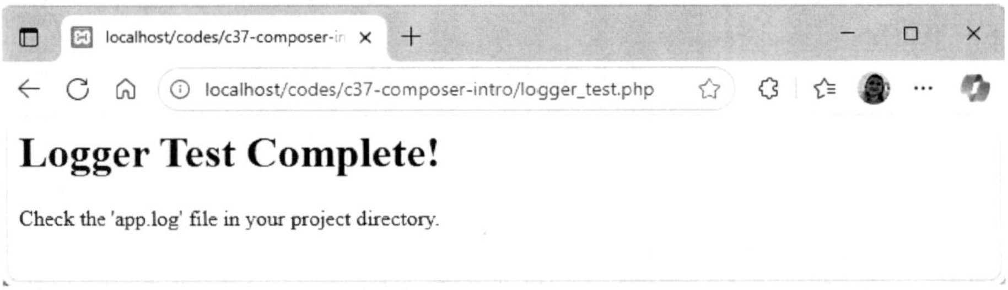

4. Now, look back at your **File Explorer** in **VS Code**. A new file, **app.log**, has been created! Open it, and you can see the two log messages we sent from our script, complete with timestamps and severity levels.

Exploring application behaviour: A practical run-through

The beauty of this approach is its robustness. If Monolog needed ten other libraries to function, Composer would have downloaded and configured them all automatically. If you were to share your project with another developer, they could simply run composer install, and Composer would read your composer.json file and install the exact same dependencies. This solves the classic **it works on my machine** problem and is fundamental to professional team-based development.

Harnessing Composer in real-world contexts

Every modern PHP application, from a small blog to a massive e-commerce platform, is built using Composer. It's the standard for managing dependencies, including entire frameworks like Laravel and Symfony, payment gateway SDKs like Stripe, and API clients for services like AWS or Gemini. Mastering Composer is a non-negotiable skill for a modern PHP developer.

The Model-View-Controller (MVC) pattern

Now that we understand how to *get* a framework (using Composer), let's talk about how they are *structured*. Most modern frameworks are built around a design pattern called **Model-View-Controller**, or **MVC**. This is a way of organizing your code to keep it clean, logical, and easy to manage. It separates your application into three interconnected parts.

- **Model:** The Model is responsible for your data. It interacts directly with your database. If your application needs to fetch a list of users, save a new blog post, or update a product's price, the Model handles it. Think of the Model as your application's data expert or librarian.
- **View:** The View is what the user sees. It's the presentation layer, typically made of HTML and CSS. The View's job is to display the data it receives from the Controller in a user-friendly way. It should contain very little logic. Think of the View as the interior designer; it makes things look good but doesn't decide what furniture goes in the room.

- **Controller:** The Controller is the "traffic cop" or project manager of the application. When a user makes a request by visiting a URL, the Controller receives it. It then tells the Model what data to fetch or modify. Once the Model is done, the Controller takes that data and passes it to the appropriate View, which then renders the final page for the user.

This separation is powerful. It means your designer can work on the View (HTML/CSS) without touching the database logic, and your database expert can optimize the Model without breaking the user interface.

Hands-on: Part 2 - "hello world" in Laravel

This exercise is designed to give you a gentle, first-hand look at a real framework in action. We're not going to build a complex application; our goal is simply to see the core structure and create a single page. We'll use Laravel, the most popular PHP framework, known for its elegant syntax and developer-friendly features.

Building the application

1. We need to install Laravel's installer tool using Composer. In your VS Code terminal (it can be in any directory for this step), run the following global command:

```
composer global require laravel/installer
```

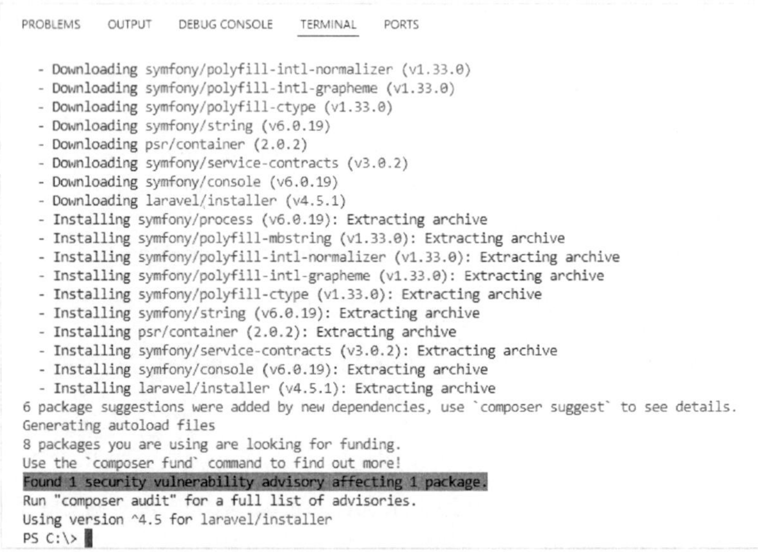

2. Once that's finished, navigate your terminal to where the Laravel is installed:

```
cd C:\Users\itsva\AppData\Roaming\Composer\vendor\bin
```

3. Now, use the Laravel installer to create a brand new Laravel project. We'll call it hello-framework. Run this command:

```
./laravel new hello-framework
```

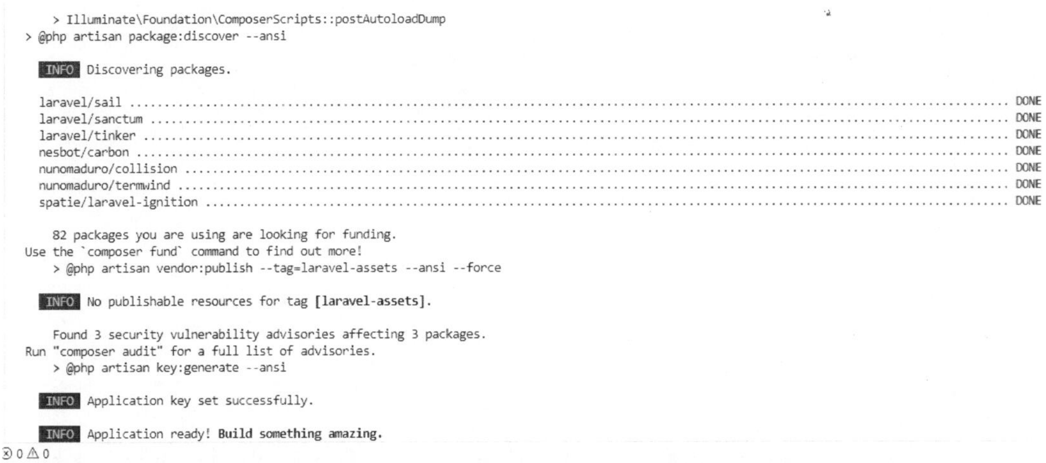

This command will take few minutes as it downloads Laravel and all of its dependencies into a new **hello-framework** folder. It's doing a lot of work for us!

4. Once the installation is complete, navigate your terminal into the new project directory:

```
cd .\hello-framework\
```

5. Laravel comes with its own convenient, built-in web server, which is perfect for development. To start it, run the following command in your terminal:

```
php artisan serve
```

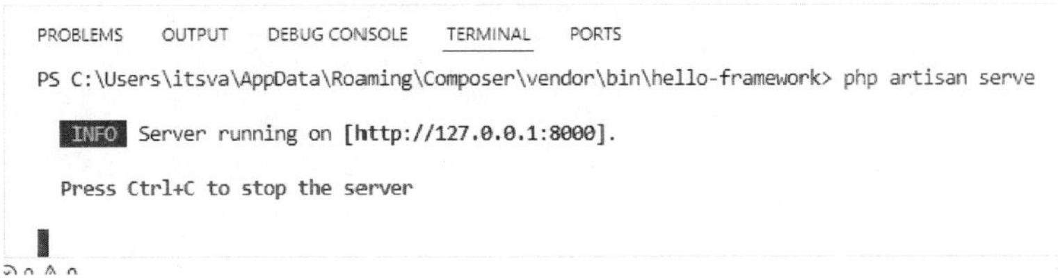

You can see a message indicating that the server has started, usually at http://127.0.0.1:8000.

6. Open your web browser and go to http://127.0.0.1:8000. You should see the beautiful default **Laravel** welcome page. This proves your installation was successful!

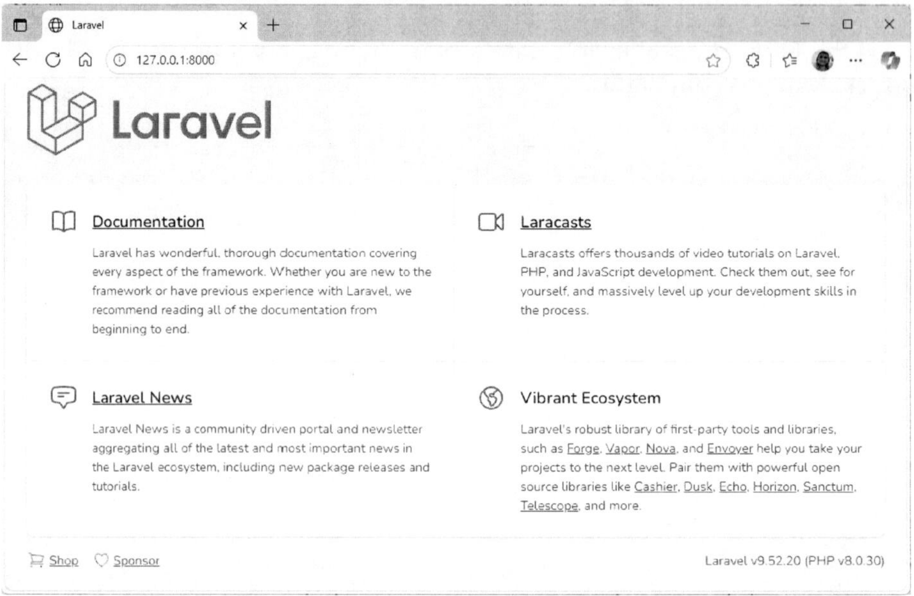

7. Let's create our own page. Go back to **VS Code**. In the **File Explorer**, open the **hello-framework** project. Find the routes folder and open the web.php file inside it.

8. This file is where you define the **URLs** (or **routes**) for your application. You can see a default route already there for the welcome page. Add the following code to the bottom of the file:

```
Route::get('/greeting', function () {
    return 'Hello from my first framework!';
});
```

This tiny block of code tells Laravel: "When someone makes a GET request to the /greeting URL, execute this function and return the string 'Hello from my first framework!' as the response."

9. The web.php file only defines the **rules** for your application's routes; it doesn't actually run the application itself. To make your application accessible and handle the new route you've defined, you need to restart the Laravel development server:

```
php artisan serve
```

Running and testing

1. With the development server still running, go back to your browser.
2. Navigate to the new URL we just created: **http://127.0.0.1:8000/greeting**.
3. You can see our simple text message displayed on the page.

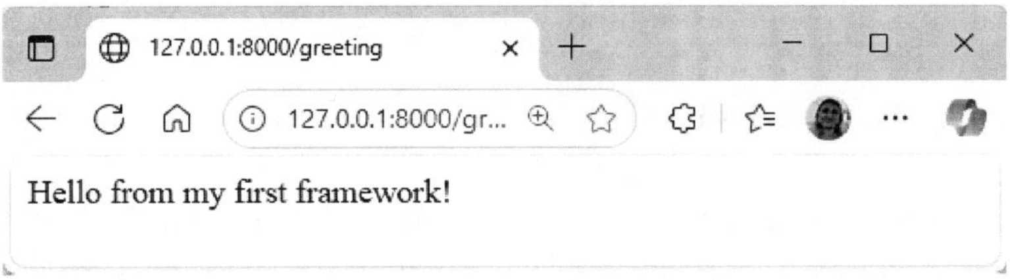

Success! You've just installed a full-featured professional framework and created a working web route.

Bridging the gap: Learned concepts and application implementation

This simple exercise touched on all the concepts we discussed.

- We used **Composer** (via the **Laravel** installer) to create our project.
- We interacted with the **Controller** layer (the routes/web.php file is the entry point for this) to define a URL.

Our controller's logic was simple—it didn't need a **Model** because it wasn't fetching data, and it didn't use a formal **View** because it just returned a simple string. But you can see the clear separation of concerns beginning to form.

Harnessing Laravel in real-world contexts

In a real project, the function in your route file would typically call a method on a Controller class. That Controller would use a Model to fetch data from the database (e.g., Recipe::all()), and then return a View, passing the data to it (e.g., return view('recipes.index', ['recipes' => $allRecipes]);). Laravel handles all the complexity of database connections, templating, security, and more, allowing developers to build massive, scalable applications like e-commerce sites, social networks, and enterprise software with incredible speed and reliability.

Wrapping up

This chapter was a major step up, bridging the gap between writing simple PHP scripts and understanding how modern, professional applications are built. Let's recap what we've covered.

- You understand why **frameworks** are essential for building fast, secure, and maintainable applications.
- You have installed and used **Composer** to manage a project dependency, a fundamental skill for modern PHP.
- You can explain the **Model-View-Controller (MVC)** pattern and the role of each of its three layers.
- You have successfully installed **Laravel**, the world's most popular PHP framework.
- You created a new **route** in Laravel, mapping a URL to a piece of code to display a custom page.
- You've seen how a framework provides a professional structure, separating concerns and solving common problems for you.

Congratulations! You have successfully stepped into the world of modern PHP development. While we only scratched the surface, you now have the conceptual foundation to understand how large-scale applications are architected. Knowing *why* and *how* frameworks like Laravel are used is a massive advantage as you continue your journey. You are no longer just learning a language; you are learning the craft of software engineering. This knowledge is your guide to taking the next steps in your professional journey. Now, it's time to put all of your skills together and start thinking about your future in this exciting field as we dive into ***Chapter 38: Your career as a PHP developer***.

Chapter 38

Section 10: Beyond the basics – Level up and stay sharp

Your career as a PHP developer

What you'll learn

- Building a portfolio
- Finding job opportunities
- The value of open source
- Continuing your education

Congratulations! You have journeyed from your first echo statement to building a full-stack, AI-enhanced web application. This is a monumental achievement. You've wrestled with variables, tamed loops, wrangled databases, and even commanded artificial intelligence. You are no longer just learning PHP; you are a PHP developer.

This final chapter is your guide to taking the next, most exciting steps in your professional journey: turning your newfound skills into a career. We'll bridge the gap from the classroom to the real world, covering how to showcase your work, find opportunities, and cultivate the mindset of a lifelong learner and professional developer.

Your portfolio: Show, don't just tell

In the world of development, a portfolio is your single most powerful asset. It's one thing to say you know PHP; it's another thing entirely to show a polished, working application that proves it. Your portfolio is a testament to your skills, your problem-solving abilities, and your dedication. It transforms your knowledge from an abstract concept into tangible proof.

The "ConnectSphere" centerpiece

The ConnectSphere application you built is the perfect centerpiece for your new portfolio. It's not just another to-do list; it's a full-stack social media platform that demonstrates a wide range of highly sought-after skills:

- **User authentication:** You built a secure login and registration system.
- **Database management:** You designed a relational database schema and performed all core CRUD operations.
- **Dynamic content:** You created a system where users can generate and interact with content in real-time.
- **AI integration:** You used modern AI to provide intelligent features, a skill that sets you apart from many other junior developers.

Before you show it to the world, take a little time to polish it. Make sure the styling is clean, fix any minor bugs you might have noticed, and maybe even add a small, unique feature of your own to make it stand out.

Creating a professional GitHub profile

In today's tech industry, your GitHub profile is your new resume. It's often the first place a potential employer or collaborator will look to see the quality of your work. A clean, well-organized GitHub profile with well-documented projects speaks volumes. The most important part of any project repository is the **README.md** file. This file is your chance to explain what your project is, why you built it, and what technologies you used.

Action item

Let's get your ConnectSphere project onto GitHub and create a professional README.md file for it.

1. **Create a GitHub account:** If you don't have one already, head over to **github.com** and sign up for a free account.

2. **Create a New Repository:**
   - Once logged in, click the "+" icon in the top-right corner and select **New repository**.
   - Give your repository a name, like **connectsphere-social-app**.
   - Provide a short description, for example: **A full-stack social media web application built with PHP, MySQL, and AI-powered features.**
   - Make sure the repository is set to **Public**.
   - Click **Create repository**.
3. **Push your code:** Follow the instructions on the next page under "...or push an existing repository from the command line" to upload your project files from your local machine to GitHub.
4. **Create the README File:**
   - In your project folder on your local machine (e.g., C:\xampp\htdocs\connectsphere), create a new file using VS Code.
   - Name this file **README.md**. The **.md** extension stands for **Markdown**, a simple way to format text.
   - Copy the following template into your README.md file and fill in the details.

```
# ConnectSphere: AI-Enhanced Social Media Platform

ConnectSphere is a full-stack social media web application designed for
users to share updates and connect with friends. This project was built
as the capstone for the "PHP for Beginners" book and demonstrates a wide
range of modern web development practices.

## Features

- **User Authentication:** Secure user registration and login system
with password hashing.
- **Friend System:** Users can send, accept, and decline friend requests
to build their social network.
- **Posting:** Registered users can create and publish short text-based
posts.

#
- **AI-Powered Friend Suggestions:** An intelligent system that suggests
new users to connect with based on various factors.
- **Dynamic Feed:** A chronological feed displaying posts from friends.
(If you built this feature).

## Technologies Used

- **Back-End:** PHP 8.3+
- **Database:** MySQL
- **Front-End:** HTML5, Vanilla CSS
```

```
- **Development Environment:** XAMPP, Visual Studio Code
- **AI Integration:** [Mention the specific AI API you used, e.g., Gemini
API]

## How to Run This Project Locally

1.  Ensure you have XAMPP (or a similar stack) installed and running.
2.  Clone this repository into your `htdocs` folder.
3.  Import the `connectsphere_db.sql` database schema into phpMyAdmin.
4.  Update the database connection details in the `config.php` file.
5.  Open your browser and navigate to `http://localhost/connectsphere-
social-app`.
```

5. **Commit and Push:** Save the README.md file and push it to your GitHub repository. Now, when anyone visits your project's GitHub page, they'll be greeted with a professional and informative overview.

Where to find opportunities

With your portfolio polished and ready, it's time to start looking for opportunities. The web development job market is vast, and there are roles suited for all skill levels. Knowing where to look is key.

Job boards

Job boards are the most direct way to find open positions. They aggregate listings from thousands of companies. Here are some of the best places to start your search for PHP developer roles:

- **LinkedIn:** The top professional networking site. Create a detailed profile, connect with recruiters, and search for junior PHP developer or web developer roles.
- **Niche Tech Boards:** Websites like Stack Overflow Jobs, Larajobs, and WeWorkRemotely often have high-quality listings specifically for developers.
- **General job boards:** Sites like Indeed, Glassdoor, and ZipRecruiter are also great resources, though you may need to filter more to find relevant roles.

The "hidden" job market

Many of the best opportunities are never posted on job boards. They are filled through networking and community engagement. This is the "hidden" job market, and tapping into it can give you a significant advantage.

- **Attend local meetups:** Search for local "PHP user groups" or "web developer meetups" in your area. Attending these events is a fantastic way to meet other developers, learn from them, and hear about opportunities.
- **Engage in online communities:** Participate in forums and discussions. Websites like Reddit (specifically the /r/php subreddit), the Laracasts forums, and Stack Overflow are places where developers help each other. Being an active, helpful member of these communities can build your reputation and lead to connections.
- **Networking:** Don't be afraid to reach out to people. If you see someone working at a company you admire, send them a polite message on LinkedIn. Ask them about their experience and for advice. The worst that can happen is they don't respond; the best that can happen is you make a valuable connection.

The power of open source

Open-source software is code that is publicly available for anyone to view, use, and contribute to. The PHP ecosystem itself—including tools like Composer and frameworks like Laravel—is built on open source. Contributing to open-source projects is one of the most respected and effective ways to grow as a developer.

Why contribute?

Contributing to open source offers several incredible benefits:

- **Real-world experience:** You get to work on real projects that are being used by people around the world.
- **Learn from experts:** Senior developers will review your code. Their feedback is like a free, high-level mentorship session.
- **Build your reputation:** A history of contributions on your GitHub profile is a massive signal to employers that you are passionate and skilled.
- **Give back:** You are helping to improve the tools that you and other developers rely on every day.

How to start

The idea of contributing to a large project can be intimidating, but it doesn't have to be. The key is to start small. Many projects have issues specifically labeled for beginners.

- **Look for "Good First Issue" Labels:** On GitHub, project maintainers often tag simple bugs or tasks with labels like good first issue, help wanted, or documentation. These are perfect entry points.
- **Fix a Typo:** The easiest way to make your first contribution is to fix a typo in a project's documentation. It may seem small, but it's a complete contribution cycle—from finding an issue to submitting a fix (a "pull request") and having it accepted.

Action item

Let's walk through the process of making your first, simple open-source contribution.

- **Find a project:** Go to GitHub and search for good first issue php. This will show you a list of issues in PHP projects that are suitable for beginners.
- **Choose a simple issue:** Look for something very straightforward, like a typo in a README.md file or a broken link in the documentation.
- **"Fork" the repository:** A "fork" is your personal copy of the project. Click the "Fork" button on the project's page.
- **Make the change:** In your forked copy, navigate to the file you want to edit and click the pencil icon to edit it directly in your browser. Correct the typo or fix the link.
- **Commit the change:** At the bottom of the page, write a short, clear message describing your change (e.g., "Fix typo in installation instructions") and save it.
- **Submit a "Pull Request":** Go back to the main page of your fork. You'll see a button that says "Contribute" or "Open pull request." Click it. This will take you to a page where you can propose that your change be merged into the original project. Write a polite message and submit it.

That's it! You've just become an open-source contributor.

Never stop learning

The web changes fast. A developer's greatest skill is not knowing a specific language but rather the ability to learn new ones. The skills you've built in this book are a powerful foundation, but they are just the beginning of a lifelong journey of learning and growth.

Your learning path

Here is a logical roadmap for what to learn next to continue advancing your career:

- **Go deeper into a framework:** You've had a taste of Laravel. Now is the time to master it, or explore another popular framework like Symfony. Frameworks are used in almost every professional PHP job.
- **Strengthen your front-end skills:** While you've used HTML and CSS, the modern web is powered by JavaScript. Learning a JavaScript framework like Vue.js (which is very popular in the Laravel community) or React will make you a much more versatile and valuable full-stack developer.
- **Understand DevOps basics:** "DevOps" is the practice of managing the infrastructure that runs your application. Learning the basics of deployment, using tools like Docker to containerize your applications, and understanding CI/CD (Continuous Integration/Continuous Deployment) pipelines will give you a huge advantage.

Resources

Here is a curated list of excellent resources to help you stay sharp and continue your education:

- **Blogs:** PHP.Watch, Laravel News, Smashing Magazine.
- **Podcasts:** The Laravel Podcast, PHP Town Hall.
- **Online courses:** Laracasts (the best resource for the Laravel ecosystem), SymfonyCasts, and courses on platforms like Udemy and Coursera.
- **Official documentation:** The single best resource is always the official documentation for any tool you are using (e.g., the PHP Manual, the Laravel Docs).

Wrapping up

This chapter was your launchpad from learning to earning. We covered the essential non-coding skills that define a professional developer.

- You have a plan to turn your project into a compelling portfolio piece.
- You know where to look for PHP jobs and how to engage with the community.
- You understand the value of contributing to open source projects.
- You have a roadmap for your continued growth as a professional developer.

Take a moment and look back at the journey. You started this book perhaps with just a flicker of curiosity. You began with a simple echo "Hello, World!";. From there, you set up a professional development environment, you mastered variables, control structures, and functions. You learned to interact with users through forms, to handle files, and to manage sessions. You didn't stop there. You conquered the database, building a full CRUD application from scratch. Then, you stepped into the future, integrating powerful AI into your work, and even made PHP and Python work together as a team. You built project after project, culminating in ConnectSphere, a complex application that is a testament to your hard work. You are not the same person who started this book. You are a builder. You are a problem-solver. You are a developer.

And think about this: you picked up a book about PHP, but you're walking away with so much more. You've gone a step further than most beginners by learning how to make PHP and Python work together, a skill usually reserved for more experienced developers. You learned the critical importance of using the right tool for the right job—leveraging PHP for its web prowess and Python for its specialized AI and data processing capabilities. This experience means you are not just a 'PHP developer'; you are a versatile problem-solver, a developer who can build bridges between technologies. Be incredibly proud of that. It's a skill that will open countless doors and set you apart in your career.

This book focused on the powerful features of PHP 8.x, but the specific version is less important than the solid foundation you've built. The core principles of programming, web development, and database interaction that you've mastered are timeless. As new versions of PHP are released, your most important skill will be your ability to learn and adapt. Make it a habit to read the "What's New" section in the official PHP documentation for each new release. Try out the new features, understand why they were added, and integrate them into your projects. This practice is what separates a good developer from a great one—the commitment to continuous growth.

The path ahead is filled with challenges, but also with incredible opportunities to create, to innovate, and to build the future of the web. Never lose the curiosity that brought you here. Keep building, keep learning, and keep pushing the boundaries of what you think is possible.

For more resources and to stay updated on our upcoming books, we invite you to visit my website at **www.sharanamshah.com**. We are always posting new content and would love for you to keep an eye on what's coming next.

Thank you for trusting us to be your guide. Now go build something amazing. The world is waiting.

Index

D

E

Q

For Books on following Subjects

- Business, Management & Finance
- Career Development, Career Guides
- Catering & Hotel Management / Recipes
- Civil Engineering
- Computers
- Communication
- Dental / Health / Medical
- Economics
- Electrical Engineering
- Electronics & Communication
- English
- Entrepreneurship
- Environmental Engineering
- Event Management
- Fiction
- Forensic Science
- General Titles
- HRD
- International Trade
- Law
- Learning Disability
- Mathematics
- Mechanical Engineering
- Media
- Mobile Computing
- Motivation & Self Help
- Parenting
- Patent
- Physics
- Project Management / Software Engineering
- Real Estate
- Statistics

Publishers We Represent

O'REILLY®
THE X TEAM
BEP BUSINESS EXPERT PRESS — Leader in applied, concise business books
FRANKLIN, BEEDLE
The MIT Press
IT REVOLUTION
PyQML
The Pragmatic Engineer
Sandiver Publishing
Make: Community
ROBERTO VITILLO
ByteByteGo
Matt Harrison
Jaewoong
TOWARDS AI
STATQUEST! TRIPLE BAM!!
James Turnbull
Nathan Hunter
sitepoint
JORGE BRASIL
Nigel Poulton
RMC LEARNING™ SOLUTIONS
Rheinwerk Computing
Kt. Academy
Pragmatic Bookshelf